A HISTORY OF INDIAN LITERATURE

A History of Indian Literature

Volume II

Buddhist and Jaina Literature

MAURICE WINTERNITZ

A new authoritative translation
from original German
by
V. SRINIVASA SARMA

MOTILAL BANARSIDASS
INTERNATIONAL
DELHI

Reprint : Delhi, 2025
Revised Edition : Delhi, 1983

ISBN : 978-93-48911-60-5 (Vol. 2)
ISBN : 978-93-48911-84-1 (3 Vols. Set)

Also available at
MOTILAL BANARSIDASS INTERNATIONAL
H. O.- 41 U.A. Bungalow Road, (Back Lane)Jawahar Nagar, Delhi - 110 007
4261 (basement) Lane #3,Ansari Road, Darya Ganj, New Delhi - 110 002
Shop No. 6 Luz Ginza Complex, 241 Luz Corner, Mylapore, Chennai - 600 004
12/1A, 2nd Floor, Bankim Chatterjee Street, Kolkata - 700 073
Stockist : Motilal Books, Ashok Rajpath, Near Kali Mandir, Patna - 800 004

Printed in India
MOTILAL BANARSIDASS INTERNATIONAL.

TRANSLATOR'S NOTE

The present edition of the German work "Geschichte der Indischen Literatur" by Moriz Winternitz (published by "K. F. Koehler Verlag, Stuttgart") has been translated from the original, incorporating the additional information as found in Mrs Ketkar's translation from which a larger part of the text (especially beginning with "The Poet Aśvaghoṣa and his School") has been reproduced here verbatim.

—Translator

CONTENTS

SECTION III

SECTION IV

APPENDIX

LIST OF ABBREVIATIONS USED IN THE NOTES

ABA = Abhandlungen der Berliner Akademie der Wissenschaften, Philol.—hist. Klasse

ABayA = Abhandlungen der Bayerischen Akademie der Wissenchaften, Phil. Klasse.

AGGW = Abhandlungen der Kônigl. Gesellschaft der Wissenchaften zu Göttingen, Philol.—histor. Klasse

AKM = Abhandlungen fur die Kunde des Morgenlandes, herausg. von der Deutschen Morgenländischen Gesellschaft.

Album Kern = Album-Kern : Opstellen geschreven ter eere von Dr. H. Kern..op zijn zeventigsten verjaardag, Leiden, 1903

AMG = Annales du Musée Guimet (Paris)

Ann. Bh. Inst. = Annals of the Bhandarkar Institute, Poona

AR = Archiv für Religionsgeschichte

ASB = Asiatic Society of Bengal

ASGW = Abhandlungen der Philol. – histor. Klasse der Königl. Sächs. Gesellschaft der Wissenschaften

ĀUS = Agamodaya Samiti

Bagchi = Prabodhachandra Bagchi, Le Canon Bouddhique en Chine, tome I, Paris 1927

BB = Bibliographie Bouddhique (Paris)

BEFEO = Bulletin de l'ecole francaise d'Extreme Orient

Bezz. Beitr. = Beiträge zur Kunde der indogermanischen Sprachen, herausg. von A. Bezzenberger

Bhandarkar, Report 1882-83 = R. G. Bhandarkar, Report on the Search for Sanskrit Manuscripts in the Bombay Presidency during the year 1882-83, Bombay 1884.

Bhandarkar, Report 1883-84 = R. G. Bhandarkar, Report etc. during the year 1883-84, Bombay 1887

Bibl. Buddh. = Bibliotheca Buddhica (Leningrad)

Bibl. Ind. = Bibliotheca Indica (Calcutta)

BSGW = Berichte über die Verhandlungen der Königl. Sachsischen Gesellschaft der Wissenschaften zu Leipzig, Philol.-histor. Klasse

BSOS = Bulletin of the School of Oriental Studies, London Institution

BSS = Bombay Sanskrit Series

Cambridge History = The Cambridge History of India, Vol, I, Ancient India, Ed. by E. J. Rapson, Cambridge, 1922.

Comm. Wogihara = Journal of the Taisho University, Vols. VI-VII, in commemoration of the Sixtieth Birthday of Professor Unrai Wogihara, Sugamo, Tokyo, the Taisho University, 1930, Part II

CUIS = Columbia University Indo-Iranian Series, New York

DJGK = Digambara Jaina Granthabhāṇḍāra, Kāśi Kā, ed. by Pannālāl Chaudhari, Benares 1924-25

DLZ = Deutsche Literaturzeitung

Duff = C. Mabel Duff, The Chronology of India, Westminster, 1899

EB = The Eastern Buddhist (Kyoto, Japan)

Eliot = Sir Charles Eliot, Hinduism and Buddhism, London, 1921

EP. Ind. = Epigraphia Indica

ERE = Encyclopaedia of Religion and Ethics, edited by James Hastings

Festgabe Jacobi = Beiträge zur Literaturwissenschaft und Geistesgeschichte Indiens. Festgabe Hermann Jacobi zum 75. Geburtstag, Bonn, 1926

GGA = Göttinger Gelehrte Anzeigen

GOS = Gaekwad's Oriental Series, Baroda.

GSAI = Giornale della societa Asiatica Italiana

Hiralal, Catalogue = Rai Bahadur Hiralal, Catalogue of Sanskrit and Prakrit MSS., published under the Orders of the Government of the Central Provinces and Berar, Nagpur, 1926

HOS = Harvard Oriental Series, ed. by Ch. R. Lanman

Ind. Ant. = Indian Antiquary

Ind. Hist. Qu. = The Indian Historical Quarterly, edited by Narendranath Law, Calcutta

Ind. Stud. = Indische Studien, herausgegeben von A. Weber

JA = Journal Asiatique

JAOS = Journal of the American Oriental Society

JASB = Journal of the Asiatic Society of Bengal

JBORS = Journal of the Bihar and Orissa Research Society

JBRAS = Journal of the Bombay Branch of the Royal Asiatic Society

JBTS = Journal of the Buddhist Text Society

JDL = University of Calcutta, Journal of the Department of Letters

JPTS = Journal of the Pāli Text Society

JPU = Sheth Devchand Lalbhai Jaina Pustakoddhāra

JRAS = Journal of the Royal Asiatic Society of Great Britain and Ireland

Km = Kāvyamālā

Lanman Studies = Indian Studies in honour of Charles Rockwell Lanman, Harvard University Press, Cambridge Mass. 1929.

LZB = Literarisches Zentralblatt

MDJG = Māṇikacandra Digambara Jaina Granthamālā.

Nanjio = Bunyiu Nanjio, Catalogue of the Chinese Translation of the Buddhist Tripiṭaka, Oxford, 1883

NGGW = Nachrichten von der Kgl. Gesellschaft der Wissenschaften, Göttingen, Philol—histor. Klasse

NSP = Nirṇaya-Sāgara Press (Bombay)

OC = Transactions (Verhandlungen, Actes) of International Congresses of Orientalists

Oldenberg, Buddha = Hermann Oldenberg, Buddha, Sein Leben, seine Lehre, seine Gemeinde. 7. Aufl. Berlin, 1920

OTF = Oriental Translation Fund

OLZ = Orientalistische Literaturzeitung

OZ = Ostasiatische Zeitschrift

Peterson, Report 1882-83 = P. Peterson, Report on the Search for Sanskrit Manuscripts in the Bombay Circle, 1882-83 (JBRAS, VOL. 16, Extra Number).

Peterson, Report II = P. Peterson, A Second Report of Operations in Search of Sanskrit MSS., etc. 1883-84 (JBRAS, Vol. 17, Extra Number)

Peterson, 3 Reports = P. Peterson, Three Reports on a Search for Sanskrit MSS. with an Index of Books (JBRAS, Vol. 18, Extra Number) 1887

Peterson, Report IV = P. Peterson, A Fourth Report, etc., 1886-92 (JBRAS, Vol. 18, Extra Number)

Peterson, Report V = P. Peterson, A Fifth Report, etc., April 1892 March 1895, Bombay 1896

Peterson, Report VI = P. Peterson, A Sixth Report etc.— April 1895 March 1898, Bombay 1899

Proc. I etc., OC = Proceedings and Transactions of the First, etc. Oriental Conferences

PSS = Punjab Sanskrit Series (Lahore)

PTS = Pāli Text Society

PTS Dic. = The Pāli Text Society's Pāli-English Dictionary edited by T. W. Rhys Davids and William Stede

RGG = Die Religion in Geschichte und Gegenwart (Tübingen)

RHR = Revue de l'histoire des Religions, Paris

RSO = Rivista degli studi orientali, Rome

SBA = Sitzungsberichte der Preussischen Akademie der Wissenschaften in Berlin

SBB = Sacred Books of the Buddhists (London, Oxford University Press)

SBE = Sacred Books of the East (Oxford)

SBJ = Sacred Books of the Jainas (Arrah)

SIFI = Studi Italiani di Filologia Indo-Iranica

SJG = Sanātana-Jaina-Granthmālā

Smith, Early History—Vincent A. Smith, the Early History of India. 4th edition, revised by S. M. Edwardes, Oxford, 1924

TSS = Trivandrum Sanskrit Series

Weber HSS Verz. = A. Weber, Verzeichnis der Sanskrit und Prakrit-Handschriften der K. Bibliothek zu Berlin

WZKM = Wiener Zeitschrift für die Kunde des Morgenlandes

YJG = Yaśovijaya Jaina Granthamālā

ZB = Zeitschrift für Buddhismus (München)

ZDMG = Zeitschrift der Deutschen Morgenländischen Gesellschaft

ZII = Zeitschrift für Indologie und Iranistik, herausg. von der Deutschen Morgenländischen Gesellschaft

ZVV = Zeitschrift des Vereins für Volkskunde in Berlin

SECTION III

THE BUDDHIST LITERATURE AND SACRED TEXTS OF THE JAINAS

The Pāli-Canon or the Tipiṭaka[1]

The Vedic literature led us into very ancient, "pre-historic" times. And for the beginnings of epic poetry also we could not have any precise dates. It is only with the Buddhist Literature that we set our foot in the bright daylight of history, and we have seen that even the darkness of the history of the Vedic and the epic literature is dispelled to some extent by this light. The age of the Buddha can be fixed and thus a beginning given from which we can calculate the origin of a Buddhistic

1. The history of the Pāli-Canon, its dating and its reliability have been dealt with at great length at first by H. Oldenberg in the introduction to his edition of the Vinayapiṭaka, Vol. I, London 1879. On this subject compare H. Jacobi and H. Oldenberg ZDMG 34, 1880, 184 ff, 751 ff, H. Oldenberg and Th. Rhys Davids in SBE, Vol. XIII, Introduction; H. Oldenberg, Buddhistische Studien in ZDMG 52, 1898, P. 613 ff; T. W. Rhys Davids, Dialogues of the Buddha, Part I (Sacred Books of the Buddhists, Vol. II, London 1899, Preface; Buddhist India, London 1903, 167 ff. Oldenberg's views were opposed by I. P. Minayeff, Recherches sur Le Bouddhisme, traduit du Russe par RHA de Pompignan, Paris 1894 (Annales du Musée Guimet, Bibliothéques d' études, t 4); A. Bath in RHR t 5, 1882, 237 ff; t 28, 1893, 241, 277 ff; t 42, 1900, 74 ff; Louis de la Vallée Poussin, Boudhisme, Etudes et Materiaux (Memoires....publié par l' Academie roy. des sciences...de Belgique, t LV) Bruxelles 1897, pp. 1 ff; Conciles Bouddhiques I, Le Muséon 1905, p 213 ff; the Bouddhist Councils, Ind. Ant. 37, 1908, 1 ff, 81 ff; Bouddhisme, Paris 1909, pp. 29 to 53, 155, 166 ff, 251 and ERE IV, p 179 ff. (Again La Vallée Poussin cf. E. J. Rapson in JRAS 1898, 909 ff). R. Otto Franke also appears extremely sceptical in his "The Buddhist Councils at Rajagraha and Vesali in JPTs 1908, pp. 1-80 (cf. A. B. Keith in JRAS 1909, p. 577 note and 1910, p. 216). A peculiar stand is assumed by K. E. Neumann in the forewords to his "Reden Gotama Buddhos" I—IV, Leipzig 1896—1905. Further, we may compare those chapters of the main work on Buddhism which relate to literature, and in particular: H. Oldenberg, Buddha, his work, his teachings and his community, 5th Edition, Berlin 1906, p. 86 ff; T. W. Rhys Davids, History of Indian Buddhism, (Hibbert Lectures 1881) 3rd Ed. London 1897; Buddhism, its History and Literature (American Lectures) 2nd Ed. New York—London 1904, p. 44 ff; Der Buddhismus (=Buddhism) translated into German by A. Pfungst, Leipzig, Reclam Un-Bibl.; R. S. Copleston, Buddhism, 2nd Ed. London 1908, pp. 45 f; 167 ff; H. Kern, Der Buddhismus

literature. Gotama Buddha was born about 480 B.C.[1] and according to a reliable tradition he lived for 80 years. As a young man of 29 years he is said to have taken to the life of a wandering ascetic and thus begun to seek the path of salvation. As a mature man after hard inner conflicts he began to proclaim what he had discovered. Thus the time between 525 B.C. and 480 B.C. might be considered as the period of the Buddha's activity, the founding and propagating of that Indian religion which was destined to become one of the three great religions of the world. The Ganges region in north eastern India was the place of his activity. Here—in the Kingdoms of Magadha (Bihar) and Kosala (Oudh)—he wandered from place to place, preaching his doctrine and gathering more and more followers around himself.

Is also writing one of his activities lasting for decades ? Certainly not. In the Tipiṭaka, the Pāli-Canon of the Buddhists most of the speeches and addresses are attributed to the Buddha himself; it is also told at length and in detail, where and on which occasion the master delivered a speech or addressed a gathering. But of all this what really originates from the Buddha can perhaps be hardly ever decided. For Gotama Buddha left behind as little in writing as Yājñavalkya, Śaṇḍilya or Śaunaka. But just as much of the speeches and addresses of these sages has really found place in the Upaniṣads, so also many speeches and addresses of Buddha have been preserved

---

und Seine Geschichte in Indien translated by H. Jacobi, Leipzig 1882—1884, Vol. II, 281 ff and Manual of Indian Buddhism (Grundriss III, 8), Strassburg 1896, p. 1 ff, 101 ff; R. Pischel, Leben und Lehre des Buddha, 2nd Edition, Leipzig 1910, p. 5 ff., 99 ff.

1. Max Mueller, General A. Cunningham and G. Buehler have fixed the year of Buddha's death as 477 B.C. (see in particular Buehler in Ind. Ant. VI, 1877, p. 149). Proceeding on different lines H. Oldenberg, A. Barth, J. F. Fleet and V. A. Smith have arrived at the dates 480 or 482 and 480-470 B.C. Divergent views are expressed by T.W. Rhys Davids (412 B.C.), H. Kern (388 B.C.) and V. Gopala Aiyer (Ind. Ant. 1908, 341 ff) who would like to assume 487 B.C. as the year of his death. Cf. also E. Hultzsch and Fleet in JRAS 1909, p. 27 & 981 ff. Although unfortunately there is no unanimity in the matter of the exact date, still the greatest probability speaks in favour of a date that cannot be far from 480 B.C.

See also Appendix I.

in the memory of his faithful disciples and have been handed down to posterity. Speeches like the famous Sermon of Benares on the "four noble truths" and the "noble eightfold path" which again and again recur word for word in the same form not only in many places of the Pāli-Canon but also in Buddhist Sanskrit texts, some of the farewell speeches occurring in the Mahāparinibbānasutta which the master is said to have addressed to the disciples before his death, some of the verses and short addresses handed down as "Words of the Buddha" in the Dhammapada, in the Udāna, in the Itivuttaka and in more or less in the same form in the Sanskrit texts of Nepal as well as in Tibetan and Chinese translations as "Words of the Buddha", we may perhaps consider as originating from Buddha without ourselves being guilty of gullibility. But Gotama Buddha has not only preached his new doctrine of the suffering and the end of the suffering but he has also founded a formal religious order; he has gathered around himself a community of disciples who lived a holy life as expected by the master according to strict rules, in order to attain the end of the suffering—the much-admired Nirvāṇa. And thus some of the rules and prescriptions for this community of monks, especially the ten commandments for the beggar-monks (daśaśīlam) and perhaps also the confessional Litany (pātimokkha) may be traced back to the Buddha.[1]

Although none of the works belonging to the Buddhist literature may originate from the time of Buddha, yet individual texts contained in these works may perhaps be considered as the words of the Buddha. Among the early disciples of the Buddha also there were certainly some excellent scholars and some of them might be the authors of a few of the speeches, sayings and poems[2] found among our collections.

1. Cf. Eliot, I, 294 f.; Oldenberg, Reden des Buddha, p. xxiii ff.

2. A great antiquity especially of the sayings in verses (gāthā) is indicated by the prosody. The metres of the Pāli-Gāthās are according to Oldenberg (Gurupūjākaumudī, p. 9 ff.) more ancient than those of the Rāmāyaṇa. Cf. however, also R. Simon in ZDMG 44, 1890, 83-97 on the Śloka in Pāli and Oldenberg "Zur Geschichte des Śloka" (Nachrichten der. K. Ges. d. Wiss. zu Göttingen, phil.-hist. Kl. 1909, p. 244).

Almost the whole of the earliest literature of the Buddhists consists evidently of collections—collections of speeches or dialogues, of sayings, songs, stories and rules of the holy order. And the Tipiṭaka is nothing but a large collection of such collections. It is evident that such collections can only be the finale of a long period of literary activity preceding them and that their constituents must belong to various epoques.

According to Buddhist tradition such a finale took place very early. For it is reported that a few weeks after the Buddha's death in the town of Rājagaha (the present Rajgir) a meeting of monks was held by the direct disciples of the Buddha—the so-called first Buddhist Council—in order to fix a canon of religion (Dhamma) and of orderly discipline (Vinaya).[1] The reliability of this information, particularly in its oldest form, as it is transmitted to us in the Tipiṭaka itself[2] is rendered already questionable by the fact that it expects us to believe too much, namely that the two large parts of the Tipiṭaka dealing with the teachings and the orderly discipline – Suttapiṭaka and Vinayapiṭaka – have existed essentially just as we find them in our Pāli canon even shortly after the death of Buddha, which is simply impossible.[3] That this tradition is entirely baseless, need not be assumed on that account. Perhaps it contains a reminiscence of the certainly not improbable fact that the elders of the community met immediately after the death of the master in order to come to an agreement about the main points of the doctrine and the orderly discipline.[4] For compiling a canon of sacred texts of the

1. Pāli "Dhamma" (i.e. Sanskrit "Dharma") is the technical expression for the religion of Buddha, Vinaya for the "orderly discipline", i.e. the rules and regulations for the order of the mendicant monks.

2. Vinayapiṭaka, Cullavagga. XI.

3. Other grounds against the credibility of the tradition of the first council have been mentioned by Oldenberg (Vinayapiṭaka, Introd. p. XXV ff, ZDMG, vol. 52, 625 f).

4. Cf. H. Kern, Manual of Indian Buddhism, p. 103; R. Pischel, Leben und Lehre des Buddha, 4 aufl., 1926, p. 11, 99 f; E. Windisch in OC XIV, I, 284 f; L. de La Valleé Poussin, Ind. Ant. 37, 1908, 2 ff; S. Levi (JA, 1915, s. 11, t. V, 401 ff) has compared the reports as to the first Council in the Pāli Vinayapiṭaka the Udāna, the Divyāvadāna, as well as the Vinaya of the Mūlasarvāstivādins and the Sarvāstivādins, and has shown that they hark back to an early age.

kind of our Tipiṭaka the time that had lapsed after the death of Buddha was, however, still too short.

More reliable is the tradition of the second council which is said to have taken place a hundred years after the death of Buddha at Vesali. But according to an earlier report[1] this meeting had only the object of removing ten false teachings concerning the orderly discipline. Only the later reports[2] claim to know that a revision of the doctrine took place simultaneously in a meeting lasting for eight months. If we follow the older report, we may accept it as a historical fact[3] that approximately a hundred years after the demise of Buddha a schism took place which raised so much controversy that a large meeting of monks was called to decide what was to be considered as right in the matter under dispute. This presupposes that in those times there was some guideline for deciding such questions and this could have been only a canon of rules for the life of the monks—of a kind that we find in our Vinaya-piṭaka. Therefore, in the course of the first century after Buddha there must have come into existence, if not a canon, at least a basic stock of texts for one such.

A real canon of sacred texts was compiled probably only during the third council, which (according to the report of the chronicles of Ceylon), although highly embellished with legends, is still in its essence certainly creditable, took place at the time of the famous king Aśoka. The Buddhist community was (as reported by these chroniclers) even in those days, already split into numerous sects[4] and, therefore, it is probable that the need was felt to compile a canon of texts for the strictly religious people—i.e. for those who wanted to be considered as followers of the original doctrine of the Buddha. No less probable is it

1. Vinayapiṭaka, Cullavagga XII, s. SBE, vol. XX, p. 409 ff.

2. Thus Dipavaṃsa V, 27 ff, Mahāvaṃsa IV.

3. Rightly has Copleston (Buddhism, p. 174 f) remarked, that the tradition of the councils would not have come into existence if at least one council had not been historical. That the Indians have imagined everything, as R. Otto Franke thinks, cannot at all be presumed.

4. 18 different schools are mentioned. We are familiar with the fact that the number 18 is a favourite number in India; hence the existing schools, whether they are numbered more or less than 18 were fitted into a scheme of 18.

however, that such a compilation took place precisely during the reign of King Aśoka, the great patron and follower of the Buddhist community. Aśoka himself expressed himself against the schismatists in some of his edicts.[1] He decrees that heretical monks and nuns shall be excommunicated.[2] Consequently, it would have been only natural for him to take an active interest in establishing what tenets constituted the true religion of Buddha. On the other hand, we find no mention in any of his numerous edicts of a council to determine the canon. It is true that he would have had no reason of doing so, because even according to the tradition, it was not the king himself but the learned monk Tissa Moggaliputta who, 236 years after the death of Buddha convened an assembly of a thousand monks in the city of Pāṭaliputra (Patna), with the object of compiling a canon of texts of the true religion or the Therāvāda, i.e. the "Doctrine of the elders," the immediate disciples of Buddha.

The school of the Vibhajjavādins,[3] to which Tissa, the President of the council, belonged, adhered to this Therāvāda, and it is the canon of this school which was compiled during the nine months' session of the Council of Pāṭaliputra. Tradition has it, too, that Tissa has also compiled the "Kathāvatthu,"

1. V. A. Smith, Aśoka, 2nd Ed. Oxford 1909, p. 195 ff.

2. Hence Aśoka had no reason to make mention of the council in his edicts. (Cf. Fleet in JRAS 1908, p. 493). But perhaps V. A. Smith is right in supposing that the third council took place between 242 and 231 B.C., after the king had issued the seven pillar edicts and that this is the ground for not mentioning the council in the edicts (ERE II, p. 126).

3. There is no distinction in the chronicles between the Therāvāda and Vibhajjavāda; but Therāvāda is probably a general term meaning merely "authentic doctrine". The word is used in this sense also with reference to the schools of Buddha's predecessors (Majjh. 26, I, 164 f). The Vibhajjavādins declared that they taught the Therāvāda. However, the same thing is also maintained by other sects,/such as the Mahissasakas and the Sarvāstivādins (s. Kern, Manual of Buddhism, p. 110 f.). In Majjh. II, 197 (99) Buddha says referring to himself that he is a Vibhajjavāda, i.e., "one who explains everything with careful distinctions," and not an ekāṃtavāda, "who answers questions from one point of view only". Cf. Majjh. III, 208 (136); Aṅgutt, III, 67 (I), p. 297 Milindap., 144f; Mrs. Rhys Davids points of Controversy, p. xl sq. M. Walleser Die Sekten des alten Buddhismus, Heidelberg 1927, p. 13 f.

a book refuting all the heretical doctrines of those times, and incorporated it with the canon.

It has been much disputed whether or not there is any historical foundation for the tradition about the councils.[1] In the nature of things it is likely that, in the course of time, the orthodox Buddhists would feel the need of compiling a canon of doctrines, monastic rules and authentic texts as a defence against the schistatics; and this could only be done by one or several meetings of monks. This would be an argument in favour of there being at least a nucleus of historical truth in these reports even though they are not attested in all their details. It has been rightly remarked[2] that the tradition about the councils would not have arisen had not the one council been a historical fact. As a matter of fact, it is possible that even more than three councils were held. Singhalese and North Indian records of a "great council" (mahāsaṅgīti) which is said to have led to the schism of the Mahāsaṅgītikas, or Mahāsaṅghikas, would seem to indicate that the council of the orthodox Buddhists at Pāṭaliputra was preceded by a great assembly of the schismatics. It is true nevertheless, that these reports contradict one not compiled at all at once, but at several meetings of the monks the most important of which was the Pāṭaliputra session.

It was also Tissa—at least if we believe the chronicler of Ceylon—who sent missionaries to north and south and paved the way for spreading Buddhism in foreign countries. And a pupil of Tissa was Mahinda, the younger brother (according to another tradition, the son) of Aśoka, who is said to have brought Buddhism and Buddhist texts to Ceylon. It is understandable that legend took control of this apostle of Ceylon. But even if we may not believe the chronicler when he says that Mahinda and the monks accompanying him came to Ceylon flying like flamingoes in the air, still we certainly need

1. Cf. Kern, Manual of Buddhism, p. 101 ff, La Vallée Poussin ERE IV 1911, 170ff.; Geiger, Mahāvaṃsa Transl., p. LI ff, Elliot I, 254ff—, Nalinaksha Dutt, Early History of the Spread of Buddhism and the Buddhist Schools, London, 1925 (Calcutta Oriental Series) pp. 225 ff, 249 ff. See also p. 1 note above.

2. By Copleston, Buddhism, p. 174 f.

not reject the whole legend[1] but we may presume that all the numerous legends have as their base the historical fact that Mahinda really introduced Buddhism into Ceylon and brought the texts of the canon along with him. These texts are supposed to have been handed down at first orally until under the Singhalese king Vaṭṭagāmani, in the first century B. C. these were committed to writing. This again sounds trustworthy.[2]

In the opinion of the Buddhists of Ceylon it is the canon which was compiled during the third council, brought to Ceylon by Mahinda and recorded under Vaṭṭagāmani that is also the same as our Pāli-canon or the Tipiṭaka as we have it even today. This Tipiṭaka—the word means "three-baskets" — consists of three so-called Piṭakas.

In the Tipiṭaka itself there is, in various places[3], mention of a division of the Canon into 9 Aṅgas or "limbs," viz., 1. Sutta, prose sermons, 2. Geyya, sermons in a mixture of prose and verse, 3. Veyyākaraṇa (Vyākaraṇa), explantions,

---

1. As Oldenberg does in Vinayapiṭaka, Introd. p. LI ff. Cf. as against this Kern, Manual, p. 116 f. When the chroniclers report that Mahinda was sent to Ceylon and Majjhima to the Himavat (Dipavaṃsa VIII, 10) and we find in the Sanchi-Stupa a shrine of relics with the inscriptions "(Relics) of Majjhima, Teacher of Himavat". This speaks very much in favour of the creditability of the chronicles of Ceylon. (Copleston, Buddhism, p. 173 f).

2. See Volume I, p. 27 ff. The Chinese pilgrim Fa-hein (s. A. Record of Buddhistic Kingdoms transl. by J. Legge, Oxford 1886, Chap XXXVI) when he travelled through North India during the years 399-414 A.D., did not as yet find any manuscripts of the Vinayapiṭaka, but only oral tradition. It was not until he came to Pāṭaliputra that he found a copy of the Vinaya in a Mahāyāna monastery.

3. Majjh. 22 (I, p. 133) and in several passages in the Aṅguttaranikāya. Cf. Milindapanha, p. 345; Sumaṅgalavilāsini I, p. 23 ff; Atthasālinī, p. 26; Gandhavaṁsa in JPTS 1886, p. 57; H. Kern Manual, p. 7; E. Senart JA 1901, S. 9, t XVII, p. 407 f. The texts dealing with Vinaya also belong to the "Sutta", whilst the Abhidhamma texts (at least according to Buddhaghosa) belong to the Veyyākaraṇa. However, they might also be included in the "Veddala." Lord Chalmers (SBE V, pp. 93, 207 ff) renders "veddala" by "miscellany". But it is doubtful whether there is any thought of Abhidhamma texts in the list of Aṅgas.

commentaries,[1] 4. Gāthā, stanzas, 5. Udāna, pithy sayings, 6. Itivuttaka, short speeches beginning with the words : "Thus spake the Buddha", 7. Jātaka, stories of former births of Buddha, 8. Abbhutadhamma, reports of miracles, 9. Vedalla, teachings in the form of questions and answers. This division[2] does not allude to a canon complete in itself, or to definite books, but it is only meant to classify the various types of Buddhist texts according to their form and contents.

The list of the Aṅgas is evidence of the fact that, at the time when the Canon was compiled in its present form, all these diverse forms of Buddhist literature were already in existence. Moreover, there are other passages of the Canon which show us that there was at that time a great mass of short texts, rules of the order, speeches, dialogues, aphorisms in verse, and even minor collections of texts,[3] which passed as "the word of Buddha" (Buddhavacanam), and were memorised and recited by the monks. They were recited as a kind of recitative, as all sorts of sacred texts are still recited to this day in India and Ceylon.[4] Among the monks there were Suttantikas, reciters of the Suttantas, Dhammakathikas, preachers of the doctrine and Vinayadharas, experts in the discipline.[5] In order to ensure the

1. In the Buddhist Sanskrit "vyākaraṇa" frequently means prophecy especially the prediction of a future Buddha; thus also in Pāli in the Nidānakathā (Jātaka ed., Faüsböll, p. 34, 44).

2. A similar division into 9 Aṅgas sometimes into 12 Dharmapravacanas is also found in Sanskrit Buddhist texts. Cf. Kern, l.c. Saddharmapuṇḍarika II, 48 (SBE, Vol. 21, p. 45); Mahākaruṇāpuṇḍarīka in SBE Vol. 10 (i), p. xxxiii.

3. Such as the Aṭṭhakavagga, which we now find in the Suttanipāta, and which is already mentioned in the Vinayapiṭaka (Mahāv. V, 13, 9) and in the Udāna V, 6, (p. 59). Cf. Dhammapada 19, 20, 102, 185, 352; Suttanipāta 87.

4. Cf. Rhys Davids, SBE Vol. 20, p. 72n. 3. The reciters (or leaders of a common recitation) were known as sarabhāṇakā "intoners". Later on, the entire Canon was divided into lessons (bhāṇavāra) for the purposes of recitation. Cf. SBE Vol. 20, p. 415 ff. In the Cullavagga V, 3, it is expressedly forbidden to sing the texts of the Dhamma to melodies as if they were songs.

5. Cullavagga IV, 4, 4, and in many other passages. Cf. N. Dutt., Early History of the Spread of Buddhism, p. 207 ff. Upāli is mentioned as one of the first Vinayadharas, Cullavagga VI 13, IX; 5, XI, I, 7ff. Cf. SBE, Vol. XIII, p. xiii.

continuance of the knowledge of the doctrine and the rules of the order, the texts had to be memorised, recited and expounded again and again. When, during the rainy season, many learned monks assembled at a place, there was an opportunity to obtain enlightenment on knotty places. It happened that some learned monk or perhaps a whole community of monks in some monastery would declare as Dhamma or Vinaya something which had first to be investigated before it could be sanctioned as being really in accord with the "teaching of the Master" (satthusāsanam).[1] This means that there must have been authoritative texts which could be consulted. It is often said of prominent monks that they are "very learned, masters of the tradition, and well versed in the Dhamma, Vinaya and the Mātikās."[2] The Mātikās are the "lists" or "tabulated summaries" of those ideas which are of importance in the doctrine and the monastic order. These Mātikās were subsequently worked into the texts of the Abhidhammapiṭaka.[3] From this it would appear that the texts of the Abhidhamma were merely in their beginnings before the Canon was compiled.

The Kathāvatthu attributed by tradition to the Tissa is found in our Pāli canon as a part of the Abhidhammapiṭaka. The Abhidhammapiṭaka can be proved to be the youngest constituent of our Tipiṭaka. For it presupposes not only the texts of the Vinayapiṭaka and of all the Nikāyas of the Suttapiṭaka, but of other books of the Abhidhammapiṭaka too.[4] Moreover, the more ancient texts speak for example in the news of the council of Rajagaha always only of Dhamma and Vinaya but never of an

1. Aṅgutt VI, 51; IV, 180; Dīghanikāya XVI, 4, 7-11. The fact that there is always mention here of the Sutta and Vinaya but not of the Abhidhamma, proves that, at the time when this Sutta was completed only two Piṭakas were recognised as authorities.

2. Vinayapiṭaka, Mahāv. II, 21,2, X, 1, 2; Cullav. I, 11, 1; XII, 1, 9f. 2, 1, Dīgha. II, p. 125; Aṅgutt. I, p. 117. The phrase is : bahussuta agatagama dhammadhara vinayadhara matidadhara.

3. In the Sanskrit Buddhist texts the corresponding word mātṛka is used for "Abhidharmapiṭaka". Cf. Kern, Manual, pp. 3, 104. Oldenberg and Rhys Davids, SBE, Vol. 13, p. 273; Mrs. Rhys Davids, Buddhist Manual of Psychological Ethics, 2nd Ed., pp. ix, cv-xiii.

4. Cf. Mrs. Rhys Davids, Points of Controversy, pp. xxix f, 401 ff.

Abhidhamma.[1] Hence it would be easily possible to suppose that while compiling the available texts the members of the third council put the books of the Abhidhama at the end as having originated at last and, to complete them, added the work of Tissa himself.

Yet we cannot concede as a matter of course to the devout Buddhists of Ceylon that the canon compiled at the third council is exactly the same as the one that lies before us in the Pāli Tipiṭaka.

First of all, the language of our Tipiṭaka can scarcely be the same as that of Canon of the third century B.C. Buddha himself spoke the dialect of his native province Kosala (Oudh) and it was most likely in this same dialect that he first began to proclaim his doctrine. Later on, however, he wandered and taught in Magadha (Bihar) he probably preached in the dialect of this province. We must, however, take into account the fact that, in the early days of Buddhism, little importance was attached to the linguistic form of texts. An utterance of Buddha has come down to us, in which he affirms that he cares not for mere wording, but only for the meaning itself.[2] When in course of time, the doctrine spread over a large area, the monks of various districts preached each in his own dialect. It is probable that monks coming from Brahmin circles also attempted to translate the speeches of Buddha into Sanskrit verses. In the Vinayapiṭaka, however, this procedure is expressly declared as a transgression against the monastic discipline, because it "Contributes neither to the conversion of the unconverted nor to the augmentation of the converts," and it is declared to be right that each one should learn the doctrine in a version adapted to

1. In addition to Dhamma and Vinaya there is also mention of Mātikās (particularly in the common usage "One who has studied the Āgamas, who knows Dhamma, Vinaya and Mātikās, Vinayapiṭaka Mahāvagga II, 21, 2; X, 1, 2; Cullavagga I, 11, 1; XII, 19 f) and these Mātikās are perhaps the "Lists or Enumerations" which are further processed in the Abhidhammapiṭaka. In Buddhistic Sanskrit texts the word mātṛka (=Pāli mātika) is used for "Abhidhammapiṭaka". Cf. Kern, Manual, p. 3 and 104.

2. Majjhimanikāya 103 (II, p. 240).

his own language.[1] The monks who compiled the Canon in Pāṭalīputra, most probably used an ancient Māgadhī dialect. Pāli[2] however, the literary language of the Buddhists of Ceylon, Burma and Siam, though called "Māgadhī" by these people themselves, deviates essentially from the dialect, otherwise known to us through inscriptions, literary works, and grammarians. On the other hand, it agrees just as little with any other dialect. The fact is that Pāli is a literary language which was exclusively as such only by the Buddhists, and like all literary languages, it developed more or less out of a mixture of dialects. Of course a literary language of this kind, even if it represents a kind of compromise between two different dialects, could at all events only have proceeded out of one particular dialect. This was very likely an old Māgadhī. The tradition which makes Pāli and Māgadhī the same, though it is not to be taken literally, has some historical background.

The time and place of origin of this literary language cannot be determined with any degree of certainty.[3] It is probable, that during the period immediately after Aśoka, when Buddhism had already spread throughout the whole of Central India and in the North west too, it developed as a compromise between various dialects spoken in this vast territory among the monks engaged in handing down the territory the Therāvāda Canon. It is for this reason that Pāli bears traces of so many different Indo-Aryan dialects.[4] When the Canon of the Vibhajjavādins was written down in the first century B.C., there was already an older and a more modern form of Pāli[5] so that, even at that early period Pāli must have been a language with a considerable development behind it. The monks of Ceylon were, however, bent on preserving and passing on the texts written in the language once established for them in India.[6] In all probability these monks

1. Cullavagga V, 33; SBE, Vol. 20, p. 1, & cf. W. Geiger, Pāli Literatur und Sprache, p. 5 offers a different explanation for this passage, s. Appendix II.

2. See Appendix II.

3. See Appendix II.

4. Cf. S. K. Chatterji, Origin and Development of the Bengali language, Calcutta, 1926, I, 55 ff.

5. Cf. Geiger, l.c., p. 1 f.

6. The fact that a Pāli Canon was known in North India as late as in the 2nd and 3rd centuries A.D., is proved by a quotation (from the Saccasaṃyutta

were just as conscientious regarding the contens as regarding the language and preserved and handed down to us the texts of the Tipiṭaka which was written down in the Pāli language, with rare fidelity during the last two thousand years. However, before they were fixed in Pāli and had reached Ceylon, they probably also passed through the changes in contents.

Thus, as regards language and contents, our Pāli Tipiṭaka, though closely approaching the canon compiled under Aśoka, is yet not identical with it. For we must admit that, in the period from the third century to the first century before Christ when the writing down took place and occasionally even still later, the texts suffered many a change that especially much was added, and that in many cases commentaries penetrated into the texts and became mixed with them. Thus the collections as well as the separate texts contained in them, must have increased in extent. The centuries have surely not passed them by without leaving traces.[1] This accounts, too, for the numerous contradictions within the Canon[2] and for the existence of

---

of the Saṃyuttanikāya?) about the "four noble truths" in an inspiration dating from this period in Sarnath, s. Konow, Ep. Ind. IX, 1908, 291 ff and Dharmananda Kosambi, Ind. Ant. 1910, 217. In inscriptions from Swat in the extreme North west of India written at the close of the first century B.C. or in the first half of the first century A.D. we find Sanskrit verses which seem to be literal translations from the Pāli of verses of the Mahāparinibbānasutta and the Dhammapada (G. Bühler, Ep. Ind. IV, 133 ff). A fragment of the Cullavagga discovered by C. Bendall (OC XIII Hamburg, 1902, p. 58 ff) would seem to prove that the Pāli Canon was in existence in Nepal in the 8th and 9th centuries. But it is possible that the MS. was taken from Ceylon to Tibet. So also, when we find that Chinese and Tibetan translations betray familiarity with Pāli texts, it is possible that the translators had been in Ceylon.

1. A comparison with the verbatim transmission of the hymns of the Ṛgveda (see vol. I, p. 34 and 242) would be improper. The Vedic hymns were protected from their ancient language which was largely different Sanskrit. Any interpolations would have been immediately recognised as such. Pāli on the other hand, remained the language of the monks who use it even today. For the Epigonians it was comparatively easy to make additions to the ancient Pāli texts in a language with which they were conversant.

2. Such contradictions have been proved for example by B. R. Otto Franke (WZKM 24, 1900, 1ff). Cf. also Minayeff, Recherches etc. p. 62 ff and Mrs. Rhys Davids, Buddhist Psychology, 2nd Ed., London, 1924 pp. 2 of, 291f.

several old and new traditions side by side with one another and for the occurrence of the same texts frequently in various collections.[1]

With these reservations and restrictions we can still say that to a very large extent the main mass[2] of our Pāli Tipiṭaka might not differ much from the Māgadhī canon of the 3rd century B.C. This is testified above all by the inscriptions of King Aśoka. Not only do these edicts breathe the same spirit as the oldest Suttas in our Pāli-Canon[3] but the language of the texts of our canon and quotations reminds us of the texts of our canon

1. See the concordance of the Gāthās by R. D. Franke in ZDMG 63, 1909, 1 ff, WZKM 24, 1910, 1 ff; 225 ff; 26, 1912, 171 ff. However, from such repetitions and contradictions occurring in them one must not at all, as Franke (ZDMG 63, 1909, 8 ff) does, at once conclude that the canon is either not authentic or not original. For if in one text a verse is attributed to Buddha and in the other to Sāriputta or if a lecture is said to have been delivered in Rājagaha according to one text and in Benares according to another, then this only shows that these legendary embellishments are not authentic, but it proves nothing against the presumption that the verses and the lectures themselves are "authentic", i.e. that they reproduce faithfully the ancient teachings of Buddha. The arguments of Franke and other critics have a crushing effect on the belief of orthodox Buddhists that every word of the Canon is genuine and can be traced back to Buddha himself; but they do not prove anything against the presumption of the European scholars who recognise a certain genuineness and reliability although in a very limited way of the canon.

2. Doubts against the Abhidhammapiṭaka are justifiable because, with the exception of the Vibhajjavādins only the Sarvāstivādins have a corresponding Abhidharmapiṭaka and the latter contains totally different texts from the Pāli Abhidhammapiṭaka. Cf. La Vallée Poussin Bouddhisme, p. 44 Farquhar, Outline, p. 68 f. Keith : Buddhist Philosophy p. 22. When in the Dīpavaṃsa V, 35-37, we are told that the great Council of the Vesali, the Mahāsaṅgita Bhikkus rejected certain passages of the Suttas and the Vinaya especially the Parivara, Abhidhamma, Patisambhida, Niddesa texts and portions of the Jātakas and wrote down other texts in their place it is noteworthy that it is precisely these texts which we too are inclined to suspect of being later additions to the Canon.

3. Parallel passages from the Dhammapada which are in accord with the Dhamma of Aśoka, are quoted by Hultzsch, Inscriptions of Aśoka, p. xlvii ff. We can only compare such texts as have reference to the morals of the laity as Aśoka had only these views and not the philosophy and dogmas of Buddhism.

and quotations.[1] But this is not all. In the edict of Bairat (or Bhabra) of the year 249 B.C. the king says to the monks of Magadha, "All that has been said by Lord Buddha is well said", but he names the titles of seven texts, whose study he recommends to them in particular. The existence of these texts, partly with the same titles and partly with similar titles, can be proved in our Suttapiṭaka also.[2]

The majority of the inscriptions on the famous stūpas of Bharhut and Sanchi are written in the same characters as the inscriptions of Aśoka and the stūpas were formerly regarded as monuments of the time of Aśoka. Nowadays, however, authorative archaeologists are inclined to ascribe the bulk of the sculptures rather to the 2nd and 1st centuries B.C.[3] The

1. Cf. G. Bühler ZDMG 48, p. 57 ff. E. W. Thomas, JRAS 1903, p. 831 ff; K. E. Neumann, WZKM 11, 1897, p. 156 ff. When the last mentioned author (in the Reden Gotama Buddhos III, p. 41 Note) speaks of Aśoka as of "educated with our texts", he has said thereby much more than can be proved. E. Hardy (JRAS 1901, 314) compares Aṅgutt III, p. 247, 340 : Yena, saddhammo ciratthitiko hoti ti, with Aśoka's Bhabhrau Edict, hevan sa dhammo cilatihitiko hasati ti.

2. See Appendix III.

3. The Stūpa at Bharhut (Bharhut, Bharaut, Barahat) was discovered by General A. Cunningham in the year 1874 and described by him in the work "The Stūpa of Bharhut", London 1879. The inscriptions have been published and translated by E. Hultzsch, ZDMG 40, 1886, p. 58 ff. and Ind. Ant. 21 1892, 225 ff., and B. M. Barua and K. G. Singh, Barhut Inscriptions, Calcutta, 1926. Cf. J. Ph. Vogel in JRAS 1927, 592 ff. According to Cunningham, the inscriptions date from the period between 250 and 150 B.C., and only the Eastern Gateway should be attributed to the 2nd or 1st century. The sculptures of the Sanchi stūpas have been described by F. C. Maisey, Sanchi and its Remains, London 1892, and Sir J. H. Marshall, A Guide to Sanchi, Calcutta, 1918. G. Bühler, On the Origin of the Indian Brāhmī Alphabet, p. 17 dates the stūpas of Bharhut and Sanchi in the 3rd century B.C. on palaeographic grounds (with repairs and additional buildings in the 2nd century). V. A. Smith, A History of Fine Art in India and Ceylon, Oxford, 1911, p. 73 ff ascribes the Sanchi stūpas to the period between 150 and 100 B.C. but in his Early History (1924) p. 173, he speaks of them as "buildings of the Aśokan period". See also A. Grünwedel, Buddhistische Kunst in Indien, Berlin, 1900, 22 ff.; A. Foucher, The Beginnings of Buddhist Art, London, 1917, pp. 29 ff., 61 ff., J. H. Marshall in Cambridge History I, 618 ff., 627 ff. Only the earliest portions of the monuments of which little has been preserved go back to Aśoka's time. Cf. Grünwedel, l.c., p. 24; Foucher, l.c., p. 34 and Marshall, l.c., p. 627; Rapson in Cambridge History, I, p. 523.

remnants of the stūpa of Bharhut are at present among the most precious treasures in the Indian Museum at Calcutta, while we are as yet able to admire the magnificent remains of the stūpas of Sanchi in their original place. The railings and gateways of the stūpas of Bharhut and Sanchi are covered with reliefs and inscriptions of inestimable value. The sculptures represent scenes from the life of the Buddha, testifying to an abundantly developed Buddha legends, such as we find in a few of the Pāli Suttas, but more especially in such works as the Nidāna-kathā, Lalitavistara and the Mahāvastu.[1] Many of the reliefs are, however, illustrations to fables and tales, the titles of which are generally mentioned in the inscriptions in the case of the stūpa of Bharhut. These inscriptions prove beyond the shadow of a doubt, that the reliefs depict Jātakas, i.e., "stories from former births of the Buddha," and most of these have also been traced in the monuments of Bharhut and Sanchi votive inscriptions in which monks are given the epithets "bhānaka", "reciter", sutaṃtika, "Sutta reciter"[2], pañcanekāyika, "knower of the five Nikāyas," peṭakin, "knower of the Piṭakas" and the dhammakathika, "preacher of the doctrine."[3]

From all this, it follows that, some time before the second century B.C., there was already a collection of Buddhist texts, which was called "Piṭakas" and was divided into five "Nikāyas" that there were "Suttas" in which the "Dhamma," the religion of Buddha, was preached that some of these Suttas agreed with those contained in our Tipiṭaka, and that "Jātakas" of exactly the same kind as those contained in the Tipiṭaka, already belonged to the stock of Buddhist literature—in short, that, at some period prior to the 2nd century B.C. probably as early as the time of Aśoka or a little later, there was a Buddhist Canon, which if not entirely identical with our Pāli Canon, resembled it very closely.

1. Cf. B. M. Barua in Ind. Hist. Qu. I, 1925, 50 ff., 245 ff.

2. In one of the Sanchi inscriptions a nun, .Sutātikinī, "female reciter of the Sutta," is also mentioned.

3. Such experts for preaching and recitation are also mentioned in the Canon, s. above p. 11. In the days of Buddhaghoṣa there were also reciters of special texts, such as Dighabhāṇakas, Majjhimabhāṇakas etc.

The oldest literary testimony for the existence of the three baskets or a trinity of Piṭakas (piṭakattayam) and of Nikāyas is found of course only in the Milindapañha[1] a work whose first part belongs presumably to the beginning of the first century A. D. But all the rest of the Buddhist literature that is there in addition to the Pāli-Canon, proves that the texts contained in the latter date back to an early time which is not far from the age of the Buddha himself and that in any case they can be considered as the most genuine testimonials of the original teachings of Buddha and of Buddhism in the first two centuries after Buddha's death.

This is proved firstly by the non-canonical Pāli literature to which belongs the dialogues of the Milindapañha, the chronicles of Ceylon Dīpavaṃsa and Mahāvaṃsa and a rich literature following the Tipiṭaka. All these works presuppose the existence of the Tipiṭaka at least as early as the early centuries of the Christian era.[2]

But even the Buddhist Sanskrit literature[3] testifies to the age and the faithfulness of the Pāli transmission. To this literature written partly in good Sanskrit and partly in "mixed

1. Ed. Trenckner, p. 22, where there is a mention of the tepiṭakā, i.e. "Knowers of the three Piṭakas" and of such of these who are pañcanekāyikā and catunekāyikā "Knowers of the five Nikāyas" and the "knowers of the four Nikāyas". There is no reason for regarding this passage as interpolated as does F. O. Schrader. Sanskrit trepiṭaka occurs in an inscription of King Kaniṣka (2nd century A.D.) s. J. Ph. Vogel Ep. Ind. VIII, 176.

2. The entire Pāli literature, canonical as well as non-canonical, is often termed as "south Buddhistic" because it is at present spread and known among the Buddhists of Ceylon, Burma and Siam. But what speaks against the use of this term is the fact that the texts of the Pāli Canon and of the Milindapañha do not contain any kind of relation to the south; they do not reveal even a knowledge of South India and Ceylon, but in all probability they were born in North India. That in some manuscript the expression "tāmraparṇiya-nikāya" occurs once does not entitle us to speak of the Sinhalese Canon, as La Vallée Poussin does (JA s. 9, t. XX, 1902, p. 237). Cf. Rhys Davids in JRAS 1896, 378f.

3. Still more important than the expression "south—Buddhistic" for the Pāli literature is the use of the term "north-Buddhistic" for the Buddhist Sanskrit literature as well as for the Buddhist literatures of Tibet, China and Japan based on it. For by this usage texts of quite different sects, such as those of the Hīnayāna and the Mahāyāna are all clubbed together.

Sanskrit"[1] belong also works of the most diverse nature and of most diverse sects. One of these sects had also its own canon, although of which only recently some fragments have become known to us. It was seen that this canon, although not translated from Pāli, still proves the faithfulness of the Pāli transmission most splendidly. For in spite of numerous deviations in the text and the arrangement there are so many verbatim concurrences between the Sanskrit Canon and the Pāli Canon that one must presume that the same transmission is the basis for both collections. But in the Sanskrit texts of Buddhists of Nepal as well as in the works of the various Buddhist sects[2] known to us only in the Tibetan and Chinese translations we find a basic stock of not only teachings but also of texts that concur with the transmission of the Pāli Canon in all essential respects. The more this Buddhistic literature is explored to us, the more deeply it is compared with the Pāli Canon, the more manifest does it become that Oldenberg is right when he says, "the Pāli Copy, although of course not perfectly infallible, must still be pronounced to be exceedingly good"[3] Moreover, there

1. See Vol. I. p. 41.

2. For comparing the Pāli texts with the Buddhist Sanskrit texts E. Windisch "Māra und Buddha" (ASGW XV, 4) Leipzig 1895 and "Buddhas Geburt" (ASGW XXVI, 2) Leipzig 1908 has rendered meritorious service. Cf. also Oldenberg, ZDMG 52, 654 ff., 662 ff.; Barth RHR t. 41, 1900, p. 166ff La Vallée Poussin and T. W. Rhys Davids JRAS 1903, p. 359 ff., 362; and M. Anesaki in OC XII, Hamburg 1902, p. 61; N. S., VI, 1905, p. 23 ff.; VII, 1906, p. 33 ff., who shows that even Pāli quotations occur in the Mahāyāna texts, E. Waldschmidt, Bruchstucke des Bhikṣuṇī Pratimokṣa der Sarvāstivādins, Leipzig 1926, has come to the conclusion after a careful and unbiased comparison of the bhikṣuni Pratimoksa in the recensions of six different schools, that "the Pāli version of the school of the Theravādins proves itself to the most faithful preserver of an earlier tradition" (p. 187). S. also Oldenberg AR, 13, 1910, 596 ff.; NGGW 1912 171 ff, Barth RHR, t. 41, 1900, 166 ff. (=Oeuvres II 300 ff); La Vallée Poussin and T. W. Rhys Davids. JRAS 1903, 359 ff. A canon similar to the Tipiṭaka is also recognised by the Mahāyāna Buddhists, s. Kern, Manual, p. 3 n 4 and La Vallée Poussin Bouddhisme p. 29 f. Also the Mahāyāna texts presuppose the existence of a canon similar to the Tipiṭaka and this canon is related to them as the Old Testament to the New Testament. (Kern, Manual, p. 3-4).

3. ZDMG 52 p. 673. A. Barth humself RHR 1900, t. 42, p. 57 (cf. Journal des savants 1899, p. 631 and RHR 1900, t. 41, p. 170) admits that the Pāli trans-

is no canon and no Buddhistic text preserved from such an early time as the Pāli Canon committed to writing in the first century B.C., in which not a single word is mentioned of the great Buddhist king Aśoka.[1] In language, style and content the Pāli texts follow most closely the Upaniṣads whereas the Buddhist Sanskrit literature reminds us by far of the Purāṇas. Lastly, the fact, that in these texts committed to writing and transmitted in Ceylon we do not find any references whatsoever to Ceylon, testifies further that we have to see in them "not a Canon of the Buddhists of Ceylon" but a canon of that Buddhist sect in India which has indeed preserved most of the ancient Buddhism and could with some justification describe the teachings as the teachings of the direct disciples of the Buddha.

But the Pāli-texts distinguish themselves from all the other products of the Buddhist literature not only as a source for our knowledge of the Buddhism but also (and this is what is more important for us than anything else) from a purely literary point of view. This might be shown by the following survey of this literature.[2]

---

mission is doubtless supported by other guarantees than the disjointed mass of the writings of the north.

1. Never have the Indians forged so carefully that if Aśoka had been mentioned, they would have eliminated the references in order to create the illusion of antiquity. Cf. Rhys Davids, Buddhist India, p. 174.

2. A complete edition of the holy scriptures of the Tipiṭaka in 39 volumes (in Siamese characters) was got printed in Bangkok by King Culālaṅkaraṇa of Siam while celebrating the silver jubilee of his reign in 1894 and distributed with remarkable generosity to all European and American libraries. Cf. R. Chalmers, JRAS 1898 p. 1 ff. and Cf. Lanman, JAOS, vol XVI, 1895, Proceedings CCXLIV ff. Most of the texts have also been published by the Pāli text Society. Extracts from the Tipiṭaka have been translated by K. E. Neumann Buddhistische Anthologie, Leiden 1892; Henry Clarke Warren, Buddhism in Translations, Cambridge, Mass 1896 (Harvard Oriental Series, vol. 3) Julius Dutoit Des Leben Des Buddha Leipzig 1906; M. Winternitz, Buddhismus in A. Bertholet Religionsgeschichtliches Lesebuch, Tübingen 1908 Einelausgabe 1911, Karl Siedenstücker, Pāli Buddhismus in Ubersetzungen, Breslau 1911, 2nd ed. 1923; H. Oldenberg Reden des Buddha, Munich 1922 E. J. Thomas, Buddhist Scriptures, London 1913 (Wisdom of the East Series), F. L. Woodward, Some Sayings of the Buddha according to the Pāli Canon, Oxford 1925.

The Vinayapiṭaka of the Pāli-Canon

The Buddhists themselves put the Vinayapiṭaka[1] at the head of the Canon and we can follow them without thereby giving expression to the opinion that this is older than the Suttapiṭaka.[2] The following texts belong to the Vinayapiṭaka :—

I The Suttavibhaṅga, consisting of 1. Pārājika and 2. Pācittiya.

II The Khandhakas, consisting of 1. Mahāvagga and 2. Cullavagga.

III The Parivāra or Parivārapāṭha.

Suttavibhaṅga means "explanation of the Suttas", and hereby Sutta[3] the individual sentences or articles of Pāṭimokkha are meant.

The nucleus of the Vinayapiṭaka is the Pāṭimokkha[4], a list of transgressions against the rules of discipline of the order,

---

1. The text of the Vinayapiṭaka has been completely published by H. Oldenberg, London 1879-1883 in five volumes.

2. Kern, Manual, p. 2 and La Vallée Poussin Bouddhisme, E'tudes et Materiaux, p. 27 considers the Vinayapiṭaka to be older. According to R. Otto Franke(JPTS 1908, pp. 8ff., 68 ff., 74)Mahāvagga and Cullavagga of the Vinayapiṭaka would be younger than Dīghanikāya. K. E. Neumann (Foreword to Vol. I and III of Reden Gotamo Buddhos) thinks that from the Suttapiṭaka gradually Vinayapiṭaka and later Abhidhammapiṭaka have partly got separated and partly developed further. In favour of this opinion is the fact that some of the Sūtras deal with Vinaya and some are just scholastic as the Abhidhamma-texts. But it is also certainly possible that the compilation of the Suttapiṭaka and that of the Vinayapiṭaka took place at the same time.

3. Rather in the sense of the old meaning of the word "Sūtra", vol. I, p. 249.

4. S. Dutt, l.c. p. 90 f. thinks that, even etymologically pātimokkha means "bond" in this sense. The PTS Dic., s.v. (also R. C. Childers, Dict. of the Pāli language, s.v.) explains it by pratimokṣya "that which should be made binding", "obligatory", "Obligation" with reference to Jātaka V. p. 25 where it explains saṃgaraṃ pāṭimokhaṃ by a "binding promise". The correct explanation of this phrase is "a promise to be redeemed." Accordingly, pāṭimokkha means "a promise to be redeemed" For other etymologies Rhys Davids and Oldenberg, SBE, Vol. XII, p. xxvii f. (Disburdening, Getting free) Oldenberg Buddha, p. 419n 1, Kern, Manual, p.74n. 5 ("a spiritual cuirass") and R. O. Franke Dīghanikāya, p. 66m. 7. The earliest etymology is the one in the old commentary Mahāvagga II, 3, 4, which was also accepted by Buddhaghoṣa, pāṭimokkha being taken as a derivative of mukhaṃ which is quite impossible.

together with the corresponding atonements. The life of the monk was regulated by this code of rules, which formed the bond[1] holding the community together. Its immense significance as regards the stability of the Buddhist order becomes evident from a speech attributed to Ānanda[2] in which he declares that though Buddha had not appointed any one of his disciples as his successor nor invested him with the supreme authority, the community of monks would continue, because the Sublime One had proclaimed the Sikkhāpada (the ten commandments for the conduct of the monks) and the Pāṭimokkha to the monks. In an oft recurring phrase, it is said that of a good monk that his life is "restrained" by the restraints of the Pāṭimokkha.[3] This code of rules was recited in the form of a confession formulary in solemn conclave of the monks, twice every month, on the new-moon and the full-moon days. After the recital of each chapter — there are eight different kinds of greater and lesser sins, the treatment of which takes up eight different chapters—the conductor of the ceremony would ask whether any one had committed the sin in question : and if this was the case, he had to confess his guilt.[4] This Uposatha ceremony, as it is called, was probably already instituted by Buddha himself, being modelled on ceremonies of a similar character among earlier sects of the ascetics,[5] and the very earliest Buddhist literature must have

1. Majjhimanikāya 108 (Vol. III, p. 9 f.).

2. Pāṭimokkhasaṃvarasaṃvuto, see Dīghanikāya II, 42; XIII, 42, XXVI, 28; cf. Dhammapada 185.

3. According to Dighanikāya XIV, 3, 22-28, at an earlier period (the legend is here dealing with the period of the former Buddha Vipassi) the Buddhist monks appear to have assembled every six years at some large centre, for the recital of the Pāṭimokkha, which then was merely a kind of confession of faith though the expression pāṭimokkhopadesāya is the same as in Majjh. 77 Vol. II p. 8 where there is mention of the fortnightly celebration.

4. At least this was the original idea, according to the wording of the formulas of the Pāṭimokkha. However, even in the Vinayapiṭaka itself the procedure was simplified and toned down, inasmuch as a monk who felt himself guilty of some transgression, had to confess it to one of the brethren *before* the Uposatha ceremony, so that he might be pure when he took his place in the assembly. Cf. Oldenberg, Buddha, pp. 381 f., 418 ff.

5. There may possibly be some historical foundation for the story told in Mahāvagga II, 1, that the heretical Paribbājakas convened assemblies for

included a Pāṭimokkha.[1] Originally it probably contained only 152 rules,[2] but they were extended to 227 at the time of the origin of the Vinayapiṭaka of the Theravādins. Though the text of these 227 rules of the Pāṭimokkha has come down independently in manuscripts, it does not, as such, form a part of the Canon, but it is included in the Suttavibhaṅga, for this last named work is nothing but an ancient commentary on the Pāṭimokkha consisting of 227 rules, a commentary which attained to the honour of being included in the Canon. Suttavibhaṅga means "explanation of the Suttas," and in this case we should take "Sutta"[3] to mean the separate clauses or articles of the Pāṭimokkha. Each Sutta, i.e. each single article, is explained word for word and in an introduction it is related, where and on

---

the recital of their Dhamma on the 14th, 15th and 8th days of each half-month, and that King Bimbisāra proposed to Buddha that similar assemblies should be organised. The Pāli word *Uposatha* is the Sanskrit Upavasatha, which means "fasting". From time immemorial, the Brahmanical Indians observed the new-moon and full-moon days by sacrifices, prayers and fasting. The Uposatha ceremony, as performed in Ceylon at the present day, is described by J. F. Dickson, JRAS 1875 (reprinted in Warren, Buddhism in Translations, p. 405 ff.).

1. This is proved by the fact that we have a Prātimokṣa (Sanskrit for Pāṭimokkha) also in a Sanskrit version, and in one Tibetan and four Chinese versions. Cf. L. Finot and Ed. Huber in JA 1913, s. 11, t. 11, p. 462 ff.; Mahāvyutpatti paragraphs 256-264; Oldenberg, ZDMG, 52, 645 f.; Kern, Manual, 74 f., 85 ff.

2. Aṅguttaranik. I, pp. 236, 230 (III, 83, 1; 87, 1) and Milindapañha, pp. 243, 272 speak of 150 Sikkhāpadas, which probably mean the rules of the Pāṭimokkha. Most likely the figure 150 is only a round number for the 152 rules remaining out of the total of 227 rules, after deducting the 75 sekhiyā dhammā which are merely rules of etiquette. The Prātimokṣa of the Sarvāstivādins gives the number of Pātayāntika dharmāḥ as 90 (in the Pāli 92 Pācittiyā dhammā), and it also gives us a total of 150, excluding the Śaikṣā dharmāḥ. The Sarvāstivādins have 113, the Mūla-Sarvāstivādins 106, the Dharmaguptas 100, Śaikṣā dharmāḥ (corresponding to the 75 sekhiyā dhammā in the Pāli), and the Mahāvyutpatti, para. 256 reads only: sambahulaḥ śaikṣadharmāḥ. Cf. Finot, JA 1913, s.11, t. II, p. 469., S. Dutt, Early Buddhist Monachism, p. 92 f.

3. In the sense of the ancient meaning of the word *Sūtra*, see. Vol. I, p. 249 f. The text of the Pāṭimokkha is published separately and translated by J. F. Dickson, JRAS 1876, p. 62 ff. and translated once again by Rhys Davids and Oldenberg in SBE, Vol. 13, p. 1 ff.

what occasion the Buddha issued the decree in question. The Mahāvibhaṅga consists of eight chapters, corresponding to the eight classes of transgressions against the discipline. By analogy with the Pāṭimokkha for the monks, a similar code was compiled later for the nuns. The Bhikkhunīvibhaṅga, a much shorter work, is a commentary on it.

The Khandhakās, i.e., "sections,"[1] which give the precepts for the various arrangements of the order (Saṅgha) and regulate the entire conduct of the monks and nuns in their daily life, form a kind of continuation and supplement of the Suttavibhaṅga. The ten sections of the Mahāvagga, i.e., the "great section," contain the special precepts for admission into the order, for the Uposatha celebrations, for life during the rainy season and for the Pavāraṇā celebration taking place at the end of the rainy season, and further, the rules for the wearing of shoes, facilities for seats and vehicles, medicine and clothing of the monks, and finally for the regulation of the legal conditions and the legal procedure within the order, especially in the case of schisms. The first nine sections of the Cullavagga, i.e. the "lesser section," deal with the disciplinary methods in lesser matters, with various atonements and penances, the settlement of disputes, the daily life of the monks, dwellings and furnishing of dwellings, the duties of monks towards one another and the exclusion from the Pāṭimokkha ceremony. Section X of the Cullavagga deals with the duties of the nuns. In the same way as the Pāṭimokkha underlies the Suttavibhaṅga, there are also, underlying the acts and ceremonies prescribed in the Khandakas, old formulae, the so-called Kammavācā, i.e., "words for the acts". These do not form a part of the Tipiṭaka any more than the Pāṭimokkha does[2] but are merely included in the Vedic

1. Translated into English by Rhys Davids and Oldenberg in SBE, vols. XIII, XVII and XX.

2. Upasampadā-Kammavācā, formularies for admission into the Order. These were first published by F. Spiegel, (Kammavākya, liber de officils sacerdotum Buddhicorum, Bonnae ad. Rh. 1841), with Latin translation, then by J. F. Dickson (JRAS 1875, p. 1 ff.) with English translation. The last-mentioned also describes the ceremony of admission, as it is still performed today in Ceylon. Other Kammavācā have been published and translated by

Brāhmaṇas and Sūtras. Sections XI and XII, in which the story of the first two councils of Rājagaha and Vesālī[1] is told, are no doubt later additions, and form a kind of appendix to the Cullavagga. As this appendix too only deals with the history of the order, we can say that the one and only subject of the books of the Vinayapiṭaka is the monastic community, or the Order (Saṅgha).

The Pāṭimokkha already indicates a fairly complicated organisation of the community.[2] The Khandakas presuppose a still more advanced organisation. We are struck by the far-reaching liberality, if not laxity, in the rules for monastic life. According to the strict regulation the monk is to live only on what he obtains by begging, but he is also allowed to accept invitations to meals. He is to clothe himself in cast-off rags, but he may also wear garments of linen, cotton and even silk. He is to live at the foot of a tree, but he may also seek a more comfortable lodging in houses, huts or caves. Urine is to be his sole medicament, but he may also take butter, oil and honey. He may even eat fish, as long as the fish have not been killed for him.[3] All this indicates that there must have been a fairly long development of the discipline of the community prior to the final compilation of the Vinayapiṭaka, and that the bulk of the rules originated, not all at once, but gradually. On the other hand, it has been shown that many of the regulations of the order of the community are identical with those which were in vogue among other sects of ascetics before Buddha.[4] Nevertheless, all the rules and regulations of the Vinaya are attributed to Buddha himself; for just as in the Suttavibhaṅga, the rules

O. Frankfurter, Handbook of Pāli, London, 1883, Herbert Baynes (JRAS 1892, p. 53 ff.; cf. also p. 380), Sarat Candra Das in JASB 63, Part I, 1894, p. 20 ff. and G. L. M. Clauson (JPTS, 1906-1907, pp. 1-7).

1. See above p. 6 ff. The fact that the last two books were added later, also appears from the title Cullavagga, "lesser section," which would only be justified if this work, like the Mahāvagga, were composed of ten parts only. Cf. Rhys Davids and Oldenberg in SBE, Vol. 13, p. xxi, n.3.

2. Cf. E. Waldschmidt "Bruchstücke des Bhikṣuṇi-Prātimokṣa der Sarvāstivādins", p. 3 f.

3. Mahāvagga, I, 30; Cullavagga, VII, 3, 14 f.

4. S. Dutt, Early Buddhist Monachism, pp. 16, 28, 37.

and regulations in the Khandakas too, are introduced by narratives recording when and on what occasion they were declared by Buddha. As regards style too, the stories in the Khandakas agree with those in the Suttavibhaṅga to so great an extent that we are bound to a sume that they belong approximately to the same time.[1] In a few cases these stories may possibly have reference to actual events. In the majority of cases, however, they were probably invented ad hoc. On the whole, they are stereotyped, and of little value as literature.

But fortunately this does not apply to all of them. Even the early chapters of the Mahāvagga[2] contain one of the oldest fragments of a Buddha-legend. In a beautiful, archaic language it is narrated here, how Gotama Buddha attained the enlightenment (Bodhi), how he resolved to proclaim his doctrine and how he acquired his early disciples. Here for example the legend of the noble youth Yasa is narrated, who grows in a life full of luxury, spends the nights in the company of a host of women who sing and dance, but wakes up once in the midst of night and catches sight of the beautiful women in various ugly postures, upon which he is seized with disgust and vexation at the pleasures of this world; he flees from the life of pleasure, rushes to the Buddha and becomes a monk. The later Buddha-legend narrates this story about Prince Siddhārtha, the later Buddha himself. A peculiar cultural picture is revealed by the story of the conversion of a host of young men who go out with their wives to enjoy themselves; one of them, who has no wife, takes a prostitute with him; this prostitute steals the valuable things of the men and runs away. While giving chase to her they come upon the Buddha and ask him whether he has not seen a women. The Buddha asks, whether it would not be better for them to seek themselves instead of a woman and seizes the opportunity to preach his doctrine to them, whereupon they all become monks. There are also plenty of stories of miracles in which snake-kings and gods play a role. The most beautiful of all these

1. If the rule dealt with in the Khandhakas is the same as the one dealt with in the Suttavibhaṅga, then the introductory story is also the same. Cf. Oldenberg, Vinayapiṭaka, Introd. p. xxii f.

2. I, 1—24, SBE, Vol. 13, p. 73 ff.

stories of conversion is however that of the conversion of the two friends Sariputta and Moggallana, who later belonged to the favourite disciples of the Buddha.[1] Also the early sermons of the Buddha—for example the "Sermon of Benares" and the "Fire-Sermon"—are included in this old report.

In a later part of the Mahâvagga[2] the story is narrated as to how Buddha visits his hometown and takes his son Rāhula into his order. Then we find in the Cullavagga the stories of the rich merchant Anāthapiṇḍaka who gifts his park to the order; of Devadatta, the enemy and rival of the Buddha who causes the first schism in the community; of the founding of the nuns' order for which Buddha gives his consent only unwillingly, on being repeatedly requested and pressed by his foster-mother Mahāpajā-pati, who finds a noble supporter in Ānanda, the disciple, and many similar stories.[3]

Even among those introductory stories which have been presumably invented ad hoc and have neither historical nor legendary value, we find some beautiful and valuable pieces. One story of this kind that is touching in its simplicity is the following one :

In those days one of the monks was once suffering from a severe attack of colic and lying in his own refuse. At that time the Lord was just on his rounds through the bedrooms accompanied by the revered Ānanda and came to the room where that monk was lying. Then the Lord saw this monk lying in his own refuse and after seeing him he came near him and spoke thus : "What is troubling you, O monk ?" "I am having colic, my Lord". "Do you have a monk to nurse you ?" "No, my Lord, I am not of any use to the monks, therefore, my Lord, they do not nurse me." Then the Lord spoke to the revered Ānanda : "Go, Ānanda, fetch water and let us bathe this monk

1. Mahâvagga I, 7 f.; 14; 15 ff.; 23 f. SBE, Vol. 13, pp. 102 ff., 116 ff., 144 ff. All these stories end with the admission of the converted people into the order. They, therefore, constitute a quite natural introduction to the part on the admission to the order.

2. I, 54; SBE, Vol. 13, p. 207 ff.

3. Cullavagga VI, 4, 9; VII, 2-4, X, 1 f.; SBE, Vol. 20, pp. 187 ff., 233 ff.. 320 ff.

here." "Yes, my Lord," said the revered Ānanda agreeing with the Lord and fetched water. And the Lord poured the water on the monk and the revered Ānanda washed him well; the Lord held him by his head and the Revered Ānanda by the feet, and they lifted him and laid him on a bed. And then, on this occasion and by reason of this, the Lord called for a meeting of the monks' order and put the monks the question : "Is here, O monks, in such and such room a monk ill ?" "Yes, O Lord." "What is troubling that monk, O monks ?" "He has colic, O Lord." "Has he got, O monks, anyone to nurse him ?" "No, Lord." "Why don't the monks nurse him ?" "This monk is not of any use to them, therefore, they do not nurse him." "You have, O monks, neither mother nor father, who could nurse you. If you, O monks, do not nurse one another, then who shall nurse you ? Whoever would nurse me, O you monks, shall nurse the sick."[1]

Other stories of this kind are valuable to us for they give us an insight into the everyday life of ancient Indians[2] : e.g. when we are told how the parents of the boy Upāli discuss what they should want the boy to become, how they consider that through writing he could get sore fingers, through reckoning breast pain and through painting he could spoil his eyes and therefore they decide to let him become a monk because it is the most comfortable way to earn one's bread.[3] Not only interesting from the point of view of the history of culture, but also full of delicious humour are the stories about the doctor Jīvaka,[4] of which at least a very small extract may be given here :

1. However much this passage (Mahāvagga VIII, 26) (transl. by Rhys Davids and Oldenberg in SBE, vol. 17, p. 240 f.) may remind us of Matth. 25, 40 ("Inasmuch as ye have done it unto one of the least of these my brethren, ye have done it unto me."), still, the situation is quite different and the similarity is certainly only by chance.

2. In this respect the Vinayapiṭaka constitutes a valuable supplement to the Brahminic Gṛhyasūtras. See Vol. I, p. 253 ff. Also for our knowledge of justice and moral in ancient India some chapters are not unimportant (e.g. for the detailed lists of thefts, sexual offences and crimes of all kinds).

3. Mahāvagga I, 49.

4. Mahāvagga VIII, 1. The stories end with Jīvaka making a gift of clothes to Buddha. Hence they constitute the introduction to the chapter on

The town of Rājagaha vies with the great city of Vesālī in fame and splendour. The magnificence of Vesālī is due in no small measure to the famous courtesan Ambapālī, who wants 50 gold coins for one night. In order to raise Rājagaha also to this level, on the orders of the king the beautiful and educated Sālavatī is employed as a courtesan and she demands a hundred gold coins for a night. She becomes pregnant but in view of her profession she conceals her pregnancy and after giving birth to a child, she abandons it in a small basket. The child is found by Prince Abhaya who orders it to be brought up and gives it the name "Jīvaka".

Jīvaka grows up and goes to a famous doctor in Takkasilā (Taxila) to study. After learning for seven years he appears for his "examination". This consists in this that his teacher gives him a spade and asks him to bring all the plants in the country around Takkasilā which cannot be used as medicinal plants. Jīvaka comes back and explains that he could not find even one such plant far and wide. The teacher is satisfied, and, giving him some money for travelling he permits him to leave.

Soon all the money is spent, and in order to earn something, he reports himself as a doctor in a town where he hears that the wife of a rich merchant is seriously ill. Jīvaka puts some melted butter into her nose. This passes into her mouth and she spits it out and then she asks her servant to collect and preserve it. Jīvaka is already worried about his fee because he considers the woman to be greedy. The woman, however, pacifies him; she is simply a prudent housewife, —the melted butter can be used by the servants as grease or for the lights. She recovers and rewards the doctor with 4,000 gold coins; also her son, her daughter-in-law and her husband give him 4,000 gold coins each; her husband gives him moreover a man and a woman as slaves and coach and horses.

So he returns to Rājagaha where he hands over to Prince Abhaya the money he had earned as payment for having brought him up. He, however, does not accept it, but wishes

---

the dress of the monks. The stories of Āmrapāli (Ambapāli) and Jīvaka also occur in the Chinese Tipiṭaka; See Ed. Chavannes "Cinq Cents Contes, III", p. 325 ff.

that Jīvaka settle down in Rājagaha. After curing the old king Bimbisāra of a very bad disease he becomes the personal doctor to the king and performs many peculiar cures. Once a big businessman of Rājagaha falls seriously ill. All doctors have given up their hopes. Then the king permits his personal doctor treat the businessman. Jīvaka fixes at first a fee of a hundred thousand gold coins for himself and an equal amount for the king, then he asks him whether he will be in a position to lie on one side for seven months and then on the other side for 7 months and finally on his back for 7 months quietly without moving. The patient answers in the affirmative, whereupon the doctor ties him to the bed, cuts open the skin of his head, removes two worms—it was these worms that had threatened the life of the merchant—and stitches the wound up. The patient is, however, not in a position to lie in each posture for seven months but he can manage it only for seven *days*. After thrice seven days, however, he is healthy. Now Jīvaka explains that he has spoken of seven months because otherwise the patient would not have managed to lie quiet even for seven days.

Many more stories are told about the artfulness and skilfulness of Jīvaka the doctor,[1] who moreover gave medical treatment to the Buddha and was a great friend of the order.

This is not the only example which shows that the authors or compilers of the Vinayapiṭaka sometimes become tired of dullness and sometimes interrupted the enumeration of prohibitions and ordinances with stories in a lighter vein. Thus Buddha narrates the following fable as introduction to the rules on giving preference to age among the monks.[2]

"There stood once upon a time, O monks, on a mountain slope of the Himalayas, a great fig tree. Under this fig-tree three friends, a partridge, a monkey and an elephant, took their

1. He was considered as an authority on child-medicine and was called the "paediatrician". Cf. Jolly, Medicin (in Grundri B III, 10), p. 68. Even later the Buddhists were very much engaged in the study of the science of medicine. (Jolly, ibid, p. 8 and 15 f.).

2. Cullavagge VI, 6, 3. Translated by Rhys Davids and Oldenberg in SBE, Vol. 20, p. 193 f.

residence. But they lived there without showing reverence or obedience to one another and without in any way regulating their common life. Then they once thought in the following way : "Let us just see, who of us is the oldest by birth. To him we will show respect, reverence, him we will honour and adore and we will follow his exhortations." Therefore, the partridge and the monkey asked the elephant : "Friend, how far back can you remember ?"

"As I was young, O friends, I strode over the tree, with this fig tree between my legs and the highest branch just reached upto my belly. Thus far, O friends, can I recall to my memory from the past."

Then the partridge and the elephant asked the monkey : "How far back, O friend, can you remember ?"

"As I was young, O friends, I sat down on the ground and ate the highest branch of this fig tree. Thus far, O friends, can I recall to my memory from the past."

Then the monkey and the elephant asked the partridge, "How far back, O friend, can you remember ?"

"There, O friends, in that clearing over there, stood a big fig-tree of which I ate a fruit and eased myself here on this place here and from the seed in the excrement is this fig-tree born. Thus, my friends, I am the oldest by birth."

Then the monkey and the elephant said to the partridge, "Yes, friend, you are the oldest of us by birth, so we will show you respect and reverence, we will adore you and follow your exhortations".

However, serious stories of purest, really Buddhistic moral are also inserted sometimes; thus for example, the touching tale of Prince Longlive who stakes everything to revenge the murder of his parents, but at the moment when the murderer, King Brahmadatta, falls into his hands, puts back his drawn out sword in the sheath and renounces the idea of revenge.[1] Finally we

1. Mahāvagga, X, 2, 3-20; SBE, Vol. 17, p. 293 ff.

Extracted and reproduced by Oldenberg, Buddha, p. 345 ff. However, it is hardly probable (as Copleston, Buddhism, p. 103, note, presumes) that the legend is influenced by the Biblical story of David and Saul (I Sam. 24).

find in the Vinayapiṭaka also the similes which play a big role in the sermons and sayings. Thus for example in the Cullavagga (IX, 1, 3 f.) in a carefully constructed simile eight properties of the ocean are compared with eight characteristics of the Buddhistic doctrine and orderly discipline. Here we come across the oft-quoted sentence :

"Just as, O monks, the great ocean has only one taste, the taste of salt, so also, O monks, has this religion and orderly discipline only one taste, the taste of redemption."

The Vinayapiṭaka texts show a certain resemblance with the Vedic Brāhmaṇas. In both we find "rule" (vidhi) and "explanation of the meaning" (arthavāda) by the side of one another and to the latter group belong in both, the narrative poems which stand out distinctly like oases in the desert of the religious technics.[1]

An insignificant, and much later product, perhaps only the work of a Singhalese monk[2] is the Parivāra, the last book of the Vinayapiṭaka. These are 19 smaller texts, catechisms, Indices, appendices, lists and similar things, just of the sort of the Anukramaṇis and Pariśiṣṭas appended to the Veda and the Vedāṅga texts. They have the form of questions and answers in common with the texts of Abhidhammapiṭaka which originated perhaps at about the same time.

The Suttapiṭaka of the Pāli-Canon

1. *Speeches and Dialogues*

Just as the Vinayapiṭaka is our best source for the Saṅgha, i.e., the institutions of ancient Buddhist order, and the life of the monks, so also is the Suttapiṭaka our most reliable source for the Dhamma, i.e. the religion of the Buddha and of his early disciples. But in the Suttapiṭaka we find also—what is most important for us here—in the prose of the dialogues and stories as well as in the sayings and songs the most significant literary works that Buddhism has produced.

1. Cf. Vol. I, p. 187 and 193.
2. SBE XIII, p. XXIV.

The Suttapiṭaka consists of five Nikāyas or "collections",[1] namely: I Dīghanikāya, II Majjhimanikāya, III Saṃyuttanikāya, IV Aṅguttaranikāya and V Khuddakanikāya. To the last one belong the following texts : 1. Khuddakapāṭha 2. Dhammapada 3. Udāna 4. Itivuttaka 5. Suttanipāta 6. Vimānavatthu 7. Petavatthu 8. Theragāthā 9. Therīgathā 10. Jātaka 11. Niddesa 12. Paṭisambhidāmagga 13. Apadāna 14. Buddhavaṃsa and 15. Cariyāpiṭaka.

The first four Nikāyas or "collections" have for their contents the Suttas[2] or "doctrinary lectures." These are either speeches of the Buddha (sometimes also of one of his disciples), which are preceded only by a short introduction, in which is narrated where and on what occasion the Buddha has delivered the speech,[3] or they are dialogues with framework narratives (Itihāsa-saṃvāda, Itihāsa dialogues) of the kind which we have already met with in the Upaniṣads and in the Mahābhārata. But the form of the Suttas is, however, as a rule prose. Only here and there in some Suttas the prose is interrupted by verses (Gāthās) which are partly quotations and partly verse insertions such as were popular at all times in Indian literature at specially important places for enhancing the prose.[4]

I. The Dīghanikāya, "the collection of long doctrinary

1. But according to Buddhaghoṣa (Sumaṅgalavilāsini, p. 22 f.) the whole Tipiṭaka (not the Suttapiṭaka) is divided into 5 Nikāyas and he reckons Vinayapiṭaka and Abhidhammapiṭaka with the Khuddakanikāya. Similarly Gandhavaṃsa (JPTS 1886, p. 57).

2. For Sutta the expression Suttanta is also used often.

3. Hence the typical beginning of every Sutta with the words: "Thus have I heard (evam me sutam) once the Lord was staying in etc. (for example in Sāvatthi in the garden of Anāthapiṇḍaka").

4. If for example, stanzas are introduced with the words, "Here the following is said, " (tatth' etam vuccati) then they can be recognised as quotations (e.g. in Dīghanikāya 30). If on the other hand, important words in verse-form are quoted as Buddha's words and these verses are introduced by sentences like, "This spoke the Master" or "The Lord addressed him in the following verses" (for example Dīghanikāya 31; Majjhimanikāya 7, vol. I, p. 39, 34) then they are verse insertions which belong to the author of the Sutta himself, at least in general because in ancient India they never made a sharp distinction between one's own literary product and that of others.

lectures"[1] consists of 34 long Suttas, of which each individual one treats intensively some particular point or points of the doctrine and could be as well considered as an independent work. The whole work is divided into three books, which differ in contents and character, but all of which contain earlier and later strata of tradition.[2] The earliest stratum is represented principally in the first book, and the later one, mainly in the third book, whilst the second book is composed of the longest Suttas some of which have grown into their present bulk owing to interpolations.[3]

In form too, the Suttas in Book I and a number of Suttas in Books II and III are written entirely in prose, there are many Suttas in Books II and III written in a mixture of prose and verse, a form so popular in India. The verses are either ballad verses (as in Nos. 16, 18, 19, 21) or momentous utterances (as in Nos. 16, 17). Elsewhere we find (as in Nos. 30, 31) a constant interchange between prose and gāthās, such as we shall frequently come across in Sanskrit and half Sanskrit Buddhist texts. Suttas Nos. 20 and 32 are almost entirely in verse.

The majority of Suttas in Book I deal with ethical questions, more especially with virtue (sīla), concentration (samādhi) and insight (paññā) which lead to the state of an arhat, the ideal of the devout life. The ethical doctrines of the Buddha are frequently set up controversially as against the teachings of the Brāhamaṇas and of other masters.

The very first Sutta, the Brahmajālasutta, the "Discourse on the Brahman net" is of the greatest significance not only for the Buddhist religion but also for the whole religious life and

1. Edited by T. W. and C. A. F. Rhys Davids and J. E. Carpenter, London PTS, vol. I 1890, Vol. II, 1903, Vol. III, 1911. The Suttas 1-25 have been translated by T. W. Rhys Davids, Dialogues of the Buddha I-III SBB vols. II-IV, London 1899 and 1910 and 1921 into German by K. E. Neumann, Munich 1907-1918. The Suttas 13, 16 and 17 have already been translated by Rhys Davids in SBE Vol. XI, p. 158 ff., 235 ff. into German by R. O. Franke, Göttingen 1913, and P. Dhalke "Suttapiṭaka" II, Berlin 1920.

2. Cf. P. V. Bapat in Ann. Bh. Inst. VIII, 1926, p. 1 ff.

3. Book I is called Silakkhandhavagga after its contents (it treats of sīla, "virtue"). Book II is called Mahāvagga after its bulk (it contains mostly Suttas, the titles of which begin with mahā "great"). Book III is called Pāṭikavagga i.e. "the section beginning with the Pāṭika-Sutta".

thinking in ancient India.[1] After laying down the rules for the moral conduct of his disciples the Buddha enumerates in long lists all kinds of occupations, entertainments, ways of living and thinking of the Brahmins and the ascetics, from which the Buddhist monks should keep aloof. There are Brahmins and ascetics who amass riches, those who find pleasure in dances, music performances, dramas and games of all kinds — the student of culture finds here an interesting enumeration of the popular sources of pleasure — others who indulge in all possible kinds of luxury, yet others who earn their livelihood through sacrifice, soothsaying and magic — we find here a list which is highly instructive for the students of ethnology — and finally many who dedicate themselves to all kinds of speculations on being and not-being, on the beginning and end of the world, on the soul, its essence and its story — no less than 62 different philosophical views are enumerated here. From all these things the disciple of the Buddha must keep aloof. Just as a skilled fisherman, casting his net with fine meshes in a pond can catch all fishes, big and small, so the Buddha can catch in the Brahman net all sophists and philosophers and show that their teachings and speculations are worthless and only obstruct the true salvation. Also the second Sutta, the Sāmaññaphalasutta, "the lecture on the reward for asceticism", is a valuable testimony to the way of living and thinking in India at the time of the Buddha; because here we get to know the views of a whole range of eminent non-Buddhistic preachers and founders of sects. A most vivid description of the visit of King Ajātaśatru to Buddha forms the introduction to this dialogue.[2] For the History of the Indian Caste System and for the view of the Buddha on the problem of caste, the Ambaṭṭhasutta (No. 3) is of a specially great significance. Through

1. These are dealt with by Rhys Davids in "Buddhism, American lectures" p. 30 ff. and F. O. Schrader, "Über den Stand der indischen Philosophie zur Zeit Mahāviras und Buddhas, Strassburg, 1902, p. 8 ff. At the conclusion the Sūtta calls itself Veyyākaraṇa ("commentary", "exposition").

2. According to Oldenberg, Zur Geschichte der altindischen Prosa AGGW XVI, 6, 1917, p. 40 note this introduction of the Yājñavalkya dialogue in the Bṛhadāraṇyaka Upaniṣad IV, 1. However, in spite of the similarity, this seems doubtful.

allusions to the history of the House of the Śākyas and to the Ṛṣi Kṛṣṇa (Kaṇha) the Sutta is of great interest to the history of the saga, perhaps even to history as such. Greatly instructive for the relationship between the old and the new religion, the Brahminism and the Buddhism, are the Suttas No. 5, Kūṭadantasutta, "the lecture on the sharp tooth[1] of the Brāmaṇas" and No. 13, Tevijjasutta, "the lecture on the knowers of the three Vedas" in which we find, (but not at all wounding) the irony with which the Brahminic cult with its bloody sacrifices and the endeavour of the Veda-knower to the union with the Brahman is mocked at; and they are contrasted with Buddhist "sacrifice" and ideals of life. The basic teaching of Buddhistic philosophy of the interlinking of causes is treated in No. 15, the Mahānidānasutta, "the great instructive lecture on the causes." One of the most important duties of the Buddhist monk is "mindfulness" The four kinds of mindfulness are treated in No. 22, the Mahasatipaṭṭhāna Sutta, "the great discourse on the various kinds of mindfulness." It also deals with the fundamental doctrines of Buddhism and closes with a detailed presentation of the "four noble truths."[2]

For Buddhistic ethics according to its popular side is No. 29 the Sigālavādasutta, "the instructive lecture : the exhortation of Sigāla" in which all the domestic and social duties of the Buddhist lay followers are described exhaustively, one of the most important texts in the Pāli Canon.

But the Sutta of the Dīghanikāya that is most significant in every respect is No. 16, the Mahāparinibbānasutta, "the great lecture on the complete Nirvāṇa"[3] (of the Buddha) that in its

1. In this Sutta as in No. 17 (Mahā-Sudassana-Sutta) we find the Jātaka type.

2. This conclusion is absent in the Satipaṭṭhāṇa-Sutta of the Majjhimanikāya (No. 10) F. Heiler, Die buddhistische Versenkung 2nd Ed., München 1923, p. 13, calls this Sutta "the exercise manual of the Buddhist monk".

3. Cf. R. C. Childers, "The Whole Duty of the Buddhist Layman," Ind. Ant. 12m, 1883, p. 23 ff.; T. W. Rhys Davids, "Der Buddhismus"(SPCK) p. 143 ff. and Mrs. Rhys Davids SBB Vol. IV, p. 168 ff.

form and content essentially differs from all the other Suttas. It is neither a dialogue nor a speech on any one or more main points of the teaching, but it is a running account of the last days, the last speeches and statements and the death of Buddha. The oldest parts of this extensive account belong certainly to the oldest stock of the Tipiṭaka and to the earliest beginnings of poetical treatment of the life of Buddha. It is particularly noteworthy that the Pāli Canon does not contain any Buddha-biography although the beginnings of such a biography are found partly in the Vinayapiṭaka[1] and partly in the Suttapiṭaka. That precisely the memory of the last days of the master and of his last speeches got firmly fixed in the minds of his disciples and that they were preserved and transmitted by them with faithfulness, full of love, is fully understandable. And we do not hesitate to see the early beginnings of a Buddha biography in the earliest parts of this sutta. But it is only a few pieces in the Mahāparinibbānasutta which can be considered really old and original. For the Sutta is by no means a unitary work but it is composed of pieces which belong to different ages. Even at a very early period—probably soon after the death of Buddha—there must have been a shorter "Sutta of the complete Nirvāṇa (of Buddha)" which in course of time swelled more and more through interpolations and additions, until it has become more "the great Sutta of the complete Nirvāṇa" that we find now in our Pāli Canon. Old and original are certainly such passages as those in the second section where the story is told of Buddha's first illness, which befell him at Belua and which he fought with the power of his will where he assures Ānanda that he is not one of those preachers "with a closed fist" who keep back something for themselves but that he has proclaimed the whole truth and where he turns down the idea that he ever wanted to proclaim himself a leader of the community. The order was never

1. Translated by Rhys Davids SBE Vol. II and SBB Vol. II, 78 ff. into German by J. Dutoit, "Leben des Buddha", p. 221 ff., K. E. Neumann, München 1911 R. O. Franke, "Dīghanikāya" 179 ff., H. Beckh, Stuttgart, 1925. Extracts from it have been translated by all books on Buddhism. Cf. also F. Müller, JRAS 1913, 1087 ff.; H. Kern OZ II 1913-14, 229 f.; P. Oltramare in RHR 66, 1912, 118 ff., Eliot I, 161 ff.

dependent on him and would, therefore, be not "without a leader" even after his demise, when it would be led only by the religion proclaimed by him. "Therefore, Ānanda, be lights unto yourselves ! Be your own refuge ! Hold on to religion as your lights, fast as to your refuge !" And equally old and original is certainly also the text in the fifth part where we read how Ānanda cannot contain himself any longer in his grief over the impending demise of the Master, he goes out and stands weeping, leaning against a door post, whereupon the Buddha summons him and says to him intrinsically good words of consolation, recognising his affectionate loyalty to him. Also the verses strewn all over the Sutta bear the stamp of very great antiquity. They contain in some parts statements of the Buddha and his disciples and in some parts they extol the most important moments of the story very impressively.[1] Whereas at all these places the Buddha speaks entirely as man to man, at other places of the same text we see him as a demigod or master magician performing miracles; indeed he boasts of his miraculous power, by virtue of which, if only he wished, he could extend his life till the end of a world epoque, and he reproaches Ānanda for not understanding the sign at the proper moment and not requesting him to continue his life (III, 34-47). Buddha's decision to die is the cause of an earthquake and he takes this opportunity to enumerate the eight causes of an earthquake and to follow it up at once by the enumeration of other things which are also likewise eight in number (III, 11-33). Here it is a case of additions and interpolations by epigones who do not have any more even the last trace of the spirit that animated the authors of the old report. In most cases it is also not difficult to prove the sources from which the additions have flowed out. For, large portions of the Sutta they constitute almost the entire Sutta, are found again in other texts of the Tipiṭaka and issue out from there evidently.[2] Nevertheless all

1. Copleston (Buddhism, pp. 46, 53) thinks that an older epic poem from which these stanzas are taken, are the basis for our Sutta. But we find in these verses rather the first beginnings of a poetic treatment of the life of Buddha (namely in the form of spiritual ballads).

2. But in some cases, also the Mahāparinibbānasutta is the source from which passages have gone to one another. The parallel texts have been

interpolations and additions have not been able to obliterate the character of this text which more than any other text of the Tipiṭaka reminds one of Christian gospels.[1]

It is evident that it was a favourite practice to utilise this famous and popular Sutta for inserting especially important texts into it, with a view to enhance their prestige by this means; thus for instance, also the Dhammādasa, or "mirror of religion," the solemn confession of faith in the Buddha, the doctrine and the community was inserted.[2]

The final editing of the Mahāparinibbānasutta, however, can have taken place at a comparatively later date. At one place, of course there is mention of the transmission and authority of the Suttas and the Vinaya texts.[3] And in the concluding part of the Sutta mention is already made even of Buddha relics[4] and the erection of Stūpas, i.e. the same Buddha whom we encounter as a simple human being and preacher even in the beautiful dialogue with Ānanda, appears here already as the object of a cult as he has been established to have become one through the monuments only after the time of Aśoka.

---

compiled by Rhys Davids in "Dialogues of the Buddha II," p. 72. Only a close comparison of the Pāli text with the Sanskrit texts which remnants of a Parinirvāṇasūtra have preserved for us and with the Tibetan and Chinese translations might show what of the Sutta is old and genuine. Cf. Windisch, "Māra und Buddha", p. 33 ff. Oldenberg ZDMG 52, 1898, p. 628, J.S. Speyer ZDMG 53, 1899, p. 121 ff.; J. Edkins JRAS 1881 m p. 66 ff. For the Chinese translations of the Mahā-Parinirvāṇa Sutras see Carlo Puini in GSAI 21, 1908, 59 ff., 22. 1909 p. 1 ff. For a comparative study of the different Parinirvāṇa texts see M. Przyluski in JA 1918-20 s. II, t. XI, 485 ff.; XII, 401 ff; XV, 5 ff.

1. Cf. Oldenberg "Literatur des alten Indien", p. 94 f.

2. II, 8-10, Cf. Saṃyuttanikāya 55, 8 (Vol. V, p. 357) and Theragāthā 395. H. Baynes has published an enlarged form of the Dhammādasa, as it is still recited at the present day at the Pāṭimokkha (WZKM 10, 1896, 242 ff.)

3. IV, 7-11, Digha Vol. II, p. 123 ff.; Cf. Aṅguttara-Nikāya, IV, 180 (Vol. II, 167 ff.) and Copleston, "Buddhism" p. 45. In IV, 10 f. (Vol. II, p.125) the knowers of the Mātikās (page 12 Note 2 above) are also mentioned.

4. Cf. J. Fleet JRAS 1906, 657 ff., who (ib. 667 ff.) tries to prove that the Sutta could not have been composed before 375 B.C. The final editing must have taken place much later.

Also No. 14, the Mahāpadānasutta or "the big discourse on the miracles (of the Buddha)" belongs to a very late period. In this "big discourse" the dogma of the six Buddhas[1] who were the predecessors of Gotama Buddha and the entire legend of the Buddha provided with numerous miracles especially the miracles of the conception and birth, are presupposed.[2]

The Lakkhaṇa Sutta (No. 30) also belongs to the same stratum of tradition. This Sutta enumerates the 32 signs of a "great man" the man who gave these physical marks must become either a ruler of the world or a saviour of the world, a Buddha. There is no doubt that Buddha, like the majority of his contemporaries, believed that by continued meditation one could attain to all sorts of supernatural powers (siddhis) and become a kind of superman. However, he expressly declared it unworthy of a monk and dangerous for the doctrine, to attempt to exert influence over a layman by means of magic of this nature, rather than by means of teaching and persuasion, and the "miracle of instruction".[3] For this reason it is certain that the main portion of the Paṭika Sutta (No. 24) in which Buddha not only takes part in a miracle working competition with other ascetics, but also boasts grandiloquently of his marvellous powers, represents a later stage of the tradition. As a matter of fact, this Sutta is a very miserable compilation in which only the beginning is ancient and all the rest is an inferior admixture.[4]

1. It is perhaps more than mere coincidence that, in this Sutta, Buddha Vipassi's favourite pupil is named Aśoka.

2. There is absolutely no foundation for the supposition of L. A. Waddell (JRAS, 1914, 661 ff.) that the title of the Sutta was originally Mahā-Padhāna-Sutta, "Sutta of the highest being". However, he may be right in assuming that this Sutta and the Lalitavistara can be traced back to a common source, and that the Sutta corresponds to the tradition of about the 3rd to the 1st century B.C.

3. Kevadha Sutta (No. 11) Vol. I, p. 214. Similarly in No. 28 (Vol. III, p. 112 f.). In the Vinayapiṭaka (Culia V, 8, s) it is declared as a Dukkata offence for a monk to perform miracles before layman for the sake of worldly gain. A monk who does this, is compared to a woman who displays her charms for money.

4. Cf. Friedrich Weller in Asia Major I, p. 620 ff.; "Der Chinesische Dharmasaṇgraha, Mit einem Anhang über das Lakkhaṇa suttanta des Dīghanikāya", Leipzig 1923.

Many Suttas are mythological (Nos. 17-21) they take us into the world of the gods and are meant to prove that even the gods owe their heavenly splendour to the fact that in an earlier birth they have been good Buddhists.[1] Most interesting of all is No. 21, the Sakkapanhasutta "the Sutta contains the questions of Sakka". Sakka is the king of gods, Indra, whose weapon is the thunderbolt. To the ancient Buddhists it must have appeared just as edifying as it appears grotesque to us, how the king of gods hardly dares approach the serene Buddha, how he sends before him one of his Gandharvas, the heavenly musicians in order to put the wiseman in a favourable mood—which is achieved by the Gandharva in a very strange manner by means of a love song,[2] how the God is received by Buddha kindly but at the same time condescendingly and now learns from the lips of the Exalted One the Great truth that the highest goals can be reached only through the religion of the Buddha and how at last, after the Master has answered all his questions, the king of the gods breaks out in an eulogy of the Exalted One. One of the best dialogues between Pāyāsi, the incredulous chieftain denying soul and the other world, and the monk Kumāra Kassapa. While otherwise in the "dialogue" of the Suttapiṭaka the occasional interrupter interrupts the main speaker who is usually Buddha himself mostly with only words of assent, here we have before us a real live dialogue which reminds us sometimes of Platonic dialogues. But this Sutta also is not original but it is an unfavourably extended Itihāsa-dialogue, which has been borrowed from another sect, presumably from the Jains.[3] That the editing of the Dīghanikāya was done at a very late

1. Just as in the Purāṇa and in some sectarian sections of the epic, Indra is presented as paying homage to God Śiva or Viṣṇu, so in these Suttas, which Rhys Davids so aptly calls "Tenderzschriften" (SBB Vol. III, p. 298) i.e. Pamphlets with a purpose, we find Indra and the other Gods and demi gods as devout worshippers of Buddha.

2. It appears that a fragment of an old non-Buddhistic poetry has been treated in the Sutta here.

3. Kumāra Kassapa wants to prove to Pāyāsi that the soul exists, although the Buddhists themselves reject the existence of a soul. Cf. E. Leumann in OC VI, Leiden 1883, III, 2, 467 ff. We also find a version of the dialogue among the Jains. Probably both sects borrowed it from an earlier source.

date, is also indicated by Suttas like No. 32 which is only a sort of warding off magic against snakes and demons, No. 26 in which the prospective Buddha Matteyya, the Buddhistic Messiah, is mentioned and the two last Suttas (Saṅgīti) and Dasuttara-Suttanta which are composed in the style of the Aṅguttaranikāya and which, like the texts of the Abhidhamma which they resemble in contents, are in the form of a catechism[1] that is usually found in the Abhidhammapiṭaka.

To anyone who has followed this survey of the contents of the Dīghanikāya, it will scarcely be credible that a prominent Pāli scholar[2] attempts to prove that this text should be regarded as a literary work which was drawn up as a uniform whole.[3] It is a matter of course that the compiler or the committe of compilers were desirous of arranging the Suttas according to some principle, classing together such Suttas as seemed to belong together by reason of association of ideas or wording;[4] but this does not prove that the whole work is the work of one author. When the same scholar seeks to trace a uniform idea underlying the whole of the Dīghanikāya namely, that Gotama Buddha was a Tathāgata, i.e. that he had trodden the path of salvation in order to encourage his disciples to tread the same path, and that the doctrine of the path leading to liberation or Nirvāṇa is the nucleus of the work, it is merely saying in other

---

Dhammapāda says (in his commentary on the Vimānavatthu) that this dialogue was written subsequently to the death of Buddha and the erection of a Stūpa over his ashes. (See Rhys Davids ŚBB Vol. III, p. 347.).

1. A text corresponding to the Saṅgīti Sutta entitled Saṅgītiparyāya appears among the Sarvāstivādins as a book of the Abhidhammapiṭaka. Cf. J. Takakusu, JPTS 1904, 1905, p. 99 ff.

K. E. Neumann (Reden Gotammo Buddho's des Suttanipato, IV, p. X) describes the Dīghanikāya particularly as a collection that is "on the whole comparatively late and often apocryphal".

2. R. O. Franke, ZDMG, 67, 1913, 409 ff. WZKM 27, 1913, 198 ff., 276 ff. Dīghanikāya, p. x ff.

3. Dīghanikāya, p. xlii.

4. However, in the Chinese translation, of the Dīrghāgama, the Sūtras are arranged in an entirely different order from that in which they appear in the Dīghanikāya; cf. M. Anesaki in "Transactions of the Asiatic Society of Japan", Vol. XXXV, part 3, 1908, p. 35 ff. The fact is that the compiler of the Sanskrit version arranged the material in a different way.

words that the alleged author wished to present the tenets of the Buddha on the ideal life. Now this comprises practically all Buddha's teaching, and, therefore, in this way, one could puzzle out a "uniform and underlying idea" in all texts of the Tipiṭaka dealing with the Dhamma and claim that they are the work of one author.[1]

If, as we have shown, the Dīghanikāya is composed of earlier and later portions, it cannot be the earliest work of the Canon, as Franke endeavours to prove[2] and there is no justification for the attempt to construct "the doctrine of Buddha in its earliest accessible form from the Dīghanikāya. It is only by comparing all the ancient Buddhist texts, which are scattered in the various collections, that we can attempt to reconstruct the doctrine of Buddha in its earliest accessible form.

The Majjhimanikāya, "the collection of instructive lectures of medium length"[3] consists of 152 speeches and dialogues which differ from those of the Dīghanikāya only in this that they are in general shorter. But in this collection also each Sutta is complete in itself and they are as different in their value as in their nature. But even by reason of the large number of the Suttas, their contents are much more variegated than those of the Dīghanikāya. Here we find discussions on almost all points of religion of the Buddha, on the four noble truths, on the Karman, on the futility of the desires, on the reprehensibility of the belief in the soul, on the Nirvāṇa, on the various kinds of meditation etc. These discussions are often only uninteresting sermons, often, however, they also have the so popular and charming form of dialogues with a longer or shorter introduction or frame-work

1. Franke's view is also repudiated by Oldenberg (AR 17, 1914, 626 f.). C. A. F. Rhys Davids (JRAS 1914, 459 ff.), Geiger (Pāli Literatur und Sprache, p. 11 f.) and Eliot 1, 278 n.1.

2. ZDMG 69, 1915, 455 ff.; 71, 1917, 50 ff.

3. Edited by V. Trenckner and R. Chalmers, London PTS 1888-1902, 3 vols. Translated by Lord Chalmes, Further Dialogues of the Buddha in SBB, Vols. V and VI, 1926-27; into German by K. E. Neumann, "Die Reden Gotamo Buddho's aus der mittleren Sammlung Majjhimanikāyo des Pālikanons. 3 vols. Leipzig 1896-1902. Selections translated by T. W. Rhys Davids in SBE, Vol. II and (into German) by P. Dahlke, Suttapiṭaka, Vol. III, Berlin, 1923.

narrative (Itihāsa-dialogues). General popularity is enjoyed by the teachings through allegories, whether an allegory is maintained through the whole speech or a chain of allegories passes through the whole speech in order to din one and the same teaching again and again. Also myths and legends, are narrated, in order to associate with them some teaching or the other as in no. 37 where the visit of Moggallāna, the famous disciple of the Buddha to the heaven of Indra is described. Here the monk Moggallāna, with his toe makes the whole palace of the heaven shake[1]—a feature that reminds us completely of the holy men of the Brahminic legends of Mahābhārata and the Purāṇas. Some of the framework-narratives give the impression of real happenings, as for instance the story of Pukkusāti, who wants to be admitted to the order and while going to fetch a mantle and a begging bowl for himself, is killed by a cow (no. 140), whereupon Buddha adds that this man has attained Nirvāṇa, although he was not a monk. Or the story of the monk Channa (no. 144) who is seriously ill and commits suicide by opening his veins which is approved by the Buddha : Suicide is blameworthy if one wants to acquire only another body (in a new rebirth) by that means, but not when one goes into Nirvāṇa. The splendid Assalāyanasutta (no. 93) also seems to have been taken from real life at the time of the Buddha. It must have been certainly very unpleasant to the proud Brahmins that Gotama taught the "purity of all the four castes". So such dialogues on the justification of the caste system as that between the young Brahmin Assalāyana and Gotama Buddha may have taken place not infrequently. And excellent is the argumentation against the claims of the Brahmins by virtue of their caste. Here Assalāyana says to Buddha :

"The Brahmins, O Lord Gotama, speak thus : "The Brahmins alone are the best caste, low is every other caste; the Brahmins alone are the white caste, black is every other caste; the Brahmins alone become pure, not the non-Brahmins; the Brahmins alone are the real sons of God Brahman, born out of his mouth, produced by Brahman, formed by Brahman heirs of Brahman. What does Lord Gotama say to this ?"

1. A feat to which there is an allusion again in No. 50.

Thereupon Buddha puts a number of questions to Assalāyana, all of which he must answer affirmatively and thereby he must admit that the views of the Brahmins are untenable. He says for e.g. :

"What do you mean, Assalāyana ? Let us suppose that an anointed king from a warrior's family summons together a hundred men from different castes : Men should come from the families of warriors, of Brahmins, of noblemen and they should take an upper friction-wood (for producing fire) of a sal-tree or salala-tree or sandal-tree or Padmaka-tree,[1] make fire by churning (in the lower friction-wood) and produce a flame. And men should come from the families of Caṇḍālas, hunters, basket-makers, cartwrights, Pukkuśas[2] and they should take an upper friction-wood from a dog-trough, a swine-trough, a washerman's trough or from a castor-trough, make a fire by churning and produce a flame. Now, will the fire[3] that the warriors, the Brahmins etc. have produced with the noble wood, have flame, splendour and light and will it be possible to use this fire for all purposes ? Will on the contrary the fire that the Caṇḍālas, the hunters etc. have made with wood from the dog-trough etc. have no flame, no splendour and no light, and will it not be possible to use this fire for all purposes ?" Assalāyana must naturally answer that between the two kinds of fire there does not exist any difference, and Gotama concludes saying that it is just the same way with the castes also.[4]

Some of the Suttas, however, are neither dialogues nor sermons, but they are simply stories. Thus No. 86 is a regular old Ākhyāna in which in prose and verse the story of the terrible robber Aṅgulimāla is told who became a monk and reached even the height of an Arhat (a holyman who is sure of Nirvāṇa) —a valuable piece of ancient Buddhist poetry. Another Sutta

1. Different kinds of quality wood.

2. Sanskrit Pukkaśas, a very low-caste.

3. From here onwards condensed.

4. Majjhimanikāya, Vol. II, p. 151 ff. A discourse on the problem of castes is also contained in the 84th Sutta. Cf. R. Chalmers, JRAS 1894, p. 341 ff.

(no. 83) tells the legend (repeated in the Jātakas also) of King Makhadeva, who lays down his kingdom on the appearance of the first grey hair and becomes a monk. One of the most magnificent pieces of this kind is the Raṭṭhapāla-sutta (no. 82). In the beautiful ancient ballad-style the following is told here : (Only a short extract is given here) :—

The young prince Raṭṭhapāla wants to become a monk. His parents do not at all consent but by going on fast he forces them to give their consent. After many years he comes as a monk to his native town and begs in front of his parents' house. His father does not recognise him and drives him away from his threshold with abuses. "By these monks with clean shaven heads our only beloved son has been misled to world-renunciation" says he. In the meanwhile the servant comes out to throw away the remnants of food. The beggar-monk begs for these remnants of food for his meal. Then the servant recognises him as the son of the family and reports this to his master, who then comes and invites him to come inside the house. He however declines saying, "I have already eaten for today". But he accepts the invitation for the next day. Then his father not only prepares a dinner but in the dining hall he heaps up gold and jewels and asks the earlier wives of Raṭṭhapāla to decorate themselves. On the next day he is received ceremoniously and his father offers him all treasures and valuables. But Raṭṭhapāla says simply, "If you want to follow my advice, father, load all the gold and jewels on a carriage and throw it into the Ganges where it is deepest. And why? Because only pain and misery, suffereing and sorrow will be caused by them". With the wives also, who fall on his feet flattering him he does not want to have anything to do. After food he goes away. Then he meets the king of the Kuru-country, who says that some one who has become old or ill or poor or who has lost his kith and kin becomes a monk, but not that someone who is young, cheerful and healthy should renounce the world. Raṭṭhapāla replies with a speech on the uselessness of life and the insatiability of desire and he convinces the Kuru King of the truth of the teaching of Buddha in a dialogue that he holds with him in a Socrates-like manner.

By the side of such splendid poetry there are most dreary

sermons in which, in the style of catechism a number of technical expression or some basic doctrine is explained—for example, Nos. 43 and 44[1]. Some of these Suttas (like for example, Nos. 127, 137, 140, 148, 151) proceed exactly like the enumerations of the Aṅguttaranikāya and of the definitions and classifications of the Abhidhammapiṭaka. And quite different from the above mentioned Ākhyānas in which the narration proceeds lively in a mixture of prose and verse, are Suttas like No. 116 where an uninteresting list of Paccekabuddhas (Hermit-Buddhas, who received enlightenment without proclaiming it to the world) is given first in prose and immediateby after that in verse. This mixing of prose and verse belongs to a much later type which we come across in Buddhist Sanskrit literature.

But apart from the fact that the Suttas of the Majjhimanikāya give us the best picture of the ancient Buddhist religion and the manner of teaching of Buddha and his early disciples, they are also of importance to us as they give us some interesting glimpses into the life and deeds of those ancient times, not only into the life of the monks themselves (as in No. 5, 21, 22, etc.) but also of that of other sections of the people. Thus No. 51 gives us clear picture of the Brahminical system of sacrifice and valuable indications regarding the connection between bloody sacrifices and regarding the classes of rulers and priests. Again and again we come across enumerations of various kinds of ascetic practices which were popular in ancient India. A real specimen of ascetic atrocities is found in No. 12 and No. 14 and also in the Suttas, Nos. 40, 45, 51 and 60 we come across all kinds of queer saints of various sects. There were in htose days for example "dog-ascetics" and "cattle ascetics" whose asceticism consisted in this that they ate and lived just like dogs and cattle. To the question what would happen to these ascetics in the future birth, the Buddha replies that the "dog-ascetic" would be born at best as a dog and the "cattle-ascetics" as cattle or that possibly they might both go to hell. Of

1. These two Suttas, which are termed the "big" and "small" Vedalla-sutta, have nothing in common except the form of questions and answers. It seems that the unexplained expression "Vedalla" refers to this form itself. Cf. p. 11 above, note and C. A. Foley (Mrs. Rhys Davids), JRAS 1894, p. 321 ff.

historical significance for the relationship of the Buddha to the sect of the Jainas are many Suttas, in particular the Upālisutta (No. 56)[1] and also No. 57, 101 and 104. References are also made sometimes to all kinds of superstitions and to social and legal conditions. Thus in No. 13 we find an enumeration of cruel penalties; of all kinds of peculiar ideas on the birth and breeding of children the 38th Sutta reports; the relationship between daughter-in-law and father-in-law is explained in No. 28 and 37 etc.

In time the individual Suttas are far removed from one another. Whereas in some Suttas of the Majjhimanikāya as well as in the ancient pieces of the Mahāparinibbānasutta the Buddha appears entirely as a human being and preacher and speaks of himself only as an ordinary mortal to whose lot a certain knowledge has fallen, and who looks forward to attaining complete Nirvāṇa, whereas he narrates his autobiography in the 26th and the 36th Sutta[2] in simple words free from all miracles, in the other Suttas (for example No. 12) all possible powers of miracles and absolutely divine properties are attributed to the Buddha. In the "Sutta of the astonishing events and miracles" (No. 123) the conception and the birth of the Bodhisatta are described with all the miracles as are known to the Buddha legend of later non-canonical works (like Nidānakathā, Lalitavistara, etc.) as we have found them already in the Mahāpadānasutta of the Dīghanikāya.[3] That the Buddha or even a holy man like Moggallāna stretches out his bent arm like a strongman or bends his stretched-out arm", disappears,

1. This is treated thoroughly by Leon Feer in OC VI, Leiden 1883 t. III, 67 ff., RHR t. 13, 1886, 74 ff. and JA 1887, s.8, t. IX, 309 ff.; 1888, s. 8, t. XI, 113 ff., 123 ff. and t. XII, 209 ff. Cf. also R. Chalmers in the JRAS 1895, p. 665 f.

2. Similarly Aṅguttaranikāya III, 38, see Dutoit, Leben des Buddha, p. 14 ff.

3. See p. 38 above. According to Windisch, "Buddhas Geburt", p. 104, Majjh. 123 is only a shorter version of the Mahāpadānasutta. Indeed the concurrence between the two is very precise, only with this difference that in the Dīghanikāya 14 there is a report on the birth of the Buddha Vipassi. Regarding the significance of the Sutta Majjh. 123 for the development of the Buddha-legend in the later texts. Cf. Windisch ibid. p. 107 ff.

to appear suddenly in the world of the gods or in Brahman's heaven is not rare in the Suttas (as in No. 37, 49 and elsewhere). One Sutta (No. 49) claims to prove that the Buddha is superior to all the gods and even the highest Brahman. And although in most of the speeches Buddha appears as the speaker, in some of the speeches the disciples of Buddha are also the main speakers (e.g. No. 15, 43, 44). Not rarely does one of the disciples answer a question, but he gets the correctness of his answer confirmed through the Buddha (e.g. No. 126). Moreover, they do not always maintain the fiction that all Suttas originated during the life of the Buddha. Thus in No. 84 and 94, on a question as to where the Buddha may be staying at the present time, a disciple gets the answer, "He has attained complete Nirvāṇa". The Sutta No. 108 tells about the time immediately, following the death of the Buddha, when Ānanda is asked whether the Buddha before dying did not appoint any monk as the head of the monastic order. Ānanda gives a negative reply but explains that the community is not, on that account, of course "without a refuge", for the religion (Dhamma) is its refuge.[1] and the order in the community will be maintained by the Pāṭimokkha-festival[2] laid down by the master. This is, incidentally, a Sutta that refers more to the orderly discipline (vinaya) than to the religion (dhamma), which also is the case sometimes (e.g. 103, 104, 142).[3]

Whether from the various methods and manners in which the individual points of the doctrine are treated in the Suttas we can also draw inferences about their earlier or later origin,[4] cannot be discussed here. If for example, in the Suttas No.

---

1. Evidently an allusion to the well known passage in the Mahāparinibbānasutta; See p. 39 above. Cf. also C.A.F. (Rhys Davids) in JRAS 1902, p. 476 f.

2. See p. 22 ff. above.

3. K. E. Neumann, Reden Gotamo Buddha's III, Introduction, bases his view on this that originally the Vinaya was contained in the Suttapiṭaka and has been shaped into an independent Vinayapiṭaka only afterwards. According to R. O. Franke (WZKM, 29, 1915, p. 136) the Majjhimanikāya is "the very earliest work of the Vinaya Literature," and he points out many passages (ib. 139 ff.) in which the Majjh. speaks of the Vinaya.

4. Cf. C. A. F. (Rhys Davids) in JRAS 1902, 474 f.

129f. and No. 135f. the doctrine of Karman is presented in a crudely sensuous way and the tortures in hell are described with such an elaborateness which finds its counterpart in the descriptions of hell in the Purāṇas, then this may indicate their later origin. It is, however, also possible that even in the earlier days had existed, by the side of the purely philosophical concept, also a rather popular picture of the doctrine of Karman. That the order had already a certain history of its own when the Majjhimanikāya was compiled, is indicated by a text in No. 65 which says that previously there were less regulations and more monks whereas now there are more regulations and less monks. The mention of the Yona-Kambojas in the Assalāyanasutta (No. 93) points to the existence of the Graeco-Bactrian kingdom, i.e. to the time shortly before Aśoka.

For the way and manner in which the collection has come into being, the Suttas Nos. 41 and 42 may be characteristic. The latter is, except for the short introduction, verbatim the same as No. 41. Even otherwise the same sermons or dialogues appear again and again in a different framework. Thus, for example, Nos. 132-134 are only different versions of one and the same sermon. These are perhaps sermons which were really delivered by the monks[1]. If a monk did not get any original idea then he repeated an old sermon with inconsequential alterations. The compilers collected then everything that they could get from the lips of any preacher.[2]

III. The third big collection is the Saṃyuttanikāya[3] "the

1. We learn from the 115th Sutta that these sermons had definite titles (and sometimes the same sermon even more than one title). In his Bhabra edict Aśoka points to such titles of individual sermons. See p. 17 above.

2. R. O. Franke has tried to trace a uniform fundamental idea and associations of thought underlying the various Suttas in the Majjhimanikāya too (WZKM 29, 1915, 134 ff. ZDMG 68, 1914, 473 ff.) with a view to proving from it, that this book too is not a collection of sermons and dialogues but the unified work of one author. The arguments in this case are, if anything, even less convincing than in the case of the Dīghanikāya. The very fact that we often find a "great" and a "small" Sutta on the same subject side by side in the Majjh. (e.g. Cula-and Mahā-Sihanāda-Sutta) is evidence that the work is in the nature of a collection.

3. Edited by Leon Feer, London PTS 1884-1898, Indexes by Mrs. Rhys Davids 1904. Translated by Mrs. Rhys Davids and F. L. Woodward (Book

collection of the preachings divided into groups". It consists of 56 groups (saṃyutta), each one of which, referring to some definite name or object, deals with various points of the doctrine. It is, therefore, not a subject-wise division but only a weak attempt at such a one. Thus the Devatāsaṃyutta (I) contains remarks by deities, but the utterances refer to most diverse objects. The Mārasaṃyutta consists of 25 Suttas, each one of which narrates a legend in which Māra the seducer appears in order to turn Buddha himself or one of his disciples away from the doctrine of salvation; but he always fails. The Bhikkhunīsaṃyutta (V) contains ten legends of nuns (bhikkhunī) whom Māra tries to seduce but in vain. The Nidānasaṃyutta (XII) consists of 92 speeches and conversations, all of which treat the subject of 12 Nidānas or the involvement of causes and effects (Paṭiccasamuppāda)[1] in unending repetitions. The Anamataggasaṃyutta (XV) contains 20 speeches, all of which begin with the words : "Without beginning and without end (anamataggo) is this Sāṃsara, O ye monks !" and explain this sentence by describing in terms of similes and metaphors which are invented from time to time the endlessness of the sufferings in the eternal cycle of transmigration from life to life. As against this the 13 Suttas of the Kassapasaṃyutta (XVI) are combined into one group only for the reason that in all of them the disciple Kassapa appears; just as the Sāriputtasaṃyutta (XXVIII) contains ten speeches of Sāriputta. Serpent-demons (Nāgas) form the subject matter of the fifty Suttas of the Nāgasaṃyutta (XXIX), which mention the various kinds of serpents and name the deeds through which one will be reborn in the form of this or that serpent. The 55 Suttas of the Jhānasaṃyutta or Samādhisaṃyutta (XXXIV) treat contemplations or meditations. (jhāna, samādhi). The

of the Kindred Sayings or Grouped Suttas) PTS, Parts I, 1917, II, 1922; III, 1925; into German by W. Geiger in ZB IV-VII, separately Vol. II, München 1925 and Volume I, 1930. The Bhikkhuni-Saṃyutta is also translated by Mrs. Rhys Davids, "Psalms of the Sisters", pp. 180-191; Mara-Saṃyutta and Bhikkhuni-Saṃyutta into German by E. Windisch, "Māra und Buddha", pp. 88 ff., 132 ff.

1. Also called "causality-formula", See Oldenberg, "Buddha," 257 ff.

34 Suttas of the Mātugāmasaṃyutta (XXXVII) deal with the strength and weakness, virtues and vices of women (mātugāma) and the destinies which await them in the next life. Legends of the great Moggallāna and some of his speeches are found in the 11 Suttas of the Moggallānasaṃyutta (XL). The hero of the Sakkasaṃyutta (XI) is Sakka, God Indra, who appears here also[1] as a pious Buddhist. How great the gap between the Veda and the Tipiṭaka must be assumed to be is shown by a comparison of the wild and furious Vṛtra-killer of the Vedic hymns with the mild Sakka of the Sakkasaṃyutta who professes that he can never become angry and who scares away the demon who seized his throne only with the polite words, "I am Indra, the ruler of the gods, my dear friend".[2] The last saṃyutta is the Saccasaṃyutta (LVI) which in 131 Suttas deals with the four noble truths (sacca) of suffering, origin of suffering, removal of suffering and the way to the removal of suffering. Here we find also (LVI, 11) the famous Dhammacakkappavattanasutta, the "Sermon of Banaras" through which Buddha set the wheel of religion (dhammacakka) in motion.[3]

We find that there are at least three different principles according to which the Suttas are compiled. The Suttas of a group either (1) deal with any main point or any main area of the Buddhistic doctrine or (2) they refer to some classes of gods, demons or human beings, or (3) in them some excellent person appears as hero or speaker. These 56 Saṃyuttas or "Groups" are also divided into 5 Vaggas or "sections" and the total number of the Suttas is 2889. In general these are much shorter Suttas than those of the Majjhimanikāya or of the Dīghanikāya. The large number of the Suttas is essentially the result of the same topic being treated thoroughly in all its aspects and variations

---

1. As in the Sakkapañha-Sutta, Cf. p. 42 above.
2. XI, 3, 2 translated by Warren, Buddhism in Translations, 426 f.
3. Cf. p. 28, Note above. Translated by many scholars, for example by Feer in JA 1870, s.6, t.X, 345 ff.; Oldenberg, Buddha 149 ff., 243 f.; Pischel, Leben und Lehre des Buddha, 28f.; Dutoit, Leben des Buddha, 81ff.; Winternitz, Religionsgeschichtliches Lesebuch, p. 219 f. Also F. L. Woodward translates it as "Some Sayings of the Buddha", p. 7 ff.

according to a fixed pattern—with continuous repetitions of the same idioms and phrases—until both the topic and the reader are thoroughly exhausted. Thus for example in the Salāyatanasaṃyutta (XXXV) not less than 207 Suttas, speeches and dialogues on the six senses are combined. With untiring monotony it is described here that the senses of seeing, hearing, smelling, tasting, touching and the organ of thinking are ephemeral and painful and have nothing to do with the self, that the sense-perceptions which correspond to the sense-organs are ephemeral and have nothing to do with the self and that the sense objects which correspond to the sense organs are ephemeral and painful and have nothing to do with the self. But the whole series of the statements are repeated verbatim for every individual sense organ, every individual sense perception, every individual sense object and every statement constitutes a Sutta in itself. That this can make us dead-tired goes without saying. However tedious we may find this multiplication of Suttas, there are sure to have been sound, practical reasons for it in the use of the Suttas for religious exercises.[1] Even in this collection, however, we find many things which are to be appreciated also from the purely literary point of view though it contains much more that is of importance only because it contributes to our knowledge of the doctrine of Buddha.

This is especially the case with the first Vagga. It comprises the Saṃyuttas I-XI and is called Sagāthavagga, i.e. "the section with the song stanzas (gāthā). Such gāthās or stanzas appear here and there in all sections—just like in the other Nikāyas but they are so numerous in the first Vagga and many of the Suttas consist entirely of verses only. Thus, in the Devatā-Saṃyutta we find many riddles and aphorisms in the form of questions and answers, e.g. the following riddles :

Hast thou no little hut? Hast thou no nest?
Hast thou no line stretched out? Art free from ties?
"Nay, never hut is mine, nor any nest.

1. It is possible that the fact "that the varying Suttas were collected from different sources, from different vihāras or even laymen", may also have been a factor in the multiplication of Suttas.

Nor line stretched out. Yea, I am free from ties."
What do I mean who speak to thee of 'hut'
And 'nest,' and 'line' stretched out and 'ties'?
"Mother thou meanest when thou speak'st of 'nest,'
And 'wife' thou meanest when thou speak'st of 'nest,'
And 'children', when thou sayest 'line stretched out,'
And men's desires, when thou dost speak of 'ties' " !
O well is thee for whom no hut doth wait !
O well is thee who hast no nest at night !
Thou hast no line stretched out—O well is thee !
And happy thou who from all ties art free ![1]

These riddles and aphorisms are not always in reference to Buddhist doctrines, as the following riddle will show :

What is the basis and support of men ?
What here below is comradeship supreme ?
What are the spirits who sustain the life
Of all such creatures as to earth are bound?
"Children are mankind's basis and support,
The wife is here below comrade supreme;[2]
The spirits of the rain sustain the life
Of all such creatures as to earth are bound.[3]

Just as, in an episode of the Mahābhārata,[4] Yudhiṣṭhira answers the questions of a Yakṣa, thereby gaining his favour, likewise in Saṃyutta X, 12, Buddha satisfies a Yakṣa by the wise answers which he gives to his questions. It is especially the ballads (ākhyānas) in verse or more often in the prose and verse form mixed as we find them particularly in the Māra-Saṃyutta and the Bhikkhunī-Saṃyutta,[5] which are of great poetical value. Some of these short ballads about Māra and the nuns which are remarkable also for the sake of their archaic

1. I, 2, 9, translated by Mrs. Rhys Davids, Kindred Sayings I, p. 13 f.
2. Cf. Aitareya-Brāhmaṇa : "A friend is the wife," s. Vol. I, p. 196.
3. I, 6, 4, translated by Mrs. Rhys Davids l.c., p. 52.
4. III, 313 see Vol. I, pp. 333 f.
5. See Windisch, "Māra und Buddha," pp. 87 ff., 132 ff., and Feer in JA 1883 s. 8, t.I 410 ff.

language,[1] are among the most beautiful productions of ancient Indian poetic art. As an example the Sutta (V, 3) of the nun Kisā-Gotamī ("Slender Gotamī") is translated here :

Thus have I heard. The Lord once sojourned at Sāvatthi in the Jeta grove in the garden of Anāthapiṇḍika. The nun Kisā-Gotamī, after she had dressed herself, went in the morning into the town of Sāvatthi with her begging bowl and robe to beg food. After she had begged in Sāvatthi and had returned with the food which she had obtained through begging, she went, after her meal, into the dark forest, in order to spend the day there. Then, when she had retired far into the dark forest she sat down at the foot of a tree to stay there for the day.

Then Māra the evil one, desiring to cause the nun Kisā-Gotamī fear, terror and horror and to disturb her deep meditation, went to the place where the nun Kisā-Gotamī was. And after he had gone there he addressed the nun Kisā-Gotamī in the verse :

"How now? Dost sit alone with tearful face,
As mother stricken by the loss of child ?
Thou who hast plunged into the woods alone,
Is it a man that thou hast come to seek ?"

Thus the nun Kisā-Gotamī thought within herself, "Who is it, human or no-human who has just uttered a verse ?" And it occurred to the nun Kisā-Gotamī : "It is Māra, the evil one, who, in order to cause me fear, terror and horror and to disturb me in my meditation, uttered the verse". But when the nun Kisā-Gotamī knew that it was Māra, the evil one, she addressed Māra, the evil one in the following verses :

"Past are the days when I was she whose child
Was lost ! Men to that past belong—for me !
I do not grieve, I am not shedding tears.
And as for thee, good sir, I fear thee not.

---

1. By their language, too, the stanzas (gāthās) occurring in the Nikāyas, at least the majority of them, prove themselves as belonging to the oldest portions of the Tipiṭaka literature. Cf. Rhys Davids and Carpenter, "Dīgha Nikāya", edited, Vol. II, Preface, p. VIII and also p. 12, note 1, above.

Lost on all sides is love of worldly joys.
The gloom of ignorance is rent in twain,
Defeating all the myrmidons of death,
Here do I bide (to rest), sane and immune."[1]

Then Māra, the evil one, knew that the nun Kisā-Gotamī had recognised him, and he vanished from the place, unhappy and despondent.

In this poetry one can hardly see anything but ecclesiastical ballads, the counterparts of those Ākhyānas, from which the epic poetry of India was born.[2] If we could, like J. Charpentier[3], view them as "small dramas", then they would be artistic creations of a refinement which we cannot imagine the Buddhist monks to be capable of; especially when we consider that in the whole Tipiṭaka there is not even the slightest trace to be found, that such ecclesiastical dramas had been enacted. On the contrary, monks – and only monks can be authors of the poetry under discussion – are often prohibited in the Buddhist texts from taking part in dramas and similar performances. Still, if there had been already an ecclesiastical drama, then our texts would have perhaps made an exception in favour of such religious performances. We shall come across these ecclesiastical ballads more often and find everywhere the same strongly dramatic element in them. The mundane and ecclesiastical ballads of this kind have certainly contributed much to the origin of the drama, but these poems themselves can be described as little as "dramas" as "epics", although both may have been born out of them. We can only doubt this, namely that the prose of these poems may be considered just as old as the verses.

---

1. The stanzas given in the translation of Mrs. Rhys Davids, l.c. p. 162 f.
2. Cf. Vol. I, pp. 291, 294, 450, 487 f. The technical term for this poetry consisting of prose and verse, however, appears to have been geyya and not ākhyāna. See p. 10 above.
3. WZKM XXIII, 1909, 33 ff. The fact, that, as we shall see, subsequently there has been a Buddhist drama, proves for that early Period just as little as the theatrical performances in the cloisters of Tibet.

IV. The fourth big collection is the Aṅguttaranikāya,[1] "the collection of doctrinal lectures".[2] The Suttas – there are at least 2308 of them[3] – are arranged here in eleven sections (nipāta) in such a way that in the first section those things are treated, of which there is only one, in the second those things of which there are two, in the third those things of which there are three etc. upto the eleventh section in which things are mentioned of which there are eleven. Thus for example in the "dual-section" there are Suttas on two things which one must avoid, on two dark and two bright things, on two grounds for the life in the fore·t, on two kinds of Buddhas etc.; in the "Section of threes" there are Suttas on the trinity of deeds, words and thoughts, on three kinds of monks (those who have absolutely no desires, those who have some and those who are free from all desires), on the three messengers of gods (age, disease and death) on three grounds on which death rules the world, on three kinds of observing silence, on three things on account of which women go to hell etc.; in the "Section of fours" there are Suttas on things which lead to redemption from life (virtue, meditation, realisation and freedom), on four things through which man goes to hell and four things through which he goes to heaven; on the four causes (namely good and bad deeds in an early life), by reason of which some women are ugly and poor, others ugly and rich, others beautiful and poor and yet others beautiful and rich etc.; in the "section of sevens" there are Suttas on seven requirements for meditation, on seven wonders,

1. Published by R. Morris and E. Hardy, London PTS 1885-1900, 5 vols., in addition to this vol. VI indexes by Mabel Hunt. An analysis of the contents is given by E. Hardy in vol. V, p. 371 ff. Translated into German by Bhikkhu Nāṇatiloka (Nyānatiloka) I, Leipzig, Buddhist. Verlag O. J., II, Breslau 1911. Cf. also E. Leumann, in GGA 1899, p. 586 ff.

2. Verbatim: "The one-more-part-collection". In the Sanskrit canon corresponding to the Aṅguttaranikāya there is an Ekottarāgama (Cf. Milinda-pañha VII, 3, 4, 8: Ekuttaranikāya), Ekottara means "still one more", is, therefore, synonymous with aṅguttara. The title "Dasuttara-Suttanta (Digha 34) means the "upto-ten-Suttanta", i.e. the doctrinary lecture, in which the Dhammas (religious concepts) of one to ten are enumerated.

3. In some cases it is not clear whether we should presume one or more Suttas. Therefore, one can make out also 2363 Suttas.

on seven kinds of wives etc.; in the "section of eights" there are Suttas on eight things through which the woman puts the man in fetters and the man the woman, on eight kinds of alms, on 8 qualities which women must have, in order to be born again as angels, on eight causes of an earthquake etc., in the "section of tens" there are Suttas on the ten powers of a Buddha, on the ten fundamental questions (a summary of the whole doctrine of the Buddha) on the ten grounds for instituting the Pāṭimokkha, on ten kinds of rich people etc. etc.

Each of these 11 sections is again divided into several classes (Vagga); and in this sometimes (and by no means always) Suttas are compiled which treat one and the same subject. Thus the ten Suttas of the first section of the "section of ones" (Ekanipāta) treats the relationship of man and woman; the contents of I, Vagga 14 are 80 Suttas in which the names of the most eminent male and female disciples and their virtues are enumerated; I, Vagga 20 contains 262 Suttas on the various kinds of meditation, which lead to Nirvāṇa; V, Vagga 18 deals in 10 Suttas with lay-disciples (upāsakas) etc. As in the Saṃyuttanikāya are the Suttas in this collection also mostly short speeches or dialogues. But longer speeches are also found in them and as in all Nikāyas, also here, the speeches are often interrupted by stanzas (gāthās). Very numerous are the suttas and gāthās, which the Aṅguttaranikāya has in common with other texts of the canon and these are sometimes specially quoted[1].

A few Suttas may be translated here as specimens of this collection. We read in the "Section of twos" (II, 4, 1-2):

"I will explain to you, ye monks, what makes a bad man

1. These parallel texts and quotations are listed by E. Hardy, vol. V, p. VIII f. From this synopsis it does not at all follow that the Aṅguttaranikāya is a later collection. Thus for example the report on the admission of women to the order or the founding of an order of nuns belongs as much to Aṅg. VIII, 51 as to the Cullavagga X, 1 of the Vinayapiṭaka. As against this, the enumeration of the eight causes of the earthquake and of the eight kinds of meetings in the Aṅgutt. (VIII, 70) is entirely in order, whereas the parallel text in the Mahāparinibbānasutta does not all fit into the context. (See p. 39 above).

and what a good man. Listen then, and attend carefully, I will speak".

"Yes, O Revered One !" say the monks and listen to the Lord. And the Lord spoke thus :

"And what is it, ye monks, that makes a wicked man ? A wicked man, ye monks, is ungrateful, he knows no gratitude. This is what one finds in wicked ones : ingratitude, thanklessness. The sum of all that makes a wicked man is this: ingratitude, thanklessness. But a good man is grateful, he knows gratitude. This is what one finds in good ones, gratefulness, gratitude. The sum of all that which makes a good man, is gratefulness, gratitude.

Two beings I mention to you, ye monks, whom one cannot adequately reward for the good that they have done. Who are they ? Mother and father. If one would, O ye monks, carry his mother on one shoulder and his father on the other and thus would become 100 years old, would live for a hundred years, and even if he would serve them by massaging their bodies and washing them and rubbing off the dirt from their bodies, and if they would even answer their calls of nature on him—even then he would not have expressed adequately his gratitude to his parents and he would not have rewarded them for their good deeds. And even if he, O ye monks, would make his parents rule over the whole earth filled with all sorts of treasures and make them supreme rulers of it, even then he would not have adequately shown his parents his gratitude and rewarded them for their good deeds. And why all this ? Much good, O ye monks, do the parents do to their children as responsible for their birth, by feeding them and by explaining this world to them.

If one, however, O ye monks, when the parents are non-believers, brings them to complete faith, inspires and strengthens them in the faith, when they are wicked, brings them to complete virtue, inspires them and strengthens their virtue, when they are greedy, brings them to complete readiness to sacrifice, inspires them and strengthens them in it, when they are ununderstanding, brings them to perfect understanding, inspires them and strengthens them in it--then O ye monks, has done good to the parents and has rewarded them for their good deeds, indeed, has more than rewarded".

Some of the Suttas of the Aṅguttaranikāya have the rare virtue of brevity. Thus we find in the "section of threes" (III, 129) the speech of Buddha which may be recommended warmly to all those who believe in the swindle of a Buddhist "secret doctrine":

"Three things, O ye monks, work secretly and not openly. Which three? Women folk, O ye monks, work secretly and not openly. The magic formulas of the Brahmins work secretly and not openly. Wrong doctrine works secretly and not openly. These, O ye monks, are the three things which work secretly and not openly.

Three things, O ye monks, shine openly and not secretly. Which three? The moon's disc, O ye monks, shines openly and not secretly. The Sun's disc, O ye monks, shines openly and not secretly. The religion and orderly discipline proclaimed by the Buddha shines openly and not secretly. These, O ye monks, are the three things that shine openly and not secretly".

Very many Suttas are concerned with women about whom the Buddhist monks have just as little good to say as the priests and holy men of other religions. Only Ānanda, the favourite disciple of the Buddha was always a zealous advocate of women. It was he, on whose recommendation the Lord, after a long resistance and only with unwillingness, permitted the founding of a nun's order—a support to women, which as tradition reports,[1] he was called to explain even at the council of Rājagaha. Once—as is told in the "section of fours" (IV, 80)—Ānanda asked the Lord like a modern supporter of women's emancipation :

"What is the reason, Revered One, what is the cause, that women have no seat in a public meeting, transact no business and do not earn their livelihood by following an (independent) occupation ?"

(Buddha replies thereupon) : "Subject to sudden spurts of anger, Ānanda, are women; jealous, Ānanda, are women;

1. Vinayapiṭaka, Cullavagga XI, I, 10. Cf. Oldenberg, Buddha, p. 190.

envious, Ānanda, are women; stupid, Ānanda, are women. That, Ānanda, is the reason, that is the cause, why women do not have any seat in an open meeting, why women do not transact any business and do not earn their livelihood by following an (independent) occupation".

One of the most beautiful speeches in the "Section of Threes" (III, 35) is that of the three messengers of gods[1]—age, disease and death—about whom King Yama in the nether-world asks the evildoer and whereupon he hands him over to the guards of hell for punishment : ideas of hell which might be perhaps older than Buddhism. However, in the Aṅguttaranikāya the number of the pieces which are valuable from the literary point of view is not large. There are a number of monotonous and endlessly uninteresting sermons here whose value by no means increases by the dry tone of enumerations. Thus we find hardly anything beautiful and exalting in the whole of "the Section of Ones." It is conspicuous that besides the numerous Suttas all of which refer to all the areas of Buddhist ethics and psychology and sometimes also of the orderly discipline (vinaya), we find also some Suttas which do not at all have anything to do with the religion of Buddha and are added only for the sake of the number-principle. Still, sometimes in such pieces there is no lack of a certain humour, which is brought about by mentioning in a series a number of things very different from one another. Thus for example in the "Section of Eights" (VIII, 27) it is said :

"Here O ye monks, there are eight powers ! Which are they ? Weeping is the power of the child, anger the power of women, weapons the power of robbers, command the power of kings, arrogance the power of fools, humbleness the power of wise

1. Similarly in the Majjhimanikāya No. 130, where, however, there are five messengers of gods. Cf. Oldenberg, Buddha 263; L. Scherman Materialien zur geschichte der indisten Visionsliteratur, Leipzig 1892, p. 60 f. Parallels from European literatures (for example Grimm's Household Tales 177, "The Messengers of Death" which was known already in the 13th century, and La Fontaine's fable VIII, 1 "La Mort et le Mourant" have been mentioned by R. Morris in JPTS 1885, pp. 62-75. Cf. also Grimm, Kinder und Hausmärchen, III Göttingen 1856, p. 249.

people, reflection the power of scholars, gentleness the power of ascetics and Brahmins".

Similar things occur sometimes in the Indian epigrammatic poetry. The idea of such enumerations is certainly old and popular among the masses and with truly Indian pedantry it has become the ordering principle of a great work only in the Aṅguttaranikāya.[1]

That the Aṅguttaranikāya was compiled at a time when the Buddha had already become a demi-god (if not God) to whom alone all truth can be traced back, is shown by the text where God Indra asks some preaching monks wherefrom they had learnt such excellent things, whether from Buddha or through their own realisation, and they reply : "If one sees people carrying corn near a granary, some of them in a basket, some in a cloth, some others in their hands, then it does not at all really matter wherefrom the corn is taken,—all that comes evidently from that big granary. Precisely so is everything, that is well said, is spoken by Buddha the Lord. This is a much greater dogmatism than what Aśoka says in his Bhabra-edict, "All that the Buddha has said is well said", indeed much greater dogmatism than the words of a later Sanskrit work,

1. The same principle is also found in the Thāṇaṅga and Samavāyāṅga Suttas of the Jainas. Exactly according to the same principle of numbers is a section on worldly wisdom (nīti) attributed to Vidura included in the Mahābhārata V, 33, 56-106. But even more antiquarian is the Brahmanic game of riddles (Mahābh. III, 134), in which Aṣṭāvakra defeats Vandin, the sophist, who knows all about the things of which there are one, two, three etc., but gets stuck up at the things of which there are thirteen; whereas Aṣṭāvakra enumerates also those things of which there are thirteen. Number-riddles and number-litanies of the same kind are found in the literatures of other nations as well. The best known of them is the so-called "Catholic Vesper" in which Christian dogmas are enumerated according to numbers from 1 to 12: "Good friend, I ask you. Good friend, what are you asking me ? Tell me, what is *one* ? *One* and *One* is God the Lord" etc. (K. Simrock, Die deutschen Volkslieder. Frankfurt a. M. 1851, p. 520 ff). A Greek fairy tale in J. G. v Hahn, Griechische und Albanesische Märchen" (Leipzig 1864) II, p. 210 f. reminds us of Aṣṭāvakra. There is a similar number litany in the Passover Hagada of the Jews. Cf. K. Kohle in "Zeitschrift fur" die Geschichte der Juden in Dentschland" 3, 1889, 234ff. and G. Léjeau in Revue celtique II, pp. 58 ff.

the Divyāvadāna : "The heavens will fall, with the moon and the stars, the earth will perish with its mountains and forests, the oceans will dry up—but the Buddha will never speak falsehood."[1]

With this dogmatism the Aṅguttaranikāya is only a precurser of the Abhidhammapiṭaka for whose texts it has probably laid the basis[2].

The large number of the Suttas in the Aṅguttaranikāya has resulted in the same way as that in the Saṃyuttanikāya[3].

Regarding the relationship of these four Nikāyas or collections of Suttas to one another–the Khuddakanikāya has a completely different character—we can say with certainty only this much, that a large series of Suttas occurs not only in one but in many of these collections and that in respect of the teachings there is absolutely no difference between the four Nikāyas. In most cases it is difficult to decide whether a Sutta was originally in this or that Nikāya. If for example the Sutta on the three properties through which women go to hell is found both in the Saṃyuttanikāya and the Aṅguttaranikāya then its proper place is in the former collection in the "Section on women" as well as in the latter collection in the "Section of Threes". On the other hand some sections of the Saṃyuttanikāya look like extensions of or explanations to the Aṅguttaranikāya[4]. The Suttas of the Dīghanikāya often give the impression that they were the result of extending shorter texts. Thus for example the 10th Sutta of the Majjhimanikāya (Satipaṭṭhānasutta) in the Dīghanikāya No 22 verbatim appears again (as Mahā-Satipaṭṭhānasutta), only with some additions, like a commentary. That the Mahāparinibbānasutta has attained its large volume probably through additions, was already elaborated. And some passages of the Dīghanikāya would better fit in the Aṅguttaranikāya.[5] We have already mentioned that the large

1. Aṅgut. vol. IV, p. 163 f. Cf. La Vallée Poussin, Transactions of the Third Internat. Congress for the History of Religions, vol. II, p. 36.

2. Cf. Hardy in vol. V of the edition, preface, p. IX f.

3. See p. 53 above.

4. Cf. Saṁy. XXXVII, 4 with Aṅgutt. III, 127 and Saṁy XXXVII, 5-9, resp. 14-24 with Aṅgutt. V, 230 resp. 115-120.

5. See p. 53 f. above.

number of the Suttas in both the latter Nikāyas is in a great measure due to the variations of one and the same motive with endless repetitions, and also that sometimes this is also the case with the Majjhimanikāya.[1] But the large volume of many speeches in the Majjhimanikāya and the Dīghanikāya is also the result of continued repetitions. In the case of all these collections one cannot help getting the impression that they owe their origin to practical needs, by having been composed for the use of the monks for religious practices—sermons, public recitations, hours of worship and devotion. That they were originally meant for oral delivery, is proved by the peculiarity of almost all of these Suttas which we have already mentioned, namely the repetitions about which we have already spoken—repetitions which are piled up to such an extent that they vex us.

These continued repetitions of the same words, sentences and whole paragraphs had the double object of impressing the speeches in the memory and of making them rhetorically more effective. As texts written down and intended for being read they would have been as dreary and even repulsive to the Indians as they are to the Europeans. In the recitation the repetitions played a considerable part "as parts of a purely musical construction" and proved no more tiring to the ears of a Buddhist audience "than the repetitions of the motifs in the musical compositions of Bach or Wagner."[2] It is almost impossible to translate these Suttas word for word with all the repetitions. Even K. E. Neumann, who with admirable patience retains in general these repetitions in his translations of the "Reden Gotamo Buddho's" and by omitting nothing, gives the German reader a good picture of the original, sometimes appears compelled to omit the one or the other repetition. For

1. See p. 51 and 53-54 above.

2. P. Tuxen in "Festgabe Jacobi" p. 98 ff., who adds that "even in individual cases the ancient authors showed a very well defined sense of musical effect when they constructed their rhythm". This would also explain the extraordinary impression made by the recitation of the Pāli texts in the monasteries on hearers who follow the recital without being able to understand a single word of the contents. Tuxen testifies to this from his own experience.

it is indeed not only, as Oldenberg[1] says, as though these Buddhist monks had not yet found the magic word "and" but it is also as though they did not know any pronouns. How powerful, and stirring for example is the following speech from the Saṃyuttanikāya (XV, 3) if we omit the repetition.

... Thus spoke the Lord: "Without beginning and end, ye monks, is this Saṃsāra; one does not know the beginning, from when the beings wander and roam about, bound by the veil of ignorance and the bonds of greed. For, what, do ye monks think, is more; the floods of tears that you have shed, while you wandered and roamed about on this long path while you bemoaned and lamented when meeting people you did not like and when leaving people whom you liked,—or in water in the four great oceans ?"

"As we, O Revered One, understand the doctrine of the Lord, is this flood of tears, O Revered One, which we have shed while wandering and roaming on this long path and while meeting people we did not like and leaving people whom we liked, is more than the water in the four great oceans."

"Well, well, ye monks, very well have you, O monks understood the doctrine proclaimed by me. Yes O ye monks, this flood of tears, that ye have shed while wandering and roaming on this long path and while meeting people whom ye did not like and leaving people whom ye liked is more than the water in the four great oceans. O monks ye experienced for a long time the death of your mother, ye experienced the death of the sons, ye experienced the death of the daughters, ye experienced loss of relatives, ye experienced loss of goods, for a long time O monks, ye experienced loss through disease, and while thus experiencing (the death of the mother, by experiencing the death of the sons, by experiencing the death of daughters, by experiencing the loss of relatives, by experiencing the loss of goods[2] and by experiencing the loss through disease is the flood of tears that ye shed while meeting people whom ye did not like and leaving persons whom ye liked is more than the water in the four great oceans. And what is the reason for this ? Without beginning

1. Buddha, p. 211. Cf. also Windisch, "Māra und Buddha", p. 38f.
2. These words are also missing in manuscripts but have to be added.

and end, o monks is this Saṃsāra, one does not know the beginning from when the beings, bound by the veil of ignorance and the bonds of greed, wander and roam about. And thus o monks, therefore, there is reason enough to loathe the things of this world, reason enough to scorn them, reason enough to free ourselves from them."

The repetitions are here however not at all so excessive as in numerous other Suttas. All the more pleasing are the short and brief speeches in which a thought is projected in all brilliance and clarity and is stated without a single superfluous word. We find such individual dialogues in all the four Nikāyas. In all the four Nikāyas there are very old elements besides comparatively younger elements. In style and language too, there is no essential difference among the four Nikāyas.[1] And if we may be perhaps justified in assuming that the shorter, less ove burdened Suttas which are not mutilated by too many repetitions are among the oldest Suttas of the canon, then we are not justified in presuming one or the other of the four compilations originated much earlier than the others, and although the Aṅguttaranikāya may be somewhat later than the other Nikāyas.[2] There is even less reason for assuming the

1. The description of the characteristics of early Buddhist prose given by Oldenberg (Zur Geschichte der altindischen Prosa, AGGW 1917, p. 39 ff) may be applied with equal truth to all the four Nikāyas.

2. M. Anesaki (Transactions of the Asiatic Society of Japan, Vol. 35, 1908, Part 2, p. 83 f) thinks that both the Pāli Aṅguttaranikāya and Ekottarāgama bear traces indicating that this collection is later than the three others. Moreover, it contains the greatest number of quotations which are given as quotations. However, the Nikāyas or other collections are never cited as such, but only separate Suttas or portions of a collection. Thus for instance, in Aṅg. X, 26, 2, a verse which occurs in Samy. IV, 3, 5, (I, p. 126) is not quoted as being taken from the Saṃy., but with the words: "Thus it was said by the Sublime one (Bhagavatā) in the questions of the daughters (of Māra)". Aṅg III, 32 quotes verses from the "Pārāyaṇa" (not from the "Suttanipāta" in which we find the Pārāyaṇa). In the same way, the quotations in Samy. 22, 4 from the "Sakkapañha" does not prove that it was taken from the Dighanikāya. Cf. Eliot I, p. 279n., 1. Rhys Davids in Cambridge History I. p. 194; Mrs. Rhys Davids in Prefatory Note to Indexes of Aṅgutt. in Ed. Vol. VI.

Dīghanikāya to be the "earliest accessible source of Buddhist writing."[1]

That all the four collections are composed of the same elements, is shown also by the qualities common to all collections. In all of them we find individual dialogues, in which the Buddha, while discussing with an opponent, whether he is a Brahmin or a follower of some other sect, does it in the same fine, skilful and yet always polite and amiable manner. At first he expresses apparently just the same view as his opponent, proceeds from the same premises as he, makes use of the same idioms and phrases as he, often also the same technical terms and—unnoticed—he leads the opponent to his contrary viewpoint. We may presume with Rhys Davids[2] that the authors of such dialogues must have had a certain remembrance of the kind of the dialogues which Buddha actually had. They give us at least just such a good idea of Buddha's method of teaching as the Platonic dialogues give of that of Socrates.

It was also certainly a part of Gotama Buddha's method of teaching, to captivate and convince the listeners by parables. A parable is certainly no argument, but on the heart and even on the mind of the listener a parable often has an effect which is more than that of a thousand arguments. Buddha was very well aware of this, he liked to embellish his speeches with allusions and his disciples followed him in this. Thus we find in the Suttas of all four collections a veritable flood of parables and it is indeed in no small measure they that lend a literary character and artistic value to these speeches.

A beautiful example of a convincing parable is found in the dialogue of the Buddha with the son of Māluṅkyā,[3] in which Buddha says to the inquisitive disciple who wants information on *being*, *not-being* and similar metaphysical questions, that answering to all these questions did not allow any time for

1. R. O. Franke ZDMG 69, 1915, 455. Eliot I, p. 278 says of the Majjhimanikāya "Taken as a whole it is perhaps the most profound and impassioned of all the Nikāyas and also the oldest".

2. Dialogues of the Buddha, I, 206 f.

3. Majjh. No. 63; Oldenberg, Buddha, p. 324 ff; Warren p. 117 ff.

finding the way to salvation, for freedom from suffering, and this he makes clear through the following parable:

A man is struck by a poisoned arrow. Friends rush to the doctor. He wants to remove the arrow from the wound. The suffering man calls out, "Stop ! I will not allow the arrow to be removed until I know who has shot it, whether a warrior or a Brahmin, a Vaiśya or a Śūdra, from which family he hailed, whether he was tall or short, of which kind and class the arrow was etc. What would happen ? The man would die before one has answered all these questions. Thus also would the disciple die, who would like to have all questions pertaining to the life beyond death and similar questions answered, before he would have recognised the truth about suffering, about the origin of suffering, about the removal of suffering and about the way to the removal of suffering.

Equally apt are the parables of the Tevijjasutta (Dīghanikāya, XIII, 15 ff) in which Buddha wants to show how foolish it is of the Brahmins that they see the path of salvation in the union with Brahman although they must admit that neither they themselves nor their teachers nor the teachers of their teachers, nor the old Ṛṣis of yore have seen this Brahman. "To me", says Buddha, it looks like a number of blind men following one another although the foremost one sees nothing, the middle one sees nothing and the last one sees nothing. And this yearning for the unknown God seems to him to be like a man longing for a beautiful damsel, but to the question who this damsel is, would not know what to answer, would not know to which caste, to which family she belongs, nor know her name, whether she is tall or short, dark or fair-complexioned, and where she lives, or like a man who wanted to construct a stair case to the balcony of a palace without knowing whether this balcony is in the east or south, in the west or north, whether it is high or low or of medium height. In a whole series of beautiful similes in the "Sutta of the Reward for asceticism" (Dīghanikāya II, 69 ff, 78 ff) Buddha compares the happiness of the monk liberated from earthly bonds to the joy of a debtor who, through fortunate enterprises, has succeeded in clearing off not only his debts but has even managed to earn more money for supporting a family;—to the joy of a patient, who, after much suffering, regains his health;—to the joy of a prisoner rotting in jail to whom at last, freedom is given; to the joy of a traveller, who wanders on a dangerous road through a jungle and at last reaches a village inhabited by people. And like a lake which receives its water from one source and into which water does not flow from any side, on which it never rains, so that it receives all its water only from the cool source and it is filled through and through with cool water,—similarly is the monk completely pervaded and permeated by blissful peace.

Numerous are also the parables, by which the futility of pleasures is sought to be described. In order to show how torturous and painful the pleasures of the senses are, seven massive pictures are projected in Sutta 54 of the Majjhimanikāya.[1]

To a dog tortured by hunger the butcher throws a paltry, meatless bone, with which it cannot pacify its hunger—like such paltry bones are the torturous and painful pleasures of the senses out of which only evil is born. As a bird of prey swoops on a piece of flesh and other birds fall on it and badly malign it,—likewise only suffering and evil are born out of the pleasures of senses. As from a pit filled with burning coal, does the wise man withdraw in fright from the pleasures of senses. Like a beautiful picture in a dream that vanishes when we wake up—like a borrowed treasure for which a man is envied by those who do not know that it is only a borrowed one,—are the pleasures of senses. A man comes to a forest, sees a tree laden with fruits, and climbs it to eat the fruits to his heart's content; there comes another man, sees the same tree and to take possession of the fruits, he begins to fell the tree : the man on the tree will be upset;—likewise only pain and torture and all kinds of evil are the result of satisfying the sensual pleasures.

Sometimes the parables fit into the given situation in a very appealing and congenial manner like for example in Sutta 58

1. In Sutta 22 of the Majjh. there is a reference to these seven similes as to something already known.

of the Majjhimanikāya. Then comes Prince Abhaya, incited by Nigaṇṭha Nātaputta, Buddha's opponent, to the Lord, in order to corner him by putting a very difficult question. He asks him whether the Buddha never speaks an unkind word. As he admits that sometimes he too must speak unkind words, Abhaya replies that in that case there is evidently no difference between him and a common man who also indulges in unkind words.

Prince Abhaya was then having on his lap (narrates the Sutta further) a small child of tender age. So the Lord said to Prince Abhaya : "Tell me, O Prince, if this child, due to the carelessness of yours or of the nurse, would put a small piece of wood or a pebble in his mouth, what would you do with him ?" "I would take it out, O Revered One. And if I could not take it out with just one snatch, then I would hold the boy's head with my left hand, and with my right hand, by bending my fingers, I would take it out, even if in doing so the child should bleed. And why that ? Because, O Revered One, I take pity on the boy". "Similarly, O Prince, although the Tathāgata does not say a single word which he knows to be untrue, incorrect, disastrous and which is moreover disagreeable and unpleasant to the others; he also speaks not a single word which he knows to be true, correct, disastrous and which is moreover disagreeable and unpleasant to the others;—but if the Tathāgata knows that a word is true, correct, salutary and is yet disagreeable and unpleasant to the others,—then the Tathāgata knows that it behoves him to speak even such a word ...And why ? Because the Tathāgatha takes pity on the beings".

A very favourite and oft used parable is that of the oil lamp, for e.g. :

"As when, O monks, by means of the oil and the wick an oil lamp would burn and a man would pour oil from time to time and renew the wick, this oil lamp thus fed and provided with fuel would burn for a very long time,—in the same way, O monks, grows the greed of him who finds pleasure in the things of this world which are only fetters"[1]

1. Saṃyuttanikāya, XII, 53.

On being asked by a senior villager, why the Buddha, although it is said of him that he is well-disposed and sympathetic towards all beings, yet preaches his religion to some thoroughly and to the others less thoroughly, he answers with the simile: As the peasant cultivates at first the good field, then the field of medium quality and finally the bad field, so the Buddha preaches his doctrine first to the monks and nuns, then to the lay followers and only at last to the non-followers also.[1]

Also humour is not lacking in these parables, when for example in Majjh. 126 it is said : If one fills a tub with sand and water and mixes it and churns it however much he wants, he will not obtain any sesame oil; if one tries to milk a cow by the horn, however much he may try, he will obtain no milk etc.; in the same way a monk will never reach the goal if he does not endeavour in the right manner.

Some similes have become an integral part of the dictum of the Buddhist texts and probably of the Buddha and of his disciples themselves. When they speak of greed which is the origin of all suffering, then they term this as "thirst", which leads beings from one life to the other. And this wandering from one life to the other, the Saṃsāra, is the "ocean" to whose "other bank" the Nirvāṇa points. Desire and sin, the whole earthly existence is a "flood", and "from the flood is rescued" he who has attained Nirvāṇa. The reward for good and bad deeds, the Karman is the "fruit" and the simile of seed and fruit is always before the eyes of the speakers when there is a talk of the "Karman". When the Buddha speaks, then he "gives out a lion's roar"[2] etc.

A favourite simile,[3] which occurs outside the Nikāyas also, is as follows :

1. Saṃyuttanikāya XLII, 7, 1-8, translated by Winternitz in the Religionsgeschichtl. Lesebuch p. 313 f. R. Otto Franke has compared with it Matth. 13, 12 ff., Mark. 4, 12 and Luk. 8, 10. (DLZ 1901, Col. 2759).

2. In a cave near Turfan A. Grünwedel (Ref: Report on the archaeological works in Idikutschari, Abh. der k. bayr. Akad. d. Wiss. 24, Bd., 1 Abt, Munchen 1906, p. 125) found a picture that represents a monk who preaches which fact is indicated by a small lion standing on a small cloud appearing before his face.

3. Majjhimanikāya, 129; Saṃyuttanikāya, 56, 47 f. The simile is very, popular also in Buddhist Sanskrit literature (S. Winternitz, WZKM 27, 1913,

"Just as, O monks !, when a man would throw a one-eyed yoke into the sea and the east wind would push it to the west and the west-wind to the east, the north wind to the south and the southwind to the north; and there were a one-eyed tortoise that rose to the surface once in a hundred years;—what do you think, O monks, would, the one-eyed tortoise put its neck into the one-eyed yoke ?" "Scarcely ever, perhaps once in a very long time". "But the one-eyed tortoise with its neck might fall into that one-eyed yoke rather than that the fool who, having once fallen into the lower forms of life will ever again be born as a human being. Why ? Because in the lower forms of life there is only mutual murdering and no good deeds".

These similes are also of the greatest importance from the point of view of the History of Culture. For, they take us right into the interior of ancient Indians—the artisans, agriculturists and merchants—of whom the Brahminical literature which deals almost exclusively with priestly and warrior circles can tell us very little.[1] We find in them parables of drivers of carts and horses, of gamblers, of the preparation of sesame oil etc. In one parable (Majjh. 140) the entire work of the goldsmith is described, in another (Majjh. 125) the whole process of taming the elephants and in yet another one (Majjh. 101) the entire process of healing when a man is wounded by a poisoned arrow.[2]

Finally although the parables and similes can be hardly admitted as real evidences still they are the best way of

43. ff.) and occurs also in the Yoga-Vāsiṣṭha (S. G. A. Jacob, JRAS 1909, p. 1120 f.). The simile has nothing in common with the "camel going through the eye of a needle," which G. de Lorenzo and K. E. Neumann (Reden Gotamo Buddho's, III, 334 note) have derived from it.

1. Cf. Mrs. Rhys Davids "Buddhist Parables and Similes" (The Open Court, Chicago, Vol. XXII, 522 ff), which rightly observes, that in these similes enough material is found for a big book which must be written. An admirable ground work has been done in this respect by Mrs. Rhys Davids who prepared the Index of the Similes ("Similes in the Nikāya, a Classified Index" in JPTS 1907 and 1908).

2. The similes of the surgeon are especially popular, as in the whole of Buddhist literature Buddha is often termed "the doctor" (cf. p. 31, Note 1 above).

argumentation that we find in the Suttas. For, as for the rest, when some doctrine or the other is to be proved we find nothing but a list of synonyms and dogmatic divisions and enumerations[1] which are indeed particularly characteristic of the Aṅguttaranikāya, but which also occur in all the Nikāyas.

The method of argumentation in our Suttas can by no means be compared with that of Plato. And as dialogues only a few Suttas can stand comparison with the Platonic dialogues. No doubt Karl Fries[2] has pointed to a number of remarkable parallels between Indian and Greek dialogues. But there is no similarity in just the most essential points. And they are certainly not conspicuous enough to compel us to think of any mutual influence. The majority of the Suttas are not "dialogues" in the proper sense of the word, but they are rather speeches of a chief speaker (usually the Buddha) which are interrupted by the other speakers only through a "yes" or "no" or expressions of approval or applause. But even the best of the real dialogues in the Nikāyas will seldom remind us of the dialogues of Plato, but on the other hand they will again and again remind us of those Itihāsa-dialogues[3] which we have come across in the Mahābhārata.

II. Stories, Songs And Sayings

The Khuddakanikāya or the "collection of smaller pieces", usually considered as the fifth Nikāya and therefore as part of the Suttapiṭaka, considered by some also as part of the Abhidhammapiṭaka, should be more properly called the "collection of Miscellania". For, in this collection we find, besides many smaller works, also some of the most voluminous books of the Pāli-canon. But in respect of content and character the texts compiled here differ largely from one another. In one

1. T. W. Rhys Davids has here the remark: "There are on the contrary many quite decent arguments and inferences." But we do not find many.

2. The philosophical dialogue from Hiob to Plato, Tubingen 1904, p. 65, 76 ff. Although in Plato's Menon K. E. Neumann (Reden Gotamo Buddhos, III, p. 85) sees "a very astonishing reflection of Majjhimanikāya, 107, clearly identifiable upto the fine details", we are not able to see anything of this "reflection".

3. See Vol. I. p. 400 ff.

very peculiar Sutta which occurs many times,[1] we read a prediction of the dangers that threaten the religion of the Buddha in the future. One of these dangers is this that the monks do not like to hear and learn any more "the profound, significant, eternal Suttantas dealing with the void"[2] but they like to lend their ears only to the heretical Suttantas embellished with beautiful words and beautiful syllables, composed by poets, and proclaimed by pupils. This leads one to think that at first the poetical pieces were not recognised in general, that their right to holiness was disputed and that they were only subsequently compiled into a Nikāya – precisely into the Khuddakanikāya. This presumption is based on the fact that the main content of this collection is composed of works of the art of poetry – like sayings, songs, poems, fairy tales and fables. It is possible that subsequently some other texts also which were not poetic but generally not recognised in their genuineness were included in this collection which was completed only at a later date.[3] It cannot be doubted that the works compiled here

1. Saṃyuttanik. XX. 7; Aṅgutt. IV, 160; V, 79, 5. Cf. Rhys Davids, Buddhist India 110 f; La Vallee Poussin, Bouddhisme, p. 149. This passage is just typical of the oral transmission of the Buddhist texts. If they were not heard and recited any more, they disappeared.

2. Sunnata "void" (devoid of independent reality). Here as in a few other passages of the Pāli Canon we already meet with the conception of the void (śūnyatā) which in later times is the central idea of the philosophy of the Mahāyāna. Cf. C. A. F. Rhys Davids, A Buddhist Manual of Psychological Ethics. p. xlii f.

3. It is typical of the not all too fixed character of the Khuddakanikāya as canonical collection that the Buddhists of Burma consider also 4 texts Milindapañha, Suttasaṃgaha (an anthology of the Suttapiṭaka) Peṭakopadesa and Netti as parts of the Khuddakanikāya, although they are not considered as canonical in Ceylon. (Mabel H. Bode, Pāli literature of Burma, London 1909, p. 4 f). That in the Siamese edition of the Pāli canon (Note 2 on p. 21 above) 7 texts of the Khuddakanikāya (Vimānavatthu, Petavatthu, Theragāthā, Therigāthā, Jātaka, Buddhavaṃsa and Cariyapiṭaka) are missing is perhaps, no pure coincidence at all. According to the Dīpavaṃsa V, 37 the Mahāsamgītikas did not recognise the Paṭisambhidā, the Nidessa and a part of the Jātaka. The Kuddhakanikāya as a whole does not appear in the Chinese Āgamas, but many of the texts are included in other collections Cf. M. Anesaki in "Transactions of the Asiatic Society of Japan," Vol. 35, part 3, 1908, p. 9.

originated at different periods and were originally not meant to form parts of a collection.[1] And although the collection as such is one of the latest compilations of the canon, yet it contains besides comparatively younger handiworks, also many of the oldest Buddhist poems. Indeed it contains all those works of Buddhist literature which are among the most significant creations of Indian poetic art. But in the following pages we will discuss the texts of the Khuddakanikāya not according to their presumed age or their importance, but in the order in which we got them transmitted by the Buddhists of Ceylon in their manuscripts.

1. At the head of this collection is the Khuddakapāṭha,[2] "the recitation of the small pieces" or "the small reader", as one could translate it somewhat more liberally. This is a compilation of nine short texts which a prospective monk must know more than any other texts and which are used in the Buddhist cult as a kind of Mantras or "prayers". Whether the compilation is meant as a manual for the novice or as a "prayer book" remains an open question. The first four pieces are quite short. No. 1 is the Buddhist confession of faith, No. 2 an enumeration of the ten commandments for the monks, No. 3 a list of the 32 parts of the body for the purpose of meditation on the loathsomeness and the futility of the human body and No. 4 contains the "Questions of the Novice". Here in ten questions ("What is one? What is two?" etc.) and answers—in the manner of the Aṅguttaranikāya—the most important Buddhist terms are explained. The remaining five pieces are short Suttas, which through their content as well as through their formula-like usages and refrains reveal themselves as serving liturgical purposes. From the earliest times the Indians have attached great importance to

---

1. Otherwise it would be unthinkable that in the small Khuddakapāṭha three Suttas (Maṅgalsutta, Ratnasutta and Metasutta) occur which appear verbatim in the Suttanipāta also, or that the same stories are told from an entirely different point of view than in the Jātaka.

2. Published and translated by R. C. Childers in JRAS 1870 pp. 309-339. Translated into German by Karl Seidenstucker, Breslau 1910, most of the pieces also by M. Winternitz in "Religionsgeschichtl. Lesebuch", p. 259f, 261 f. 295-300

Maṅgalas, i.e. to all sorts of possible things and ceremonies which are considered as good omens or which are supposed to bring luck. Such Maṅgalas like good wishes, blessings, feeding of Brahmins, wreaths of flowers, music, chanting etc. were indispensable at every sacrificial festival, at every celebration of wedding, birth and similar events. In the Maṅgalasutta[1] (No. 5) Buddha teaches what he considers as the best Maṅgalas. He says, for example :

"Respecting the parents, affectionately caring for wife and children and a peaceful occupation : this is the best Maṅgala.

Generosity, pious living, affectionately caring for kith and kin and irreproachable deeds, : this is the best Maṅgala.

Renouncing and avoiding evil, abstaining from drinking intoxicating drinks and observance of the injunctions of religion : this is the best Maṅgala".

The same spirit of a higher ethics permeates also the remaining Suttas. This is the case with the Ratnasutta (No. 6) with which in the traditional way the three Ratnas or "gems"[2] are venerated. Similarly the 7th Sutta also which is devoted to the cult of the dead and of which even today some verses are recited at the time of cremating dead bodies in Ceylon and and Siam. On a still higher plane are the 8th Sutta of "the hidden treasure" in which it is said that a treasure of good deeds is the best treasure that the Buddhist may collect, and above all the splendid "Mettasutta" (no. 9), in which wishing the welfare (metta) of all beings is praised as the true Buddhist cult.

Seven of these nine texts are used even today at the time of the Buddhist Parittā-ceremony or of the "Pirit" as it is called by the Buddhists of Ceylon. The word Parittā means "protection, defence" and is used even in the Tipiṭaka in the sense of

---

1. Copleston, Buddhism, p. 140, says of this Sutta: "It is repeated nowa-days again and again by the monks of Ceylon and it is a pity that nobody understands it". In Burma, when there is an epidemics this Sutta is sung by white-clad old men and women before the images of Buddha at cross-roads. Ind. Ant. 8, 1879, pp. 82 and 329.

2. These are: Buddha, Dhamma (religion) and Saṅgha (monks' community).

"Pirit' or "conjuring formula, blessing". "Today by Parittā (Sinhalese Pirit) one understands in Ceylon the recitation (or reading out) by the Bhikkhus of some thirty texts belonging to the canon in order to expel the effect ofevil powers. The Parittā ceremony is performed on all possible occasions, for example while building a house, at the time of death, disease etc.[1]" We can only agree with K. Seidenstücker when he sees in the Suttas 5-9 old songs of exorcism, and as the first four pieces are composed in the form of formulas, we consider it as not improbable, that the Khuddakapāṭha was compiled for similar purposes, as the Parittā textbook used at present in Ceylon.

2. The Dhammapada[2] ("words of religion"[3] is the most widely known work of the Buddhist literature and also the

---

1. Seidenstucker ibid p. 3. cf. M. Grimbolt and Leon Feer, Extraits du Paritta in the JA 1871, s. 6, t. XVIII, 225 ff. In Burma also there is a small collection of texts from the Suttapiṭaka called Paritta or Mahāparitta which is used for exorcisms and is more popular among the people than any other Pāli book (M. H. Bode ibid p. 3 f).

2. Dhammapadam, Palice edidit, latine vertit V. Fausboll, Huaniae 1855. The Dhammapada being a collection of moral verses in Pāli, edited a second time with a literal Latin translation by V. Fausboll, London 1900. Translated into German by A. Weber (ZDMG 14, 1860 and Indische Strefen, Vol. I, 1868) by L. v. Schroeder ("Worte der Wahrheit" Leipzig, 1892) and by K. E. Neumann ("Wahrheitsfad", Leipzig 1893) into English by F. Max Muller (Introduction to Buddhaghosa's Parables translated by T. Rogers, London 1870, and SBE Vol. X, Part I, from this English translation translated into German by Th. Schultze, 2nd edition Leipzing 1906). The work has been translated into French by Fernando Hu(Paris 1878) and into Italian by P. E. Pavolini (Milan 1908) and Testi di morale buddhistica, Lanciano 1912, pp. 1-80). Pavolini (JGAI 25 1912, p. 324 also mentions a Russian translation by N. Gerasimov).

3. According to the different meanings of pada and of dhamma, the title has been translated variously as "Footsteps of Religion", "Path of Religion", "Path of Virtue", "Sentences of Religion", "Worte der Wahrheit," etc. The title means certainly only a "collection of words (Texts, Sentences) on religion" This is also according to R. C. Childers "Dictionary of the Pāli Language, London 1875 p. 117 f. Cf- Max Muller, SBE Vol. 10, Part 1, p. xlv ff,; L. v. Schroeder, Transl. p. 131. ff.; R. O. Frauke. ZDMG 46, 1892, 734 f.; WZKM 15 1901, p. 396; PTS Dic., s. v. There is no doubt that the "Dhammapada" is used in a collective sense, like "Udāna," "Itivuttaka etc., and that it means "Collection of Words or Verses on Religion", "Dhamma Words" or "Religious Sentences."

work that is known longest which has also been translated repeatedly into the European languages. It is also oft quoted in all works on Buddhism and always esteemed very highly by virtue of its profound moral content. In Ceylon the book has been used for centuries down to our times by the novices as a text-book which they must have studied before they can receive the higher orders (upasampadā). For this reason there is not a monk in Ceylon who cannot recite his Dhammapada from beginning to end from memory. Buddhist preachers often take verses from the Dhammapada as the text of their sermons.[1] It is an anthology of sayings which refer mainly to the ethical teachings of Buddhism. Of the 423 stanzas every 10-20 are put together in one section (Vagga) on the basis that they deal with the same subject that a simile (for example of the flower in the 4th Vagga, the "flower-section"), or sometimes even a refrain runs through all the verses of such a section. The compiling and the ordering in Vaggas is of course the work of the compiler. But often many verses actually form together a small poem, as for example the verses 197-200. :

> Ah, how do we live so happily, without hatred among those full of hatred :
>
> Among those full of hatred we do live without hatred.
>
> Ah, how do we live so happily among invalids free from infirmity !
>
> Among invalid men we do live free from all infirmity.
>
> Ah, how do we live so happily without greed among greedy ones !
>
> Among greedy men we do live without greed.
>
> Ah, how do we live so happily we who actually nothing possess !
>
> Blissfully we feed on joy, like the gods in radiant splendour.

Especially popular are the verse-pairs that form together a whole, for example the verses 335 f :

---

1. Cf. Sumangala Thera in the Foreword to his edition.

Whom she vanquishes, the wild greed, the pleasure of senses
His worry grows, like wild weeds shooting suddenly up.
He who vanquishes her, the wild greed, who is hard to be vanquished,
His worry vanishes like the drop from the lotus-leaf.

Many of the most famous Buddhist sayings are found in the Dhammapada. Thus the beautiful verses (153f) which Buddha is supposed to have spoken after he attained enlightenment :

"Of many births I have gone through the cycle restlessly
Seeking the house-builder. Full of suffering is eternal rebirth.
House-builder, you are detected ! You will not build the house anymore.
Your rafters are broken, the roof of the house destroyed
Free is my heart, accomplished the destruction of all desires.

A simple and yet splendid metaphor : the greed, the world-pleasure is the "house-builder" who again and again builds up a new house, i.e. a new body on a new rebirth. In the sayings we come across such simple but impressive metaphors and similes again and again. Thus the equanimity of the wise man is compared with a deep, mirror-smooth lake or with an unshakable rock (81f), or it is said :— just as the ladle does not have any taste of the soup, so also the fool has nothing from his contact with the wise men; only the wise man benefits from the contact with wise men, as it is only the tongue that enjoys the taste of the soup (65 f). Whoever speaks or acts with an impure heart, is followed by suffering as the foot of the animal drawing a cart is followed by the wheel; whoever speaks or acts with a pure heart, is followed by joy as by his own shadow (1 f). Or : "Not fast, as the milk curdles does the evil deed one has done break up into its consequences; burning it follows the fool like fire that is covered with ash".[1] We come across such metaphors at every step and they appear in pairs. There is, however, also no lack of more artistic sayings with those plays on-words (e.g. 344) for which Indians have a preference from times immemorial.

More than half of all verses of the Dhammapada are also found in other texts of the Pāli-canon and it can hardly be doubted that the compiler of our anthology has, in general, taken them from those texts where we find them even today.[1] However, in the collection such sayings have also included, as are originally not Buddhistic but have been taken from that inexhaustible fountain of Indian sayings of wisdom, from where also they found their way into Manu's lawbook, into Mahābhārata, into the texts of the Jainas and into the tales of the Pañcatantra etc. It is generally almost impossible to decide where such sayings were placed originally.[2]

3. While the Dhammapada is only a collection of verses and only later on stories were added in the form of a commentary not belonging to the canon any more in which we are told on what occasion the individual verses were pronounced, the Udāna,[3] the collection of the "enthusiastic pronouncements" consists of verses and stories. The work is divided into 8 vaggas or "sections", each of which contains 10 Suttas. These Suttas are very short stories, which tell some experience from Buddha's time and end with a pronouncement of Buddha, which stimulated by this experience, Buddha is said to have "breathed out", i.e. given out himself in his enthusiasm. Just such an enthusiastic pronouncement is called Udāna i.e. literally "expiration" and it is usually a verse (Śloka, Triṣṭubh or Jagatī), more seldom a prose saying. These "enthusiastic pronoucements" serve mostly to glorify the Buddhistic ideals of life, the deep

1. Cf. Rhys Davids in JRAS 1900, 559 f., and the concordance by R. O. Franke, in the appendix to his Translation, pp. 93 ff.

2. Sometimes, we may be reminded of Brahminical sources. This verse 109 is probably only a quotation from a Brahminical text that is given so as to serve as a connecting link to the following verses (110-115).

3. Edited by Paul Steinthal, London PTS 1885. Translated into English by D. M. Strong, London 1902; into German by K. Seidenstucker (1920). See also E. Windisch in JPTS 1890, p. 91 ff.; K Seidenstucker, Das Udāna, I. Teil : Allgemeine Einteitung, Leipzig 1913; B. C. Mazumdar, JRAS 1911, p. 197 ff.

delightful peace of mind of the holy man (Arhat) severed from all that is earthly things, the unending blissfulness of the Nirvāṇa.

The Book of the Udānas contains only a section of the "pithy sayings" ascribed to Buddha. In other books of the Tipiṭaka also, there are utterances of this kind, called "Udāna", which are not always attributed to Buddha, but sometimes to a king, a deity or some other personage.[1] Quite a number of Suttas as well as of separate Udānas (without the Suttas belonging to them) are common to the Udāna and other collections.[2] In particular, it contains several Suttas relating to the life of the Buddha, which are in agreement with the biographical texts of the Vinayapiṭaka and the Mahā-Parinibbāna-Sutta. However, they were probably not borrowed from these collections, but were based on earlier traditions on which the various collections have drawn.

It is an open question whether, as Seidenstucker thinks,[3] the majority of the Udānas in this collection are really "authentic words of the Master". We are safe, however, in granting that most of these short[4] and beautiful utterances certainly bear the stamp of antiquity and that many of them are possibly the actual words of Buddha himself or of his most prominent disciples. On the other hand, there can be no doubt that the utterances themselves, are as a rule older, than the narratives into which they are inserted. Though a few of them may have come down from the very beginning in association with an introductory story, yet in the majority of cases it was the compiler who appended such a story to an old Udāna. This is why many of the Suttas only contain very simple, in fact sometimes silly stories, inappropriate to the pathos of the utterances themselves. For instance, in one pithy saying (III,7) we are told

1. For instance, Vinayap. Mahāv. I, 1, 5 Dighanikāya XV 3, 10 Saṃyuttanik. I, 3, III, 3, VII, 1, XXII, 55.

2. Cf. Seidenstucker Allg. Einleitung p. 62f.

3. l. c. p. 36. Seidenstucker is probably right in saying that the metrical irregularities which Mr. Mazumdar has pointed out in some of the Udānas must not be corrected but are rather a sign of antiquity.

4. Only III, 10 and VI, 8, are not short sayings but short homilies.

that even the gods envy the saint who is free from desire. To illustrate this, a story is told how Sakka and the other gods actually envy the Arhat Mahākassapa. Another pithy saying (VI, 9) compares people who are engrossed in worldly life and do not strive after that which is essential with moths rushing into a flame. The corresponding story relates that Buddha once sojourned in Sāvatthi, and noticed a number of moths flyin into the burning oil lamps and being burnt.

Or, again, the Buddha sees, for example, how the venerable Sāriputta teaches another monk through a lecture. That suffices to make him make the "enthusiastic pronouncement" (VII, 5)

> As he is free from all desires, is the wheel[1] broken;
> Dried up is the river[2] and runs not any more; no more
> Does the broken wheel roll,—suffering's end is reached.

Or, of Sāriputta and Moggallāna, the two great disciples of the Buddha the following edifying story is narrated :

The venerable Sāriputta is sitting in a moonlight night with clean-shaven head in the open, engrossed in meditation. Then a Yakṣa, a giant demon in jest gives him a blow on his head. "But with one such stroke one could strike down an elephant seven or eight and a half cubits tall or smash to pieces a big mountain peak." Scarcely has he given the blow, when he sinks down to hell crying," I am burning, I am burning". The venerable Moggallāna sees all this with his superhuman eye, rushes to Sāriputta in order to make enquiries about his welfare. "Are you well, friend, are you feeling well ? Have you no pain ?" he asks and Sāriputta replies, he is quite well, only he has a little headache. At this the friend expresses astonishment mixed with admiration, whereupon Sāriputta on his part gives expression to his wonderment that Moggallāna, by virture of his miraculous power, has seen the giant demon, wheras he himself has not even once seen even a "dust particle of a spirit." Buddha hears

---

1. & 2. The "wheel" is the wheel of consecutive rebirths; the "river" are the desires of the senses. To the Buddhists these metaphors are so familiar that they have become a part of the diction of their language. Cf. also the parables, p. 68 ff.

this wonderful conversation with his superhuman ear and gives out the "enthusiastic pronouncement" (IV, 4).

Whose sense is firm as a rock and does not shake,
Free from desire for everything whatever causes desire,
Who does not grow angry, whatever may cause anger,
To him, who has such a sense, can suffering never happen.

If there is a certain kind of humour in this story it is perhaps not an intentional one. Another story tells of a holy man who attains complete Nirvāṇa by flying up into the air and burning there in such a way that of him neither coal nor smoke is left behind, which makes Buddha make the "enthusiastic pronouncement" (VIII, 10) :

Nobody knows, where the fire has gone,
When by the whizzing down iron-hammer
Off the spark springs and slowly dies out,
Thus of the fully liberated one, who from the fetters of the senses,
Who from the floods of desires, has fled, who the Nirvāṇa's Bliss has reached – knows no one, where he has gone.

How badly does the childish legend fit into the beautiful and profound Buddha's sayings ! There are also instances where "enthusiastic pronouncement" does not at all harmonise with the story, for example, V, 5 and VII, 10. There are a few Suttas, in which the narrative is more interesting and more significant than the "pithy saying". For instance, III, 2 tells the story of Nanda, the half brother of Buddha, who, though a monk still harbours thoughts of the wife he has left behind, and is taken by the Lord to Indra's heaven, where he sees the heavenly nymphs, and observes that, besides these, his wife only looks like a wretched she-ape. Then Nanda only practises his monastic vow so as to gain possession of the beautiful heavenly women, but finally Buddha puts him on the right path.[1] The story in II, 8, is of interest because it shows that in comparatively olden times loving devotion (bhakti) to Buddha was regarded

1. Translation (rather free) by D. M. Strong, p. 129.

as productive of miracles. The parable of the blind men and the elephant in VI, 4, is famous :

Some ascetics and Brahmins once met together and began to quarrel. Some said : "The world is eternal," and the others "The world is not eternal". Some declared: "The world is finite," and the others: "The world is infinite;" again some taught : Body and soul are separate," and others : "Body and soul are but one". Some said : "the Perfect man is after death," Others maintained : "The perfect man is not after death" and so forth. Finally all this leads to a quarrel and to harsh and insulting words. The monks tell Buddha of this quarrel, and then he tells them the following parable :

There was once a king, who had all those who were born blind brought together. When they were assembled, the king commanded an elephant to be shown to them. An elephant was brought, and they made some feel his head, others his ear and others his tusk, others his trunk etc., and the last one the elephant's tail.[1] Then the king asked them : "How does the elephant look ?" Then those who had touched the elephant's head, said : "An elephant is like a pot", those who had touched the ear, said : "An elephant is like a winnowing basket" those who had touched the tusk declared: "An elephant is like a ploughshare", those who had touched the trunk said : "An elephant is like the pole of the plough" etc. and those who had touched the tail maintained: "An elephant is like a broom". A great tumult arose. Each one maintained "An elephant is like this, and not otherwise; he's not like that, he is like this," until at last they came to blows at which the king was mightily amused.

Even so, concluded Buddha, is the case of the ascetics and Brahmins, each of whom has only seen a portion of the truth and who then maintain "Thus is truth, and not otherwise, truth is not thus, but thus."[2]

1. The text reads: "He showed them the head, "etc, but the meaning is of course that he told them to feel the elephant's head etc.

2. The parable was also familiar to the Brahmanical philosophers among whom the rule of the blind men and elephant (andhagajanyāya) has become proverbial. Cf. G. A. Jacob, "A Second Handful of Popular Maxims", Bombay 1902, p. 53 and JRAS 1902, p. 174 T. W. Rhys Davids JRAS 1911, p. 200 f. It occurs also in the Jaina Syādvādamañjarī. (See V. S. Ghate Ind. Ant. 42, 1913, p. 251).

In the light of the aforesaid we see, that only the Udāna verses belong to the genuine poetry of ancient Buddhism, while the prose-stories have been partly invented by one or more commentators and partly taken over from other texts. Some of the stories are evidently fragments of the Buddha and of the Vinayapiṭaka.[1] That they were included in the canon may be due to the reason that they are perhaps older than the stories of the Dhammapada commentary; but the reason may perhaps also lie in this that these short pronouncements appeared to need elaboration through introductory stories.

4. Like the Udāna the Itivuttaka[2] ("Thus spoke Buddha"[3]) also consists of prose and verse. But here the relation between the two is essentially different. Here we do not have any narrative prose, but the same idea, whether it be a teaching or a warning, is delivered partly in prose and partly in verse. And obviously in many cases—in about 50 of the 112 short pieces of which the work consists—some idea is first pronounced briefly in prose and then again repeated in verse—deviating only so much as is required by the metrical form.[4] In some cases only one verse has a counterpart in prose while many verses follow to which nothing in the prose relates. And these cases are followed by the numerous cases in which prose and verse complement each other, in such a way that the prose forms only a very short introduction to the thoughts pronounced in the verse or that thought is treated from one angle in the prose and from a different angle in the verse. In all these cases the spirit of the prose and that of the verse is to a large extent the same and it is not seldom that a thought is expressed in prose more sharply and emphatically and perhaps even more

1. Thus I, 4; II, 1; VI, 1; VII, 9; VIII, 5 and 6.

2. Edited by Windisch, London PTS 1889. Translated into English (Sayings of Buddha, with an Introduction and Notes) by J. H. Moore, New York 1908; into German by K. Seidenstucker, Leipzig 1922; into Italien by Pavolini, Testidi morale buddistica, Lanciano 1912, pp. 97-111.

3. The title means literally, "The speeches beginning with the word thus was spoken (by the Lord)". Each piece begins obviously with the words "This was spoken by the Lord".

4. On the metre of the Itivuttaka, refer J. H. Moore in JAOS vol. 28, 317-330.

beautifully than in the verse. Yet even in the latter there is no lack of formalised usages and of repetitions so characteristic of Buddhist Suttas and the style is in general free from excessive verbosity. They are almost all short pieces. The language is in the prose as well as in the verse, simple, natural and not all too metaphorical. There are no developed similes. Yet beautiful individual metaphors occur. Thus the generous man who gives liberally to pious beggars is compared to the rain-yielding cloud that pours out its water on hill and dale (no. 75). The wise man avoids evil company, for through a poisoned arrow the pure quiver is also rendered impure (no. 76). The senses are the gates which must be guarded well (no. 28 and 29). Buddha calls himself the incomparable healer and surgeon and the monks his children and successors (no. 100). The language of the prose attains its most exalted height in the piece no. 40 about wishing well of all beings (metta) :

"All deeds conditioned by existence, through which man acquires merit, O monks, all of them are not worth even the sixteenth part of the well-wishing (metta), that frees the mind; but the well-wishing radiates, shines and illuminates by excelling them as mental freedom. Just as, O monks, all the lights of the stars are not equal to the sixteenth part of the moonlight, but that the moonlight excelling them all, radiates, shines and illuminates,—just in a similar way, O monks, are the deeds conditioned by existence, through which man acquires merit, not equal to the sixteenth part of the well-wishing, that frees the mind, but the well-wishing radiates, shines and illuminates by excelling them as mental freedom. Just as, o monks, when, in the last month of the rainy season, in autumn, the sky is clear and cloudless, the sun rises on the sky and, chasing away the darkness which fills the whole space, radiates, shines and illuminates,—just in a similar way, O monks, are all etc ... excels. And just as, O monks, at dawn, when night has passed, the morning star radiates, shines and illuminates, just in a similar way, O monks, are all etc ... excels.[1]

Sometimes the prose has a personal note which is lacking in the verses. Thus Buddha says in no. 30 f, that two things pain

1. Cf. Pischel, Leben und Lehre des Buddha, p. 76 f.

him, namely when a man has done no good and when a man has done evil; and that two things please him, namely when a man has done no evil and when a man has done good. The verses say only that he who has done evil in thought, word and deed goes to the hell after his death, while the virtuous man who does good in thought, word and deed will attain heaven. In the prose of no. 92 Buddha says most beautifully : Even if a monk holds the ham of my robe and follows me at every step, and is thereby avaricious, passionate, wicked etc., then he is far from me and I am far from him. But if a monk lives a hundred miles away from me and is not avaricious, not passionate and not wicked etc., then he is still close to me, I am close to him. Following this there are verses composed in a dull commonplace manner, in which it is said that the avaricious man, the wicked man, the discontented man is far from the wise man who has attained peace; whereas the good man, the quiet man, the selfless man is very close to the good, the quiet and the selfless. It seems almost that here a compiler has welded together two texts, one in prose and the other in verse, although they have nothing in common than that in both the words "far" and "close" appear.

Indeed, cases are not seldom, where the prose represents an independent Sutta and the verses that follow have to the prose only a distant relation that is caused by the sound of words. There are really some pieces where prose and verse do not at all have anything to do with each other or even contradict each other. In all these cases it is a matter of later additions. That an idea was first expressed in prose and then clothed in verse or that a teaching was begun in prose and then continued in verse, —this seems to be an old form of Buddhistic poetry. As these texts which had this form were then compiled in the Itivuttaka, —perhaps immediately after the first compiler, or perhaps only later—other texts in prose and verse which were taken from somewhere were also combined according to the same pattern and added to the collection. The fact is that in the Chinese translation of the Itivuttaka made by Hiuen-Tsiang, many of the last pieces of our collection are missing.[1] and that

1. Cf. Watanabe, Chinese collection of Itivuttakas, in JPTS, 1907, p. 44 ff. Cf. A. J. Edmunds, Buddhist and Christian Gospels, I, 209 ff. On

some of these last pieces are again found in the Aṅguttaranikāya. It is highly probable that they have been taken from there. If to this we add that a number of verses, combined with different prose pieces, appear twice, then there is no doubt that even in this very small collection earlier and later pieces are combined. Among the additions there are also some pieces, where the prose appears to be a sort of a commentary to the verses. In the old and genuine pieces however[1] the prose is not inferior to the verses in value as well as in age. And in the later additions also it can happen that an old prose piece has been combined with later verses.

5. If it can be presumed that in all the books of the Khuddakanikāya mentioned till now some pieces of the oldest Buddhistic poetry are contained, then the same thing can be said with a greater degree of certainty in the case of the Suttanipāta[2] (the "small collection of doctrinal lectures").[3] For, though not the whole collection as such, still some pieces of its important constituents can be proved to belong to the oldest

---

the other hand the Chinese Itivuttaka has 137 songs against 112 in the Pali text. Cf. Seidenstucker, ib. p. xvi ff.

1. Moore wrongly considers the prose in general to be of later origin. That some of the oldest pieces of the Itivuttaka originate from Buddha himself, is probable. But much too optimistic is A. J. Edmund when he says, "If the Itivuttaka be not the words of Buddha, nothing is" (Buddhist and Christian Gospels, I, p. 83). Seidenstucker also sees in the prose the nucleus of the work. It is probable that in the oldest passages of the Itivuttaka there is much that can be traced back to Buddha himself.

2. Edited by V. Fausboll, London PTS 1885 and 1893 and translated by himself into English in SBE Vol X, Part 2, 1881, from this translation again translated into German by K. E. Neumann (Die Reden Gotamao Buddhos aus der Sammlung der Bruchstucke Suttanipāta des Pāli Kanons", Leipzig 1905, 2nd edition, 1911, as Vol IV of "Reden Gotamo Buddhos") Cf. also A. Pfungst," "Aus der indischen Kulturwelt", Stuttgart 1904, p. 62-85 H. Oldenberg, "Aus dem alten Indien", Berlin 1910, pp. 25-64. New edition of the text by Dines Anderson and Helmer Smith London PTS 1913. Cf. Rhys Davids, Buddhist India, p. 177ff.

3. Nipāta is a small section of a bigger collection; the sections of the Aṅguttaranikāya are called so. Hence it is translated as 'small collection". Neumann translates them as "fractions", Oldenberg (ibid p. 25), "Isolated occasional speeches."

of what we possess of ancient Buddhistic poetry. The Suttanipāta is a collection of poetical Suttas in 5 sections. The first 4 sections (Uragavagga, Cūlavagga, Mahāvagga Aṭṭhakavagga) contain 54 shorter poems, while the 5th section (Pārāyaṇa) is a long, independent poem consisting of 16 shorter pieces. Of these 5 sections, two, Aṭṭhakavagga and Pārāyaṇa, are mentioned with their titles and quoted both in other texts of the Pāli-canon as well as in the Buddhistic Sanskrit texts.[1] To these two sections there is a commentary which has been included in the canon (as the 11th book of the Khuddakanikāya) under the title "Niddesa". Further, individual Suttas and numerous Gāthās (and that from all the 5 sections) can be found in the other texts of the canon.[2] Among the texts which King Aśoka especially recommends for study in the Bhabra-edict are three texts which probably belong to the Suttanipāta.[3] On the grounds of language and contents also we find that some of these Suttas date back to the beginnings of Buddhism and many might have been originated at least in the circles of the earliest disciples of Buddha, not long after his death.

As generally recognised as the hoary past of this poetry is also its significance for the knowledge of the old doctrine of Buddha. And the Suttanipāta is, besides the Dhammapada, perhaps the most frequently quoted text in all works on

---

1. The same two texts also occur in the Chinese Tipiṭaka, while the Suttanipāta as a whole has not been translated into Chinese. For this, see, M. Anesaki in JPTS 1906-7, p. 50 f Le Museon N. S VII, 1906 p. 33 ff. and Transactions of the Asiatic Society of Japan XXXV 1908, Part 3, p. 8 ff. Fragments of an Arthavargiya-Sūtra in Sanskrit have been discovered in Central Asia. s. A. F. R. Hoernle JRAS 1916, 709 ff.

2. Cf. R. Otto Franke in ZDMG 63, 1909, p. 1 ff, 23 ff, 255 ff, 551 ff.; 64, 1910, 1ff, 760 ff.; 66, 1912, 204 ff, 699 ff Franke (WZKM 28, 1914, 261 ff) endeavours to prove that the Suttanipāta has borrowed the Sela-Sutta (III, 7) and the Vāseṭṭha-Sutta (III, 9) from the Majjhimanikāya (No. 92 and No. 98). This proof is not conclusive. But even if were, it would only follow that the collection of the Suttanipāta is later than the collection of the Majjhimanikāya. As neither the Majjmanikāya nor the Suttanipāta is a unified work, it does not follow that all the separate portions of the Suttanipāta are later than the Majjhimanikāya.

3. Cf. Neumann, Reden Gotamo Buddho's I, 567 IV, 71 f., 226 and Dharmānanda Kosambi, Ind. Ant, 41, 1912, p. 37 ff.

Buddhism. In short, the Suttas of this collection are esteemed generally also as works of poetic art.

We have here verse groups, sometimes short, sometimes long, which are combined into one poem by means of the same idea and often also by means of the same refrain. Side by side with prose sermons into which occasional verses are inserted, we also find sermons in verse but with a prose framework.[1] We also find the forms popular since early ages, namely the pure dialogue as well as the Ākhyāna or the ballad, in which the stanzas of dialogues alternate with those of narration, and finally we find the Ākhyāna[2] forms, a mixture of prose and verse which we have already seen in the old Brāhminic and epic poetry. Again and again the Brāhminic ideas are taken up and pursued, or references are made to them. The Brāhmaṇadhammikasutta (19), the "poem of the pious ones among the Brahmins" could be found as well in an old Purāṇa. It describes how the Ṛṣis of ancient times who were the "true Brahmins" lived in abstinence in every respect; how they were attracted by the wealth and the luxurious life of the kings and longed for such pleasures themselves, got beautiful women and riches as gifts from King Ikṣvāku and how from this the bloody animal sacrifices ensued during which even the innocent cow was killed. Caste-mixing and moral decadence were the results of this. Thus Buddhism is presented here as a return to true "Brahminism". Also in the Selasutta (33) which tells the conversion of Sela, the Brahmin, there are texts which very much resemble verses of the Bhagavadgītā and the Anugītā.[3] Thus in many poems also the Buddhist monk who is true to his vow is described as the "true muni".[4] The idea that we came across already in an old piece

1. E.g. Sundarikabhāradvāja-Sutta, Bela-Sutta and Others. Cf. Oldenberg, "Zur Geschichte der altimdischen Prosa", p. 77 ff.

2. There is no reason why we should use the expression "ākhyāna" only for the latter form of narrative poetry and not for the ballad in general. According to Buddhaghoṣa the Suttanipāta consists of Gāthā, Geyya and Vyākaraṇa (Paramatthajotikā, Introd.)

3. Cf. Suttanipāta 568 f with Bhagavadgītā IX, 30 and Anug. 28, 2, 29, 1.

4. Muni, the silent one, the ascetic, who has vowed to be silent is first of all a term used for a Brahminical ascetic.

of the Mahābhārata,[1] that true Brahminism consists not in birth but in good conduct is beautifully elaborated in the Vāsettha-sutta (35) in 63 verses with the refrain "Him do I call a true Brahmin". In other poems however, in a subtle polemic manner the Buddhistic ideal of life is contrasted with the Brahminical one and is shown to be superior to it. Thus in the Āmagandha-sutta (II, 2) a Brahmin to whom observance of food regulations is the highest moral commandment and enjoyment of forbidden flesh is the most reprehensible impurity, is told by Buddha that true impurity consists not in the enjoyment of flesh, but

"Torturing living beings, murdering, killing, enslaving,
Thieving, lying and cheating, enjoying the neighbour's wife—
This is impurity and not enjoyment of flesh".

"Being cruel and harsh, slandering, betraying,
Being merciless, proud and greedy, giving nothing —
This is impurity and not the enjoyment of flesh".

By means of a poem like the Kāśibharadvājasutta (I, 4) we feel ourselves transported to the early beginnings of Buddhism when the monk was sometimes still looked upon as an idler by the working people, by peasants and herdsmen. Here Bharadvaja the Brahminical agriculturist mocks and sends away the begging Buddha saying that he who does not work shall also not eat. Thereupon Buddha shows him that he too works and what his "ploughing" consists of. And in the Dhaniyasutta, (I,2) one of the most beautiful of these old poems, the pleasant happiness of the wealthy herdsman who finds delight in his wealth and happy family life is contrasted with the quiet happiness of the Buddha who wanders devoid of all possessions but who is free from all earthly bonds. In a splendid dialogue the rich Dhaniya and Buddha speak one verse each alternately with the same refrain, "Rain, heaven, when you want".

1. See Vol. I, p. 377 f. The theme of "the true Brahmin" is also dealt with in the Dhammapada (Chapt. 26=383-423), in the Udāna I, and similarly in the Jinistic Uttarājjhayaṇa XXV. Cf. Charpentier, WZKM 24, 1910, 62 ff.

These poets find again and again new melodies to sing the old song, that only the secluded monk who has and wants to have no connection with wife and children and with the joys and sorrows of this world, is truly blissful. What is told in the form of a lively dialogue in the Dhaniyasutta is found in the Khaggavisanasutta (I, 3), in the "Rhinoceros-Poem", in 41 powerful stanzas with the refrain "May he wander alone, like the rhinoceros", expressed with a seriousness and pathos, which cannot fail to impress even those who are absolutely far from the monastic view of life.

The dialogue-form is combined sometimes—in the Ālavaka-sutta (10) and Sūcilomasutta (17)—with the ancient form of riddle-poetry which we have already come across in the Vedas and the epics. Just like in the Mahābhārata[1] here too a Yakṣa appears as questioner and a wise man answers the questions by delivering speeches on the ethical teachings of Buddhism.

But the Suttanipāta contains not only didactic but also individual narrative dialogues. Of these, three—Nālakasutta (37), Pabbajjasutta (27) and Padhanasutta (28)—are of special importance to us. For, they are precious remnants of that ancient spiritual ballad-poetry, from which has originated the later epic presentation of the life of Buddha like the heroic epics from the mundane ballads or Ākhyānas.[2] The main peculiarity of these ballads is the dialogue-form. Speech and counter-speech would be sufficient mostly to picturise to the listeners the course of a story. Where however that was not the case; often short formulas in prose, a short introduction or a few short sentences in prose were introduced. It was one further step in development that between dialogue-stanzas they inserted stanzas also. This last stage in the development of the ancient Indian Ākhyāna, the stage actually preceding the epic, we find in the above-mentioned three ballads of the Suttanipāta dealing with the story of Buddha's youth. The main features of the later Buddha-legend are, as we see, already prepared here. The Nālakasutta occurs immediately after the birth of the child Buddha :

1. See Vol. I, p. 333 ff.
2. See p. 39, note 1, 57 and Vol. I, p. 294. Cf. also Windisch, Māra und Buddha, p. 3 ff, 222 ff, 245 ff and Oldenberg, Aus dem alten Indien 45 ff.

The gods in heaven are in joyous excitement. The heavenly seer Asita notices their outbursts of joy and upon his asking, he is told, that just then in the town of the Sakyas in the Lumbinī-grove Buddha is born for the good of the world. Then the wise man, descending from the heaven, goes to the palace of Suddhodana and wants to see the new born boy. And as he sees the boy, who "like a fire, like the brightest of the stars, like the autumn sun in a cloudless sky" radiates, while divine beings fan him with coolness, then he takes the child in his arms and exclaims ! "This is the incomparable, the highest of men". In the same moment however he thinks of his own impending end and breaks out in tears. Astounded, the Sakyas ask him whether some disaster threatened the boy. The wise man pacifies them and says that the boy will attain the peak of perfect enlightenment. But he himself will not live to hear sermon of the Exalted One; that is what made him sad. Before departing he however enjoins his nephew Nālaka to follow Buddha as soon as his fame resounds.[1]

The second of these poems, the Pabbajjāsutta, describes the "departure" (pabbajjā) of the youthful Gotama from his native place, and the encounter which he had with the King of Rājagaha while wandering about as a mendicant ascetic. A later episode—how Māra the wicked one, after he has followed Gotama at every step for seven years, once again takes up the fight and wants to bring him who is struggling for knowledge back to worldly life and how Māra is disgracefully defeated in this fight—is described in the third ballad, the Padhānasutta.[2] Although, as we see, these ballads too are certainly rich in legend-like features and mythical paraphernalia, still compared to the exaggerations of later Buddha biographies, they may be said to be simple and factual.

1. This legend has been often compared with that of Simeon in Lucas 2, 25 ff; and it is indeed one of the most conspicuous Buddhist parallels, to the gospels. Cf. especially Pischel, "Leben und Lehre des Buddha" p. 23 ff. E. Windish (in "Festschrift Kuhn", p. 6 ff) has discussed the variants of the legend and traced Asita Devala back to Brahminical literature. Windish regards it as "not absolutely proved that the Simeon of St. Luke owes his existence to the Asita of Buddhist legend.

2. Here too, a comparison has been made with the Christian legend of temptation.

Nevertheless, even in the form in which they are found in the ballads of the Suttanipāta, these legends cannot belong to the oldest layer of Buddhistic tradition. They already presuppose a long history of the Buddha-legend. To a later layer belongs perhaps the Pārāyaṇavagga, the last section of the Suttanipāta—at least in the form in which it has come down to us. This section begins with a frame-work story in verses : To the Brahmin Bāvarī, who, in his generosity, has gifted away everything, so that he does not possess anything more, comes another Brahmin and asks for 500 gold pieces. As he does not get them he spells out the curse on Bāvarī, that after seven days his head shall be split into seven pieces. Bāvarī is greatly frightened, but a deity advises him to turn to the Buddhas. Here follows a hymn to Buddha in which the 32 marks of his bodily features are praised; among these are also the long tongue with which he can cover his whole face and the part enclosed by a sheath. Thereupon Bāvarī sends his 16 pupils, all of them excellent scholars and famous Brahmins, to Buddha and each of them puts one question to Buddha and he answers it. The 16 questions and answers form the actual nucleus of this poem. The last question is followed by a piece of prose on the importance of these questions and answers, which—quite in the manner of certain Buddhistic Sanskrit texts—is repeated in Gāthās. A second hymn to Buddha closes the poem, without the frame-work-story actually coming to a close. Since the Pārāyaṇa, as mentioned above (p. 90) has been proved to be old, it is perhaps to be presumed, that the frame-work-story has been handed down to us not in its original form, but mutilated by means of additions.

And the same can be said perhaps of some of the prose frame-works in the pieces mixed prose and verse. Fausboll[1] has declared that all prose passages are later additions. That is perhaps hardly correct. But when K. E. Neumann in his translation simply omits some of the prose verse pieces, by considering them, as he said once rather strongly, "priestly trash of the commentators", we think that in most cases he is right. When for example in the prose of the Selasutta Buddha is glorified as

1. Preface p. vii to his edition, "editio princeps" of the text.

Cakravartin and the 32 marks of his bodily features are enumerated at length,[1] or when in the Sabhiyasutta (32) there is a mention of the institutions of sects, or when a Yakṣa or a deity appears often in a very superfluous and highly clumsy manner in order to introduce a dialogue, such things may perhaps be rightly called additions[2] of the commentators. At all events the Sutta-Nipāta too, is a collection made up of earlier and later texts and is certainly not a unified work[3] even though a few of the poems included in the Sutta-Nipāta such as perhaps the 12 Suttas of the Uragavagga, may be the work of the same author.

6.7. To the youngest layer of the literature united under the Pāli Canon belong certainly Vimānavatthu and Petavatthu[4] the "stories of gods' palaces" and the "ghost stories" both of them highly displeasing and fortunately not so voluminous works. The truly great and profound doctrine of Karman, which has found expression in so many beatiful sayings and legends[5] in Brahminical as well as Buddhistic texts is explained through examples most inartistically in these small stories in which what is poetical is only the metrical form. The stories are all stereotyped. In the Vimānavatthu some divine being is asked by Moggallāna how he has attained this or what divine place (vimāna) with all its splendours.[6] In reply the deity reports briefly the good deed which he performed in his previous life, as a result of which the heavenly happiness has been awarded

1. La Vallee Poussin, Bouddhisme p. 246 ff compares the Saddharmapundarika of the Mahāyāna-literature to the Selasutta. But the verses of the Salasutta also presuppose the worship of Buddha. The verses 314 ff, and 324 prove the existence of religious texts and religious teaching.

2. See for example I, 6, 10, II, 4, 5, III, 10.

3. Cf. R. O. Franke in "Festschrift Windisch" p. 194 ff.

4. The Vimānavatthu, edited by E. R. Gooneratne, London PTS 1886. Petavatthu edited by J. Minayeff London PTS 1888. Cf. L. Schermann, "Visions literatur" p. 56 ff. L. Feer in JA s. 8, t.III, 1884 pp. 109 ff. 138 ff, Oldenberg, "Buddha" 354 Note. W. Stede, "Die Gespenstergeschichten des Petavatthu," Leipzig 1914, and Bimala Charan Law, "The Buddhist Conception of Spirits", Calcutta 1923 (Calcutta Oriental Series).

5. Cf. Vol. I 239 f, 396 f, 423 f, 537 f.

6. According to E. Kuhn and R. Garbe (Indien und das Christentum, p. 142) the Vimānavatthu is the source for the palace in the legend of Saint Thomas.

to him. In the Petavatthu some Peta (Sanskrit Preta, ghost of a dead one, which wanders about in the vicinity of the earth, restlessly and tortured) appears and is asked by Nārada to which evil deed he has to attribute his misfortune, whereupon he speaks of it in short. One example (Petavattu I, 2) will suffice:

(The wise Nārada speaks to a ghost)

Quite golden is your body radiating far through the whole world,

Yet your mouth is that of a pig. What is the deed that you have done ?

(Thereupon replies the ghost):

Well bridled was I in deeds, unbridled only in words,

That's it, why you, O Nārada, are seeing me in such ugly form.

So do I say to you, O Nārada, as you yourself have seen it,

Nothing bad do with your mouth that you may not get a pig's mouth.

That in the Petavatthu (IV, 3)a King, Piṅgalaka by name, occurs, who, according to the commentary of Dhammapāla, is said to have ruled in Surat 200 years after Buddha, proves that even the commentators of a later time push these texts to a period considerably removed from the time of Buddha's life. Even if one admits that the notions of heaven and hell have already existed in ancient Buddhism side by side with the Arhat- and Nirvāṇa-ideals, these "poems" cannot be considered to be very old.[1]

8.9. How disorderly the jumbling up of the texts of the Khuddakanikāya is, is shown by the fact that immediately following the two texts mentioned just now which belong to the

1. According to E. Hardy ZDMG 53, 1899, 25ff., Petavatthu and Vimānavatthu could have borrowed material useful for their purposes from other works of the Khuddakanikāya like the Jātakas; Cf. also E. Hardy in "Introduction to the edition of Vimānavatthu commentary", London PTS 1901, p. xi. But the contrary viz. that the Jātaka book has borrowed from Petavatthu and Vimānavatthu is equally possible. And in Jātaka No. 243 Vimānavatthu is quoted in particular.

most desolate and dullest products of monastic poetry, there are the Theragāthā and Therīgāthā,[1] the "monks' and nuns' songs"[2] —spiritual poems which can stand with dignity by virtue of their power and beauty by the side of the best products of Indian lyric—right from the hymns of the Ṛgveda upto the lyrical poems of Kālidāsa and Amaru.

The Thera-and Therigāthā are two collections, of which the first one contains 107 poems with 1,279 stanzas (gāthās) and the second 73 poems with 522 stanzas, which are attributed by tradition to some particular Theras and Therīs whose names are also mentioned. This tradition is vouchsafed not only by the manuscripts but also by the commentary of Dhammapada which was written probably in the 5th century A.D. and which contains also stories in which is told a kind of biography of each of these Theras and Therīs. But the stories are partly adaptations of the verses and they are partly also purely invented or extracted from various narrative works. There is no credibility attached to them. Even the tradition of the names of the Theras and Therīs as the authors of the verses does not in general deserve any credibility.[3] Yet tradition is right in assuming

1. Edited by H. Oldenberg and R. Pischel London PTS 1883, translated by Mrs. Rhys Davids, "Psalms of Early Buddhists I", "Psalms of Sisters II," "Psalms of the Brethren," London PTS 1909, 1913, into Germam by K. E. Neumann, Berlin 1889, Index to the Pādas of Thera-and Therī-Gāthā by W. Stede JPTS 1924-27, p. 38 ff. Cf. E. Muller JRAS 1910, 536 f. Maria E. Julius van Good, De Buddhistische Non Le den 1915, p. 142 ff.

2. The translation is however not quite correct, because by Theras and Theris, to whom these songs are attributed, not monks and nuns in general, but especially the earliest and most famous male and female disciples of Buddha himself are meant, and then particularly old (the word thera, fem. therī corresponds to Sanskrit sthavira and means actually old) and venerable monks and nuns. Thera and Therī are however only titles which are not associated with any honorary office (Cf. Pischel Leben des Buddha p. 99 and also T. W. Rhys Davids, ERE Vol. 5, p. 252 f.

3. If among the verses attributed to Ānanda (Therag. 1018-1050) we find also verses which refer to Ānanda, among others, verses praising Ānanda, or if into the verses attributed to Moggallāna (verses 1146-1208), the legends of Moggallāna narrated in the Majjhimanikāya 50 are also interwoven and if we find more such things, then we see that the monks who ascribed these verses to any particular Theras or Theris knew of the real authors of the songs just as little as the compilers of the Anukramaṇis knew of the authors of the Ṛgveda hymns (Cf. Vol. I, p. 52 f.).

that these poems were written not by one but by many authors and certainly also in this that it lets the songs be composed partly by monks and partly by nuns. It may be that some songs which are ascribed to various authors may belong in reality to only one author, and conversely some of the stanzas originating from various authors may be ascribed to one and the same poet, it may also be that among the "nuns' songs" some songs written by monks are found and perhaps also among the "monks' songs" some songs written by nuns are found,[1]—but in no case can these poems have originated from one head. If the same usages of language recur and the tone of the poems is the same in many respects, then this only proves that they all bear the stamp of the Buddhist spirit, but not as K. E. Neumann[2] thinks, that "one man has put the stamp of his mind to the whole".

It is beyond any doubt, that a great majority of the "nuns' songs" have been composed by women. In particular, the monks would never have shown so much sympathy for the female members of the community that we could expect of them that they would have composed the songs which come directly from the hearts of women folk. We need only recall to our minds the difficulty which, according to tradition, Gotama gave to his foster mother when she wanted to found a nuns' order, and the reproaches which were made against Ānanda in several places of the canon on account of his attitude favouring women. For the same reason it would have never occurred to the monks to ascribe songs to women, if an incontestable tradition had not pointed in this direction. Mrs. Rhys[3] Davids has pointed the differences in

1. The editing is not at all a careful and clever one. We often find verses separated which decidedly belong to one poem and sometimes verses which are not connected with one another included in one poem. We find also quite often the same verses repeated, word for word, at different places. And some verses were torn asunder and, on the basis of purely external indications, they were included, some in the Theragāthā and some in the Therīgāthā.

2. In the foreword to his translation of the "Songs of the Monks and Nuns", p. vii, Also what R. O. Franke says in WZKM 24, 1910, p. 15 f only proves that individual parts are unitary poems, but not that the whole work has only one author.

3. Psalms of the Sisters, p. xxiii ff.

language, feeling and tone between the monks' and nuns' songs. We need only read the two collections one after another to believe that in the nuns' songs often even a personal note is struck which is unknown to the monks' songs, that in the nuns' songs we hear more often of external experiences, and that in the monks' songs nature-descriptions dominate whereas in the nuns' songs life-pictures do so.[1]

Common to both collections are the religious ideals that are held high and the moral teachings that are proclaimed. All these monks and nuns know nothing higher than that profound peace of the soul for which the gods envy even the holy men and which is attained through the extinction of passion, hatred, delusion and through liberation from all sensual urges and inclinations and which gives foretaste of that supreme bliss, the Nirvāṇa, the end of all suffering in the consciousness of not-being born-again. Blissful is the monk who is equally insensitive to joy and sorrow, who feels neither hunger nor cold. Blissful the nun, who can say of herself (Therīg. 76) :

All longing, for earthly or heavenly pleasures,
Is destroyed, – discarded I have folly and worldly pleasure,—
Have found peace, highest bliss : Nirvāṇa.

These ideals, as well as the ethical teachings—the noble fourfold path, tenderness and kindness towards all beings (metta), not-injuring (ahiṃsā), self-control etc.—are in these songs the same as in the sayings of the Dhammapada and the poems of the Suttanipāta. The monks' and nuns' songs differ in this that they are self-confessions or describe self-experiences. There a monk says proudly how wife and children tried in vain to disturb his peace—"the fetters have I broken" (Therag. 299 ff). Blissfully another monk praises himself, that he has at last freed himself from his wife although slowly, "like the bud gets separated from

1. Oldenberg, Literature of Ancient India, p. 101 Note, might be right, when he explains the domination of nature-descriptions in the monks' songs saying that the nature, of which mention is made in the songs, is the forest-nature and the hermitage-life in the forest naturally played a greater role with the monks than with the nuns. But this again speaks in favour of this that the nuns' songs were composed by the nuns themselves.

the stalk". (Therag. 72). And yet another recalls to his mind the courtesan, whose enticements he has resisted. (Therag. 459 ff). Numerous are the attacks in the monks' songs on the woman, the temptress—this noose, this fetter—that again and again threatens to distract the monk from his sacred life.[1] Howsoever many women may come, boasts a monk they shall not entice me (Therag. 1211). The cause of all suffering is the woman, only he who stays firmly away from her, can become a true hero (Therag. 738ff). One monk describes in a particularly disgusting way how he is led to the truth by the sight of the decaying corpse of a woman (Therag. 315ff 393ff.). These ugly pictures are again confronted with some beautiful ones. We hear for example of a monk whom his own mother has led to the truth and for which he thanks her in beautiful words.[2] In another song a monk consoles his mother saying that he is indeed not dead. (Therag. 44). Another narrates how he as a poor devil lived by gathering faded flowers, came to Buddha and found salvation. (Therag 620ff.). Yet another narrates how he led his life in wealth and arrogance as the son of a court priest until he saw Buddha and was converted. (Therag 423ff.) A king having become a monk, compares his present mendicant life with his earlier pompous court life (Therag 842ff.). We find also robbers who have become monks and recall to their mind their earlier life as robbers. But in the monks' songs such references to the external experiences are comparatively rare. In general they describe only the inner life of the monks mostly in short poems of a few verses. Still we have in the verses ascribed to the Thera Talaputta[3] also a marvellous lengthy poem, the monologue of a monk struggling for holiness. Some of the Monks' songs deal neither with introspective self-expression nor eternal experience but are merely verse sermons of general content.[4]

---

1. Cf. Therag. 267 ff., 279 ff., 453 ff., 459 ff., 1150 ff.

2. Therīg 204-212, where the Thera Vaddha is inspired by his mother to become a monk and Therag. 335-339, where Vaddha thanks his mother, belong evidently to one poem. Cf. Note 1 on p. 99 above.

3. Therag. 1091-1145 ref. Oldenberg "Literatur des alten Indien", p. 101 f.

4. Cf. Mrs. Rhys Davids, "Psalms of the Brethren", p. xxxi ff.

Much more numerous than in the monks' songs are as already remarked above the pictures from the real life in the nuns' songs. Mad with sorrow at the loss of a child, a mother wanders about until consoled and enlightened by Gotama Buddha himself, she is admitted to the order. And more than once it happens that women are led to the nuns' order through the loss of their children.[1] In one song we hear of poor widow, who (involuntarily) goes begging from house to house and by chance comes to the nuns, by whom she is received sympathetically and enlightened and becomes out of her own will, a beggar, who through her kind teacher Paṭācārā also soon finds the path to Nirvāṇa. We hear repeatedly of erstwhile courtesans who became nuns and the contrast between the life and conduct of the mistress and the calm self-possession of the nun has a great artistic effect. In the midst of jubilation and festivities, in festive decoration comes a beautiful woman to a cloister and is enlightened and converted by Buddha. Here also the contrast between the wild festive joy and the calm of the Nirvāṇa is very effective.[2] But we also hear of young girls from noble families, of matrons in advanced age, of a mother of ten children, who—enlightened either by Buddha himself or by a revered nun—seek the path to Nirvāṇa and find it. We hear also often, how relatives try in vain to dissuade their daughters from their resolve to become nuns. The sons of rich men and even princes are interested in the beautiful daughter of a rich man and one of them sends the father of the girl the message : "Eight times as much as she weighs, will I give in gold for her and treasures of precious stones moreover". But she has heard Buddha and prefers the life of a mendicant nun. Also tragedies are not wanting. While Kisā-Gotamī[3] is lying in pains on the road, her husband dies, and also her son, her daughter, mother, father and brother die—this need not be an exaggeration, when we think of such frequent outbreaks of hunger and pestilence—, she does not however despair, but attains salvation through

1. Therig. 133-138, 51-53, 127-132, 312-337.
2. Therīg. 122-126, 25, 72-76, 145-150.
3. Mrs. Rhys Davids (Psalms of the Sisters, p. 109) thinks that Kisā-Gotamī is here not relating her own fate, but attending to that of Paṭācārā, as told in the legend of the commentary to Therig. 112 ff.

liberation.[1] After the tragedy, a comedy : The woman, who is glad, through her conversion, to be free from the thrashing of rice and an unwanted husband, what she expresses not without humour, saying, that she is now free from "three crooked things" —mortar, pestle and the hunchback husband.[2]

What significance these pictures of life have for our knowledge of social conditions, especially for the social position of the woman in ancient India, is self-evident. It need hardly be mentioned how great the contribution of such pictures is for the enlivening of these poems which are for the non-Buddhist reader, so monotonous[3] in their actual thought-content. In the monks' songs however, the monotony is often interrupted through charming nature-descriptions. The delight in nature, which we have already seen as an excellent feature of Indian poetry in the Rāmāyaṇa, which we will admire in the ornate-epic and in the love-lyric of India and indeed even in its didactic epigrams, was not unknown to these monks in spite of all their renunciation of the world and its charms. With great delight they devote themselves, more as poets than as monks, to descriptions of landscapes with mountains and forests in the midst of which the sage in his loneliness pursues his meditations. When thunder rolls and from dark clouds torrential rain pours down, the liberated monk sits blissful in his cave. And also the holyman uninfluenced by pleasure and pain does not fail to describe the spring.[4]

Delight in nature finds expression in some beautiful similes also. The wise man is compared to a rock that does not shake or to an elephant. Like the monkey in lion's skin is the monk who is proud of his monk's robes. Like the lion in his den[5] sits the

1. Therig. 151-156, 16 f, 69, 102 ff, 338-365, 213-223.

2. Therig. 11, perhaps a counterpart to Therag. 43, where a monk is glad that he is free from "three crooked things" (sickle, plough and spade).

3. Mrs. Rhys Davids (Psalms of the Brethren p. 1) contests the very suggestion of monotony because, as she has pointed out (Psalms of the Sisters, p. xxxvii f. Psalms of the Brethren p. xlii ff.), the one Arhat ideal is treated in various aspects.

4. Therag. 537 ff, 1062 ff, 1135 ff., 189 f. 522 ff, 307 ff., 527 ff. Cf. C. A. F. Rhys Davids, "The Love of Nature in Buddhist Poems"; The Quest Review, April 1910.

5. Therag. 692 ff. 1000, 1080, 1081

monk with self-control. Similes are artistically heaped in one of the nuns' songs (Therīg. 112 ff.) : As the peasant ploughs the field, sows the seed and reaps, so will the nun attain Nirvāṇa, washing her feet she sees the water tickling down from the rock and stimulated to contemplation by this sight, she controls her heart as one tames a noble horse; then she goes to the monastery, takes the lamp and with a needle pulls down the wick and as the light of the lamp goes out, so she attains Nirvāṇa. This artful entwining of similes reminds us already of the embellishments (Alaṃkāras) of ornate poetry, as also while incidentally artificial play on words occurs. Artfully constructed is also a beautiful song ascribed to Ambapāli, the erstwhile courtesan (Therīg. 252 ff.). Here the poetess describes in the first two lines of every stanza the beauty of her body; in the third line what has become of this youthful pretty body in old age where upon the refrain follows : "The truth-proclaimer's word is not belied".

The refrain and the repetition of typical phrases are a characteristic feature of these poems.[1] In these songs also the dialogue-form is very popular. Thus one of the nuns' songs (Therig. 271 ff.) is a conversation between daughter and father; in which the daughter analyses the good points of monastic life and converts the father. Another of these songs (Therig. 291ff.) shows us a man—he was at first a monk, became then a hunter, produced a son and now wants to become a monk once again —in a conversation with his wife who tries to dissuade him from his resolve; she threatens to kill the child if he goes away; he however remains firm :

> "And if you would throw the child away to be eaten by jackals and dogs—
> Me you will not bring back for the child's sake, you wretched woman !".

This is already a kind of ballad. And we find in the monks' and nuns' songs, especially in the latter ones, a very large number

1. Cf. W. Stede in JPTS 1924-1927, p. 34 ff. Stede's "Synoptical Table of Repeated Pādas or 'Repertory' Phrases", ib. p. 197 ff. shows how numerous these repetitions are.

of real ballads, both with and without narrative stanzas. One of the longest of these ballads, which is extraordinarily dramatic, is found among the nuns' songs (Therīg. 312-337). In astonishment a Brahmin asks his wife, how is it that she does not weep, although she has lost her seven children, while previously she mourned day and night for the dead ones. She replies that she has learnt from Buddha how one escapes life and death. Then the Brahmin goes to Buddha and becomes a monk. He sends back his carriage-driver and informs his wife that he has become a monk. As reward for the good news the wife wants to present the carriage-driver with horse and carriage and a thousand gold pieces more. But he says, "keep the horse and carriage and the gold, I too will become a monk". The daughter also, whom the woman wants to instal as her successor to inherit the great treasures of the family renounces and says she wants to become a nun. Perhaps the most beautiful of these ballads is that of the nun Subhā, who, is pestered in the forest by a rogue with declarations of love. In glowing terms he praises her beauty, paints the terrors of the forest to her, and tries to seduce her. She turns him down saying :

"Where there is no way or path, there you want to go,
Want to have the moon for a toy,
Want to jump over the gods' mountains—
You, in your longing for Buddhas' daughter".

All worldly-desire, says she, she has thrown off like burning coals, like poison. She describes the futility and ugliness of the body, even the eye is only a wretched ball of flesh. With these words she pulls out her eye[1] and holds it out for the man. The man is overwhelmed with remorse and begs to be excused. The

1. When in Christian legends the holy Lucy and the holy Brigitta pull out their eyes because young people fail in love with them on account of their beauty, this can be perhaps a mere chance coincidence. We need only think of Matth. 18, 9, to see that a Buddhistic influence can be hardly presumed, as E. Muller (Archiv fur Religionsw. III, 1900, p. 233) thinks. Cf. C. H. Tawney, "Kathāsaritsāgara," Transl., I, p. 248 note; R. Garbe, "Indien und das Christentum," p. 116; E. W. Burlingame, "Buddhist Parables", New Haven 1922, p. 325 ff and H. Gunter, "Buddha in der abendlandischen Legende ?" Leipzig 1922, p. 220 f.

nun however goes to Buddha and as soon as he sees her, her eye shines brightly as before (Therīg. 366-399).

Some of these ballads—dialogues between Māra and the nuns[1]—are partly side-pieces, partly other versions of those which we have found in the Bhikkhunīsaṃyutta of the Saṃyuttanikāya. Also the ballad of the robber Aṅgulimāla, which we have found in the Majjhimanikāya[2] reappears verbatim in the Theragāthā (866 ff.). And it can be also proved that a number of other songs and verses of our collection are found in the four Nikāyas, in the Dhammapada and in the Suttanipāta. At one place (Therag. 445) even similes of the Nikāyas are assumed to be already known and hence even quoted. But even if we would presume that in all these cases they were quotations or borrowings, that would hardly prove the later origin of both the collections as such; for the concerned pieces could also have been inserted later.

Certain it is that in both the collections there are also a considerable number of poems, which must be of later origin. When for example a monk tells that simply because he has presented a single flower, he has wandered through the heaven for eighty hundred million years and finally has attained Nirvāṇa, then this presupposes a Buddha-cult as we will see it fully developed in the later Mahāyāna texts. Also when a seven year old holy man works miracles, when a monk multiplies himself thousandfold and flies through the air, when the gods in heaven receive Sāriputta and offer respects to him,[3] and there are many more such miracles—then such pieces hardly belong to the oldest layer of Buddhist poetry and thought. And only centuries after the founding of the order and as I would believe, after the time of Aśoka can both the poems[4] have originated, in which there is mention of the decadence of religion. In the first poem the monks' life of the "present day" is contrasted with the simple and pious life of the monks of the

1. Therīg. 182 ff., 189 ff., 196 ff.
2. No. 86, s. p. 46 above.
3. Therag. 96, 429 ff, 563 ff., 1082 ff.
4. Therag. 920-948 and 949-980, where Neumann has compared with Aṅguttara nikāya V, 79 and 80.

past. "They, who once upon a time had forsaken riches, wife and children, now do evil for the sake of a spoonful of rice", eat what pleases them, have unholy conversations, expect rich presents in return for nothing that they offer to the people, gather herbs like doctors, dress up like courtesans, are cunning, crafty and false. And in the second poem Phussa, in reply to a question as to how the monks of the future will be, draws up a picture of which one might think that that would apply best to the monks of Tibet. The monks, it is said there, will be filled with anger and hatred, jealousy and obstinacy, will know nothing of truth, will twist the word of the Lord, accept gold and silver, they will despise virtuous and true monks, monks and nuns will live licentiously etc. — a strange picture that would not have possibly come down from ancient times. To the same period of decadence does also the song of Isidāsī in the nuns' songs appear to belong. Here it is presumed in particular as self-evident that a girl becomes a nun only as a consequence of some misfortune. And, that one becomes a monk, discards the monk's robes in order to marry, and after a fortnight again goes back to the life of a monk—although this appears to have been taken from real life, yet it was taken out perhaps from life at a time when Buddhism had already passed through some crisis. Also the last nun's song (Therig. 448-521) is either a later addition or a poem that has been mutilated with later additions and overburdened with quotations.[1]

If therefore K. E. Neumann says of our songs that they "have been collected and carefully preserved even during Gotama's lifetime and were reasonably fixed soon after his death", this is not only an assertion that cannot be proved but cannot be possibly said of some of the songs and is improbable in case of the rest. Yet it is possible that some of the songs have been composed by the earliest disciples of Buddha. Thus the line so often recurring in the monks' songs: "I am not glad to die, I am not glad to live[2]", may have been very well spoken by one of the earliest disciples. It is possible that Mahāpajāpati,

1. Also Mrs. Rhys Davids (Psalms of the Sisters, p. xviii ff) considers the last two nuns' songs to be products of later ornate poetry.

2. Therag. 196, 607, Cf. 20, 1002.

Gotama's foster mother, has really sung the panegyric on Buddha (Therīg. 157-162) ascribed to her. And the verses (Therag. 981-994) in which the ideal of monk's life is described so elaborately, can very well have been composed by Sāriputta. The beautiful words: "May striving for perfection be your

Eternal concern: this I enjoin you.
Well now, I depart, disappear,—
Quite freed I am, freed from all".[1]

could have been handed down in reality as Sāriputta's testament, his last entreaty to the disciples. And the famous lines which recur at many places in the Pāli-canon and in our collection are ascribed to the great Moggallāna:

Ah transitory are the things all,
As they become, so must they perish
Hardly born, are they destroyed
To be free from them — is bliss".[2]

are certainly so old that Moggallāna or another of the first disciples of Buddha can have composed them. Here too, as in all collections of the Tipiṭaka, old and new is combined and investigations will have to fix the age of each piece separately.

10. This is also true particularly of the collection of the Jātakas included in the Khuddakanikāya called "Stories from

1. Therag. 1017, translation by Mrs. Rhys Davids, "Psalms of the Brethren", p. 349. The verse is ascribed to Revata the brother of Sāriputta in 658. Perhaps the verse is only an enlargement of the last words of the Buddha (Mahā-Parinibbāna-Sutta, Dighanikāya XVI, 6, 7: appamādena sampādetha).

2. Therīg. 1159. In the Mahāparinibbānasutta VI, 10, the words are attributed to the god Sakka, In the Jātaka Vol. I, p. 392, Saṃyutta-Nikāya Vol. II, 193; I, 6, 158 and 200 they appear again, "This famous saying is so popular that it was recited to me in Colombo by a servant in pure Pāli and, what may perhaps mean much more in this case, excellently interpreted as is understood properly. K. E. Neumann (Lieder der Monche und Nonnen p. 242.)

the earlier births (of Buddha)[1] "or "Bodhisatta-stories", as we may shortly call them.

A "Bodhisatta" is, in the Buddhist dogma a being (Pāli satta, Sanskrit sattva), who is destined to attain enlightenment (bodhi), i.e. to become a Buddha.[2] Gotama the Buddha, (i.e. the "Enlightened one") is called "Bodhisatta" upto the moment when he attained enlightenment, but not only in his last earthly life, but also in all the innumerable existences which—he as human being, as animal or as God—has passed through before he was reborn, for the last time, as son of the Sakya prince. Now a "Jātaka" is a story in which the Bodhisatta in one of his earlier existences lays a role, whether as the hero of the story or as a subordinate figure or even as a spectator. Every Jātaka therefore begins with the words : "At such and such a time (for example as Brahmadatta was ruling) was the Bodhisatta reborn in the womb of this or that being (for example of the queen or of a female-elephant)"—and then follows the story. In this way it was possible to transform into a Jātaka any arbitrary story that was told by the people to one another or that was known to the people from world-literature. It was enough to make some human, animal or divine being that occurred in the story to make the Bodhisatta. And thus could every mundane story, however far from Buddhistic ideas become a "Buddhistic" story. But Buddhistic monks would not have been Indians if they had not taken into account the need of story-tellers and listeners which is deeply rooted in the soul of the Indian folk and if they had not used this for winning followers for their religion. Indeed not only the Buddhist monks but also the preachers of all sects in India have always done the same thing, as centuries later the Christian monks of the occident did. To these Christian monks had already Gregory the Great recommended the use of the "example", of the story serving the purpose of proof, "quite nonnunquam mentes audientium plus exempla fidelium quam

1. This is the usual and probably correct explanation of the word "Jātaka" that is derived from "Jāta" (birth). H. Kern, "Der Buddhismus" I, 328 translates "Jātaka" by "small story". This finds the approval of Speyer, "Jātakamālā", p. xxii. Ref. Oldenberg as against this in DLZ, 1896, C. 261.

2. Others explain Bodhisatta by "One whose essence (Sattva) is perfect knowledge" Cf. La Vallee Poussin ERE, II, p. 739.

docentium verba convertunt".[1] Also the monks in India adhered to this principle. And just as later the Christian preachers, so also the Buddhist monks have pressed into the service of their purpose all possible stories, fairy tales, fables, anecdotes etc. Books like the "Gesta Romanorum" or Wesselski's "Monchslatein" in which the stories from the sermons of the clergy of several centuries are collected, with their variety of contents, with pious legends side by side with very mundane stories, give us a clear idea of our collection of the Jātakas. For a long time the strictly Buddhistic Theras of ancient times may have perhaps revolted against approving this story-telling of the monks. In many places of the canon[2] the monks are even forbidden from narrating stories of kings, robbers, ministers, arms, wars, women, gods and ghosts, marine adventures etc. But soon they yielded and even in one of the earlier Buddhist Sanskrit texts[3] we read that Buddha tells many pleasant and didactic stories through which people not only find pleasure in religion in this life but also attain bliss after death.

In ancient times it was not yet found necessary to give to the stories the form of "Jātakas". In those times we still find individual stories, for example that of Dīghâvu ("Prince Long-life") narrated in the Vinayapiṭaka,[4] without the hero being identified with the Bodhisattta. Only later was it made into a Jātaka. Yet we also find individual real Jātakas in the collections of the Suttas[5] and they prove that the Buddhist monks, just like their Christian colleagues in the middle ages have told these stories in their sermons or have used them as sermons.

1. Alb. Wesselski, Monchlatein, Leipzig 1909, p. ix.

2. Vinayapiṭaka, Mahāvagga V, 6, 3; Dīghanikāya I, 17; IX, 3; XXV, 2, 21.

3. Saddharmapuṇḍarika II, 44 and V (SBE, pp. 45, 120).

4. See p. 32 above, cf. Jātaka no. 371 and 428. Similarly the fable quoted above on p. 31 is not a Jātaka as yet, whereas in Jātaka no. 37 in the same story the Bodhisatta is the partridge. Cf. Rhys Davids, Buddhist India, p. 195. E. W. Burlingame, JAOS, Vol. 38, Part 4 gives a list of ten Jātakas which are taken from the canon. Rhys Davids, JRAS 1919, p. 231, adds another three to the list. See also Burlingame, "Buddhist Parables," p. 59 ff.

5. So are Kūṭadantasutta and Mahāsudassanasutta in Digha—and the Mahādevasutta in the Majjhimanikāya Jātakas.

But not all Jātakas have they included in the canon, as they began to combine them into a book.[1] Indeed, it is difficult to determine how much of the Jātaka book, as we have it, belongs to the canon, for we do not possess the original canonical Jātaka, but merely a commentary on it. In this commentary, every single Jātaka consists of the following parts : (1) An introductory story, Paccuppannavatthu, i.e. "story of the present time," relating on what occasion the Buddha himself told the monks the Jātaka in question; (2) a prose narrative, Atītavatthu, i.e. "story of the past," in which a story of one of the former births of the Buddha, in other words a Bodhisatta story, is told; (3) the Gāthās, i.e. stanzas, which, as a rule, form part of the "story of the past," but, which are very often, too, a part of the "story of the present time";[2] (4) short commentary (Veyyākaraṇa) in which the Gāthās are explained word for word and (5) the "connexion" (Samodhāna)[3] in which, finally (again by Buddha himself) the personages of the "story of the present" are identified with those of the "story of the past." This huge narrative work in the form of a commentary, the Jātakaṭṭhavaṇṇanā, or elucidation of the meaning of the Jātakas[4] is the work of an unknown Singhalese

1. Majjhimanikāya, Sutta 81, is a Jātaka which does not occur in the Jātaka book. In the Milindapañha two or three Jātakas are mentioned, which cannot be traced in the collection; in the Dhammapada commentary, too, as well as in the Buddhist Sanskrit texts, there are some Jātakas which are absent in the collection. See also L. Feer, JA ser. 7, t. V, 1874, 417 ff.; VI, 1875, 244 ff. It is probable, though not yet proved "that a Book of Jātakas, as contained in the Pāli Canon was not the exclusive possession of this particular school, but belonged to ancient Buddhism in general". (Oldenberg, NGGW, 1912, p. 195).

2. The commentary generally calls these verses Abhisambuddha-Gāthās, i.e., "verses spoken by the Buddha after his enlightenment." Cf. Senar, JA 1901, ser. 9, t. XVII, p. 385 ff.

3. As a rule the Samodhāna is in prose, but verses occur here and there.

4. Standard edition by V. Fausboll, Vols. I-VII (Vol. VII: Index by D. Andersen), London 1877-1897. A new edition, in Siamese characters, has been issued by their Majesties Queen Aunt and Queen Suddhasinninath of Siam in 1925 (10 vols.). Translations: Buddhist Birth Stories, or Jātaka Tales, translated by T. W. Rhys Davids, London, 1880 (contains Nos. 1-40). The Jātaka or stories of the Buddha's Former Births, translated from the Pāli by various Hands under the Editorship of E. B. Cowell, Vols. I-VI,

monk[1] who took his materials from an earlier commentary on the Jātakas, the Jātakatthakathā.

This last-named work, as indeed the Aṭṭhakathās in general, is said to have been written in Pāli immediately after the canon, brought to Ceylon with the canon itself, there translated into the Old Singhalese language, and then translated back again into Pāli by the compiler of the Jātakaṭṭhavaṇṇanā.[2] It is only the prose, however, which was translated into Singhalese and

---

Cambridge 1895-1907 (the translators are R. Chalmers, W. H. D. Rouse, H. T. Francis, R. A. Neil and Cowell himself): Vol. VII contains the Index. A considerable number of Jātakas have been translated by R. Morris in Folk-Lore Journal II-IV and Paul Steinthal, "Zeitschrift fur vergleichende Litteraturgeschichte", N. F. VI, 1893, pp. 106 ff., VII, 1894, pp. 296 ff., X, 1896, pp. 75 ff., XI, 1897, pp. 313 ff. and "Studien zur vergleichenden Litteraturgeschichte" I, 1901, pp. 475 ff., II, 1902, pp. 265 ff.; A Grunwedel, "Buddhistische Studien I", Berlin 1897 gives 55 Jātakas partly in extract, and partly in translation. Selections have been translated by Else Luders, "Buddhistische Märchen, mit einer Einleitung von H. Luders", Jena 1921. A complete German translation by Julius Dutoit was published in Leipzig in 1908 ff. Literature on Jātakas: Leon Feer, JA 1875, s.7, t. 5. pp. 357 ff., t. VI, pp. 243 ff.; 1895, s.9, t.V, pp. 31 ff., 189 ff.; 1897, s.9, t.IX, pp. 288 ff.; S. d'Oldenburg JRAS 1893, pp. 301 ff.; R. O. Franke, in "Bezz. Beitr." 22, 1897, pp. 289 ff., WZKM 20, 1906, pp. 317 ff.; T.W. Rhys Davids, "Buddhist India", pp. 189 ff.; Album Kern, Leide 1903, pp. 13 ff.; Oldenberg, "Litteratur des alten Indien", pp. 103 ff.; NGGW 1912, pp. 183 ff.; 214 ff.; 1918, pp. 429 ff.; 1919, pp. 61 ff. and "Zur Geschichte der altindischen Prose" (AGGW 1917, p. 79 ff.); S. Levi, "Les Jātakas (Conferences du Musee Guimet XIX, 1906)"; W. Geiger, "Pāli Literatur und Sprache", pp. 20 f.; Winternitz in ERE, Vol. II, pp. 491 ff. See also Gokuldas De in "Calcutta Review", June 1929, 265 ff.; August 1929, 246 ff.; January 1930, 78 ff.; July 1930, 65 ff.; Feb. 1931, 278 ff.

1. According to the Gandhavaṃsa (JPTS 1886, p. 59), Buddhaghoṣa (5th century A.D.) is said to be the author of Jātakaṭṭhavaṇṇanā. T. W. Rhys Davids, in "Buddhist Birth Stories," p. lxiii ff., had already, on good grounds, questioned the authorship of Buddhaghoṣa. E. W. Burlingame (Buddhist Legends, HOS, Vol. 28, pp. 49, 59 f.) adds that both the language and the style of the Jātaka commentary differ from those of the authentic works of Buddhaghoṣa. See below.

2. Burlingame (JAOS 38, 1918, pp. 267 f.) declares this tradition to be unreliable as it has been shown that Pāli sources were used for the commentary. But it is difficult to understand how and why so definite a statement could have been made without any historical background. It is quite feasible, in fact perfectly natural that, when translating into Pāli, the compilers

then translated back again; the Gāthās were preserved unchanged in Pāli. According to tradition, it is only these Gāthās, the stanzas, which were included in the canon.[1] This tradition is probably correct insofar as both prose and verse originally came down orally; but the prose naturally had a less stable form than the stanzas, so that when the canon was compiled, and later on, when it was written down, only the verses retained their original form, whilst, in the case of the prose, the rendering of it was at first entrusted to the reciters, and it was only at a later period committed to writing by the commentators.

The majority of Jātakas, in fact, belong to that type of literary work which consists of a mixture of prose and verse, a type which is such a favourite in Indian literature. It was ever a favourite method in ancient India to enliven narrative prose by verses, and to introduce or garb narrative verses by explanatory prose passages. The teller of fairy-tales would insert into his story such fairy-tale verses as those familiar to us from our own fairy-tales. The writer of fables would give the moral or the point of the fable in one or two verses. The ballad poets and the singers, who recited their songs in alternating stanzas

---

should have accepted both canonical and non-canonical Pāli texts in their original Pāli form, without taking the trouble of translating the texts from the Singhalese.

1. Cf. Rhys Davids, Buddhist Birth Stories, p. lxxvii. It was hitherto thought that this Jātaka, which consists entirely of verses, had been preserved in manuscripts. But F. Weller (ZII 4, 1926, pp. 46 ff.) examined 3 manuscripts of Jātaka verses, and concluded that these manuscripts only contain extracts from the Jātaka commentary, but not the ancient verse Jātaka which belongs to the canon. This serves to confirm the hypothesis of Hertel (ZDMG 64, 1910, 58; WZKM 24, 1910, 23). Weller (l.c; p. 54) raises the question as to whether a verse Jātaka ever existed at all. In the commentary itself, however, a distinction is often made between Pāli and Aṭṭhakathā, and in this case 'Pāli' cannot refer to anything but the verse Jātaka. Moreover, the fact that the principle of division of the Jātaka Book in 22 sections (Ekanipāta etc.) is based upon the verse Jātaka and no longer agrees with the number of verses in the Jātaka commentary (see below), is further proof of the existence of the canonical verse Jātaka. Senart (JA 1901, s. 9, t. XVII, pp. 385 ff. Oldenberg NGGW 1911, p. 447) adduces still further arguments in favour of the verse Jātaka, arguments which have not been confuted by Weller. See Winternitz in Ind. Hist. Qu. 4, 1928, 1 ff.

to correspond to the speeches of the dialogue, must often have prefaced them by a prose introduction, sometimes inserting explanations in prose, if occasion required it.[1]

We should, however, be mistaken in supposing that all the Gāthās which are included in the Jātaka commentary, belong to the canon. In accordance with a system of classification popular in India,[2] the Jātaka book is arranged according to the number of verses contained in them. The entire book consists of 22 sections, (Nipātas), of which the first contains 150 stories of one verse each, the second 100 stories of two verses each, the third 50 stories of three verses each, etc. In each subsequent section the number of verses increases, whilst that of the stories decreases.[3] Now, the number of Gāthās does not by any means always tally with the title of the sections in question. Thus, for instance, in the "section of one," we find stories of 4, 5, 6, 10 and 11 stanzas, in the "section of two" there are some stories of 3 to 10 stanzas, in the "section of twenty" there is one case of 44, in the "section of seven" there are only two stories, one of 92 and the other of 93 Gāthās, in the "section of eighty" stories of 103 and 123 stanzas occur, and so forth. The only explanation of this is, that the classification is based on the verse-Jātaka, and not on the Jātaka commentary, and that the verse-Jātaka of the canon contained a far smaller number of Gāthās.

---

1. Cf. Vol. I, p. 93 and Oldenberg, "The Prose-and-Verse Type of Narrative and the Jātakas" (translated from NGGW 1911), in JPTS 1910-1912, pp. 19 ff. F. W. Thomas (JRAS 1903, pp. 402 f.) says: "The conjunction of a text in itself brief and obscure with an indispensable commentary is, one might say, the prevailing one in all periods of Indian literature down to the present.... The figure of the poet who recites his verse in the middle of a prose narrative is still familiar in all parts of India and may have been familiar to the earlier age."

2. For instance, the Theragāthās are also classified according to the number of verses.

3. In the original verse-Jātaka the number of verses must have tallied exactly with the title of the section (Eka-Nipāta, Duka-Nipāta etc.), otherwise the Pakiṇṇaka-Nipāta, "Section of mixed (number of verses)" would not have been inserted after Section XIII, neither would the Mahā-Nipāta, "Great Section," which contains only 10 stories, each consisting of a very large number of Gāthās, have been placed at the end, as Section XXII.

Even from this story of Jātakaṭṭhavaṇṇana it follows that the prose of the Jātakas cannot be considered as so old and original as the Gāthās. It is not covered by the arguments which have been brought forth for the age of the canon. Further, whereas the Gāthās remained unchanged in Pāli, the prose has been translated from Pāli into Sinhalese and from this again into Pāli. There cannot be any doubt that both the translation and the retranslation have brought about various changes and additions even if some had undergone a completely new edition—which is highly probable. In many cases the prose reveals itself as a very late handiwork. It contains references to Ceylon. Very often it contradicts even the Gāthās.[1] Also the language of the Gāthās is more antiquarian than that of the prose, which however can be explained by the fact that the Gāthās have not been translated and retranslated. The "stories of the present" cannot be distinctly separated from the "stories of the past" as appears from Fausboll's edition and both are the works of one and the same commentator.[2] But this commentator must have

1. Lüders has proved in NGGW 1897, p.40ff., that the prose of the Dasrathajātaka has nothing to do with the Gāthās and in ZDMG 58, 1904, 689ff, that the Kṛṣṇa saga appears in the prose of the Ghaṭajātaka "in a savage condition", "as such a complicated saga, uprooted from its native soil is bound to become in course of time". Also Hertel in ZDMG 60, 1906, 399ff. and Charpentier in ZDMG 62, 1908, 725 ff. have proved contradictions between prose and verse. But such contradictions are found at every step. In No. 128 the prose narrates the fable of a jackal whereas in the verse as well as in the title there is mention of a cat. That Jāt. no. 253 occurs in the Vinayapiṭaka with the same Gāthās but with different kinds of prose only proves that the prose of the Jātakas has in general no claim to genuineness.

2. In his edition, Faüsboll differentiates the Paccuppaṇṇavatthus from the Atītavatthus by printing the former in smaller type. But this distinction cannot by any means be maintained throughout. It is often clear that both were written or compiled at the same time. It is possible that the word for word explanation of the Gāthās was the work of a still later commentator. Cf. R. O. Franke in "Bezz. Beitr" 22, 1897, 289 ff.; Senart, JA. 1901, s.9 t.XVII, p. 406 f. It is perfectly natural that the "Stories of the present" tell chiefly of Kosala and sometimes of Magadha i.e. those districts where Buddha taught; on the other hand when the scene of most of the Atītavatthus is laid in Benaras, it is merely the result of a stereotyped convention. (It is only rarely that

used good and old materials. Hence it is that we find especially in the prose of the shorter fables and fairy tales a large number of excellently narrated stories whereas in the other Jātakas, particularly in those which need no prose, the prose narration is very much inferior and tasteless and in many respects not at all in harmony with the Gāthās. We can hardly believe that the same commentator has narrated once skilfully and wittily and at another time in a stupid, tasteless and unintelligent manner, but we must presume that when he has narrated well he has followed good old models or traditions. Therefore, much that is old can have been preserved in the prose.

That this is actually the case and that even in regard to the content of the prose some of the Jātakas belonged to the Buddhistic tradition at least as early as in the 3rd century B.C. is proved by the reliefs on the stone walls of the Stūpas of Bharhut and Sanchi[1] which are so very important to the history of the Jātakas. On these valuable Buddhistic monuments, which on epigraphical grounds are ascribed to the 3rd or 2nd century B.C., we find scenes from the Jātakas represented, among them also scenes, which occur only in the prose and in Bharhut even the titles of the Jātakas are written above them.[2] These reliefs prove therefore that a number of stories which are also found in our Jātaka book were given the technical term "Jātaka" as early as in the 3rd century B.C. and were accepted as Bodhisatta-stories.

Taxila is the scene of the story; very occasionally the scene is laid on other cities of India and once in Ceylon). There is no justification for Fausböll's statement (Jātaka Ed., Vol. VII, p. viii) that the Atītavatthus are necessarily earlier on this account.

1. See above p. 17, Note 3 and also compare S. d'Oldenberg, JAOS XVIII, 1897, p. 183 ff. and E. Hultzsch, JRAS 1912, p. 399 ff; B. M. Barua, Ind. Hist. Qu. II, 1926, 623 ff. and Calcutta Review, Dec. 1926, pp. 430 ff.

2. In our Jātaka book every Jātaka has a title which is coined after the hero of the story (usually the Bodhisatta) or after another person, or the initial words of the first stanza. But the same Jātakas also occur under various titles. Cf. Dines Andersen in Vol. VII, p. XV of the Jātaka-edition. Also on the Stūpa of Bharhut the titles are sometimes the same as in our Jātaka book, and sometimes also different. By this the identification is rendered difficult. A list of 27 or 29 Jātakas of the Stūpas of Bharhut identified till now is given by Rhys Davids in Buddhist India, p. 209 and Hultzsch JRAS 1912, p. 406. See also A. Coomaraswamy in JRAS 1928, 390 ff.

They prove that in those days already many mundane stories, which were found by the Buddhistic monks were "buddhisised", that accordingly they must have been known in India even from a long time before that and could have possibly belonged to the pre-Buddhistic period.

If, therefore, some eminent researchers[1] have presumed that the Jātakas present to us a picture of the narrative literature and the cultural conditions at the time of Buddha or at a still earlier period, this holds good only in a restricted sense. It may be that some of the poems and some prose stories may be old. It may be, that some sayings and legends may belong to the pre-Buddhistic ascetic-poetry. But for the large volume of the verses our conscience does not permit us to consider and certainly we cannot prove, a date earlier than the 3rd century B.C. And much of the prose belongs certainly only to the centuries after Christ. We have already mentioned that not even all the Gāthās belonged to the canonical Jātaka. Now the Jātaka book is not the work of a single, individual author, but is the product of the labours of compilers.[2] The compilers arranged the verses

---

1. Thus G. Buhler on the Origin of the Indian Brāhmī Alphabet 2nd Ed., Strassburg 1898 p. 16 ff; R. Fick, "Die soziale Gliederung im nordostlichen Indien zu Buddhas Zeit", Kiel 1887 (English translation by S. Maitra: "The Social Organization in North-east India in Buddha's time", Calcutta 1920) T. W. Rhys Davids, "Buddhist India", 201 ff. and Mrs. Rhys Davids, "Notes on Early Economic Conditions in Northern India," JRAS 1901, 859 ff. B. C. Sen, "Studies in the Buddhist Jātakas," Calcutta 1930, still takes the whole of the Jātaka book as evidence for the "history" of the time of Buddha. Gokuldas De, "Jātaka Gleanings bearing on Ancient Indian Culture and Civilisation," (Calcutta Review, Sept. 1931, p. 361ff.) Oct. 1931, p. 106 ff.) is more cautious in taking his "gleanings" from the Gāthās only.

2. It is quite impossible for the Jātaka Gāthās to be, as is the opinion of Franke (WZKM 20, 1906, p. 318, cf. ZDMG 63, 1909, p. 13), "when considered as a whole, the personal production of a single author" who "not only put them together, but very often composed them himself, adapted, altered and patched them up, and in fact endowed the complete work with the stamp of his own individuality". If we change the word "author" into "compiler" or "editor", there is some truth in these words of Franke; for the compilers of Indian literary collections have never scrupled to alter the verses of other poets and to add verses of their own composition, to them.

in such a manner as they thought proper, in order to form a narrative. Such procedure must have entailed an error.[1]

From all this it only follows that the same is the case with our Jātaka book as with the Mahābhārata.[2] Not only every big section and every single story, but also every simple Gāthā will have to be examined in itself with regard to its age. Some of the Gāthās may possibly date back to the Vedic period,[3] others should perhaps be regarded as a preliminary stage of epic

---

1. Thus we may doubt whether the verses of Jāt. 61-65 were really intended as Gāthās for 5 different stories. The Gāthās of No. 377 and No. 487 probably belonged to one story, and in the same way those of Nos. 523 and 526. Cf. Lüders In "Festschrift Windisch", pp. 228 ff. and NGGW 1897, 1 Jāt. No. 203 with 5 Gāthās, though it is included in the Section of two, is a snake incantation, in which, besides Buddha, Dhammma and Saṅgha the "Seven Buddhas" are also worshipped though it is absurd to imagine that Gotama Buddha could have been worshipped as the seventh Buddha in the Atītavatthu, that is, at the period of one of his previous existences !

2. Cf. Vol. I, p. 450f. The manifold relations between the Jātakas and the epics (cf. Vol. I, p. 385 Note 387, 395, Note, 400 Note, 451, 452 Note, 487) do not give us any help for fixing the time as the age of the epics is much too uncertain. It does not also help us in any way that numerous Jātakas are mentioned and quoted in the Milindapiṭaka and that in the V book of the same work in addition to Dīgha and Majjhima reciters also Jātaka reciters are mentioned. For, these books belong to the later portions of the Milindapañha missing in the Chinese translations, which have therefore originated only after the 4th century. That in the Milindapañha IV even verses of fairy tales which do not at all contain anything Buddhistic are quoted as "words of Buddha" only proves that a few centuries after Christ these verses were canonical and every word of the canon was taken for Buddha's word, But that even in these later books of the Milindapañha there are deviations from our Jātaka book in the Jātakas quoted, shows the inexactness that crept in during transmission. That some Jātaka verses are found in Patañjali's Mahābhāṣya and the language of the latter shows points of contact with the language of the Jātakas (F. Kielhorn JRAS 1898, 17 ff and R. G. Bhandarkar in OC IX London 1892, I, 421 ff.) would indicate that some Jātakas have originated in the 2nd century B.C.

3. For instance, if Luders (Festschrift Windisch, pp. 228 ff.) has proved that some of the Gāthās of Jātakas Nos. 377 and 487, having reference to Śvetaketu, who is familiar to us from the Upaniṣads, date back to the Vedic period, then the statement is only true of these particular Gāthās, and we are *not* warranted to make the generalisation that the Gāthā poetry of the Jātakas forms "the connecting link between the Vedic Ākhyāna and the epic poetry."

poetry[1] but the collection as we find it in Jātakaṭṭhavaṇṇanā, cannot as such be the "earliest" collection of Indian fables, fairy tales and narratives, as has often been affirmed.

Yet we cannot but proceed from this Jātakaṭṭhavaṇṇana, the only one known to us till now, when we report in the following pages about the contents of the collection of Buddhistic stories which is of very great importance not only for the history of Indian literature but also for the history of world-literature. However we can safely ignore the "stories of the present". They are partly only doublets of the "stories from the past" and partly simple and absolutely worthless inventions and at best stories which have been borrowed from other parts of the canon —for example the Vinayapiṭaka, Suttanipāta, Apādāna—or also from other commentaries. The actual Jātakas or the "stories from the past" are, therefore, all the more valuable.

Among the Jātakas of our collection whose number exceeds 500,[2] all kinds and forms of narrative poetry find representation. As far as the form is concerned we find :[1] Stories in prose with insertions of fable-verses, story-stanzas or moral-sayings. Prose and verse are fused into each other here so well and thus constitute such a beautiful whole, that we must presume that the Jātakaṭṭhavaṇṇana has used in these cases also good old traditions for its prose;.[2] Ballads (a) in dialogue form,[3] (b) in a

1. Oldenberg in his researches as to the style of the Jātakas (NGGW 1918, 429 ff., 1919, 61 ff.) comes to the conclusion that the Jātaka Gāthās represent a more ancient type of poetry than epic. He is compelled to admit however that it is not possible to decide for certain whether that type which is more primitive as regards development is at the same time also the earlier as regards actual chronology.

2. The number of items in the Jātaka Book is 547. But because in some of these items more than one story are put together. While others contain only references to later Jātakas, and because sometimes the same stories also recur in various versions the number 547 does not correspond exactly to the actual number of Jātakas. The Culla Niddesa (p. 80) speaks of 500 Jātakas. Fahein too (Record of Buddhist Kingdom transl. by J. Legge, Oxford, 1886, p. 106) speaks of pictures illustrating "500 Jātakas" which he had seen in Ceylon. Cf. B. M. Barua, Ind. Hist. Qu., II, 1926, p. 623 ff.

3. Dramatic as many of these Ballads are—L. Feer (JA 1895, s. 9, t. V pp. 47 ff.) for instance calls the Chaddanta Jātaka (No. 514) "Un veritable drame," and the same could be said of many other Jātakas—we can scarcely

mixture of dialogue verses and narrative stanzas.[1] The prose that we find in our Jātakaṭṭhavaṇṇana is in these cases in general a very superfluous and tasteless handiwork of commentators and is very often even in contradiction with the verses; 3. longer stories, which begin in prose and continue in verse, or in which prose narration alternates with narrative and conversational verses. Here prose is indispensable, but the prose of the Jātakaṭṭhavaṇṇana is not a true picture of the original prose but it has been enlarged and modified manifold[2] by means of commentary additions; 4. collections of sayings on some theme and 5. real epic or epic fragments. In the last two cases the prose in our book is again only a superfluous and mostly also unintellectual commentary.

With regard to the contents we find in the Jātakas : 1. Fables, most of which, like the Indian fable in general, have the object of teaching Nīti, i.e. worldly wisdom. Only a few of them have a moral tendency of the manner of ascetic poetry,[3] and only very few are genuine Buddhistic in character. 2. Fairy tales, including four with animal figures in them, mostly quite in the nature of European popular fairy tales and without any relation to Buddhism. Only in some cases they have been provided with a Buddhistic tendency, they have been so to say "Buddhisised"

---

look upon them as "dramas" in the true sense of the word. What has been said above, p. 57 ff. regarding ballads of the Saṃyuttanikāya may be applied to these ballads also.

1. To distinguish the narrative verses from the conversational verses the commentary calls the former verses by the name Abhisambuddhagāthās i.e. Verses spoken by Buddha after his enlightenment which means nothing "but verses spoken by the narrator" for the narrator of the canonical Jātaka (consisting of verses only) is Buddha himself. Cf. Senart JA 1901, s. 9, t. XVII p. 383 ff.

2. It is not possible to reject the type of poetry consisting of prose and verse for the Jātakas, as A. B. Keith does (JRAS 1911, 979ff.; 1912, 435ff.); it is also not possible to speak of a "prosaic-poetic type triumphing almost alone" in the Jātakas as Oldenberg does (NGGW 1911, p. 441ff., but cf. p. 444, note 3), even if that "almost" is stressed. And we cannot also agree with Charpentier (ZDMG 66, 1912, p. 41f.), when he says that the Jātaka prose is based "in general" on old tradition; but only this much can be said, that this is the case "sometimes". Charpentier (WZKM, 1913, pp. 92 f.) repeats his opinion, though without putting forward any new grounds.

3. See vol. I, p. 300 and 391 f.

and a few may also be purely Buddhistic invention; 3. short anecdotes, witty tales and short anecdotes which do not at all have anything Buddhistic about them; 4. short stories and full fledged novels with many adventures and sometimes with a large or small number of stories inserted in them. In these also there is nothing Buddhistic except that the hero is Bodhisatta; 5. moral stories; 6. sayings and 7. pious legends, all of which are only in part of Buddhist origin, whereas many of them belong to the common possession of Indian ascetic poetry. We will not be wrong if we say that far more than half of all Jātakas, if we omit the commentary, are not of Buddhistic origin. The explanation of this fact is not far to seek. The Buddhist monks were recruited from all classes. Hence, there were among them many who were very well familiar with the popular stories, and anecdotes of the workers, craftsmen and especially the merchants, others who knew well the old ballads and hero-songs of the warriors and yet others who had often heard the pious legends and myths of the Brahmins and hermits. When they became monks they tried to associate these familiar things, as far as was possible, with the monastic and purely religious tradition. Just on account of this are these Jātakas all the more significant for the history of Indian literature. Like a huge sack the Buddhist monks who preached stuffed the Jātaka book with everything that they and their listeners liked. And as with regard to content and form so also with regard to volume the Jātakas are very different[1] from one another. By the side of small stories which hardly fill half a page in print, we find voluminous poems of many many pages of which some could as well be termed

1. In our Jātakaṭṭhavanna the Jātakas are arranged purely externally according to the number of stanzas (Gāthās) contained in them. The book consists of 22 sections (Nipātas) of which the first 150 stories contain only 1 stanza each, the second 100 stories with 2 stanzas each, the third 50 stories with 3 stanzas each etc. In each subsequent Nipāta the number of the Gāthās increases and that of the stories decreases until in the last sections we find very long poems with hundreds of verses. This division was in existence already in the canonical Jātaka stanza collection and is not a work of the commentator. Cf. Senart JA 1901 s.9, t. XVII, p. 402f.

independent books.[1]

In the earlier sections which contain the less voluminous Jātakas we find most of the fables. Here we come across the cunning cat which eats up the mice by pretending to be a pious ascetic.[2] Here we find also many fables which recur in other Indian story-books like Tantrākhyāyikā, Pañcatantra etc. and many of those fables of world-literature whose nativity is difficult to fix, because they have equally taken roots in the east as in the west. How lion and bull, the two friends are separated by the jackal and kill each other, tells the Jātaka no. 349 agreeing with the framework-story of the first book of the Tantrākhyāyikā. Of the interesting story of the monkey which outwits the crocodile, the framework-story of the fourth book of the Tantrākhyāyikā, the jātaka-book knows several variations.[3] As in Aesop's fable the donkey in the Jātaka No. 189 has a lion's skin hanging around whereas the Tantrākhyāyikā gives it a panther's skin and the Pañcatantra and the Hitopadeśa give it a tiger's skin. Other well known fables are that of the jackal which praises the sweet voice of the crow and in this way gets a good bite;[4] of the ox which envies the swine for the good

1. The numerous allusions in the Jātaka book, of one Jātaka to another, preceding as well as later ones seems to confirm that the single Jātakas were in existence as independent texts long before they were combined to form a large collection. The long Jātaka of the last books, in particular, which in their turn are divided into sections and to which references is often made in earlier short Jātakas were surely originally independent poems. Cf. J. Dutoit, "Jatakazitate in den Jatakatexten," in "Festschrift Kuhn", 345 ff.

2. Jāt No. 128 The stanza: "If one always holds high the banner of religion like the banner of an inn held high but secretly commmits sins, then that is called a cat's vow" agrees verbatim with Mahābh. V 160, 13 and has also found entrance into the books of law. (Manu IV, 195, Viṣṇu 36, 8) Cf. Vol. I p. 391 f.

3. No. 57 208, Benfey, Pantschantantra, I, 420 ff. R. O. Franke has proved the existence of this fable among the Suahelis. (WZKM, 7, 1893, 215 f., 384 f.). Also the framework-story of the II book of the Tantrākhyāyikā has a parallel in the Jātaka No. 206 for which there is a beautiful relief on the Stūpa of Bharhut. (Cunningham, Pl. 27, Fig. 9).

4. Jāt. No. 294. In No. 295 it is conversely the crow which flatters the jackal and thus gets a bit of an ox carrion. In La fontaine's fables I, 2, the ox praises the crow's sweet voice and thus gets the cheese.

feed until it learns that the swine is fed well only to be slaughtered;[1] of the cunning crane of stork which pretends to bring the fish to a beautiful pond but eats up all of them until at last it gets from the crab the penalty it deserves;[2] of the parrot which has to keep watch on the chastity of a frivolous wife and is killed on account of its indiscretion.[3] The fable of the dancing peacock which through its shameless dance loses its bride, the daughter of the king of birds.[4] As this fable has been represented on a relief of the Stūpa of Bharhut as early as in the 3rd century B.C. it must have been already a Jātaka at that time. Another relief on the same Stūpa is an illustration to the Jātaka No. 383, which narrates in four verses, how the cat wants to get the cock under its control by flattering and telling it that it will be its obedient wife. But the cock sees through the trick and chases it away. From this in three verses the moral is drawn which is truly Buddhistic: As the cat, so do also cunning women when they want to seduce men, but the wise man is invincible to them, as the cock is to the cat. One of the few fables of decidedly Buddhistic origin is no. 278. Here the

1. Jāt. No. 30 variant No. 286, Benfey, Pantschatantra I, 228 f. I. Scheftelowitz in ZB VII, 1926, pp. 284 f.

2. Jāt. No. 38, Benfey, Pantschatantra I, 174 ff.; Tantrākhyāyikā I, 5; La fontaine, Fables, X, 4. A gipsy version ZDMG 42, 122 f.

3. Jāt. No. 198; is found again in "Arabian Nights", in "Gesta Romanorum" in "Sindbad" (Sindbad or the seven wise masters, Syrian and German by F. Baethgen, Leipzig 1879, p. 15) and in Chaucer (Wife of Bath, I, 231). Cf. JRAS 1890, p. 504.

4. Jāt. No. 32. This fable seems to have wandered very early via Persia to Greece, where Herodotes (VI, 130) has woven it into the story of Hippokleides. C. H. Tawney (Journal of Philosophy XII, 1883, p. 121) presumes that the story was brought to India by the Greeks when they ruled over Bactria, but this is improbable because it is more easy to explain that a fable is extended to human conditions than that from out of an anecdote a fable is made. Also the peacock which while dancing reveals its hind part is proverbial in India as an example of shamelessness. Cf. Bohtlingk, "Indische Sprüche" No. 5233; Benfey, Pantschatantra I, 280; J. G. v. Hahn, Sagwissenschaftliche Studien, Jena 1876, p. 69. S. J. Warren, in "Hermes", Vol. 29, 1894, pp. 426 f. says "The details of the story as told by Herodotus are exceptional, they are so reminiscent of an Indian svayaṃvara where the maiden or the father selects a husband from among the assembled suitors that one would assume oriental origin were it not for the fact that Herodotus narrated it with such convincing certainty as if it had actually taken place".

Bodhisatta is reborn as a buffalo and as such shows limitless patience: An impudent monkey climbs on his back, defiles him, holds him by the horns and does all kinds of mischief with him. But then the monkey behaves in the same way with another buffalo and is killed by it. In this way, as the prose commentator expressly says, the Bodhisatta retains his virtue of patience and the monkey is of course punished.[1]

Closely related to the fable is the animal fairy-tale that finds some beautiful representatives in the Jātaka book. A delicious humour is found in the story of the jackal Allzahm (Sabbadāṭha):

This jackal uses a magic formula which he has heard by chance, to make all quadrapeds subordinate to him. In his arrogance he resolves to march against the king of Benares. On the backs of two elephants a lion had to stand and on the back of this lion the jackal sat with his jackal-wife whom he had made the first queen and thus he marched in great pomp against the town of Banares. With impudence he demands the king to give him his kingdom, all are in great fright, but through a trick of the royal priest (this is the Bodhisatta) the jackal perishes with its army of animals. Then the people of Banares rush to the city gate in order to fetch flesh—which the Bodhisatta, in a highly un-Buddhistic way, asked them to do—, and what they cannot eat, they dry. "At that time, it is said", thus the Jātaka closes in a genuinely fairy-tale-like manner, "the drying of flesh started."[2]

More numerous than the fairy tales with purely animals are the fairy tales with animals and human beings, in which the animals as a rule fare better than human beings. Thus it is in the fairy tale of the wise partridge which has learnt the Vedas from a famous teacher. Many youths come to him for learning. Lions and tigers are among his friends. He lives in a golden cage and is guarded by a lizard. One day a wicked ascetic

1. This Jātaka is also found illustrated in a mural painting of a cave-temple of Ajantā; see John Griffiths, The paintings in the Buddhist Cave-Temples of Ajantā, London 1896, I, 12 f., Fig. 27, p. 13.

2. No. 241. Translated and discussed by Alb. Grunwedel, Buddhistische Kunst in Indien, 2nd Ed., Berlin 1900, p. 53 ff.

comes, who has gone through an interesting career (he was previously carrier of lords, pedlar, juggler, hunter, fencer, bird-catcher, corn-measurer, gambler and hangman's servant), kills the lizard and the partridge and as punishment for this is torn to pieces by the tiger.[1] Here we find also in particular the fairy tales of grateful animals and ungrateful men which are so wide spread in world literature and many of which are found in our collection. One of the most beautiful ones is No. 73[2]:

Once upon a time there was a king, he had a wicked son called Prince Villain. He was like a poisonous snake, spoke to no one a kind word and was to the people like a dust particle in the eye. Once as he wants to bathe during a big storm, the people bring him out into the river to drown him. But he saves himself together with a snake, a rat and a parrot by climbing on a tree-trunk. All the four are pulled out of water by an ascetic who then brings them home, where the pious man nurses at first the animals as they are the weaker ones and only then the prince. The prince is angry at this. All the three animals promise the ascetic to show their gratefulness; so also the prince, who however, inwardly swears vengeance. After a while the ascetic wants to test the beings saved by him. The three animals show their gratefulness immediately, but the prince, who has become king in the meanwhile, as soon as he recognises him, orders him to be whipped and wants to get him beheaded. On being whipped each time the ascetic says the verse:

"True is the proverb which says: A lump of wood, washed ashore by water, is often better than some men".

Asked by the people, what he is saying, he tells the story. Thereupon the whole folk gathers, they catch hold of the tyrant, kill him and make the ascetic their king.

Among the fairy tales of world literature is also that of the ungrateful wife :

1. No. 438. Cf. E. Windisch in Gurupūjākaumudī, pp. 64 ff. and Frick, Soziale Gliederung etc. p. 193. (Social Organisation in North-East India, p. 301 f.)

2. Cf. also no. 482 and 516. Benfey, Pantschatantra I, 193 ff. (where also the versions of Rasavâhinī, Ch. 3 and the Tibetan Karmaśataka are translated), 286, 603; II, 128 ff; Kathâsaritsâgara 65, 45 ff.

Once a man saved the life of his wife by giving her his own blood to drink. But she falls in love with a wretched cripple. In order to entirely belong to him she pushes her husband down a precipice. The husband however is saved by a lizard and in a strange way he becomes king in which capacity he has the opportunity to see again and to punish his unfaithful wife with her crippled lover.[1]

Worldwide popularity is also enjoyed by the humorously narrated fairy tale of the king, who understands the languages of animals :

He may not reveal the magic formula to anyone; for if he does, he must die. One day the king laughs at the funny conversation between ants and flies. The queen wants to know the cause of his laughing and pesters her husband to tell her the magic formula, although he tells her, that that would be his death. The king is about to yield to his inquisitive wife's urges when Sakka the king of the gods appears in the form of a he-goat and advises the king to give his wife a good thrashing; then she will give up her desire for the magic-formula, he says. The king follows the advice and is successful.[2]

Reminiscent of the German fairy tale of the magic table is the fairy tale of the three brothers of whom the first has a magic axe which he need only to stroke, in order to get firewood, the second has a drum with the help of which he can defeat his enemies, and the third has a whey pot, out of which flows out a stream of whey when it is turned.[3] A similar tale is that of the

---

1. Jāt. No. 193. Cf. Benfey, Pantschatantra I, 436 ff.; II 303 ff. and Gaston Paris in the Zeitschrift des Vereins für Volkskunde XIII, 1903, who pursues the story in oriental and romantic fairy-tale literature; Chavannes, Cinq Cents Contes No. 12.

2. Jāt No. 386. Similarly in the Arabian Nights (Cf. Orient and Okzident II, 138 ff.) and Gesta Romanorum (Grasse II, p. 190 ff). Regarding this story so widespread in the literature of the world see also Hertel, "Das Pancatantra", p. 284 f. J. J. Meyer, "Das Weib im altindischen Epos", 376. Zachariae also refers to Kuhn, "Barlaam und Joasaph", p. 81 R. Kohler Kl. Schriften II, 610 f. III, 539; "Linguistic Survey of India", VIII, 1, pp. 410 f and others.

3. Jāt No. 186 Cf. Grimm, "Kinder-und Hausmarchen," No. 36, and 54.

youth, who has wasted his whole wealth and to whom his dead father who is reborn as god Sakka presents a pot which grants him all his desires but which he must guard carefully, because only as long as the pot exists will he not be wanting in money. Once the youth, in intoxication, hurls the pot many times into the air to catch it again, but soon the pot lies broken to pieces on the ground. This moment is the end of his fortune; he now becomes so poor that he at last remains lying near the wall as a beggar clad in rags and there he dies.[1]

Although many fairy tales have found their way from India into the west, there can be hardly any doubt that some foreign tales have also come to India. This for example might be the case with the seafarers' tales, which tell about ship-wrecks and all sorts of peculiar adventures on the sea. The female demons (Yakkhiṇīs) which entice shipwrecked people to approach them and favour them with love in order to kill them then and eat them up remind us instinctively of the sirens and of beings like Circe and Calypso.[2] A strange mixture of popular fairy tale and moral story is the Jātaka of Mittavindaka who experiences wonderful adventures on the sea, enjoys himself with ghostly women in splendid palaces on islands in the midst of the ocean finally on account of his insatiable greed, or, according to a second version, on account of ill treatment of his mother, comes to a hell where a wheel with sharp knives revolves on his head incessantly.[3]

---

1. M. Gaster, JRAS 1897, p. 379 f. and Alfred Forke, "Die indischen Marchen und ihre Bedeutung fur die vergleichende Märchenforschung", Berlin 1911, p. 8 f. Compare with this Uhland's wellknown ballad "Das Gluck von Edenhall".

2. Valāhaka-Jātaka, No. 196. The shipwrecked men are rescued by a winged horse (the Boddhisatta). Cf. Divyāvadāna, p. 120; 524 ff; Karaṇḍa-vyūha p. 52; Nayadhammakahão IX; Charpentier J. A. 1910, s.10, t.XVI, p. 606, 608, WZKM, 27, 1913, p. 93. Other mariners' tales are No. 463 (of the clever Suppāraka, who, in spite of his blindness, is made the first pilot and acquits himself splendidly) and no. 360 (of Garuḍa who plays dice with the king and seduces his wife, with whom then the royal singer enjoys himself after he has suffered a shipwreck and cast on to the shore of the island of Garuḍa).

3. No. 439 with all its variations and fragments, nos. 41, 82, 104 and 369 have been treated by L. Feer while summing up the various Pāli and Sanskrit versions of the tale. (JA 1878, 2.7, t.XI, p. 360 ff., 1892 s.8,t. XX, p. 185 ff.)

In the tales of man-eaters also there is a mixture of truly popular motives for fairy tales with moral tendencies. These tales of man-eaters are connected with the name of king Kalmāṣapāda, well-known in the Brahminical literature. He has become a man-eater as a result of a curse. But the actual Buddhistic story culminates in this, that Sutasoma, the pious king, is caught by this man-eater and is again set free by him in order to keep the promise he gave to a Brahmin. But then again he comes back to the monster as per the promise to be eaten up by him whereupon the man-eater moved by so much love for truth, is converted.[1]

Superhuman beings of all kinds, serpent-and bird- deities (Nāgas and Garuḍas) Yakṣas, Kinnaras[2] etc. play a great role in the fairy tales. Some of these Jātakas have been formed into voluminous poetry of fairy tales. Jātakas, like No. 504, of the Kinnara couple that is deeply mourning because it was separated for a single night, or No. 485 of the Kinnara woman who mourns for her lover, whom the king has shot dead, so long that he is brought back to life by means of elixir of life, are actually lyric-dramatic poems of fairy tales, in which the lyrical element dominates. A greater work of fiction in prose and verse with enclosed stories is the Jātaka No. 432 where the Bodhisatta is reborn as the son of a horse-headed, man-eating Yakkha woman. A great work of fiction in a mixture of prose and verse from the world of the Nāgas and Garuḍas, a strange mixture of popular fairy tale-motifs and Buddhist dogma, is the Jātaka

---

1. K. Watanabe has treated in JPTS 1909 (p. 236 f.) in detail the numerous Buddhistic versions of this Jātaka in the literatures of Pāli, Sanskrit, Chinese and Tibetan and its forerunners in the epic-puranic tradition Cf. Charpentier in WZKM, 23, 1909, p. 161 note 3, 24, 1910, p. 396 note. Pavolini (GSAI, 25, 324) also refers to H. Kern in Versl en Meded der Kon. Akad von Wetensch. Afd. Letterk. IV, 11, pp. 170 ff. J. S. Speyer, and after him R. Garbe (contributions of Buddhism to Christianity, Chicago 1911, p. 42 ff.) try to connect the legend of St. Christopher with this Jātaka. The two legends have however nothing in common except a man-eating monster. Of the actual essence of the Buddhistic tale we do not find anything in the Christian legend. See also H. Gunter, "Buddha in der abenlandischen Legende," Leipzig 1922, pp. 19 ff.

2. Kinnaras are half-human winged beings. On their representation in Buddhistic art, ref. Grunwedel, "Buddhist Kunst in Indien," p. 44 ff.

No. 543, which can be recognised as an independent work even by the division into 8 sections (Khaṇḍas). And a veritable epic in 6 sections (khaṇḍas) is the Vidhurapaṇḍitajātaka,[1] whose hero is the wise Vidhura, the minister of the Kuru king. This Vidhura recurring many times in the Jātaka book is none else than the Vidhura known to us from the Mahābhārata, the half-brother and councillor of Dhṛtarāṣṭra who appears even in the epic as well-versed in fables, parables and wise sayings.[2] Both through this name and through a lively description of the game of dice this Jataka is in a certain way related to the Mahābhārata and is hence of special interest. But even in itself it is an epic work of fairy tales of no mean poetic worth.

Much less than the fables and fairy tales have the numerous, often very witty anecdotes of the Jātaka book originally to do with Buddhism. That the Indians also enjoyed various foolish pranks as the Germans do their Swabian pranks is testified by stories like that of the son who wants to kill the fly on the head of the sleeping father and in doing so smashes the father's skull to pieces;[3] or of the monkeys who were to water the trees and do this in such a way that they pull them out with roots in order to see which tree needs more water and which less.[4] The stupid one is often a priest or a monk. Thus a Brahminical mendicant monk comes to a place where two rams are fighting with each other. As he sees one ram spring back, he imagines that the ram knows manners and wants to pay respects to him. A merchant warns him that the ram was only making a start for an attack; but the animal comes in the meanwhile running and throws the monk down who then cries wailing, "Help, help,

---

1. Jātaka No. 545. English translation by Cowell and Rouse, Vol. VI, pp. 126-156. In its somewhat different version of Burma this Jātaka was translated by R. F. St. Andrew St. John in JRAS 1896, 441-475. It is also to be found in the Chinese Tripiṭaka, see Chavannes, Cinq Cents Contes, III, p. 100.

2. Cf. Vol. I, p. 392 ff. and 451. Vidhura occurs also in Theragāthā 1188 and Majjhimanikāya 50.

3. Jāt. No. 44, and variation No. 45. Cf. Benfey, Pantschatantra I, 283, 292 f; II, 154 ff; La Fontaine, Fables VIII, 10.

4. Jāt. No. 46, illustrated on the Stūpa of Bharhut.

a holy man is being killed."[1] A grim humour is hidden in the story of the wicked king Mahāpiṅgala (No. (240).

This Mahapingala was a bad tyrant. When he died, entire Banaras rejoiced—only a doorkeeper weeps. The Bodhisatta asks him for the reason and he replies, "I am crying, not because Mahāpiṅgala is dead, for every time he came down from the palace and went up there he gave me eight blows on my head, as with a hammer. Now, when he is in the other world, I am afraid. he will do the same thing to Yama, and the latter will send him back to the earth; but I shall again get my eight blows with the fist as before, so I am weeping." The Bodhisatta consoles him saying, "the dead one will not come back, he has been properly cremated. the pyre extinguished with water and the earth around has been filled up."

Full of subtle satire is the anecdote of the monkey who has stayed for a long time in the palace of a king and then has been set free by him. As he comes back to his comrades, they surround him and would like to learn from him how all went in the world of human beings, of whose life and activities he must have seen much. The monkey however describes the activities of human beings in the two verses:

"The gold is mine, the wealth is mine, so they cry by day and by night,
The word of truth,—that they know not, the human beings in their folly.
In every house are two masters, no beard has one of them,
But hanging breasts, long plaits, big rings in the ears,
For much money he is bought, and yet he pesters all people."

Then the monkeys do not want to hear any more, close their ears tightly and run away (Jāt. No. 219). Of special importance on account of its relationship to Greek literature is the anecdote

1. Jāt. No. 324. A crude farce in which the greed of Brahmins is mocked at is the Jātaka No. 113. That good advices are not useful for everyman, realises an all too clever ascetic to his detriment in Jāt. No. 376.

of a woman whose husband, son and brother are to be beheaded, and to whom the king grants a wish that she might choose to save one of them. She decides for the brother with the argument that she can easily get a husband and a son, but not again a brother. The same anecdote is told by Herodotus about the wife of Intaphernes, and Sophocles makes Antigone argue in the same way. But the same idea occurs again in India in the Rāmāyaṇa also namely in connection with an old Indian proverb which says that one can have in the world anything more easily than a blood-brother. Therefore, the anecdote is very old in India as well as in Greece; but it has in itself as little that is characteristically Indian as is specifically Greek, so that it will be hardly possible to decide where to look for its actual native place. Only this much appears to be certain that it cannot have originated twice.[1]

The anecdote mentioned just now is one of a class of stories which are just as popular in the narrative literature of all folks as those of fools' pranks, that is of stories of very great intelligence or skill which is expressed in intelligent answers, especially answers to riddles, or in wise judgements or in making wonderful pieces of art. Numerous stories of this kind are found in the Jātaka book and many of them belong to world-literature. Of this kind is also for example the story of the wise judge who gives all kinds of witty "Solomonic" judgements and thus helps a poor fellow come out of his difficulties—this poor man has, without any guilt on his part, rendered a horse lame, caused premature childbirth to a pregnant woman and similar things—and solves at the same time several riddles given by animals and men.[2] An artist who is a match on every occasion is the hero of the charming Kuśajātaka (No. 531).

---

1. Jāt. No. 67. Cf. Herodotus III, 119. Sophocles, Antigone 909 to 912. Pischel in Hermes, Vol. 28, 1893, 465 ff. believes in the Indian origin. Th. Noeldeke ibid, Vol. 29, 1894. 155 f in the Persian and C. H. Tawney in the Ind. Ant. X, 1881, 370 f. in the Greek origin of the anecdote.

2. Jāt. No. 257, poetically translated by J. J. Meyer, Kāvyasaṃgraha, p. 46 ff. The same story retold as per the Tibetan Dsanglun in Benfey's Pantschatantra, I, 393 ff. and followed, through world literature upto Shakespeare's "Merchant of Venice". Cf. also Tawney in the Journal of Philology, XII, 1883, 112 ff.

Kusa, the son of king Okkāka is as ugly as clever and wise. As he wishes to marry, he makes a beautiful image of a woman in gold and says that he will marry only a girl who is as beautiful as the image. The image is taken from town to town until it comes to the town where Pabhāvatī, the daughter of the Madda king, is found to be as beautiful as the image. She is promised to Kusa for wife. But on account of the ugliness of the prince, the mother of Pabhāvatī makes it a condition that till the time of conception the couple may meet each other only at night. But they cannot resist the desire to see each other and through various means they at last succeed in seeing each other which finally leads to the consequence that the princess goes back to her parents because she cannot stand such an ugly man. But Kusa is filled with a yearning for his wife and is determined to win her back at all costs. He sets out for Sāgala where the princess is staying. There he draws the attention of the king first as a troubadour through his sweet music on the lute, then through his wonderfully shaped figures as a potter, after that as a basket-maker through his valuble fans, then as a gardener through a splendid wreath and at last as a cook by making a preparation with a bone in such a way that a pleasant odour spreads in the town, attracts the attention of the king, advances upto the princess, but is rejected by her every time with mockery and scorn. Then Sakka sends seven kings who court Pabhāvatī and king Madda is greatly embarassed; for if he would give his daughter to one of the kings in marriage, the others would fight against him. Therefore, he tells his daughter that he will cut her into seven pieces, to give each of the seven kings a piece of her. In her fear she flees to Kusa who is staying as a cook in the palace and falls at his feet on the dirty floor of the kitchen. Kusa the artist proves his mettle even now as a great hero. In no time he defeats all the seven kings and takes them prisoner. But as he is as kind as he is clever, he makes the king give his seven unmarried daughters in marriage to them. He himself goes home with his wife Pabhāvatī whom he has won back.[1]

In a shorter story the Bodhisatta is a master in the art of

1. A Sinhalese treatment of this short story has been translated by Th. Steele into English under the title "An Eastern Love Story", London 1871.

smithy and wins the beautiful daughter of a smith for wife by making a wonderful needle that is surrounded by such fine needle-cases, that the smiths in the village take the cases for the needles.[1] But a veritable rallying point for such stories of extraordinary intelligence and artistry is the Mahā-Ummagga Jātaka (No. 546). This is an entire novel with numerous anecdotes, riddles and stories shoved in, a true chapbook of the kind that we find in India even today which is specially interesting because it shows points of contact with the stories of the wise. Ahiqar (Haikar or Heykar) in "Thousand and One Nights" and with the "Life of Aesop" by Planudes.[2]

The hero of this Jātaka is Mahosadha, who, even as a boy, gives proof of his wonderful wisdom and establishes himself as a clever judge in particular. Thus like king Solomon he decides the question to which of the two quarrelling women the child belongs, by making mother's love decide the issue. He draws a line on the floor and places the child in the middle, ordering that one woman shall pull the child over the line by the hands and the other by the feet and the child shall belong to that woman who pulls the child to herself. They begin to pull and the child cries. Then the true mother lets the child loose which naturally settles the dispute.[3] Whatever riddles and puzzles the

1. Jāt. No. 387. In a Chinese version of the story the artisan Smith makes such fine needles, that they swim on the water, as in the Sanskrit Divyāvadāna. Cf. A. Schiefner, Indische Kunstleranekdoten, Melanges asiatiques, VII (1875), p. 519 ff.

2. Cf. Benfey, Kleine Schriften II, 192 ff. and B. Meissner, ZDMG 48, 174 ff.

3. This "Solomonic judgement" constitutes the essence of the Chinese drama "Hoei-lan-ki" or the chalk circle. That this anecdote and the Solomonian judgement of 1. Kon, 3, 16-28 cannot have been originated independent of each other, can perhaps be considered to be certain. A. Weber in his "Indische Streifen," III, p. 60 considers it as entirely wrong to suppose that the jews had borrowed it from the Indians; so also Garbe, in "Contributions of Buddhism to Christianity, Chicago 1911, p. 12, Note 16. As against this, Hugeo Cressmann (in Deutsche Rundschau, Vol. 33, 1907, p. 212 ff.) has advanced very good grounds for their Indian origin. Cf. also Th. Benfey, "Kleine Schriften" II, 170 f; R. Kohler, "Kleinere Schriften" I, 531 ff; H. Gaidoz, Melusine, t. IV, R. Engelmann in Hermes, Vol. 39, 1904, 148f; T. W. Rhys Davids, Buddha's Birth Stories, XLIV ff. Zachariae, "Kleine Schriften," pp. 150 ff.

king gives, Mahosadha is never in a fix. By placing a pole in water and seeing where the heavier end is, he decides where the trunk and where the top of the tree was out of which the pole has been made. Like a modern anthropologist, by observing the stitches he distinguishes a masculine skull from a feminine one. Masculine and feminine snakes too he can distinguish from each other. As the king once asks for a white bull with horns in its legs and a hump on the head, which raises its voice after three notes, no one knows except Mahosadha that the king wants a white cock. The king orders that they should bring him cooked rice under the following conditions : it must have been cooked without rice, without water, without pot, without oven, without fire and firewood and may be carried over the street neither by a man nor by a woman; then Mahosadha accomplishes this also. The king wants a rope of sand for his swing. Mahosadha says that he is prepared to make one such, only, he asks for a specimen of the old sand-rope in order to be able to make it equally thick and long. He can also guess the thoughts of animals, for example, of a chamelon. The wise Mahosadha, who by means of an intelligence-test, has managed to become one of the king's councillors, selects for his wife only a clever-girl[1] who understands all his riddles. She manages very cleverly to deal with the ministers persecuting her and jealous of her husband. Mahosadha proves to be a clever councillor in politics, in the fight against external enemies and lastly also as a splendid architect who builds a tunnel, whose description reminds us of the artistic Indian cave-constructions like those of Ajantā.[2]

This strange novel, which represents indeed an independent book[3] closes with a glorification of Mahosadha, who of course, is

1. Cf. Benfey Kleine Schriften II, 156-223; "Die kluge Dirne, die indischen Märchen von den klugen Rātsellosern und ihre Verberitung über Asien und Europa" and R. Kohler, "Kleinere Schriften," I, 445 ff.

2. The description presupposes in any case that the narrator knew splendid underground constructions.

3. An elaborated and worsened Tibetan version of this Jātaka is reported by A. Schiefner from Kanjur in "Indische Erzahlungen" (Melanges asiatiques

the Bodhisatta. And except for the fact that Mahosadha has his great wisdom and skilfulness only as Bodhisatta, there is nothing Buddhistic in the whole of the long novel.

One will find little that is Buddhistic also in the robber-stories and other stories of the Jātaka book in which robbers, tramps, gamblers and courtesans are the chief characters. All these stories are very interesting from the point of view of cultural history. Twice is the Bodhisatta himself a highway man.[1] One of these stories tells how a Brahmin causes a rain of precious stones by means of a magic formula, how two bands of robbers begin to fight for the treasure thus obtained and kill one another so that only two are left behind and how these two also, each in trying to take possession of the treasure kills the other—just like the tramps in the "story of the Seller of Indulgences" by chance.[2] Numerous are the stories which treat the wickedness of women—a theme so inexhaustible with the Indians. A whole series of such stories is found in the Jātakas Nos. 61-66, while in No. 536 a whole collection of stories and sayings on this topic is included within a framework. In an endless variety of ways, through several kinds of stories which are partly highly artful, attempts are made to prove that every woman is inclined to commit adultery if only there is a man available to seduce her. The story is told with particular artifice as to how a Brahmin, in order to be quite sure, brings up a girl in his house from the moment of her birth, and after she has grown up and become his wife, has her strictly guarded in a tower surrounded with seven

---

VII, 1876, 673 ff). The Singhalese version "Ummagga Jātaka" (The Story of the Tunnel) has been translated from the Singhalese by J. B. Yataware London, 1912.

1. Jāt. No. 279 and 318, Cf. No. 419, 91, 193 360. Cf. R. Fick in Harden's "Zukunft", Vol. 27, 1889, 565 ff. (Unehrliche Leute im alten Indien"). We hear of organised robber bands, and of entire robber villages. Cf. R. Fick, "Social Organisation in North East India", p. 274 and J. J Meyer in the Introduction to his German translation of Daṇḍin's Daśakumāracarita pp. 14 ff., 32 ff.

2. Jāt. No. 48, Chaucer's Works translated by A. V. During III, p. 172ff; R. Morris in "Contemporary Review", May 1881; C. H. Tawney in "Journal of Philology", XII, 1883, 203 ff.

ramparts and yet, in the end, she turns unfaithful to him; she however denies her unfaithfulness and even subjects herself to a divine judgement which she manages to falsify.[1]

In the Kuṇāla-Jātaka, we find, among others, the story of Kaṇhā (i.e. Kṛṣṇā or Draupadī) who, not content with her five husbands, commits adultery with a hunchback dwarf, which causes the Pāṇḍavas to renounce the world and retire to the Himālayas.[2] This Jātaka, the greater part of which is merely a sermon on the wickedness of woman-kind, attributed to Buddha himself, also abounds in sayings against women, of which we may quote a few especially characteristic ones :

"Like poisoned draught or robber fell, crooked as horn of stag,
Like serpent evil-tongued are they, as merchant apt to brag.
"Murderous as covered pit, like Hell's insatiate maw are they.
As goblin greedy or like Death that carries all away."

"Women like flames devour their prey,
Women like floods sweep all away,
Women are pests, like thorns are they,
Women for gold oft go astray."[3]

Such stories which were at all times immensely popular in India could of course easily have a "Buddhistic" tendency tacked on to them and be incorporated in Buddhist sermons. For

1. Jāt No. 62 translated into German and discussed by Pischel in "Philology. Abhandlugen Martin Hertz zum 70. Geburtstag", Berlin 1888, p. 74 ff. Cf. Chavvanes, "Contes bouddhiques" I, No. 116 and J. J. Meyer, "Isoldes Gottesurteil", Berlin 1914, pp. 112 ff.

2. Cf. above Vol. I, p. 452. The composition of the Kuṇāla-Jātaka is very confused, "Stories of the Present" and "Stories of the Past" being jumbled together, and the style, which is in part veritable ornate prose with very long compound words, is most peculiar and reminds us of such works as the Divyāvadāna. Cf. Oldenberg in JPTS 1910, 1912, p. 26, note 3.

3. Translated by H. T. Francis.

it was only a grist to the monks' mill if by such narratives they could prove what a snare and danger every woman is to man and how very carefully one must protect oneself against these temptresses.

Thus these stories, which were often very immoral, constitute the transition to the moral stories of the Jātaka book. A longer moral story in a ballad form, which is so unusually dramatic that one could very well call it also a small drama, is the Jātaka No. 527.[1]

A prince sees the beautiful wife of the general Ahipāraka and falls passionately in love with her. But as he learns that she belongs to another one she is inaccessible to him. In a melancholic, tender lamentation he gives vent to his feelings. Ahipāraka, although deeply in love with his wife, is ready to give her to the king, and he is anxious of the latter's health. But the king declines to commit a sin. In an excellent, extraordinarily dramatic dialogue the king and his general surpass each other in nobleness. Finally virtue triumphs and the king renounces.

Some of the moral stories (just like some of the fables) have a pronouncedly didactic object and look as if they had been composed for children. Of this kind is for example No. 484 of the Bodhisatta as a wise parrot which not only eats rice from the field, but also carries it away in its beak and to the question, why it does so, answers, "A debt I am repaying, a credit I am giving, a treasure I am putting by", by which it means, that it is taking fodder for its old parents, it is feeding its children and is giving fodder to other weak birds.

A special kind of moral stories are the "consolation stories" of which we have already seen some in the Mahābhārata.[2] We may give here shortly the contents of only two of them :

No. 352 : A man is perturbed on the death of his father. Then his son stands in front of a dead cow and gives it grass and water. The father considers him mad. But he says, "Here at least there exist still head, feet and tail, so that finally the cow could at least get up; but of grandfather, there, exists neither head nor hand nor foot, you seem to have lost your

---

1. Ummadanti-Jātaka, cf. Zachariae, Bezz. Beitr. 4, 375 ff.
2. See vol. I, p. 380 ff, 398 f.

senses as you are again and again weeping at the grave. By this the father is consoled."[1]

No. 454 : Kaṇha (the Kṛṣṇa of the saga) is perturbed on the death of his son. Then his brother Ghata pretends to be mad and runs through the town crying, "Give me the hare !" Kaṇha asks what he wants actually. Ghata replies, "The hare in the moon." Kaṇha shows him that his demand is impossible to be met, but Ghata tells him that he too is wishing for the impossible when he is bemoaning the death of his son and wants to have him back. Through these words Kaṇha is healed of his sorrow as a father.[2] The same object as by these stories of consolation namely consoling the mourners of dead people—is also followed by the consoling sayings of Rāma in the Daśaratha-Jātaka (No. 461), which have been probably taken from an old Rāma-ballad.[3] And just as this Jātaka when we exclude the the prose commentary, is not a story at all, but contains only didactic sayings, so is also for example, the Jātaka No. 512 nothing but a collection of sayings. Although the prose narrates a saga of the origin of the vice of drinking this is only a foolish invention of the commentator. Old are only the sayings in which for advising a king the terrible consequences of drinking spirituous drinks are described in very strong words—in verses which can give joy to every opponent of alcoholic drinks. But the refrain "therefore buy a full mug of this drink" used ironically seems to have been taken from an old drinking song. To the epigrammatic poetry belongs also the dialogue between the Kuru-king Yudhiṭṭhila (Yuddhiṣṭhira) and his wise councillor Vidhūra (Vidura) on the question, who is a "true Brahmin",

---

1. This is a dialogue between father and son in eight verses whose meaning is quite clear even without the prose. On the Stūpa of Bharhut can be seen on a very beautiful relief(Cunningham, Stūpa of Bharhut, Pl. 47, Fig.13), how the youth gives the cow grass to eat and his father stands behind him. The same story in the Commentary to Petavatthu, see Bimala Charan Law, The Buddhist Conception of Spirits, Calcutta 1923, pp. 21 f.

2. This too is a ballad in dialogue form. The prose which contains a bowdlerised form of the Kṛṣṇa saga is only the commentary. Cf. p. 115 Note 1 and Vol. I, p. 451. A consolation story is also No. 372.

3. See Vol. I, p. 465 f and Cf. also E. Senart, Essai sur la legende du Buddha, 2. ed., Paris 1882, p. 317 f. On Chinese-Buddhist versions of the Daśaratha-Jātaka and the Rāma story, see Vol. I. p. 492.

which could as well be found in the Suttanipāta.[1] With the Maṅgalasutta the commentator connects the Mahāmaṅgala-Jātaka (No. 453), but in reality it is a collection of sayings, which answer not the question, "What is the best Maṅgala ?" but the question, "What is happiness".[2] The sayings are also not at all wholly Buddhistic, but they correspond more to the Brahminical ideal of life. So also are the sayings in answer to the question, how can one recognise a true friend, in the Jātaka No. 473 not at all Buddhistic, but rather of the kind, that is found in the Sanskrit epigrammatic-poetry.[3]

The greatest volume of the Jātaka-book, especially in the last few books is filled by the legends. Some of these are, just as some dialogues of the Upaniṣads and especially the Itihāsa-dialogues of the Mahābhārata[4] simply framework for the speeches and sayings. Of this nature is also the extremely interesting dialogue of the Jātaka No. 544, an extract of which may be given here :

King Aṅgati of Videha summons his three ministers together and asks for counsel. Alāta, the general, counsels a vigorous and hilarious war. Sunāma says a war is not necessary, it is better to enjoy music, dance and pleasures. But Vijaya suggests that he may hear what a pious ascetic or a Brahmin says. And on the suggestion of Alāta the king has the nude ascetic Guṇa Kassapa summoned. This Guṇa Kassapa appears and proclaims crudely materialistic doctrines like the following : There is no Karman, there are no manes, no parents, no teachers, all beings are equal and have their fate predestined; making gifts does not serve any purpose, reward and punishment in the other world are meaningless. Alāta declares that these teachings are acceptable to him and says, "I remember my previous births : I was a cow-killer, a hunter and have killed many beings, and yet I am

1. Jāt. No. 495, translated by Fick, Soziale Gliederung u.s.w., p. 140 ff. who has also already compared the Vāseṭṭhasutta of the Suttanipāta.

2. In the commentary the "Mahāmaṅgalasutta is mentioned and not Khuddakapāṭha or Suttanipāta, in which the Sutta occurs. See p. 76, Note 1 and p. 77 above.

3. That in the Jātaka-book some old Dharmaśāstra sayings are also found, has been proved by Lüders, in ZDMG 61, 1907, p. 641 ff.

4. See Vol. I, 390 f. 400 f.

reborn in a respectable family, am now a general". Agreeing with him Bījaka the slave who is there sighs saying, "I was in a previous birth good and generous and yet I am reborn as the son of a prostitute, am now a slave. I am losing in the gamble of life, Alāta is winning like a skilful gambler". King Aṅgata is convinced by these speeches and begins a life full of mirth, thinks thereafter only of pleasures and lets the kingdom be ruled by others. Then appears his good and pious daughter Ruyā and proclaims the true doctrine : "He who moves with bad people becomes himself bad. As the ship of a merchant with too heavy a freight sinks, so sinks the man into hell who has loaded upon himself gradually too heavy a burden of sins. Then she narrates about her previous births, in which she as a young man frivolously seduced women and afterwards, many times reborn in the world of men and animals and in hell, suffered terrible tortures, Then comes Nārada from heaven and teaches like Ruyā, that there is a Karman and the other world. But the king says, "If there is the other world, then lend me a hundred gold pieces; I shall give you a thousand in the next world". Nārada replies, "I would certainly lend you the hundred gold pieces, but who gives me the guarantee that you will give it if you are in hell ? Even in this world one lends money only to a trustworthy man". Then he gives an elaborate description of hell with its tortures. He concludes with a simile of a cart with which the human body is compared[1] and at last converts the king.

A similar Itihāsa-dialogue which can be read rather like a piece of an old Purāṇa, is Jātaka No. 530. Here king Brahmadatta is told that the holy Saṃkicca, his earlier family-priest has come. The king receives him and asks him about the lot of sinners in the other world. Saṃkicca replies with a sermon which contains a detailed description of the hell. Also in the legend of the two friends, who are reborn as caṇḍālas, antelopes, sea-vultures and at last as Citta, the priest's son and Sambhūta the prince (No. 498), are the speeches on the main point. In these speeches Citta praises the life of an ascetic while recalling his earlier births and he exhorts the king, his old friend to rule

1. Regarding this simile, compare also Ait. Ār. II 3, 9; Śvet. Up. II, 9; Kaṭh. Up. I, 3 ff; Sanatsujātiya, VI; Anugita, 36.

justly even if he cannot renounce the world, always remembering that he who is now a king, has been once poor and low.[1]

Almost all these legends have the form of ecclesiastical ballads already known to us. A very large number of these poems tells of kings who through some minor event were stimulated to contemplate, gave up the throne, renounced the world, and as hermits[2] in the Himālayas led a contemplative life. A king sees a mango tree robbed of its fruits, is reminded by this of the ephemeral nature of all that is earthly and renounces the world. Another is reminded by the clinging of two bangles on the arm of a girl that only the lonely one finds peace; a third one learns on seeing vultures which fight for a piece of flesh and tear one another to pieces, how contemptible greed is, a fourth man sees how a raging bull rushes towards a cow and is gored to death by a second one mad with love, and learns to despise the pleasures of love. The result is always the same.[3] There is also the legend of king *Makhādeva* (No. 9), who, when he sees his first grey hair, is made to renounce the world. The most beautiful of these poems, however, is the Mahājanaka-jātaka (No. 539), whose hero is that wise king Janaka of Videha, whom we have met many times in the Upaniṣads and the Mahābhārata. He is supposed to have said his famous words: "When the whole city of Mithila burns, nothing of mine burns"[4] when the queen showed him the town in flames, in order to make him go back. How Janaka takes the decision to renounce the

1. E. Leumann has (in WZKM V, 1891, 111 ff. and VI, 1892, 1 ff.) proved the existence of this beautiful piece of ascetic poetry in other versions with the Jainas also. To the ascetic poetry belongs also Jātaka No. 497 to which Charpentier (ZDMG 63, 1909, 171 ff.) has proved the existence of a Jaina parallel.

2. In the Buddhistic dogma they are called Paccekabuddhas, i.e. 'Enlightened ones, who have attained enlightenment through themselves (without a teacher) and for themselves (not for acting as teachers)".

3. No. 408, 529, 539. Cf. P. E. Pavolini, sulla leggenda dei quattro Pratyekabuddha, OC XII, Rom 1899, I, 129 ff. and J. Charpentier, Studien zur indischen Erzahlungslitteratur, I. Paccekabuddhageschichten (Uppsala universitets Arsskrift 1908, Filosofie, Sprakvetenskap och hist. vet. 4), Upsala 1908 and ZDMG 66, 1912, p. 38 ff.

4. See Vol. I, p. 400 f.

world, how he remains firm on the balcony of his palace at first in deep contemplation, but soon realises that he must go away into loneliness with the earthern begging bowl instead of the golden coronation bowl, how his wives try to hold him back, how he remains more and more firm in his decision, how his mind does not waver, and finally how he goes his way alone—all this is described with such overwhelming power that is inspired only by the deepest inner conviction combined with no less poetical talent.

All these legends belong to that common property of ancient Indian ascetic poetry which is the source as we have seen,[1] for some of the most beautiful legend-poems in the Mahābhārata and the Purāṇas. That the poem on Ṛṣyaśṛṅga (he is known as Isisiṅga in Pāli) is found again in the Jātaka-book and that in the Nalinikājātaka (No. 526) the older form of this legend is still preserved was already mentioned.[2] A doublet of the same legend is preserved in the Jātaka No. 523, where the celestial nymph Alambusā seduces the young holyman Isisiṅga who has never seen a woman just like Śāntā did the Rṣyśṛṅga of ancient poetry. In the prose introduction to this Jātaka it is said how Isisiṅga was born to an antilope. This introduction must be old, for already on a relief of Bharhut the scene is portrayed, depicting a baby born to an antilope being picked up by an ascetic (the father of Isisiṅga).[3]

But in particular among the legends there are many, whose Buddhistic origin is unmistakable. One of the most beautiful of these legends shows points of contact with the tragic story which King Daśaratha tells on his death-bed.[4] This is the ballad of

1. Cf. Vol. I, p. 294, 394 f. 453 and also M. Winternitz, "Some Problems of Indian Literature", Calcutta 1925, p. 21 ff.

2. See Vol. I, p. 384 ff., 452, 498, 516: J. Hertel, WZKM XVIII, 1904, 158 f. and L. v. Schroeder, "Mysterium und Mimus im Ṛgveda" Leipzig, 1908, p. 292 ff. have tried to prove that the Ṛṣyaśṛṅga poem is a "cultic" drama. We can see in it, as in many other conversational poems of the Jātaka book, only a ballad in which, however, there is a strongly dramatic element.

3. Cunningham Stūpa of Bharhut, Pl. 26, Fig. 7.

4. Rāmāyaṇa II, 63, 25 ff. Cf above Vol. I p. 462 and Charpentier WZKM 24, 1910, p. 397 Note 2, 27 p. 94. Oldenberg (NGGW 1918, 456 ff.)

the pious youth Sāma (No. 540) whose contents are given below:

Sāma is a pious hermit-boy who lives in the forest with his blind parents and is devoted entirely to their service. While fetching water for them one day he is struck with a poisonous arrow that was shot by king Pilyakkha of Banaras in the arrogance of his hunting bout. Not a curse, not an evil word comes from the lips of the lad, but only melancholic lamentation on the fate of his poor parents who are now robbed of their support. Full of remorse the king consoles him and promises to take over the responsibility for his parents. Sāma tells him the direction in which the cottage of his parents lies and uttering words of thanks he falls into unconsciousness. Filled with bitter remorse the king breaks out in lamentation and is consoled by a forest-spirit who tells him that he will be freed from his grave sin if he goes to Sāma's parents to care for them like a son. Lamenting he then takes the water mug and goes to the cottage of the parents. On hearing the footsteps of the approaching king the old father recognises that this is not the expected son. Piliyakkha says who he is and the blind old man welcomes the king with kind reverence and offers water and fruits as presents to his guest. The king asks him wherefrom he got the fruits as he himself cannot gather them. And the old father replies, "We have a dear son, young and beautiful, it is he who brings us water and fruits. Then the king proclaims the terrible news, "your dear son is dead, I have killed him. Gentle but full of painful lamentation are the words of the father. But the mother breaks out in loud lamentation and cannot understand the gentleness of her husband who does not wish the king ill. The king consoles the parents and requests them to accept him in the place of their son, he would take care of them as Sāma has done. But the parents beg him only to take them to the corpse of their son, and the king does so although unwillingly. Before the dead body the parents break out in moving lamentation which however ends with swearings.[1] The mother says, "If it is true that Sāma has

---

has compared the epic tale with the Jātaka as regards style, and has shown that in the Jātaka the story is told with greater simplicity and less subtlety than in the Rāmāyaṇa.

1. Such swearings or Saccakiriyas (literally "Confirmations of truth") which consist in a person appealing to his virtues and through this working

always lived a virtuous life, then the poison shall disappear and he shall stand before us again alive." The father repeats this on the strength of his wife's and his own virtues. The forest spirit also swears in a similar way. Then Sāma gets up, stands fresh and healthy in front of his parents and welcomes the astonished king. He says that he has been only unconscious; for those who honour father and mother enjoy even in this world the support of the gods and go to heaven after death. The King surrenders himself to the care of Sāma and the latter gives him a lecture on the virtues which a king shall practise.[1]

Limitless kindness and gentleness and a self-sacrifice exceeding by far all natural limits are characteristic of these legends of purely Buddhistic inventions. We have already pointed to the legend of King Sivi (Sanskrit Śibi) who gifts his eyes away.[2] Of Prince Kaṇha who gifts away all that he possesses, in order to go to the Himālayas as a hermit tells us Jātaka No. 440. To the pious hermit Sakka grants boons, but he does not desire any thing but peace, freedom from hatred, greed and longing and the truly prettiest of all boons:

"If you want to show me a favour, God Indra, Lord of the creatures, then, may for my sake never and nowhere a being have suffering. In body and soul, this, Indra, is the best of favours, this is my wish".

The moral of loving one's enemies proclaimed in a very simple way in the legend (No. 151) of the two kings who meet each other at a narrow pass. They are both equally old, equally just, equally famous, equally powerful and the question is, who should give way to the other. As one of them not only returns good for good

---

miracles are not rare in Buddhistic legends; we also meet with them in the epic (thus in the Nalopākhyāna, Mahābhārata III, 63) and frequently in the later sections. Cf. E. W. Burlingham JRAS 1917, p. 429 and N. M. Penser, New Edition of C. H. Tawney's Translation of "Kathāsaritsāgara", I, 166 f., II, 31 ff., III, 179 ff.

1. This legend is found already in the 3rd century B.C. in a relief on the Stūpa of Sānchi. A whole series of scenes is represented in the Gandhāra sculptures of Jamālgarhi. Cf. A. Foucher L' art greco-boudhique du Gandhāra I, 279 ff

2. See Vol. I p. 395, and Winternitz, "Some problems of Indian Literature", p. 38.

but also good for evil, he is given preference. Another genuine product of Buddhism is the Khantivādi-Jātaka (No. 313), the Jātaka of the "patience preacher" in which the Bodhisatta is whipped and mutilated by an enraged king, but he endures it all with patience, and forbears from any thoughts of revenge.[1] In not a few of these legends—which we may call the "animal legends"—the Bodhisatta is a good and noble animal. To these belong also legends like that of the self-sacrificing male gazelle, who is prepared to give up his life for the sake of a pregnant gazelle, is also able to persuade the king not only to spare the herd of gazelles but also to totally give up hunting,[2] of the hare who himself jumps into the fire in order to offer himself as food for his guest. (No. 316)[3] of the monkey chieftain who

1. The frequent occurrence of this legend in Buddhist literature and art bears witness to its great popularity among the Buddhists of all nations. Cf. A. Attenhofer in "Festschrift Kühn", pp. 353 ff.

2. Nigrodhamiga-Jātaka (No. 12). The Christian legend of Saint Placidus or Eustachius, who is said to have been converted through a stag, on whose forehead the sign of the cross was shining, is traced back to this Jātaka by some scholars. Cf. M. Gaster, JRAS., 1894, 335 ff.; J. S. Speyer in "Theolog. Tijdskrift", 40, 1906, 427 ff.; E. Kühn in "Beil. Allg. Ztg.", 9th Nov. 1906; R. Garbe, "Contributions of Buddhism to Christianity", p. 30 ff.; "Indien und das Christentum", pp. 86 ff.; W. Bousset in NGGW1916, 469 ff.; W. Meyer, ibid. pp. 762 ff.; Clemen, "Theolog. Literaturzeitung", 42, 1917, 257 ff.; H. Günter, "Buddha in der abendländischen Legende", Leipzig 1922, pp. 7 ff. There does not seem to be any connection between them .

3. Just as, in memory of this act of self-sacrifice, Sakka draws a hare in the moon, using a mountain as his pencil, so the Kalmuks have preserved the legend of "Sakimuni" as the "hare in the moon," s. T. W. Rhys Davids, "Buddhism", London SPCK., 1890, p. 197. The "hare in the moon", however, is not familiar only in India, Tibet, Burma, China and Japan, but also in America. In India the idea is most likely earlier than Buddhism, at least as early as the Śatapatha-Brāhmaṇa XI, 1, 5, 3 and Śvetāśvatara-Upaniṣad II, 11.Cf. Benfey, "Pantschatantra" I, 348 f.; A. Pfungst, "Aus der indischen Kulturwelt", Stuttgart 1904, pp. 122 ff.; I. Schefterlowitz, ZB., VII, 1926, pp. 270 f.; H. Kunike, "Amerikanische und asiatische Mondbilder" (Mythologische Bibliothek VIII, 4, 1916, pp. 24 ff.); E. Seler in "Zeitschrift für Ethnologie," 39, 1907, p. 10. Just as in Tantrākhyāyikā III, 3, so in a Hottentot story, the hare appears as a messenger of the moon. Cf. W. H. I. Bleek, "Reineke Fuchs in Afrika", Weimar 1870, pp. 54 ff.; "A Brief Account of Bushman Folklore," London, 1875, pp. 9 f.

constitutes himself as a bridge over the Ganges in order to save his camp-followers[1], of the monkey who saves a man fallen into an abyss and whom the man, fond of monkey flesh, wants to kill on account of which he has had a bad attack of leprosy (No. 516) or the legend of the elephant who shows the way out of a forest to a wanderer who lost his way and even gifts his teeth to him, whereupon the man in his greed cuts and takes out even the roots of the elephant's teeth and causes him torturous pain but is immediately swallowed by the earth and sinks into hell (No. 72).[2] Animal legends like the last two make it highly probable that the fairy tales already mentioned, of grateful animals and ungrateful men, are all of Buddhistic origin.

Perhaps the most famous and the most popular of all these legends in the whole of the Buddhistic world is the last one in our Jātaka. Collection, the Vessantara Jātaka (No. 547). It is in reality a regular epic, for the prose is here nothing but a commentary and one can point out effortlessly how the commentator in a way revealing lack of sense and taste has diluted the story wherever it was possible. Nevertheless the hero of this epic is no warrior and no conqueror, but a hero of generosity.

Prince Vessantara has taken the vow, not to refuse anything to any one, whatever one may ask of him.

"My heart and eye, my flesh and blood, my whole body—should one ask them of me, I will give them away."

As he gifts away a wonderful elephant, without any consideration for the good of his country, he is sent into exile where his wife Maddi and his two little children follow him. They have already given away all they possess. On a carriage drawn by

---

1. Jāt. No. 407, illustrated on the Stūpa of Bharhut (Cunningham, Pl. 33, Fig. 4). H. Kern (Gurupūjākaumudi, pp. 93 f.) compares the old Cymric legend from the Mabinogi, in which King Bran makes himself into a bridge, over which his army reaches the bank of a river. In this case, however, the agreement, though certainly striking, seems to be merely accidental.

2. The elephant is in general very popular in the animal-legends. Cf. Feer in the JA 1895, s.9, t.V, 31 ff, 189 ff and Foucher on the Chaddantajātaka (No. 5 14) in Mélanges d'indianisme offerts á M. Sylvain Levi, Paris 1911, p. 231 ff.

four horses, their last possession, they leave the country. But soon they come across a mendicant Brahmin to whom Vessantara presents horses and carriage. They continue to wander by foot, carrying the children, and at last reach a hermitage in the forest, where they put up a cottage to live in. There appears Sakka in the guise of a wicked and ugly Brahmin who asks for the children as his slaves and gets them also. At last he wants the wife too and only after Vessantara does not refuse even her, does Sakka disclose his identity. And every thing finds a happy end.

The legend is told in 786 stanzas in truly epic elaborateness. The description of Vessantara's leaving the country to go into exile reminds us of that of Rāma in the Rāmāyaṇa. Also the numerous and long nature-descriptions like that of the forest and the hermitage remind us of the Rāma-epic. With particular delight the poet elaborates while narrating how the children are gifted away, who are treated so cruelly by the wicked Brahmin, how the little children lament, and while describing the wailings of the mother in her vain search of her children. No wonder that there seems, in the course of their recitation or performance on the stage – for in Tibet and Burma the Vessantara legend forms the topic of theatrical performances – something that even to-day moves the audience to tears.[1]

The hero of the Vessantara-Jātaka, as in the last-mentioned purely Buddhistic legends in general, is the Bodhisatta of Buddhistic dogma, to whom are attributed a particular number

1. We meet with the legend of Vessantara in pictorial representations also. Cf. Foucher, "L'art greco bouddhique", I, 283 ff. The Chinese traveller Song Yun relates that he saw a picture of Shahbaz-Garhi reproducing the Vessantara legend, and that, whenever, they saw this picture, the barbarians shed tears of pity for the pious man who had given away his children to the wicked Brahmin. Chavannes, "Cinq Cents Contes", t. I, p. x P. Dahlke (ZB., I, 1914, p. 9) says : "This Vessantara legend is a favourite decoration in Buddhist temples. We find it represented from Ceylon to Cambodia. In the Wesak season it is produced on the stage of the people's theatres, and never does it fail to produce its effect." R. Fick (Festgabe Jacobi, p. 145 ff) has compared the various versions of the Vessantara legend with a view to tracing its original form. He shows that the Jātakamālā probably used an earlier version than that of the Pāli Jātaka. A Soghdian version of the Jātaka has been published by R. Gauthiot (JA 1912, s. 10, t. XIX, p. 163 ff.)

of "perfections" – Pāramitās[1] as the technical expression is called – and who already possesses certain superhuman gifts like the memory of previous births, extra-ordinary physical strength or mental powers and similar things. But it is this image of Bodhisatta as of a higher being which otherwise in the texts of the Theravāda sects of the Hīnayāna whose canon is the Pāli-Tipiṭaka, plays only an insignificant role, which however has become all the more highly developed. It is therefore no chance coincidence that the Jātakas belong to the Mahāyāna as well as to the Hīnayāna and one could raise the question whether their actual place of origin is not the Mahāyāna-Buddhism rather than the Hīnayāna-Buddhism. In reality we find Jātakas in the texts of all Buddhist sects. Probably they belonged originally to no particular sect; but like all the sects they were an important means of propaganda and as they carried the popular Buddhism in regard to which there would have been little difference between the various sects, so also they penetrated deep into the folk along with Buddhism. No book finds, even to the present day, so much favour as the Jātaka with the peoples who follow Buddhism. Even to-day the Sinhalese listen with great attention throughout the night when the Jātakas are recited without even the slightest trace of the tiresomeness and with fervent delight. In Burma also the Jātakas are and have been for centuries the charm of scholars and masses, of clergy and laity alike.[2] And it is the same everywhere, where-ever Buddhism has penetrated. We have an idea of the huge

1. Pārami or Pāramitā, "highest perfection" is the technical expression for the ten (or six)perfections which a Bodhisatta possesses, namely: Generosity, virtue (i.e. obedience to the commandments) renunciation of the world, wisdom, energy, patience, truthfulness, determination friendliness towards all creatures, equanimity. Cf. R. Spence Hardy "Manual of Buddhism", 1860, pp. 98, 101 ff., Kern, "Manual", p. 66. The expressions pārami, pāramitā do not appear in the earliest texts, or in the Jātaka Gāthās but in the Jātaka commentary (eg. Nos. 515, 528, 529) it is expressely stated that the Lord told the story with reference to one of the "perfections". In other instances (eg. Nos. 407 547) the hero is clearly presented as the Bodhisatta endowed with the "perfections". Cf. Rhys Davids, JRAS, 1913, pp. 482 f.

2. Cf. R. Spence Hardy, Manual of Buddhism, London 1860, p. 101; M. H. Bode, Pāli Literature of Burma, London, 1909, p. 81.

wealth of Tibetan literature in Buddhist stories from A. Schiefner[1] and of the Chinese Buddhist stories from Ed. Chavannes.[2] But the Jātakas have also enriched the literatures of many other nations directly and indirectly and have thus become greatly important for the literature of the world on the whole. To-day we may not believe any more as Th. Benfey did that the entire fairy-tale literature of the world is of Buddhist origin. But, however much Brahmins, Jainas and other sects may have contributed to Indian fairy-tale literature, yet it is only Buddhism alone which as a world-religion has penetrated beyond the frontiers of India and has therefore spread Indian cultural and literary products in all the countries of east and west.[3] But it was also Buddhism, which brought the Indians more than ever in contact with other peoples; and it is not probable that they always narrated stories to the other peoples; they too may have received some from them—especially from peoples like the Greeks, the Persians and the Semites who were intellectually so highly developed. Most probably the Greek artists who came to India in large numbers after Alexander's campaigns and helped build and embellish so many Buddhist monuments of art, have also brought with them many Greek stories and motifs of stories. This is all the more probable as precisely the Jātakas were pictorially represented on Buddhistic monuments in several ways. For like

1. Indische Erzählungen, Bulletin de l' Academie Imperiale des Sc. de St. Petersbourg 1876 and 1877 (Melanges asiatiques VII and VIII); Mahakatjajana und Konig Tschanda Pradyota, ein Zyklus buddhistischer Eizahlungen (Memoires de l' Academic imp. des Sc. de St. Petersbourg, 1875). Cf. Cf. also W. R. S. Ralston, Tibetan Tales derived from Indian Sources, London 1882, and W. W. Rockhill, Tibetan Buddhist Birth-Stories, Extracts and Translations from the Kandjur, JAOS, XVIII, 1897, p. 1 ff.

2. Cinq cents contes et apologues extraits du Tripitaka Chinois et traduit en Francais, t. I-III, Paris 1910-1911. But if we find here in the books which have been translated into Chinese in the 5th century A.D. many Jātakas which also occur in our Jātaka-book, then from this it does not at all follow that they are translated from this . Jātaka-book or from any Sanskrit collection corresponding to this book.

3. Chavannes, Cinq Cents Contes I, p. xvi still considers that Buddhism may be called "le plus vaste receptacle de contes qu'ily ait eu au monde." Charpentier (Festschrift Kuhn pp. 228 ff) supposed that a collection of Jātakas may have been the source of the Greek Physiologus. H. Günter, "Buddha in der abendlandischen Legende", pp. 65 ff. raises objection to this theory.

literature so also Indian and foreign art was impregnated by the Jātakas. They are among the oldest motifs which were pictorially represented in India and even to-day they yield favourite models for sculptors and painters in all Buddhist countries. We find them in the 3rd and 2nd century B. C. or the stone walls of Bharhut and Sānchi, in the 2nd century A. D. on those of Amaravati and still later in the caves of Ajanta.[1] When the Chinese pilgrim Fahien in the year 412 A.D. travelled in Ceylon he saw how during a great festival the King of Ceylon had got the 500 Jātakas represented through painted figures resembling living persons placed on both sides of the streets through which the procession passed. And Hiuen-Tsang speaks of Stūpas which he had seen, and which were erected in various parts of India to remind the people of the deeds of the Bodhisatta reported in the Jātakas.[2] Many hundreds of reliefs which contain Jātaka portrayals decorate the temples of Boro Budur in Java (9th century),[3] of Pagan in Burma (13th century)[4] and of Sukhodaya in Siam (14th century).[5]

And just as per literature and art, so also for the history of Culture the Jātakas are of inestimable value. Although they

1. Cf. In addition to the works of Cunningham and Maisey mentioned in Note 3 on p. 17 also A. Grunwedel, "Buddhistische Kunst in Indien," 2nd Edition, Berlin 1900, p. 38 f, 59 and A. Foucher, "L'art greco buddhique du Gandhāra" I, Paris 1905, p. 270 ff.

2. Cf. L. Feer, Les Jātakas dans les memories de Hionen Thsang, OC XI, Paris 1897, I, p. 151 ff. and also J. Legge, "Record of Buddhistic Kingdoms being an account of the Chinese monk Fa-hein of his Travels in India and Ceylon", transl. Oxford, 1886, p. 106-

3. A list of the jātakas illustrated in Bharhut, Ajanta and Bore Budue is given by S. d'Oldenberg in JRAS 1896, 623 ff and JAOS XVIII, 1897, 183 ff. In the reliefs of Boro Boudur d' Oldenberg believes (ibid p. 196 ff., by quoting also C. Leemans, Boro-Boudour dans l'ile de Java, Leide 1874 for support) that he finds 34 jātakas arranged in the order of the Sanskrit poem Jātakamālā. See also Foucher in BEFEO IX, 1909 p. 1 ff.

4. More than a hundred reliefs of the Maṅgala cheti-temple of Pagan are in the possession of the Berliner Museum fur Vokkerkunde. They have been discussed by A. Grunwedel in Buddhistische Studien I (Publications from the K. Museum für Volkerkunde V, Berlin 1897).,

5. L. Fournerau, Le-Siam ancien, Zeme partie, Annales du Musee Guimet Paris 1908. The order of the pictures is that of the Pāli-jātaka collection.

may not be decisive for the cultural conditions at the time of Buddha, but almost for the period of the 3rd century B. C. and to a great part—especially in their prose only for the period after Christ, yet in India so much has remained unchanged that the cultural image of the Jātaka can still be considered as very "old". However, the stories of the Jātaka book enable us to have a look at the life of popular circles in India about which we learn anything only rarely from other works of Indian literature.[1]

This extraordinary significance of the Jātaka book in every respect must be enough justification for our devoting such a long time to this work. Accordingly we may devote shorter time to those books of the Tipiṭaka which we have yet to mention.

11. Niddesa,[2] "Explanation," is the title of a commentary, which has already been mentioned on sections of the Suttanipāta. It consists of the Mahā-Niddesa, the "Great Explanation" containing the commentary on the Aṭṭhakavagga, and the Culla-Niddesa, the "Short Explanation," which explains the Khaggavisāṇa-Sutta (Suttanipāta I, 3) as well as the Pārāyaṇa. The inclusion of this commentary in the canon can certainly be due merely to its great antiquity in comparison to other Pāli commentaries. Indeed, we learn from the Niddesa how the sacred texts were explained at the lessons, in ancient times.[3] Grammatical and lexical explanations go hand in hand with instruction in the dogma. Important technical expressions are explained with reference to the doctrine, and passages from canonical texts are frequently quoted for this purpose. In order to explain a word, a long list of synonyms is given, and this is repeated every time the same word occurs. It is easy to understand how, in this way, these lists of words were impressed on

1. For this reason the illustrations of cultural history by R. Fick and Mrs. Rhys Davids in the note on P. 117 above are very valuable, although chronologically a different view has to be taken in judging them.

2. Mahā-Niddesa, ed. by L. de la Vallee Poussion and E. J. Thomas, PTS. 1916 and 1917; Culla-Niddesa, ed. by W. Stede, PTS, 1918. On the relation of this old commentary to Buddhaghosa's commentary, see M. H. Bode in JRAS 1918, pp. 574 ff. See also B. Ch. Law in Ann. Bh. Inst. 12, 1931, p. 173 f.

3. Cf. E. J. Thomas, Ind. Hist. Qu. II. 1926 pp. 495 ff.

the memory. Probably they formed the foundation for later dictionaries.

12. The Patisambhidāmagga,[1] "the Path to Analysis" consists of three large sections, each containing ten treatises on some important point of the Buddhist doctrine. Thus, for instance, I, 1 deals with the 73 kinds of knowledge, among which, to give an example there is the knowledge of the great pity of the Tathāgata; I, 3 deals with the regulating of the breath as an aid to mindfulness (sati) I, 7 deals with the Karman, II, 2 with the four noble truths, II, 4 with the love towards all creatures (mettā), III, 2 with the miraculous powers (iddhi) of the saints and so on. All these subjects are treated in the form of questions and answers, after the fashion of the Abhidhamma texts. The work appears in the Suttapiṭaka, however, and not in the Abhidhammapiṭaka because, at least in part, its form is that of the Suttas, as some sections begin with introductory stories ("Thus I have heard" etc.) and the address "O monks" (bhikkhave) is to be found here and there as in the case of Suttas.[2]

13. Vast as the Jātaka book is, and abundant as are its contents, it does not by any means contain the entire wealth of Buddhist tales. Another narrative work which is just as copious as the Jātaka, though of lesser value from a literary point of view, is[3] the collection of "Apadānas" in the Khuddakanikāya, known as the Apadāna. The word apadāna (Sanskrit avadāna) means "heroic deed, glorious deed," the sense being extended also to glorious deeds of self-sacrifice and piety; and the Apadānas like the Avadānas which are their counterpart in the Buddhist Sanskrit literature, are "tales of the heroic deeds," i. e., the pious works of the saints (which often consist of very commonplace actions performed in adoration of a Buddha). The Apadānas, too, like the Jātakas, have a "Story of the present" and a "Story of the past." Whereas the Jātakas always describe a previous exis-

1. Ed. by Arnold C. Taylor, PTS, 1905 & 1907 Cf Rhys Davids, JRAS, 1906, pp. 238 ff.

2. On archaisms in the text, s. Kosambi in Ind. Ant. 41, 1912, p. 38 note.

3. Ed. by Mary E. Lilley, PTS—, 1925 and 1927. Cf. L. Feer in JA, 1883, s.8, t.I, 408, 433 ff.; E. Muller in OC X, Geneve 1894, I, 165 ff.; T. W. Rhys Dzvids, ERE, Vol. I, p. 603.

tence of the Buddha, the Apadānas, as a rule, deal with that of a saint, an Arhat. These stories are, therefore, legends of saints. The collection of Apadānas, written entirely in verse, begins with a Buddhāpadāna, containing a glorification of the Buddhas, of the "innumerable kings of the Dhamma, endowed with the 30 perfections,"[1] and Buddha himself is made to pronounce this glorification. Next comes the Paccekabuddhāpadāna, a glorification of the Paccekabuddhas, who go their solitary way, "like the rhinoceros". The entire "Sutta of the Rhinoceros" (Khaggavisāṇa-Sutta from Suttanipāta I, 3 is inserted here. The main portion of the work, however, is the Thera-Apadāna, "the Glorious Deeds of the Elders," in 55 sections (vagga) consisting of 10 Apadānas each.[2] The last part is the Therī-Apadāna, "the Glorious Deeds of the Lady Elders," in 4 sections, consisting of 10 Apadānas each.[3] The "glorious deeds" are always related by the saint in question himself. The first heroes of the Thera-Apadāna are the most famous disciples of Buddha: Sāriputta, the great Moggallāna, the great Kassapa and Anuruddha; side by side with these and other well-known names such as Upāli, Ānanda, Rāhula and Raṭṭhapāla[4] among the Theras, and Mahāpajāpatī Gotamī, Khemā, Paṭācārā, Kisā-Gotamī, and others among the Theris, we meet with a far larger number of names which are only types and not real personages, e. g., the Theras "Dispenser of fans," "Dispenser of clothes," "Dispenser of mangoes," "Worshipper of foot-prints," "Waterworshipper" (i. e., the Thera who worshipped Buddha with a gift of water), Theras who are named after some flower offering, such as Kiṁsukapuphiya, and

1. As each of the 10 Pāramitās or "perfections" is divided into three grades, i.e., ordinary, superior and pre-eminent, there are 30 Pāramitās in all. (R. Spence Hardy, "Manual of Buddhism," p. 101).

2. Vagga 34 has only 7 Apadānas, hence the total of 547 instead of 550.

3. Extracts from the Therī Apadāna have been published by E. Müller in his edition of the commentary on the Therīgāthā (PTS. 1892). The Apadāna of Mahāpajāpati Gotami has been translated into Dutch by Maria E. L. van Goor, "de buddhistisch non," pp. 204 ff.

4. The legend of Raṭṭhapāla in the Apadāna, who is familiar to us from the Majjhimanikāya, no. 82, has been compared with that in Buddhaghosa's commentary, by Mabel Bode in "Mélanges Levi", p. 183 ff.

the like. Most of these legends are made on one and the same plan. First of all thera (or Theri) tells of the adoration which he (or she) had offered to one of the previous Buddhas, the predecessors of Gotama Buddha, then he (or she) declares the prophecy uttered by that previous Buddha that he (or she) would hear the doctrine of the future Gotama Buddha, and finally relates how this prophecy has come true, and how he (or she) attained to the dignity of an Arhat. Only few of the Apadānas deviate from this stereotyped plan, for instance, the very remarkable Buddhāpadāna (No. 387) with the secondary title Pubbakammapiloti, "the Interweaving of the Previous Deeds," in which the Buddha tells of his previous bad deeds in consequence of which he had to suffer countless reincarnations in hells, and the remains of which deeds caused him many an unpleasant experience even in his last existence.

The Apadāna is certainly one of the very latest works of the Khuddakanikāya and of the canon generally, if we are really justified in including it in the canon. At all events, judged by its general character, it is much more closely allied to the Sanskrit Avadānas than to the remaining works of the Pāli canon.[1] We must leave it to future research to find out, by means of a detailed comparison between the Apadānas and the Buddhist Sanskrit texts,[2] what place they occupy in the chronology of the history of Buddhist literature.

1. Not very many instances of actual agreement have been traced so far. Avadānaśataka VIII relates stories of ten holy women, but only three names coincide with those in the Therī-Apadāna. Cf. L. Feer, JA, 1884, ser. 8, t. III, p. 32.

2. E. Muller (Gurupūjākaumudi, pp. 55 ff.) after comparing the Dipankara legend in Apadāna No. 486 with the other versions of the same legend, has come to the conclusion that some of the Apadānas are later than the Sanskrit Avadānas. S. Levi (JA, 1908, ser. 10, t. XII, pp. 167 ff.) concludes from the comparison of Therī-Apadāna No. 17, of Mahāpajāpatī Gotamī, with Kumāralāta's Kalpanāmaṇḍitikā ("Sūtrālaṅkāra") No. 68, that the author of the Apadāna must have been familiar with the Sanskrit poem. This is not convicing. As we have a plain story in the Apadāna, and elaborate one in the Kalpanāmaṇḍitikā, it is just as likely that the last-mentioned work used the raw material, either in the Apadāna or in a Sanskrit version corresponding to it, and created a work of art from it, as that the author of the Apadāna used the work of art, and made a dry extract of it.

14. One of the less voluminous books of the Khuddakanikāya is the Buddhavaṃsa.[1] These are poetical legends of the 24 Buddhas who are said to have preceded Gotama Buddha in the last 12 world-epoques (Kalpas). After an introductory chapter one chapter is devoted to each one of the 24 earlier Buddhas.[2] In a somewhat dreary manner it tells of each Buddha, how he set the "wheel of the religion" in motion and how — with minor deviations — the chief events in the life of Gotama Buddha took place in the case of each one of the earlier Buddhas. Gotama Buddha himself is made to tell the story and he says, speaking in the first person, who he was under each of the preceding Buddhas[3], how he worshipped the Buddha and how his own future Buddhahood was prophesied by the Buddha of that time. Somewhat stronger and more poetic is only the second chapter,[4] which speaks of Dīpaṅkara the first Buddha.

Gotama Buddha was at that time a rich Brahmin called Sumedha, and he narrates in verses (7-27), which remind us of the Therīgāthās, how one day he got disgusted with the world and casting off his wretched body as if it were filth withdrew into a hermitage in the Himālayas. Precisely at that time Dīpaṅkara the Buddha was on his victorious march through the world and men and gods were venerating him. Sumedha the hermit also comes that way and at a marshy place he unties the knot of his plaited hair and spreads it as well as his hempen role and his fur-mantle on the dirty earth and lies down with

---

1. Edited by R. Morris,London PTS 1882.

2. On the dogma of the plurality of Buddhas cf. Oldenberg, "Buddha," 370 ff. and Kern, "Manual of Buddhism," 62 ff. Even Aśoka mentions in one of his edicts that he got restored a Stūpa of Buddha Konākamana (i.e Koṇāgamana of the 23rd Buddha of the Buddhavaṃsa) (Buhler, 152 KM, 9, 1895, p. 175 f.)

3. Usually he was a Brahmin or a warrior but once also Sakka the king of gods, another time a lion, the king of the animals, two times the king of the Nāgas, once a Yakṣa and many times an ascetic.

4. Translated by Warren, "Buddhism in Translations," p. 5-31. Translated from the Chinese (Abhiniṣkramaṇa Sūtra) by S. Beal in JRAS 1873, pp. 277 ff. E. Muller (Gurupūjākaumudī p. 54 ff.) has compared the various versions of the Dīpaṅkara legend.

his head turned downward[1] animated by the desire that the exalted Buddha Dīpaṅkara with his host of disciples may march over him so that their feet may not be made dirty by the mud. Lying on the floor he resolves to become Buddha later and bring salvation to the world. Dīpaṅkara comes there and prophesies the future greatness of Sumedha. The inhabitants of the ten thousand worlds raise a cry of jubiliation and there appear omens and miracles, as is always the case when a future Buddha is predicted. But Sumedha resolves to realise within himself all the ten perfections (Pāramitās) in order to fulfill the prerequisites for the future Buddhahood.

Thus this piece is actually a kind of background-story for the autobiography which Gotama Buddha gives them in the 26th chapter by summarising briefly the main events of his last earthly existence in 25 verses. The book ends with a list of the Buddhas upto Metteyya, the future Buddha and a report on the distribution of the relics of Buddha.

The commentator of the Buddhavaṃsa says that the work was proclaimed and delivered by Gotama Buddha himself and was transmitted further down by an unbroken series of Theras upto the time of the third council and similarly from then onwards by an unbroken series of teachers and pupils. We will not believe what the commentator says because the older texts know only 6 predecessors of Gotama, but we will have to count the Buddhavaṃsa as belonging to the latest products of the canonical Pāli literature. It is indeed full of that worship and deification of Buddha which is not known to the oldest Tipiṭaka texts, but which is in full bloom in the Buddhist Sanskrit Literature, especially that of the Mahāyāna.

15. The last book of the Khuddakanikāya is the Cariyāpiṭaka'.[2] This is a collection of 35 Jātakas, in verse, which pursue the express purpose of showing how the Bodhisatta possessed

1. This scene is often protrayed on Buddhistic monuments ; see Foucher, "L'art Greco bouddhique" I, 273 ff.; A. Grünwedel, "Bericht über archaolog. Arbeiten in Idikutsari (A. Bay. A 24, I, 1906), p. 90 f.

2. Edited by R. Morris, PTS 1882 (Devanāgari script; Introduction by Bimala Charan Law, Lahore, 1924.)

the Pāramitās or "perfections"[1] in several of his earlier births. To each of the first two perfections, generosity and virtue, one whole chapter consisting of 10 stories is devoted, while the third chapter contains 15 stories as examples for the remaining Pāramitās.[2] Buddha himself is made to narrate the stories. In short, scanty words he reports an event, sometimes only thus hinting at it so barely that a familiarity with the event is already taken for granted and we are to be only reminded of the same. Most of the stories are such as also occur in the Jātaka-book. Here only what is essential for the explanation of some particular pāramitā is narrated. Every trace of poetry is lacking, every trait of humour is scrupulously avoided. The stories are subjected to manifold mutilations so that they may serve as illustrations for a "perfection". We may compare for example the fable of the crocodile that is outwitted by the monkey.[3] In Jātaka No. 208 we are told (as in the Pañcatantra) how the crocodile whose wife covets a monkey's heart, lies in wait for the monkey, lures him in order to kill him and is outwitted by the monkey who says he does not carry his heart with himself but lets it hanging on a tree on the bank. Somewhat less witty is the version of the same fable in Jātaka No. 57. But every trace of wit is destroyed in the Cariyāpiṭaka III, 7, where the Buddha says:

"When I was a monkey who lived on the bank of the river in a cave, then once threatened by a crocodile I could not tread my usual path. At exactly the same point where I used to stand in order to jump to the other bank, sat the murderous enemy, the crocodile, terrible to look at. He said to me, "Come". I said to him: "I am coming" and standing on his head I reached the other bank. I told him no lie, acted as per my word. In the love of truth I have no equal. Such was my complete perfection of truthfulness."

---

1. See above p. 148

2. The concluding verses prove that in reality all the ten Pāramitās were to be illustrated in the Cariyāpiṭaka. Perhaps the three missing ones (wisdom, energy and patience) are supposed to be included with the others, in Chapter III.

3. See above p. 122.

The fable has shrunk down here to an empty skeleton without content and the main point is the moral which (as in Jātaka No. 57 where also we find it is most ill-suited). Thus appears also the Vessantara Jātaka—in jātaka-book an epic of 786 verses – in the Cariyāpiṭaka I, compressed into 58 dry verses in which the entire stress is laid on the miracles like the quaking of the earth and similar things. Only five verses of the Vessantara epic are also found word for word in the Cariyāpiṭaka.

We can imagine the relationship between Cariyāpiṭaka and the Jātaka book in two possible ways. It might be, that at first the purpose of the Jātakas was only to explain the "perfections" and there was at the beginning only a small collection of 34 or 35 stories[1] which were later increased so much that gradually the Jātaka book with its 550 stories originated, in which the original purpose was more and more neglected. The Cariyāpiṭaka might be a resumé of such an older Jātaka book. The second possibility is that the stories, as we find them in our Jātaka book appeared to be too mundane to one school of more serious monks and therefore they endeavoured to connect the Jātakas more intimately with the Buddhist dogma. Therefore they made a selection of Jātakas, which they arranged with reference to the ten Pāramitās and modified them according to their purpose. We would consider the second possibility to be more probable and believe that our Jātaka collection shows already traces of having been influenced by a Cariyāpiṭaka[2], but that originally it did not have anything to do with the Pāramitā theory. For in the majority of the stories of the Jātaka book to which, as we have seen, the Buddhist role fits in general only loosely, there is no mention of the "perfections" of the Bodhisatta.

It is a different question, whether we have the Cariyāpiṭaka now in the same form in which it was incorporated in the canon in the 3rd century B.C. Indeed in the introduction to the

1. This seems to be the view of Pischel (Leben und Lehre des Buddha, p. 58f), when he says that there was an older Jātaka with only 34 stories.

2. See p. 148 above.

Jātaka book the "Nidānakathā"[1] to which we will again refer later, we find a resumé of a Cariyāpiṭaka that is essentially different from our texts. It consists of 34 stories of which only 21 agree with those of our Cariyāpiṭaka. This shows that there were various recensions of the Cariyāpiṭaka. However, that through a comparison of the two recensions and of the Jātakamālā[2] arranged as per the same principle of the Pāramitās, it should be possible to produce a sort of "Original Cariyāpiṭaka" as Charpentier[3] has attempted, is highly doubtful. The same scholar has also tried to prove that our present Cariyāpiṭaka is a "late, incomplete handiwork, that was compiled—of course with the help of the old work—according to the present Jātaka text, probably only in the period after the translation into Pāli, i.e. about 430 A.D." But the agreements and tones between the Jātakas of our Jātaka collection and those of the Cariyāpiṭaka on which this view is based, can also be explained easily if we presume that the time when the canon was concluded there were many Jātakas out of which one school of monks with somewhat more liberal views compiled the collection forming the basis of our Jātakaṭṭhavaṇṇanā and another, stricter school compiled the Cariyāpiṭaka. In any case, the Cariyāpiṭaka[4] is the work of a righteous monk who was anything but a poet, whereas among the authors of the Jātakas as they appear in our

1. Jātaka, ed. Fausboll, I, 45-47; Rhys Davids, Buddhist Birth stories, pp. 54ff.

2. In this connection see the chapter on Buddhist Sanskrit Literature below.

3. In his valuable work "Zur Geschichte des Cariyāpiṭaka" in WZKM 24, 1910, 351 ff.

4. The two recensions of the Cariyāpiṭaka have only 21 Jātakas in common with each other, and there are only 12 of these which they share with the Jātakamālā too. The fact that 34 was the original and traditional number is proved not only by the Jātakamālā but also by the name or epithet of Buddha Catustriṃśajjātakajña, "knower of the 24 Jātakas" in Hemachandra's Abhidhānacintāmaṇi 233 in the commentary of which the old lexicographer Vyāḍi is quoted who enumerates a list of Jātakas the majority of which occur in the Jātakamālā. Cf. Kern Manual, p. 66. The hypothesis suggested by some scholars (thus Rhys Davids, l.c p. liii f. but see Charpentier l.c. p. 406 f) that it was originally intended to elucidate each Pāramitā by 10 Jātakas, has no foundation whatsoever.

Jātaka book, apart from some good monks and bad poets, there were also individual poets who were very important.

Thus we see again and again, combined in the Khuddakanikāya, books of various epoques and certainly of various schools and also books of all sorts whose canonical dignity was doubted.

THE ABHIDHAMMAPIṬAKA BUDDHIST SCHOLASTICISM

As the word Abhidhamma means "higher religion," or the "higher subtleties of religion,"[1] it is used sometimes to be translated by "metaphysics". In reality however, Abhidhamma has nothing to do with metaphysics, and as to philosophy, it has no more and no less connection with it than the Dhamma as taught in the Suttapiṭaka. Indeed, the only difference between the books of the Abhidhammapiṭaka and those of the Suttapiṭaka is, that the former are most circumstantial, drier, more learned, in a word, more scholastic. Both treat of the same subject. We shall look in vain for originality and profundity in the Abhidhamma books. Definitions and classifications are their strong point. The definitions, however, valuable as they are for the dictionary and the knowledge of Buddhist terminology, are disappointing in that they only turn on an endless series of synonyms. The classifications too, however, estimable for the attempt at creating a psychological basis of ethics which they contain, are rarely penetrating analyses of psychical processes; much more frequently they are many enumerations, unduly protracted or arbitrarily created or banal categories. As a rule, all this yields nothing but dogmatism, hardly ever is there a trace of any research which could be called scientific. The form of these works is mostly that of questions and answers, after the style of a catechism.

The texts of the Abhidhamma, the beginnings of which are already to be found in the Suttapiṭaka (e.g. Majjhimanikāya

---

1. Buddhaghoṣa explains the abhi ("higher") in the word "Abhidhamma" as referring, not to the contents, but merely to the more detailed mode of treatment. Cf. A. C. Taylor, in JRAS, 1894, pp. 560 f. and Rhys Davids in SBE, Vol. 36, p. 237 note.

137 and 140, and in many of the Suttas of the Aṅguttaranikāya), are probably merely extensions of the Mātikās or "lists," (viz., of the philosophical and ethical conceptions treated in the Suttapiṭaka) which are already mentioned in the Vinayapiṭaka.[1]

Book I of the Abhidhammapiṭaka, the Dhamma-Saṁgaṇi[2] "Compendium of Dhammas," deals with the classification and definition of the Dhammas, i.e., the psychical conditions and phenomena. Now, as in ancient Buddhism, ethics and psychology are just as inseparable as are philosophy and religion,[3] the English translator of this work, Mrs. Rhys Davids, is quite right in calling it "A Buddhist Manual of Psychological Ethics."[4] In the extremely valuable introduction to her translation,[5] this excellent authority on the philosophy of the Pāli texts, has been successful in her attempt to present the philosophy of ancient Buddhism in its main characteristics as contained in the doctrine of the Nikāyas, and classified and summarised in this catechism, whose bare structure of enumerations is so difficult of comprehension, and to assign to that philosophy its rightful place in the general history of philosophical thought. It is not the intention of the Dhamma Saṃgaṇi itself to give any systematic presentation of ethics or psychology; it presupposes a knowledge of the Dhamma and only claims to be a manual of study for advanced monks. In spite of the fact that it is a purely learned work, and anything but popular, it has been held in great regard in Ceylon. Evidence of this can be found

1. The Dhamma-Saṃgaṇi begins with a Mātikā of this nature, and Mrs. Rhys Davids (Buddhist Manual of Psychological Ethics, 2nd Ed., pp. ix, cv-cxiii) believes that this one should be regarded as the sole source of the Abhidhammapiṭaka. The Puggalapaññati and the Dhātukathā, however, also begin with Mātikās. The passages in which Mātikā is mentioned (e.g. dhammadharo vinayadharo mātikādharo paṇḍito, Cullavagga I, 11, 1, XII, 1,9) indicate that the word does not mean any one definite text, but, as in the case of dhamma and vinaya, a class of texts.

2. Edited by E. Müller, PTS 1885.

3. Cf. Mrs. C. A. F. Rhys Davids, "Buddhist Psychology" 2nd Ed., London 1924 p. 138. Buddhist Manual 2nd Ed., p. xxxviii ff.

4. Translation of the Dhamma Samgaṇi (Compendium of States or Phenomena) on OTF 1900, 2nd Edition 1923.

5. Also in her work "Buddhist Psychology" 2nd Ed. London 1924. Cf. also A. B. Keith, Buddhist Philosophy, pp. 187 ff.

in the report about a king of Ceylon in the 10th century, who had a copy of the work engraved on gold plates studded with jewels, and took it in grand procession to a vihāra he had built, where he worshipped it with offerings of flowers.[1]

By way of appendix to the Dhamma Saṃgaṇi, an old commentary to Book III of the work has also been included in the canon, and tradition has even ascribed this commentary to Sāriputta.[2]

Book II of the Abidhammapiṭaka the Vibhaṅga,[3] "Classification," is merely a continuation of Book I. It presupposes the formulas and categories of the Dhamma-Saṃgaṇi, but new ones are added. Section I deals with the fundamental conceptions and fundamental truths of Buddhism, with which the Dhamma-Saṃgaṇi begins. Section II deals with the knowledge of the sense impression up to the highest knowledge of a Buddha and Section III with the things which hinder knowledge. The last section, which deals with the various conditions in human and non-human existences, contains a considerable mythological element.

Book III of the Abhidhammapiṭaka, called Dhātukathā[4] "Discourses on the Elements" is a short text of 14 chapters, in questions and answers on the elements of psychical phenomena and their mutual relations.

In form and contents, Book IV, called Puggalapaññatti,[5] "Description of Human Individuals", is the book which is most closely allied to the texts of the Suttapiṭaka. In form it differs but little from the Saṅgīti-Sutta of the Dīghanikāya, and Sections 3-5 are for the most part to be found in the Aṅguttaranikāya too. Some chapters here read exactly like Suttas in one of the Nikāyas and stand out favourably from their environ-

---

1. Mrs. Rhys Davids, "Buddhist Manual" 2nd Ed, p. xxv.
2. Buddhaghosa calls this appendix (Text p. 234 ff. cf. Mrs. Rhys Davids, l. c. p. 334 ff) a commentary (aṭṭhakathākāṇḍam or atthuddhāra). In the text itself, it has no special title as though it were a part of the work.
3. Edited by Mrs. Rhys Davids, PTS. 1904.
4. Edited by E. R. Gooneratne, PTS 1892.
5. Edited by R. Morris, PTS 1883 translated into English ("Designation of Human types") Bimala Charan Law, PTS 1923, into German by Bhikkhu Nyānatiloka ("Das Buch der Charaktere") Breslau, 1910.

ment. We occasionally come across pretty similes. For instance (V,3) five kinds of warriors, and the simile, as is so often the case in the Majjhimanikāya, is carried on to the minutest detail. But it is only rarely that we come upon such passages of undeniable literary value. Generally speaking, even the parables are as barren and as tedious as the remaining parts of the book, the object of which is to classify individuals according to their ethical qualities. A few examples will suffice to give an idea of the spirit and style of the work, and of the type of definitions and classifications to be found in those portions which genuinely partake of the nature of the Abhidhamma.

"What sort of person is angry? What then is anger? That which is anger, being angry, and the state of being angry, hatred, hating, hatefulness, malice, the act of being malicious, maliciousness, hostility, enmity, rudeness, abruptness, resentment of heart – this is called anger. He who has not got rid of this anger is said to be an angry person."

"What sort of person is crafty? What is meant by craftiness? Here a person becomes crafty and cunning, that which is craft, craftiness, state of being crafty, hardness, toughness, counterfeit, sham (– this is called craftiness)[1] the person in whom craftiness remains unremoved is said to be a crafty person. What sort of person is one having low inclination? Here is a person, who, himself morally wicked and evil by nature, serves, follows, and worships another person who is also wicked and of evil disposition: – this is said to be a person having low inclination."

"What sort of person is one having good inclination? Here is a certain person who, morally good and of virtuous habits, serves, follows and reveres another person of the same nature: – he is said to be a person having good inclination."[2]

Book V of the Abhidhammapiṭaka, the Kathāvatthu[3] "Sub-

1. Missing in Law's translation.
2. II, 1, 4, 25 f. Translation by B. Ch. Law.
3. Edited by A. C. Taylor, PTS 1894, 1897. Translated ("Points of Controversy or Subjects of Discourse") by Shew Zen Aung and Mrs. Rhys Davids, PTS 1915. For an analysis of the work, see T. W. Rhys Davids, in JRAS 1892.

jects of Discourse," is that book which more than all others in the Abhidhammapiṭaka, is of importance from the point of view of the history of Buddhism, and is the only work of the canon which is ascribed to a definite author.[1] As already mentioned above (p. 8 f) it is said to have been compiled in connection with the Third Council, by Tissa Moggaliputta, the president of the Council. This tradition handed down by the chroniclers of Ceylon, has been accepted as historical by prominent scholars whilst others reject it as being entirely unauthentic.[2] Now as the Kathāvatthu in its present form is a patch work,[3] it is quite possible that Tissa Moggaliputta might have compiled a Kathāvatthu in the 3rd century B.C., but that the work was augmented by additional portions every time a new heresay cropped up.[4] The work, as we have it at present, and as Buddhaghosa commented it in the 5th century A.D. consists of 23 sections, each of which contains 8-12 questions and answers, in which the most diverse false views are presented, confuted and rejected. (The Commentary tells us which schools taught these false doctrines). We find such questions as, for instance, the following:

1. In the days of Buddhaghosa it was indeed believed that Buddha himself had proclaimed the outlines of the work, and that Tissa had only elaborated the details. On the other hand, in the introduction to the Atthasālinī i. e. the commentary on the Dhammasaṁgaṇi Buddhaghosa mentions that there were schools which did not acknowledge the Kathāvatthu as canonical.

2. For the tradition : Oldenberg ZDMG 52, 1898, 633 f· T. W. Rhys Davids in Cambridge History I, 194, Mrs. Rhys Davids, "Points of Controversy," pp. 30 f., "Buddhist Manual of Psychological Ethics", (1923) pp. xxiv f. Geiger, "Pāli Literature und Sprache," pp. 6 and 16, Dwijendra Lal Barua in Ind Hist. Qu. 7, 1931, 368 ff. Against the tradition I. P. Minayeff, "Recherches śur le Bouddhisme", pp· 81 ff S00 ff.; Barth in RHR 4, 1900, pp. 72. f.=Oeuvres III, 355 and Keith, "Buddhist Philosophy," 18 f. Max Walleser who formerly (Die buddhistische Philosophie in ihrer geschichtlichen Entwicklung I. Heidelberg 1904, (1925) pp. 20 ff, 95, f) placed absolute reliance on the tradition has now come to the conclusion (Die Buddhist. Philosophie. IV, Die Sekten des Buddhismus 1927. p. 12) "that this text is very considerably later than the historical legend would have us believe"

3. Mrs. Rhys Davids, "Points of Controversy", p. xxxi, speaks of "the patchwork quilt appearance" of this work.

4. Cf. La Vallee Poussin, ERE IV, p. 184. See also B. Ch. Law in Ann. Bh. Inst. 12,1931, p. 177f.

"Is there such thing as a person (an individual soul) which can be regarded as a real or absolute substance? Does everything exist? Are there two kinds of cessation (of suffering)? Do the pupils of Buddha share in his superhuman powers? Can a householder be an Arhat? Can an Arhat lose his Arhat-hood as a result of Karman? Is virtuous behaviour unconscious? Can a person who has arrived at the right view (i.e. at the true faith) intentionally commit a murder? Is it correct that the Buddha lived in the world of human beings? Were the excrements and urine of the sublime Buddha more fragrant than all other fragrant things? Can animals be reborn among the gods etc. ?"

All these themes are discussed in questions and answers with an imaginary opponent; the final answer is in the negative, the opposite opinion being declared false. For the refutation of false doctrines, which, in the majority of cases, are differences of opinon among schools, and not so much the heresies of various sects, many passages are quoted from the Vinayapiṭaka and the Suttapiṭaka.[1] which shows that the Kathāvatthu is at any rate later than these Piṭakas. It also refers to passages in the first two books of the Abhidhamma, and to subjects which are treated in the Paṭṭhānas, but it quotes neither the Dhātukathā nor the Puggalapaññatti, nor the Yamaka.

Even though the Kathāvatthu in its present form cannot be regarded as a work of the 3rd century B.C., it nevertheless throws interesting light on the development of Buddhist dogmatics during the later centuries. As far as the history of the Buddhist schools and sects is concerned, the information contained in the Kathāvatthu and the commentary on it, is only of value if taken in conjunction with the Chinese and Tibetan records of the schisms.[2]

We should be inclined to think that the Kathāvatthu formed the conclusion of the Abhidhammapiṭaka, but in the traditional enumeration of the texts, it comes fifth. The sixth is the

1. For a list of these passages, see Taylor's edition, pp. 633 ff.

2. Cf. La Vallee Poussin, JRAS 1910, pp. 413 ff.; Wallesser, "Die Sekten des alten Buddhismus," Heidelberg, 1927.

Yamaka[1] the "book of double questions," so called because all thc questions are presented and explained in two ways.[2] This work which is very difficult to understand, is intended to dispel any doubts which might still arise after the first five books of the Abhidhamma.

The seventh and last book of the Abhidhammapiṭaka is the Paṭṭhāna-Pakaraṇa the "Book of Causal Relationships," or the Mahā-Pakaraṇa, "The Great Book," the first part of which is the Tika-Paṭṭhāna and the second part the Duka-Paṭṭhāna.[3] The entire work deals with the investigation of the 24 kinds of relationships which are assumed between the (corporal and psychical) phenomena: causal relationship, relationship of the subject and object, relationship of the ruler and the ruled, contiguity, co-existence, etc. With the sole exception of Nirvāṇa which is absolute, there is nothing which is not in some sense relative, i. e. which is not related to something else in one of the 24 ways.[4] Mrs. Rhys Davids recommends the historian of Buddhistic ideas, and of logical and philosophical ideas in general to study the first part of the Tika-Paṭṭhāna, in which these 24 kinds of relationships are enumerated, calling it "the one noteable constructive contribution to knowledge in the Abhidhamma" though, in general, she speaks rather sceptically about the value of this work of pure scholasticism.[5]

---

1. Edited by Mrs. Rhys Davids assisted by Cecilia Dibben Mary C. Foley Hunt and May Smith, PTS 1911 and 1913.

2. Not even the title of the work is clear, s. Introductory Note, p. xv f. Mrs. Rhys Davids took great pains to obtain light on the meaning and method of the work, from the learned monks in Burma. The answers to her questions are incorporated in a Pāli essay by the Thera Ledi Sadaw of Mandalay in the Appendix to the edition.

3. Tika-Paṭṭhāna, Parts I-III ed, by Mrs. Rhys Davids, PTS 1921-1923 Duka-Paṭṣṭhāna i, ed. by Mrs. Rhys Davids, PTS 1906. The contents of the continuation of the Duka-Paṭṭhāna are given in the Tika-Paṭṭhāna, Part III, p. 336 ff.

4. Cf. Ledi Sadaw on the Philosophy of Relations in JPT 1915-16, p. 21 ff.

5. Cf. Foreword to part I, p. v and Editorial Note to Part II, of the Tika-Paṭṭhāna.

And Mrs. Rhys Davids, who has devoted years of patient and scholarly labour to the investigation of the texts of the Abhidhamma yet concludes a general survey of the work accomplished with these words of resignation: "As we leave this house of cloistered lives, of a closed tradition, of a past dominating present and future, we have a sense of rooms, swept and garnished clean and tidy, of sealed windows, of drawn blinds, of no outlook towards the dawn."[1]

If we give credence to the tradition which dates the Kathāvatthu away back in the 3rd century B.C., we are compelled to date the earlier texts of the Abhidhamma still further back, and to assume that the scholastic activity of the monks, began very early, immediately after the texts of the Suttapiṭaka. However, the authenticity of the Abhidhammapiṭaka is not universally recognised. It is disputed by the Sautrāntikas of the Hīnayāna, and the Sarvāstivādins have an Abhidhammapiṭaka in Sanskrit, the books of which differ entirely from those of the Pāli Abhidhammapiṭaka, though as in the case of the latter they are seven in number.[2] As even the report of the First Buddhist Council in the Vinayapiṭaka (Cullavagga XI) only mentions Vinaya and Dhamma but not Abhidhamma there are still doubts both as to the authenticity and as to the age of the Abhidhammapiṭaka.[3]

Among those sects, however, which recognise the Abhidhammapiṭaka as canonical, it is held in great esteem. In Milindapañha it is related as a great marvel that young Nāgasena was so very clever that he could at once be instructed in the seven books of the Abhidhamma without having first learned the Suttas. In an inscription of about 262 A.D., engraved on a

---

1. JRAS 1923, p. 250

2. Cf. La Vallee Poussin, "Bouddhisme, Etudes et Materiaux." p. 55; "Bouddhisme," p. 166. Kern, "Manual of Buddhism," p. 126. Walleser (Buddhistische Philosophie, I, 17 ff) tries to identify certain texts of the Pāli Abhidhammapiṭaka with similar ones in Sanskrit, but can only take his stand on mere conjectures.

3. Eliot, "Hinduism and Buddhism," I, 276 Note 1, 291 f., thinks it is possible, though not proved, that the Abhidhammapiṭaka was compiled in Ceylon, and not earlier.

rock in the neighbourhood of the temple of Mihintale in Ceylon, we read along the rules for the monks, of the monastery: 12 cells are to be allotted to expounders of the Abhidhammapiṭaka, 7 to preachers of Suttapiṭaka, and 5 to readers of the Vinayapiṭaka.[1]

The study of the Abhidhamma is continued, especially in Burma, even at the present day, and numerous works have been written on it in the course of centuries.

The Non-Canonical Pali-Literature[2]

The Pāli texts included in the canon, except for later supplements, for the most part, originated in India, and have been carried to Ceylon only later. However, the huge volume of the non-canonical Pāli literature is the work of the monks of Ceylon. The only exception is the Milindapañha[3], the Questions of Milinda," the most important of all of them. This

1. R. Spence Hardy, "Easterm Monachism," London 1860, p. 156.

2. Cf. Geiger' "Pāli Literatur und Sprache", p. 17 ff. G. P. Malalasekara, "Pāli Literature of Ceylon," London 1928, and B. Ch. Law in Ann. Bh. Inst. 12, 1931-32, pp. 97-143.

3. Ed. by V. Trenckner, London 1880; Vol. I of an edition in Siamese characters has been issued by Their Majesties Queen Aunt and Queen Suddhasinninath of Siam, in 1925; translated into English by T. W. Rhys Davids in SBE Vols. 35 and 36; into German (only the genuine parts) by F. O. Schrader, Berlin s. a. (1905) and (complete) by Bhikkhu Nyāṇatiloka, München 1919; Books I-III into French by L. Finot, Paris 1923 (Les Classiques del) Orient VIII). Extracts (similes and short parables) are translated by E. W. Burlingame, "Buddhist Parables," p. 201 ff. Cf. Barth in RHR 28, 1893, 257 ff.=Oeuvres II, 170 ff; R. Garbe, "Beiträge zur indischen Kulturgeschicte," Berlin, 1903, p. 95 ff.; T. W. Rhys Davids in ERE VIII, 1915. 631 ff. The title of the work is given in Mss as Milindapañham (neut.) or Milindapanha (plur.), but the Buddhists of Ceylon generally say Milindapanho (masc). Trenckner Ed., p. vi. A new theory on the composition of the Milindapañha has been suggested by Mrs. Rhys Davids, "The Milinda Questions—An Inquiry into its Place in the History of Buddhism with a Theory as to its Author," London, 1930. She thinks that there is one author of the book who first edited the conversation between Milinda and Nāgasena, which she considers to have actually taken place, then—about ten years latter—wrote the dialogues on the Dilemmas, and still later, as "a grey-haired man," "the book of the Similes." For an analysis of the work see also B. Ch. Law in Ann. Bh. Inst. 13, 1931-32, pp., 105-22.

work must have originated in north-western India, only where the great and wise ruler Milinda can have remained so well in the people's memory that he was made the hero of a poem. For this Milinda is none else than the Greek king Menandros, the most distinguished among the rulers of Graeco-Indian kingdom which got separated from the Graeco-Bactrian kingdom in the 2nd century B.C. He reigned probably in the first century B.C.,[1] and ruled over a big kingdom that included not only the whole of Indus country including Gujarat but also the Ganges valley. Whether a historical event the meeting and talking of the Greek king with a famous Buddhistic preacher gave rise to the birth of the Milindapañha or the author of the dialogue followed only the example of so many Upaniṣadic and Itihāsa dialogues in showing the great king in a conversation with a wise man: in any case Milinda-Menadros, even if he were not himself a Buddhist[2] must have maintained close contact with the Buddhistic community. We can also presume as certain that the author of the Milindapañha, whose name is however not known to us, has lived at a time when people's memory of the Greek king was still fresh. But as there was an end to Greek rule over India soon after the death of Menandros,

1. A. V. Gutschmid Geschichte Irans und seiner Nachbarlander. Tübingen 1888, p-104 gives the approximate dates of Menander's reign as 125-95 B. C. According to Smith, "Early History' pp. 227 ff., 239 258, Menander invaded India in about 155 B. C. but," Gardner places him about 110 B. C." H. Raychaudhuri (Political History of Ancient India) Calcutta 1923, p. 204 ff, 209 whose view is shared by L. D. Barnett (Calcutta Review, Feb. 1924, p. 250) places Menander in the first century B. C., and (according to Benoytosh Bhattacharya "The Indian Buddhist Iconography," Oxford 1924 p. xxi) R. C. Mazumdar is said to have proved "that a date prior to 90 B. C. cannot be assigned to Menander." (Bhattacharya gives no reference, so Mazumdar's arugments are not known). See also Rapson, "Cambridge, History" I, 547 ff.

2. This could be supported by the interesting news of Plutarch that after Menander's death several Indian towns fought for his ashes which were at last divided, whereupon every town erected a monument on his share of the ashes. Exactly the same thing happened according to the legend, when Buddha died (Garbe ibid p. 102 and 112f; Schrader ibid, p. xvi) But it is also possible that Menandros sympathised only with the Buddhists and made liberal gifts to the order. Any way, the coins of Menandros also show the Buddhistic wheel (see Levi in RHR 23, 1891 p. 43 f.).

it can be hardly presumed that he would have been remembered for more than one century. Accordingly the work might have been composed by about the beginning of the Christian era.[1] In favour of such high antiquity is also the fact that the Milindapañha dialogue differs so little from the canonical dialogues,[2] that it would not at all be conspicuous if it stood as a Sutta in the Suttapiṭaka. Also Buddhaghosa, the famous commentator of the 5th century, quotes in his support the Milindapañha as a high authority which high esteem he shows otherwise only to the canonical texts.[3] But in respect of literary value our text can be compared only with the best dialogues of the Suttapiṭaka. Indeed only few of the canonical dialogues are conducted with such freshness and liveliness as the Milindapañha, that very well stands comparison with the Dialogues of Plato.[4]

Nevertheless this praise and the dating presumed by us applies not for the entire work as it is found in the Pāli text before us,

1. According to Garbe ibid. p. 106 who follows perhaps Trenckner (in the foreword to his edition, p. vii) the work has originated probably in the second century A. D.

2. The themes discussed show remarkable similarity with those which play a prominent part in the Kathā-Vatthu. Cf. Rhys Davids in SBE Vol. 36, pp. xx-xxvi. The allusion to the Thera (p. 71, SBE Vol. 35, p. 110) "a master in the art of writing," who is said to have died many years before and "of whom people know only by his writings" would seem to point to a considerable, though not unduly protracted, interval of time between the author of Milindapañha and Tissa Moggaliputta (if it is he who is meant) who lived in the 3rd century B. C.

3. E. G. Atthasālinī, pp. 112, 114, 119, 120, 122, 142: Visuddhi Magga p. 87, all these references are to passages in Books I-III of the Mil. P. Rhys Davids in SBE Vol. 35, p. xiv ff.

4. A. Weber, (Die Griechen in Indien) (SBA 1890, p. 927) has raised the question whether the Milindapañha is not connected with the Platonic dialogues more closely, whether it does not represent, so to say, an intentional Indian 'double stakes' against them. This is improbable even due to the fact that the Milindapañha has so many models in the dialogues of the Upaniṣads, in the ascetic poetry of the Mahābhārata and in the Tipiṭaka that there is no need to think of a Greek model. Further, there is no trace of the knowledge of the Greek language or of the world of Greek thoughts in the Milindapañha (Cf Garbe, ibid p. 114. Finot, too (Introduction to his French translation, p. 14) thinks that the style of the Milindapañha shows traces of Greek influence.

but only for the work in its original form. For there can be no doubt that of the seven books of which our text consists, only a small portion of the first Introductory Book and the II and the III Book are old and genuine. Even in the III Book some later additions have crept in. By far the largest portion of the Book-more than five-sixths—has been added only later in Ceylon. The most striking proof for the spuriousness of Books IV-VII is their absence in the Chinese translation, which is said to have originated between 317 and 420 A.D..[1] But even in their content, the Books IV-VII are essentially different from the preceding ones whereas in the old and genuine dialogue only the most general and important questions of religion are discussed i.e. basic questions which are of interest for every layman, with the IV Book there begins a Buddhistic apologetics which could be of any interest only to those who knew the canonical texts. In these later works dilemmas are raised with great fondness which are the outcome of mutually contradictory texts confronting one another. Thereby every word of the canon—including the most unimportant remark in the most profane stories of the Jātaka book—is viewed as a sacred word of Buddha which must

1. Cf. Ed. Specht et S. Levi. "Deux traductions Chinoises du Milindapañhe" OC, IX, London 1892 Vol. I, 518 ff. The date of the Chinese translation (According to Schrader ibid., p. 119 there is only one translation in two editions, not two different translations.) is not quite certain, because the name of the translation is not known and because in a catalogue of Chinese Books of the Year 520 A. D. this work does not find a place yet. On the other hand, in support of a higher antiquity for the Chinese translation is the fact that in a Chinese Buddhistic Avadāna—work of the year 472 A. D. the introductory book of the Milindapañha appears, embellished with anecdotes as an independent story, which appears like a later echo of the old dialogue. (Cf. J. Takakusu) in JRAS 1896, pp. 1-21 and Ed. Chavannes, Cinq Cents Contes du Tripiṭaka Chinois III, 120 ff, No. 418). L. A. Waddell (in JRAS 1897, p. 227 ff) has tried to make it appear, on the basis of very doubtful Tibetan dates, that this Chinese Avadāna is closer to the original work and that originally not Milinda but a king Nanda of Magadha was the hero of the book. But "Nanda" is certainly only a Sanskrit version of the Greek Menandros. Cf. Pelliot, l. c. p. 380 f. Rhys Davids (ERE VIII) 632 thinks that it is possible that the Indian work, which was translated into Chinese, consisted of seven books and that the concluding books were omitted by the Chinese translator. This appears to be most unlikely.

certainly be true and good. If in some one of his earlier births of which the Jātakas speak, the Bodhisatta had mistakes and vices, then the author of the V book of the Milindapañha endeavours to purify him by washing it off. Because, for him the Bodhisatta is quite identical with the perfect Buddha. Of this kind of view there is not a single trace to be found in the genuine books (as also in the Tipiṭaka). Similarly, in literary respects also the later books are essentially different from the genuine portions of the work. Of course even in these later books we find here and there beautiful parables and ingenious remarks, but they do not come anywhere near the beauty and originality of the earlier books. Finally, the end of the third Book constitutes also a good conclusion to the work which every one would consider to be complete if the Books IV-VII did not follow.[1]

The old poem began probably with the splendid description of the town of Sāgala, the residence of king Milinda.[2] Then it was said how the learned and mighty king of Greece one day after inspecting his army, expressed a desire for a declamatory tournament. But the king was such a formidable opponent in declamation that it was not easy to find a Brahmin or an ascetic who dared argue with him. At last his courtiers took him to Monk Āyupāla who lived in a hermitage near Sāgala. But he too was embarassed through even the first question of the king

1. Cf. Garbe, l. c. p. 136 ff. F. O. Schrader (Introduction to his translation, p. xxiii f.) assumes that there were seven different recensions or revisions of this work. It is, however, more probable that there were gradual interpolations and additions rather than revisions. There are no sufficient reasons for declaring the whole of Book III to be spurious, as do Garbe and Schrader. Senart (JA 1892 sur 8, t. xix p. 343) and Barth (Oeuvres II, p. 171) already declared the end of Book III (Trenckner's ed. p.89) to be the final portion of the original work. Similarly, Pelliot JA s. II, t. IV, 1914, p. 418.

2. The Pāli work begins with some introductory verses and towards the end of the introduction also we find some verses. Schrader (p. XXVI, XXXII) believes that these verses are the remnants of a Pāli poem originated in Ceylon. It appears more reasonable to believe that only Gāthās are of the kind as are found too often in the Suttas of the Tipiṭaka also and as were always used with special preference for embellishing prose in India. Cf. above, pp. 34, 39 and 113 above.

so that Milinda exclaimed: "Ah, nothing is in India ! Ah, the whole of India is empty prattle. There is no ascetic or Brahmin who would be in a position to debate with me and clear my doubts !" At that time it so happend that the highly learned and wise Buddhist monk – Nāgasena – was going through the villages and towns and begging. He was famous throughout the country for his wisdom and in debate none could resist him. He had just then arrived in Sāgala and taken abode in a hermitage. To him the courtiers brought the king who was very strongly impressed at once by the personality of the wise man.[1]

Connected very skilfully to the above situation, even the first dialogue takes us straight way into the main teachings of Buddhism, King Milinda asks the wise man his name. The latter says, he is called Nāgasena, but that is just a name,—an "I", a person does not exist thereby. Thereupon the wise man and the "King get entangled in an admirably conducted dialogue at the end of which the" King must admit that there is no permanent "I".[2]

This fundamental teaching of Buddhism, that there is no "I" no soul[3], but only an eternal change of physical and psychic phenomena can be reconciled only with great difficulty with the belief in a cycle of rebirths as was also presumed by Buddha,

---

1. The passages which may be regarded as decidedly spurious in Book I, are the following : paragraph 3 (a table of contents, which refers to the entire Pāli work), paragraph 4-8 (a Jātaka, which tells of the former births of Milinda and Nāgasena, and ends with a prophecy of Buddha), 11-14 (already recognised by Rhys Davids as a clumsy interpolation) and 16-36 (conception, birth, youth, conversion and attainment of Arhatship of Nāgasena).

2. Cf. Oldenberg, Buddha, p. 292 ff.; Radhakrishnan, "Indian Philosophy," I, 391 f.

3. This is certainly the standpoint of the author of the Milindapañha. In the Canon we find sometimes a decided denial of the ego, at other times the doctrine that an ego does exist in a certain sense, and frequently the agnostic point of view that it is impossible to say either that there is a soul, or the contrary. Cf. M. Walleser, "Die philosophische Grundlage des alteren Buddhismus" I, 111 ff.; Mrs C. A. F. Rhys Davids, "Buddhist Psychology" (1924), pp. 156 ff., 278 ff.; Radhakrishnan, l. c., 382 ff., 390 ff.; Keith, "Buddhist Philosophy," pp. 75 ff., 191 ff.

and with still greater difficulty with the doctrine of Karman, the doctrine of the results of action, a doctrine that is so important for the entire ethics of Buddhism. The first of these two questions is the topic of the following dialogue[1] which is reproduced here because it shows how the author of our verses knows how to deal with the most difficult problems in a very learned manner and through appropriate parables.

The King said: "O Nāgasena, is the one who is reborn the same or a different person?" The Thera spoke: "Neither the same nor another." "Give me a parable." "What you think, O great King, are you now, as a grown-up man, the same as you were at that time, when you were a gentle baby, as a small child kicking with legs ?" "No, sir, another was that gentle baby, that small child kicking with legs, and another am I now as grown up".

"If it is so, O great King, then you have perhaps no mother, no father, no teacher, then you have been never taught, have never learnt the commandments, never acquired wisdom. How then O King is the mother of the embryo in its four stages a different one every time, is the mother of the small child different from the mother of the grown up person ? Is it a different person that is taught and a different one that has learnt something? Is it a different person who commits a crime and a different one whose hands and feet are cut off?" "No Sir, but what would be your answer to the question ?" The Thera spoke: "I myself, O Great King, was the gentle baby, the small child with kicking legs and I myself am now grown up. Through one and the same body all these are condensed into one unit." "Give me a simile." "If O great King, a man would light a lamp, would it burn the whole night ?" "Indeed, Sir, it would." "How then, O great King, is the flame in the first quarter of the night the same as in the second quarter ?" "No, Sir" "And is the flame in the second quarter of the night the same as the flame in the last quarter ?" "No, Sir", "How great king, was then the lamp in the first quarter of the night another, in the second quarter of the night another and again another one in the last quarter of the night ?" "No, Sir, by means of one and the same (fuel)

1. Ed. Trenckner, p. 40; SBE, Vol. 35, p. 63. ff. Cf. Oldenberg, "Buddha," p. 301; Keith, "Buddhist Philosophy", p. 169 f.

did the lamp shine through the whole night" "Exactly in the same way, O great king, is the continuity of the phenomena[1] brought about : it is a different one who is born, a different one who dies, but at the same time there was something that unites them and hence a man in his last union with consciousness[2] enters neither as the same one nor as different one."

A whole series of parables is supposed to explain, why man is responsible for his actions although there is no permanent "I". One of these parables is the following one.[3]

"Let us suppose that one man has stolen another man's mango fruits. The owner of the mango tree catches him, brings him before the king and says: "Your Majesty, this man has stolen my mango fruits"; if now the thief would say, "I, your Majesty, have not stolen this man's mango fruits; it was other fruits that this man had planted and others which I have taken; I need not be punished", then would this man get his punishment, O great king?" "Yes, Sir, he would get his punishment." "And why so?" "Whatever the man may object, he would get his punishment because of the latter mango fruits which undeniably would not have been there without the earlier ones."

The II Book has an abundance of excellent parables like this one. In the genuine portion of the third Book also we find some beautiful parables. When for example Nāgasena answers a question of the king saying that the end of the suffering is brought about not only by renunciation in this life but that in this respect efforts in earlier births were also necessary, he comments on this by asking the king whether he will have a well dug only when he feels thirsty, or whether he will make people plough, sow and reap only when he is hungry or whether he will make his men dig ramparts, erect walls and build fortresses only when the enemy stood before the gate.

These specimens justify adequately our calling the first and genuine part of the Milindapañha a true masterpiece of ancient

1. i. e. of the beings which are in reality only changing phenomena.
2. That is in his last rebirth, for the "consciousness" (viññāṇa) is it, through which a new individual is born in the womb. Cf. Oldenberg, "Buddha", 255 ff; Pischel, "Leben und Lehre des Buddha," p. 67; Keith, "Buddhist Philosophy," p. 78 f.
3. II, 2, 6; Edition Trenckner, p. 46; SBE, Vol. 35, p. 72.

Indian prose. In Book II and the greater part of Book III, only such questions are raised, as relate to the most important points of Buddhistic ethics and psychology, fundamental questions which are of interest to any layman. Book IV, on the other hand, contains a system of apologetics which could not possibly be of interest to any but thorough-going scholars of the canonical texts. The dilemmas which are discussed in this work frequently turn to very petty subjects of dogmatics, but especially to the person of Buddha, e.g., what is the use of the veneration of relics, if the Buddha has passed away utterly? How can the Buddha be omniscient, when we are told that he pondered? why did Buddha receive Devadatta into the order, even though he knew that this monk would cause a schism etc. ? The reason for these dilemmas is the juxtaposition of contradictory texts. At the same time, every word of the canon, even the most casual remark in the profanest stories in the jātaka-Book, is regarded as a sacred word of Buddha, which must of necessity be true and good. If, in any of his former births, related in the Jātakas, the Bodhisatta had any faults or vices, the author of Book IV of the Milindapañha does his best to exonerate him. For, in his eyes, the Bodhisatta is entirely identical with the perfect Buddha. The authentic books do not bear the slightest trace of such a conception (neither does the Tipiṭaka). The question as to whether the Buddha ever existed at all,[1] which had already been broached in Book III, is again raised in Book V, and Nāgasena answers it by saying that his existence may be inferred from his teachings. This idea is worked out in a lengthy, very ornate and detailed parable making up the greater part of the Book, in which Buddha, who has created his religion, is compared with a master-builder, who builds up a large city. Book VI presents a dilemma, which had already been brought up for discussion in Book IV, but had not found any very satisfactory solution;[2] it is this: If, as the scriptures say, even laymen can attain to the state of an Arhat, why should a man take upon himself the strict monastic vows ? The answer given here is, that laymen can attain to the state of an Arhat and Nirvāṇa only because they

1. Ed. Trenckner, pp. 70, 73; SBE, Vol. 35, pp. 109, 113.
2. Ed. Trenckner, p.242 ff.; SBE, Vol. 36, p. 56 ff.

have already fulfilled the strict vows in former births. These strict vows, the thirteen Dhutaṅgas,[1] are then described in detail, and their exceptional value explained. This is apparently the real purpose of Book VI. In all the books of the Milindapañha the questions raised are generally answered in parables. Book VII is entirely a book of parables; there are no less than 67 parables[2] illustrative of the qualities essential for the monk who desires to attain to the state of an Arhat. Many of these parables already appear in the Tipiṭaka.

In Books IV-VII we find, on the one hand, a liberal sprinkling of quotations from the canon, and on the other, frequent allusions to traditions divergent from those embodied in the canon, and most likely belonging to a latter period, and especially allusions to legends which appear only in the commentaries, in the commentary on the Jātaka and in those on the Vimānavatthu and Dhammapada.[3] These legends are permeated with a low conception of the doctrine of Karman, exaggerated cult of the Buddha (Buddha-Bhakti) and a somewhat crude belief in miracles, which would seem to indicate a later period.

A work which is probably as early as the earliest portions of the Milindapañha, and which also possibly dates far enough back to have been written in India, is the Netti-Pakaraṇa, also

1. They are very advantageous for a holy life, but are not compulsory for all monks. They are discussed in Section I of Buddhaghosa's Visuddhi-Magga. The term Dhutaṅga (or Dhutāṅga) is not yet to be found in the Tipiṭaka, except in the Parivāra of later date (Vinayapiṭaka, ed. Oldenberg, Vol. V, p. 193, cf. p. 131). Cf. Kern, "Manual of Indian Buddhism," p. 75 f.

2. The book begins with a table of contents (mātikā), which gives an additional 38 parables. The entire book was probably appended to the Milindapañha even later than the preceding books, and remained incomplete.

3. Cf. E. W. Burlingame in HOS, Vol. 28, p. 60 ff. Burlingame is wrong in concluding from these references that Books IV-VII of the Mil. "are as late as the beginning of the sixth century A. D." Not only is it not proved, but, in view of sundry deviations, it is unlikely, that the author of Books IV-VII of the Mil. derived his knowledge of the legends referred to, from these commentaries,. Cf. also Rhys Davids, SBE., Vol 35, pp. xl ff., 196, 284 ff., 297 f., Vol. 36, pp. 43 ff., 143 note. The authentic parts of the Mil. contain only such quotations as could, for other reasons too, be regarded as belonging to the earliest part of the Canon. The enumeration of the seven books of the Abhidhamma (I, 26) appears in the spurious part of the introduction.

called Netti-Gandha, on simply Netti, "The Book of Guidance" (viz., to the True Religion).[1] This is the earliest work which offers a connected treatment of the whole of the teaching of Buddha; it is possibly earlier than the last two books of the Abhidhammapiṭaka,[2] and is ascribed to no less a person than Mahākaccāna, the disciple of Buddha, who, as far back as in the Majjhimanikāya, was proclaimed to be the best expounder of the word of the Buddha.[3] The same Mahākaccāna is also said to have composed the Peṭakopadesa, "Instruction of the students of the Piṭakas,"[4] a continuation of the Netti, and most likely not much later than this last-named work. A commentary on the Netti was written by Dhammapāla (probably in the fifth century A.D.).

Just as the spurious part of the Milindapañha is also the whole of the remaining non-canonical Pāli literature the work of scholarly monks. These monks studied most fervently in their cloisters the canonical texts whose relatively faithful transmission we owe to them. However, they did not content themselves with learning and teaching these texts but endeavoured even from the beginning to explain them. This gave rise to a voluminous commentary literature of which some pieces have of course already been included in the canon itself.[5] And even if we cannot believe the orthodox Buddhists of Ceylon when they say that the Aṭṭhakathās, i.e. the "sense-explanations" or "Commentaries" handed down together with the texts of the Tipiṭaka

---

1. With Extracts from Dhammapāla's Commentary ed. by E Hardy, PTS 1902. For an analysis of the contents of the Netti, see B. Ch. Law. in Ann. Bh. Insti. 13, 1931-32, p. 105.
2. Cf. Mrs Rhys Davids, JRAS, 1925, p. 111 f.
3. Majjh. 18 (I, 110 ff.), 133 (III, 194 ff.), 138 (III, 223 ff.)
4. Not yet published, but see Rudolf Fuchs, "Specimen des Petakopadesa," Berlin, Diss., 1908. Cf. Shwe Zan Aung in JPTS 1910-1912, p. 120; B. Ch. Law in Ann. Bh. Inst., 1931-1922, p. 105.
5. B. Ch. Law, "Life and Work of Buddhaghosa," p. 53 ff. The Sutta-Vibhaṅga in itself is a kind of commentary on the Pāṭimokkha. The Udāna and the Suttanipāta contain prose passages in the nature of commentaries. The Niddesa is an early commentary on parts of the Suttanipāta. A commentary ascribed to Sāriputta found its way into the Abhidhammapiṭaka as an appendix to the Dhamma-Saṅgaṇi.

since the time of the first Council have been translated by Mahinda into Sinhalese, recorded under Vaṭṭagāmani and have been rendered into Pāli[1] by Buddhaghosa (5th century A.D.), still the exegetic and poetic activity of the monks began immediately after the compilation of the texts already in India and that too in Pāli, the language of the canon. But as the Theravāda-school itself was more and more dislodged by other Buddhistic sects and schools, it was the cloisters of Ceylon[2] in which the study of the Theravāda texts found a permanent nursery. What was available of Pāli-commentaries was translated into Sinhalese. Only the verses partly memorial verses and partly verses of narrative pieces were left unchanged in Pāli. But the monks of Ceylon continued to work in this direction, wrote Sinhalese commentaries, tried their hand at Pāli also, especially at writing Pāli verses and reached such a perfection in it that Buddhaghoṣa writes already in the 5th century an elegant Pāli and also begins to translate or to re-translate the Sinhalese commentaries into the holy Pāli language. But the exegetic and literary activity of the monks covered all the "three gems"; the Buddha, the religion (Dhamma) and the monk's community (Saṅgha). The Buddha legend was elaborated; they were not contented with the ballads and incidental details of the Tipiṭaka, but they wanted to have a description of the lord. The religious texts were commented upon and explained and in the same way as was usual at the time of the Brāhmaṇas themselves, not only grammatically and lexically but also by means of stories

1. Cf. L. Comrilla, "Vijasinha" and R. C. Childers in JRAS 1871, p. 289 ff., Kern, "Manual of Indian Buddhism," p. 8 f.; Th. Foulkes in Ind. Ant. 17, 1888, 123 f.; Dipavaṃsa 20, 20 f.; Mahāvaṃsa, 33, 100 ff.; Geiger, Pā i Literatur und Sprache, p. 17 (para. 18).

2. Various monasteries had their own commentaries; besides the Mūla- or Mahā-Aṭṭhakathā of the "great cloister" of Anurādhapura, also one of the "northern Cloister" (Uttaravihāra) in the same town of Ceylon, and an Andha-Aṭṭhakathā in Kancheepuram in South India among others. Cf. Mrs. Rhys Davids, "Buddhist Manuals of Psychological Ethics," p. XXII. In the later commentaries there are references to the Aṭṭhakathā also often only shortly with the "Porana", i. e, "the old ones." Cf. Mrs. Rhys Davids, "Buddhist Manual of Psychological Ethics", 2nd Ed., p. xxviii.

and legends.[1] Like the Brahmins in their Vedic schools, so also were the monks in their cloisters true Indians in this that they found unlimited joy in telling stories. The numerous stories that the canon contained were not enough for them. They elaborated and supplemented, they appended what they received additionally by oral transmission, they inserted what was known to them from other literary circles by reshaping them to suit Buddhists line of thinking and they also composed something new imitating old models. They collected also the legends on the birth of the monks' community and made recordings of the monks' community whose order they treated in the commentaries to the Vinayapiṭaka so that the Atthakathās also contained the beginnings of an ecclesiastical history.

But in respect of the Buddha legend we have seen that the canon did not contain any actual biography of Buddha but it contained only the beginnings of one such. In the Vinayapiṭaka, in the individual speeches and in some antiquarian ballads of the Suttanipāta we found already partly more or less reliable reports of the true life of the Lord and partly the earliest beginnings of a Buddha legend and of a Buddha epic. In the Buddhavaṃsa we found in a way a previous history of a biography of Buddha and in its 26 chapters a short summary of the same. The Cariyāpiṭaka and Jātaka also, in narrating about the previous lives of Buddha, contain – at least for the devout Buddhists — contributions to the story of the life of Buddha.[2] But a cogent biography of Buddha is found in the Pāli literature only in the Nidānakathā,[3] the "Story of Beginnings"[4] which

1. The Aṭṭhakathās contain Jātakas and other stories like the Arthavāda of the Brāhmaṇas (Cf. Vol. I, p. 193) Itihāsas and Ākhyānas.

2. Cf. Rhys Davids, "Cambridge History," I, 196 f.; J. Dutoit, "Das Leben des Buddha", Leipzig 1906. E. H. Brewster, "The Life of Gotama the Buddha." (Compiled exclusively from the Pāli Canon) With an introductory Note by C. A. F. Rhys Davids, London 1926.

3. The text is found in Fausboll's Jātaka edition, Vol. I, pp. 1-94, translated by T. W. Rhys Davids, Buddhist Birth Stories, pp 1-133; a free reproduction of the content of the Nidānakathā in Kern, Der Buddhismus I, pp. 24-140, a translation of Durenidāna and Avidurenidāna in Warren, Buddhism in Translations, pp 5-83. Two smaller pieces translated by J. Dutoit, Leben des Buddha, p. 5ff, 18ff.

4. i. e. of the beginnings of the career of Buddha, Nidāna means "Cause" hence also "Beginning"

precedes the Jātakavaṇṇana, our Jātaka commentary and forms a part of this great commentary work.

This Nidānakathā consists of three sections: 1. the story of the "Beginnings in the distant past" (Durenidāna), which extends from the existence of the later Buddha as Sumedha up to the time of Buddha Dīpaṅkara up to his rebirth in the heaven of Tusita-gods; 2. the story of the "Beginnings in the not very distant past" (Avidurenidāna) which begins with the descent of Buddha from the heaven of the Tusita gods and ends with the attainment of the Bodhi, i.e. the enlightenment; and 3. the story "of the Beginnings of the nearest past" (Santikenidāna), which narrate the events from the enlightenment of Buddha up to the story of the generous gifting of the merchant Anāthapiṇḍika.

The first section follows immediately the Buddhavaṃsa and the Cariyāpiṭaka and is in essence nothing but a commentary to an extract from these two texts. Completely included is only the story of Sumedha from the II Chapter of the Buddhavaṃsa. We have already seen how the future Buddha lived unenumerable aeions ago as Sumedha pays his respects to Dīpaṅkara the Buddha of those days and resolves to attain the ten "perfections" in order to be worthy of Buddhahood.[1] After resolving thus, he endeavours in unenumerable rebirths again and again to fulfil these highest "perfections" — of these narrates the Cariyāpiṭaka which is quoted by the author of the Nidānakathā here[2] — until finally in his life as Vessantara he has attained the peak of perfection by means of his limitless self-sacrificing generosity and then is reborn in the heaven of the Tusita-gods.

Whereas in the first section the prose is interrupted again and again by the Buddhavaṃsa—and Cariyāpiṭaka—verses, the two later sections contain only a few incidental verse quotations. The second section begins with a "Buddha-uproar" in the heaven. The Tusita-gods assail the Bodhisatta saying that he might be reborn on the earth for the welfare of the world and he agrees to this after a long contemplation. Then follow the

1. p. 156 above.
2. Nevertheless, as remarked already on p. 159 in a recension different from ours.

well-known legends of the conception of the Bodhisatta who as a white elephant appears to enter the womb of the dreaming Queen Māyā, of his wonderful birth in the Lumbinī grove[1], of the welcome given to the new born baby and the prophecy of his future greatness by Sage Asita, of the miracles of childhood and boyhood, of the prince's encounters through which he gets to know old age, disease, death and renunciation of the world, of the night-scenes in the harem, which strengthens in him the decision to renounce the world, of his departure from the palace accomplished with numerous miracles and the cooperation of the gods and the transition to the state of mendicant monk, of his great asceticism, of Sujāta's preparation of milk-rice with numerous miracles by which (milk-rice) he acquires new strength, of the meditation under the Bodhi-tree and the assaults of Māra and at last the attainment of Bodhi, the highest knowledge which is accompanied by numerous miracles.

In the third section also which deals mainly with the earliest conversions, and is less suited for introducing miracles, there is no lack of these. Buddha spends a week, immersed in meditation, under the Bodhi-tree and the gods begin to doubt whether he has really attained enlightenment. In order to dispel their doubts he performs a few miracles, rises in the air, stands beside his "throne" looking towards the east and stays like that for a whole week without winking his eyes. Here the Nidānakathā inserts the remark that at this place later the Animisacetiya, i.e. the "Not blinking-sanctuary" has been put up. And at several other places also sanctuaries are mentioned which are supposed to remind us of events in the life of Buddha and which will have even existed in reality. The Vinayapiṭaka (Mahāvagga I, 4) already narrates about the two merchants Tapussa and Bhallika into lay disciples. But the Nidānakathā adds that these early lay disciples of Buddha also received somc hairs over which they constructed shrines as relics. There is a very detailed report on

1. In all this the Nidānakathā has embellished a little only the miracles reported in the Dīghānikāya 14 and Majjhimanikāya 123. However the "white elephant" does not yet occur in the Pāli-canon; but it is found already in the sculptures from the time of Aśoka. Hardy, Aśoka, p. 56 Windisch, Buddhas Geburt, p. 5 ff, 155 ff.

Buddha's visit to his home town of Kapilavastu during which also there is no lack of miracles. The story of the big merchant Anāthapiṇḍika also occupies a lot of space This Anāthapiṇḍika made a gift of the Jetavana — grove to the order of monks. With this story the Nidānakathā ends abruptly without making it in any way clear why an abrupt end is made here.

That it is not sheer chance that the Nidānakathā is given precedence over the Jātaka commentary but that it constitutes an essential part of the same follows from the fact that in the "Present stories" (Paccutpannavatthu) sometimes there are references made back to the Nidānakathā. But because the author of the latter says at one place[1] expressly that he deviates from the Jātakaṭṭhakathā, and supports himself on the "other Aṭṭhakathās", it follows that he has not simply translated the Sinhalese commentary but has modified it freely by using other commentaries. Unfortunately, we do not have any clue to fix clearly the date of the Jātaka commentary and hence that of Nidānakathā. But one thing is certain. The numerous agreements between the Buddha legend as it is narrated in the Sanskrit sources and the Nidānakathā proves that the latter is based on the same Indian transmission as the former and can perhaps be traced back to the commentaries which were brought to Ceylon from India and that at a time before the Mahāyāna literature was developed in India. For the Nidānakathā, however, represents a still earlier phase in the development of the Buddha legend than Lalitavistara and similar Sanskrit works, even if the latter must be ascribed to an earlier period.

According to the Gandhavaṃsa "History of Books" composed in Burma probably in the 17th century, Buddha is the author of the Jātaka-commentary. If these were correct, he would belong to the 5th century A.D. For although we know very little of this commentator[2] as famous in Ceylon as in Burma, this much

1. „Jāta· "Ed Faūsboll. P. 62.

2. Cf. Bimala Charan Law, "The Life and Work of Buddhaghosa, Calcutta and Simla 1923, (Calcutta Oriental Series, No. 9, B. 3); Max Muller in SBE 10 (I) pp. xii-xxiv; Minayeff, Recherches, 189ff.; Thos. Foulkes in Ind Ant, 19, 1890, p. 105-122 and T. W. Rhys Davids in ERE

we can believe tradition that he lived during the reign of King Mahānāma of Ceylon who ascended the throne in 413 A.D. Although we find this information only in the continuation of the Mahāvaṃsa written about the middle of the 13th century, still it is testified by the fact that a work of Buddhaghosa was translated into Chinese as early as in 489 A.D.[1] And from all these legend-like reports we have about this scholar, this much might be concluded as a historical fact that he studied with great fervour in the first half of the 5th century in the "great cloisters" of Anurādhapura in Ceylon the texts of the Tipiṭaka and the Sinhalese Aṭṭhakathās or "Commentaries" which were preserved there, that as the first fruit of his studies he then wrote a Systematic work on the Visuddhimagga[2], the doctrine of the Buddha, and later on revised the commentaries to the main texts of the Tipiṭaka[3] in the Pāli language. It is

---

II, 885 ff. The "biography" written by the monk Mahāmaṅgala in Burma, perhaps in the 14th century (cf. Geiger, Pāli, Literatur und Spreache" p. 31 para 40) and published by James Gray, Buddhaghosuppti or the Historical Romance of Buddhaghosa, London 1892 is purely legendary.

1. The Chinese translation in the Samantapāsādikā is the earliest work of which it has been proved, that it was translated from Pāli into Chinese. Before this only those Chinese translations were known which were from Sanskrit (J. Takakusu in JRAS 1896, 415 ff.)

2. There is a tradition that he wrote a book (which has not come down to us) Ñāṇodaya ("the dawning of knowledge") and the Atthasālini in India, before departing for Ceylon. If there is any truth in this tradition this aṭṭhasālini could only have been the rough plan of his commentary on the Dhamma Saṅgaṇi; for the Aṭṭhasālinī which has come down to us., presupposes the Vissuddhi-Magga which was written in Ceylon. Cf. Mrs. Rhys Davids, "Buddhist Manual of Psychological Ethics" 2nd Ed., p. xxvii.

3. He tells us himself (introduction to the Samantapāsādikā) that he not only translated the commentaries of the Mahāvira from the Singhalese but compared them with the commentaries of other monasteries, abbreviated and freely revised them. Burlingame (JAOS 38, 1918, 267 f.) pronounces the tradition according to which the Aṭṭha-Kathās were translated from Pāli into Singhalese and translated back again from Singhalese into Pāli by Buddhaghosa and others to be "unreliable and misleading" because Buddhaghosa and the compiler of the commentary on the Dhammapada availed themselvers of common Pāli originals, though independently of each other,

not impossible that as the legend reports he came from a Brahmin family near Bo-Gaya, acquired great Brahminical learning already in his early youth but following a debate he was converted to Buddhism by the monk Revata and was inspired by his master to go to Ceylon to study the Sinhalese commentaries.[1] It is certain that he composed many of the works ascribed to him which made his name so famous that he was considered as the commentator par excellence and later on also commentaries were ascribed to him which were written by some others or which were written by unknown authors. He himself calls himself the author of the Visuddhimagga, of the Samantapāsādika (commentary to the Vinayapiṭaka), of the Sumaṅgalavilāsinī (commentary to the Dīghanikāya),[2] of the Papañcasūdanī (commentary to the Majjhimanikāya), of the Sārathapakāsinī (commentary to the Saṃyuttanikāya) and of the Manorathapuraṇī (commentary to the Aṅguttaranikāya). Moreover, in the Gandhavaṃsa the commentaries Kaṅkhāvitaraṇī (to the Pātimokkhas), Paramatthakathā (to the seven books of the Abhidhammapiṭaka) and the commentaries to the Khuddakapāṭha, to the Dhammapada, to the Suttanipāta, to the Jātaka and to the Apadāna are ascribed to him.[3]

There is scarcely any doubt that Buddhaghosa is also the author of the commentaries on the Abhidhammapiṭaka, or at least of the Atthasālinī (commentary on the Dhamma-Saṅgaṇī) the Sammoha-vinodanī (commentary on the Vibhaṅga) and the commentary on the Paṭṭāna-Pakaraṇa and most likely of the Kaṅkhāvitaraṇī and the Paramattha-Jotikā (commentaries on the Khuddaka-Pāṭha and the Suttanipāta.[4]

---

and because both Dhammapāla and the compiler of the Jātaka commentary copied from Buddhaghosa's commentaries. Nevertheless, it is possible, indeed probable, that the 5th century translators, though translating from the Singhalese, used available Pāli texts as well (eg., of legends and tales).

1. On Buddhaghosa's date and life see Appendix IV.

2. Edited by T. W. Rhys Davids and J. Estlin Charpentier I, London PTS 1886.

3. Gandhāvaṃsa JPTS, 1886 p. 59 f.

4. The Khuddaka-Pāṭha commentary has been proved to be work of Buddhaghosa, by Burlingame in HOS, Vol. 28, p. 51 f. An edition in Siamese characters of all the commentaries of Buddhaghosa (23 vols) and of his

But it is highly improbable[1] that Buddhaghosa was really the author of the commentaries to the Jātaka and to the Dhammapada. Actually in the case of these two works the term "Commentary" is indeed as ill-suited as the expression "author". For in both these works only very little space is taken by the "Commentary", i.e. the grammatical and lexical explanation of the verses, whereas stories—more precisely "sermons" in the form of of stories[2] form the main consitutent. And Buddhaghosa, or whoever it might have been, to whom we owe the Jātakaṭṭhavaṇṇanā and the Dhammapada-commentary, could at best be called the compiler who collected and edited these sermons or stories.

The Dhammapada-commentary[3] constitutes indeed a valuable addition to the Jātaka-commentary and contains like the

Visuddhi-Magga (3 vols) issued by H. H. the Supreme Patriarch of Siam, Prince Vajiryana, in 1920-1922, has been generously presented to scholars by H. R. H. the Prince of Chandaburi. The following commentaries have up to now (1927) been published by the PTS : Samanta-Pāsādika ed. by J. Takakussu assisted by M. Nagai, 1, 1924, II, 1927; Sumaṅgala-Vilāsinī ed. By T. W. Rhys Davids and J. E. Charpenter, I' 1886; Papañcasūdanī ed. by J. H. Woods and D. Kosambi, I, Suttas 1-10, 1922. Manoratha-Pūraṇī I, Eka-Nipāta ed. by Max Walleser, 1924; Paramattha-Jotikā I. Khuddakapāṭha Commentary, ed. by Helmer Smith from a Collation by Mabel Hunt 1915; Paramattha-Jotikā II, Suttanipāta Commentary ed. by Helmer Smith 1916, 1918. Aṭṭhasālinī ed, by Muller, 1897; translated ("The Expositor") by Maung Tin, ed. and revised by Mrs. Rhys Davids, 1920-21; Sammohavinodaṇī, ed. by A.P. Buddhadatta Thera 1923, Commentary to Patthānapakaraṇa in the edition of the Tikapaṭṭhāna by Mrs. Rhys Davids 1921-1923; Puggalapaññatti Aṭṭhakathā ed., by G. Landsberg and Mrs Rhys Davids in JPTS 1913-1914 p. 170 ff.; Kathāvatthuppakaraṇa-Aṭṭhakathā ed. by J. p. Minayeff in JPTS 1889; Yamakappakaraṇātthakathā ed. by Mrs. Rhys Davids in JPTS 1910-1912, p. 51ff. Editions of Buddhaghosa's commentaries have also been published in Ceylon and Burma. See Geiger, "Pāli Literatur und Sprache," p. 19 f., para 22. There is no mention in any Pāli source, of Buddhaghosa's having written a Sanskrit epic Padyacūḍāmaṇī also (see below in the chapter on Buddhist Sanskrit Literature).

1. Cf. Rhys Davids, Buddhist Birth Stories, p. LXIII ff. Burlingame in HOS, Vol. 28, pp. 49, 59., Law, 'Life and work of Buddhaghosa' p. ix f.

2. Both in the Jātaka as well as in the Dhammapada-commentaries the stories as "Dhammadesanā", i. e. "religious teachings" or "Sermons" are made to be narrated by Buddha himself.

3. Edited by H. C. Norman, 5 Vols. (Vol. 5 Indexes by Lakshmaṇa Shastri Tailang) PTS, 1906-1915. Translated (Buddhist legends) by Eugene Watson

latter, many old, popular narrative materials, some of which have crossed the frontiers of India and are known to world-literature. Thus we find here the story of a King of Banaras, who like Harun al Rashid goes about the town in the night, and the tale of "Doctor All-knowing" etc. Here we find also the famous story of Kisā-Gotamī, the mother who, with her dead child in her arms, wanders about desparately and comes to Buddha who tells her he can bring her child back to life if she bring to him a mustard corn; but this mustard corn must be brought from a house in which there has never been a death. In vain does the mother wander from house to house until she at last realises that the Lord wanted only to teach her the great truth about the law of death, and consoled thus, she joins the community of the Buddha. The legend proves itself to be truly Indian even by the fact that it belongs to the type of the "Consolation-stories." Hence if we find a similar anecdote in the Alexander-saga in some versions of the Pseudo-callisthenics as well as in Arabic, Jewish, Persian and Coptic stories about Alexander—then it is more probable that the Buddhistic legend has influenced the Greek saga than that as Rohde thinks, it has originated on Greek soil.[1] But when we read in the novel of Udena and Vāsuladatta,[2] how King Pajjota, in order to

---

Burlingame with important introduction in HOD Vols. 28-30, Cambridge, Mass, 1921. Extracts have been edited by V. Faūsboll in his edition of the Dhammapada (Hauniae 1885). Selections of tales have been translated by Warren, "Buddhism in Translations", p. 222 ff., 264 ff., 380ff, 430 ff. 451 ff., into French by L. De La Vallée Poussin and G. de Blonay in RHR 26, 1892, 180 ff., 29, 1894, 195 ff., 329 ff., from a Burmese version by T. Rogers, "Buddhaghosa's Parables", London 1870. Cf. Burlingame, "Buddhaghosa's Dhammapada Commentary and the Titles of its three hundred and ten Stories, together with an Index thereto and an Analysis of Vaggas I-IV," in Proceedings of the American Academy of Arts and Sciences Vol. 45, 1910, pp. 467-550. On the subject matter and motifs of the stories s. Burlingame in HOS Vol. 28, p. 29 ff.

1. The story is told in connection with Dhammapada 114, Ed. Norman II, 272 ff translation Burlingame in HOS, Vol, 29, p. 257 ff. Cf. E. Rhode in "Verhandlugen der 30, Versammlung deutscher Philologen und Schulmänner zu Rostock", 1875, p. 68 f J. H. Theisen, "Die Legende von Kisāgotami," Breslau, 1880, and above Vol. I, 380 f., 397 f, Vol. II, p. 137.

2. "Udānavatthu on Dhammapada," 21-23 ed. Norman I, 161-231 transl. Burlingame in HOS, Vol. 28, 62 f, 247 ff. Cf. A. Weber, "Indische Streifen," I, 370, note and III, 16, and Rhys Davids, "Buddhist India", p.4ff.

trap Udena and get him under his control, ordered a wooden elephant to be made, in which he had hidden 60 warriors, then we see in this rather an echo of the saga of the Trojan horse which has penetrated as far as India.

The plan of the work is as follows: In the case of every verse or group of verses it is said that the master has delivered "this sermon" (dhammadesanā)—the verse or the group of verses along with the story is meant thereby—at such and such place and with reference to such and such person or persons or incident. This is then followed by the story which ends with the verse or verses which are then explained word for word. All these story, verses and word-explanations are made to be said by Buddha himself. In conclusion it is said then usually that after this sermon or after these Gāthās a person occurring in this story or "many" or "hundred thousand" persons (or monks) entered the path of sacredness or attained a higher level of sacredness. Often also regular Jātakas are introduced or joined in which there are reports of the deeds or destinies of the heroes of the story in an earlier birth. The stories themselves are of varied nature. Beside regular long stories told with elaboration we find short edifying legends which have been only invented in a sober, simple way only for explaining a verse and on the other hand also highly interesting tales and stories drawn from the sources of popular literature. The chief doctrine which the stories want to drive home is that of karman. Characteristic is the story of Moggallāna's death which is also of interest because like some other stories of the Dhammapada it points to a very antagonistic attitude to the "nude asceties", i.e. the Jaina monks.[1]

A sarcastic remark against the "nude ascetics" is also contained in the story of Visākhā[2] which is interesting in many respects, but whose moral culminates in only this that this rich and pious lay follower is blessed with great wealth because in an earlier birth she has venerated the Buddha of those times and that even in her new existence she acquires a good karman by utilising

1. On Dhammapada 137, Translated by Warren ibid 221 ff., Ed. Norman, III, 65 ff, tranal. Burlingame, HOS 29, 304 ff.

2. On Dhammapada 53, Cf. Warren, ibid 451 ff., Ed. Norman, I, 384ff.; transl. Burlingame. HOS 29. 59 ff.

her wealth for making great gifts to the community of Buddhistic monks. Some of the stories are only versions of those which already occur in the books of the Tipiṭaka. Thus for example the story of the Godhika[1] the holyman, who cuts his throat in order to dive into Nirvāṇa, whereupon Māra seeks in vain for a trace of his, only a slightly deviated form of the legend told in the Saṃyuttanikāya.[2] But that in this collection, just as in the Jātaka book, sometimes humour also gets its due share, is proved by the fable of the stubborn donkey[3] told in the form of a Jātaka, whose contents may be given here briefly.

A merchant goes with an ass from Banaras to Taxila in order to sell earthen ware. While the man is selling his goods the ass is grazing outside the town. There he chats with a she-ass, who however pities him that he has to carry such heavy loads for many miles and has got nobody who would massage his legs and back when he comes home. By these speeches the ass becomes obstinate and refuses to go back to Banaras. Even the threats with the whip prove of no avail. At last his master sees the she-ass and guesses that she is responsible for the obstinacy of the ass and he resolves to bait him through the eternal female. He promises him to provide a pretty she-ass as his wife. Highly pleased the ass trots home willingly. But after a few days he reminds his master of his promise. The latter says, "I will not break the word that I have given you, I shall get a wife for you, about food I can give only for you, whether that will be sufficient for you or not when you are two, you alone must know, through the cohabitation of you both, children also will be born, whether that will be sufficient for you all or not when you are so many, you alone must know." Hardly had the master ended his words than the ass lost all the desire for a spouse. Quite a number of stories in this commentary on the Dhammapada have their parallels in the commentaries of Buddhaghosa, and over 50 stories are common to the commentaries on the Dhammapada and Jātaka respectively. In some cases there is a word

1. On Dhammapada 57, Cf. Warren ibid 380 ff., Ed. Norman, I, 431ff.; transl. Burlingame, HOS 29, 90ff.

2. IV, 3,3, translated by Windisch, Māra and Buddha, p. 113 ff.

3. On Dhammapada 13 f (Ed. Norman I, p. 123 ff), transl. Burlingame, HOS 28, 224 f.

for word identity, in others we find varying versions of the Jātaka tales. The commentaries of Dhammapāla have borrowed about 25 stories from the commentary on the Dhammapada[1] There is of course, also the possibility that all these commentaries did not copy from one another, but made use of common sources. Burlingame, however, has succeded in making it appear fairly likely that the Jātaka commentary is later than the commentaries of Buddhaghosa, the commentary on the Dhammapada is later than that on the Jātaka, and that those of Dhammapāla are still later. Nevertheless, it is probable that none of these commentaries was separated from the rest by any very cousiderable period of time.[2]

In the authentic commentaries of Buddhaghosa, too similes and parables and valuable traditions and tales occur frequently, as for instance in the Aṭṭhasālinī,[3] the Papañcaspandanī,[4] Sumaṅgalavilāsinī[5] and especially in the Manoratha-pūraṇī.

The Sumaṅgalavilāsinī contains in the commentary to Brahmajālasutta a remarkable report on the daily life of Buddha. Here Buddha appears on one hand already as a kind of demigod like in the Mahāyanasūtras when he starts on his begging rounds, gentle winds clean the floor before him, clouds wipe off the dust with a light shower and spread over his head like a canopy, uneven place become level. and lotus flowers sprout up under his foot-steps, rays in six colours emanate from his body etc. but on the other hand he leads completely the life of men-

1. Burlingame, HOS 28, 45 ff.

2. Burlingame l. c. p. 57 f., dates Buddhaghosa's commentaries as 410-432 the Jātaka commentary somewhat later, the Dhammapada commentary about 450 and Dhammapāla's commentaries towards the close of the 5th century (s. Appendix IV) the other commentaries would have to be placed in the 6th century.

3. Parables of the man who sleeps beneath a mango tree with his head covered up, of the blind and the lame man, and others in Atthasālinī, ed. Muller pp. 271 ff, 279 ff translation ("The Expositor") p. 359, 367 ff, 555.

4. Tales, eg. I, pp. 201, 230 f. Three tales from the commentary on the Upāli-Sutta (Majjhimanikāya 56) translated into French by L. Feer in RHR, 13, 1886, p. 77 ff and JA 1887 ser, 8, t. IX, p. 309 ff.

5. Cf the parables in the commentary to Dīghanikāya 22, s. Warren, "Buddhism in Translations" p. 353 ff.

dicant monk[1]. Stories of the doctor Jīvaka are woven into the commentary to the Sāmaññaphalasutta (I, p. 132 ff). And in the commentary to the Ambaṭṭhasutta (I,p.259 ff) we find the family saga of the Sakyas and the Koliyas which is of extraordinary interest to the cultural history of the century. The following may be given as an extract:-

The princes of the House of Ikṣvāku (Pāli Okkaka), who had built Kapilavatthu, are so proud that they do not find any princes who would be worthy of marrying their sisters. Out of fear from degrading their family they therefore installed their eldest sister as their mother and cohabited with the remaining sisters. Then the eldest sister has an attack of leprosy, she is brought into the forest and put in a pit. At the same time Rāma, a king of Banaras also has an attack of leprosy and goes into the forest after leaving the kingdom to his eldest son. In the forest he cures himself by means of herbs and takes up residence in the cavity of a tree. One day a tiger comes to the pit where the the princess is living. She raises a cry of alarm. King Rāma hears this and goes to the pit. He wants to pull her out, but in spite of her misery she is so proud that she lets herself be pulled out by him only after he has explained that he too is of royal blood. Then he cures her and makes her his wife. However, he does not go back to his country, but he builds a town for himself in the forest. With the Sākya princess he begets many sons. As these sons grew up their mother sent them Kapilavatthu so that there they might take the daughters of their maternal uncles as wives. They go there and rob the princesses. As the Sākyas hear that the robbers of their daughters are their relatives, they do not have anything against that. Thus was born the clan of the Koliyas[2]).

Buddhaghosa's commentary to the Aṅguttaranikāya, the Manorathapūraṇi contains about a hundred legends. Among

1. Sumaṅgalavilāsinī I, p. 45 ff; Warren, Buddhism in Translations, p. 91 ff.

2. The same saga is also told in the Paramatthajotikā, the commentary to the Suttanipāta, and from this text conveyed by Fausboll, it has been translated into German by A. Weber (Ind. Stud. V, 412-437, Ind. Strefen I, 233-244)

them we find for example 13 extremely interesting stories from the life of the Therīs, the early women-disciples of Buddha, which are very valuable to us as additions to the Therīgāthās.[1] The wreath of legends with which the Buddhistic narrators have surrounded their female saints certainly throws some light on the real life and feelings of those women who gave up the world in order to follow Buddha. The section begins with the life-story of the Mahāpajāpati Gotamī, the aunt and foster-mother of Buddha who became the first nun. Her story is of course told already in the Vinayapiṭaka. After this story which gives the impression of a true happening, follows the wonderful legend of Khemā the queen, proud of her beauty, who does not even take cognizance of the existence of Buddha for a long time; but one day Buddha makes appear before her the phantom of a charming, beautiful goddess who, before her eyes, becomes older and older until she stands before her as an infirm old woman and at last falls down dead; then Khemā too is reminded ofher impending fate and begs the king for permission to enter the community of the nuns.

Another one, Uppalavaṇṇā, is so marvellously beautiful that the princes of the whole of India want to marry her, and the father is greatly embarrassed, and the daughter solves the problem by becoming a nun. The legend of Kisā-Gotamī and of the mustard-corn comes here again. Most touching of all is the story of Paṭācārā whose contents may be retold here in short.

Paṭācārā is the daughter of a rich merchant in Sāvathi. She falls in love with a worker employed in her house and allows him to seduce her. After becoming pregnant she would like to come back to her parents. The husband agrees, but puts off the departure from day to day, until at last she departs alone. He follows her and joins her just at the moment when, having pains on the way, she gives birth to a child. Then they come back to their house. The same thing is repeated at the birth of their second child. But while she delivers the child on the way

1. Some of these have been translated by Burlingame, "Buddhist Parables" Chapter. IX.

2. Cf. Mable Bode, Women Leaders of the Buddhist Reformation in JRAS 1893, pp. 517-566.

there is a big storm. Her husband makes a protective roof for her with twigs of trees. While he is cutting grass to cover it, he is bitten by a snake and dies. The sorrowing mother continues her journey with her two childern. She comes to a river which she cannot cross with both her children at the same time. So she leaves back the older boy on the bank, carries the younger one to the other bank, lays him down and comes back to the older boy. While she is in midstream a hawk comes flying to the younger child. She raises her hands to scare away the hawk. This the older boy sees who thinks that his mother is signing him to come to her. So he gets into the water and is washed away. In the meantime the hawk has flown away carrying the younger child.[1] Full of grief the woman continues her journey to Sāvatthī. Arriving there she learns that her parental home has been destroyed by a cyclonic storm and that her parents have died. They are just about to be burnt on the pyre. The wretched woman breaks out wailing and lamenting, tears her clothes from off her body and wanders about for many days naked and mad. One day at last she comes across Buddha who is just preaching. And the Lord lets his feeling of benevolence flow on her and says, "Sister, come back to your senses.: Sister, come back to your senses." As soon as she hears the words of the Lord she is overwhelmed with the feeling of shame. A man throws a piece of clothing at her and she covers herself. Through one verse of Buddha she is fully converted and she has become later one of the most highly esteemed nuns of the community.[2]

In some of these stories we find motifs of fairytales which belong to the common property of world literature, whether they have wandered out of India or they have been taken over by Indians from foreigners. Thus Uppalavaṇṇa was in earlier birth the Buddhist narrators are never content with describing the events in the life of their saints only in their last

1. In the Zeitschift fur Volkskunde S. Singer has pointed to a similar episode in a poem of Guillaume d' Angletere in Old French (ZVV 4, 1894, p. 73) Cf. W. Bousset and W. Meyer in NGGW 1916, 501 ff 768 ff., 1917, 80 ff, 703 ff.

2. Text ed.,, Wallesser, l. p. 356 fl. transl. Burlingame, Buddhist Parables," p. 94 ff.

birth the girl Padumāvatī born from a lotus-bud. When she walked, lotus flowers sprouted under her footsteps. As she is the favourite queen of the king of Banaras her co-wives became jealous of her. When the king is away fighting a battle they rob her of her new born babies in whose place they place a bloody block of wood. On his return from the battle-field the King is told that Padumāvatī is a monster and has given birth to a block of wood. She is driven away, but soon the babies who have been put in a wooden box are fished out and the truth is discovered. Similar stories are current in the literature of these fairy tales of cast and west.[1] At another place of the Manorathapūraṇī we find the story of Ghosaka the merchant. This story appearing again and again in India and wide-spread in the whole world, tells of a boy of poor circumstances but born under a lucky star who, in spite of all attacks on his life, at last attains a high position through the help of young girl who falls in love with him and replaces a letter which is meant to bring death upon him with another letter by which his marriage with herself is brought about. A second attack on the life of the young man is foiled like in Schiller's ballad of "Gang nach dem Eisenhammer", by making the abettor of the murder of his son die[2] in accordance with the proverb "The biter will be bitten"

1. The same story is also found in the Therīgāthā-commentary. Cf. Ed. Muller in the Archiv fur Religionswissenschaft III, 1900, 217 ff.

2. The story is also found with the Buddhists in the Dhammapada-commentary, see E. Hardy in JRAS 1898, 741 ff; with the Jainas in Campakaśreṣṭhikathānaka (A. Weber in SBA 1883, p. 567 ff) and in the Kathākośa (translated by CH. Tawney, London 1895, p. 169 ff); also in the Brahminical Jaimini Bhārata, see Weber in the Monatsber. der Berliner Akademi 1869, p. 14 ff, who has already pointed to the numerous parallels in the fairy-tale literatures of Orient and of Occident, where however often only one of the two motifs occurs which are combined here, either only that of the lucky child and the replaced Uria's letter (for example in the legend of the birth of Henry III in Grimm, Deutsche Sagen II, No. 480 and Gesta Romanorum, Kap 20 and in Grimm's "Kinder und Hausmärchen 29) or only the Fridolin-motif ("Gang nach dem Eisenhammer "and its French source). Also in the Indian Kathāsaritsāgara (XX, 194 ff) we find only the second motif Cf. also Benfey, Pantschatantra I, 321; E. Kuhn in Byzantin, Zeitschr, IV, 242 ff. The Buddhistic story in Chinese version by Chavannes, "Cinq Cents Contes et apologues, t I, No. 45.

The majority of the stories are however, only edifying stories. One of those, for example, tells of a merchant whom Māra in the guise of Buddha tempts in order to teach him a false doctrine, but the merchant recognises him as Māra, since Buddha cannot have taught something like that.[1]

In his commentaries Buddhaghosa makes frequent reference to his Visuddhi-Magga and in the introductions to some of them,[2] he states expressely that he does not wish to repeat anything which has already been explained in that work. It would seem, therefore, that Buddhaghosa regarded the Visuddhi-Magga[3] or "The Path to Complete Purification," as a preparation for his commentatorial labours. The author himself explains the title of the the work, when he says : Visuddhi here means the Nirvāṇa which is wholly and thoroughly purified, and freed from dirt of every description and the path which leads to this purification is called Visuddhi Magga. He says that it is his intention to expound this "Path to Complete Purification" in accordance with the teachings of the Mahāvihāra, i.e. the traditions preserved in the "great monastery" of Anurādhapura. For the present, however, it is impossible for us to decide whether he had some definite work before him, which he merely revised[4] or whether

1. E. Hardy (in JRAS 1902, 951 ff) compares with it a Christian legend in which Satan assumes the form of Christ in order to teach a false doctrine to a monk, and Garbe (Indien und das Christentum, p. III f) holds that the Christian legend is Buddhist in origin. However, the resemblance seems not very striking.

2. To Atthasālini, Papañcasūdani, and Manorathapūraṇi.

3. Edited by C. A. F. Rhys Davids, 2 vols. PTS 1920-21 A short table of contents by J. E. Charpenter in JPTS 1890, p. 14 ff, a detailed analysis and considerable extracts in English translation by H. C. Warren in JPTS 1891-1893 pp, 76-164 and "Buddhism in Translations", pp. 285, ff 291 ff, 315 ff 376 ff, 384 ff. Bhikku Nyānatiloka has translated "The Reflection on Death" from Chapter 8 into German in ZB VII, 1926 p. 75 ff Cf. Law, "Life and work of Buddhaghosa," p. 70 ff. "Buddhaghosa's monumental work, the Visuddhimagga ('The Path of Purity'), is an anthological Aṭṭhakathā and forms an indispensable text book in Burma" (Shwe Zan Aung in JPTS 1910-1912. p. 121)

4. If we are to believe the Japanese scholar M. Nagai (JPTS 1917-1919, p. 69 ff), the Visuddhi-Magga is not the work of Buddhaghosa, but merely the revised version of a work written by a Thera Upatissa in the first century A. D. entitled Vimuttimagga, "The Path of Release," which was translated

we should give him credit for being the first to offer a systematic presentation of the entire doctrine of Buddha, on the basis of interpretations and explanations which had been handed down in the Mahāvihāra. Should the latter theory be correct, the clear, and systematic arrangement and classification of the subject matter according to the three points of view, morals (sīla) meditation (samādhi) and wisdom (paññā), would be his own work, whilst generally he was content to collect together with great diligence and industry, all that had accumulated during the course of the centuries, by way of explanation of the doctrine and legendary traditions. His style is clear and lucid, and, as in his commentaries, in the Visuddhi-Magga, too, he frequently, enlivens the dry elucidations by occasional parables and often by legends too. These last are not his own inventions, but he must have taken them from older sources. In style and contents, some of these legends are strongly reminiscent of the Tipiṭaka, and some do actually occur in canonical texts while most of the narratives, it is true, date from a later period when Buddha worship was just as highly developed in the Hīnayāna as in the Mahāyāna. It is the spirit of the old Arhat ideal as it is illustrated, for instance, in the prose of the Udāna, by many legends; the same spirit is also found in narratives such as the legend of the Thera Mahā-Tissa, who is reminded of the impurity of the human body by the sight of the teeth of the beautiful woman while laughing, and by this thought, attains to the highest stage of holiness; that of an Arhat;[1] or that of the monk who lived for sixty years in his hermitage without noticing that the walls were covered with paintings; or of the monk who is so unworldly that for three months he goes daily begging for food and eating it in the house of his mother who is longing

---

into Chinese between 505 and 520 A.D. by the Cambodian monk Saṅghapāla. Though very ingenious, the arguments of Nagai are not convincing. Until we are better acquainted with the Chinese translation of this work, it appears to be quite possible, that it is merely a Chinese version of Buddhaghosa's work. According to Nagai himself, the contents of the Chinese Vimuttimagga bear a general resemblance to the Visuddhi-Magga but are not free from Mahāyāna influence (l. c, p. 79). Like "visuddhi" the word "vimutti" also means "Nirvāṇa".

1. Edition Mrs. Rhys Davids I, p. 20 f; Warren, "Buddhism in Translations" p. 297 f.

to see him but does not recognise him in his monk's robe, without once saying: "I am your son, and you are my mother."[1] On the other hand, we find, especially in Part II, many legends which testify to a Buddha-worship recall the Kṛṣṇa-Bhakti. For example, a frog hears the voicc of Buddha who is preaching on the bank of the river, listens and being trodden on by a shepherd, is literally transported to a better world; for he is immediately reborn as a god in a golden palace in the heaven of the thirty-three gods.[2] In this work we also find numerous miracle-tales intended to show how saints attain miraculous and magic powers by meditation. A monk rescues a snake which is fleeing from a bird; he does this by quickly creating a hill, in which the snake disappears. The monk Bakkula is swallowed by fish, but remains safe and sound, as he is destined to become an Arhat. Sañjīva was in the state of utter absorption, was taken for dead and laid on the pyre, but the flames could not burn him. The nun Uttarā, absorbed in meditation, was not even injured by boiling oil. The snake Nandopanandā had wound herself around tne mount Meru and stretched her heads up to the second heaven, then the holy Moggallāna came, transformed himself into a still larger snake, wound himself around Nandopanandā and crushed her and the mount Meru in the bargain. Chapter 13[3] gives a long and circumstantial account of the ages of the world and the destruction and restoration of the worlds, reminiscent of the Purāṇas—fancies, which would scarcely have come from Buddhaghosa's brain, but are most likely faithful reproductions of earlier traditions.

As far as the dogmatical and philosophical contents of the Visuddhi-Magga and the commentaries are concerned, it is surely an exaggeration to set Buddhaghosa up as a philosopher who cut out new paths and made an original contribution to Buddhistic philosophy.[4] He was a man of astonishing erudition and of most extensive reading who to this day enjoys a well merited reputation among the Buddhists of Ceylon, Burma and

1. Ed. Mrs. Rhys Davids I, 91 ff; Warren l. c. p. 434 ff.
2. Ed. Mrs. Rhys Davids I, 208 f; Warren l. c. p. 301 f.
3. Ed. Mrs. Rhys Davids, II, 411 ff.; Warren l. c. p. 315 ff.
4. R. Ch. Law, l. c. 135 ff.

Siam, but it is going too far to call him "a great teacher of mankind."[1] There is a difference of opinion as to how far he is reliable in his commentaries as an expounder of the canonical texts. K.E. Neumann says on one occasion: "The moment the Buddhist patres ecclesiae and doctores profundi try their hand at elucidating profound and obscure passages in the canon they simply talk moonshine."[2] We cannot follow them blindly, and yet, on the other hand, we must admit, that they do help us over difficulties and if we neglected them, we should be depriving ourselves of one of the means of explanation.[3] Mrs. Rhys Davids appears to be right when she says: "Buddhaghosa's philology is doubtless crude and he is apt to leave cruces unexplained, concerning which an Occidental is most in the dark. Nevertheless his work appears to be not only suggestive, but also a mine of historic interest. To put it aside is to lose the historical perspective of the course of Buddhist philosophy."[4] Even if Buddhaghosa had no original contribution to make, we should yet be indebted to him for his faithful preservation of ancient traditions.

Not long after Buddhaghosa, Dhammapāla wrote his commentary Paramattha-Dīpanī, "Elucidation of the True Meaning," on those texts of the Khuddakanikāya which Buddhaghosa had not explained: "the Itivuttaka, Udāna, Cariyāpiṭaka, Thera-Gāthā, Vimāna-Vatthu and Peta-Vatthu.[5] Padaratittha on the southern coast of India nearest Ceylon, is mentioned as his native town, but in any case he must have studied at Anurādhapura too; for, like Buddhaghosa, he refers to the Aṭṭha-Kathās of the "great monastery" of Anurādhapura. Moreover, both commentators have similar conceptions throughout and follow the same method

1. B. Ch. Law, l. c. 174.

2. Reden Gotamo Buddho's aus der mittleren Sammlung I, 1896, Preface.

3. Cf. what has been said on Sāyaṇa in Vol. I.

4. A Buddhist manual of psycholc gical ethics, 2nd ed., p. xxxi.

5. This is the order in which they are enumerated in the Sāsanāṃsa (ed. by M. Bode PTS 1897) p. 33 where the commentary on the Netti is also ascribed so him. The following parts of the Paramāttha-Dipanī have up to now been published by the PTS: The commentaries on the Peta-Vatthu ed. by E. Hardy 1894; on the Vimāna Vatthu, ed. by E. Hardy, 1901; on the Therigāthā ed. by E. Muller, 1893; On the Udāna by F. L. Woodward, 1926.

of explanation. For this reason, it is impossible that any considerable period of time could have elapsed between these two.[1] In the commentary on Therī-Gāthās we find a few legends about Theris which are also to be found in the Manoratha pūraṇī; portions of the Therī-Apādāna are included in this commentry, and it contains some traditions which are certainly very old. The legend of Bhaddā-Kuṇḍalakesā, for example, is reminiscent of conditions such as we imagine must have been prevalent at the time of the Buddha and his first disciples when the adherents of various sects travelled about from place to place in order to challenge scholars and ascetics to philosophical contests:

Bhaddā is the daughter of the royal treasurer. One day she sees a robber who is being taken for being hanged, and she falls in love with him. Her father manages, through bribing, to get the robber released in order to get him married to his daughter. The robber however is interested only in the jewels of the girl. He takes her to a lonely place to rob her. But she sees his intention and while pretending to embrace him she pushes him down a precipice. After this adventure, however, she does not like to go back to her father's house but becomes a jaina-ascetic. Nevertheless she is not satisfied with the teachings of the Jainas and goes therefore to places where famous scholars live, in order to debate with them. But as she does not find any one who could match her in disputation, she goes from place to place and at the entrance to every village and every town she places a twig of a rose-apple on a heap of sand telling the children, "If any one wants to enter into a dialogue with me he shall trample this twig." The children were to report to her if it happened. If the twig stood upright even after one week, she took it and continued wandering. In this way she comes to Sāvatthī also where the

---

1. On Dhammapāla cf. T. W. Rhys Davids in ERE Vol. 4 p. 701 f.; Gandhavaṃsa in JPTS 1816, pp. 57, 60; Burlingame in HOS Vol. 28 p. 56 f. Law, "Life and work of Buddhaghosa", p. 101 ff. The Dhammapāla who wrote commentaries on the Visuddhi-Magga and on the Dīgha., Majjhima-, and Saṃyuttanikāyas (Sāsanavaṃsa, p. 33) is probably a different man. At all events, the Dhammapāla with whom we are concerned is not the same as the Dharmapāla, who lived in the monastery of Nalanda, and was the teacher of Hsuan Tsang; s. Hardy in ZDMG 51, 1897, 105 ff.

great Sāriputta enters into a debate with her and converts her into Buddhism. Buddha himself consecrates her as nun.[1]

Although some of these stories may be beautiful (and the commentary may be valuable because it quotes many texts of the Apādānas, yet the stories are often also very stupid, very often they are made up only of old verses and sometimes so factual and tasteless that compared with the Therīgāthā-verses they work like only a cold-shower.

The commentaries to the Petavatthu and to the Vimānavatthu[2] are, like the Jātaka commentary and the Dhammapada-commentary[3] arranged by the fact that they explain and enlarge the verses through long-winded stories in prose. There are several valuable legends among them. We find a few interesting Consolatory Stories in the commentary on the Peta-Vatthu.[4]

In some cases the stories in the commentary on the Vimāna-Vatthu are even of greater value than those in the Vimāna-Vatthu itself. As regards Dhammapāla as a commentator what has been said of Buddhaghosa might be applied to him also.[5]

The work of the monks in the cloisters of Ceylon did not stop, however, with the collection of legends and the explanation and interpretation of canonical texts, but they also began very early to record as a chronicle also the chief events in the history of the community of Buddhist monks. Indeed even the report on the councils in the Cullavagga of the Vinayapiṭaka reveals a historical interest as also the representation of the sects and schools in the Kathāvatthu. And the commentary to the latter[6]

1. Therīgāthā-commentary, p. 107 ff. Cf. Mrs. Rhys Davids, Psalms of the Sisters, p. 63 ff where also many other stories from the Therīgāthā-commentary find a place and also Maria E. Lulius van Goor, "De buddhistische Non", p. 142ff. The same story also in the "Manorathapūraṇī" translated by Burlingame, "Buddhist Parables". p. 151 ff.

2. Edited by. E. Hardy, London PTS 1894 and 1901.

3. This is quoted in the Vimānavatthu commentary, p. 165, and must therefore be in any case older.

4. Legends from the Petta-Vatthu Commentary have been translated by B. Ch. Law, "The Buddhist Conception of Spirits," 1923. For the Consolatory Stories (Law l. c., 29 ff., 33, 64 ff.) cf. above Vol. I, pp. 380 f., 398 ff.

5. Cf. Mrs. Rhys Davids, "Psalms of the Sisters," p. xvi f.

6. Buddhaghosa is not mentioned as the author, either at the beginning or in the colophons of the Commentary. At the beginning, a long passage is cited word for word from the Dīpavaṃsa (ed. Oldeberg p. 36).

in particular is of very great importance for the history of sect divisions of the oldest Buddhists' community. But even those Sinhalese Aṭṭhakathās mentioned already quite often which had been fervently studied by Buddhaghosa and also used by Dhammapāla, contained sections on ecclesiastical history. These constituted presumably the introduction to the Aṭṭhakathās which treated the Vinaya. Buddhaghosa followed them and drew from them when he prefaced his Samantapāsādikā, the commentary to the Vinayapiṭaka by a historical introduction.[1] But they also formed the basis for the historical and epic Pāli poetry of Ceylon. For not only as actual works of history but also as "historical poetry" can we term the Pāli chronicles of Ceylon, Dīpavaṃsa and Mahāvaṃsa.[2]

Indians have never made any distinction between saga, legend and history and writing of history was in India always a kind of epic poetry. Thus for the Buddhists, all legends on the Buddhas of earlier times and the earlier births of Gotama Buddha in the Buddhavaṃsa,[3] in the Cariyāpiṭaka and the Jātaka-book are also history just like the whole Buddha legend. As per the pattern and model of this legend-poetry and connected with them the monks of Ceylon also narrated in the histori-

1. Published by Oldenberg in his edition of the Vinayapiṭaka, Vol. III, 281 ff.

2. The Dipavaṃsa, edited and translated by H. Oldenberg, London 1879. The Mahāvaṃsa was first published and translated by G. Turnour (Vol. I containing the first 38 chapters) in 1837 and the translation again printed in The Mahāvaṃsa, Part II, translated by L. C. Wijesiṃha, Colombo 1889. We owe the first critical edition to Wilk. Geiger, London PTS 1908, Also an English translation of the Mahāvaṃsa (London PTS 1912) by the same author has appeared now. Cf. H. Jacobi in GGA 1880, 851 ff; W. Geiger, Dīpavaṃsa and Mahāvaṃsa und die geschichtliche Uberlieferung in Ceylon, Leipzig 1905 and ZDMG 63, 1909, 540 ff against R. O. Franke, Lit. Zentralblatt 1906, Sp. 1272 ff.; WZKM 21, 1907, 203 ff; 317 ff. Cf. also Oldenberg, Aus dem alten Indien, Berlin 1910, 69 ff.

3. The title means "Story of Buddha". For the Pāli word Vaṃsa (Sanskrit vaṁśa) means "genealogy, generation, order", hence also the "chronicle" or the "story" of a house, a dynasty, an order of teachings etc., and hence in general a "history" going back to the earliest beginnings in titles like Buddhavaṃsa, Dīpavaṃsa, Mahāvaṃsa, Thūpavaṃsa, Dāṭhāvaṃsa etc., as also in the Sanskrit titles of Harivaṃśa, Raghuvaṃśa, etc.

cal sections of the Aṭṭhakathās the story of the introduction of Buddhism into the island. They invented stories[1] which were supposed to connect the Buddhist community of Ceylon not only with that of India but also with Buddha himself—edifying stories in which it was narrated how the Enlighted One visited the island inhabited in those days only by demons and serpent-deities by flying there accompanied by gods in order to make the light of his doctrine radiate and prepare the future grandeur of the church of Ceylon. To the pious legends of this nature were added saga-like reports on the earliest kings of Ceylon and further quasi-historical informations on Aśoka, Mahinda, the councils and the conveyance of the sacred texts to the island. As these recordings approached historical times more and more, really historical informations began to dominate more and more, but the legendary character of the works never retreated to the background completely. Only, to the ecclesiastical traditions were added also popular, worldly stories and anecdotes.[2] Thus the historical sections of the Aṭṭhakathās, which of course have been lost, but whose contents described here can be understood from the Pāli chronicles and Pāli commentaries, became collecting centres for spiritual and worldly traditions of all kinds as well as for actually historical informations.

The first attempt, although yet very imperfect, to shape into an epic the traditions stored up in the Sinhalese Aṭṭhakathās, is found in the Dīpavaṃsa, the "History of the Island". The author, whose name has not been told, but who has written his work probably between the beginning of the 4th and the first third of the fifth century A.D.[3] reveals himself as lacking in skill in the use of language and prosody. Numerous are the violations of the rules of grammar and metre. We see that for the Cey-

---

1. But only some stories are inventions of the Singhalese monks. To a great extent the historical as well as legendary traditions of the Aṭṭhakathās go back to Indian sources (s. above p. 179) Sten Konow (in "Festgabe Garbe" p. 33 ff) has shown this with regard to certain narratives (Dīpavaṃsa XVII) Mahāvaṁsa which a priori would have been considered to be Singhalese in origin.

2. For the same reason for which also so many worldly stories found access into the Jātakas and the commentaries in general.

3. Oldenberg, Dīpavaṃsa, Intro. p. 8 f.

lonese, it is still an unusual thing to write Pāli verses. He follows like a slave the models before him. His verses are hammered into shape depending on his memory of the Tipiṭaka, especially of the Buddhavaṃsa, Cariyāpiṭaka and Jātaka.[1] But his main source for the material was the historical section of the Aṭṭhakathā[2] preserved in the "great cloister" of Anurādhapura, although he might have used one or two other Aṭṭhakathās in addition to this. Hence, it is perhaps that quite often the same object is treated twice or thrice in different versions. Thus immediately after a short and more sketchy report on the three councils we have a more complete, a more even report. In such cases an interpolation is out of question, but the author has found several versions and as he considered them all of equal value, has transmitted them further. Naturally a poet would not have done that. But even otherwise the composition is as imperfect as language and metre. The narrator jumps abruptly from one theme to another. Often the description is also incomplete. Some episodes are treated like ballads while others are only almost hinted at. Indeed in individual cases we find only memorial verses in which the main points of story or description are enumerated in catch-words. Evidently there were such verses in the Aṭṭhakathās where it was left to the reciters to do wellknown scenes by themselves. On many occasions the method of the primitive epic[3] is followed and speech and counter-speech are arranged one after another. In some cases it follows from the context who the speaker is, as it

---

1. This has been proved very well by Franke in WZKM 21, 1907, 203ff, however only for the forms. Of the material he could take only the least part from the Tripiṭaka as this does not tell anything about Ceylon. Cf. Geiger, ZDMG 63, 1909, 543.

2. This section of the Aṭṭhakathā which was also a source of the Mahāvaṃsa, is quoted in the commentary to the latter as Sihalaṭṭhakathā-Mahāvaṃsa i. e. the great history (of the island of Ceylon) belonging to the Sinhalese commentary and is termed even in the proemion of the Mahāvaṃsa as "the (Mahāvaṃsa) composed by the ancients", According to Geiger Dīp. and Mah., p. 71 it was an independent work of chronicle, according to Oldenberg (Dīpavaṃsa, Introd. p.4) with whom we have to agree, a historical introduction to a theological commentary.

3. Cf. Volume I, p. 303.

happens so often in the case of the ancient ballads. But sometimes we must presume that the reciter established the relationship between the speeches through connecting prose narratives. In this also the author perhaps followed only his models which were meant to be delivered by monks when people assembled in large numbers.[1]

While the Dīpavaṁsa is thus connected closely with its sources even in its form, and represents only a feeble attempt to write an epic, the Mahāvaṃsa probably the work of a poet Mahāmātra who has lived in the last quarter of the 5th century A.D.[2] is already a completed epic. The poet wanted to write a work of art, a kāvya and makes this remark expressly in the proemion with which he prefaces his work. He says that the historical work that the ancients have written[3] is in some places too extensive and again at other places too short and contains also many repetitions. He says he has avoided these mistakes and endeavoured to present the material that he has received transmitted in such an easily understandable way that it causes feelings of joy or sorrow at the appropriate places. In the Mahāvaṃśa not only language and prosody are employed indeed with great skill-which perhaps lies not only in the talent of the poet but is perhaps also due to the fact that the literary activity of Buddha

1. At two places, IV, 47 and XII, 30-33, we also find prose and verse mixed as we have to presume in the case of the Aṭṭhakathā.

2. This follows with a high degree of probability from the Mahāvaṃsaṭikā, Geiger, Dip. and Mah. 44 ff· Cf. V. A. Smith ind. An.. 31, 1902,. 192 ff.

3. It seems doubtful that this means the Dīpavaṃsa, as is assumed by Geiger (Mahāvaṃsa Transl. p. xi). It certainly gives a false idea of the epic Mahāvaṃsa, if we designate it as a "commentary" on Dīpavaṃsa as is done by Fleet (JRAS 1909, p. 5) whose view is supported by Geiger (Mahāvaṃsa transl. p. xi f. "Pāli Literatur und Sprache," p. 24) Fleet's explanation of the passage in Mahāv. 38, 59 (ed Turnour, p. 257 f. Cūlavaṃsa ed. Geiger I, p. 26) to which he refers is erroneous. There is no question of the composition of a "Dīpikā" or a commentary, but it is merely related that King Dhātusena made a donation of 1,000 pieces of gold and commanded that, at the great Bodhi celebration in front of the memorial temple of the Mahāthera Mahinda, the monks assembled there should always expound the Dīpavaṃsa (in Singhalese) in return for which they should receive sweetmeats.

ghoṣa so important for the Pāli literature of Ceylon coincides with the period between the origin of the Dīpavaṃsa and that of the Mahāvaṃsa, but the poetry also leaves nothing to be desired. In it we find no disturbing gaps and no repetitions. Where the Dīpavaṃsa is too short, Mahāvaṃsa has added and elaborated, in other cases also condensed the matter. The Mahāvaṃsa is, as Geiger[1] says, "a piece of art, created by a man who richly deserves the name of a poet and who managed the material that was in many respects dry and brittle, not with genius but with taste and skill.

Dīpavaṃsa and Mahāvaṃsa show on the other hand a large concurrence in the matter of material and its arrangement and they even have a large number of verses in common. Both epics begin with the story of Gotama Buddha, narrate about his three visits to the island of Ceylon which was at that time inhabited by demons-Rākṣasas, Yakṣas, Piśācas and serpents-and report how the Exalted One surveyed the whole world with his "Buddha-eye" and saw the beautiful island, how a terrible war broke out between the serpent kings, Big-belly, and small-belly which threatened to destroy the island, how Buddha in his boundless kindness took pity, accompanied by gods flew over to Ceylon and made the light of his doctrine radiate, whereupon scores of serpents and other demons embraced the pure doctrine. Then the genealogy of Gotama's father is traced back to a mythical king of primeval times and the history of Buddhism in India is told especially that of the councils. Both epics deal at length with Aśoka the great, patron of Buddhism. With the report on the third council and the sending of Mahinda to Ceylon, the scene of action changes and is now entirely shifted to Ceylon. Out of the union of an Indian princess with a lion two children are born—Sīhabāhu and Sīvalī. The marriage between the brother and sister results in the birth of Vijaya with whom the history of the kings of Ceylon begins. This wild prince is banished from his native country, sets out to see with his 700 companions land after several adventures on Ceylon and becomes its king. The history of Vijaya and his early successors is told in the Dīpavaṃsa much more briefly than in the Mahāvaṃsa. Both works deal at length

1. Dīp. and Mah., p. 19.

with King Devānāṃpiyatissa who ruled over Ceylon at the time of Aśoka, under whom Mahinda (of course flying through the air) came to Ceylon, founded there the religion of Buddha and established the earliest cultures of Buddhist cult. Saṅghamitta, the sister of Mahinda brings a branch of the Bodhi-tree whose transplantation to Ceylon is described in great detail. Then the history of the kings of Ceylon - among them that of Vaṭṭagāmani somewhat more detailed, who got the Tipiṭaka with the commentaries recorded is traced upto Mahāsena with whose death (352 A.D.?)[1] the story is cut short both in the Dīpavaṃsa and the Mahāvaṃsa; for the authentic work of Mahānāma ends with 37,50. Everything which comes after that, is generally known in Ceylon as the Cūlavaṃsa,[2] "the little history," and consists of a series of addenda serving as a continuation of the Mahāvaṃsa and written by various authors. The first appendix is written by the Thera Dhammakitti, who lived during the reign of King Parākramabāhu (1240-1275).[3]

Although the subject-matter of the Mahāvaṃsa moves within the same frame-work as that of the Dīpavaṃsa, yet Mahāvaṃsa has included within this frame-work much new material. In particular,

1. This is the view of Geiger, "The Mahāvaṃsa", Transl., P. xxxviii· 302 used to be assumed as the year of the death of Mahāsena. The chronology is by no means certain.

2. Cūlavaṃsa, being the more recent part of the Mahāvaṃsa, ed. by W. Geiger, I, PTS 1925. Cūlav. 37, 215 ff. deals with Buddhaghosa. Chapter 39 has been edited and translated by T. W. Rhys Davids (JRAS 1875. p. 191 ff. 201 ff. "The Reigns of Kaśyapa the Parricide and of Moggallāna the First"). In some MSS. the work consists of 90 chapters, and in others of 100 or 101. The title Cūlavaṃsa is nowhere to be found in the MSS. In 99, 76, the kings of Ceylon are divided into those of the "Great Dynasty" (mahāvaṃsa) and those of the "Lesser Dynasty" (cūlavaṃsa).

3. Cf. M. de Z. Wickremasinghe in JRAS 1896, 200 ff.; Geiger, Dīp. und Mah., p. 19. The coincidence of both the Dīpavaṃsa and the ancient part of the Mahāvaṃsa breaking off precisely at the Death "Mahāsena, can only be explained by the fact that the "Mahāvaṃsa" of the Aṭṭhakathā, the common course of both the epics, was discontinued after the destruction of the "Great Monastery" of Anurādhapur which took place under Mahāsena, though Mahāsena has the monastery rebuilt. Cf. Mahāvaṃsa, 37; Dīp. 22, 66 ff.; Geiger, "Dīp. und Mah.," p. 71. It is now probable that an older Thera Dhammakitti (I), who lived in the reign of Parākkamabāhu I, was the author of the first part of the Cūlavaṃsa ending with the death of

out of the story of King Gāmani the Wicked (Duṭṭhagāmani), to which in the Dīpavaṃsa only 13 verses are devoted, he has made an independent hero-poetry in eleven cantos (22-32)-Geiger calls this the "Duṭṭha-gāmani-Epic." In the first part he describes the war-deeds of this mighty king and only in the second part he makes him a religious hero who makes amends for the rivers of blood that he has caused to flow, by erecting sacred buildings, especially the Mahāthūpa, "the great Stūpa", about whose construction tales of wonder are told. Mahānāma has also adapted in his poetry some materials from fairy tales and short stories of which some belong to world-literature. Whereas in the Dīpavaṃsa it is simply said that Vijaya landed with his companions on the coast of Ceylon, founded there towns and a kingdom, in the Mahāvaṃsa we are told (**7**,9ff) fairy tale-like adventures of Vijaya and the magician Kuveṇi which remind vividly of the experiences of Ulysses with Circe. Very interesting is the legend of King Elāra (21, 15 ff):

This righteous king had a bell fixed to his bed whose string was led into the open so that every one to whom injustice was done could ring the bell.[1] At first the string is pulled by a cow whose calf was run over by the son of the king. The king lets his own son be crushed by the wheels of the same chariot. Then a bird seeks the King's help because a snake has killed its young one and the king lets the snake be killed. The bell rings

Parakkamabāhu I in 1186 A. D., while chapters 80 ff. were written by another Dhammakitti (II), who may be the same who wrote the Dāṭhāvaṃsa in 1211 A. D. The second part of the Cūlavaṃsa deals with the period 1186-1333 A. D. and the third part, probably composed by the Thera Sumaṅgala in the second half of the 18th century, with the period from 1333 to 1781 A. D. See W. Geiger in Ind. Hist. Qu. 6, 1933, 206ff.

1. "When the emperor Charlemagne . . . lived at Zurich, he had a pillar erected with a bell attached to it, so that anyone who desired administration of justice would pull it whenever the emperor was seated at his midday meal." Grimm, "Deutsche Sagen II, No. 453. Here, as in the similar legend of the sage Theodosius (Gesta Romanorum 105) it is a snake which demands and obtains justice against a toad. Cf. also the poem "Die Leidglocke" by F. Ruckert in "Brahmanische Erzalungen;" E. Hultsch in JRAS 1913, 528ff., who, amongst other things, has traced a Tamil version of this story, and cites other parallels given by Th. Zachariae. See also Benfey, Pantschatantra I, 168 f.

for the third time and an old woman pulls the string. She has spread out rice for drying and a rain falling at an improper time has spoilt it. In this the king sees his punishment for an offence committed by him shortly before. He makes penance by fasting whereupon Sakka orders Pajjumna the rain-god to cause rain fall only at a particular time of the night once a week.[1]

It is perhaps to be presumed that Mahānāma has taken all these materials which are missing in the Dīpavaṃsa from the old Aṭṭhakathās, above all, from the Sihalaṭṭhaka-Mahāvaṃsa which was his main source, although he has known and used the Dīpavaṃsa in addition to that. That both epics rest on the historical sections of the old Aṭṭhakathās also speaks very much for the fact that we cannot deny to them a certain reliability as sources of history. Of writing history in the real sense of the term we cannot think either in connection with the Dīpavaṃsa or the Mahāvaṃsa. It is enough to point that neither of the two works even mentions the name of Alexander the Great, about Aśoka the great they can tell us nothing but a few miracles and that this mighty conqueror is in their descriptions more a religious than a worldly hero. Even Gāmani the Wicked is glorified above all as a religious hero. Both epics claim to edify and the Mahāvaṃsa claims to be a Kāvya. Yet one does injustice to these works if one paints their authors as wanton falsifiers and liars as some critics have done with an indignation not completely free from humour. Certainly they were not so. What they narrate, is what they considered to be true history, but we, however, must consider all that in many respects as saga, legend and poetry. As they did not make any intentionally wrong reports, we may believe much of what they report on historical times and on periods not far from their own life-times. Of course it was they who first gave information about Candragupta, the grandfather of Aśoka

1. Many other tales from the Mahāvaṃsa, which are of importance from the point of view of folk-lore, have been traced by Geiger, "Dīp. und Mah.", pp. 23-28. Some of these interesting parallels. On the sources of Mahāvaṃsa see also W. Geiger in ZII 7, 1929, 259 ff., who shows that Mahānāma probably also used a chronicle of Rohaṇa, and Puññapotthakāni (books containing lists of pious foundations), besides popular oral traditions.

2. Cf. Oldenberg, Aus dem alten Indien, 77ff.

which although not entirely in agreement with the particularls by the Greeks, still can be reconciled with them to such an extent that with their help the year of Buddha's death could be calculated and with that the most important date in the history of Indian literature could be arrived at. And by a comparison of Chinese annals with our Sinhalese chronicles Sylvain Levi[1] has found that the latter beginning from the 4th century B.C. are as historical sources "solide, sinon impecable".

Of the Mahāvaṃsa we have a very enlarged recension—in 5791 verses as against the 2915 verses of our text—which although as a piece of art quite insignificant, is for the history of literature very informative. For it shows how in India (Sinhalese authors followed only Indian models) epics were enlarged through the addition of more and more new materials.[2] More important is the Mahāvaṃsa-Ṭīkā the commentary to our Mahāvaṃsa, written between 1000 and 1250 A.D. This is evidently not just an exegetical and dogmatic commentary, but it contains also numerous sagas, fairy tales and legends as additions to the content of the epic. These are drawn partly from monastic and partly from popular tradition. Popular are for example the specially interesting sagas of Candragupta and Cāṇakya[3], which as

1. Journal des savants 1905, p. 539. The reliability of the chronicles is also supported by Max Mueller SBE, Vol. 10 (I), pp XIII-XXV; Rhys Davids, Buddhist India, p. 274 f; H. C. Norman, JRAS 1908, 1 ff. In his investigations into the history of the Canon (see above Note 1 on p. 3) Oldenberg has several times quoted the authority of the particulars given by Dip. and Mah. Fleet (JRAS 1909, pp. 987 and 1015) says that the Dīpavaṃsa rests on local recordings from the time of Aśoka, and that in the Mahāvaṃsa 32 actually the last words of Duṭṭhagāmani are contained. Very poor opinion of the reliability of the chronicles as sources of history is expressed by V. A. Smith (Ind. Ant. 32, 1903, p. 365f) and R. O. Franke JPTS 1908, p 1. Against Franke, see Geiger ZDMG 63, 1909, p. 550. "The Mahāvaṃsa Transl.", pp. XII ff., XV ff., XX ff. Hultsch (JRAS 1913, p. 517 ff.) has succeeded in tracing synchronisms even between the later additions to the Mahāvaṃsa (for the period from the 10th to the 12th century) and the inscriptions. On Mahāvaṃsa and Cūlavaṃsa as sources of history, see also. Geiger in Ind. Hist Qu. VI, 1930, 208ff.

2. The enlarged Mahāvaṃśa has been found by E. Hardy (JPTS 1902-1903, p. 61 ff) in a Cambodian manuscript and discussed by Geiger, Dip. and Mah. p. 28 ff.

3. On these and other stories refer Geiger, Dīp. und Mah. pp. 37-44, where also analogies especially in the Cyros saga are pointed.

the commentator himself says, he has taken partly from the Aṭṭhakathā of the "northern cloister". But for this he too has drawn mainly from the Aṭṭhakathā of the "great cloister" and also used the commentaries Sumaṅgalavilāsini and Samantapāsādikā of Buddhaghoṣa and a number of other works, among which a certain Sahassavatthaṭṭhakathā, "Commentary to the thousand stories" which is quoted very often, is specially important.[1]

All the later works of Ceylon dealing with ecclesiastical history are based finally also on the Aṭṭhakathās. Buddhaghoṣa drew upon them for his historical introduction to his Samantapāsādikā[2] already mentioned. This, the Nidānakathā and the Mahāvaṃsa again formed the basis for the historical works—if one may call them so, because they contain more of legend than of history Bodhivaṃsa, Dāṭhāvaṃsa and Thūpavaṃsa, which in later centuries were translated into Pāli or modified following Sinhalese models. The Mahābodhivaṃsa or Bodhivaṃsa[3], "the story of the Bodhi-tree" is a prose work—only at the end of the chapters and towards the end of the whole work do we find Gāthās—, that was written by Upatissa, a monk, by about the end of the 10th century. The Dāṭhāvaṃsa, "the history of Buddha's tooth"[4] is an epic in five cantos in Sanskritised Pāli (with long compositis) by Dhammakitti, the monk, composed at the beginning of the 13th century. Similarly, the Thūpavaṃsa[5] "the History of the Relic Shrines" is also a work of the 13th century. This work is available in Sinhalese as well as in the Pāli language. Vācissara

1. Cf. Geiger, Dīp. and Mah. p. 52ff.
2. See p. 201 above.
3. Edited by S.A. Strong, London PTS 1891, Cf. Geiger, "Dip and Mah." p. 84 ff; "Pāli Literatur und Sprache", p. 25.
4. Edited and translated by Coomaraswamy; edited by Rhys Davids and R. Morris JPTS 1884, p. 109ff edited and translated by Bimalacharan Law together with a Note on the Positions of the Dāṭhāvaṃsa in the "History of Pāli Literature" by W. Stede, Lahore 1925 (PSS No. 7) Cf. J. Gerson da Cunha, "Memoir on the History of the Tooth relic of Ceylon". JBRAS XI, 1875, p. 115 ff. and Geiger, "Dip. und Mah.," p. 8 ff. The Dāṭhadhātuvaṃsa mentioned in the continuation of the Mahāvaṃsa 37, 93, is probably (See Geiger p. 19) the same work.
5. Two editions have appeared in Colombo. Cf. Geiger, "Dip und Mah, p. 92ff.

claims to be its author. All these works are stereotypes, they begin with the history of the earlier Buddha Dīpaṅkara, then of the Gotama Buddha, of the three councils etc. until finally they narrate the history of the cult-centres treated by them. In Burma also similar works have been written, like the Chakesadhātu-vaṃsa[1] "the history of the six shrines of Hair-relics. Even a quite modern work, the Sāsanavaṃsa, the history of the Doctrine"[2] written by monk Paññasāmi in Burma in 1861 follows completely the old stereotype. But it is interesting to see from this work how the Pāli language continues to exist even in our present day. Both, the Sāsanavaṃsa as well as the Gandha-vaṃsa, "the history of the books"[3] which is also equally modern and written by a certain Nandapañña in Burma are very valuable for the history of the Pāli literature. In five chapters the Gandhavaṃsa gives a description of the canon according to the three Piṭakas and nine Aṅgas, the titles and sometimes the names of the authors of the later Pāli works, a description of the authors' birth-places, informations about the occasions on which on the books were written and finally a report on the written recording of the canon.

We can treat very briefly the remaining modern Pāli literature of Ceylon and Burma. For the most part it is a scholarly, theological literature which is closely connected to the canonical texts, yet there is no lack of single poetical work. From the time of Buddhghoṣa upto the renaissance of Pāli literature in the 12th century we have in Ceylon nothing but a few authors'

---

1. Edited by Minayeff in the JPTS, 1885. Cf. of ecclesiastical content is also the Sīmāvivādavinišchayakathā, ed. by J.P. Minayeff, JPTS 1887, 17 ff.

2. Edited by Mable H. Bode, London PTS 1897. This work was the main source for M.H. Bode, "The Pāli Literature of Burma," London 1909, Cf. by the same author, "A Burmese Historian of Buddhism, " London 1898 and Geiger, " Dip und Mah.", p. 98 Note.

3. Edited by Mina yeff, Recherches, pp. 235ff and once again in JPTS 1886 pp. 54-80. To this, an index by Mabel Bode JPTS 1896, p. 53ff. According to M.H. Bode (Pāli Literature of Burma pp. X) it is a work of the 17th century. The work is called Cullagandhavaṃsa, "Small History of the Books" Therefore there might be also a Mahagandhavaṃsa. Cf. E. Hardy in ZDMG 51, 1897, p. 111.

names and titles, whereas in Burma before the 11th century there is not even the least talk of a Pāli literature.

Buddhadatta is said to have been a contemporary of Buddhaghosa. It is claimed that he, too, was born in India and lived at various times both in Ceylon and at Kāncīpura and other places in South India. It is, however, questionable whether the legends about the meeting of Buddhadatta and Buddhaghosa were not merely invented with a view to enhancing the reputation of a much later writer. This later Buddhadatta is the author of a commentary on the Buddhavaṃsa and of comprehensive works on the Abhidhamma and Vinaya: the Abhidhammāvatāra, Rūpārūpavibhāga and the Vinaya-Vinnicchaya.[1]

The poem Anāgatavaṃsa[2] "the History of the Future One," i.e., the future Buddha, is, as regards its contents, a sequel to the Buddhavaṁsa, the story of the past Buddhas, and perhaps belongs to an earlier period. The earliest description of the paradise of the future Buddha Metteyya, where human beings will attain the mature age of 80,000 years, and where the maidens will be marriageable at the age of 500, when India will be teeming with human beings, like a poultry yard swarming with fowls, etc., is already to be found in the Dīghanikāya (No. 26). The Anāgatavaṃsa gives a more detailed treatment of this Metteyya and his contemporary the Cakravartin, world ruler, Saṅkha in the form of a prophecy which is made to issue from the lips of Gotama Buddha.[3]

1. Buddhadatta's Manuals or Summaries of Abhidhamma, Abhidhammāvatāra and Rūpārūpavibhāga ed. by A. P. Buddhadatta, PTS1915. Cf. Geiger, "Pāli Literature und Sprache", p. 22 para 25; B. Ch. Law, "Life and Work of Buddhaghosa", p. 96 ff. and Ann. Bh. Inst. 13, 1931-32 p. 122 ff., There is of course the possibility that there was more than one Buddhadatta. A paper on Buddhadatta by S. Jambunathan in Journal of Or. Res. Madras, April 1928, pp. 111-17 is quoted in BB. I, No. 130.

2. Ed. by J. Minayeff in JPTS 1886, p. 33 ff., and by E. Leumann "Maitreya-Samiti, das Zukunftsideal der Buddhisten," Strassburg 1919, p. 177ff (with explanatory notes)

3. According to the Gandhavaṃsa (JPTS 1886 m pp. 61, 72) Kassapa is the author of the work, and Upatissa the author of the Aṭṭhakathā on it. Now both Kassapa and Upatissa are names of Theras and writers of various periods. Cf. Geiger, l.c. p. 25 para 29. Visuddhi-Magga p.434, and Attha-Sālinī, p. 415, as well as Anāgatavaṃsa V, 96, say of the future Metteyya,

A short summary of the rules of the Vinayapiṭaka is contained in the Sikkhas, the Mūla-Sikkha by Mahāsami and the Khudda Sikkha by Dhammasiri.[1] According to Burmese history books these compendia are supposed to have been written by 440 A.D., but are in all probability much more recent.[2] These Sikkhas together with the so-called Dvematika (consisting of Bhikkhu and Bhikkhuni Patimokkha) and the Kaṅkhavitariṇi are considered in Burma as sufficient for those who have no time to learn the complete Vinayapiṭaka.[3] Compendia which deal with the doctrine are the Dhammasaṃgaha of Dhammakitti[4] and the Sārasaṃgaha[5] of Siddhatta (a pupil of Buddhappiya), which probably belong to the end of the 13th and the beginning of the 14th century[6] are compendia which deal with the doctrine. The headquarters for the study of the Abhidhamma is Burma. Also the most important manual of Buddhistic psychology and ethics, the Abhidhammatthasaṃgaha has been written there by the monk Anuruddha (probably in the 12th century).[7] Even today

---

that the name of his mother is Brahmavathī and that of his father Subrahmā. It is not clear however, that Buddhaghosa quotes from the Anāgatavaṃsa as is assumed by Mrs. Rhys Davids (Visuddhi-Magga, Ed., pp. 761, 764) Hence we are not in a position to prove that the Anāgatavaṃsa is earlier than Buddaghosa. As a matter of fact, there is also a recension of the Anāgatavaṃsa which is written in the mixed prose and verse style, and yet another Anāgatavaṃsa which diverges from our work and tells the story of the ten future Buddhas. (Minayeff JPTS 1886, pp. 33 ff., 39f.)

1. Ed. by Ed. Müller in JPTS 1883, p. 86 ff. At the end of the Khudda-Sikkhā itself, Dhammasiri from Ceylon is mentioned as the author. Cf. Gandhavaṃsa in JPTS 1886, p. 61

2. Rhys Davids (JPTS 1883, p. xiii f) considered them to be earlier than Buddhaghosa; Ed. Müller ascribes them to the 6th or 7th century; Geiger (Pāli literature und Sprache," p. 24 para 27) thinks that judged by their language, they could scarcely have been written prior to the 11th century.

3. Bode ibid 5 f.

4. Ed. by N. Saddhananda in JPTS 1890.

5. "Des Sārasamgaha erstes Kapitel," Text and German Translation by K.E. Neumann, Leipzig 1891.

6. Cf. Geiger, l.c., p. 30

7. The text was published by T.W. Rhys Davids in JPTS 1884. A translation appeared under the title, Compendium of Philosophy being a translation of the Abhidhammattha—Saṅgaha with the Introductory Eassay and Notes by

it enjoys in Ceylon as well as in Burma the greatest respect and and has been commented and translated in Burma more than any other Abhidhamma text. Anuruddha is also the author of the Nāmarūpapariccheda, a philosophical poem of 1,885 verses.[1]

Of scholarly poems which treat poetically one or more points of Buddhistic doctrinary system, the following may be mentioned in particular. The Pañcagatidīpana, the "Illumination of the five ways[2] is a poem of 114 verses. There the five big and the five small hells and the remaining worlds are described and the actions enumerated through which men are reborn in one of the five states of existence, namely as hellish beings, as animals, as spirits, as human beings or as gods. With the same topic is also the Lokadīpasāra concerned which was written in the 14th century in Burma by Medhaṃkara.[3] In the 14th century a certain Dhammakitti wrote the Pāramitāmahāśataka, a Pāli poem on the ten Pāramitās.[4] The Saddhammopāyana, "Means and Ways of the Good Religion"[5] deals in 629 verses with the basic teachings of the Buddhist religion in general and especially the ethical teachings. A small poem in praise of the Buddha is the Pajjamadhu, "the Verses-honey"[6] that was composed by Buddhappiya by about 1100 A.D. In 104 beautiful stanzas of Sanskritised Pāli the magnificence of Buddha is described here and his wisdom praised. An ornate poem on the good religion of Buddha are also the Telakaṭāhagāthā, "the Oil-Cauldron Verses".[7] The poet is supposed to have been a monk who was

Sewe Zan Aung, revised and edited by Mrs. Rhys Davids, London PTS 1910, Cf. Bode ibid 61 f. German transl. by E.L. Hoffmann in ZB 7, 1926, 175 ff, 316 ff.

1. Ed. by A.P. Buddhadatta in JPTS 1913-14 pp. 1-114.

2. Ed. by Feer in JPTS 1884 and translated into French in the "Annales du Musee Guimet", t. V, 1883, 514 ff. Cf. B.C. Law in "Ann. Bh. Inst." 13, 1931-32 p. 141 ff.

3. Bode, ibid 35 f.

4. There were no less than five Theras by the name of Dhammakitti who lived in the 13th and 14th centuries. Cf. M. de Z. Wickremasinghe in JRAS 1896, 200 ff.

5. Edited by R. Morris in JPTS 1887, 35-98.

6. Edited by E.R. Gooneratne in JPTS 1887, 1 ff. The poet is also the author of the Pāli grammar "Rūpasiddhi".

7. Edited by E.R. Gooneratne in JPTS 1884, 49 ff.

unjustly suspected by King Tissa of Kalyāṇī of an intrigue with his wife and was condemned to be thrown into a Cauldron with boiling oil. This was done, but the monk rose from the Cauldron and sang the 100 verses. Before dying he recollected his earlier existence when he was a herdsman and had thrown a fly into a pot with boiling milk. The "Hundred Verses" are in our poem 98 verses in artistic, Sanskritised Pāli in which however there is no allusion to the legend. King Tissa of Kalyāṇī reigned in the 3rd century B.C. but the poem might be, judging from its language, scarcely older than the 12th century A.D.[1]

A piece of downright ornate poetry is the Jinālaṅkāra of Buddharakkhita,[2] a poem of 250 stanzas in which the Buddha legend is treated in bombastic Kāvya-style and which was written in the year 1156 A.D. There we find verses which can be read equally forwards and backwards, a stanza in which no other consonant than *n* occurs and many more such tricks. Not only the style but also the content makes this probable. For the poem is saturated with Mahāyāna-teachings and full of Purāṇa-like exaggerations.

A very mediocratic poem on the life of Buddha in simple, unartificial but also in not a beautiful language is the Jinacarita[3] of the poet Vanaratna Medhaṃkara[4], who lived under Bhuvanaka Bāhu I (1277-1288 A.D.). It looks almost like a somewhat unskilled verification of the Nidānakathā. A

1. The legend is told briefly in the Mahāvaṃsa 22, 13 ff and more elaborately in the Rasavāhinī.

2. Edited with notes and Translation by James Gray, London 1894. According to the Gandhavaṃsa (JPTS 1886, pp. 69, 72, cf. 65, 75) a Jinālaṃkāra was written by Buddhadatta and commented on by Buddharakkhita. A work like the Jinālaṃkāra with which we are concerned could not have possibly been written by a contemporary of Buddhaghosa (see above p. 212 on Buddhadatta). The date "1, 700" years after the death of Buddha" figures in the concluding verses of the poem, where Buddharakkhita refers to himself as the author. Cf. Geiger, l.c. p. 28.

3. Edited and translated by W.H.D. Rouse (JPTS 1904-5, p. 1 ff)

4. According to Saddhamma-Saṃgaha IX. 22 (JPTS 1890, p. 63) and Gandhavaṃsa (JPTS 1886, p. 62, 72).

Buddha-biography from a more recent period (1773), the Mālālaṃkāravatthu has become known only through the English translation[1] of a Burmese translation from Pāli.

Also narrative works have been written in Pāli till most modern times. The most important of these works is the Rasavāhinī[2] a collection of 103 stories of which the first 40 take place in India and the remaining 63 in Ceylon. The book was written originally in the Sinhalese language, then translated by a certain monk named Raṭṭhapāla into Pāli and even later improved (between 1320-1347) by the Thera Vedeha[3]. In spite of this "improvement" it is still written in bad Pāli—Prose and verse alternate each other—and in an extremely careless style. Many of the legends are very stupid, although very edifying for Buddha-worshippers. The Buddha-worship in some of the legends does not distinguish itself in any way from that of the Mahāyāna and from the Bhakti for Viṣṇu among the Bhāgavatas, for instance in the story of the snake, which is tamed by the single word "Buddha". But there are, in the collection, also some important stories which are interesting partly also through their parallels in world literature. Thus we find here again the widely spread stories of grateful animals and ungrateful men which we have already come across in the Jātaka.

The Jātaka book was the inexhaustible source from which Buddhistic poets, writers and compilers have drawn again and again. Thus the poet Sīlavaṃsa of Ava wrote in the 15th

---

1. By Bishop P. Bigandet, Life or Legend of Gaudama the Buddha of the Burmese, Rangoon 1858, 3rd ed. London 1880. Cf. Rhys Davids SBE, Vol. 11, p. XXXII.

2. Selected stories have been edited and translated into German by F. Spiegel, "Anecdota Palica," Leipzig 1845; Sten Konow in ZDMG 43, 1889, 297 ff.; the second decade by Magdalene and W. Geiger in SBayA 1918, into Danish by D. Anderson, Kopenhagen 1891, into Italian by E. Pavolini in GSAI 8, 1894, p. 179 ff., 10, 1896, p. 175 ff into English (Legends of Asoka) by Lakshmana Sastri (with a "Prefatory Note" by H.C. Norman) in JASB 1910, p. 57ff. Cf. Gooneratne in PTS 1884, p. 50f., Pavolini in GASI 11, 1897, p. 35 ff.

3. He is also the author of Samantakūṭavaṇṇanā, a description of the Adam's Peak, published in the Journal of the Buddhist Text Society, May 1893.

century a poem, Buddhālaṃkāra, based on the Sumedhakathā in the Nidānakathā. By about the same time the poet Raṭṭhasāra of Ava wrote a few poetical adaptations of the Jātakas. Tipiṭakālaṃkāra who was born in 1578 in Burma wrote as a novice of 15 years of age a poetical adaptation of the Vessantarajātaka.[1] Moreover, for the Rājādhirājavilāsinī, a prose work written on the order of the Burmese King Bodopāyā, who ascended the throne in 1782, the Jātaka book is the chief source, although in order to show his scholarliness, the author has diligently used the whole literature from the Suttas up to the latest commentaries as also all sorts of learned Pāli and Sanskrit works on grammar, astronomy and other sciences.[2]

Buddhistic Literature in Pure and Mixed Sanskrit

However greatly rich and vast the Pāli literature of India, Ceylon and Burma may be, it represents only the literature of one particular Buddhist sect namely, Theravādins. In addition to it even in India — apart from other Buddhist countries — several sects have produced their own literary works, whose language is partly Sanskrit and partly a Central Indian dialect,[3] resembling Sanskrit which we will call, like Senart, "Mixed Sanskrit"[4]. In the North and North-West of India there were great centres of learning, such as the universities of Nālandā and Takkasilā (Taxila) where for hundreds of years not only all branches of secular knowledge, especially medicine, but also the philosophical and theological literature of the Buddhists were

1. Bode ibid 43f., 53.
2. Bode ibid 78 ff.
3. According to Vinītadeva (8th century (A.D.) the Sarvāstivadins used Sanskrit, the Mahāsaṅghikas Prākrit, the Sammitiyas Apabhraṃśa and the Sthaviravādins (i.e., Theravādins) Paiśāci. Cf. Ryukan Kimura, "A Historical Study of the Terms Hīnayāna and Mahāyāna and the origin of Mahāyāna Buddhism", Calcutta, 1927, p. 7; R. Pischel in SBA 1904 p. 808.
4. Previously it was usually called "Gāthā dialect" (see Vol. I, p. 41 f) which is all the more inappropriate as it is also widespread in inscriptions. Cf. E. Senart, JA 1882, 7, t. XIX, 238 ff. 1886 s. 8, t. VIII, p. 318 ff; Kern SBE 21, p. XIV ff; Buhler Ep. Ind. I, 1892, 239, 377; II, 34; Hoernle and Bhandarkar, Ind. Ant. 12 1883 pp. 89 f: 205 f, 139 ff.; 17, 1888, p. 36ff.; J. Wackernagel, "Altindische Grammatik" I, Gottingen 1896, p. XXXIX ff.

cultivated with great zeal. Indian Pandits went thence to Tibet and China, learned Tibetan and Chinese, and translated Sanskrit works into these languages. Chinese pilgrims like Hsuan-Tsang learnt Sanskrit at Nālanda, and translated Buddhists texts into Chinese.[1] Some of the Sanskrit works which were produced there, and the originals of which are lost, would not be known to us, but for the Tibetan and Chinese texts. The finds of manuscripts in Central Asia include fragments not only of Sanskrit texts, but also of translations of Indian works in Central Asiatic languages.[2]

---

1. Cf. Phanindranath Bose, "Indian Teachers of Buddhist Universities," Madras, 1923; "The Indian Teachers in China," Madras, 1923; and Prabhatkumar Mukherjee, "Indian Literature Abroad,"in Ind. Hist. Qu., Vols. I-III, 1925-1927. Buddhist texts are known to have been translated into Chinese already in the second century A.D. if not earlier. The earliest Tibetan translations date from the second half of the eighth century A.D. see A.H. Francke, "Antiquities of Indian Tibet," Vol. II, "The Chronicles of Ladakh and Minor Chronicles" (Archaeological Survey of India, New Imp. Series, Vol. 50), Calcutta 1926, p. 86.

2. Thus fragments of Buddhist texts have been found in two languages hitherto unknown, which are now termed "Kuchean" and "Khotanese" after Kucha and Khotan, the places in Eastern Turkestan where they were discovered, as the names "Tokharian", "North Aryan", "East Indian" and "Sakian" suggested by various scholars have not been generally accepted (Cf. Sten Konow in "Festschrift Windisch," p. 96 f.; Hoernle, "Manuscript Remains," I, p. IX ff.) Fragments in "Kuchean" have been published by S. Levi, in JA 1911, s. 10 t. XVII, 138 ff., 431 ff., t. XIX, 1912, 101 ff; JRAS 1913, 109 ff, and in Hoernle, "Manuscript Remains", I, pp. 357 ff., 365ff. Fragments in "Khotanese" by Konow and Hoernle, "Manuscript Remains" I, pp. 214 ff., 289ff., 395 ff., also by E. Leumann, "Zur nordarischen Sprache und Literatur," Strassburg, 1912, Maitreyasamiti, Strassburg 1919, and "Buddhistische Literature, Nordarisch und Deutsch", I, Leipzig 1920, (AKM xv, 2) A Soghdian version of the Vessantara-Jātaka has been edited and translated by R. Gauthiot in JA 1912. s. 10, t. XIX, pp. 163 ff., 430 ff; see also Le Sūtra des causes et des effects du bien et du mal, ed. et trad. d' apres les textes sogdiens, chinois et tibetains par R. Gauthiot et P. Pelliot, Paris (Mission Pelliot) I, 1920; II 1926. Buddhist texts in the Uigurian language have been published by H. Stonner in SBA 1904, P. 1282 ff and F.W.K. Müller, Uigurica I and II in ABA 1908 and 1910. E. Sieg and W. Siegling, to which scholars is due the credit of having proved "Tokharian" ("Kuchean") to be an Indo-European language (SBA 1908, p. 915 ff) have published fragments of Buddhist Sanskrit texts from the finds of Turfan : "Tocharische Sprachreste I, Die Texte," Berlin and Leipzig 1921.

By far the greater part of this literature written in pure and mixed Sanskrit—we call it briefly Buddhist Sanskrit literature —belongs either to the Mahāyāna or has been certainly more or less influenced by it.[1] For understanding this literature it is therefore necessary by way of an introduction, to make a few remarks on the division of Buddhism into its two great sections—Mahāyāna and Hīnayāna.

---

1. For our earliest knowledge of this literature, which is preserved chiefly in Nepal, we are indebted to Brian Houghton Hodgson, who lived in Nepal from 1821 to 1843, and rendered equally signal services as a statesman, geographer, zoologist, ethnographer and investigator of Indian languages and antiquities. He was instrumental in procuring numerous Buddhist manuscripts for Indian and European libraries and especially for Paris, where they were turned to excellent use by Eugene Burnouf (Introduction a L' Histoire du Buddhisme Indien, 2 ed., Paris. 1876) At about the same time (1824) as Hodgson made his discoveries which so essentially promoted the knowledge of Buddhist literature, the celebrated Hungarian Alexander Csoma de Koros, after wandering on foot from Hungary to Tibet, had just begun to open up the Buddhist literature of Tibet. Shortly afterwards, the Pāli literature of Ceylon, too, was opened by George Turnour. Information regarding the contents of numerous manuscripts of Buddhist Sanskrit literature is given by Rajendralala Mitra, "The Sanskrit Buddhist Literature of Nepal," Calcutta 1882; C. Bendall, "Catalogue of Buddhist Sanskrit Manuscripts in Cambridge," Cambridge 1883; and Haraprasada Sastri, "A Descriptive Catalogue of Sanskrit Manuscripts in the Government Collection under the care of the Asiatic Society of Bengal "I, Buddhist Manuscripts," Calcutta, 1917. The Tibetan translation in the Kan-jure are described by. A Csoma de Koros, "Asiatic Researches." Vol. 20, Calcutta 1836, and Feer, in AMG, t. 5, Paris 1883. Cf. also H. Beckh, "Verzeichnis der tibetischen Handschriften I, Handschriftenverzeichnis der Konigl. Bibl. zu Berlin, Bd. 24," Berlin, 1914. A considerable amount of information about the later literature of Buddhism from Tibetan sources is afforded us by Taranatha in his work "History of Buddhism in India" completed 1608, translated from the Tibtan into German by A. Schiefner, St. Petersburg, 1869, translated from the German in Ind. Hist. Qu. 3, 1927. On the Chinese translations, see Bunyiu Nanjio's "Catalogue of the Chinese Translations of the Buddhist Tripiṭaka," Oxford, 1883; E. Denison, Ross, "Alphabetical List of the Titles of Works in the Chinese Buddhist Tripiṭaka', being an Index to Bunyiu Nanjio's Catalogue and to the 1905 Kioto Reprint of the Buddhist Canon," Calcutta 1910, and Probodhchandra Bagchi, "Le Canon boudhique en Chine, les traductions," I, Paris 1927. Sino-Indica Publications de l 'Universite de Calcutta, 1. Among the most famous translators are Dharmarakṣita 265-313 A.D., Kumārajīva, 344-431 A.D. Hsuan-Tsang, 700-712. On Kumārajiva s. S. Levi in JA 1913, s. 11 t. II, p. 334 ff. translated by Phanindranath Bose, Calcutta 1922, and J. Nobel in SBA 1917, 206 ff.

The oldest Buddhist schools whose main teachings coincide with those of the Theravāda as handed down in the Pāli canon, saw in ones' own salvation, in Nirvāṇa, the highest salvation and in the state of the Arhat who, even in his life time, has a foretaste of Nirvāṇa, the goal of all endeavour,—a goal that can be reached only by a few with the help of knowledge that can be acquired by leading a monk's life. This doctrinary system is not rejected by the followers of Mahāyāna, but is recognised as having originated with Buddha,[1] although termed as Hīnayāna, i.e. as the lower (hīna), the inadequate "vehicle" (yāna), that is not enough to take all beings to the end of their suffering. What they teach is the Mahāyāna, the "big vehicle", that is suited to ferry the large number of human beings across the sufferings of the world. This new doctrine, which rests, as those who profess it claim, on a profounder interpretation of the old texts or on later mythical revelations of Buddha, replaces the ideal of the Arhat with that of the Bodhisattva. Not only the monk, but every man can have the ideal of being reborn as a Bodhisattva, a "being of enlightenment", i.e. a "candidate for enlightenment", in order to bring salvation to all human beings. But if this goal is to be accessible to all, there must be more easy means of attaining it than are thought of in the Hīnayāna. Thus, therefore, according to the teachings of Mahāyāna, salvation can be attained also by the householder fully engrossed in life—by the merchant, the artisan, the king and even the worker and the Pariah—on the one hand by showing sympathy and kindness to all beings, by extreme generosity and self-denial and on the other hand by pious and fervent worship of Buddha, of the Buddhas and of the Bodhisattvas.[2] Although as we have already

---

1. Hsuan Tsang gives a classification of the sacred writings of the Mahāyāna in which the Śrāvaka-Piṭaka i.e. The Canon of the Hīnayāna is also included. Cf. S. Levi and Ed. Chavannes in JA ser. II, t. VIII, 1916, p. 5ff.

2. We see here the influence of the doctrine of Bhakti, known to us from the Bhagavad-Gītā and it is most probable that it was the Bhagavad Gītā itself which influenced the development of the Mahāyāna Cf. above Vol. I, p. 413 ff. Kern, "Manual of Buddhism". p. 122. Some scholars assume that outside influences, too, contributed towardes the moulding of Mahāyāna; but a hypothesis of this nature is not necessary and cannot be

seen, Buddha is in the Pāli-canon very often only a human being, still, he has become a super human being who was able to achieve some miracles and he finally sank into Nirvāṇa. And only his doctrine, and in any case his relics are left behind as objects of worship. The Lokottaravādins also belonging to the Hīnayāna went still further and saw in the Buddhas no ordinary human beings but superhuman (lokottara) beings, who come down to the earth for a certain time to partake of all human experiences. In the Mahāyāna on the contrary, the Buddhas are, from the beginning, nothing but divine beings and their wanderings on the earth and sinking in Nirvāṇa nothing but a sport or delusion. And while in the Hīnayāna there is already mention of a number of Buddhas, of predecessors of Śākyamuni in the earlier world-epoques, the Mahāyāna speaks of thousands, even millions of Buddhas. And as divine beings are also numberless millions ofBodhisattvas—beings of enlightenment endowed with "perfections" (Pāramitās) who out of sympathy for the other beings renounced the Nirvāṇa worshipped by the Mahāyāna Buddhists. To these were added also Hindu deities, especially from the sphere of Śiva who joined the Buddhas and Bodhisattvas and with them filled the Buddhist pantheon. This new-born mythology, the new Bodhisattva ideal, and the Buddha-worship (Buddha-Bhakti) which was becoming even more prominent constitute together the popular side of the Mahāyāna. Just as the Mahāyāna was already prepared in the Hīnayāna but developed further under the influence of Hinduism, so also the philosophical side of the Mahāyāna only a further development of the teachings of the Hīnayāna under the influence of Brahminical philosophy. Ancient Buddhism had explained the origin of suffering or the discords of existence

---

proved. Cf. S. Levi, "Mahāyāna Sūtrālaṃkāra" II, p. 16 ff Kennedy JRAS 1902, p. 377 ff. Eliot, "Hinduism and Buddhism" III, p. 445 ff A.B. Keith, "Buddhist Philosophy" p. 217. On the Hīnayāna and Mahāyāna in general, see La Valee Poussin in ERE VIII, 1915, 330 ff and R. Kimura, "A Historical Study of the Terms Hīnayāna and Mahāyāna", Calcutta 1927. Nalinaksha Dutt, Aspects of Mahāyāna Buddhism and its relation to Hīnayāna, London 1930 (Calcutta Oriental Series, No. 23.).

by the Paṭiccasamuppāda,[1] i.e. the formula in which it is shown that all the elements of being originate only in mutual interdependence. The Hīnayāna derives from this formula the doctrine of Anattatā, of the "Non-Self" i.e. the doctrine that there is no corporeal and physical phenomena which change every moment. The Mahāyāna derives from the same formula the doctrine of Śūnyatā i.e. the doctrine that "all (is) void" (sarvaṃ, śūnyam) meaning "devoid of independent reality."[2]

But the Buddhistic Sanskrit literature is by no means exclusively Mahāyānic. There are also a number of important Hīnayāna texts, which are exclusively written in pure and mixed Sanskrit.

Remnants of the Sanskrit Canon

In the first place, the Sarvāstivāda school[3] of the Hīnayāna which had its adherents more especially in Kashmir and Gandhāra, and spread thence to Central Asia, Tibet and China, had a Sanskrit Canon of its own. Though no complete copy of this canon has come down to us, we know it firstly, from many fragments, large and small, which have been discovered among

1. Sanskrit Pratītya-samutpāda, "the dependently-coordinated-origination" (Stcherbatsky). The usual translation "formula of causality" is not quite correct, for the doctrine is not of a succession of cause and effect, but it is that of a mutually interdependent conditionality. The established formula runs thus : "If there is this, then there appears that." Cf. Th. Stcherbatsky, "The Conception of Buddhist Nirvāṇa", Leningrad, 1927, p. 39 ff.

2. Stcherbatsky (l. c., pp. 40 f., 42f.) renders "Śūnyatā" by "relativity", because, according to this doctrine nothing real can be stated of objects, but only relations. Max Walleser ("Die buddhistische Philosophie", Vol. II, Heidelbrg 1911, p. III) calls this doctrine "negativity" because it simultaneously denies the existence and non-existence.

3. The literal meaning of Sarvāstivāda is "the all-is doctrine," the doctrine that everything exists permanently. I-tsing (A record of the Buddhist religion, transl. by J. Takakusu, Oxford 1896, pp. XXIV 8 ff, 20) calls it Āryamūlasarvāstivāda and he mentions the schools of the Mūla-Sarvāstivādas, the Dharmaguptas, the Mahiśāsakas and the Kāśyapiyas as its sub-divisions. The relationship between the Sarvāstivāda and the Mūla-Sarvāstivāda is, however, by no means clear. Cf. Takakusu ERE XI, p. 198 ff. Levi in T 'Qung Pao, ser. 2. t. VIII, 1907, p. 114 f., N. Dutt, "Early History of the Spread of Buddhism and Buddhist Schools", p. 271 and table to p. 224. In the Buddhist dictionary Mahāvyutpatti, para 275, a list of the schools begins with: Āryasarvāstivādaḥ, Mūlasarvāstivādaḥ.

the manuscripts and block-prints brought from Eastern Turkestan by M.A. (Sir Aurel) Stein, A. Grünwedel, A. von. Le Coq, P. Pelliot, and others;[1] further from quotations in other Buddhist Sanskrit texts (like Mahāvastu, Divyāvadāna and Lalitavistara) and finally from Chinese and Tibetan translations.[2] The main texts of the canon of the Mūlasarvāstivādins were translated from Sanskrit into Chinese by the Chinese pilgrim I-tsing in the years 700-712.[3] There are, however, Chinese translations of single texts dating from the middle of the 2nd century onwards, and there were adherents of the Sarvāstivāda in India as early as the 2nd century B.C.[4] In wording and in the arrangement of the texts, the Sanskrit Canon envinces greats imilarity to the Pāli Canon, but on the other hand, there are many points of difference too. A feasible explanation of this is that both canons had a common source, probably the lost Māgadhī Canon, from which first the Pāli Canon branched off in one part of India, and then, later on, the Sanskrit Canon in another district.

---

1. Cf. W. Geiger, "Die archaeologischen und literarischen Funde in Chinesisch Turkestan und ihre Bedeutung fur die orientalistische Wissenschaft", Erlangen (Rede beim Antritt des Prorektorats) 1912; H. Oldenberg in NGGW 1912, 171 ff.; H. Luders, "Uber die literarischen Funde von Ostturkestan" in SBA 1914, p. 85 ff.; A. F. Rud. Hoernle, "Manuscript Remains of Buddhist Literature found in Eastern Turkestan", I, Oxford, 1916.

2. Cf. Oldenburg in ZDMG 52, 1898, 654 ff.; M. Anesaki in OC XIII Hamburg, 1902, p. 61; Le Museon, N. S. VI, 1905, p, 23 ff.; VII, 1906, p. 23 ff.; JRAS 1901, p. 895 ff.

3. J. Takakusu, "A Record of the Buddhist Religion by I-tsing", translated, p. XXXVII. Cf. Ed. Huber in BEFEO, VI, 1906, pp. 1 ff.; S. Levi in "T'oung Pao", ser. 2, t. V, 1904, p. 297 ff.; t. VIII, 1907, p. 110 ff. The Chinese "Tripiṭaka," though also divided into a Vinaya, Sūtra, and Abhidharma, does not, however, mean the same as the Pāli Tipiṭaka, for it contains many non-canonical texts besides the canonical ones, in fact even Brahmanical philosophical treatises (s. Takakusu in JRAS 1896, p. 415). In the Tibetan Kanjur, too, which is also designated as a "Tripiṭaka" and consists of a Vinaya, Sūtra and Abhidharma, much is included which does not admit of comparison with the Tipiṭaka, and was certainly not a part of the Canon.

4. A Sarvāstivādin ācārya Buddhila is mentioned in inscriptions on the lion-capitol in Mathura dating from the 2nd century A.D. F. W. Thomas Ep. Ind. 9, 1907-8 p. 135 ff.

Fragments of the Prātimokṣa-Sūtra of the Sarvāstivādins as well as other texts of the Vinayapiṭaka of the Sanskrit Canon, have been found in Central Asia (Eastern Turkestan), and a few in Nepal too. It is also possible to reconstruct the Prātimokṣa-Sūtra from Chinese and Tibetan translations. Both the Sanskrit Canon of the Sarvāstivādins and the Vinayas of the Mahīśāsakas, Dharmaguptas and Mahā-Saṅghikas, show manifold divergences in separate details from the Pāli Canon and from one another; not only as regards the rules of the Prātimokṣa but also as regards the rules of the Vinaya in general. Nevertheless, the original stock of rules is one and the same.[1] It is in the stories prefaced to the rules in order to relate on what occasion the Buddha proclaimed the rules in question, that the texts show greater divergences. The Mūla-Sarvāstivāda Vinaya contained many legends having reference to the conversion of Kashmir and North western India to Buddhism.[2] Some of these legends are also to be found in the Divyāvadāna, which borrowed a large portion

1. The Sanskrit text of the Prātimokṣa-Sūtra has been edited by L. Finot on the basis of the fragments of manuscripts found by Pelliot in Central Asia, and has been translated into French, with the Chinese version of Kumārajiva by Ed. Huber in JA SER. 11 t. II, 1913, pp. 465-558; a fragment from M. A. Stein's collection by La Vallee Poussion in JRAS 1913, p. 843; a fragment in the Kuchean language, by S. Levi in JA s. 10, t. XIX 1912, 101 ff.; JRAS 1913, p. 109 ff.; Hoernle, "Manuscript Remains", p. 357 ff.; E. Waldschnidt, Bruchstücke des Bhikṣuṇi-Prātimokṣa der Sarvastivadins", Leipzig 1926, has edited the fragments of manuscripts of the Prātimokṣa of the nuns, which were found at Turfan, and compared them with the corresponding texts of all the other schools. For the Tibetan version of the Prātimokṣa, see G. Huth, "Die tibetische Version der Naiḥsargika-prāyascittikadharmāḥ", Strassburg 1891. See also Oldenberg in ZDMG 52, 1898, p. 644 ff.

2. Cf. J, Przyluski and S. Levi in JA s. 11, t. IV, 1914, p. 493 ff. In addition, the reign of Kaniṣka is prophesied, the seven-day week is mentioned, among other things, from which Levi (T'oung Pao, s. 2, Vol. VIII, 1907, p. 115 f.) concludes that the Mūla-Sarvāstivāda-Vinaya was not completed before the 3rd century A. D. However, as there were already Sarvāstivādins at a much earlier period (see also p. 223 above), it is most likely that there was an earlier Sarvāstivāda-Vinaya too, and possibly the Mūla-Sarvāstivāda-Vinaya was merely a later version of that work. On the legendary matter, Jātakas and Avadānas, in the Mūla-Sarvāstivāda Vinaya, see also J. Przyluski in Ind. Hist. Qu. 5, 1929, p. 1 ff.

portion of its tales from the Vinayapiṭaka of the Mūla-Sarvāstivāda.[1] The Vinayapiṭaka also includes the Śikṣās and Saṅghakarmans corresponding to Pāli Sikkhās and Kammavācās, and fragments of these have been brought to light in Central Asia.[2]

The Nikāyas of the Pāli Canon find their parallel in the Āgamas of the Sanskrit Canon; the Dīrghāgama corresponding to the Dīghanikāya, the Madhyamāgama to the Majjhimanikāya, the Saṃyuktāgama to the Saṃyuttanikāya, and the Ekottarāgama to the Aṅguttaranikāya. Fragments of various Sūtras of the Dīrghāgama (Saṃgīti-Sūtra, Āṭanātiya-Sūtra), of the Madhyamāgama (Upāli-Sūtra, Śuka-Sūtra), of the Saṃyuktāgama and the Ekottarāgama, have been found in Central Asia.[3] These fragments are not always in agreement with the corresponding Pāli texts. The comparison of the Chinese Āgamas with the corresponding Pāli Nikāyas, has also shown both agreement to a considerable extent, and notable divergences.[4] In the first

1. Fragments corresponding to the Mahā-Vagga of the Vinayapiṭaka, found in the Stein collection, have been edited by La Vallee Poussin in JRAS 1913, p. 550 ff. A fragment of a Buddhist ritual of ordination, corresponding to the Culla-Vagga X, 17, in Sanskrit, was discovered by C. Bendall in Nepal and edited in Album Kern, p. 373 ff. Various fragments of the Vinaya, ed. by Hoernle, "Manuscript Remains", pp. 4-16. A fragment of the Bhikṣuṇikā-dharma-vacana, ed. by Miss C. M. Ridding and La Vallee Poussin in BSOS I, 1920, p. 123 ff. See also S. Levi, T'oung Pao, s. 2, Vol. VIII, 1907, p. 110 ff.; N. Dutt, "Early History of the Spread of Buddhism and the Buddhist Schools," p. 280 ff.

2. Cf. La Vallee Poussin in JRAS 1913, 843 ff.; Luders in SBA 1922, p. 243.

3. Fragments of the Āgamas of the Sanskrit Canon were discovered amongst the remains of MSS. found in Eastern Turkestan, and edited by R. Pischel in SBA 1904, pp. 808 f., 1138 ff.; JRAS 1911, p. 764 ff.; L. De La Vallee Poussin in JRAS 1911, p. 772; the Śroṇa-Sūtras of the Saṃyukta-Āgama (cf. Saṃyuttanikāya 22, 49 f.= Vol. III, p. 48) has been edited by La Vallee Poussin from Mss. of cecil Bendall's collection in JRAS 1907, 375 ff. Quotations from the Saṃyukta and Ekottara Āgamas have been traced by S. Levi in the commentary on Asaṅga's Mahāyāna-Sūtrālaṃkāra (ed. Levi, on XVI, 21 f. 75). V. A. Smith and W. Hoey found Buddhist Sūtras in Sanskrit, written on bricks, in the ruins of Gopalpur, together with inscriptions which are dated between 250 and 400 A.D. (JASB, proceedings 1896, p. 99 ff.).

4. See especially M. Anesaki, "The Four Buddhist Āgamas in Chinese", in Transactions of the Asiatic Society of Japan, Vol. 35, Part 3, 1908, and

place there is no agreement as regards the order of the Sūtras in the separate Āgamas. In the Saṃyuktāgama the division into Vargas and Saṃyuktas is totally different, and there are Saṃyuktas in the Pāli which are missing in the Chinese version; on the other hand, there are some in the Chinese which do not occur in the Pāli.[1] The greatest differences are those which we find between the Ekottarāgama and the Aṅguttaranikāya. On the whole it may be said that the points of agreement and the divergences prove that the Sanskrit Āgamas and the Pāli Nikāyas were compiled from the same materials but were arranged in different ways in the different schools. Now in the Chinese Tripiṭaka there are also texts which, though bearing the same titles as the corresponding Pāli texts, are nevertheless essentially different. Thus there is a Brahmajāla-Sūtra, which was translated into Chinese by Kumārajīva, and is held in high esteem in China and Japan but which teaches Buddhist ethics in the spirit of the Mahāyāna. On the other hand, there are in the Abhidharma-Kośa-Vyākhyā, several quotations from a Brahmajāla-Sūtra, which must have corresponded to the Pāli text.[2] The Chinese Tripiṭaka contains ten different translations of the Mahā-Parinirvāṇa-Sūtra. Three of these translations belong to the Hīnayāna and seven to the Mahāyāna; and the only thing they have in common is the

---

above, p. 223. The Chung-Tsi-King (Chinese version of the Saṃgītisutta) of the Dīrghāgama has been translated into German and discussed by Siegfried Behrsing in Asia Major 7, 1931, pp. 1-149, Cf. above, p. 43.

1. The Sagāthavarga in the three Chinese versions of the Saṃyuktāgama contains 318 Sūtras, out of which 244 coincide with those of the Pāli text. It is impossible to determine whether the quotations traced by Anesaki (Le Museon, N. S. VII, 1906, 38 ff.) in the Chinese Mahā-Prajñā-Pāramitā-Śāstra, are derived from a Pāli or Prākrit text of the Saṃyutta and Suttanipāta. For the Saṃyukta-Āgama, see also Levi in T'oung Pao, s. 2, Vol. V, 1904, p. 297 ff.

2. Cf. La Vallee Poussin in JRAS 1903, 359 ff., Anesaki in ERE, Vol. V, p. 452. The Chinese "Fan wang King" or "Brahmajāla-Sūtra." a Vinaya work of the Mahāyāna, translated by Kumārajīva from an unknown Sanskrit text, has been edited and translated into French by J. J. M. De Groot, Le Code du Mahāyāna en Chine, son influence sur la vie monacale et sur le monde laique (Verhandlingen der Kon. Akademie van Wetenshappen te Amsterdam, Afd. Lett. Deel I, No. 2) 1893. Another Brahmajāla-Sūtra in the Tibetan Kanjur, corresponds to the Pāli text in the Dīghanikāya.

external form, inasmuch as they contain speeches which the Buddha is supposed to have uttered prior to his death (parinirvāṇa).[1]

The Sanskrit Canon also contained a "Kṣudraka" corresponding to the Khuddakanikāya.[2] We do not know whether this included all those texts which in the Pāli Canon are counted as belonging to the fifth Nikāya; but we do know that the Sanskrit Canon also contained the Sanskrit texts Udāna, Dharmapada, Sthavira-Gāthā, Vimāna-Vatthu and Buddha-Vaṃsa. In the Chinese Tripiṭaka, it is true, there is no single text to correspond to the Suttanipāta; but more than half of the texts included in the Suttanipāta occur in the Āgamas, for instance the texts corresponding to the Aṭṭhaka-Vagga and the Pārāyaṇa. Fragments of the Sanskrit version of the two last-mentioned have been found in Eastern Turkestan too.[3] A collection corresponding to the Itivuttakas was translated into Chinese by Hsuan Tsang in about 650 A.D.[4] Considerable quotations, forming a parallel to

---

1. Cf. F. Max Müller in SBE, Vol. 10 (I), p. xxxi, note; J. Edkins in JRAS 1881, p. 66 ff.; R. Kimura, in JDL 4, 1921, 188 f. note, and Historical Study of the Terms Hīnayāna and Mahāyāna, p. 94 note. The Hīnayāna includes the translation of Po-fa-tsu (290-306 A.D.) and that of Fa-hien (between 317 and 420 A.D.); translated into Italian, after the last-named, by Carlo Puini in GSAI 21, 1908, p. 59 ff.; 22, 1909, p. 1 ff. The earliest Vaipulya-Parinirvāṇa-Sūtra was translated into Chinese by Dharmarakṣita (between 205 and 316 A.D.). Specimens of it are given by S. Beal in Ind. Ant. 5, 1876; p. 222 ff. and SBE. Vol. 19, p. 365 ff.

2. A Kṣudraka is mentioned by Hsuan-Tsang as the fifth Āgama of the Śrāvakapiṭaka, s. Levi in JA, s. 11, t. VIII, 1916, p. 20. Nevertheless, the "four Āgamas" are especially emphasised as the real Āgamas, as for instance, when the Divyāvadāna makes frequent mention (pp. 17, 331, 333) of the āgamacatuṣṭayam, cf. Oldenberg in ZDMG 52, 654 f.

3. Cf. M. Anesaki in JPTS 1906-7, p. 50 f.; Hoernle in JRAS 1916, p. 709 ff.; 1917, p. 134. In the Sanskrit version of the Aṭṭhaka-Vagga (it is mentioned as the arthavargīyāṇi Sūtrāṇi in the Divyāvadāna, p. 20) prose narratives precede the verses, but there are none such in the Pāli. There are also other divergences from the Pāli text. The Sanskrit text is shorter.

4. K. Watanabe in JPTS 1906-7, p. 44 ff. In the Chinese Tripiṭaka there is a work Ṣaṭpāramitā-sannipāta-Sūtra (translated in 222 A.D.) which is a kind of Cariyāpiṭaka: s. R. Kimura, "A Historical Study of the Terms Hīnayāna and Mahāyāna", p. 129, note 1.

passages from the Khuddaka-pāṭha, the Vimāna-Vatthu, Buddha-Vaṃsa and Dhammapada, are to be found in the Mahāvastu.[1]

We glean from one of the Mahāvastu quotations,[2] that there was a Dharmapada in the Sanskrit Canon, divided into Vargas, after the style of the Pāli Dhammapada. This Sanskrit version was not identical with that of the Pāli Canon, but both versions had an original stock of verses in common, and were arranged on one and the same principle. The collection of verses which belonged to the original Canon, also served as a prototype and as a foundation for more comprehensive anthologies, which were compiled in later times, and were widely propagated in Central Asia, Tibet and China. Thus, for instance, there is a Chinese anthology with the same 26 sections (Vargas) as the Pāli Dhammapada though it has 13 additional sections.[3] Fragments of a Sanskrit anthology have been found in Central Asia, which were at first regarded as passages from recensions of the Dhammapada, but which in reality belong to the Udāna-Varga, which is known to us from a Tibetan translation. This anthology was compiled by Dharmatrāta, who, according to Tārānātha, is supposed to have lived in King Kaniṣka's day. In the Tibetan version, it contains only 375 verses, corresponding to verses of the Dhammapada, but also the greater part of the verses of the Udāna, and numerous verses which have parallels in the Suttanipāta and other portions of the Pāli Canon.[4] Another anthology was written in a Prākrit dialect, which is a later form of

1. Mahāvastu, ed. Senart, I, 290 ff.; II, 191 ff.; 250 ff.; Quotations from "the Dharmapada" (sing) or "the Dharmapadas" (plur.); II. 212; III, 91, 156, 434 ff.

2. III, 434 ff. Here a Sahasravarga is quoted from "the Dharmapadas"; it contains 24 verses, whilst the Sahassa-Vagga in the Pāli consists of only 16 verses. On the Dharmapada in Nepal, Tibet and China, s. Oldenberg in ZDMG 52, 1898, p. 662 ff.

3. Cf. Max Müller in SBE, Vol. 10 (1), p. 2 ff.; S. Beal, "Texts from the Buddhist Canon commonly known as Dhammapada", London 1902; and the important study on the Dharmapada recensions by S. Levi in JA., s. 10, t. XX, 1912, pp. 203-294.

4. Fragments of the Udānavarga, from finds in Central Asia, have been published by R. Pischel, "Die Turfan-Recensionen des Dhammapada", SBA 1908, p. 968. ff.; S. Levi and La Vallee Poussin in JA s. 10. t. XVI, 1910, p. 444 ff.; XVII, 1911, 431 ff.; t. XIX, 1912, p. 311 ff.; JRAS 1911. p. 758 ff.;

the North-west Indian dialect familiar to us from the Shāhbāzgarhī rock edicts of Aśoka, and compiled after the pattern, and with the help of the Dhammapada or some similar verse collection of the Sanskrit Canon, or the original Canon. Fragments of this anthology have come down to us in a few leaves of a manuscript written in the Kharoṣṭhī script, which M. Petroffsky and J. L. Dutreuil de Rhins had found at Khotan, and brought to Europe.[1]

It is a certainty that there were Jātakas too, in the Sanskrit Canon; but it must remain an open question whether this Canon ever included a Jātaka Book or a large collection of Jātakas of its own. It is doubtful, too, whether the collection of "seven Abhidharmas," which is translated in the Chinese

---

1912, p. 355 ff. The Tibetan version of the Udānavarga has been translated into English by W. W. Rockhill, London 1883, and the Tibetan text was published by H. Beckh, Berlin 1911. Cf., A. Schiefner, "Über Vasubandhus Gāthāsaṃgraha", in Malanges Asiatiques VIII (Bulletin XXV, 1878), pp. 559 f., 590 ff.; La Vallee Poussin in GGA 1912, 191 f.; Luders in SBA 1914, p. 102; and Seidenstücker, "Das Udāna", I, 1913, pp. 37, 71 ff. A voluminous anthology, about five times as large as the Pāli Dhammapada, is the Dharmasamuccaya by Avalokitasiṃha, who has also drawn from Mahāyāna sources; on a MS. of this work, found in Nepal, see Dharma Āditya Dharmācārya in Ind. Hist. Qu. 1, 1925, 422 ff., 677 ff. Fragments of Udānavarga translations in Kucean language are discussed by E. Sieg and W. Siegling in BSOS VI, 2, p. 483 ff.

1. The old Kharoṣṭhī manuscript, important from the points of view both of language and palaeography, has been edited by Senart in JA s. 9, t. XII, 1898, pp. 193 ff., 545 ff. This edition was the foundation for the new edition by Benimadhab Barua and Sailendranath Mitra, Calcutta 1921. The fragments found by Petroffsky were identified by S. d' Oldenburg, St. Petersburg 1907. On the "MS Dutreuil de Rhins," cf. "Comptes rendus de l' academie des inscriptions," 14. mai 1895 et 15. avril 1898, Senart, OC XI Paris 1897, I, 1 ff.; G. Bühler, "On the Origin of the Indian Brāhmi Alphabet", 2nd Ed., Strassburg 1898, p. 122 ff.; Lüders in NGGW 1899, p. 474 ff.; T. W. Rhys Davids in JRAS 1899, p. 426 ff.; R. O. Franke in ZDMG 60, 1906, p. 477 ff.; M. A. Stein, "Ancient Khotan", Oxford 1907, I, 188; Jules Block, JA ser. 10, t. XIX, 1912, p. 331 ff.; Konow ("Festschrift Windisch", p. 85 ff.) is of opinion that, though this anthology is composed in a dialect originating in the North-west of India, it was written in the neighbourhood of Khotan. Like Bühler (l. c.) he ascribes it to the 1st century A.D., whilst Lüders (SBA 1914, p. 101) thinks it was written in the 3rd century A.D. It is probably the earliest Indian manuscript which has been discovered so far.

Tripiṭaka, is also derived from the old Canon, for these Abhidharmas have nothing in common with the Abhidhammapiṭaka of the Pāli Canon save the number seven and a few titles.[1]

The Canon of the Mūla-Sarvāstivādins has thus only come down to us in an incomplete way, but as regards the other Buddhist sects, we do not know whether they had any set Canon at all. As far as we can see, each sect merely has one or several texts which pass as especially sacred, being regarded as a kind of "Bible," and which partly assimilated and partly displaced the old texts of a Tripiṭaka which they, too, acknowledged in principle.

The Mahāvastu

One of the most important works which still belongs to the old school of the Hīnayāna is the Mahāvastu[2] or Mahāvastu-Avadāna.[3] The work calls itself a book "of the Vinayapiṭaka

1. J. Takakusu, JRAS 1905, p. 3 ff. and JPTS 1905, p. 67 ff. See also p. 167 above.

2. The text has been edited by E. Senart in 3 volumes, Paris 1882-1897, with detailed surveys of the contents in the Introductions and a valuable commentary. A survey of the contents has also been given by Rajendralala Mitra "Sanskrit Buddhist Lit. of Nepal", pp. 115-161. See also A. Barth, in RHR 11, 1885, 160 ff.; 42, 1900, 51 f. (=Oeuvres I, 376 ff.; II, 334) and Journal des savants 1899, 459 ff., 517 ff., E. Windisch, "Die Komposition des Mahavastu", in ASGW XXVII, 1909, 467-511; Oldenberg in NGGW 1912, 123 ff.; L. de La Vallee Poussin in ERE VIII, 328 ff.; Haraprasad Sastri in Ind. Hist. Qu. 1, 1925, 202 ff. See now also Bimala Charan Law, "A Study of the Mahavastu", Calcutta and Simla 1930, and Supplement.

3. This is the title of the work in most of the colophons. In the text itself and also in some of the colophons, it is called Mahāvastu. Mahāvastu means "The Great Subjects," i. e., the main subjects of the Vinaya, that is to say the admission to the order, etc., and corresponds to the Mahā-Vagga of the Pāli Vinayapiṭaka and the Vinayavastu (beside Kṣudrakavastu, corresponding to the Culla-Vagga) of the Vinayapiṭaka of the Sarvāstivādins. Cf. La Vallee Poussin, l. c., Mahāvastu-Avadāna means "The Legends pertaining to the main Subjects of the Vinaya." H. Zimmer (in ZII 3, 1925, 201 ff.) seeks to prove that "avadāna" means the same as "nidāna", "origin", "original causes," and he explains "mahāvastu" as the "great fact of salvation." This, however, seems to be erroneous. The fact that the Chinese translators occasionally confused *nidāna* and *avadāna* (cf. S. Levi in

according to the text of the Lokottaravādins belonging to the Mahāsāṅghikas." The Mahāsāṅghikas, i.e., the followers of the Mahāsaṅgha, the "great community", are, it is generally agreed, the earliest schismatics. A sub-section of them are the Lokottaravādins, i.e., those according to whose doctrine the Buddhas are "above the world" (lokottara) and follow the worldly life only externally.[1] Exactly in agreement with this doctrine the biography of Buddha is told as an "Avadāna" a miracle-story. Of course it does not differ much from the texts of the Pāli canon which deal with the life of Buddha. In both we hear miracles which accompany conception, birth, enlightenment and the first conversions of Buddha. The Mahāvastu concurs with the Nidānakathā in this that it treats the life of Buddha in three sections[2] of which the first begins with the life of the Bodhisattva at the time of the Buddha Dīpaṅkara (I, 193 ff) and tells of his life at the time of the other earlier Buddhas. The second section (II, 1 ff) takes us to the heaven of the Tuṣita-gods where the Bodhisattva who is reborn there, decides to take rebirth in the womb of Queen Māyā and tells of the

---

JA 1912, s. 10, t. XX, p. 219) is no proof that these two expressions are identical. Moreover, in the Vinaya literature, "vastu" has the definite meaning of "subject of the Vinaya" and the "event" related in connection with this subject.

1. "The perfectly enlightened ones have nothing in common with the world, but with the great Ṛṣis everything is exalted above the world," Mahāvastu I, 159, 2. "They wash their feet, though no dust clings to them, they sit in the shade, though the heat of the sun never oppresses them, they take nourishment, though hunger never troubles them, they use medicine, though they have no illness, etc;" Windisch, l. c., p. 470. According to Mahāv. I, 2, the Lokottaravādins belong to the "middle land" (madhyadeśa), i.e. to the "sixteen countries" of Northern India. Cf. Mahāvastu I, 198. Mm. Haraprasada Sastri (Calcutta Review, Sept. 1930, p. 441 f.) would translate: "Vinayapiṭaka according to the text of the Mahāsaṅghikas who declare the Buddha to be lokottara." For, he says, all the Mahāsaṅghikas believe the Buddha to be lokottara, and in the list of the eighteen sects "Lokottaravādins" are not mentioned. But Vasumitra and Bhavya mention the Lokottaravādins as a sect of the Mahāsaṅghikas. See Mrs Rhys Davids, "Points of Controversy", p. xxxvi f. and Max Walleser, "Die Sekten des alten Buddhismus." Heidelberg 1927, pp. 28, 78.

2. See also p. 181 above. However, the expressions Durenidāna, avidurenidāna and santikenidāna are not to be found in the Mahāvastu.

miracles of the conception and birth of the prince, of his exit from his native town, his fights with Māra and the enlightenment which he accomplishes under the Bodhi tree. The third section (in Vol. III) narrates at last, concurring with the Mahāvagga of the Vinayapiṭaka[1] in its main features, the history of the earliest conversions and the origin of the community of monks. And this is also the reason why the Mahāvastu describes itself as belonging to the Vinayapiṭaka, although—except for a few remarks on the admission to the order—it contains practically nothing about the actual Vinaya, the rules of the order. It corresponds to that part of the Vinayapiṭaka which tells the history of the origin of the order.[2]

But when we say that the Mahāvastu mainly narrates the story of life of Buddha for the Lokottaravādins, with that we have not by any means exhausted the contents of the work, nor given an idea of its composition. For, far from being a piece of literary art, the Mahāvastu is rather a labyrinth in which one can discover the thread of a connected story of the life of Buddha only with great difficulty. This narrative is again and again interrupted through other topics, especially through numerous Jātakas and Avadānas as well as dogmatic Sūtras. We cannot recognise any principle of arrangement. We find often that not even an attempt is made to establish at least a loose connection between the various constituents. Moreover, very often one and the same story, whether it is an episode from the life of Buddha or a Jātaka is told two times one after another, at first in prose and then—more or less deviating from it—in verses.

1. Cf. Windisch, l. c., 467 ff.

2. See p. 26 above, and Windisch, l. c., pp. 473, 476 ff. Probably it is only this portion of the Vinayapiṭaka which has come down to us in the Mahāvastu. Cf. Oldenberg in NGGW 1912, 152. T. W. Rhys Davids (SBB III, 256 f.) advances the less likely theory that the Lokottaravādins revised only the introduction, because they took over the rules of the Vinaya themselves in their Pāli form, or in some form resembling the Pāli, just as they were, without any change, H. Zimmer, l. c., 209 ff., thinks that the presentation of Buddha's life with the preliminary conditions in previous existences, constitutes a "Vinaya" for those who wish to attain Buddha-hood (in the sense of the Mahāyāna, which, he says, is already foreshadowed in the Mahāvastu). There is no evidence anywhere for this use of the word "vinaya".

But even at different places the same episodes recur again and again with small deviations from one another. Thus the legend of Buddha's birth is told not less than four times.[1] There is also no uniformity in the language. Although the whole work, prose as well as verse is written in "mixed Sanskrit" this dialect approaches the Sanskrit language in varying degrees. When it is not so close to Sanskrit it is more ancient.[2] As regards style, too, earlier and later portions of the work can be clearly distinguished.[3]

In spite of all this and although we learn from this work hardly anything that is new on the teachings of Buddha not even anything on the special teachings of the Lokottaravādins, it is of the greatest importance because it contains many old traditions and old versions of the texts which also occur in the Pāli-canon. Thus the exit of Prince Siddhārtha from his home town (abhiniṣkramaṇa) is told in a most antiquarian way—similar to the Majjhimanikāya (26 and 36).[4] Similarly we find in it old versions of the "Sermon of Banaras", of the Mahāgovindasutta (Dīghanikāya 19), of the Dīghamakkhasutta (Majjhimanikāya, 74) of the Sahassavagga from the Dhammapada, of the Khuddakapāṭha, of the Pabbajja, Padhama and the Khaggavisana—Suttas from the Suttanipāta and individual pieces of the Vimāna vatthu and of the Buddhavaṃsa.[5] The poems on the birth of Buddha are also composed in the antiquarian style of ballads. They are remnants of that ballad-poetry of ancient Buddhism that we have already seen in so many places.

1. Windisch, Buddha's Geburt, p. 106, 124 f.

2. Oldenberg, ZDMG 52, 663. Haraprasad Sastri (Ind. Hist. Qu. I, 1925, 204 f.) rejects the term "vernacularized Sanskrit" or "Sanskritized vernacular" as applied to the language of the Mahāvastu. He regards it as a dialect which was actually spoken in Northern India in the 2nd century B.C.

3. Cf. Oldenberg in NGGW 1912, 123 ff.

4. II, 117. This is followed immediately by a second, later version of the same Abhiniṣkramaṇa-Sūtra.

5. Cf. Oldenberg, ZDMG 52, 659 ff., Windisch, "Mara and Buddha", 316 ff., 322 ff.; J. Dutoit, Die duṣkaracarya des Bodhisattva, Strassburg 1905; J. Charpentier in WZKM 23, 1909, 33 ff. (Māra-Saṃyutta und Mahāvastu); Rhys Davids, SBB III, p. 256 ff. (on the Mahā-Govinda-Sutta).

But of very special value is the Mahāvastu as a treasure-house of Jātakas[1] and other stories. A good half of the work consists of Jātakas which are told partly in pure prose, partly in prose with interspersed verses, sometimes first in prose and then once again in verses. Here again we meet the Bodhisattva sometimes as a king ruling over the whole world, sometimes as the son of a merchant, or as a Brahmin and also as a Nāga prince, as a lion, elephant etc. Many of the Jātakas are versions of the same stories that we find in the Pāli Jātaka-book, sometimes concurring almost word for word, sometimes with smaller or bigger deviations. Thus the Śyāmakajātaka (II, 209ff) the pathetic story of the son of a Brahmin whom the king Peliyakṣa kills with an arrow, is only another version of the Sāmajātaka known to us. The Kinnarījātaka (II, 94 ff) corresponds in its character if not content, to the Kinnara tales of the Jātaka book. The Kuśajātaka appears once (II, 420 ff) in a recension considerably differing from the Pāli one, a second time (III, 1 ff) in a metrical version which shows concurrences with the Pāli Gāthās.[2] The story of Nalini who seduces Ekaśṛṅga (i.e. "unicorn") has been watered down to a very pious legend in the Mahāvastu (III, 143 ff) which however has still preserved antiquarian features which have disappeared in the prose of the Pāli-Jātaka of Isisiṅga.[3]

But there are also many Jātakas and Avadānas in the Mahāvastu which have no correspondences in Pāli. They glorify very often the extraordinary readiness to sacrifice and generosity of the Bodhisattva. As King Arka, for example, gifts to the

1. They have been compiled by S. d' Oldenberg in JRAS 1893, p. 335 ff. and A. Barth in the Journal des savants 1899, p. 625 ff. Charpentier shows how the text of the Mahāvastu can often be corrected with the help of the Pāli text. Paccekabuddhageschihten 2 ff., 12 ff., 25 ff., and in Le Monde oriental III, 1909, p. 34 ff.

2. See above p. 143, 128f, 131 f. The story of Amarā, the daughter of the Smith (II, 283 ff) corresponds to the Pāli Jātaka No. 387. The Markaṭa Jātaka (II, 246 ff) is the fable of the monkey and the crocodile (Jāt. No. 208), above p. 122, 157 f. The Syāmaka-Jātaka translated from the Chinese Tripiṭaka by Ed. Chavannes, Cinq Cents contes, t. I, p. 156 ff. On the Kusa-Jātaka in the Mahāvastu see Charpentier in WZKM 27, 1913, 94 f.

3. Lüders, NGGW 1901, p. 20 ff., and above p. 142 ff.

Buddha of his time 80,000 grottoes (cave-temples) made of the seven kinds of precious stones (I, 54). Again he gifts his wife and child only to learn a wise saying (I, 91 f). As a potter he is more pious than King Kṛkin as he kills no living being and puts up his pots at crossroads in order to fill them with rice and beans for hungry people, and when he hears that during his absence his parents have gifted to Buddha the straw with which he had covered his hut a short while ago, he rejoices for a month (I, 317 ff). Some of the stories bear more Brahminical or Purāṇa-like character; for instance, the story of Brahmadatta who is childless and turns to the ṛṣis for help, whereupon three birds are born to him which speak with human voice and give out very wise sayings (I, 272 ff).[1] The Rājavaṃśa, the "History of the Kings" (to whose dynastry Śākyamuni belongs), begins precisely in the nature of the Purāṇas with a report on creation (I, 338 ff). The spirit of the Purāṇas pervades also the Jātaka (I, 283 ff) in which a ṛṣi Rakṣita, the Bodhisattva as a hermit attains such miraculous powers that with his hands he can touch the sun and the moon. The spirit of the Mahāyāna is much similar to that of the Purāṇas, and some of the stories of the Mahāvastu exhibit that special love for phantasmagoria-splendid and enchanting illustrations which are to portray the miraculous powers of the holyman as well as to serve the glorification of Buddha—which is so characteristic of the Mahāyāna texts. Of this nature are also for example the "umbrella-stories" (Chattavastu I, 253 ff). After Buddha has freed the town of Śrāvastī from a terrible pest caused by the Yakṣas, gods and spirits hold an umbrella over the Exalted One to show him their respect. He however makes, in his usual kindness, by his powers of magic, one Buddha appear under every umbrella so that

1. The story reminds us of the beginning of the Mārkaṇḍeya-Purāṇa, Cf. Vol. I, p. 535f. Also the description of the hell at the beginning of Mahāvastu shows allusions to the same Purāṇa (L. Scherman, Visionslitteratur, p. 36). The visit of Maudgalyāyana (Pāli Moggallāna) to the eight hells, as also his wandering through the animal world, the world of the Pretas, of the Asuras and of the various classes of gods is also rooted in the Pāli tradition in which similarly Moggallāna is a holy man who wanders through heaven, hell and all the worlds.

every god believes that the Buddha is sitting under his umbrella.

And although the Mahāvastu belongs to the Hīnayāna and contains much that could likewise occur— or even actually occurs—in the Pāli texts of the Theravādins, still it also contains something that makes it come closer to the Mahāyāna. The reason for many such traits is probably that the conception of Buddha prevalent among the Mahāsaṅghikas and the Lokottaravādins does actually represent a transition to the Mahāyāna. In other cases, however, we are most likely right in assuming that interpolation took place.[1] Thus we find in the first volume (I, 63-193) a big section on the ten Bhūmis or steps, which a Bodhisattva must go through and the description of the virtues which he must possess in each of the ten steps.[2] Included in this section is a Buddhānusmṛti (I, 163 ff), i.e. a hymn on Buddha which is not different in any way from the stotras on Viṣṇu or Śiva in the Purāṇas. It also represents the spirit of the Mahāyāna when (II, 362 ff) it is said, that the purity of Buddha is so great that even the worship of the Exalted One already suffices for attaining Nirvāṇa and that one earns unlimited merit when one simply saunters around a Stūpa and worships it with gifts of flowers etc. That from the smile of the Buddha rays go out which light up the entire Buddha-field (Buddha-kṣetra) (III, 137 ff) occurs in the Mahāyāna texts times without number. It is also Mahā-

1. Thus, for instance, the Avalokita-Sūtra (in two versions, II, 293 ff., 297 ff) is cited as an independent Sūtra, in Śāntideva's Śikṣā Samuccaya (ed. Bendall, pp. 89f, 297 ff., with the title Avalokana-Sūtra) and in the Tibetan too, it appears as an independent work. Hence it is probably interpolated in the Mahāvastu, the more so because, in the colophon at the end of the second version it is called parivāra ("accessory," see above p. 33, the Parivāra of the Vinayapiṭaka) See Senart, II, P. xxvi, note 3). Though the text in the Śikṣā Samuccaya agrees in the main with that of the Mahāvastu, there are nevertheless such striking divergences of particular passages, that it cannot possibly be an extract from the Mahāvastu.

2. The presentation of the Bhūmis in the Mahāvastu diverges from that in the texts of the Mahāyāna, hence this is prabably a transition form the Hīnayāna to the Mahāyāna. A Tibetan Mahāyāna author, whose object is to prove that the doctrine of the Bhūmis was not a Mahāyānistic innovation alludes to the fact that they already occur in the Mahāvastu. Cf. La vallee Poussin in ERE II 743 ff., VIII,.330 Note; J. Rahder, "Dasabhūmika-Sūtra, Leuven 1926 p. iii ff.

yānic when there is a talk of a large number of Buddhas and when it is said that the Bodhisattvas are not born to father and mother but that they are born directly through their properties.[1]

The way the Mahāvastu is composed makes it difficult to fix the time of its composition. Many factors like its belonging to the Lokottaravāda-school and its language indicate that it is very old. That the work is written entirely in "mixed Sanskrit" whereas in the Mahāyāna texts this dialect alternates with pure Sanskrit, is an indication of its greater antiquity. For as Barth[2] says, Sanskrit is only an intruder in Buddhist texts. Also those numerous pieces which are common to the Mahāvastu and the Pāli canon and which can be traced back to a common source are certainly old. So the Gāthās of the Khaḍgaviṣāṇasūtra (I, 357 ff.) may be older than those of the corresponding ones in the Khaggavisāṇasutta of the Pāli Suttanipāta. But if in the Mahāvastu these verses are sung of 500 mortal Pratyekabuddhas, then it appears peculiar enough when they sing the refrain, "He wanders lonely like the rhinoceros" and it is not probable that the prose framework is just as old as the Gāthās. Also the Mahā yānic features already mentioned point to the early centuries A.D. as also some texts which appear to be influenced by the sculptures of the Gandhāra art.[3] We are brought up to the 4th century by the allusions to the Mahāyāna sects of the Yogācāras (I,120), to the Huns, to the Chinese language and script and the description of astrology as "Horāpāṭhaka" (III, 178).[4]

---

1. Cf. Windhish, "Buddha's Geburt", p. 97 note, 100 f. and 193 f.

2. Journal des savants 1899, p. 459.

3. When for example during a flower miracle the lotus-flowers fall round the halo of Buddha in the form of a circle. The halo has been introduced in India only through Greek artists. Cf. A. Foucher JA 1903, s 10, t II, p. 208 f. and L'art greco-bouddhique du Gandhāra, t. I, Paris 1905, p. 622. Also the several Buddhas under the umbrellas (above, p. 235) remind us of monuments of art.

4. According to Senart (I, p. 469 f) we should regard Mahāvastu I, 120 as an allusion to the Mahāyāna school of the Yogācāras, which would indicate the 4th century. It is possible however, that Yogācāra which is used merely with its general meaning of "practising Yoga." Cf. La Valee Poussin

But the nucleus of the work is old and has originated already in the 2nd century B.C. although enlarged even as late as in the 4th century A.D. and even still later through additions and interpolations. For the Mahāvastu has only borrowed the embellishments from the Mahāyāna and contains only a weak sprinkling of actual Mahāyāna teachings and nothing of the Mahāyāna mythology.

The Lalitavistara

While the Mahāvastu describes itself as a work belonging to the Hīnayāna but which as taken up some features of the Mahāyāna, the Lalitavistara[1] is considered as one of the holiest texts of the Mahāyāna, describes itself as a Vaipulyasūtra ("elaborate teaching text")—a common term for Mahāyāna Sūtras—and exhibits all features of a Mahāyāna Sūtra although the work originally contained the description of Buddha's life for the Sarvāstivādins belonging to the Hīnayāna.[2] But even the title Lalitavistara i.e., "the exhaustive story of the sport (of Buddha)" corresponds to the Mahāyāna ideas. The life and work of Buddha on the earth is thus described as the "sport" (lalita) of a supernatural being.[3] And as an exalted, divine being Buddha appears in the introductory chapter also. It

in ERE VIII, 329 note 4, Haraprasad Sastri in Ind. Hist. Qu. I, 1925, 205. See also B. Ch. Law, "A Study of the Mahāvastu", supplement p. 17 f., and A. B. Keith, "A note on the Mahāvastu in Law's book", p. vii.

1. First edition by Rajendralala Mitra in Bibl. Ind. 1877 (very faulty), a better edition by S. Leffmann, Halle a. S. 1902 and 1908. Even this edition however needs correcting. Cf. Friedrich Weller, "Zum Lalita Vistara", Diss, Leipzing 1915, p. 8 ff. The English translation by Rajendralala Mitra (Bibl. Ind. 1881-1886) only goes as far as Chapter XV. Chapters I-V translated into German by S. Lefmann, Berlin 1875; a complete French Translation by Ph. Ed. Foucaux in AMG t. 6 et 19 (Paris 1884, 1892).

2. This is according to Chinese tradition. Cf. S. Beal, The Romantic Legend of Sakya Buddha from the Chinese-Sanskrit, London 1875, Introd.; Foucaux, Lalitavistara tradut, t II, Introd. Beal's "Romantic Legend" is a condensed translation from Chinese of the Abhiniṣkramaṇa-sūtra that is not preserved in Sanskrit but has been translated from Chinese in 587. It is said to be the Buddha-biography for the sect of the Dharmaguptas.

3. Cf. on the title Lefmann, translation, p. 70 ff, II edition, p. VI f.; Foucaux, t. II, p. 3 and Winternitz, WZKM 1912, p. 244. The work calls itself also as a Mahānidāna, i.e. "a great Sūtra dealing with the beginnings

begins certainly in the manner of the Pāli Suttas with the words: "Thus have I heard: Once the Lord was staying at Śrāvastī in the Jeta-grove in the garden of the Anāthapiṇḍada". But while in the Pāli texts after this or similar stereotyped introductory words in which the Lord is presented to us as surrounded by some disciples or at most by a retinue of "five hundred monks", immediately the actual Sutta begins, in the Lalitavistara as in all the Vaipulyasūtras of the Mahāyāna first one more picture is drawn of Buddha bathed in the light of divine splendour. He is surrounded by 12,000 monks and not less than 32,000 Bodhisattvas, "all of them bound to just one more rebirth, all born with the perfections of a Bodhisattva, all enjoying the knowledge of a Bodhisattva, all in possession of the insight into the texts of miraculous powers" etc. While he sits in midnight vigil engrossed in deep meditation a ray of light shoots up emanating from his crown and penetrates into the heavens transporting all gods into excitement. These gods then begin immediately to sing a song in praise of the exalted Buddha and soon appear Īśvara and other gods before him and beg him, for redeeming and blessing the world, to reveal the eminent Vaipulyasūtra, called Lalitavistara, praising in bombastic words the excellent qualities of this text which was also revealed already by earlier Buddhas. Not saying one word, Buddha gives his assent. After this longwinded introduction that fills a whole big chapter, the actual story, the biography of Buddha begins which forms the content of the work. And in fact it begins where the second chapter (avidurenidāna) in the Nidānakathā begins:

The Bodhisattva lives in the heaven of the contented (Tuṣita) gods in a magnificent divine palace (The Bodhisattva receives over a hundred attributes and the divine palace in which he lives over a dozen). Under the deafening noise of 84,000 drums he is requested to come down to the earth to begin his work of salvation. After prolonged consultations in the course of which the advantages and disadvantages of a large number of royal families are discussed, the Bodhisattva decides to take

(of the life of Buddha)" and as "Lalitavistara-Purāṇa", a term, which is appropriate inasmuch as the style of the work is not unlike that of the Purāṇas.

rebirth in the house of King Śuddhodana, in the womb of Queen Māyā as she has all the qualities of a Buddha-mother. As perfect as her beauty (described with the minutest details) are her virtue and purity. But she alone, of all the women of India, is also capable of bearing the future Buddha, as she possesses the strength of ten thousand elephants. With the aid of gods the conception takes place after the Boddhisattva has decided to penetrate into her womb in the form of an elephant. The gods not only provide a celestial house as maternity chamber for Māyā but they also create a palace with precious stones in her womb so that the Bodhisattva may not be made impure during the ten months in his mother's womb. In this palace of precious stones he sits with admirable gentleness. But his body shines in splendid beauty and a light spreads for miles from the body of his mother. People afflicted with diseases come to Māyā Devi and are freed from their sufferings as soon as she places her hand on their head. "And whenever she saw to her right, she saw the Bodhisattva in her womb, just as one saw one's own face in a pure plain mirror." Even when he is in his mother's womb the unborn Bodhisattva delights the gods through pious preaching, and god Brahman is at his beck and call.[1]

Just like the conception of the Bodhisattva so also his birth takes place to the accompaniment of mighty miracles and omens. In the Lumbinī grove he is born to Māyā in the well known manner portrayed in numerous sculptures, however not as an ordinary human child but as an omniscient exalted being, as a "Mahāpuruṣa", a "great spirit". While lotus flowers sprout up under his footsteps, the new born baby, announcing his greatness, takes seven steps in each of the six cardinal directions.[2]

Here the story is interrupted by a dialogue between Ānanda and Buddha[3] in which there is a passionate declamation

1. Chapt 2-6. The beginning of Ch. 6 has been translated by Windisch, "Buddha's Geburt", p. 162 ff.

2. As Puruṣa and Mahāpuruṣa the creator Prajāpati is described in the Brāhmaṇas and Upaniṣads, later also as Brahman and Viṣṇu. The seven steps of the new born Buddha child are also to be explained from the myth of the seven steps of Viṣṇu.

3. Ch. 7, ed. Lefmann, pp. 87-91.

against those infidels who do not want to believe in the miraculous birth of Buddha. But belief in Buddha is taught as an essential constituent of religion. And we are reminded of the Kṛṣṇa of Bhagavadgītā when Buddha says here:

> "To all who believe in me, I do good. Like friends are those to me who seek refuge in me. And many friends has the Tathāgatha. Those friends of Tathāgata however speak always the truth, nothing false...To believe, O Ānanda, shall be your endeavour. This I enjoin you."

It is certainly not purely by chance that this dialogue is inserted here, but the reason for this is that precisely in respect of the legends of the conception and birth of Buddha the Lalitavistara differs very much from the reports of other schools through its exaggeration of the miraculous element. This is not the case any more with the later course of the story. Indeed we find here very often an extraordinarily close concurrence with the oldest Pāli reports, for example those in the Mahāvagga of the Vinayapiṭaka[1] where occasionally the Gāthās of the Lalitavistara appear to be more antiquarian than the corresponding Pāli texts. In such cases the two texts are not dependent on each other but both of them originate from a common and older tradition. But here also the Lalitavistara has something more that is totally missing in the older reports. Two episodes deserve special mention in this context. One of them (Ch. 8) tells how the Bodhisattva is brought by his foster-mother as a boy to the temple and the statues of all gods rise from their pedestals in order to fall at his feet. The other (Ch. 10) describes Bodhisattva's first visit to the school.

With a retinue of 10000 boys, with huge pomp and participation of all gods—8000 divine damsels strew flowers in front of him—the tiny Bodhisattva marches into the school to learn writing. The poor schoolsmaster cannot stand the splendour

1. The relationship of the Pāli tradition to Lalitavistara is treated by Oldenberg in OC V, Berlin 1882, Vol. 2, p. 107-122. Cf. also Windisch, "Māra und Buddha" and "Buddhas Geburt", as well as Kern SBE, Vol. 21, p. XI ff. Also already Burnouf, Lotus de la bonne Loi, p. 864 ff.

of the Bodhisattva and falls down to the floor. A god raises him and pacifies him saying that although the Bodhisattva is omniscient and has no need to learn anything, yet following the usual way of the world, he has come to the school. In the meantime the Bodhisattva surprises the schoolmaster by asking him which of the 64 ways of writing he will teach him. And he names them all—including the scripts of the Ciṇas (Chinese) and the Hūṇas (Huns)—scripts whose names the teacher has not even heard once. At last he begins to teach him and the 10,000 boys the alphabets. While learning every letter of the alphabet however the Bodhisattva gives by himself some saying of wisdom beginning with that particular letter.[1]

Also chapters 12[2] and 13 contain episodes which are missing in the other biographies of Buddha. The further course of the narrative (Chs. 14-26) deviates only very little from the legends known from other sources—when it speaks of the four encounters by which the Bodhisattva makes acquaintance with old age, disease, death and renouncement of the world, of the escape from the palace, of the encounter with King Bimbisāra, of Gotama's apprenticeship and his futile ascetic exercises, of the fight with Māra, of the final enlightenment and the proclamation of his teaching on a request of God Brahman.[3] But the last chapter (27) is devoted—quite in the manner of the Mahāyānasūtras—to the glorification of the Lalitavistara itself and to the enumeration of the merits and advantages which one earns by propagating and worshipping it.

When we consider all this, it appears probable that our Lalitavistara is an edition of an older Hīnayāna text, the

1. E. Kuhn (Gurupūjākaumudī, p. 116 ff) has proved that these two legends of the young Buddha have served as models for the apocryphal gospels which tell similar stories of the young Jesus.

2. Cf. Winternitz WZKM, 1912, p. 237 ff.

3. Also through traditions the Lalitavistara distinguishes itself in many ways. While for example Gotama spends four weeks after his enlightenment meditating under various trees according to our oldest report (Mahāvagga I, 1-4; Dutoit, "Leben des Buddha," p. 66 ff) in the Lalitavistara (ed. Lefmann, p. 377) in the second week he takes a "long stroll" through thousands of worlds and in the fourth week a "short stroll" which extended from the eastern to the western ocean.

Buddhabiography of the Sarvāstivāda-school, enlarged and embellished in the spirit of the Mahāyāna. This presumption also explains the character of our text which evidently is not at all the unitary work of one author but an anonymous compilation in which very old and very modern pieces are found by the side of one another. Indeed even in its form the work consists of dissimilar parts—of a continuous narrative in Sanskrit prose and many long metrical pieces in "mixed Sanskrit".[1] Only seldom do these verses form a part of the story, generally they are insertions which reproduce what has been narrated in prose in shorter and simpler form and some times also with some changes in content. Some of these insertions in verse—for example the birth-legend and the Asita-episode in the VII Chapter, the Bimbisāra-story in the XVI chapter, the dialogue with Māra in the XVIII chapter etc.—are beautiful old ballads which originate from the same sources as the poems of the Suttanipāta mentioned above (p. 93 f). They belong to the ancient religious ballad-poetry of the early centuries after Buddha. Even many prose-pieces like the Sermon of Banaras (Ch. 26) belong to the oldest layer of Buddhist traditions. On the other hand the later parts are found not only in prose but also in the Gāthās of which many are composed in artistic metres.[2]

When the final editing of the Lalitavistara took place, we do not know. That the work was translated into Chinese as early as in the 1st century A.D.[3] was erroneously maintained previously. In fact we do not even know whether the Chinese biography of Buddha, Phu-Yau-King originated about 300 A.D., the alleged "second translation of the Lalitavistara" is

1. F. Weller, "Zum Lalita Vistara I, Uber die Prosa des Lalita Vistara", Leipzig, Diss. 1915, has made it seem probable that even the prose in Lalita-Vistara was not originally written in Sanskrit but in a dialect akin to the prose of the Mahāvastu and that it was not sanskritized until later.

2. Thus Vasantatilakā and Śārdūlavikrīḍita are considerably frequent. Cf. the list of metres in Lefmann's translation, Vol. II, p. 227 ff and introduction p. XIX ff.

3. By B. Nanjio, who regarded the Fo-pen-hing-king (68 A.D.) which has been lost long ago as a translation of the Lalita-Vistara; but there is no proof whatsoever for such an assumption. Cf. Bagchi l. c. p. 6. I.

really a translation of our text.[1] An exact translation of the Sanskrit text is the Tibetan one ,[2] which was made only in the 9th century. It may be presumed as certain that one version which did not deviate much from our Lalitavistara was known to the artists who about 850-900 A.D. decorated with their sculptures the famous temple of Boro-Budur in Java. For these magnificent sculptures present scenes from the Buddha-legend in such a way as if the artists had worked just on the basis of a Lalitavistara-text. And for explaining the sculptures M. Pleyte[3] has simply reproduced whole content of the Lalitavistara.

But even the artists who have decorated the Graeco-Buddhist monuments of North India with scenes from the life of Buddha are well conversant with the Buddha-legend as it is narrated in the Lalitavistara. However they worked not as per texts but on the strength of living, oral transmission. The concurrence between sculptures and texts is very often of such a nature that one must presume that the literary transmission was also occasionally influenced by art. Art and literature influenced each other.[4] Whereas the ancient Buddhist art of the times of Aśoka (reliefs of Bharhut, Sānchi etc.) does not know any pictures of Buddha but puts only symbols (for example the wheel) for the person of the founder of the religion, portrayal of Buddha is a chief object of the Gandhāra

1. It contains only 8 chapters. See Winternitz, WZKM 20, 1912, 241 f., and Bagchi, l. c. I, p. 87 f.

2. It is published and translated by Ph. E. Foucaux into French (Rgya-tcher-rol-pa, Version tibetaine du Lalitavistara) Paris 1847-48.

3. C. M. Pleyte, "Die Buddhalegende in den Skulpturen des Tempels von Boro Budur", Amsterdam 1901, and N. J. Krom, "The Life of Buddha on the Stupa of Barabudu according to the Lalitavistara Text", the Hague 1926, have given extracts from the Lalitavistara in translation by way of explanation of the sculptures. Cf. Speyer Le Museon, NS IV, 1903, p. 124 ff; F. C. Wilsen, "Die Buddha Legende auf den Flachrelief der ersten Galerie desStūpa von Boro Budur, Jāva, verkleinerte Wiedergabe der Umrisszeichnungen", Leipzig 1923 (Veroffentl des Forschungsinstitutes für vegleichende Religionsgeschichte.)

4. Cf. A. Foucher, "L'art greco bouddhique du Gandhāra", t. I, Paris 1905 p. 324 f. 616ff., Grünwedel, "Buddhistische Kunst in Indien", p. 98 104 f, 184, Senart OC XIV, Alger 1905, I, 121ff and T, Bloch ZDMG 62, 370ff.

art. Is it not connected with the development that in the meanwhile Buddha became an object of Bhakti and the Buddhaworship the essence of Buddhism ? Thus everything supports the view that the age of the Gandhāra art whose golden age was in the 2nd century A.D. was also the age of the older Mahāyāna texts treating the Buddha-legend.[1]

It is therefore only correct that we find in the Lalitavistara both very old transmissions as well as transmissions which are a few centuries younger about the Buddha-legend. It is an important source for ancient Buddhism only where it agrees with the Pāli-texts and other Sanskrit texts like the Mahāvastu. But it is wrong to consider the whole Lalitavistara as a good old source for our knowledge of Buddhism, as especially E. Senart has done in his Essai sur la legende du Buddha[2] which is as ingenious, as it is out of place. Even about the "popular Buddhism" of the olden days the Lalitavistara does not give us any information as Louis de La Vallee Poussin maintains,[3] but perhaps it gives information—and thus the work is of immense value to the history of religion—about the development of the Buddha-legend from its earliest beginnings when only the main events in life of the great founder of the religion were associated with miracles to that boundless deification of the Lord when he appears from the beginning till the end of his life only as god and above all gods. But for the History of Literature also the Lalitavistara is one of the most

---

1. Scholars are practically unanimous in assuming that the Graeco Buddhist art of Gandhāra began shortly before the birth of Christ and attained its perfection in the 2nd century A.D. especially during the reign of Kaniṣka See G. Bühler in "Anzeiger der Kais, Akademie der Wissenschaften in Wien, Phil. hist. KI 1896", p. 66 f.; A Grünwedel, "Buddhistische Kunst in Indien", Berlin 1900, p. 81; A. Foucher, "L'art greco boudhique du Gandhara I" Paris 1905 p. 40 ff., II, 1918, p. 401 ff, 486 ff, V. A. Smith, "Early History of Fine Art in India and Ceylon", Oxford 1911, p. 99 ("It is quite safe to assume that the works of good quality belong to the first 3 centuries of Christian era") L. A. Waddell in JRAS 1914, p. 140 f Sir J. H. Marshall in JRAS 1909, 1056 ff. Cambridge History I, 1922, p. 648.

2. 2nd Ed., Paris 1882, pp. XXXI f., 456 f.

3. "Bouddhisme, Etudes et Materiaux", p. 37 and 42 f. Through the Pāli texts we get acquainted, says La Vallee Poussin, only as "aristocratic and philosophic Buddhism."

important works of Buddhist Literature. Although it is not yet an actual Buddha-epic it contains all the germs to one such. Out of the ballads and episodes as preserved in the Lalitavistara in the oldest constituents if not out of the Lalitavistara itself, Aśvaghoṣa, the greatest poet of the Buddhists created his marvellous epic, the Buddhacarita, the "Life of Buddha."[1]

The Poet Aśvaghoṣa,[2] and his School

Until the year 1892, when the French scholar Sylvain Levi Published the first chapter of the Buddha Carita, little more than the name of Aśvaghoṣa was known in Europe. Today we know him as the most prominent predecessor of Kālidāsa, and as the creator of epic, dramatic and lyrical compositions; but of his life we know little. The traditions embodied in the Chinese and Tibetan sources agree in asserting that Aśvaghoṣa was a contemporary of King Kaniṣka (2nd century A.D.).[3] Pārśva or his pupil Puṇyayaśas is mentioned as his teacher, and he is generally enumerated among the leaders or founders of the Mahāyāna.[4] In the Chinese lists of the Buddhist patriarchs in India, he always appears after Pārśva and Puṇyayaśas, and *before* Nāgārjuna and Āryadeva. It may be taken as certain that he was of Brahmin family, and had enjoyed a thorough Brahminical education before he went

1. Sylvain Levi, "Le Buddhacarita d' Asvaghoṣa", JA 1892, s 8 t. XIX pp. 201 ff. (But we cannot agree with Levi when he calls here on p. 202 the Buddhacarita "un abrege substantiel du Lalita-vistara". At least in its present edition the Lalitavistara cannot have been the basis for Aśvaghoṣa).

2. On Aśvaghoṣa in general see S. Levi in JA 1892, ser 8 t. XIX, p. 201 ff., 1908, s. 10, t. XII, p. 57 ff.; T. Suzuki Aśvaghosha's Discourse on the Awakening of Faith, Transl., Chicago 1900 Introduction M. Anesaki in ERE II, 1909 p. 159 f., and F. W. Thomas, Kavīndravacanasamuccaya, Bibl. Ind. 1912, p. 25 ff. A purely legendary biography of Aśvaghoṣa was translated into Chinese by Kumārajiva between 401 and 409 A.D., it is published in extracts by W. Wassiljew, "Der Buddhismus", St. Petersburg 1860 p. 231 f.

3. According to Chinese sources, Aśvaghoṣa was the spiritual counsellor and Caraka was the medical adviser of King Kaniṣka. Cf. Levi in JA 1896, s. 9, t. VIII, p. 447 f. On the period of Kaniṣka, s. Appendix V, and Vol. I, p. 491.

4. Perhaps this is only based on the fact that the authorship of the Mahāyāna-Śraddhotpāda was attributed to him.

over to Buddhism. As a Buddhist he probably associated himself first with the Sarvāstivāda school,[1] but laid great stress on the Buddha-Bhakti and thus prepared the Mahāyāna. Sāketa (*i.e.* Ayodhyā, the present-day Oudh) is generally given as his birthplace or home; but Benares and Patna are also mentioned. His mother was called Suvarṇākṣī. The Tibetan biographer of Aśvaghoṣa says of him: "There was no question which he would not have solved, no imputation which he would not have rejected; he overcame his opponents as frequently as a strong wind breaks rotten trees." According to the same account, he was also an excellent musician, who himself composed pieces of music and travelled about with a band of male and female singers in the bazaars. He played and sang with his choir melancholy songs about the vanity of existence, and, attracted by the beautiful melodies, the crowd stood still and listened. In this way, he won many over to the religion.[2] The Chinese pilgrim I-tsing, who travelled through India in 671-695 A.D., speaks of the learned monks, who oppose the heretics with great success, promote the religion of the Buddha, and therefore receive respect above gods and men, and says that "of such persons in every generation only one or two appear," such men as "Nāgārjuna, Deva, Aśvaghoṣa of an early age."[3] I-tsing also relates that at his time in India, among other songs which were chanted at Buddhist sanctuaries, there was a collection of sacred texts compiled by Aśvaghoṣa. He mentions him also as a composer of songs, of the Sūtrālaṃkāra and of the Buddha-Carita.[4]

Of the Buddha-Carita[5] I-tsing says that "this extensive

1. See Levi, JA 1908, s. 10, t. XII, pp. 90 ff., 184, and H. Lüders, Bruchstücke buddhistischer Dramen, Berlin 1911, p. 65. According to Vasubandhu he is supposed to have assisted Kātyāyaniputra with commentary on the Abhidharma.

2. A. Schiefner in ABA 1859, p. 259 ff.

3. Hsüan-Tsang (Si-yu-ki, Buddhist Records of the Western World, transl. by S. Beal, II, p. 302 f.) calls Aśvaghoṣa, Deva, Nāgārjuna and Kumāralabdha "the four suns that illumined the world."

4. I-tsing, Record transl. by Takakusu, pp. 152 f., 165. 181.

5. The text has been edited by E. B. Cowell, Oxford (Anecdota Oxoniensia, Aryan Series, Vol. I, Part VII) 1893, and translated by the same scholar in SBE, Vol. 49. Translated into German by C. Cappeller, Jena 1922

work......relates the Tathāgata's chief doctrines and works during his life, from the period when he was still in the royal palace till his last hour under the avenue of Sāla-trees." And he adds: "It is widely read or sung throughout the five divisions of India, and the countries of the Southern Sea.[1] He clothes manifold meanings and ideas in a few words, which rejoice the heart of the reader so that he never feels tired from reading the poem. Besides, it should be counted as meritorious for one to read this book, inasmuch as it contains the noble doctrines given in a concise form."[2] We gather from the words of I-tsing that he knew the Buddha-Carita in the form in which it appeared in the Chinese translation,[3] where the epic consists of 28 cantos, and the narrative is continued

---

(Religiose Stimmen der Volker) and R. Schmidt, Hagen 1924; into Italian by C. Formichi, Aśvaghoṣa, poeta del Buddhismo, Bari 1912. Contributions to the critical restoration of the text and explanation of the Buddha-Carita by O. Bohtlingk in BSGW 1894, 160 ff.; F. Kielhorn in NGGW 1894, p. 364 ff.; J. S. Speyer in Verslagen en Mededeelingen der Kon. Akademie van Wetenschappen, Afd. Lett., 3de Reeks, Deel XI, Amsterdam 1895, and JRAS 1914, p. 105 ff.; L. Finot in JA 1898, s. 9, t. XII, p. 542 ff.; Formichi, l. c, pp. 289-400, 409. E. Leumann, in WZKM 7, 1893, 193 ff.; NGGW 1896, 83 ff.; Lüders in NGGW 1896, 1 ff.; K. M. Joglekar, Ashvaghosha's Buddha-Charita, cantos I-V with a scholium by Dattatraya Shastri Nigdukar, and Introduction, Notes, and Translation, Bombay, 1912; A. Gawronski, Gleanings from Aśvaghoṣa's Buddhacarita, in Rocznik Oryentalistyczny I, Krakow 1914-15, I ff.; and Studies about the Sanskrit-Buddhist Literature. Krakow 1919, pp. I ff., 27 ff.; E. Hultzsch in ZDMG 72, 1918, 148 ff.; C. Cappeller in ZII 1, 1922, p. 1 ff.; E. H. Johnston in JRAS 1927, 209 ff.

1. This means the Malay Archipelago (Sumatra, Java and the neighbouring islands). Takakusu, l. c., p. xxxix.

2. I-tsing, l. c., p. 165 f.

3. This is the Fo-sho-hing-tsan-king, translated from Sanskrit into Chinese between 414 and 421 A. D. by Dharmarakṣa, and translated into English by Samuel Beal in SBE, Vol. 19. T. W. Rhys Davids (JRAS 1901, p. 405 f.) has asserted that this Chinese work is not a translation of Aśvaghoṣa's Buddha-Carita at all. Else Wohlgemath, however (Über die chinesische Version von Aśvaghoṣas Buddhacarita, Diss. Leipzig 1916), has shown that the Chinese version is undoubtedly based on Aśvaghoṣa's poem, though some things have been added and others omitted, and that the recension on which it is based differed from the one which we know.

down to the Nirvāṇa of the Buddha. As the Tibetan translation[1] also consists of 28 cantos, we must assume that the Sanskrit text, which consists of 17 cantos, and ends with the conversions in Benares, only represents a torso. In any case the work is a torso, for even of these seventeen cantos, only the first thirteen are old and authentic. The work was completed by a certain Amṛtānanda, who copied it at the beginning of the 19th century, and added the conclusion, because (as he himself admits) he could find no complete manuscripts.[2]

However, even with the mere torso which has come down to us, we can fully endorse what the Chinese pilgrim has said in praise of the Buddha-Carita. Here we have indeed for the first time an actual epic of Buddha, created by a real poet, a poet who, filled with intense love and reverence for the exalted figure of the Buddha, and deeply imbued with the truth of the Buddha doctrine, is able to present the life and doctrine of the Master in noble and artistic, but not artificial language. His Sanskrit is faultless, even though it does not always comply strictly with the rules of Pāṇini.[3] The Buddha-Carita calls itself a Mahākāvya, or "great poem," *i.e.*, an ornate epic poem in the technical sense, and it is composed in the so-called Kāvya style, the beginnings of which we have already found in the Rāmāyaṇa.[4] Vālmīki and his immediate successors were the predecessors of Aśvaghoṣa, in the same way as the latter himself is a predecessor of Kālidāsa. All these three great poets have one thing in common: they are still very moderate in their use of the Alaṃkāras or "embellishments." Aśvaghoṣa

1. The Tibetan translation of the 7th or 8th century is far more accurate than the Chinese one, but on the other hand it does not (at least in the first canto) reproduce the original text of Aśvaghoṣa. Cf. E. Leumann inWZKM 7, 1893, p. 193 ff. and Friedrich Weller, Das Leben des Buddha von Aśvaghoṣa, Tibetisch und Deutsch, Leipzig, 1926 (Gesang I-VIII übersetzt; in Veroffentlichungen des Forschunginstituts für vergleichende Religionsgeschichte an der Universität Leipzig, II, 3) ; Part II, 1928.

2. Also a manuscript of the Buddha-Carita discovered by Haraprasāda Sastri only goes as far as the middle of Canto XIV (JASB, N. S., Vol. V, 1909, p. 47 ff.),

3. Cf. Sukumar Sen in Ind. Hist. Qu. II, 1916, p. 657 ff.

4. Cf. above, Vol. I, pp. 454 ff., 477, 485.

is not only moderate in language and style, but he also uses restraint in the presentation of miracles in the Buddha legend. He always keeps himself far removed from such exaggerations as we find, for instance, in the Lalita-Vistara. In contrast to the chaotic disorder in texts like the Mahāvastu and the Lalita-Vistara, we find in the Buddha-Carita a well-planned, artistic arrangement of the material. Although the poet is quite familiar with the older sacred texts, he nevertheless assumes a certain amount of freedom in his attitude towards them. Not that he has made any alterations in the traditions; but he has the art of clothing the old familiar legends in a new poetical garment,[1] and of imparting original expression to the well-known doctrines of the Buddhist Sūtras. Aśvaghoṣa is always more of a poet than a monk, at least in the Buddha-Carita.

How different from the Lalita-Vistara is, for instance, the highly poetical description of the excursions of the young prince in Cantos III and IV !

First of all, there is a beautiful description of how, on hearing that the prince is going out, the women of the city, full of curiosity, hasten from their rooms to the house-tops and the windows. Hampered by their falling girdles, they scamper up in the greatest haste, pushing and jostling one another, and scaring away the birds on the roofs by the clattering of the girdles and rings. The lotus faces of the fair ones, leaning out of the windows, look as though the walls of the houses were decorated with real lotus blossoms.[2] Beautifully the poet then describes the encounter with the old man, whom the gods cause to appear. In consternation the prince asks:

> "Who is the man who here approaches, O charioteer,
> With white hair, and eyes sunk deep in their sockets,
> Bent down on his staff, his limbs trembling ?—
> Is it a process of Nature, or the sport of destiny ? "

---

1. As Windisch (Māra und Buddha, p. 205) says, Aśvaghoṣa seems "almost intentionally to have avoided any resemblance to the wording of older texts."

2. In the Raghuvaṃśa (VII, 5-12) Kālidāsa imitated this description of Aśvaghoṣa (Buddha-Carita III, 12-24), as has already been pointed out by Cowell (Buddha-Carita, Edition, Preface).

Whereupon the charioteer replies :

"It is age which has broken him,—Age,
The thief of beauty and destroyer of strength,
The source of care and the end of joys,
The foe of the senses, the vanishing of memories.
He, too, has sucked at the mother's breast
As a little child, learned walking in the course of time,
Gradually he grew big and strong, a youth,
Gradually age has overtaken him."

After the prince, on his three excursions, has become acquainted with age, disease and death, he takes no more pleasure in anything. It is in vain that the family priest, at the King's request, invites the women and girls of the palace to apply all the arts of love in order to inveigle the prince and to drive away his sad thoughts. The prince remains unmoved by all the sweet temptations. He only marvels at the gay doings of these women, and exclaims (IV, 60 f.) :

"How senseless seems to me the man who has seen
his neighbour ill and old and dead,
And yet remains happy and is not shaken by fear.
Thus, when a tree which, quite bereft of blossoms
and of fruits,
Is felled or falls,—the neighbour tree cares not."

The presentation of love scenes is one of the indispensable elements of an ornate court poem. The poet fulfils this requirement by describing the blandishments of the beautiful women, by which they seek to tempt the prince (IV, 24-53) ; and in in the highly-coloured description of the night scene in the harem, which is the cause of the prince's flight from the palace,[1] the poet reveals his knowledge of the science of love. But a court poet must also be versed in the doctrines of Nītiśāstra,

1. V. 48-62, This scene is related in its original version with regard to the youth Yasa in the Vinayapiṭaka (see above, p. 27). It has already been stated (see above, Vol. I, p. 470, note 2) that the similar scene in Rāmāyaṇa, V, 9, 11, was composed in imitation of Aśvaghoṣa

state-craft. Such doctrines are recited to the prince by the family priest (IV, 62-82), in order to distract him from his thoughts. Lastly, an ornate poem is not complete without a description of battle scenes. Our poet fulfils this requirement also, in Canto XIII, in which he gives an animated description of the battle of Buddha with Māra and his hosts.

The Saundarananda-Kāvya.[1] a second poem by Aśvaghoṣa, also belongs to the same class of ornate court poetry. This work, too, is connected with the life story of the Buddha, but it amplifies those scenes and episodes in particular which receive scanty attention or none at all, in the Buddha-Carita. Thus, in Canto I, the story of the founding of Kapilavastu is related in minute detail. The actual theme of this poem, however, is the story of the love-lorn Nanda, the half-brother of the Buddha, who is ordained as a monk against his will by the Buddha :

Just as Sundarī, the beautiful wife of Nanda, mourns and laments for her lost husband, so Nanda, too, longs to be back with his beloved. Vain are the attempts of the other monks to calm him. Even Buddha's words fail to change his mood. Then the Master takes him by the hand, and ascends with him to heaven. On the way they see in the Himālaya an ugly, one-eyed female ape, and Buddha asks him whether Sundarī is more beautiful than this, which Nanda of course enthusiastically affirms. Soon they see in heaven the Apsaras, the heavenly nymphs, and Nanda thinks that the difference between the last-named and his wife, is just as great as between her and the

---

1. The poem was discovered by Haraprasāda Śāstrī, and was also edited by him, Bibl. Ind., Calcutta 1910. A new critical edition, with notes, by E. H. Johnston, has just been published in the Punjab University Oriental Publications, Oxford University Press, London, 1928. Cf. Haraprasāda Śāstrī in JASB 5, 1909, p. 165 f.; F. W. Thomas in JRAS 1911, p. 1125 f.; A. Baston in JA 1912, s. 10, t. XIX, p. 79 ff; La Vallee Poussin in BSOS 1918, p. 133 ff.; A. Gawronski, Studies about the Sanskrıt Buddhist Literature, Krakow 1919, p. 56 ff.; Notes on the Saundarananda, Critical and Explanatory, Second Series (Prace Komisji Oriental. Polskiej Akad. Um. Nr. 6.) W. Krakowie 1922; E. Hultzsch in ZDMG 72, 1918, p. 111 ff.; 73, 229 ff.; 74, 293 ff.; C. W. Gurner in JRAS 1928, p. 131 f. From the concluding verses we may perhaps (with Hultzsch, ZDMG 72, 121 f.) assume that Aśvaghoṣa wrote the Saundarananda first and the Buddha-Carita afterwards.

one-eyed ape. From that moment he has an ardent desire for the heavenly women, and, on his return to earth, devotes himself diligently to ascetic practices in order to reach heaven. Then Ānanda teaches him that even heavenly pleasures are empty and vain. At last Nanda is convinced, and goes to Buddha, in order to tell him that he no longer desires the heavenly women. Buddha rejoices greatly at this, and preaches to him (in several cantos) the principles of his doctrine. Now Nanda retires into the forest, practises the four great meditations, and becomes an Arhat. Thankfully he goes to Buddha and pays homage to him, but the Master exhorts him, now that he has attained his object, to preach the good doctrine to others, out of pity, and so as to lead them to liberation.[1]

In the concluding verses, the poet states emphatically that he has written his work, the aim of which is liberation, not for the sake of delectation, but with a view to perfect peace; he has given it the form of an ornate poem, only so as to be able to win over non-Buddhist hearers to Buddha's doctrine, and to make this doctrine palatable to them, just as one mixes a bitter medicine with honey to make it drinkable. Much space in the Saundarananda is accordingly devoted to preaching, in which the poet makes use of much the same expressions which are familiar to us from the Tipiṭaka. The joys of solitude and meditation are extolled in this poem just as in other Hīnayāna works.[2] Nevertheless the Saundarananda also alludes

1. In the Vinayapiṭaka (Mahāvagga 1, 54) and the Nidāna-Kathā (Jātaka ed. Fausboll, I, p. 91: Rhys Davids, Buddhist Birth Stories, p. 128) it is only related that Nanda was ordained as a monk by Buddha against his will. The legend of Nanda's ascent to heaven and his yearning for the Apsarases is told in Udāna III 2, and in the Dhammapada Commentary I, 9 (Buddhist Legends, transl. by Burlingame, HOS, Vol. 28, p. 217 ff.). See also Spence Hardy, Manual of Buddhism, p. 204: and Kern, Der Buddhismus, I, 155 f. Some scenes from the Nanda legend are also to be found on reliefs, s. Foucher, L'art greco-bouddhique, 1, p. 464 ff.

2. The recommendation of yogācāra in XIV, 18, and XX, 68, does not refer to the yogācāra school of the Mahāyāna, but only to the advantages of the practice of Yoga (Haraprasāda Śāstri, preface p. xii). Moreover, the tendency of the Hīnayāna, is seen clearly when Nanda pays homage to Buddha, and Buddha restrains him by saying that worship is due not to him, but to the Dharma (XVIII, 22).

to doctrines which are peculiar to the Mahāyāna. Nanda is filled with the "great pity," which makes him search his heart, in deep commiseration, for means whereby he may release the beings from suffering (XIII, 8). Whilst the Tipiṭaka teaches often enough that everything is "transitory, without self, and full of suffering," Nanda attains to the realisation that everything is "transitory, empty (śūnya), without self, and full of suffering."[1] And at the end, it is not enough for Nanda himself to become a saint who attains to Nirvāṇa : he must also become an apostle.[2]

In the Buddha-Carita, too, Aśvaghoṣa's teaching is in the main that of the Hīnayāna, though traces of the Mahāyānā are not wanting. Book XVI contains the "Sermon of Benares," which is only a poetical and expanded version of the text known from the Tipiṭaka, but it also speaks of the body as "empty, without a self" (śūnyam anātmakam, XVI, 28), calls the Buddha not only "the Self-born" (Svayambhū), "the Overlord of the Whole Dharma," but even the "Lord of the World" (XVI, 64 ; 69). And he even says that he has attained the Great Vehicle, the Mahāyāna, that has been set forth by all the Buddhas for establishing the welfare of all beings (XVI, 75 ; 85). Thus Aśvaghoṣa probably belongs to the period of the beginning of the Mahāyāna.

Both in the Buddhacarita and the Saundarananda there are abundant allusions to Brahminical legends and epic narratives, which serve to confirm the tradition that Aśvaghoṣa was of Brahmin family.

The Vajrasūcī or "Diamond Needle,"[3] which is sometimes ascribed to Aśvaghoṣa, also reveals an intimate knowledge of

1. XVII, 16-22 Cf. Vidhusekhara Bhattacharya in JRAS 1914, p. 747 f.

2. However, the Hīnayāna, too, valued highly the duty of instruction and conversion: this is shown, for instance, by the Sutta quoted above, on p. 60 f., from the Aṅguttaranikāya.

3. Wujra Soochi or Refutation of the Arguments upon which the Brahmanical Institution of Caste is Founded, by the learned Boodhist Ashwa Ghoshu (published by Lancelot Wilkinson with the translation by B. H. Hodgson, which had already appeared in 1829 in the Transactions of the Royal Asiatic Society, Vol. III), also the Tunku by Soobajee Bapoo, being a Reply to the Wujra Soochi, 1839. A. Weber, "Uber die Vajrasūcī" (ABA

Brahminical literature. Unfortunately there are grave doubts as to whether he was actually the author of this little work, which is certainly interesting in any case. This work refutes the Brahminical caste system very cuttingly. The author's method is extremely effective, for he takes up the Brahminical standpoint, and seeks to prove from the Brahminical texts themselves, by quotations from the Veda, the Mahābhārata and the law-book of Manu,[1] how frail the claims of the Brahmin caste are. When B. H. Hodgson published a translation of this work, as far back as the year 1829, and L. Wilkinson edited the text in 1839, they were quite charmed with the democratic spirit with which the author defends the equality of all classes of men, "as they are equal as regards joy and sorrow, life, intellect, profession and trade, death and birth, fear and sexual love." For the sake of the quotations from Brahminical texts, if on no other grounds, this work would be of great importance in the history of literature, if only we had any certain data about the author and the date of the work. There are some serious objections to ascribing the authorship to Aśvaghoṣa. The Vajrasūcī is not enumerated either by I-tsing or in the Tibetan Tanjur among the works of Aśvaghoṣa; and in the catalogues of the Chinese Tripiṭaka a Vajrasūcī, which is said to contain "a refutation of the four Vedas," and which was translated into Chinese between 973 and 981 A.D., is ascribed to a man named Dharmakīrti.[2]

Among the lyrical poems which are ascribed to Aśvaghoṣa, the only one we know is the Gaṇḍīstotra-Gāthā, which A. von

---

1859, p. 205 ff., and Indische Streifen, I, 186 ff.). Cf. also B. H. Hodgson, Essays on the Languages, Literature and Religion of Nepal and Tibet, London 1874, p. 126 ff.; E. Burnouf, Introduction ā l'histoire du Bouddhism Indien, 2ieme ed., Paris 1876, p. 192 f., and S. Levi, in JA 1908, s. 10, t. XII, p. 70 f.

1. In the same way in Kumāralāta's Kalpanāmaṇḍitikā ("Sūtrālaṃkāra" No. 77) the Brahminical system is refuted by quotations from the law-book of Manu.

2. Bunyiu Nanjio, Catalogue of the Chinese Translation of the Buddhist Tripiṭaka, No. 1303. Chinese Fa-shang is the translation of Sanskrit Dharmakīrti. For the philosophical work Mahāyāna-Śraddhotpāda, which has been erroneously ascribed to the great Aśvaghoṣa, see below in the chapter on "The Masters and Poets of the Mahāyāna."

Stael-Holstein[1] has attempted to reconstruct in the Sanskrit original on the basis of the Chinese transliteration. It is a beautiful poem, worthy of Aśvaghoṣa both in form and contents.

The scanty fragments, which are all that is left of his Śāriputra-Prakaraṇa show us that as a dramatist too, Aśvaghoṣa was a worthy predecessor of Kālidāsa.[2] This drama treats of the conversion of Śāriputra and his friend Maudgalyāyana, which is already related in one of the most beautiful stories in the Mahāvagga of the Vinayapiṭaka.[3]

Chinese authors also ascribe to Aśvaghoṣa a work entitled "Sūtrālaṃkāra" which was translated into Chinese by Kumārajīva in about 405 A.D., but which was really written by Aśvaghoṣa's junior contemporary Kumāralāta, and which, in Sanskrit, bore the title Kalpanāmaṇḍitikā or Kalpanālaṃkṛtikā. We glean this from the fragments of the work, which H. Lüders discovered in the finds of Manuscripts in Turfan.[4] Valuable though these fragments are, they are unfortunately so few in number, that even now we can only judge the work on the

---

1. Bibliotheca Buddhica XV, St. Petersburg 1913. Cf. F. W. Thomas in JRAS 1914, p. 752 f.

2. H, Lüders (Das Śāriputraprakaraṇa, ein Drama des Aśvaghoṣa, in SBA 1911, 388 ff.) discovered these fragments in palm leaf MSS. from Turfan. It is uncertain whether the fragments of two other Buddhist dramas discovered by Lüders (Koniglich Preussische Turfan-Expenditionen, Kleinere Sanskrit-Texts I, Berlin 1911) were written by Aśvaghoṣa. For further information on this matter, see Vol. III in the chapter on the drama.

3. See above, p. 28. The disciples are called Sāriputta and Moggallāna in Pāli.

4. H. Lüders, Bruchstücke der Kalpanāmaṇḍitikā des Kumāralāta (Kon. Preuss. Turfan-Expeditionen, Kleinere Sanskrit-Texte II), Leipzig 1926. Both Kalpanāmaṇḍitikā and Kalpanālamkṛtikā appear as titles in the colophons. Both adjectives mean the same, and it is probable that Dṛṣṭāntapaṅktiḥ followed after them, so that the meaning of the title is: "A Series of Examples adorned by Poetic Invention." See Lüders, l. c., pp. 19, 26, and S. Levi in JA, t. 201, 1927, p. 95 ff. The Chinese did not understand the somewhat extraordinary title, and (owing to the word alaṃkṛtikā) made a "Sūtrālaṃkāra" out of it. Lüders (l. c.) has advanced the hypothesis "that Aśvaghoṣa did actually write a work entitled Sūtrālaṃkāra, which was not translated into Chinese, but soon got lost, and was subsequently confused with the Kalpanāmaṇḍitikā which was known by the similar sounding title

strength of the French translation of the Chinese version.[1] The Kalpanāmaṇḍitikā is a collection of pious legends after the manner of the Jātakas and Avadānas, and they are told in prose and verse in the style of ornate poetry. Some of the legends are old acquaintances, for instance that of Dīrghāyus ("Prince Live-Long") and that of King Śibi. An old parable, which appears already in the Tipiṭaka, namely, that it is as difficult to be reborn as a human being, as for a one-eyed tortoise to put its neck into the hole of a yoke cast into the ocean, is several times met with in this work, and one of the tales (No. 38) has been invented for the special purpose of elucidating this parable.[2] Other legends breathe rather the spirit of the Mahāyāna, or at least reveal a Buddha-worship which is more on the side of the Mahāyāna. An instance is No. 57, which is at the same time one of the most beautiful legends in the collection.

A man comes to the monastery, and desires to be admitted into the order. The disciple Śāriputra examines him, and finds that the man cannot claim to have done even the slightest good deed in any of his existences throughout aeons, and he therefore declares him unworthy of being admitted into the order. Weeping, the man leaves the monastery. Then he meets Lord Buddha himself, whose heart is full of pity, and who desires to convert that man "like a mother, who loves her son." He lays his hands on the head of the rejected one, and asks: "Why do you weep ?" The man tells him that Śāriputra has rejected him. Then the Buddha comforts him "with a voice that sounded like distant thunder," and declares that Śāriputra is not omniscient. The Lord himself brings the man back into the monastery, and before the assembled monks he tells of the Karman, the good deed which has entitled the man

Chuang-yen-lun=Alaṃkāraśāstra." We are not convinced that this is the solution of the riddle. S. Levi (l. c., p. 126 f.) tries another solution and thinks it is still possible that Aśvaghoṣa may be the author of the work.

1. Sūtrālaṃkāra traduit en francais sur la version chinoise de Kumārajiva par Ed. Huber, Paris 1908. Cf. La Vallee Poussin in Le Museon, N. S, X, 1909, 86 ff.

2. Cf. Winternitz in WZKM 27, 1913, 43 ff.

to liberation. Once in a former birth this person was a poor man, wandering about on the wooded hills to gather wood, when a tiger rushed upon him. Full of terror, he cried : "Honour to the Buddha ! " For the sake of these words, the man shall participate in liberation. Buddha himself ordains him as a monk, and he soon becomes an Arhat.[1]

According to Hsūan-Tsang,[2] Kumāralāta was the founder of the Sautrāntika school, and came from Taxila. In the work itself, the masters of the Sarvāstivādins are honoured, and many of the stories in the Kalpanāmaṇḍitikā are taken from the Canon of the Sarvāstivādins.[3] King Kaniṣka plays a part in two narratives, and he appears as a king of a past age.[4] Hence the work must have been written some considerable time after the death of Kaniṣka, and the poet could not have lived earlier than the end of the second century, when Aśvaghoṣa was already a very old man.[5] As far as we are able to glean from the few fragments extant, the language of the work is perfectly correct Sanskrit, and there are seldom deviations from grammar. It is a curious thing that, in one passage,[6] there are two Āryā verses in Prākrit in the midst of the Sanskrit verses. At all events it is very regrettable that we no longer possess the

1. Another example of genuine Mahāyānistic Buddha-Bhakti is No. 68, where Gautamī attains Nirvāṇa through the grace of the Buddha, whereupon she actually worships him. Mortals and gods also hasten to worship the Buddha (and also Buddha's mother).

2. Si-yu-ki, transl. by S. Beal, II, p. 302 f. Cf. Luders, l. c., p. 21. According to K'ouei-Ki, a pupil of Hiuan-Tsang, Kumāralāta was called master of parables," Cf. Levi, l. c., p. 95 f. "Kumāralabdha" is only a wrong retranslation of the Chinese name given for Kumāralāta. See Lüders, l. c., p. 20

3. Cf. S. Levi in JA 1908, s. 10, t. XII, 91 ff., 184. Huber (in BEFEO, 4, 1904. pp. 709 ff.) has traced three stories in the Divyāvadāna. The Sautrāntikas originated with the Sarvāstivādins, and it is therefore no contradiction for Kumāralāta, as a Sautrāntika, to honour the Sarvāstivāda teachers. (Cf. Lüders. l. c., p. 22).

4. No. 14 and No. 31 Cf. Levi in JA 1896, s. 9, t. VIII, 444 ff.

5. If Harivarman, a pupil of Kumāralāta, was really a contemporary of Vasubandhu, then Kumāralāta should be placed not earlier than the end of the 3rd century, and could not be a contemporary of Aśvaghoṣa, Cf. J. Nobel in SBA 1927, 229 ff.

6. In the 43rd story. Cf. Lüders, l. c., p. 45.

greater portion of the Kalpanāmaṇḍitikā in the original. It is not only in itself a work of literary distinction, the merits of which (as Levi rightly remarks) are still recognisable even after two processes of translation ; but also from the point of view of the history of ancient Indian literature and culture, its importance should not be undervalued, for it mentions the epics Mahābhārata and Rāmāyaṇa, it confutes the philosophical doctrines of Sāṃkhya and Vaiśeṣika and the religious views of the Brahmins and Jainas, and it contains all kinds of references to script, art and painting.

Just as the Chinese ascribed one of Kumāralāta's works to Aśvaghoṣa, some poems by Mātṛceṭa have likewise been ascribed to Aśvaghoṣa in Tibet, and, according to the Tibetan historian Tāranātha, Mātṛceṭa is merely another name for Aśvaghoṣa.[1] It is probable that Mātṛceṭa was a somewhat senior contemporary of Aśvaghoṣa, and belonged to the same school of poets, and was therefore confused with him. King Kaniṣka at whose court it is generally assumed that Aśvaghoṣa lived, also invited the poet Mātṛceṭa to the court. Mātṛceṭa replied in a letter, called the Mahārāja Kanika-lekha,[2] which has come down in the Tibetan language ; he asks the king to excuse him, as he is unable to come owing to his great age. The letter is a poem of 85 verses, containing chiefly admonitions to lead a moral life in the spirit of the Buddha. In verses running over with pity, the poet ends by imploring the king most earnestly to spare the creatures of the forest, and to give

---

1. Ed. Huber (Sūtrālaṃkāra, pp. 63, 82) thought he had found a confirmation of the identity of Mātṛceṭa and Aśvaghoṣa, in the fact that Mātṛceṭa, too, cites the parable of the tortoise and the yoke in the ocean. However, even at the time, Huber's argument was not convincing (s. Winternitz in WZKM 27, 1913, 46 f.) and now that we know that Aśvaghoṣa is not the author of the "Sūtrālaṃkāra" at all, his argument falls to the ground entirely. See F. W. Thomas in OC XIII, Hamburg 1902, p. 40; ERE VIII, 1915, 495 ff.; Hoernle, Manuscript Remains, I, p. 59; Lüders in SBA 1914, p. 103.

2. Translated by F. W. Thomas in Ind. Ant. 32, 1903, 345 ff. We agree with Thomas in thinking that Maticitra, who is mentioned as the author of the letter, is identical with Mātṛceṭa, and that the King Kanika of the Kuṣa dynasty is identical with the Kuṣāṇa King Kaniṣka, although both points are disputed by S. C. Vidyābhūṣaṇa (JASB) 1910, p. 477 f.).

up the chase. When the Chinese pilgrim I-tsing (in the 7th century) was travelling in India, Mātṛceṭa was a very famous poet, and his hymns to Buddha were sung far and wide. The following legend, which I-tsing heard in India, testifies to his fame. Once when Buddha was walking through the forest, a nightingale began to sing sweet melodies, as though she were praising the glory of the Lord, whereupon the Buddha said to his disciples that this nightingale would once be reborn as Mātṛceṭa. His most famous hymns are the Catuḥ-Śataka Stotra, "the Hymn of Four Hundred Verses," and the Śata-pañcāśatika Stotra, "the Hymn of One Hundred and Fifty Verses." Fragments of both of these have come down to us in Central Asian manuscripts.[1] They are poems in ślokas, in simple and unadorned, but beautiful, language, and they evidently impressed the faithful more by their pious thoughts than by their form. It is delightful, says I-tsing, to hear his "Hymn of 150 Verses" or "Hymn of 400 Verses" recited in the assembly of monks. "These charming compositions," he says further, "are equal in beauty to the heavenly flowers, and the high principles which they contain rival in dignity the lofty peaks of a mountain. Consequently in India all who compose hymns imitate his style, considering him the father of literature. Even men like the Bodhisattvas Asaṅga and Vasubandhu admired him greatly. 'Throughout India everyone who becomes a monk is taught Mātṛceṭa's two hymns as soon as he can recite the five and ten precepts (Śīla). This course is adopted by both the Mahāyāna and the Hīnayāna schools." I-tsing cannot find words sufficient to extol the merits of these poems, and he adds that there have been many commentators and imitators too. Thus the "Bodhisattva Jina" (an honourable title of the logician

1. W. Siegling has succeeded in reconstructing about two-thirds of the text of the Śatapañcāśatika-Stotra from the fragments of manuscripts from Turfan, and we are obliged to him for permission to peruse his manuscript which he was preparing for the press. Fragments from the collections made by pelliot and Sir Aurel Stein have been published by S. Levi (JA 1910, s. 10, t. XVI, 450 f.), La Vallee Poussin (JRAS 1911, 764 ff.) and Hoernle, Manuscript Remains, I, p. 58 ff. A few fragments of a "Tokharian" translation of the Buddha-Stotra are published by E. Sieg and W. Siegling, Tocharische Sprachreste I, pp. 216, 230 ff.

Dignāga) composed one verse to be placed before each of the one hundred and fifty verses of the Śatapañcāśatika Stotra, and in this way compiled a hymn of 300 verses, known as the "mixed Hymn of Praise."[1] I-tsing himself translated the "Hymn of 150 Verses" into Chinese, and there are Tibetan translations of both hymns.[2] A few specimens from the Śatapañcāśatika Stotra will serve to give the reader an idea of this pious poetry :

"How should I not, first of all, praise thee, and the great Compassion, by which thou, knowing its ills, hast been detained in mundane existence so long ?"

"In laying the dust of passion thy speech acts as a raincloud; it acts like Vainateya (i.e. Garuḍa) in expelling the serpent of hatred.

Ever anew it acts as the midday in dispelling the darkness of ignorance; it acts as Śakra's (Indra's) thunderbolt in splitting in pieces the mountains of self-conceit."

"Towards an enemy intent on injury, thou art a friend intent on beneficence; towards one perpetually searching for faults, thou art bent upon searching for merits.

When there was an invitation to thee accompanied with poison and with fire: then there was visiting on thy part, with kindliness and with nectar.

Revilers are conquered by thee with forbearance, and injurers with blessing; and with veracity detractors, with friendliness the revengeful."[3]

The Maitreyavyākaraṇa, "the prophecy about Maitreya," or the Maitreyasamiti, "the Meeting with Maitreya," by the

1. I-tsing, Record transl. by Takakusu, pp. 156, 157, 158, 166.

2. In the Tibetan version the Catuḥ-Śataka is called Varṇanārhavarṇana, "The Praise of Him Who Deserves Praise." The title is also found in Central Asian fragments in colophons (s. Hoernle, l. c., pp. 76, 81, 83). F. W. Thomas has translated the first half of the poem from Tibetan (Ind. Ant., 24, 1905, 145 ff.). A list of the works which are ascribed to Mātṛceṭa in Tibetan, is given by Thomas in Kavindravacana-Samuccaya, p. 27, and Ind. Ant. 32, 346 f.

3. Verses 59, 73 f. 122-124; for the text see Hoernle, l. c., pp. 66. ff. 71; translation by Hoernle with slight alterations.

Vaibhāṣika Āryacandra, belongs to the same period, and perhaps also to the same schools of poets, as the above-mentioned works. There is only one incomplete manuscript of this[1] work, but it was translated repeatedly into Chinese, into the languages of Central Asia, and also into Tibetan, and it must have enjoyed great popularity for a long time, at least beyond the confines of India.[2] In the form of a dialogue between Gotama Buddha and Śāriputra (in other versions Ānanda) the work contains the prophecy about the coming of the future Buddha Maitreya, his birth, his appearance and the paradisaic life under him. In Central Asian versions it is sometimes called a "drama" (nāṭaka), and it seems to have been adapted for dramatic performances in Central Asia (perhaps at religious festivals).[3]

The Jātakamālā[4] by the poet Śūra or Āryaśūra,[5] resembles the Kalpanāmaṇḍitikā very closely as far as style is concerned. "Jātakamālā" or "Garland of Jātakas," is however, really a

1. Haraprasāda Śāstrī, Descriptive Catalogue of Sanskrit MSS. in the Asiatic Society of Bengal, I, Calcutta 1917, p. 13 f. The name of the author is not mentioned here, but only in the colophons of Tokharian and Uigurian fragments, cf. F. W. K. Müller and E. Sieg in SBA 1916, 396, 414 f.; E. Sieg and W. Siegling, Tocharische Sprachreste, I, p. 125.

2. E. Leumann, Maitreya-samiti, das Zukunftsideal der Buddhisten, Strassburg, 1919, gives the text and German translation of the version in the language which he terms "North-Aryan" (called by others "Tokharian"). The Chinese versions by Dharmarakṣa (between 255 and 316 A.D.), by Kumārajīva (about 402 A.D.) and by I-tsing (701 A.D.) have been translated into German by K. Watanabe (see Leumann, l. c., p. 227 ff.). The Kanjur contains three lives of Maitreya translated from the Sanskrit and one from the Pāli. See H. Beckh, Verzeichnis der tibetischen Handschriften, p. 188 f. and E. Abegg. Der Messiasglaube in Indien und Iran, Berlin und Leipzig, 1928, p. 132 ff. Fragments in "Tokharian" have been published by E. Sieg and W. Siegling, Tocharische Sprachreste, I, 107, 119, 125 ff., 155 ff., 164 ff., 254 f. (reviously, too, in SBA 1908, 915 ff.), in Uigurian by F. W. K. Muller and E. Sieg in SBA 1905, p. 958; 1916, 395 ff.

3. See Sieg and Siegling, Tocharische Sprachreste, I, pp. 125, 255, and SBA 1916, 398. Expressions such as "interlude" and "all go out" in the Central Asian versions, do not, however, constitute a proof that the Sanskrit original was an actual drama. It is most desirable that Haraprasāda Śāstrī should give us further information about the contents of MS. No. 4806 in the Asiatic Society's collection.

4. Ed. by H. Kern in HOS, Vol. I, 1881; translated by J. S. Speyer in SBB, Vol I, 1895. Cf. Kern in Festgruss an Bohtlingk, Stuttgart 1888, p. 50 f.; S. d' *Oldenburg* in JRAS 1893, 308 ff.; A. *Barth* in RHR 1893, t. 28, p. 260; K. *Watanabe* in JPTS 1909, p. 263 ff.; A. *Gawron'ski*, Studies about the Sanskrit Buddhist Literature, Krakov 1919, p. 40 ff.

5. According to *Tāranātha* this, too, is only another name of Aśvaghoṣa.

generic term. Various poets have written Jātakamālās, *i.e.*, they have produced free renderings of selected Jātakas in ornate poetical language, in a mixture of prose and verse. Āryaśūra, too, does not trouble to invent new stories, he re-tells the old legends in ornate, elegant language. The style, both in the prose and the verse, is the Kāvya style, but lofty and refined, more artistic than artificial. In the same way as the Jātakas were intended for the use of the monks in their sermons, so the Jātakamālā, too, is intended for the purposes of the preachers. Yet the poet, who was perhaps himself a court preacher, certainly had in view only monks who preached in court circles in which Sanskrit poetry was understood and appreciated. The work contains 34 Jātakas, which, like the 35 Jātakas of the Cariyāpiṭaka, are intended to illustrate the Pāramitās, or "perfections" of a Bodhisattva. Almost all the narratives occur also in the Jātaka book,[1] and 12 in the Cariyāpiṭaka. Among the few stories which are not found in the Pāli collection of Jātakas, is the first one, which tells how the Bodhisattva sees a hungry tigress who is about to devour her young ones, and kills himself so as to provide food for her. This very characteristic story is given here in brief extracts :

"Even in former births the Lord had shown his spontaneous and highest affectionateness towards all creatures, and had identified himself with all beings. Therefore one must cherish the greatest love for Buddha the Lord. Thus for instance, the following great feat of the Lord in a former birth is related, a deed which is praised by my revered teacher, a worshipper of the three jewels, who satisfied his teacher with his wisdom and virtue, and was a past master in the investigation of the virtues. At that time the Bodhisattva, who afterwards became the Lord, who in fulfilment of his extraordinary promises, had mercy on the world by gifts, words of love, acts of help, and other faultless streams of pity gushing forth from wisdom and

1. Some verses coincide with the Pāli Gāthās. See the table in *Speyer's* translation, p. 337 ff., S. d'*Oldenberg* in JRAS 1893, 328 ff.; J. *Charpentier* in ZDMG 64, 1910, 67 ff.; *Oldenberg* in NGGW 1918, 464 ff. R. O. *Franke* (Indogerm. Forschungen V, 1895, Anzeiger, p. 31 ff.) has also traced Pālicism in the language of the Jātakamālā.

love, was reborn in a very learned, powerful Brahmin family, devoted to the fulfilment of their duties, and distinguished for the purity of their conduct." He grew up, and soon gained great mastery in all arts and sciences. Great wealth and honours fell to his lot. But he took no pleasure in the worldly life, and he soon retired into solitude. He lived in the forest as a pious hermit. One day, accompanied only by a pupil, he was wandering about on the hills. Then he saw in a rock cave a young tigress, exhausted by hunger, about to devour her young ones, which approached her confidingly for the milk in her udders.

"When the Bodhisattva saw her,
Then he trembled, brave though he was,
Full of pity for another's pain,
As the lord of the hills[1] in an earthquake.
Wonderful, how the pitiful
Remain brave, even when
Great sorrow comes upon themselves,
Yet at another's woe,
Though it be less, they are shaken."

Then he sends his pupil away to fetch meat, but this is only an excuse for remaining alone ; for he has already resolved to throw himself over the precipice, in order to save the lives of the tiger-cubs, and to serve as food for the tigress. His reason for this resolve is that this vain earthly body has no other value than that of being sacrificed for others. Moreover, by this means, he will afford an encouraging example to those who desire to do good in the world; he will put to shame the selfish, point the way to heaven to well-doers, and himself attain perfect enlightenment immediately. He desires nothing else :—

"Not from ambition, nor desire for fame, not for
the joy of heaven, nor to win sovereignty,
Not for the sake of my own eternal bliss do I
do this,—no, only to benefit another.

1. That is, Mount Meru.

As this is true, so may I always have the power of taking
away the sorrow of the world,
And bringing happiness to it, as the sun always brings
the light and drives away the darkness."

With these words he casts himself down into the rock cave. The tigress is attracted by the sound, leaves her young ones, and throws herself upon the corpse of the Bodhisattva to devour it. When the pupil returns and sees this, he is deeply moved, and utters some verses full of worship for the Lord. Men, demi-gods and gods express their admiration for the Lord by throwing garlands of flowers, jewels, garments and sandalwood on the remaining bones.

The boundless pity of the Bodhisattva is also glorified in most of the other narratives.

I-tsing praises the Jātakamālā (or Jātakamālās) among the works which were particularly popular and much read in India at his time. Among the frescoes of the caves of Ajantā there are illustrations to the Jātakamālā with verses by Āryaśūra in inscriptions. Paleographically, these inscriptions belong to the 6th century A.D. As another work by Āryaśūra was already translated into Chinese in 434 A.D., the poet probably belongs to the 4th century A.D.[1]

A work of ornate poetry which deals once more with the life of Buddha, and which concludes with the same episode as Book XIII of the Buddha-Carita, is the Sanskrit epic Padyacūḍāmaṇi,[2] ascribed to a man named Buddhaghoṣa. The author of this Mahākāvya (in 10 Sargas) is certainly not the famous commentator, but some Buddhaghoṣa, who knew the epics of Aśvaghoṣa and Kālidāsa, and made liberal use of

1. *I-tsing*, transl. by *Takakusu*, p. 162 f., H. *Luders*, NGGW 1902, p. 758 ff.; B. *Nanjio*, Catalogue of the Chinese Tripiṭaka, No. 1349; Th. *Zachariae*, GGA 1888, p. 850; F. W. *Thomas* in Album Kern, p. 405 ff. Though the Chinese translation of the Jātakamālā mentions Āryaśūra as the author, it only contains 14 stories, see A. O. *Ivanovski* in RHR 1903, t. 47, p. 298 ff. In the Tibetan Tanjur five other works besides the Jātakamālā, are ascribed to Āryaśūra; s. *Thomas*, Kavindravacana-Samuccaya, p. 27 f.

2. Ed. by M. *Ranga Acharya* and S. *Kuppuswami Sastri*, with a commentary by Pandits K. *Venkatesvara Sastri* and D. S. *Satakopa Acharya*, Madras, 1921.

them,[1] or perhaps an anonymous writer, who simply assumed the name of Buddhaghoṣa.

The Avadāna Literature

The Jātakamālā is also called "Bodhisattvāvadānamālā," for "Bodhisattvāvadāna" is synonymous with Jātaka; and, indeed, the Jātakas are nothing but Avadānas the hero of which is the Bodhisattva. Thus, works like the Kalpanāmaṇḍitikā and Jātakamālā often coincide with the texts of the Avadāna literature, and numerous Jātakas are also contained in the Avadāna books.[2] Like the two above-mentioned works of Buddhist narrative literature, the Avadāna texts also stand, so to speak, with one foot in the Hīnayāna literature, and the other in that of the Mahāyāna.[3] The earlier works still belong entirely to the Hīnayāna; though they already exhibit that Buddha worship which is also met with in the later works of the Pāli Canon (Buddhavaṃsa, Apadānas) they as yet eschew the exaggerations and the mythology of the Mahāyāna, whilst the latest works of the Avadāna are already completely Mahāyānistic.

The word avadāna[4] means a "noteworthy deed,"

---

1. See *Kuppuswami Sastri's* "References to descriptions of same or similar things in Raghuvaṃśa, Buddhacarita, and Padyacūḍāmaṇi," prefixed to the Edition. The name of the author is mentioned only in the colophons. See B. Ch. *Law*, Life and Work of Buddhaghosa, p. 85 ff.

2. On the Avadāna literature in general, see E. *Burnouf*, Introduction a l'histoire du Bouddhisme, p. 207 ff.: L. *Feer* in the introduction to his translation, and J. S. *Speyer* in the foreword to his edition, of the Avadāna-Śataka, Vol. II.

3. We know through *I-tsing* (transl. *Takakusu*, pp. xxii f. and 14 f.) that the boundaries between Hīnayāna and Mahāyāna were often uncertain.

4. In Pāli apadāna, see above, p. 152 f. In Sanskrit, too, the secondary form apadāna is found. See *Burnouf*, Introduction a l'histoire du Bouddhisme Indien, p. 57; *Feer*, l. c., p. ix ff.; *Speyer*, l. c., p. 1 ff. The Chinese translators sometimes confuse *avadāna* wtth *nidāna*, but we must not, as H. *Zimmer* (ZII 3, 1925, 205 ff.) does, interpret *avadāna* as being synonymous with *nidāna* in the sense of "actions which causally determine as their consequences certain events which take place later in time." In the sense of "deed," "great deed," *avadāna* occurs not only in Jātakamālā I, beginning; III, 23; IV, 2, but also in the Rāmāyaṇa, in works of Kālidāsa and in other works written in classical Sanskrit. Cf. Winternitz in Comm. Wogihara, p. 7 ff.

sometimes in a bad sense,[1] but generally in the good sense of "a heroic deed," "a feat," with the Buddhists a "religious or moral feat" and then also the "story of a noteworthy deed, or feat." Such a "feat" may consist of the sacrifice of one's own life, but also merely of a gift of incense, flowers, ointments, gold and precious stones, or the erection of sanctuaries (Stūpas, Caityas, and so on). As these stories are, as a rule, intended to show that "black deeds bear black fruits, and white deeds white fruits," they are also Karman stories, which show how the actions of one existence are very closely connected with those of former or future existences. It is, of course, only from our standpoint that they are "legends" : the Buddhists regard them as actual events, related by the Buddha himself, and are just as authentic as "words of the Buddha" (buddhavacana) as a Sūtra. Like the Jātakas the Avadānas, too, are a kind of sermons. It is therefore usually told, by way of introduction, where and on what occasion Buddha related the story from the past, and at the end, the lesson is deduced from the story by Buddha. A regular Avadāna, then, consists of a story of the present, a story of the past, and a moral. If the hero of the story of the past is the Bodhisattva, this kind of Avadāna can also be called a "Jātaka."[2] There is a special kind of Avadānas, namely those in which the Buddha, instead of telling a story of the past, gives a prophecy of the future. Like the usual story of the past, this story of the future serves to explain the present Karman.[3] There are also Avadānas in which both kinds of stories are combined, and finally also such in which a Karman already shows its good or bad fruits in the present existence.

All these kinds of Avadānas also occur sporadically in the Vinaypiṭaka and in the Sūtrapiṭaka, but are mostly to be found in large collections, which were compiled either purely for the purpose of edification or with literary ambitions as well.

---

1. For instance in Avadāna-Śataka V.
2. On Jātakas in the Avadāna literature, see S. d'*Oldenberg*. JRAS 1893, p. 304, and *Feer*, Les Avadānas Jātakas, JA 1884, s. 8, t. IV, p. 332 ff.
3. Hence the name Vyākaraṇa, "explanation," for the prophetic Stories of the Future.

The Avadāna-Śataka, or "the hundred Avadānas,"[1] is a work of the former category, presumably the oldest of these books. As it was already translated into Chinese in the first half of the 3rd century A.D., and on the other hand as the dīnāra is mentioned, we can, with a considerable degree of certainty, ascribe it to the 2nd century A.D.[2] The character of the narratives, and the fact that the Stories of the Present contain passages from a Parinirvāṇa-Sūtra and other Sūtras of the Sanskrit Canon of the Sarvāstivādins, are sufficient evidence that this work belongs to the Hīnayāna.[3] Though Buddha-worship plays a prominent part in the legends, there is no trace of the Bodhisattva cult and of Mahāyānistic mythology.

The Avadāna-Śataka consists of ten decades,[4] each of which deals with a certain subject. The first four decades contain narratives which are intended to show by which actions one can become a Buddha or a Pratyeka-Buddha.[5] All the narratives of the first decade and for the greater part also of the third decade, are of the nature of prophecies (Vyākaraṇas). The story is told of a pious deed by which a person, a Brahmin, a princess, the son of an usurer, a rich merchant, a gardener, a king, a ferryman, a little girl, and so on, worships the Buddha ; a miracle usually takes place, and the Buddha proclaims smilingly that this person will, in a future age of the world, be a Buddha or (in Book III) a Pratyeka-Buddha. On the other hand, the stories in the second and fourth decades are Jātakas. The pious, virtuous and wonderful deeds are explained by the fact that the hero of these narratives is none other than the Buddha

1. Edited by J. S. *Speyer* (Bibliotheca Buddhica III), St. Petersburg 1902-1909. Translated into French by L. *Feer* (AMG., t. 18), Paris 1891. *Feer* had already previously translated and discussed separate sections of the work in a series of treatises (JA 1878-1884).

2. *Speyer*, Vol. II, Preface, p. xv. Works in which the Roman denarius is mentioned as dīnāra, could not have originated before the Ist century A.D., and were probably written later, see above, Vol. I, p. 445, note 2.

3. *Speyer*, l. c., p. xvi ff., and ZDMG 53, 1899, p. 120 ff.; *Oldenburg* ZDMG 52, p. 672, NGGW 1912, p. 168 ff.

4. This division into Vargas (Pāli Vagga) of ten pieces each, is very popular in the Pāli texts, and therefore seems to be ancient Buddhist.

5. *i.e.*, Pāli Paccekabuddha, see above, p. 141, note 1.

himself in one of his former births. Book V is a kind of Preta-vastu, corresponding to the Pāli Petavatthu. A saint, usually Maudgalyāyana, looks around in the world of ghosts, and observes the sufferings of one of the (male or female) ghosts (Pretas). He asks the cause of his or her sufferings. The ghost refers him to the Buddha, who then relates the story of the "black deed," the refusal to give alms, the abuse of a saint, and so on, committed by that being in a former existence. Book VI relates stories of men and animals who, by means of some pious deed, are reborn as gods in heaven. The four last decades contain narratives which are to show which deeds qualify a person to become an Arhat. The Arhats of Book VII are all of the race of the Śākyas, those in Book VIII are women, those in Book IX men of blameless conduct, and those in Book X men who formerly did bad deeds and suffered for them, and only then attained the stage of an Arhat by means of a pious deed.

The tales in this collection are not only classified and compiled on a definite plan, but they are also narrated after one stereotyped pattern. This conventionality goes so far that certain phrases and descriptions of situations occur again and again in exactly the same words.[1] Thus every narrative begins with the following words :

"Buddha the Lord, honoured, highly esteemed, held in honour and praised by kings, ministers, rich people, citizens, masters of guilds, leaders of caravans, gods, Nāgas, Yakṣas, Asuras, Garuḍas, Kinnaras and great snakes, worshipped by Devas, Buddha the Lord, the famous, highly meritorious one, accompanied by a community of disciples, and receiving as alms all necessary clothing, food, bed and shelter, refreshments and medicaments, went to......and sojourned in......"

Every narrative, too, concludes with the words : "Thus spake the Lord, and with enraptured hearts the monks applauded the words of the Lord." When the moral of the story is summed up, it is always in the words :—

1. Cliches of the same kind, also occur in Bengali poems, s. Dinesh Chandra *Sen*, History of Bengali Language and Literature, p. 585 f.

"So, O monks, the fruit of quite black deeds is quite black, that of quite white deeds quite white, that of mixed deeds is mixed. Therefore, O monks, give up the black and the mixed deeds, and take pleasure only in the quite white deeds..."

In the same way, a pious man, a rich man, a powerful king, a happy marriage, the education of a young man, the appearance of a former Buddha, and so on are always described in exactly the same words. That is, indeed, not only the case with a few short sentences, but even with long passages extending over several printed pages. One of the longest stereotyped pieces is, for instance, the description of the smile with which the Buddha utters the prophecy that somebody will become a Buddha; for, before the Buddha prophesies the future, he invariably smiles. And when he smiles, blue, yellow, red and white rays burst forth from his mouth. Some of these rays descend to the hells, the others ascend into the worlds of heaven. And after they have travelled round the thousands and thousands of worlds, they return again to the Buddha from behind, and disappear in some part of the Buddha's body, which varies according to the subject of the prophecy. All this is very circumstantially described; and this circumstantiality and prolixity is characteristic of the method of narration of the Avadāna-Śataka in general. Nevertheless, besides many commonplace and tedious, though always edifying, stories, it also contains many valuable narratives and noteworthy variants from the passages of Buddhist narrative literature familiar from other texts. Only a few examples can here be quoted in extracts, in order to give an idea of the character of the collection.

No. 28. A poor girl anoints the feet of the Buddha with ointment made of sandalwood oil. In consequence of this, the whole town is filled with the perfume of sandalwood. The girl is delighted with this miracle, falls at the Buddha's feet, and prays that she may become a Pratyeka-Buddha in a future birth. Buddha smiles, and prophesies that she will one day be a Pratyeka-Buddha named Gandhamādana ("Perfume-delighter").

No. 34 is a version of the legend of King Śibi, who gives

away all his possessions. But it is not enough for him to satisfy human beings, he also wants to do good to the small creatures. Therefore he cuts his skin with a knife, and stands there to let the stinging flies satisfy themselves with his blood. Śakra sees this from his heaven, and, in order to put him to the test, appears before Śibi in the from of a vulture, as though he were about to attack him. The king only looks at him with friendliness, and says : "Take, my friend, whatever part of my body you require, I give it to you." Thereupon the god transforms himself into a Brahmin and asks the king for both his eyes. Śibi says : "Take, great Brahmin, what you will, I will not hinder you." Then Śakra assumes his true form, and prophesies that Śibi will attain perfect enlightenment.

No. 36 is the legend of Maitrakanyaka, a version of the Pāli Jātaka of Mittavindaka. But in this case the story takes quite a different turn from the Pāli version, owing to the fact that the Bodhisattva is the hero. Here, too, he goes to hell as a punishment for having offended his mother, and a glowing iron wheel revolves on his head. But while he suffers the dreadful torments, and it is foretold to him that he will have to bear the wheel for 66,000 years, until another shall come who has committed a similar sin, he feels pity for the creatures, and in order that nobody else shall have to suffer the same pains, he determines to bear the wheel on his own head for all eternity. In consequence of this merciful thought, the wheel vanishes from his head.[1]

No. 54. At the suggestion of his wives, King Bimbisāra has caused a Stūpa to be erected in his harem over some hairs and nail-parings which the Buddha had given him. The women worshipped this with incense, lamps, flowers, etc. But when Ajātaśatru murdered his father Bimbisāra, and ascended the throne himself, he issued the strict command that no woman shall dare, on pain of death, to worship the Stūpa. Śrīmatī, however, one of the women of the harem, takes no notice of this command, and places a garland of lamps around the Stūpa. The enraged king kills her, she dies thinking of the Buddha, and is at once reborn in the heaven of the gods.

1. See above, p. 127, and *Scherman*, Visionslitteratur, p. 69 ff.

No. 100. Whilst the heroes of all the other Avadānas are contemporaries of the Buddha, the hero of this last story is a contemporary of King Aśoka. The link with the time of Buddha is established by the initial mention of a report of the passing away of the Buddha.[1] King Aśoka lived a hundred years after the passing of the Buddha. Aśoka had a son named Kuṇāla, who was so handsome that the king believed there could not be his equal in the whole world. One day, however, he hears from some merchants from Gandhāra, that a still handsomer young man exists. In their country, they say, there lives a youth named Sundara ("Beautiful") who is not only of faultless beauty, but wherever he goes, a lotus pond and a garden arise. The astonished King Aśoka sends messengers for Sundara, and convinces himself of this miracle. The king then asks what Karman has given the youth his advantages, and Upagupta,[2] one of the elders, replies as follows : At the time when the Buddha had just attained complete Nirvāṇa, the present Sundara had been a poor farmer, who prepared a refreshing bath and food for Mahā-Kāśyapa and his retinue of 500 monks when they went to the burial of the Lord and were bowed down with grief at the passing of the Master, and were quite exhausted by their long wanderings. He is now enjoying the fruit of that good deed.

Many of the narratives of the Avadāna-Śataka recur in other collections of Avadānas, and a few also in the Pāli Apadānas.[3]

The Karma-Śataka ("A hundred Karman stories"), is an old work which is very much like the Avadāna-Śataka, and

---

1. This account is a passage from a Parinirvāṇa-Sūtra, and agrees fairly closely with the Pāli Mehā-Parinibbāna-Sutta. Another passage on the Parinirvāṇa is the introduction to No. 40.

2. Upagupta here takes over the role of the Buddha in the other Avadānas.

3. Thus, for example, the legend of Rāṣṭrapāla (No. 90) which corresponds partly to the Raṭṭhapāla-Sutta of the Majjhimanikāya, and partly to Raṭṭhapāla-Apadāna. See Mabel *Bode* in Melanges Levi, p. 183 ff. Frequently it is only the titles which are identical, and the Apadāna shows great variations. See *Feer*, Avadāna Śataka, pp 240 f., 313 f., 335, 340 ff., 354 f., 360 f., 372 f., 439 f.

has a number of narratives in common with it, but unfortunately it has only come down in a Tibetan translation.[1]

The Divyāvadāna ("The Heavenly Avadānas"),[2] is a later collection than the Avadāna-Śataka, but it also includes some very old texts. Though it begins with the Mahāyānistic benediction "Om, honour to all the exalted Buddhas and Bodhisattvas," and contains just a few obviously later additions in the spirit of the Mahāyāna,[3] as a whole it decidedly belongs to the Hīnayāna school. The Sanskrit Canon and single canonical texts such as Dīrghāgama, Udāna, Sthavira-Gāthā, and so on, are frequently quoted.[4] Some narratives begin and end exactly as in the Avadāna-Śataka, and a number of the stereotyped phrases and descriptions so characteristic of this book, also recur literally in the Divyāvadāna. They are probably derived from the Vinayapiṭaka of the Mūla-Sarvāstivāda school, from which, as S. Lévi[5] has shown, more than one-half of the stories is borrowed.

1. *Feer,* l. c., pp. xxix f., 442 ff.; *AMG.*, t. V, 382 ff., 404 ff., and JA 1901, s. 9, t. XVII, pp. 53 ff., 257 ff., 410 ff.; *Speyer*, l. c., p. xix f. Another Tibetan Avadāna book translated from the Sanskrit but the Sanskrit original of which is no longer extant, is the narrative work Dsanglun, well-known in universal literature, and translated into German with the title "Der Weise und der Tor" by I. J. *Schmidt* (St. Petersburg 1843). (On a Chinese version of this work, s. *Takakusu* in JRAS 1901, p. 447 ff.).

2. Edited by E. B. *Cowell* and R. A. *Neil*, Cambridge 1886. Long passages from it were translated by *Burnouf* in his "Introduction a l'histoire du Bouddhisme Indien." Four tales have been translated into German by H. *Zimmer*, Karman, ein buddhistischer Legendenkranz, München 1925. Critical notes on the text of the Divyāvadāna by J. S. *Speyer* in WZKM 16, 1902, 103 ff-, 340 ff. "Studies in the Divyāvadāna" by James R. Ware in JAOS 48, 1928, 159 ff. The title of the work is not certain; it is only found in the colophons of some of the manuscripts. *Rājendralāla Mitra*, Nep. Buddh. Lit., pp. 304 to 316, describes a manuscript entitled "Divyāvadānamālā," which diverges greatly from our edition. Also a Paris manuscript descript described in the Edition, p. 663 ff., only partly agrees with our Divyāvadāna.

3. Thus Chapter 34 calls itself a "mahāyānasūtram" (Ed., p. 483) and the ṣaḍakṣarā vidyā, i.e., om maṇipadme huṃ, is mentioned in Chapt. 33 (Ed., p. 613 f.). See *La Vallee Pousin,* Bouddhisme, p. 381.

4. See above, p. 224 f. and *Oldenberg,* ZDMG 152, 1898, pp. 653, 655 f., 658, 665. The four Āgamas are mentioned in Divyāvadāna, p. 333.

5. "Les elements de formation du Divyāvadāna" in T'oung Pao, s. II, Vol. VIII, 1907, 105 ff.

The composition of the work is, in fact, very confused and disconnected. There is no sign of any principle of arrangement. The language and style, too, are by no means unified. Most of the legends are written in good, simple Sanskrit prose, only interrupted here and there by Gāthās. In a few of the pieces, however, we also find the metres of ornate poetry and the genuine Kāvya style with its long compound words.[1] The compiler thus seems to have simply taken over the passages literally out of other texts. As a matter of fact, almost all the stories in the Divyāvadāna have been traced to other works. In addition to the Mūla-Sarvāstivāda-Vinaya, the compiler of the Divyāvadāna also made use of a "Book of King Aśoka,"[2] of thc Saṃyuktāgama (which is known by the Chinese translation Tsa A-han King), and of Kumāralāta's Kalpanāmaṇḍitikā.[3] It stands to reason that, when the Divyāvadāna was compiled in this fashion, the various parts of the work belong to different periods. There are some passages which must certainly have been written prior to the 3rd century A.D. However, the collection as a whole, could not have been in existence earlier than the 4th century A.D.; for, not only are Aśoka's successors, the kings of the Śuṅga dynasty down to Puṣyamitra (about 178 B.C.) mentioned in this work, but the dīnāra occurs several times, and this brings us at least to the first century A.D. and probably nearer to 400 A.D.[4] and lastly, some time must have elapsed after Kumāralāta, who lived a considerable

1. *Oldenberg* in NGGW 1912, 156 ff., has shown that, in the Divyāvadāna, just as in the Mahāvastu, there are two distinct styles, an earlier canonical one, and a later style.

2. It is not certain what the Sanskrit title of this work was. It was translated into Chinese as A-yu-wang-ch'uan (approximately Asokarājāvadāna) by the Parthian Fa-k'in between 281 and 306, and in a shorter version as A-yu-wang-king (approximately Asokarāja-Sūtra) in the year 512 by a certain Saṅghabhara or Saṅghabhaṭa.

3. See J. *Przyluski*, La legende de l'empereur Aśoka (Aśoka-Avadāna) dans les textes, Paris 1923 (AMG, Bibl. d'Etudes, t. 31); Ed. *Huber* in BEFEO 4, 1904, 709 ff.; 6, 1906, I ff. and *Speyer*, Avadānaśataka II, Preface, p. xvi f. A. *Gawron'ski*, Studies about the Sanskrit-Buddhist Literature, p. 49 ff., thinks that in the Aśoka cycle of the Divy. he is able to trace an acquaintance with Aśvaghoṣa's epics too.

4. See above, Vol. I, p. 445, note 2.

time after Kaniṣka,[1] for a compiler to make such extensive use of his Kalpanāmaṇḍitikā.

However, it is valuable to know that precisely one of the most interesting legends in the Divyāvadāna, the Śārdūlakarṇāvadāna,[2] was translated into Chinese in 265 A.D. The substance of this Avadāna, remarkable in several ways, is as follows :—

When the Master was sojourning in Śrāvastī, Ānanda was in the habit of going daily to the town to beg for food. One day when he was returning from the town, he was thirsty, and saw a Cāṇḍāla girl, named Prakṛti, fetching water from the well. "Sister," he said to her, "give me some water to drink." Thereupon, Prakṛti replied : "I am a Cāṇḍāla girl, honourable Ānanda." "Sister," said Ānanda, "I did not enquire about your family and your caste, but if you have water left, give me some, I want to drink."[3] Then the girl gave him a drink, and fell deeply in love with the saint. She declares to her mother that she will surely die if she cannot get Ānanda as her husband. Then her mother, who is a great sorceress, prepares a potent love-charm,[4] and bewitches Ānanda by means of mantras. The spell is successful, and Ānanda comes to the house of the Cāṇḍālas, where the delighted Prakṛti has already prepared the couch. But at the moment of the greatest danger, Ānanda bursts into tears, and in his dire need prays to the Buddha. Buddha comes to his aid with his mantras ; and Buddha's mantras render those of the sorceress powerless. Ānanda leaves the Caṇḍāla house, and returns to his monastery. The great

1. See above, p. 258f.

2. Edition, p. 611 ff. See also *Rāj Mitra,* Nep. Buddh. Lit., p. 223 ff. J. Przyluski in J. A. 210, 1927, p. 115 ff.

3. The resemblance to St. John IV, 7 ff. (Jesus and the woman of Samaria) is certainly striking, but the whole of the rest of story is so very different in the Gospel, that we can scarcely assume any connection between the two.

4. She does this in the same way as such magical rites were performed according to the Kauśika-Sūtra of the Atharvaveda (see above, Vol. I, p. 261) from time immemorial, and as they are familiar to witchcraft among all nations. See *Winternitz* in WZKM 26, 1912, 248 ff.

sorceress explains to her unhappy daughter that the spells of Gautama are stronger than hers. But Prakṛti, the Cāṇḍāla girl, was not cured of her love. She went into the town and now followed Ānanda daily when he went on his begging rounds. Again Ānanda, in his distress, appealed to the Master for help. Buddha sends for Prakṛti, and appears to agree to her desire of marrying Ānanda, but with great delicacy, he is able to induce her to take the vow of chastity, and become a nun. She not only has her hair cut off and assumes the garb of a nun, but she also enters into the complete understanding of the four noble truths, and entirely comprehends the religion of the Buddha.

Now when the Brahmins, warriors and citizens of Śrāvastī heard that Buddha had ordained a Cāṇḍāla girl as a nun, they were very angry ; they reported the matter to King Prasenajit, and the king immediately went to the Master in order to complain of this procedure. Many Brahmins, warriors and citizens of Śrāvastī were also assembled there. Then the Buddha told the story of Triśaṅku, the Cāṇḍāla chief, who wished to marry his very learned son Śārdūlakarṇa to the daughter of the proud Brahmin Puṣkarasārin. The Brahmin rejects him with scorn. Now a most interesting dialogue is developed, in which Triśaṅku severely criticises the caste system and the Brahminical ethical teachings. He points out to him that such differences as exist among the different kinds of animals and plants, cannot be shown among the castes. Moreover, according to the theory of the transmigration of souls and of Karman, there cannot be any castes, as everyone is reborn according to his actions, and so on. Finally Puṣkarasārin is convinced of the learning of Triśaṅku, whereupon he consents to the marriage. Now the Brahmin's daughter was none other than Prakṛti, the Cāṇḍāla girl, in a former birth. The Buddha himself was at that time Triśaṅku and Śārdūlakarṇa was Ānanda.[1]

---

1. Richard *Wagner* became acquainted with this legend by means of *Burnouf's* translation (Introduction, p. 205 ff.) and based the outline of his "Sieger" upon it. *Cf.* the sketch in Richard Wagner, Nachgelassene Schriften und Dichtungen, Leipzig, 1895, p. 161 f. How keen Wagner was to put Ānanda and Prakṛti on the stage, is shown by his letters to Matilde *Wesendonk* (21st edit., Berlin, 1904, p. 59 ff., 98, 197 and 242). As is well known, the "Sieger" finally became "Parsifal."

Chapters XXVI to XXIX should certainly be counted among the oldest portions of the Divyāvadāna : they contain a cycle of legends centering around the person of the great king Aśoka, and are based upon an ancient "Book of King Aśoka." This book probably originated in Mathurā between 150 and 50 B.C.,[1] but is no longer extant in its original form. We only know it from two different Chinese versions.[2] The Divyāvadāna did not only draw on the "Book of King Aśoka," which was already augmented at that time, but it also made use of the Kalpanāmaṇḍitikā.[3] These legends scarcely contain anything of much historical value;[4] but they are all the more valuable from the purely literary standpoint. Above all, we find here the exceedingly dramatic legend of Upagupta and Māra. It is an extremely bold idea to allow Māra, the evil one, the tempter, to be converted by a Buddhist monk. The idea is still bolder when the saint Upagupta, who longs to see, face to face, the Buddha who had entered Nirvāṇa a hundred years before, beseeches Māra, whom he had converted, to appear in the guise of the Buddha, and when Māra does indeed, like a skilful actor, represent Buddha in so life-like a manner, that the saint sinks down before him in prayer. The whole of this story is so dramatic that we might believe it to be simply a Buddhist drama retold here. This passage is taken almost word for word from Kumāralāta's Kalpanāmaṇḍitikā, and in language, style and metre, it is one of the best productions of ornate poetry.[5] One of the most beautiful legends in the Aśoka

---

1. *Przyluski*, l. c., pp. 13 ff., 92 f., 166.

2. See above, p, 274, note 2.

3. For a detailed treatment of the mutual relationship of the Kalpanāmaṇḍitikā, Divyāvadāna, A-yu-wang-ch'uan and A-yu-wang-king, s. H. *Lüders*, Bruchstücke der Kalpanāmaṇḍitikā des Kumāralāta, p. 71 ff.

4. Unless there is a historical nucleus underlying the persecutions of Jain monks, mentioned in Divy., p. 427, and the persecutions of Buddhist monks under Puṣyamitra, mentioned on p. 433 f. See *Rhys Davids*, JPTS 1896, p. 88 f.

5. Divyāvadāna Ed., pp. 356-364, transl. by *Windisch*, Māra und Buddha, p. 161ff. *Cf.* Ed. *Huber*, Aśvaghoṣa, Sūtrālaṁkāra traduit en Français, p. 263ff. and BEFEO 4, 1904, p. 708 ff. *Lüders*, l. c., 77 ff. A Pāli form of this legend, quite inartistic and undramatic, has been published by C *Duroiselle* (BFFEO

cycle is the touching story of Kuṇāla, the son of Aśoka, whose lovely eyes are poked out at the instigation of his wicked stepmother, without his feeling one moment's anger or hatred towards her who has done him so much injury.[1] The Divyāvadāna has many legends in common with the Pāli Canon. Thus Chapter XVII contains a passage from a Mahā-Parinirvāṇa-Sūtra.[2] Chapter III relates of the advent of the future Buddha Maitreya, combined with the legend of King Praṇāda.[3] In this it partly coincides with Dīghanikāya 26. The story of Pūrṇa, who goes as an apostle to the savage and violent Sroṇaparāntakas, determined to accept it with equanimity and gentleness if they despise him, strike him, or even want to kill him, corresponds to a familiar Pāli Sutta.[4] The story of the young son of a merchant, who gradually acquires enormous riches all on account of his having sold a dead mouse, corresponds to Jātaka No. 4.[5] The vadāna of Rūpavatī is reminiscent of the legends of the Jātakamālā: Rūpavatī cuts off her breasts in order to nourish with her flesh and blood, a woman who is near starvation and is about to devour her child. We see in her the Mahāyāna ideal of a Bodhisattva

4. 1904, p. 414 ff.) from the Burmese work Lokapaññatti. It is curious that the monastery in which Upagupta, who later became Aśoka's teacher, lives, is endowed by the brothers Naṭa ("actor") and Bhaṭa ("soldier"), and is therefore called Naṭabhaṭika. *Levī* (Toung Pao 1907, p. 120) is not wrong in calling the Aśokāvadāna a kind of Māhātmya of the Naṭabhaṭika monastery of Mathurā.

1. Divyāvadāna, p. 406 ff. ; rendered in extracts by *Oldenberg*, Buddha, p. 348 ff., and E. *Hardy*, Aśoka, p. 65 ff.

2. Divy., pp. 200 ff., 706; s. *Windisch*, Māra und Buddha, pp. 35 ff.; 43 ff.; *Oldenberg*, ZDMG 52, p. 658 f.

3. Divy., p. 55 ff.; s. E. *Leumann*, Maitreya-samiti, pp. 4, 173 ff. and E. *Abegg*, Der Messiasglube in Indien und Iran, 1928, p. 153 ff.

4. Divy., p. 36 ff. L. de *La Vallee Poussin*, Bouddhisme, Paris, 1909, p. 275 ff., sees in Pūrṇa the type of the Mahāyānist Bodhisattva. However, both in the Divy. and the Pāli Saṁyuttanikāya 35, 88 (IV, p. 60 ff.) and the Majjhimanikāya 145 (III, 267 ff.) the stress is laid on the mildness and equanimity which characterise the perfect saint, the Arhat; and therefore it shows rather the Hīnayāna ideal of an Arhat.

5. Divy, p. 498 ff. A counterpart to the story of Dick Whittington and his cat. Also in Kathā-Saritsāgara, I, 6.

when, in reply to an enquiry for the motive of her action, she answers :

"As true as it is that I sacrificed my breasts for the child's sake, not for sovereignty, not for enjoyments, not in order to attain heaven, not to become an Indra, not in order to rule a kingdom as a ruler, but for no other reason than to attain the highest perfect enlightenment, that I may tame the untamed, liberate the unliberated, comfort the uncomforted, and lead the unredeemed to the perfect Nirvāṇa,—as true as this is, may my female sex vanish, and may I become a man !" Scarcely had she uttered this, than she was transformed into a Prince Rūpavata, who later became king and reigned for sixty years. Reborn as a Brahmin, he sacrifices himself for a tigress.[1]

Chapter XXXVIII, which contains an ornate version of the Maitrakanyaka Avadāna after the Avadāna-Śataka (No. 36), is related in the same Kāvya style as the Jātakamālā.[2] It is in passages like this, that the Divyāvadāna resembles the Avadānamālās.

Poetical versions of Avadānas, partly selected systematically from the Avadāna-Śataka, partly taken from other sources, are the Kalpadrumāvadānamālā ("Wishing Tree Avadāna Garland," i.e., a garland of Avadānas which grant all wishes), the Ratnāvadānamālā ("Jewel Avadāna Garland"), and the Aśokāvadānamālā ("Avadāna Garland of King Aśoka").[3] The Kalpadrumāvadānamālā begins with a version of the last narrative of the Avadāna-Śataka. And as the Sthavira Upagupta[4] appears in conversation with King Aśoka, so all the legends in the Avadānamālās are inserted into the framework

1. *Cf.* Jātakamālā I, above, p. 263 ff. In the Chinese Tripiṭaka, Rūpavatī is rendered by "Silver-white," see S. *Beal* in Ind. Ant. 9, 1880, 145 ff.

2. Divy., p. 586 ff. *Cf. Speyer*, Avadāna-Śataka, Ed II, p. xii, and above, p. 271.

3. *Cf. Feer*, l. c., p. xxiii ff. *Speyer*, l. c., pp. xii ff., xxi ff.; Rāj. *Mitra*, Nep. Buddh. Lit., pp. 6 ff., 197 ff., 292 ff.; C. *Bendall*, Catalogue, p. 110 ff., and *Przyluski*, l. c., p. xiv f. A legend from the Ratnāvadānamālā is translated by Mahendra Lal *Dās* in the Journal of the Buddhist Text Society, 1894, Part 3.

4. Upagupta is another name of Tissa Moggaliputta, the teacher of Aśoka (see above, p. 8, *cf.* A. *Waddell*, JASB proceedings 1899, p. 70 ff.).

of a dialogue between Aśoka and Upagupta. The first part of the Aśokāvadānamālā contains legends of Aśoka himself; after these follow instructions in the form of stories which Upagupta relates to Aśoka. All the three collections differ from the Avadāna-Śataka, not only because they are written entirely in epic ślokas, but especially because they decidedly belong to the Mahāyāna, and recall the Purāṇas both in style and language. They possibly belong to the period in which the sectarian Purāṇas came into being.)[1]

Another book, which has drawn liberally on the Avadāna-Śataka, is the Dvāviṃśatyavadāna ("The Avadānas in 22 sections"). Here too, Upagupta appears in conversation with Aśoka, but both of these soon give place to Śākyamuni in Maitreya. In this case, however, the legends are told in prose (with verses interspersed) and divided into sections according to the moral they teach ("meritorious actions," "hearing of the sermon," "generosity" and so on).[2]

The Bhadrakalpāvadāna ("Avadānas from the good age of the world") is a collection of 34 legends, which Upagupta relates to Aśoka. Like the Avadānamālās, it is entirely in verse. However, in plan and contents it is said to resemble the Mahāvagga of the Vinayapiṭaka to some extent.[3]

In the same way as, in the sectarian Purāṇas, there are large sections and entire works (Māhātmyas) consisting of legends which were invented to explain the origin of some

---

1. About the 6th century A.D. and later. According to *Speyer*, l.c., p. xxxvi, who places them between 400 and 1000 A.D., they used the Jātakamālā. The *Mahājātakamālā* (or Bṛhajjātakamālā) excerpted by E. *Lang* (JA 1912, s. 10, t. XIX, p. 520 ff., *cf.* S. *Levi* in Festschrift Wilhelm Thomsen, Leipzig, 1912, 162 ff.) also appears to belong to the Avadānamālās.

2. *Feer*, l.c., pp. xix f., xxvii; *Bendall*, Catalogue, p. 36. A specimen of it translated by *Feer* (AMG t. 5, 1883, p. 544 ff.). See also Rāj. *Mitra*, Nep. Buddh. Lit., p. 85 ff. The language of the Dvāviṃśatyavadāna is a popular Sanskrit, s. R. L. *Turner* in JRAS 1913, 289 ff.

3. *Bendall*, Catalogue, p. 88 ff.; *Feer*, l.c., p. xxix; Rāj. *Mitra*. l. c., p. 42 ff.; *Speyer*, l. c., p. xxxvi. According to S. d'*Oldenberg*, who has translated the 34th tale, a version of Jātakamālā 31 (Jātaka No. 537) (JRAS 1893, p. 331 ff.), it is later than Kṣemendra (about 1040 A. D.).

feasts or rites (Vratas), so there are also similar Buddhist texts. A collection of such legends is the Vratāvadānamālā, "Garland of Avadānas on the origin of festivals or rites," which has only the framework of the dialogue between Upagupta and Aśoka in common with the previously mentioned Avadāna collections.[1]

The Vicitrakarṇikāvadāna is a collection with the most varied contents, containing 32 narratives, a few of which come from Avadāna-Śataka, and others belong to the type of the Vratāvadānas. The language, too, is as varied as the contents, now a barbaric Sanskrit, again good Sanskrit verses, and sometimes even Pāli.[2]

All these works are so far accessible only in a few manuscripts. Others are known only through the Tibetan and Chinese translations.[3] Not only books of Avadānas, but many single Avadānas of considerable length, however, have come down in manuscripts as well as in Chinese and Tibetan translations. An instance is the Sumāgadhāvadāna, the legends of Sumāgadhā, the daughter of the merchant Anāthapiṇḍada, who alienates her husband from the Jain monks, and, by a miracle, converts the whole town to the religion of the Buddha. In a former existence she had been the daughter of King Kṛkin, famous for his ten marvellous dreams.[4]

Lastly, mention must here be made of the extensive Avadāna book of the Kashmirian poet Kṣemendra, the Avadāna-Kalpa-

1. Rāj. *Mitra*, l. c., pp. 102 ff, 221 ff., 231, 275 ff. Other texts of the same kind : *Ibid*, pp. 229 f., 232 f., 265 ff., 269 ff., 280ff. L. *Feer*, Suvarṇavarṇa-Avadānam et Vratāvadānamālā, OC XII, Rome, 1899, I, p. 19 ff. These are obviously quite late Mahāyāna works.

2. *Speyer*, l. c., pp. xciii-c.

3. Based on Chinese Avadāna books (*cf. Feer*, l. c., p. xxx f.) are the "Contes et Apologues Indiens" by Stanislas *Julien*, Paris, 1860, transl. into German by A. *Schnell*, Rostock, 1903.

4. These dreams belong to universal literature. *Cf.* Jātaka No. 77, 8. d'*Oldenberg* in 1893, p. 509 ff., and Tsuru-Matsu *Tokiwai*, Studien zum Sumāgadhāvadāna, JRAS Diss. der Universität Strassburg 1898; Rāj. *Mitra*, l. c., p. 237. In Yaśomitra's Abhidharmakośavyākhyā the same Avadāna is quoted "from a Vinaya text."

latā,[1] which was completed in 1052 A.D., and which is held in great esteem especially in Tibet.[2] Kṣemendra is a prolific writer and a verse-maker of astonishing fertility. We shall meet with him again in other places, for his activity was most versatile. Yet he is distinguished not so much by genius and taste, but by an iron determination. The huge collection of legends, too, in which Kṣemendra has recast the Buddhist Avadānas in the style of ornate court poetry, contains more edifying stories than skilfully and tastefully narrated ones. The Buddhist tendency to self-sacrifice is here brought to a climax with such subtlety, the doctrine of Karman is applied so clumsily, and the moral is pointed in such an exaggerated manner, that the story often achieves the reverse of the desired result. The collection consists of 107 legends, to which Somendra, Kṣemendra's son, has added not only an Introduction but also a 108th narrative (Jīmūtavāhana-Avadāna.[3] The legends are mostly known already from the older Avadāna books and also from other sources.[4]

The Mahāyāna-Sūtras

The whole of the Buddhist Sanskrit literature discussed so far, belongs to the borderland which forms the transition between

1. The text, with the Tibetan transl., is published in Bibl. Ind., Calcutta, 1898 ff, by Sarat Chandra *Dās* and Hari Mohan *Vidyābhūṣaṇa*. A number of legends are translated in the Journal of the Buddhist Text Society, Vols. I-V, 1893-1897. *Cf.* also Rāj. *Mitra*, l. c., p. 49 ff.

2. Some Tibetan scholars, however, do not recommend this work, seeing that it was written by a layman; for Kṣemendra was not a monk.

3. Somendra is an even worse poet than his father. In addition to the Bṛhatkathāmañjari, IX. 18-1221, he also made use of Harṣa's drama Nāgānanda. See F. D. K. *Bosch*, de legende van Jimūtavāhana in de Sanskrit-Litterature, Leiden, 1915, p. 115 ff.

4. Thus the Padmāvati-Avadāna (No. 68) corresponds to the stories, familiar from the Pāli commentaries, of Padmāvatī, under whose feet lotus blossoms spring forth, and the Ekaśṛṅga-Avadāna (No. 65) corresponds to the Ṛṣyaśṛṅga legend which is so well known to us. Both are to be found also in the Mahāvastu, and *Lüders* (NGGW 1901, p. 26) shows that Kṣemendra recast the Ṛṣyaśṛṅga-legend on the model of the Mahāvastu. The Avadāna of Kṣemendra has been rendered in German verse by Hermann *Francks* (Ekasriṅga Prinz Einhorn, Leipzig, 1901).

Hīnayāna and Mahāyāna Buddhism. We shall now turn to those works which belong entirely to the Mahāyāna.

The Mahāyāna does not possess a canon of its own, and cannot possess one, for the simple reason that the Mahāyāna does not represent one unified sect. There is, indeed, an account of a council which is supposed to have assembled under King Kaniṣka, but it is doubtful whether any canon was established at all at this council, and if so, in which language and by which sect.[1] It is true that a Chinese text translated by Hsuan-Tsang[2] makes mention of a "Bodhisattvapiṭaka" consisting of a long list of Mahāyāna texts, a Vinayapiṭaka and an Abhidharmapiṭaka, and the same text enumerates a lengthy list of Mahāyāna-Sūtras. However, as the text goes on to say that "there are hundreds of myriads of similar Mahāyāna-Sūtras," we are scarcely justified in regarding this as an attempt at a classification of "the Mahāyāna Canon." The so-called "nine Dharmas"[3] are not the canon of any sect, but a series of books which were compiled at different times, and which belonged to different sects, but which, at the present day, are all held in great honour in Nepal. The titles of these nine books are : Aṣṭasāhasrikā Prajñā-Pāramitā, Saddharma-Puṇḍarīka, Lalita-Vistara, Laṅkāvatāra or Saddharma-Laṅkāvatāra, Suvarṇa-Prabhāsa, Gaṇḍavyūha, Tathāgataguhyaka or Tathāgataguṇa-jñāna, Samādhirāja and Daśabhūmīśvara.[4] All these works are also called "Vaipulya-Sūtras."

---

1. The object of the alleged council of Kaniṣka was not to establish a Canon, but to collect explanations (commentaries). According to J. *Takakusu* (JRAS 1905, 414 f.) this council dealt with the Hīnayāna, and not the Mahāyāna.

2. See S. *Levi* and Ed. *Chavannes* in JA 1916, s. 11, t. VIII, p. 5 ff. The Buddhist dictionary Mahā-Vyutpatti (Bibl. Buddh. XIII) 65, mentions 105 separate Mahāyāna texts, No. 12 of which is a "Bodhisattva-Piṭaka." This is also quoted in the Śikṣā-Samuccaya, pp. 190 and 311.

3. "Dharma" is here probably only an abbreviation of "Dharma-Paryāya" (religious texts). In Nepal a regular divine service is consecrated to these nine books (*Hodgson*, Essays, p. 13), a bibliolatry which is characteristic of the Buddhism of Nepal, and is also very conspicuous in the texts themselves.

4. *Hodgson*, l. c. ; *Burnouf*, Introduction, pp. 29 ff., 60 f., *Kern*, Der Buddhismus, 11, 508 ff.

The most important Mahāyāna-Sūtra, and certainly the one which stands foremost as a work of literature, is the Saddharma-Puṇḍarīka, "the Lotus of the Good Religion."[1]

He who wishes to become acquainted with Mahāyāna Buddhism, with all its characteristic peculiarities, with all its advantages and defects, should read this Sūtra. There is not much of the *man* Śākyamuni left in this work.[2] The Buddha now is actually nothing less than a god above all gods, an infinitely exalted being, who has lived since countless aeons in the past, and will live for ever. "I am the father of the world," he says of himself (XV, Gāthā 21), "the self-existent (Svayambhū), the physician and protector of all creatures, and it is only because I know how perverse and deluded the fools are, that I, who have never ceased to exist, pretend to have passed away." Thus it is only out of pity for the beings, out of consideration for the weakness of human understanding, that he pretends to have entered Nirvāṇa. He is like that physician with many sons who were once attacked by a severe illness during their father's absence. The physician returns and prepares medicines for them. Only a few of his sons however, take them, the others reject them. In order to persuade these also to take the medicines, he goes to distant parts, and gives out that he is dead. The children, who now feel deserted, take the prescribed medicines, and recover their health. Buddha has recourse to a similar artifice when he apparently enters Nirvāṇa, but yet returns again and again in order to preach.[3] It is his preaching which forms the link between him and the human beings. The Buddha of the "Lotus" does not, however, preach like the

---

1. Edited by H. *Kern* and Bunyin *Nanjoi*, Bibliotheca Buddhica X, St. Petersbourg, 1908 ff. Transl. into French ("Le Lotus de la bonne Loi") by E. *Burnouf*, Paris, 1852, into English by H. *Kern* in SBE, Vol. 21, 1884. The title is explained in the following manner by M. *Anesaki* (Buddhist Art in its Relations to Buddhist Ideals, (1914, p. 15 f.) : "The lotus is a symbol of purity and perfection because it grows out of mud but is not defiled,—just as Buddha is born into the world but lives above the world; and because its fruits are said to be ripe when the flower blooms,—just as the truth preached by Buddha bears immediately the fruit of enlightenment."
2. See *Anesaki* in ERE IV, p. 839; *La Vallee Poussin* in ERE VIII, 145 f.
3. Chapt. XV, SBE 21, p. 304 ff.

Buddha of the Pāli Suttas, who wanders from place to place as a mendicant monk, in order to proclaim his doctrine; on the contrary, he sits on the Gṛdhrakūṭa hill in a large assembly of monks and nuns, and in the midst of a still larger host of thousands of Buddhas and Bodhisattvas, gods and demi-gods; and when he is about to "pour down the great rain of the religion, to sound the great drum of the religion, to raise the great banner of the religion, to light the great torch of the religion, to blow the great shell trumpet of the religion, to beat the great kettledrum of the religion," a ray of light bursts forth from the hair between his eye-brows; this ray of light illuminates eighteen thousand "Buddha-lands" with all the Buddhas and all the beings in them, and permits the Bodhisattva Maitreya to see wonderful visions; for the Buddha of the 'Lotus' is also a powerful magician, who loves to work upon the senses of his audience by means of splendid phantasmagorias.

The doctrine of this Buddha differs just as greatly from that of the Hīnayāna, as his personality differs from that of the Buddha of the old texts. Though it is true that he, too desires to lead the beings to the "Buddha knowledge," to enlightenment, he gives them a single 'vehicle,' the 'Buddha-vehicle,' which carries them to their goal. Everyone who has merely heard the Buddha's preaching, who has performed any kind of meritorious actions, who has led a moral life, can become a Buddha. Moreover, even those who worship relics, erect Stūpas, construct any kind of images of Buddha, whether jewelled marble or wooden statues or frescoes, even children who in play make Stūpas of sand, or scribble figures of Buddha on the wall, those who offer flowers or perfumes at Stūpas or make music before them, even those who only by chance, have on some occasion thought of the Buddha with the thought "honour to the Buddha,"—all these will attain to the highest enlightenment.[1] It is only in appearance that there are three 'vehicles,' namely that of the disciples, that of the Pratyeka-Buddhas, and that of the Bodhisattvas, by means of which Nirvāṇa can be attained. In reality it is only by the mercy of the Buddha that all of them alike attain to enlightenment and become Buddhas.

1. Chapt. II, Gāthās 61 ff., 74 ff SBE 21, p. 47 ff.

This is illustrated by one of those beautiful parables which are not rare in the Saddharma-Puṇḍarīka :

In a ruined old house lives a father with his children. Suddenly the house is on fire. The father is troubled about his children. It is true that he is strong, and could take the little ones in his arms and escape from the house with them. But the house has only *one* door. The children, unconscious of the danger, run about in merry play, and do not pay heed to his cry of warning. It is to be feared that he and his children will all perish in the fire. Then a good plan occurs to him. Children love play-things. He calls out to them that he has all sorts of beautiful toys for them, little bullock-carts, little goat-carts, little antelope-carts, in front of the house. No sooner do the children hear these words, than they all rush out of the door and are saved. Now they ask their father for the promised little carts of three kinds. However, the father is a rich man, and gives them splendid, beautifully decorated bullock-carts instead. The children are merry and happy. Who will accuse the father of deception, because he promised the children three kinds of inferior carts, and only gave them the carts of the one, most splendid kind ? Even so does the Buddha deal with men : by the promise of the three "vehicles" he lures them away from the burning, ruined house of this world, he rescues them, and gives them the one 'vehicle,' the most precious of all, the 'Buddha vehicle.'[1]

Again, in the parable of the 'prodigal son,' the Buddha is represented as the good, wealthy father, who means well towards his sons, the human beings :

A rich man has an only son, who roams about in foreign lands for fifty years. While the father grows richer and richer, and has become a great man, the son lives in foreign parts, poor and in reduced circumstances. As a beggar, he at last returns to his home, where his father has been yearning for him all the time. The beggar comes to the house of his father, whom, however, he does not recognise in the great man, who, like a king, surrounded by a great retinue, sits before his mansion.

1. Chapt. III, SBE 21, p. 72 ff.

When he sees the pomp and splendour, he flees for fear that he, the ragged beggar, might be ill-treated. His father, however, recognised him at once, and sends out servants to bring the beggar in. Trembling and shaking with fear, he is dragged in, and he falls unconscious. Then his father commands that he shall be released. Gladly the beggar gets up, and goes to the poor quarter of the town. Now the rich man thinks out a plan whereby he may win the confidence of his son. He sends workmen to hire him for the humblest work in his house; he sometimes chats with him and gradually becomes intimate with him. In this way twenty years pass, without the father's making himself known. Not until the hour of his death does he cause all his relatives to assemble, and announce that the beggar, who has now become a trusted servant, is his own son; and he makes him the heir to all his wealth. The rich man is Buddha; the son who was lost and is found again, represents the human beings, whom Buddha, as the wise father, gradually draws to himself, and finally appoints as his fortunate heir.[1]

The Buddha is also compared to a physician, as often as to a loving father. There is an especially detailed parable, in which the human beings are compared to persons born blind, whose eyes are opened by Buddha, the great physician.[2] The fact that the Buddha knows no partiality, but is an equally good father and physician to all, is shown by two beautiful similes : Even as a mighty rain-cloud gathers, and waters and refreshes by its moisture all the grasses, herbs and trees, even as the latter absorb the moisture of the earth and blossom forth in renewed vigour, so the Buddha appears in the world and refreshes all creatures, bringing them blessed repose. Again, even as the sun and the moon send down their rays equally over all the world, on the good and the bad, on the high and

1. Chapt. IV, SBE 21, p. 98 ff, *Cf. La Vallee Poussin,* Bouddhisme, p. 317 ff. The parable of the "prodigal son" in the Gospel of St. Luke, 15 has such a very different tendency, that we do not believe that there is any connection between the two. *Cf. Garbe,* Indien und das Christentum, p. 46 and Carlo *Puini* in GSAI 17, 1215, 129 ff.

2. Chapt. V, SBE 21, p. 129 ff.

the lowly, so the preaching of the Buddha is for all the world alike.[1]

All these similes and parables would be still more beautiful, if they were not spun out to such length and with such verbosity, that the pointedness of the simile suffered from it. This verbosity is very characteristic of the whole work. It is a veritable whirl of words with which the reader is stunned; and the idea is often drowned in the flood of words. The *numbers* are, however, still more immoderate and extravagant than the words. For instance, there was a Buddha who lived "forty hundred thousand myriads of tens of millions of ages of the world, as many as there are grains of sand in the river Ganges, and after he had attained to complete Nirvāṇa, his true religion still lasted hundreds of thousands of myriads of tens of millions of ages of the world, as many as there are tiny specks of dust in the whole of India, and a copy of the true religion after that, still lasted hundreds of thousands of myriads of tens of millions of ages of the world, as many as there are tiny specks of dust in the four continents," and there arose consecutively in the world "twenty hundred thousand myriads of tens of millions" of similar Buddhas.[2] The Buddha is glorified in the most extravagant manner, immoderate both in words and in numbers, especially in the splendid phantasmagoria of Chapter XIV, where, by the magic power of the Buddha, the earth opens and there suddenly appear from all sides many hundreds of thousands of myriads of tens of thousands of Bodhisattvas, each with a retinue as numerous as the sand of sixty Ganges rivers. While these countless Bodhisattvas pay homage to the Buddha, fifty ages of the world pass, during which great silence prevails, but which, by the magic power of the Lord, seem but a single afternoon. The Buddha tells the astonished Maitreya that all these countless Bodhisattvas were his pupils. The glorification of the text itself is equally immoderate and extravagant; for, strange as it is, the text refers at every turn to Buddha's preaching and expounding of the text,

1. Chapt. V, SBE 21, pp. 119 ff., 122 ff., 128 ff.
2. Chapt. XIX, Text, p. 376 f., SBE 21, p. 355.

and to its propagation by the preachers. Thus (in Chapter XI) Śākyamuni causes a wonderful Stūpa to appear in mid-air, and from the interior of the Stūpa sounds the voice of a Buddha, who had died myriads of ages previously : "Excellent, excellent, Lord Śākyamuni, the religious discourse called 'Lotus of the Good Religion' has been well expounded by thee. Yes, so it is, Lord Buddha (Sugata)." The same chapter relates : The Bodhisattva Mañjuśrī proclaimed the "Lotus of the Good Religion" in the kingdom of the Nāgas at the bottom of the ocean, and the youthful daughter of the Nāga king heard the sermon, and understood all the doctrines. As a result she attains to enlightenment and changes her sex on the spot.[1] The merit of the preacher of the 'Lotus' and of the faithful hearing of this sermon is praised again and again. Thus it is said in Chapter XXII :

"The religious discourse called 'Lotus of the Good Religion' is like a tank for the thirsty, like a fire for those who suffer from cold, like a garment for the naked, like the caravan leader for the merchants, like a mother for her children, like a boat for those who ferry over...like a torch for the dispelling of darkness."[2] Whoever writes down this book, or causes it to be written down, acquires endless merit. A female being who hears it, has lived as a female for the last time. He who, at the hearing of the sermon of the "Lotus" expresses his acclamation, will always exhale from his mouth sweet breath as from a lotus, and sandal-perfume will emanate from his limbs.

All these extravagances, and in particular all these glorifications of the texts in the texts themselves, are just as characteristic of all the Mahāyāna-Sūtras[3] as they are of the Purāṇas.

1. SBE, Vol. 21, p. 250 ff.

2. SBE, Vol. 21, p. 388.

3. Amitāyurdhyāna-Sūtra 28 (SBE, Vol. 49, Part 2, p. 195) is significant : "If there be any one who commits many evil deeds, provided that he does not speak evil of the Mahāvaipulya Sūtras, he, though himself a very stupid man, and neither ashamed nor sorry for all the evil actions that he has done, yet, while dying, may meet a good and learned teacher who will recite and laud the headings and titles of the twelve divisions of the Mahāyāna scriptures. Having thus heard the names of all the Sūtras, he will be freed from the greatest sins which would involve him in births and deaths during a thousand Kalpas."

In fact, it is the spirit of the Purāṇas of which we are reminded by every line of the Saddharma-Puṇḍarīka.[1] At times the Buddha of the Saddharma-Puṇḍarīka reminds us of the Kṛṣṇa of the Bhagavad-Gītā.[2] This does not, however, enable us to draw any conclusion as regards the chronology, as we cannot determine any sure date, either for the beginning of the Kṛṣṇa-cult, or for the Purāṇas.

It is altogether difficult to fix any definite period for the Saddharma-Puṇḍarīka as it contains sections belonging to various epochs. The prose in pure Sanskrit, and the Gāthās in "mixed Sanskrit" could not possibly have originated at the same time,[3] because, in contents, they often diverge from one another. Both the prose and the Gāthās several times mention the work as a metrical composition. Probably it originally consisted only of verses, with *short* prose passages inserted by way of introduction and as a means of connecting the verses. The short prose passages were later enlarged, especially as the dialect of the verses had become obsolete. Without being actually a commentary, the prose served as an explanation.[4] It is significant that precisely those chapters which contain no Gāthās, have, on other grounds too, proved to be later additions. These are Chapters XXI-XXVI, which are devoted more to the adoration of Bodhisattvas, while the Saddharma-Puṇḍarīka on the

1. The few points of agreement between the vocabulary of the Saddharma-Puṇḍarika and that of the Śatapatha-Brāhmaṇa, which are pointed out by *Kern*, SBE 21, p. xvi f., are by no means sufficient to connect the work in any way with Vedic literature.

2. It seems to be, however, risky to assume that the 'Lotus' was directly influenced by the Kṛṣṇa-cult, the Vedānta and the Bhagavad-Gītā, as has been assumed by J. N. *Farquhar*, Outline of the Rel. Lit. of India, p. 114 f.

3. H. *Lüders* (Hoernle, Manuscript Remains, p. 161 f.) is of opinion that the original text was written in Prākrit, and was gradually Sanskritised.

4. We cannot, however, simply say that the prose is a resume of the Gāthās, or that the Gāthās are an amplification of the prose. For instance, supposing that in Book I, we had only the prose, we should glean a meaning from it, whereas the Gāthās by themselves would remain inexplicable in some cases. In Book II, the main content is included in the Gāthās. In Book III (the parable of the father and the children), the prose diverges somewhat from the Gāthās, but the Gāthā narrative presents a better meaning.

whole serves for the glorification of the Buddha Śākyamuni. One of these Bodhisattvas is Bhaiṣajyarāja, the "Prince of the art of Healing" who in Chapter XXI utters protecting magic formulas (Dhāraṇīs) and in Chapter XXII, after he has, for twelve years, eaten sweet-scented substances and drunk oil, wraps himself in heavenly garments, bathes in oil, and burns himself. During twelve thousand years his body burns without ceasing ; and the sole purpose of this magnificent sacrifice and splendid firework display, is to do honour to the Buddha and the Saddharma-Puṇḍarīka. Chapter XXIV is devoted to the Bodhisattva Avalokiteśvara, the great redeemer. He who invokes him is delivered from every danger. The executioner's sword is shivered into fragments, if he who is sentenced to death prays to him. All fetters are loosened if his name is but uttered. He rescues the shipwrecked and the caravan which is attacked by robbers. A woman who desires a son or a beautiful daughter, needs only to invoke Avalokiteśvara, and her wish is fulfilled. The chapter also contains a Gāthā passage of considerable length for the glorification of Avalokiteśvara. This, however, is also of more recent date ; not *all* the Gāthās are earlier than the prose : some were added later.[1]

However, though the work contains later and earlier parts, it presents a much greater uniformity of character than, for instance, the Mahāvastu or the Lalita-Vistara. Whilst both the last-mentioned works contain many a passage which harks back to the very earliest period of Buddhist doctrine and poetry, the *whole* of the Saddharma-Puṇḍarīka only gives expression to a later phase of Buddhism.[2] Nevertheless we shall most probably be right in placing the nucleus of the work as far back as the first century A.D., as it is quoted by Nāgārjuna, who probably

1. *Kern*, SBE 21, p. xviii f. Though the old Chinese translation contains Chapters. XXI-XXVI, they appear in a different order from that of the Sanskrit text. This proves that they are Pariśiṣṭas, Appendices, which did not originally belong to the work. *Kern.*, l. c., p. xxi f.

2. It is significant that *Kern* SBE 21, p. X ff., in order to prove that the Saddharma-Puṇḍarīka and the Lalita-Vistara contain materials which belong to the earliest period of Buddhism, can quote examples only from the Lalita-Vistara.

lived towards the end of the 2nd century A.D.[1] The work was first translated into Chinese in 223 A.D. This translation has not come down to us, but we have those of Dharmarakṣa (286 A.D.) and Kumārajīva (about 400 A.D.) and that of Jñānagupta and Dharmagupta (601 A.D.).[2] In the preface to the last-named translation it is stated that Dharmarakṣa and Kumāragupta made their translations according to two different texts.[3] Moreover, the fragments of the Saddharma-Puṇḍarīka which have been found in Eastern Turkestan, and which present a text diverging from that of the Nepalese manuscripts, afford a proof of the fact that there were two recensions of the work. On the whole, it is a shorter text, and yet it contains some passages which are missing in our (Nepalese) text.[4] Whatever the exact date of the work in its original form may be, one thing is certain : the nature of the work as we know it, implies a mature development of Mahāyāna Buddhism, especially in the direction of Buddha-Bhakti and the cult of relics and image worship, and above all also an advanced stage of Buddhist art. When there is such frequent talk of thousands or myriads of tens of millions of Stūpas, which are erected over the relics of a Buddha, or of hundreds of tens of millions of Vihāras, which are described as splendid buildings, furnished with the greatest comfort and luxury, there must have been at least many hundreds of Stūpas and Vihāras

---

1. See *Eliot*, Hinduism and Buddhism, II, 52.

2. See B. *Nanjio*, Bibliotheca Buddhica X, 5, 1912, Preface, p. ii f.; *Bagchi*, 1, pp. 87, 150, 186, 310, 322, 409; and N. D. *Mironov* in JRAS 1927, p. 252 ff.

3. *Kern* in SBE, Vol. 21, p. xxi note.

4. The Central Asiatic fragments have been published by *Hoernle* and *Lüders* in *Hoernle*, Manuscript Remains, pp. 132 ff., 138 ff., 162 ff. See also *La Vallee Poussin* in JRAS 1911, 1067 ff.; *Kern* in Preface to edition (Bibl. Buddh. X), p. v. ff.; *Hoernle* in JRAS, 1916, p. 269 ff. According to N. D. *Mironov* (JRAS 1927, 252. ff) there are two groups of fragments, one of which should, on palaeographic grounds, be ascribed to the 5th and 6th centuries, and the other to the 7th century. Moreover, fragments of an Uiguric translation of the Saddharma-Puṇḍarīka have been found in Central Asia s. F. W. K. *Müller*, Uigurica II. in ABA 1911, p. 14 ff.; *Lüders* in SBA 1914, p. 99. *Bendall* ascribes a Nepalese MS. of the Saddh., which he discovered, to the 4th or 5th century (JRAS 1901, p. 124 note).

(topes and monasteries) in the land, and these must have been furnished with pictures of Buddha made of jewels, statues of Buddha made of wood and metal, and with reliefs and frescoes.[1] On the other hand, the Saddharma-Puṇḍarīka inspired Buddhist art.[2] It has always ranked foremost as a book of edification, among the Buddhists of China and Japan. The Chinese pilgrim I-tsing relates that the "Lotus of the Good Religion" was the favourite book of his teacher Hui-hsi ; during a period of more than sixty years he read it through once daily, so that he read it twenty thousand times.[3] Even at the present day it may be found in every Buddhist temple in Japan : it is the most sacred book of the Hokke-shū or "Saddharma-Puṇḍarīka sect," founded by Nichiren in 1252 A.D., and one of the principal works upon which the Tien-tai School in China, and the Tendai sect in Japan also take their stand.[4]

The whole of a long Mahāyāna-Sūtra is also devoted to the Bodhisattva Avalokiteśvara, who is glorified in Chapter XXIV of the Saddharma-Puṇḍarīka. The complete title of this Mahāyāna-Sūtra is Avalokiteśvara-Guṇakāraṇḍa-Vyūha, "the detailed description basket of the qualities of Avalokiteśvara," but it is usually briefly called Kāraṇḍa-Vyūha. There are two versions of this work; an earlier one in prose and a later one in Ślokas.[5] The latter is based on a theistic view of the world. It relates how, at the beginning of all things, Ādibuddha, the "first Buddha,"

1. See particularly Chapt, II, Gāthās 77 ff., SBE Vol. 21, p. 50 f.

2. See M. *Anesaki,* Buddhist Art in its Relations to Buddhist Ideals, p. 16 f.

3. I-tsing, transl. by J. *Takakusu,* p. 205.

4. *Cf.* B. *Nanjio,* Short History of the Twelve Japanese Buddhist Sects, Tokyo, 1886, pp. 68 ff., 132 ff.; Yamakāmi *Sogen,* Systems of Buddhist Thought, Calcutta, 1912, p. 4; K. J. *Saunders,* Epochs in Buddhist History, Chicago, 1924, p. 60 ff., 120 ff., 146 f.; Timothy *Richard,* The New Testament of Higher Buddhism, Edinburgh, 1910, p. 127; and W. M, *McGovern,* An Introduction to Mahāyāṇa Buddhism, London, 1922. pp. 208 f., 222, Extracts from the Chinese translation of the Saddh., which are said to contain the nucleus of the work, have been translated by T. *Richard,* l. c., pp. 147-261.

5. The prose text is published by Satyavrata *Sāmaśramī,* Calcutta, 1873. (An edition which appeared in Serampore in 1872, is mentioned in the Catalogue of the Library of the India Office.) Cf. *Burnouf,* Introduction, pp.

also called Svayambhū, "the self-existent," and Ādinātha, "the First Lord, appeared and created the world through meditation. Out of his spirit arose Avalokiteśvara, who also takes part in the work of creation, creating the gods out of his own body. Not only does this introduction remind us forcibly of the Purāṇas, but the language and style of the metrical Kāraṇḍa-Vyūha are entirely those of the later Purāṇas. Now we know that in the fourth century A.D. there were already Buddhists who believed in Ādibuddha as God and Creator.[1] The cult of Avalokiteśvara, too, was already prevalent at that time, for the Chinese pilgrim Fa-hien, who came to India in the year 399 A.D., prayed to this Bodhisattva for deliverance, when he was overtaken by a storm on the voyage from Ceylon to China. The earliest pictures of Avalokiteśvara date from the 5th century.[2] For this reason it is possible that the metrical Kāraṇḍa-Vyūha was in existence even prior to the 4th century A.D., though this is not probable, since the Tibetan translation in the Kanjur, which originated in 616 A.D.,[3] is based upon the prose version which makes no mention of Ādibuddha. The prose version that contains a large section in the style of the Tantras, is probably not very old either.[4]

196-206,; Rāj. *Mitra*, Nep. Buddh. Lit., p. 95 ff.; 101 f.; *Bendall*, Catalogue, p. 9 ff.; Haraprasāda *Śastrī*, Catalogue of... MSS. belonging to the Darbar Library, Nepal, Calcutta, 1895, p. 89; *La Vallèe Poussin*, ERE II, p. 259 f.

1. This is proved by Maitreyanâtha who says in the Mahāyāna-Sūtrālaṃkāra IX, 77: "There is no Ādi-Buddha." Cf. *La Vallée Poussin* in *Garbe*, Indien und das Christentum, p. 182.

2. L.A. *Waddel*, JRAS, 1894, p. 57. *Cf.* A. *Foucher*, etudes, sur l' iconographie Bouddhique de l'Inde (Bibl. dc l'ecole des hautes ėṭudes, t. 13), Paris, 1920, p. 97 ff.; and *La Vallée Poussin*, ERE II, p. 256 ff.

3. Thus according to *La Vallèe Poussin*, ERE II, p. 259.

4. Unfortunately, we are unable to determine whether the Ratna-Kāraṇḍa-Vyūha-Sūtra, which was translated into Chinese by Dharmarakṣa in 270 A.D. and by Guṇabhadra between 435 and 468 A.D., (s. B. *Nanjio*, Catalogue No. 168 f.; *Bagchi* 1, 96, 380; Alfred *Forke*, Katalog des Pekinger Tripiṭaka. Ostas. Sammlungen der k. Bibliothek zu Berlin, 1916, Nos. 623, 1069) is identical with the "Kāraṇḍa. Vyūha Sūtra", translated between 980 and 1001 A.D. (*Nanjio*, No. 782: *Forke* No. 548), and with one of the Sanskrit versions. A Ratna-Kāraṇḍa-Sūtra is quoted in the Sikṣā-Samuccaya (pp. 6, 356), and mentioned in Mahā-Vyutpatti, 65, 84. In the Kanjur, the Kāraṇḍa-Vyūha and the Ratna-Kāraṇḍa are, two different works, s *Cosuma* de *Koros* in AMG II, 243, 246.

The fundamental idea, the glorification of the wonderful redeemer Avalokiteśvara, the "Lord who looks down," *i.e.*, who looks down with infinite pity on all beings,[1] is the same in both versions of the Kāraṇḍa-Vyūha. Avalokiteśvara here appears as the typical Bodhisattva, who refuses to assume Buddhahood until all beings are redeemed. Avalokiteśvara's one and only one task is to bring the doctrine of salvation to *all* beings, to help all sufferers, to save them from every distress, and to exercise infinite pity that does not even shrink from sin,[2] and does not stop at the gates of hell. The early chapters of the Kāraṇḍa-Vyūha describe how he descends into the terrible hell Avīci, in order to release the tortured ones from their torment. No sooner has he entered, than the burning heat is transformed into a pleasant coolness; in place of the cauldron in which millions of the damned boil like pulse, a refreshing lotus-pond appears. The place of torture becomes an abode of joy.[3]

---

1. The name is thus explained in the Kāraṇḍa-Vyūha itself, *Burnouf*, Introduction, p. 201 f. Other explanations of the name are also possible; see *La Vallée Poussin* ERE II, p. 256 f. H. *Zimmer*, ZII I, 1922, 73 ff. shows up the difficulties presented by all explanations of the name which have hitherto been suggested, but his own explanation: "The Master of Enlightenment, *i.e.*, he who has attained to perfect enlightenment, and yet does not become a Buddha, but remains a Bodhisattva until such time as all beings shall be released," is not at all convincing, for we ask ourselves in vain how Avalokita can possibly have the meaning of samyaksambodhi. On pictorial presentations of Avalokiteśvara, see A. *Foucher*, L'Iconographie Bouddhique de l, Inde, p. 97 ff.; Alice *Getty*, The Gods of Northern Buddhism, Oxford, 1914, p. 54 ff.

2. Avalokiteśvara is made to say that it is better for a Bodhisattva to commit sin in the exercise of mercy, and to suffer in hell, than to disappoint any being in the hope which it has reposed in him. ERE II, p. 257 f.

3. *Cf.* E.B. *Cowell*, Journal of Philology VI, 1876, p. 222 ff. (reprinted also in Ind. Ant. VIII. 249 ff.); L. *Scherman*. Visionsliteratur, p. 62 ff. *Cowell* compares the apocryphal gospel of Nicodemus, and derives the Indian legend from the Christian one. Our own opinion is that the points of agreement are not sufficiently great to warrant the likelihood of any historical connection. Similarly, *Garbe*, Indien und das Christentum, p. 77 f. Avalokiteśvara's visit to hell is the prototype of the legend of King Vipaścit in the Mārkaṇḍeya-Purāṇa, see above Vol. I, 537 ff., and J. *Charpienter*. Paccekabuddhageschichten I, 118. The beautiful poem by the Austrian poetess Betty *Paoli*. "Der gute Köning in der Hölle" (Gedichte, Auswahl und Nachlass, Stuttgart 1895, 217 ff.) is based upon the Buddhist legend.

From hell Avalokiteśvara goes to the abode of the Pretas and refreshes these ghosts, which are eternally tortured by hunger and thirst, with food and drink. One of his wanderings takes him to Ceylon, where he converts the cannibal witches (Rākṣasīs), thence he goes to Benares, where he preaches the doctrine to beings born as insects and worms, and then to Magadha, where he miraculously rescues the inhabitants from a dreadful famine. In Ceylon he appears as the winged horse Balāha, in order to bear away from the island the shipwrecked ones who had been allured by the witches, and to rescue them from destruction.[1]

Avalokiteśvara is not only a helper full of loving kindness, but he is also a cosmic being, out of whose body all the gods have come forth. "The sun and the moon came forth from his eyes, Maheśvara from his brow, Brahman and other gods from his shoulders, Nārāyaṇa from his heart, Sarasvatī from his two corner teeth, the winds from his mouth, the earth from his feet, Varuṇa from his stomach" (p. 14 f.). We see him as a genuine Bodhisattva, however, when his excellent qualities are praised : Hear O sons of a noble race ! The Bodhisattva Avalokiteśvara, the Great Being, is a lamp for the blind, a sun-shade for those who are scorched by the great heat of the sun, a river for those who are dying of thirst; he gives safety to those who are in fear of dangers, he is a physician to those who are tormented by sickness, he is a father and mother to the unfortunate, he points the way to Nirvāṇa to those who have descended into hell. This is the nature of the qualities of this Exalted One. Fortunate are those beings in the world, who are mindful of his name. They escape from all suffering of Saṃsāra (from the first) to the last. Those people are very wise, who always honour Avalokiteśvara with gifts of flowers and incense" (p. 48f.).

The major portion of Section II of the prose version of the Kāraṇḍa-Vyūha is after the style of thc Tantras, and is devoted to the glorification of the "knowledge of the six syllables," *i.e.* the protecting and benedictory prayer formula "Om maṇipadme hum." This famous prayer, which even at the present day

1. *Cf.* Jātaka No. 196, where the winged horse is identified with the Buddha of a former birth. In the Kāraṇḍa-Vyūha the merchant Siṁhala, cast adrift to Ceylon, is the Buddha Śākaymuni in former birth.

is on every one's lips in Tibet, and which is written on all praying wheels and praying banners, is praised in the most extravagant manner in this work. We read :

"This great knowledge of the six syllables is the profound secret of Avalokiteśvara, and he who knows the profound secret, knows release (p. 67).

"Whoever will give me the great knowledge of the six syllables" says a Bodhisattva, "to that man I will willingly give the four continents, filled with the seven kinds of precious stones. O Lord, if there be no birch barks on which to write it down, no ink, and no quill, let him use my blood as ink, let him strip off my skin and use it instead of the birch bark let him split my bones and make a quill of them. O Lord, this would not hurt my body. He will be a father and a mother to me, the teacher above all teachers (p. 69).

"O noble youth, I can count every single grain of sand in the four oceans, but it is not possible for me to count up the sum of merit which one acquires by a single recitation of the great knowledge of the six syllables." (p. 70).[1]

The Bodhisattva Avalokiteśvara is very closely related to the Buddha Amitābha, who is glorified in the Sukhāvatī-Vyūha, "Detailed Descriptions of the Blessed Land," in much the same manner as Śākyamuni in the Saddharma Puṇḍarīka and Avalokiteśvara in the Kāraṇḍa-Vyūha. Two works have come down to us in Sanskrit, one of considerable length and the other much shorter; both are entitled Sukhāvatī-Vyūha,[2] and diverge widely from each other, though both of them describe "the blessed land" of the Buddha Amitābha or Amitāyus [3] Not only the intro-

1. Cf. *La Vallée Poussin* in ERE II, 259; H. *Zimmer*, Kunst-form und Yoga im indischen, Kultbild Berlin, 1926, 167 ff. Om maṇipadme hum is probably a mode of addressing Maṇipadmā, the female counterpart of Avalokiteśvara ; s. F. W, *Thomas* in JRAS 1906, 464, and *Eliot*, Hinduism and Buddhism, III, 396 f.

2. Both texts have been published by Max *Müller* and Bunyiu *Nanjio* (Anecdota Oxoniensia, Aryan Series, Vol. I, Part II, Oxford. 1883) and translated by Max *Muller* in SBE, Vol. 49. Part II. The shorter Sukhāvatī-Vyūha has been translated into French from Kumārajīva's Chinease version, by *Ymaidoumi* and *Yamata* in AMG II,39 ff.

3. On Amitābha, cf. *La Vallee Poussin* in ERE I.98 f. ; *Grunwedel*, Buddhistische Kunst in Indien, p. 169 f.; and Alice *Getty*. The Gods of Northern Buddhism, Oxford. 1914, p. 36ff.

duction to the shorter text, but certain traits in the description of Sukhāvatī are different, and there is also an essential difference in their tendency. The longer Sukhāvatī-Vyūha teaches that those who have accumulated a large pile of good works, who direct their thoughts to enlightenment and think of Amitābha in the hour of death, go to the "blessed land," although those who merely direct their thoughts to Amitābha and his Buddha-land, may possibly also reach Sukhāvatī. On the other hand, the shorter text teaches that the "blessed land" is not the reward for good works, but that anyone who merely hears the name of Amitāyus and thinks of it in the hour of death, will be born in this Buddha-land. There seems to be no doubt that the longer text is the earlier one.

In the longer Sukhāvatī Vyūha, Śākyamuni appears in Rājagṛha on the Gṛdhrakūṭa hill, surrounded by thousands of monks, disciples and Bodhisattvas. In conversation with Ānanda, he enumerates 81 Buddhas of the past. The last of these, named Lokeśvararāja, instructs the monk Dharmākara regarding the perfections of the Buddha-lands. It is this Dharmākara who, by prayers (praṇidhāna) in a former life, and by faithfully practising the virtues of a Bodhisattva through countless aeons, was re-born in the Sukhāvatī world in the West as Buddha Amitābha. There he radiates immeasurable light (hence his name Amitābha) and his span of life is immeasurable (hence his other name Amitāyus). In his "Buddhaland," the Sukhāvatī paradise, there is neither hell nor animal birth, nor Pretas, nor Asuras. This Blessed land is filled with infinitely sweet scent. Jewel trees in many hundreds of thousands of colours grow there, also wonderful lotus blossoms. There are no hills there, the country is as flat as an open hand. Delightful rivers yield pleasant, sweet water, and the rippling of the water is the most glorious music. The beings who are born in Sukhāvatī are all endowed with the most beautiful qualities, physical and mental, and enjoy all imaginable pleasures. There is no difference between men and gods. There is no question of day and night. There is no darkness. Here Amitābha is continually praised. And whoever thinks of this Buddha with awe, whoever pays heed to the increase of his good deeds, whoever directs his thoughts to enlightenment, whoever prays reverently to be re-born in that world, to him Amitābha appears in the hour of his death, and he is born again in the blessed land. Indeed, even those who only think of Amitābha with one thought, are 'born' there. The beings in Sukhāvatī are not, however, born of woman : they appear seated on lotus blossoms if they have firmly believed in Amitābha, or resting in the cups of lotus blossoms if their faith had not been quite firm. The beings in that blessed world live in happiness and calm, in perfect wisdom and sinlessness.

In the Sukhāvatī-Vyūha the splendour of Amitābha and his paradise are described with the same verbal extravagance and the same numerical immoderation as we find in all the Mahāyāna-Sūtras.

Of the twelve Chinese translations of the longer Sukhāvatī-Vyūha which are said to have existed, five have come down to us in the Chinese Tripiṭaka, the earliest of which was made between 147 and 186 A.D. The shorter Sukhāvatī Vyūha was translated into Chinese three times, by Kumārajīva (402 A.D.), by Guṇabhadra (420-479 A.D.) and by Hsūan-Tsang (about 650 A.D.).[1] A third work, the Amitāyur-dhyāna-Sūtra,[2] which has come down only in the Chinese translation, deals less with the description of the blessed land, but devotes more space to the recommendation of meditations (dhyāna) on Amitāyus, by means of which one may reach that land. The loss of the Sanskrit original of this text is all the more regrettable, because it contains an interesting introduction, in which the story of Ajātaśatru and Bimbisāra is told, a story with which the Pāli accounts are also familiar.[3] For centuries, the three works on

1. Most of the Chinese translations bear titles, to which "Amitāyus-Sūtra" or "Amita-āyuṣa-vyūha" would correspond in the Sanskrit. Cf. Sukhāvati-Vyūha ed. Anecdota Oxonlensia, p. iv ff. ; B *Nanjio* Catalogue, Nos. 23 (5), 25-27, 199. 200, 863; *Forke*, Kat. des Pekinger Tripiṭaka, Nos. 42, 429 f., 562, 639 and p. 179; and *Bagchi* I,24,76 f., 192, 287. In the Tibetan Kanjur the title Amitābha-vyūha appears as well as Sukhāvati-vyūha. s. *Csoma de Koros* in AMG II, 214, 243, 245.

2. Translated from Chinese by J. *Takakusu* in SBE, Vol. 49, part 2 p. 159ff. Cf. *Saunders*, Epochs of Buddhist History, p.85ff.

3. Cf. *Kern*. Der Buddhismus, I, 243 ff.; Spence *Hardy*, Manual of Buddhism, 1860. p. 317 f.

Amitāyus and Sukhāvatī have formed the basis of the faith of the majority of Buddhists in China and Japan, who found consolation and comfort in the belief in 'Amida,' as Amitāyus is called in Japan, and in the hope of the blessed land. This is especially true of the numerous adherents of the two Japanese sects Jodo-shu and Shin-shu.[1]

Just as the Sukhāvatī-Vyūha describes the blessed land of Amitābha, the Akṣobhya-Vyūha gives an account of the land of Buddha Akṣobhya,[2] and in the same way the Karuṇā-Puṇḍarīka, "the Lotus of Mercy,"[3] gives an account of the wonderland Padma of Buddha Padmottara, whose life lasted for thirty ages of the world. The Sūtra, which also contains legends after the style of the Avadānas, was translated into Chinese twice between 385 and 433 A.D. and once again in 558 A.D.[4]

Whilst the Mahāyāna-Sūtras which have so far been mentioned, are devoted mainly to the glorification of the Buddhas and Bodhisattvas, there is a series of other Sūtras which are rather in the nature of philosophical treatises. The earliest of these Sūtras, those which are regarded with the greatest reverence, and which are of the greatest importance

---

1. B. *Nanjio,* Twelve Japanese Buddhist Sects, pp. 104ff., 122 ff., and Anecdota Oxoniensia, Vol. I, Part II, p. XVIII ff. See also H. *Haas.* "Amida Buddha unsere Zuflucht", Urkunden zum Verständnis des japanischen Sukhāvatī-Buddhismus, Leipzig, 1910, and *Saunders,* l.c., 176 ff.

2. This Sūtra has only come down in the Chinese translations by Lokakṣema (178-188) and Bodhiruci (693-713) and in the Tibetan Kanjur, and is counted as a part of the Ratnakūṭa s. *Nanjio* No. 28; *Bagchi* I, 43; Csoma de *Koros,* AMG II, 214. The same Ratnakūṭa also contains, a Mañjuśri-Buddhakṣetra-guṇa-Vyūha, "Description of the qualities of the Mañjuśri Buddha-land" which is lost in the Sanskrit; s *Forke* Pekinger Tripiṭaka, p. 181; *Koros,* AMG II, 215. On Mañjuśrī s. *La Vallee Poussin* in ERE VIII, 405 f.

3. Rāj. *Mitra* Nep. Buddh· Lst., p. 285 ff.; *Bendall,* Catalogue, p. 73. The text published by the Buddhist Text Society, Calcutta, 1898f is unfortunately not accessible. A legend of the Karuṇā-Puṇḍarika the Tokharian (Kuchean) language, has been discovered and published by S. *Levi* (Festscrift Wilhelm Thomsen, Leipzig, 1912; p. 155ff).

4. *Nanjio* No. 142; *Bagchi.* I, 217 f., 239, 271. The introduction to the Tibetan version has been translated into French by L. *Feer* (AMG V, 1883, 153 ff.); see also *Koros* AMG II, 239 ff.

from the point of view of the history of religion, are the Prajñā-Pāramitās, "the (Mahāyāna-Sūtras of the) Wisdom Perfection."[1] They treat of the six "perfections" (Pāramitās)[2] of a Bodhisattva, but especially of Prajñā-Pāramitā, the highest perfection, called "wisdom." This wisdom consists of the knowledge of Śūnyatā, "emptiness,"[3] *i.e.*, the unsubstantiality of all phenomena, implying the conviction that all Dharmas or objects of thought, are only endowed with a conditional or relative existence.

There is evidence of the fact that the Prajñā-Pāramitās belong to the earliest Mahāyāna-Sūtras. Firstly, the ancient dialogue form, which is familiar to us from the Pāli Suttas, is still more conspicuous in these than in other Mahāyāna-Sūtras, and secondly, Buddha (called Bhagavān, "the Lord") generally appears in conversation with one of his disciples, especially Subhūti.[4] In other Mahāyāna-Sūtras Buddha usually talks to a Bodhisattva. A Prajñā-Pāramitā was already translated into Chinese as early as 179 A.D. The Prajñā-Pāramitās appear to have originated in the South, and afterwards spread to the East and the North.[5]

According to a Nepalese tradition, there was first of all a Prajñā-Pāramitā-Mahāyāna-Sūtra of 125,000 "Ślokas,"[6] and

1. Prajñā-Pāramitā means both the perfection of 'wisdom', and the writings treating of it.

2. Though in the Mahāyāna, as in the Hīnayāna, there are sometimes ten Pāramitās enumerated, yet more frequently there are only six, namely : charity, moral conduct, patience, energy, meditation and wisdom (Dharma-Saṃgraha 17; see above, p. 148 n. 1).

3. See above, p. 222 In the Chinese life-story of Kumārajiva, the believer in Śūnya is compared to that foolish person who desires a thread so fine that it cannot be seen and is not content until the artisan points into the air and says : 'Here is the thread.' *Cf.* J. *Nobel* in SBA, 1927, 216 f.

4. On Subhūti in the Mahāyāna and in Pāli literature, see M. *Walleser*, Die Streitlosigkeit des Subhūti, Heidelberg (Akad.) 1917.

5. We are justified in drawing this conclusion, from the prophecy which Buddha is made to utter (Aṣṭasāhasrikā, p. 225 f.) : "These Sūtrāntas, in which six Pāramitās are taught, will be current in the South after the passing away of the Tathāgata, from the South they will go to the East again, and from the East again to the North." *Cf. Anesaki* in ERE IV, 838, (where 'west,' instead of 'east' is an error).

6. The Prajñā-Pāramitās are prose works, but it is customary in India to give the size of prose texts too, by 'Ślokas,' i.e. units of 32 syllables.

this is supposed to have been abridged successively to similar Mahāyāna-Sūtras of 100,000, 25,000, 10,000 and 8,000 'Ślokas' respectively. According to another tradition, however, the Sūtra of 8,000 'Ślokas' is the original one, and was gradually enlarged more and more.[1] The latter tradition appears to be the likelier one. At any rate, a considerable number of Prajñā-Pāramitā texts of all lengths were already in existence in India, and their number increased even more in China and Tibet. Hsūan-Tsang translated 12 different Prajñā-Pāramitā-Sūtras in his Mahā-Prajñā-Pāramitā-Sūtra : the longest is that of 100,000 'Ślokas,' and the shortest that of 150. In the Chinese Tripiṭaka, the first large section is made up of the Prajñā-Pāramitās.[2] In the Tibetan Kanjur, in which the Prajñā-Pāramitā texts constitute the Śer-phyin section in 21 books, there are translations. of the Prajñā-Pāramitās of 100,000, 25,000, 18,000, 10,000, 8,000, 800, 700 and 500 'Ślokas,' of the Vajracchedikā (with 300 'Ślokas') right down to an Alpākṣarā or Svalpākṣarā Prajñā-Pāramitā, 'Prajñā-Pāramitā of (very) few syllables', and even a Bhagavatī-Prājñā-Pāramitā-sarva-Tathāgata-matā Ekākṣarī, 'the sacred Prajña-Pāramitā of One Syllable, of the mother of all Tathāgatas', in which the perfection of wisdom is concentrated in the one sound 'a.'[3] The following have come down to us in

1. *Cf.* Rajendralāla *Mitra* Aṣṭasāhasrikā Ed., p. IV f.; *Burnof*, Introduction, p, 414; Haraprasāda, Report I, 19f. and Ind. Hist. Qu. 1, 1925, 211 ff.

2. The Daśasāhasrikā Pr. ("Pr. of 10,000") was translated into Chinese for the first time in 179 A.D., and then repeatedly till the 10th century; s. *Nanjio*, Nos. 5-8, 927; *Bagchi* I, pp, 40, 156. 186 f., 289. There are three translations of the Pañcaviṃśati-Sāhasrikā Pr. (" Pr. of 25,000"), (286, 291 and 404 A.D.), s. *Nanjio*, Nos. 2-4, *Bagchi* I, 86, 185 f. A Saptaśatikā Pr. ("Pr. of 700"); was translated between 502 and 557 A.D., s *Nanjio*, Nos. 21, 22; a Pañcaśatikā Pr. ("Pr. of 500") between 428 and 479; s. *Nanjio* No. 16; *Bagchi*, I, 404; an Ardhaśatikā Pr. ("Pr. of 150") several times between the 7th and 10th centuries, s. *Nanjio*, Nos, 18, 879, 1933 f. The Vajracchedikā Pr. was translated first by Kumārajīva (405 A.D.) and then often, s. *Nanjio*, Nos 10-15 *Bagchi* I, 192, 258, 255, 425. For other Prajñā-Pāramitās, s. *Nanjio* No. 17; *Bagchi* I, 44 ff. Apart from the numerous Chinese translations of Indian texts, there is a still greater number of original Chinese works dealing with the Prajñā-Pāramitās; s. O *Franke* in OZ 4, 1915-16, 207 ff.

3. *Cf.* Csoma de *Koros* in Asiatick Researches, Vol. 20 (1836), p. 393 ff. and AMG II. 119 ff. For a bibliography of Chinese and Tibetan translations of Prajñā-Pāramitās, s. *Walleser*, Prajñā-Pāramitā, p. 15 ff.

Sanskrit: Prajñā-Pāramitās of 100,000 'Ślokas' (Śatasāhasrikā),[1] of 25,000 (Pañcaviṃśatisāhasrikā),[2] of 8,000 (Aṣṭasāhasrikā),[3] of 2,500 (Sārdhadvaisāhasrikā),[4] of 700 (Saptaśatikā),[5] the Vajracchedikā Prajñā-Pāramitā, "the diamond cutter Prajñā-Pāramitā," *i.e.*, the Prajñā:Pāramitā,[6] cutting as sharp as a diamond and also the Alpākṣarā Prajña-Pāramitā[7] and Prajñā-

---

1. Edited by Pratāpacandra *Ghoṣa* in Bibl. Ind. 1902-1914 (19 fasc.; more did not appear until 1926). Cf Rāj *Mitra*, Nep. Buddh. Lit. 177 ff.; *Bendall*, Catalogue, pp. 143-148· On Central Asiatic fragments of the Śatasāhasrikā Pr. in Chinese and Khotanese, s. *Hoernle*, E. *Chavanes* and S. *Levi* in Hoernle, Ms. Remains I, 387 ff. Fragments of a Prajñā-P., which corresponds to the Śatasāhasrikā, but appears to be a shorter version, have been published by Pandit B. B. *Bidyābinod*, Fragment of a Prajñāpāramitā Ms. from Central Asia (Memoirs of the Archaeological Survey of India, No. 32), 1927.

2. Rāj. *Mitra*, l.e. 193 f.; *Bendal*, l.c. 144 f.; Haraprasāda *Sāstrī* Descriptive Catalogue of Sanskrit MSS. in the... Asiatic Society of Bengal, 1, p. 10 f.

3. Edited by Rājendralāla *Mitra* in Bibl. Ind. 1888; Chapt. XVIII translated by Haraprasāda *Śastrī* in J.B.TS. II, 1894; Extracts translated into German by Max *Walleser* Prajñāpāramitā, die Vollkommenheit der Erkenntnis, nach indischen, tibetischen, und chinesischen Quellen, Quellen der Religionsgeschischte, Göttingen 1914. In the Śikṣā-Samuccaya there are quotations from the Aṣṭasāhasrī Pr., as well as from a Mahati Pr., an Arya-Pr. and a Bhagavati Pr.; s. *Bendall*, Śikṣāsamuccaya Ed., p. 369 and JRAS 1898, 870ff.

4. *Bendall*, Catalogue, p. 123 f.

5. Bendall, l.c., p. 5f.

6. Edited by F. Max *Müller*. in Buddhist Texts from Japan, Anecdota Oxoniensia, Aryan Series, I, 1, 1881, and translated by the same scholar in SBE Vol. 49, part II, pp. 109-144; translated into French by C. de *Harlez* in JA 1891, s. 8, t. XVIII, 440ff.; into German by *Wallser* l.c. pp. 140-158. Complete MSS. of the Sanskrit and of the Khotanese versions were discovered by Sir Aurel *Stein* in Eastern Turkestan, and the Sanskrit version has been edited and translated by J. E. *Pargiter*, the Khotanese version by Sten *Konow* (in Hoernle. MS. Remains I, pp. 176-195. and 214-288). The first fragments have been published, together with an Adhyardhaśatikā. Pr. (in a Sanskrit recension interspersed with Khotanese sections) by E. *Leumann* (Zur nordarischen Sprache und Litteratur, 56 ff., 84 ff.). The Tibetan version has been edited and translated into German by T. Y. *Schmidt* in Memoires de l' Acad. de St. Petersbourg t. IV, 1837. C. de *Harlez* has published and translated the Manchu version in WZKM 11, 1897, 209, ff., 331 ff.

7. Haraprasāda *Sāstrī*, Descriptive Catalogue of Sanskrit MSS..in the Asiatic Society of Bengal, I No. 16; Chinese translation, s, *Nanjio* No 797; Tibetan translation in the Kanjur, s. *Koros*, AMG II, 202.

Pāramitā hṛdaya-Sūtras,[1] which are only used as protecting magic formulas (Dhāraṇīs).

In all probability the earliest of these writings is the Aṣṭasāhasrikā-Prajñā-Pāramitā, which was, on the one hand, expanded into the larger works, and the contents of which were, on the other hand, condensed in the shorter texts.[2]

The Aṣṭasāhasrikā contains in 32 chapters dialogues between Buddha and his disciples Subhūti, Śāriputra and Pūrṇa Maitrāyaṇīputra, and frequently Śakra, the prince of the gods, and sometimes a Bodhisattva joins them. The work begins with introductory verses, in which the Prajñā-Pāramitā, the perfection of wisdom, is personified and praised as "the sublime producer and the beloved mother of all heroes, she whose mind is fixed firmly on the highest goal", "as the kind grandmother of all beings" etc.[3] In the very first chapter we have an example of the dialectics which remind us of the Greek sophists, and which are characteristic of the Prajñā-Pāramitās. We read (pp. 4-6) :

Then through the power of Buddha, the venerable Subhūti spoke thus to the Lord : "Now as to what you have said, O Lord : 'May it become clear to you, Subhūti, with regard to the wisdom-perfection of the Bodhisattvas, of the Great Beings,[4] how the Bodhisattvas, the Great Beings, are able to advance

1. Edited by F. Max *Müller* and B. *Nanjio* in Anecdota Oxoniensia, Aryan Series, Vol. I, Part III, 1884, and translated by Max *Müller* in SBE Vol. 49, Part II, p. 145 ff.; also by Shaku Hannye in EB II, 1922, I63 ff. Translated from the Tibetan by L. *Feer*. in AMG V, 177 ff. See below in the section on the Dhāraṇīs.

2. In the Abhisamayālaṃkāra-Kārikās it is said that the Aṣṭasāhasrikā was remodelled into the Pañcaviṃśati-sāhasrikā; s. Haraprasāda *Śāstrī*, Descriptive Cat. of Sansk. MSS. in the As. Soc. of Bengal, I, p. 7 and Ind. Hist. Qu. I. 1925, 212. The Chinese translation of the Daśasāhasrikā is said to differ but little from the Aṣṭasāhasrikā. s. Haraprasāda *Śāstrī*, Descriptive Cat. p. 3; Ind. Hist. Qu. l.c.; *Wallser*, Prajñāpāramitā, p. 18.

3. S. *Levi* L'Inde et le monde, Paris, 1928, p. 46, compares the Gnosis of the Gnostics, to this personified Perfection of Wisdom. We also think of the personification of Pistis Sophia. It is doubtful, however, whether these are more than coincidences.

4. Mahāsattva, "the Great Being," usual epithet of the Bodhisattva.

until they attain to 'wisdom-perfection'—when there is constantly mention of 'Bodhisattva, Bodhisattva,' to what manner of object (dharma), Lord, does the term 'Bodhisattva' correspond? I do not see any object, Lord, which might be called 'Bodhisattva'. Neither do I see that object which is called 'wisdom-perfection.' Therefore, Lord, as I cannot find, perceive or see either a Bodhisattva or a Bodhisattva-object, and moreover, as I cannot find, perceive or see the wisdom-perfection,—what manner of Bodhisattva am I to teach, instruct, and in what manner of wisdom-perfection? Is it not, O Lord, perhaps precisely when his power of thought does not sink down, does not melt away, is not exhausted, does not become weak, when his mind does not lose all stability, does not entirely break down, when it does not take fright, does not tremble, does not grow fearful, on hearing such sermons and on receiving such doctrine and instruction, that he is a Bodhisattva who is fit to be instructed in wisdom-perfection ? It is precisely this which is to be understood by the wisdom-perfection of a Bodhisattva, a Great Being. That is the instruction in wisdom-perfection, when he conducts himself thus, and his teaching, his instruction consists of this. Furthermore, O Lord, a Bodhisattva, a Great Being, who walks in the wisdom-perfection, who lives and has his being in the wisdom-perfection, must be trained in such a way that, as a result of this training, he should not think anything by this thought which is fixed on enlightenment. And why is this so ? Because it is so, that the thought is a non-thought, that the nature of the thought is shining in purity (*i.e.*, free from all contamination with non-real phenomena)."

Then the venerable Śāriputra said to the venerable Subhūti: "Venerable Subhūti, does such a thought which is a non-thought exist."

To these words the venerable Subhūti replied to the venerable Śāriputra in the following words : "But, venerable Śāriputra, in the case of that which is non-thought, is there either a being or a non-being found or perceived?"

Śāriputra said : "No, venerable Subhūti."

Subhūti said : "If it is true, venerable Śāriputra, that neither a being nor a non-being is found or perceived in that which is non-thought, is there any sense in the question when the venerable Śāriputra says : "Does such a thought which is a non-thought exist?"

At these words the venerable Śāriputra addressed the venerable Subhūti in the following manner : "But, venerable Subhūti, what is this non-thinking?"

Subhūti said : "This non-thinking, venerable Śāriputra, is without change, without alternation."

Furthermore, we read in the same chapter (p. 20 f.) :

The Lord said : "Here, O Subhūti, a Bodhisattva, a Great Being, thinks thus : 'Immeasurable hosts of beings are to be led to complete Nirvāṇa by me, innumerable beings are to be led to complete Nirvāṇa by me.' Now neither those who are to be led to Nirvāṇa, nor those by whom they are to be led, do exist. He leads so many beings to complete Nirvāṇa, and there is no being which has attained to complete Nirvāṇa, and there is no one by whom such a being has been led to complete Nirvāṇa. And why so? That, Subhūti, is precisely the true nature of phenomena ;[1] they are based upon deceptive appearances. Now, Subhūti, supposing a skilful magician or magician's apprentice were to conjure up a large crowd of people at a cross road, and after he had conjured up this large crowd of people, he were to cause it to vanish again,—what do you think, Subhūti, would anyone have been struck down, killed, destroyed, or caused to vanish, by anyone?"

In Chapter II Subhūti instructs the gods (p. 39 f.) :

"O sons of gods, the beings are like an illusion (māyā), O sons of gods, the beings are like a dream. No, illusion and beings are not two different things, and do not form a duality; and dreams and beings are not two different things, and do not form a duality. Furthermore, O sons of gods, all objects of thought are like an illusion, like a dream. He, too, who has just entered the stream, (*i.e.*, the new convert) is like an illusion, like a dream...He, too, who is completely enlightened, is like an illusion, like a dream; the condition, too, of him who is completely enlightened, is like an illusion, like a dream...O

1. Literally : "The Dharma-hood of the Dharmas."

sons of gods, even Nirvāṇa itself is like an illusion, like a dream, I say, how much more then every other object of thought."

Then the sons of gods said : "Noble Subhūti, you say that Nirvāṇa is like an illusion, like a dream?"

The venerable Subhūti said : "Yes, O sons of gods, if there were another, more excellent object of thought than Nirvāṇa, I should still say that it is like an illusion, like a dream. No, O sons of gods, illusion and Nirvāṇa are not diverse, they do not form a duality, and also dreams and Nirvāṇa are not diverse, they do not form a duality."

The entire book continues in this strain. We are assured over and over again, that all phenomena are without being (śūnya), that even Buddhas, Bodhisattvas and the perfection of wisdom itself have no reality; but, at the same time, the Bodhisattva ideal is extolled time and again, as for instance, in the beautiful words (p. 321 f.) which the Lord is made to say :

"O Subhūti, a Bodhisattva, a Great Being, who desires to advance to un-surpassable complete enlightenment, must behave alike towards all beings, must cultivate the same mind towards all beings; he must support the other beings with an impartial mind ; he must support the others with thoughts of love, with kindly..., with friendly thought..., with thought which is free from pride..., he must support the others with thought which is not hostile, free from thoughts of harm..., he must support the others with thoughts free from injury. He must transfer to all beings the idea of the mother; he must support all beings, transferring to them the idea of the father, the idea of the son, the idea of the daughter (*i.e.*, he must look upon them, as if they were his mothers, his fathers, his sons, his daughters). In this way, therefore, Subhūti, a Bodhisattva, a Great Being, who desires to advance to unsurpassable complete enlightenment, must behave towards all beings : in this way he must train himself in being a protector of all beings. And he himself must be steadfast in suppressing all evil, he must give alms, observe the moral law, train himself in patience, he must show himself energetic, must devote himself to meditation and achieve the victory in wisdom, he must contemplate the formula of the causally conditioned origination both in regular and in inverted order, he must teach it to others, extol it in their presence, and enable them to take delight in it."

While in reading the numerous long epistemological and metaphysical discussions on Śūnyatā, we often wonder what all this has to do with religion, such passages about the Bodhisattva as the above, remind us of the fact that the text before us is, after al', a religious book. This religious character of the book is emphasized also in several chapters, in which the great merit to be acquired by the hearing and understanding, the reading and writing, and the learning and teaching of the Prajñā-Pāramitā, is praised over and over again in extravagant fashion.[1]

As it was considered so great a religious merit to read and write these sacred books, it need not surprise us greatly that, as a result of endless repetitions and phantastic embellishments of the scenes which introduced the speeches, more and more new works of this type, each one more voluminous than the last, came into existence.

Whilst the Aṣṭasāhasrikā relates in a few sentences that Buddha sojourned in Rājagṛha on the Gṛdhrakūṭa hill, surrounded by a host of monks, who were all arhats, the Śatasāhasrikā-Prajñā-Pāramitā begins with a grandiose description of the scene on the Gṛdhrakūṭa hill :

The Lord is seated with his body erect and his legs crossed, ready for meditation, and becomes absorbed in that meditation which is called "King of all meditations," in which all absorptions are included. And after he had arisen, mindful and with a clear consciousness, from this absorption, he glanced over

1. In the Vajracchedikā, Chapt. 13, Buddha is made to say words to the effect that he who "selects merely one four-footed verse here from this sermon (the Vajr. contains 2 Gāthās in Chapt., 26 and one Gāthā in the last chapter) and explains it to others," acquires greater religious merit than a person who might sacrifice his life day by day for aeons, *cf. Walliser.* Prajñāpāramitā, p. 146 f., 149 ff. In the fragment of the Adhyardhaśatikā Pr. from Khotan (*Leumannur* nordarischen Sprache und Litteratur, p. 89) it is even said that he who "even while still in the womb" hears this section of the Pr., is freed from all attack and dangers, and never goes to hell or is reborn in any other evil form of existence.

this Buddha-land with his heavenly eyes, and while so doing, he let a radiant light shine forth from the whole of his body and from every pore in his skin and this radiant light illumined all the continents brilliantly. And all beings by whom this radiance was seen, became clear-sighted through it, and they were all confirmed in the unsurpassable complete enlightenment. Then the Lord thrust forth his tongue through the opening of his mouth, and produced a smile, and many hundreds of thousands of millions of milliards of rays of light emanated from his tongue. On each ray there arose lotuses of jewels, shimmering like gold, with a thousand petals, brightly hued, and beautiful to look upon, sweet, golden, with a pleasant scent, delicate and soft as Kācilindika.[1] And upon these lotuses sat the embodied Tathāgatas and preached the doctrine of the six perfections. But all beings by whom this doctrine was heard, were confirmed in the unsurpassable complete enlightenment. He again became absorbed in the Buddha-meditation which is called "lion's play." In this moment, hell, animal birth, and all evil forms of existence, were suspended in all the innumerable continents. All human beings and gods remembered their former births, approached the Lord and did homage to him. And at the same moment, those who had been born blind, in all the innumerable continents, recovered their sight, the deaf recovered their hearing, the insane had their sanity restored to them, etc.

All this is not stated in such sentences, but is related with an endless mass of detail. We have already met with the peculiarity of the continual repetitions in the Pāli Suttas. This characteristic is exaggerated to such a degree in the longer Prajñā-Pāramitās, that it would be quite possible to write down more than one half of a gigantic work like the Śatasāhasrikā-Prajñā-Pāramitā from memory, as the same sentences and expressions constantly recur literally. For instance, in the introduction it is not only said that rays of light shine forth from the whole body of Buddha, and shed an infinite radiance of light over the whole world, but it is said of the

1. According to Mahā-Vyutpatti, 262, 39, a kind of garment.

toes, the ankles, and every limb and every little part of the body, that rays of light shine forth from them, and shed an infinite radiance of light over the eastern part of the world, the western part of the world, and so on—and the whole set of phrases is repeated for each part of the world, in the same words. In the same way the writer is not content to say merely : "All is only name," but this 'all' is amplified in minute detail, in never-ending series of sentences, until the whole of creation is completely exhausted. We can well comprehend people's holding the view that the world is not real and that everything is empty and vain, and that nothing can be expressed in words, and that 'no' is the only possible reply to all questions :—but we would really regard it as an impossibility for book upon book, and for thousands of pages to be written from the standpoint of such a categorical negation of anything and everything : and yet, in the Prajñā-Pāramitās, the impossibility has become a reality. Our sole explanation of this verbosity for the sake of verbosity, is that these monks wrote so much, because it was regarded as a religious merit to write and read as much as possible of these sacred texts.[1] The substance of their writing did not matter. The actual doctrine is the same in the "Hundred-thousand Prajñā-Pāramitā" as in the Vajracchedikā-Prajñā Pāramitā, a little work of but a few pages, in which the content of these texts appears in its most condensed form. In this work, too, we come across the same paradoxes as in the Aṣṭasāhasrikā-Prajñā-Pāramitā and the longer Prajñā-Pāramitās. Thus for instance, we also read in :—the Vajracchedikā (Chapt. 13).

"The perfection of wisdom which has been proclaimed by Buddha, the same has been proclaimed by Buddha as a non-perfection also. What do you think, Subhūti, is there any doctrine (Dharma) which has been proclaimed by Buddha ?" Subhūti said : "No, Lord, there is no doctrine which has been proclaimed by Buddha..." The Lord said : "What do you think, Subhūti,

1. The same principle of repetition also appears in art, when entire rocks and caves are covered all over with pictures of Buddha. *Cf. Grünwedel*, Buddhist. Kunst in Indien, pp. 172, 182.

can Buddha, the saint, the completely enlightened one, be recognised by the thirty-two characteristics of a great man ?" Subhūti said : "No Lord, Buddha, the saint, the completely enlightened one, cannot be recognised by the thirty-two characteristics of a great man. And why not ? Because the thirty-two characteristics of a great man, which have been proclaimed by Buddha, were proclaimed by Buddha as non-characteristics. Therefore, they are called the thirty-two characteristics of a great man."

There are probably just as many (non-Buddhist) readers who will see a profound meaning in such utterances as there are those who will regard them as pure nonsense.[1] In reality, they are probably neither one nor the other, but views which frequently crop up in the history of philosophy, and which only become intelligible if we distinguish between a higher, transcendental, and a lower, empirical truth, as expressly taught by the Mahāyāna philosopher Nāgārjuna.

The great philosophers of the Mahāyāna, Nāgārjuna, Vasubandhu and Asaṅga, wrote bulky commentaries on the Prajñā-Pāramitās, which have, however, only come down to us in the Chinese Tripiṭaka and in the Tibetan Tanjur. Nevertheless it is very difficult for us to imagine that the immense sanctity which is attributed to these texts, can really be due to a valuation and an understanding of the metaphysical doctrines which they propound. It is more probable that it is precisely the dark and incomprehensible element in the doctrines taught by these texts, which has contributed to make them sacred. *Omne obscurum pro magnifico.*[2]

1. Among the latter is probably *Barth,* who says (RHR, t. 5. 1882. p. 117 Oeuvres I, 326) that, in our text the Prajñāpāramitā is glorified, "transcendental wisdom, which knows that things are neither existent nor non-existent, that there is no reality which is not also a non-reality, wisdom which has proclaimed and will be proclaimed by an infinity of myriads of Arhats and Bodhisattvas who have been and have not been, who will be and will not be; who, thanks to their knowledge of Buddha, and their view of Buddha, are perceived apperceived, known of Buddha, who himself is neither existent nor non-existent." On the doctrines of the Prajñāpāramitās, *cf. Burnouf,* Introduction pp. 111, 390, 404ff., 412ff, 430; W. *Wassiljew,* Der Buddhismus, p. 157 ff. and M. *Anesaki,* ERE IV, p. 837f.

2. According to the Ādikarma-Pradipa (s. *La Vallée Poussin,* Bouddhisme, E'tudes et Mate.iaux Memoirs Ac. Belgique. 1897, p. 227), the reading and Sunwise circumambulation of the Prajñāpāramitās and similar books are part of the

In the Buddhist dictionary Mahā-Vyutpatti (64, 4), a work called Buddhāvataṃsaka[1] is mentioned in a list of Mahāyāna-immediately after the Śatasāhasrika, Pañcaviṃśatisāhasrika Sūtras and the Aṣṭasāhasrikā-Prajñā Pāramitās. Both in the Chinese Tripiṭaka (Section IV, Hua-yen) and the Tibetan Kanjur,[2] there is a large body of writings entitled thus. It is the sacred scripture of the Avataṁsaka school which arose in China between 557 and 589 A.D., and of the Japanese Kegon sect.[3] According to Chinese sources, there are supposed to have been six different Avataṃsaka-Sūtras, the longest of which contained 100,000 Gāthās and the shortest 36,000. The latter was translated into Chinese in 418 A.D. by Buddhabhadra together with other monks. Śikṣānanda made a translation in 45,000 Gāthās, between 695 and 699 A.D.[4] Though no Avataṃsaka or Buddhāvataṃsaka Sūtra has come down in Sanskrit, there is a Gaṇḍavyūha-Mahāyāna-Sūtra,[5] which corresponds to one of the Chinese translations of the

---

Buddhist cult. Fa-hien, who visited India in the year 399A.D., already mentions that the Prajñāpāramitās were an object of divine worship at his time; s. S. *Beal,* Si-yu-ki Buddhist Records of the Western World I. p. xxxix. In the Nepalese chronicle Vaṃśāvali it is related, that during the reign of King Śaṅkaradeva (12th century) on the occasion of a fire in a village, a widow fled to Patna, taking nothing with her except a small model of a Caitya, a manuscript of the Prājñāpāramitā, which is said to have been written in the year 188 A.D. in golden letters, and her little son; s. *Bendall* in OC Berlin, 1881, II, 190.

1. The title means : "Buddha Ornament; avataṃsaka is given as a synonym of alaṃkāra, in Mahā-Vyutpatti, 237, 48.

2. Section III, s. Csoma de *Koros*. AMG II, 208ff.

3. *Cf.* B. *Nanjio,* Twelve Japanese Buddhist Sects, p- 57 ff.; *Eliot,* Hinduism and Buddhism, III, 282 f.; Y. *Sogen* Systems of Buddhist Thought, 287 ff.

4. *Cf. Nanjio.* l.c. and Catalogue, Nos. 87-89: *Bagchi* I, 343 f.; *Forke,* Pekinger Tripiṭaka, Nos. 1053, 1054. Isolated sections of the Avataṃsaka were translated into Chinese by Lokakṣema (178-188 A.D.), Dharmarakṣa (291-297 A.D.) and others, s. *Bagchi* I, 42, 89 f., 97, 220, 237, 286, 405; *Forke,* l.c., Nos. 1054-1057, 1059-1065 for commentaries and explanatory writings on *Froke,* l.c., Nos. 1058, 1060.1064; Avataṃsaka Sūtra (according to Buddhabhadra's translation) epitomised by Japanese scholars and translated into English by D.T. *Suzuki* in EB I. 1ff., 146 ff.

5. The text is not yet published. For table of contents, see Rāj. *Mitra,* Nep. Buddh. Lit., p. 90 ff.; *cf Bendall,* Catalogue, pp. 23, 102; *Burnouf,* Introduction. p. 111; *Wassiljew,* Der Buddhismus, p. 171 ff.

Avataṃsaka.[1] The main contents of the Gaṇḍavyūha are the wanderings of the youth Sudhana, who travels all over India on the advice of the Bodhisattva Mañjuśrī, in order to attain to the highest knowledge essential for enlightenment. He wanders from land to land, seeking instruction from various persons, monks and nuns, lay adherents both male and female, from a merchant, a king, a slave, a body, also from the goddesses of the night, from Gopā, the wife of Śākyamuni and from Māyā, the mother of Śākyamuni,[2] until finally, by the favour of Mañjuśrī, he attains to perfect knowledge, through the instrumentality of the Bodhisattva Samanta bhadra.[3]

The Gaṇḍavyūha is quoted fairly frequently in the Śikṣāsamuccaya, whilst the "Avataṃsaka" is not quoted. For instance, there is a long quotation in Gāthās, in praise of the Bodhisattva who is resolved to become a Buddha, in order to show love and pity towards the beings and release them from suffering, to make hell empty, and to point the way to heavan. Another passage (in prose) treats of the cleansing of the city of the mind (citta-nagara) which a Bodhisattva must always bear in mind. In yet another passage we find Gāthās on the rare and blessed good fortune of seeing and hearing a Buddha.[4]

---

1. Dr. *Takakusu* compared the text of the Gaṇḍavyūha in the India Office with the text of the "Avataṃsaka-Sūtra in 40 chapters" (in Nanjio's Catalogue), and (in a letter of 4th Sept., 1912) he communicated the contents of the work, which coincides in the main with the table of contents given by Rāj. *Mitra*. According to D.T. *Suzuki* (EB 1, note), the third Chinese translation is "practically the same as the Nepalese Gaṇḍavyūha" whilst Śikṣānanda's translation 'also' contains the Gaṇḍavyūha and the Daśabhūmika. According to S. *Levi* in JA, t. 203, 1923, p. 6ff., the Gaṇḍavyūha is the last section of the Avataṃsaka. *Cf* also *Watanabe* in JRAS 1907, 663; *Pelliot* in JA 1914, II, p. 118 ff.; *Eliot* Hinduism, and BuddhismI II, 54 f.; III, 283.

2. There is a remarkably large number of women among these teachers.

3. This is according to Rāj *Mitra*'s table of contents. However, in the communication of Dr. *Takakusu* from the India Office MSS. (mentioned above in note) it is said : "At last he meets Samantabhadra who directs him to the one Buddha Amitābha of the West, from whom the earnest youth learns the highest truth and gets enlightened. In one text this last Amtiābha section is omitted."

4. Śikṣās. 101 ff., 122 f., 310 f.

At the end of the Gaṇḍavyūha, both in manusc·ipts and in Chinese and Tibetan translations, we find the Bhadracarī-praṇidhāna-gāthāḥ, "the Prayer Verses concerning the Pious Life,"[1] a prayer in 62 melodious Dodhaka stanzas,[2] which ranks among the most beautiful expressions of Buddhist piety, and has been used for purposes of worship in all countries of Mahāyāna Buddhism ever since the 4th century A.D.[3] It is also found as an independent text, and was translated into Chinese several times in the 4th and 8th centuries, and into Tibetan in the 9th century. The language is a Prākrit with a strong leaning towards Sanskrit.

The prayer opens with verses in which homage is paid to all Jinas. Then come the pious wishes (praṇidhāna), in which the believer, after having renounced all evil, requests all the Buddhas to allow the wheel of the doctrine to revolve throughout ali the aeons, in which he wishes good fortune and blessing for all beings and prays on his own behalf, that he may ever lead a pious life, direct his thoughts to enlightenment, and that he may one day, as a Buddha, make an end to the sufferings of the world. In particular, he implores the Bodhisattvas Samantabhadra and Mañjuśrī, whom he strives to imitate, and in conclusion he expresses the hope that he may at some future time behold Amitābha and attain to the Blessed Land (Sukhāvatī).

The Daśabhūmaka or Daśabhūmika-Sūtra or Daśabhūmīśvara,[4] is also regarded as a portion of the Avataṃsaka, but it is found

---

1. Cf. K. *Watanbe*, Die Bhadracarī, eine Probe buddhistisch-religioser Lyrik untersucht und herausgegebn (mit deutscher Ubersetzung von E. *Leumann*) Diss. Strassburg, 1912. According to Watanabe, Bhadra is an abbreviation of Samantabhadra, and the title should be translated : "The verses in which the pious wishes that distinguished the religious life of Samantabhadra, find expression." In the Śikṣā-Samuccaya it is quoted with the title Bhadracaryā (Gāthā).

2. On this metre (four Pādas of eleven syllables ——vv—vv—vv—) so popular with the Mahāyāna Buddhists, s. *Watanabe*, l.c., p. 24 ff.

3. *Watanabe*, l.c., p. 10 ff. According to *La Vallee Poussin* in ERE II, 259 note, it belongs to the sacred books of the Sautrāntikas, but in ERE XII, 194, he counts it among the Tantras.

4. The Sanskrit text has been edited and the chapter on the seventh Bhūmi translated into English, by Johannes *Rahder*, Diss. Utrecht 1926 (J.B. Istas, Leuven). Chapter VII also in Acta Or. IV, 214 ff. The text in Sanskrit

just as frequently as an independent work. The subject-matter of this work is a discourse on the ten steps (daśabhūmi) by which Buddhahood may be attained. The speaker is the Bodhisattva Vajragarbha, who gives himself up to a deep meditation in a vast assembly of gods, Buddhas and Bodhisattvas, and is then invited by Śākyamuni to explain the "ten steps," while rays of light emanate in all directions from all the Buddhas present. Chapter I also contains Gāthās (in Sanskrit, not in the Gāthā dialect), though the actual treatise on the Bhūmis is entirely in prose. The doctrine of the "ten steps" is to be found in an earlier form in the Mahāvastu, but in the Mahāyāna it is a principal feature,[1] and the Daśabhūmaka is the most important work which treats of this doctrine. It was translated into Chinese in 297 A.D. by Dharmarakṣa.[2]

Like the Avataṃsaka, the Ratnakūṭa or "Heap of Jewels" also constitutes a large section both of the Chinese Tripiṭaka (II,

---

and Tibetan with a French translation of Chapters I-VI (on the first six Bhūmis) had already previously been edited by *La Vallee Poussin* in Le Mussón 1907. 1910 and 1911; Chapt. VI also in Bouddhisme, Etudes et Materiaux, Theorie de douze causes (1913), p. 115 ff. *La Vallee Poussin* says (ERE II, 744) that Daśabhūmīśvara is the title of a recension augmented by Prākrit verses. *Rahder* does not make this distinction, but merely remarks that some MSS. have Gāthās in the last chapter. In the colophon in *Rahder*'s edition, the title reads : Daśabhūmīśvara Mahāyānasūtraratnarāja. *Cf.* also Rāj. *Mitra*, Nep. Buddh. Lit., P. 81 ff.; Bendall, Catalogue, p. 4f. It is frequently quoted in the Śikṣā-Samuccaya.

1. The doctrine of the Bhūmis is also to be found in the Lalita-Vistara, in the Aṣṭasāhasrikā-Prajñāpāramitā XVII ff., in Candrakīrti's Mādhyamakāvatāra and in Maitreyanātha's Mahāyāna-Sūtrālaṃkāra XX, XXI. For a detailed treatment s. T. Suzuki Outlines of Mahāyāna Buddhism, Ch. 12, and especially *La Vallee Poussin* in ERE II, 743 ff. VIII. 329 f.

2. Apart from this, it was translated into Chinese by Kumārajīva (406 A.D.), Bodhiruci (500-516) and Śīladharma (789). Kumārajīva also translated the Daśabhūmika-vibhāśā śāstra, a commentary on the first two Bhūmis, by Nāgārjuna. Cf. *Nanjio*, Nos. 88 f., 105, 110, 1180, 1194; *Bagchi* I, 87, 103, 186, 197 f., 253, 257; K. *Watanabe* in JRAS 1907, 663 f. A *Daśabhūmikleśāvachedika-Sūtra,* which is said to have been translated as early as in the year 70 A.D., has not come down, but the translation by Fo Nien (388-417) is extant, s. *Nanjio*, No. 375; *Bagchi* I, 171 f.: *Rahder*. l.c. pp. iii, viii, 217 f. The work treats of the same subject as the Daśabhūmaka, but is not identical with it.

Pao-chi)[1] and of the Tibetan Kanjur (IV, Kon-ts'egs).[2] In these works it is a collection of 49 Sūtras, including, among others, the long Sukhāvatī-Vyūha, the Akṣobhya-Vyūha, the Mañjuśrī-Buddhakṣetra-Guṇa-Vyūha, and also a Bodhisattva-Piṭaka, Pitāputrasamāgama, "Meeting of the son (Śākyamuni) with his father (Śuddhodana),"[3] the Kāśyapa-Parivarta, and many Paripṛcchās, "Questions" (with the corresponding answers).

We may take it that there was a Ratnakūṭa in Sanskrit too. According to Tāranātha the Ratnakūṭa-Dharma-Paryāya in 1,000 sections, it had its origin during the reign of Kaniṣka's son.[4] On the other hand, the various single texts which are mentioned as portions of the Ratnakūṭa in the Chinese and Tibetan works, only occur as independent works in Sanskrit.[5] The Chinese and the Tibetan books agree in giving the Kāśyapa-Parivarta as section 43 of the Ratnakūṭa. Valuable fragments of the Sanskrit original of this work were found in the neighbourhood of Khotan, and have been published by *Baron* A. *von Stael Holstein.*[6] It appears,

1. Collected by Bodhiruci in 706-713 A.D.; s *Nanjio*, No. 23, *Forke*, Pekinger Tripiṭaka, p. 179 ff. There is in Chinese also a short Ratnakūṭa-Sūtra, which treats of the Ratnakūṭa-samādhi; s. *Forke*. l.c., No. 846. Many shorter sections of the Ratnakūṭa were translated into Chinese from the 3rd to the 6th century A.D., s *Bagchi* I, pp. 24, 41-43. 96 f.. 104 f., 210, 220, 252, 258, 350 f., 391. See also *Wassiljew*, Der Buddhismus, p. 167 ff.

2. *Cf.* Csoma de *Koros* in AMG II, 212 ff. and Marcelle Lalou in JA 1927, Oct. Dec., p. 233 ff.

3. Extracts from it in the Śikṣā-Samuccaya.

4. *Eliot*, Hinduism and Budduism, II, 56 f.

5. Maitreyanātha quotes the Ratnakūṭa in his Mahāyāna-Sūtrālaṃkāra XIX, 29. The Ratnakūṭa is mentioned in Mahā-Vyutpatti 65, 39, but the single texts, too, are enumerated as independent works. Similarly, in the Śikṣā-Samuccaya, both the Ratnakūṭa and the works which it comprises, such as the Rāṣṭrapāla-Paripṛcchā, Ugra-Paripṛcchā, Akṣayamati-Parīpṛcchā and others, are cited. When the Śikṣa. quotes the Ugra-Paripṛcchā, then the *Rastrap. Pal.* and the Ratnakūṭa side by side on pp.146, 196,or when in Śikṣ., p. 54 first the Rāṣṭrapāla-Sūtra, and then again the Ratnakūṭa are quoted, it follows that Śāntideva did not know the Ugra-Paripṛcchā and the Rāṣṭrapāla-Paripṛcchā as parts of the Ratnakūṭa.

6. The Kāśyapaparivarta a Mahāyānasūtra of the Ratnakūṭa class edited in the Original Sanskrit, in Tibetan, and in Chinese (The Commercial Press Ltd.. Shanghai. 1626).

moreover, that the Kāśyapa-Parivarta is identical with the original Ratnakūṭa.[1] The work was entitled Kāśyapa-Parivarta, because Kāśyapa the Great, Buddha's disciple, is the principal speaker.

In this work, which is said to have been translated into Chinese as early as between 178 and 184 A.D.,[2] the prose and the verses alternate in such a way that the verse portions (in Sanskrit with occasional Prākritisms) repeat what has already been said in prose. As far as we can glean from the fragments which have come down, the ideal of the Bodisattva, and doctrine of unreality (śūnyatā) are proclaimed again and again in the Kāśyapa-Parivarta in many a parable in the conversations between Buddha and Kāśyapa.

The first 22 fragments are reminiscent of the section of four in the Aṅguttara-Nikāya. Four good and four bad qualities, four good and four bad friends, etc., of a Bodhisattva are enumerated. The first of the four good qualities is love of truth : "Not even in order to save their lives, do they utter a falsehood" (p. 8) Then come the comparisons (p. 56 ff). As the vast earth is useful to all living creatures, unchanging and without seeking a reward, so also is the Bodhisattva. "As the element of water, O Kāśyapa, enables all the grasses, shrubs, herbs, and trees to grow even so the Bodhisattva, who is pure of heart, enables all beings to blossom forth, by the manifestation of his love (maitra), and continuing thus, enables all the luminous qualities of all beings to mature" (p. 58). In similar fashion the Bodhisattva is compared to fire, the wind, the moon, the sun, a lion, an elephant, a lotus, etc. There is a series of other similes in the explanation of Śūnyatā. Even as a physician heals the sick man, the Śūnyatā. is a remedy for all who are entangled in heresies (p. 97.) Then come fresh similes having reference to the Bodhisattva. "O Kāś-

1. *Bendall*, Śikṣāsamuccaya Ed., p. 52 note 1, and *Stael-Holstein*. l.c.. p. ff. xiv. There is no colophon in the fragments, but the title Mahā-Ratnakūṭa-Dharmaparyāya occurs in a few fragments (pp. 82, 217, 227). However, the title "Kāśyapa-Section" remains unexplained, if the Ratnakūṭa and the Kāśyapa-Parivarta are one and the same work.

2. Three other translations were made between 265 and 420 A.D., 350 and 431 A.D., and at the close of the 10th century, s. A. *von Stael Holstein* l.c., pp. ix f., xxi; *Nanjio*, Nos. 57, 1363; *Bagchi* I.26 f., 41, 239.

yapa, just as the new moon is worshipped, and the full moon is not worshipped to the same degree, even so, Kāśyapa, a Bodhisattva should be honoured far more than a Tathāgata, by my followers. And why? Because the Tathāgatas arise from the Bodhisattvas" (p. 129).

Among the numerous Paripṛcchās which are included in the Chinese and the Tibetan Ratnakūṭa,[1] there is also the Rāṣṭrapāla-Paripṛcchā, or Rāṣṭrapāla-Sūtra.[2] The Sūtra consists of two parts, the first of which is more dogmatic and contains Buddha's reply to "Rāṣṭrapāla's question" on the qualities (Dharmas) of a Bodhisattva, while Part II relates the Jātaka of Prince Puṇyaraśmi, whose story has a few features in common with the Buddha legend. Even in Part I, however, Buddha gives a brief account of his actions in former births, by way of elucidating the Bodhisattva-Dharmas, and fifty Jātakas are mentioned. Following abruptly after these Jātakas, is a prophecy of the future decay of the religion,[3] and this is the most interesting part of the Sūtra : for the picture here sketched in a very life-like and accurate manner, must necessarily reflect actual facts, and must contain a satirical description of the lax morals of the Buddhist monks. It says, for instance :

"My monks will be without shame and without virtue, haughty, puffed up and wrathful...intoxicating themselves with alcoholic drinks. While they bear the banner of the Buddha, they will only be serving the householders...They themselves will have wives, sons and daughters like householders...'You are not to indulge in sensual pleasures, in order that you may not be born again as animals, ghosts or beings of hell,' thus they will preach to the householders, but they themselves will be uncontrolled, and so on."

---

1. *Cf. Nanjio*, Catalogue, p. xiii ff.; *Koros* in AMG, II, 564 f.

2. Rāṣṭrapālaparipṛcchā, Sūtra du Mahāyāna, publié par L, *Finot*. (Bibliotheca Buddhica II,) St. Petersbourg 1901. *Cf. La Vallee Poussin*, Le Museon N,S: IV, 1903, p. 306 ff. This Sūtra has nothing in common with the Raṭṭhapāla-Sutta (see above, p, 47 f) except the name Rāṣṭrapāla (= Pāli Raṭṭhapāla).

3. *Finot*, l.c., p. ix ff., 28ff.

This prophecy reminds us of similar ones in the Thera-Gāthās (see above, p. 107). The Chinese translation of the Rāṣṭrapāla-Paripṛcchā made between 585 and 592 A.D.,[1] proves that the conditions here described, already existed in the 6th century. The Sūtra is probably not much earlier than the Chinese translation as is shown by the barbaric language, which particularly in the Gāthās is a mixture of Prākrit and bad Sanskrit, and by the elaborate metres and the careless style.

Many of the Paripṛcchās which are counted as belonging to the Ratnakūṭa, are also quoted in the Śikṣā-Samuccaya, thus for instance, the Ugra-Paripṛcchā or Ugradatta-Paripṛcchā. "Questions of (the householder) Ugradatta,"[2] from which, for example, a long passage on the advantages of a forest hermit's life is cited, the Udayana-Vatsarāja-Paripṛcchā, "Questions of the Vatsa king Udayana" (No. 29 in the Ratnakūṭa of the Kanjur), the Upāli-Paripṛcchā, "Upāli's Questions on Discipline,"[3] and others. It is interesting that women are made to ask quite a number of "questions," thus for instance, there is a Candrottarā-Dārikā-Paripṛcchā, "Questions of the Girl Candrottarā" (Śikṣ. p. 78 ff., on the evil consequences of lust), Dārikā-Vimalaśraddhā-Paripṛcchā (No. 40 in the Ratnakūṭa of the Kanjur), Sumati-Dārikā-Paripṛcchā (No. 30 in the Chinese Ratnakūṭa), etc.

Just as the Prajñā-Pāramitās proclaim first and foremost the Śūnyavāda, the doctrine of unreality, the Saddharma-Laṅkāvatāra-Sūtra, "the Revelation of the Good Religion in Laṅkā (Ceylon)," generally called briefly Laṅkāvatāra,[4] teaches princi-

1. *Forke*, Pekinger Tripiṭaka, p. 111; *Nanjio* No. 23 (18). A second translation was made between 980 and 1000 A.D., s. *Nanjio*, Nos. 873.

2. Translated into Chinese as early as in 181 A.D. and then again in 252 A.D., s. *Bagchi* I. 47, 104; f.; *Forke*, Pekinger Tripiṭaka. Nos. 283, 1207. Śikṣās. pp. 198 ff., 367.

3. Vinaya-viniścaya-Upāli-paripṛcchā in the Kanjur (s. M. *Lalou* in JA 1927. Oct. Dec., p. 252). Upāli is the expert of the Vin aya. at the council of Rājagṛha (Vinaya-Piṭaka, Culla-Vagga XI, 1,7).

4. Edited by Bunyiu *Nanjio*, Kyoto 1923 (Bibliotheca Otaniensis, Vol. 1). An analysis of the doctrines contained in the Laṅkāvatāra Sūtra, especially in their relation to the Japanese Zen Buddhism, is given by D. T. *Suzuki* in EB IV, 199-298. *Cf.* G *Tucci* in RSO X, 1923, 567 ff. and Memorie R. Acc.

pally a modification of the Śūnyavāda, the Vijñānavāda, the "Doctrine of Consciousness," *i.e.*, that doctrine which, though it also denies the reality of the external world, does at the same time recognise that the phenomena of consciousness have a subjective reality.

In the form in which we have it, the work is either a very careless compilation, or else it has suffered very badly in coming down to us; moreover, it consists of portions which belong to various periods. It was translated into Chinese three times, by Guṇabhadra in 443 A.D., by Bodhiruci in 513 and by Śikṣānanda in 700 -704.[1] In the first translation Chapters I, IX and X are missing, so that we may be justified in assuming that these three chapters were not written until between 443 and 513 A.D. The last chapter (Sagāthakam) consists entirely of verse, while the rest of the book is in prose with occasional Gāthās interspersed.[2]

Chapter I gives a very detailed description of the meeting of Buddha with Rāvaṇa, the king of the Rākṣasas in Laṅkā. Encouraged by the Bodhisattva Mahāmati, Rāvaṇa asks Buddha questions about the difference between true and false doctrine (Dharma and Adharma). With Chapter II which has no connection whatsoever with Chapter I Mahāmati, after he has praised Buddha and obtained permission to ask him questions, begins to ply Buddha with a long series of over one hundred questions; these questions bear on all the details of the doctrine, on release ("Whither does the released one go? Who is bound ? By whom is he released?)", on Ālaya,[3] Manovijñāna and

---

Lincei, ser, V, Vol. XVII, fasc. V, p. 170ff.; J.W. *Hauer*, Das Laṅkāvatāra-Sūtra und das Sāṃkhya (Beiträge zur indischen Sprachwissenschaft und Religionsgeschichte 1927) ; and *Schaye* in ZB 8, 1928, 249 f. In the colophon of Chapt. II, the Sūtra is called Saṭtriṃśatsahasra, "consisting of 36,000 (Ślokas)."

1. *Nanjio* Edition, Preface, p. viii f.; *Bagchi* I, pp. 254, 380.

2. Though Chapts. II-VIII appear in all the three Chinese translations, *Hauer*, l.c., p. 3, doubts whether Chapt. VIII, which is devoted entirely to the condemnation of meat-eating, belonged to the original work. As the question as to whether meat-eating is permissible is already discussed in II, 45, it is possible that Chapt. VIII too may have belonged to the nucleus of the work.

3. "The store-room of all ideas." *Cf.* O. *Resonberg* Die Probleme der buddhistischen Philosophie, Heidelberg, 1924, p. 235; Th. *Stcherbatsky*, Central Conception of Buddhism, pp. 65, 67, 100; *Strauss*, Indische Philosophie, p. 256.

other main notions of the Vijñānavāda on Śūnyatā, enlightenment, etc. But we also find such questions as : "How do food and drink of all kinds come into existence? How does copulation come about? What is the nature of a king, a ruler of the world (Cakravartin), a ruler of a district (Maṇḍalin)?... How is it that you are descended from the Śākya race, through whom and how are you a scion of Ikṣvāku?...Why are you alone seen in all lands?," etc. Buddha does not only deal with these questions and give his assent to them, but adds many more questions to the list, having reference to general knowledge (medicine, the arts, geography, etc.) which Mahāmati should have asked.[1] Then comes an enumeration of 108 subjects which have been explained by former Buddhas. The main portion of Chapters II-VII is entirely philosophic in content, and actually treats of the whole system of the Buddhist doctrine, mainly from the standpoint of the Vijñānavāda. The question : "What is Nirvāṇa?" and the various opinions on it, are discussed in two places.[2] In Chapter III, we find, among other things, a discussion on the paradoxical utterance of Buddha : "Between the night during which the Tathāgata attained to enlightenment, and the night during which he will be completely extinguished, in that time not one syllable was spoken by the Tathāgata, and he will not speak a single syllable : the Buddha word is a non-word" (p. 142 ff.). In the same chapter (p. 192 f.) we also come across a remarkable list of names of Buddha. We are told here that, just as in other cases there are several names for one and the same thing, *e.g.*, Indra and Śakra, hasta and pāṇi (both of which mean "hand" etc., similarly, there are countless names for Buddha too; some call him Tathāgata, others Svayambhū, Nāyaka, Vināyaka, Pariṇāyaka, Buddha, Ṛṣi, Vṛṣabha, Brāhmaṇa, Viṣṇu, Īśvara, Pradhāna,[3] Kapila,[4] Bhūtānta (the end of the beings, death), Ariṣṭanemi,[5] Soma (moon), Bhāskara (sun), Rāma, Vyāsa, Śukra,

1. Here there is a repetition of some questions which had been asked previously. It is clear that the text is in disorder.

2. Pp. 98 ff., and 182 ff. *Cf.* Th. *Stcherbatsky*, The Conception of Buddhist Nirvāṇa, p. 31 note; *Burnouf*, Introduction, p. 459 f.

3. Original matter, a term of the Sāṃkhya philosophy.

4. The founder of the Sāṃkhya philosophy.

5. A Jain saint.

Indra, Bali, Varuṇa and others again : Anirodhānutpāda (non-destruction and non-originating), Śūnyatā, Tathatā, Truth, Reality, Highest Being, Dharmadhātu, Nirvāṇa, That which is Eternal, the Four Noble Truths, etc. Chapter IV treats of the ten Bhūmis.

In Chapter VIII,[1] (Mahāmati begs of the Lord to explain to him what is good or bad in the practice of eating meat, "so that we, I and the other Bodhisattvas, the Great Beings, may in the future and in the present so preach the doctrine that the beings who are still affected by the impressions surviving from a previous existence as a beast of prey, and who for that reason are greedy for meat, may renounce their greed for (the) taste (of meat), and in order that the meat-eaters may cast from them the greed for the taste (of meat), and that, as a result of a longing for the taste of the doctrine, they may treat all beings with a love as strong as that felt towards an only son, and thus gain the great Love (mahāmaitrī)." The eating of flesh is forbidden even by the adherents of false doctrines, and they themselves eat no meat, whilst under the Completely Enlightened One, who is all pity, people eat meat, and the eating of meat is not forbidden. Buddha's reply to this, is that the eating of meat should be avoided for innumerable reasons, first and foremost being the fact that every being is at some time or other connected with all other beings by rebirth as a father, brother, son, and so on. Legends are told, as evidence of the evil consequences of eating meat. In the Gāthās which follow the prose, not only meat, but also intoxicating drinks, onions and garlic are prohibited. Buddha admits that, in the future, there will be meat-eaters who will declare that the eating of meat is allowed by Buddha.[2] The Buddha however, forbids any kind of meat-eating, whether it be as a medicine or as a food, and he accounts it tantamount to eating the flesh of a son.

1. It begins with the words : "Then the Bodhisattva, the Great Being, Mahāmati, questioned the Lord in the Gāthās." However, what follows is only prose; the verses seem to have been dropped.

2. *Hauer*, Das Laṅkāvatāra-Sūtra, p. 3 f., regards these passages as allusions to Tantric cults. This is a possible, but not a necessary assumption. The practice of meat-eating may have arisen among Buddhists in the Northern districts even before there were Tantric cults.

Chapter IX is a Dhāraṇī, a magic formula protecting people against snake-demons and ghosts of all kinds.[1]

The whole of Chapter X is a long philosophical treatise in 884 verses.[2] In this case, too, the doctrines put forth, are those of the Vijñānavāda. It is, however, expressly emphasized again and again, that all phenomena are unreal like a fata morgana, an illusion, a delusion. We are frequently reminded of the language of the Vedānta. As in the Gauḍapādīya-Kārikās, in which the Vedāntist doctrine of Māyā is first developed, this work (v. 443) also illustrates the non-reality of the world by the simile of the circle of fire, which originates when a burning stick is twirled round. Again and again we come across the instances of the "horn of a hare" the "ring-like apparitions before the shut eyes," and similar fictions and delusions of the senses, which are intended to show that everything is only illusion and that nothing is real, not even release (verse 623)[3]. Sāṃkhyas, Vaiśeṣikas, naked sophists, and the theists, are mentioned as adherents of false doctrines (verse 723). The speaker in Chapter X is not Śākyamuni, but one of his predecessors, a Buddha of an earlier age, who says of himself : "I am descended from the family (gotra) of Kātyāyana, and have come from the Śuddhāvāsa heaven. I preach to the beings the doctrine which leads to the city of Nirvāṇa. I and those Tathāgatas have pointed to this very ancient path as leading to Nirvāṇa, in 3,000 Sūtras (v. 772f.). "And my mother is Vasumatī, my father is the Brahman Prajāpati, I am descended from the family of Kātyāyana, and my name is Jina the Pure (Viraja Jina). I was born in Campā, so were my father and my grandfather also. The latter was called

1. Translated by J. W. *Hauer*, Die Dhāraṇi im nordlichen Buddhismus (Beitrāge zur indischen Sprāchwissenschaft and Religionsgeschichte, 2, 1927), p, 2 ff, Haraprasāda *Śāstrī* in JASB Proceedings, 1900, p. 100 ff., describes a "Laṅkāvatāra" Tantra, which, however, has nothing in common with the Mahāyāna-Sūtra.

2. The prose sentence at the beginning : "Then Mahāmati, the Bodhisattva, the Great Being, spoke to the Lord thus," is an absurd interpolation : for it is evident that a Buddha is made to say these verses.

3. X, 558-623, translated into German by *Hauer*, Das Laṅkāvatāra. Sūtra, p. 7 ff.

Somagupta, and was descended from the dynasty of the moon" (v.798. f).[1]

A few passages in Chapter X might possibly be of historical significance, if they were clearer ; in particular the prophecy (X, 784 ff.) : "Vyāsa, Kaṇāda, Ṛṣabha, Kapila, the Śākya leader, these and others will be there after my passing away. A hundred years after I have passed away, the Vyāsa who is well known from the (Mahā-) Bhārata, and also the Pāṇḍavas, the Kauravas, Rāma and then the Maurya (Chandragupta is meant) will live, and after that, the Mauryas, Nandas and Guptas, and then the barbarians, the meanest of the kings. At the end of the reign of the barbarians, there will be armed riots, and after they are ended, the Kali-Yuga will come, and at the end of the Kali-Yuga, the Good Religion will not be promoted by the people." In another passage (X, 813 ff.) the coming of Pāṇini, Akṣapāda, Bṛhaspati, of the teachers of Lokāyata, of Kātyāyana the writer of Sūtras, of Yājñavalkya, Vālmīki, Masūrākṣa, Kauṭilya and Āśvalāyana, is foretold.

Whilst the last-named list is anything but chronolgical,[2] and can scarcely be of service in fixing any date, we are most likely justified in taking it that the passage about the Guptas, and the one about the succeeding reign of the barbarians, refer to the Hun invasions at the close of the 5th century.[3] From this we could infer that Chapter X was written not long before the time of the second Chinese translation (513 A.D.). The philosophy of the Vijñānavāda, which is taught in all parts of the Laṅkāvatāra, coincides with the doctrines of Maitreyanātha, Asaṅga, and the Mahāyāna-Śraddhotpāda, which may be ascribed to the 4th century A.D. at the earliest. It is, therefore, probable that the Laṅkāvatāra-Sūtra, even in its earlier form, was not in existence more than 50 or at the very most, 100 years before the Chinese translation of 443 A.D. At all events, from the point of view

1. S. Ch. *Vidyābhūṣaṇa* (JASB 1905, p. 161; JRAS 1905, p. 833 ff.) took these verses to be the words of the author of the book. His opinion is shared by *Hauer*, l. c., p. 4. Strange as this passage is, and it does really sound as though it were spoken by an author, this view is nevertheless impossible.

2. *Cf.* E. H. *Johnston* in JRAS 1929, p. 86. ff.

3. *Cf.* above, Vol. I, 501 f.

of the history of Indian philosophy from the 4th to the 6th century A.D., the importance of this work, which contains such numerous allusions to other systems of philosophy should not be undervalued.[1]

Among the latcr Mahāyāna-Sūtras there is also the Samādhirāja, "(the Sūtra about the) King of Meditations," or the Candrapradīpa-Sūtra, as it is called after the principal speaker.[2] Here, in a dialogue between Candrapradīpa (or Candraprabha) and Buddha,it is shown how a Bodhisattva can attain to the highest knowledge by means of the various meditations, especially the highest of all, the "King of Meditations," and which preliminary conditions are necessary in order to prepare the spirit for this highest stage of meditation. Such preliminary conditions are the worship of the Buddhas, complete renunciation of the world, gentleness and goodness towards all beings, entire indifference as to one's own life and one's own health if there is a question of sacrificing them for others, and lastly the knowledge of the non-reality of the world, the steadfast belief in the unreality (śūnyatā) of all phenomena. Passages of moral contents, mostly in Gāthās, are quoted by Śāntideva in the Śikṣā-Samuccaya, as for instance the beautiful verses about peace of mind (Śikṣ., p. 242f.) :

He will never depart from the doctrine of the Blessed Ones (Sugatas *i.e.*, Buddhas), *that* hero will never fall into the power of women, *he* takes a delight in the commandment of the Blessed Ones—he who understands that real peace of mind is the true nature of Religion.

---

1. Haraprasāda *Śāstrī* (Ind. Hist. Qu, 1, 1925, 208 f.) speaks of the Laṅkāvatāra as a work belonging to the period before Kaniṣka. This is probably based upon the erroneous statement of Rāj. *Mitra*, Nep. Buddh. Lit., p. 113, that the work was already translated into Chinese in 168-190 A.D. H. *Śāstrī* (l. c.) calls attention to a paper published by Harinath *De*, "in which 20 different systems of thought were culled from the Laṅkāvatāra."

2. We do not know of any edition of the work. We only know it from quotations in the Sikṣā-Samuccaya and from the table of contents given by Rāj. *Mitra*, Nep. Buddh. Lit., pp. 207:221; s. *Bendall*, Catalogue, p. 22 f.; Śikṣā-Samuccaya, ed. Bendall, p. 368.

He will soon become a prince of men here, *he* will be a healing physician, a giver of good fortune, *he* will pull out completely the thorn (of pain) of the unfortunate,—he who understands that real peace of mind is the true nature of Religion.

He shines forth among the people, like the moon, by the power of his mildness, *he* is not angered, though he be ill-treated with clods of earth and with sticks, *he* remains unmoved, though he be pulled to pieces limb by limb,—he who understands that real peace of mind is the true nature of Religion."

In the Śikṣā-Samuccaya (p. 134) a verse is cited from the Jñānavatī section of the Samādhirāja, according to which the eating of meat which is otherwise prohibited, is allowable by way of medicine. In a prose passage of some length, it is explained that it is more likely for a man who is burning from head to foot, and who is still alive, to think of sensual pleasures, than for a Bodhisattva to find rest, as long as there are still human beings in distress.[1] Legends are also told of saints who were successful owing to the "King of Meditations." This Sūtra corresponds to the Chinese Yūehteng-san-mei-ching, which was translated in 450 and 557 A.D.[2]

The last work to be mentioned among the later Mahāyāna-Sūtras, is the Suvarṇa-Prabhāsa or "Splendour of Gold,"[3] the contents of which are partly philosophical and ethical, and which

1. Śikṣ., p. 166. A long passage on morality is quoted on p. 100 f., and a passage on the advantages of a hermit's life, on p. 193 ff,; a beautiful verse on maitrī, love, which is to be esteemed far above any cult, is quoted on p. 318. In the Sikṣ. the title is always Candrapradipa-Sūtra.

2. Thus according to K. *Watanabe* in JRAS 1907, 663; *Nanjio*, No. 191. Both titles also occur in the Tibetan Kanjur, s. *Koros.* in AMG II, 249. The Śūraṅgamasamādhi, which is also quoted in the Śikṣā-Samuccaya, is a different work from the Samādhirāja.

3. Edited by Rai Sarat Chandra *Dās*, Bahadur, and Pandit Sarat Chandra *Śāstrī*, fasc. 1, Calcutta 1898 (Buddhist Text Society of India). More does not seem to have been published. The complete title reads thus in the colophons : Suvarṇaprabhāsottama-sūtrendrarāja. The fascicule contains Chapts. I. XV. Rāj, *Mitra*, Nep. Buddh. Lit., p. 241 ff., gives the contents of 21 chapters. *Cf. Burnouf*, Introduction, pp. 471 ff., 490; *Bendall* Catalogue, p. 12 f.; M. *Anesaki* in ERE IV, p. 839. An edition of the Suvarṇa-Prabhāsa was prepared by the late Bunyiu *Nanjio*, and is being made ready for the press by his pupil Hotoku *Idzumi*, s. J. *Takakusu* in The young East, May 1928, p. 404.

also contains many legends, but which, for a great part, already bears the stamp of a Tantra.

In Chapter I the Brahmin Kauṇḍinya begs for a relic of Buddha, even though it might not be larger than a grain of mustard. The Licchavi prince Sarvalokapriyadarśana replies to him in the following verses : "When flowers will grow in the floods of the Ganges, when crows are red and Kokilas are the colour of conch-shells, when the Jambū tree bears palm nuts and the date tree mango blossoms,—then there will be a relic the size of a grain of mustard. When people will be well protected against the winter's cold with coats made out of the hairs of the tortoise, ...When the feet of a mosquito will afford a firm support which will not waver ... When people will make a firm ladder out of a hare-horn, whereby to climb up to heavan,...When a mouse will climb up this ladder, and having eaten the moon up, will run around Rāhu,...When an umbrella made of Palāśa leaves will be large enough to protect people from the rain,...When ocean ships will career around upon the dry land with sail and mast, when owls will carry away Gandhamādana hill with their beaks[1], then there will be a relic." The Brahmin himself states the reason: It is impossible to find a relic of Buddha, even as small as a grain of mustard, as there is neither bone nor blood of Buddha's body, for the Completely Enlightened Tathāgata has only a Dharmakāya,[2] and consists only of the Dharma element, *i.e.*, he has only an immaterial 'body' consisting of the absolute and he is composed only of ideas, of spiritual (non-sensual) phenomena. A Buddha was never created and never passes away; only in order to bring the beings to maturity, he causes the vision of the complete Nirvāṇa to appear.

---

1. This list of impossible things is to be found, in part word for word, in Jātaka No. 425 (Aṭṭhāna-Jātaka, "the Jātaka of the Impossibilities"). *Cf.* Th. *Zachariae*, Kleine Schriften, Bonn 1920, p. 70 f.; She-Rab Dong bu or Prajuya Daṇḍa by Lu-Trub (Nāgārjuna ed. and transl. by W. L. *Campbell*, Calcutta 1919, p. 98 (vs. 194); and *Penzer-Tawney*, The Ocean of Story, IX, 152.

2. On the Mahāyāna doctrine of the three bodies (trikāya) of the Buddha, *viz.*, dharmakāya (absolute), sambhogakāya (the superhuman body with which the Buddhas enjoy their glory, virtue and wisdom and nirmāṇakāya (the assumed body, which the Buddhas assume, in order to carry out their

Chapter IV is on a lofty ethical plane, and contains many a beautiful passage such as the confession of sins,[1] and the praise of love (maitrī) towards all beings.[2] The doctrine of Śūnyatā is developed in Chapter VI. The major portion of the work consists, however, of a glorification of the Suvarṇa-Prabhāsa itself, and the merit ofreading this book is extolled over and over again. In Chapter VIII the goddess Sarasvatī appears, and in Chapter IX Śrī Mahādevī, the great goddess Śrī, in order to magnify the Suvarṇa-Prabhāsa as a Dhāraṇī.[3] Chapter XIII is a kind of manual for kings (rājaśāstra), called Devendrasamaya, which Baladaketu recited to his son Ruciraketu when he was anointed as king.[4] Among the legends which are related in the Suvarṇa-Prabhāsa, there is also one about a prince who kills himself in order to serve as food for a hungry tigress,[5] whereupon the prince's father has his son's remains preserved in a golden casket and has a Stūpa erected over them. In other places, however, Tantric ritual is also taught, and female deities, Hārītī, Caṇḍikā, etc., are mentioned.

The Suvarṇa-Prabhāsa enjoys a great reputation and is popular in all countries where Mahāyāna Buddhism prevails. In Central

---

work of releasing the beings on earth), see *La Vallée Poussin* in ERE I, 97 f.; M. *Anesaki* in ERE IV, 839 f.; P. *Masson-Oursel* in JA 1913, ser, 11, t. I, p. 581 ff.; *Rosenberg*, Die Probleme der buddhistischen Philosophie, p. 236 ff.; W. Montgomery *McGovern*. An Introduction to Mahāyāna Buddhism, London 1922, p. 75 ff. I-tsing's Chinese translation of the Suvarṇa-Prabhāsa has a chapter on the doctrine of Trikāya, which does not appear in the Sanskrit text, and which, in the opinion of *Anesaki* (l. c.) was probably interpolated by an adherent of Vasubandhu. On Dharmadhātu see Th. *Stcherbatsky*, Central Conception of Buddhism, pp. 59, 97.

1. P. 12 ff., quoted in Śikṣā-Samuccaya, pp. 160-164. This passage has been published by H. *Stānner* (SBA 1904, 1310 ff.) from a block print found in Idikutschari (Eastern Turkestan).

2. P. 19 ff., quoted in Śikṣā-Samuccaya, p. 217 f.

3. It is justified to a certain extent, when *La Vallée Poussin*, Bouddhisme, E'tudes et Materiaux, Memoires etc., 1897, p. 127, describes the Suvarṇa-Prabhāsa as a Māhātmya of Dhāraṇis.

4. It is not easy to see how this section crept into this pious work. It reminds us of similar sections in the Purāṇas.

5. See above, p. 263 f. According to a Mongolian version translated by I. J. *Schmidt*, Grammatik der mongolischen Sprache, St. Petersburg 1831, p. 142 ff.

Asia, too, fragments of this work have been discovered.[1] It is said to have been explained in China by Kāśyapa Mātaṅga as early as during the reign of Ming-ti (58-75 A.D.).[2] If this statement is not a mere fiction with a view to extolling the work, there must have been a Suvarṇa-Prabhāsa in those days which diverged widely from the present text. The Chinese translation by Dharmakṣema (414-433), Paramārtha and his pupils (552-557) and I-tsing (703) have come down to us.[3]

The Masters and Poets of the Mahāyāna

Tāranātha[4] says that the adherents of the Hīnayāna declare the Śatasāhasrikā-Prajñā-Pāramitā to be the latest of the Mahāyāna-Sūtras, and the work of Nāgārjuna[5] and it is not impossible that this Prajñā-Pāramitā is indeed an apocryphal Sūtra which was produced by Nāgārjuna's school. It is more likely, however, that this statement is due to a confusion between the text of the great Prajñā-Pāramitā and the Prajñā-Pāramitā Sūtra-Śāstra which was ascribed to Nāgārjuna, *i.e.*, the commentary on the Pañcaviṃśati-Sāhasrikā-Prajñā-Pāramitā. At all events Nāgārjuna cannot possibly have been the founder of the Mahāyāna, as was so often

1. A passage from it in the language of Khotan, s, in E. *Leumann*, Buddhist, Lit. Nordarisch und Deutsch, 1920, p. 53 ff. A few Central Asiatic fragments of the Sanskrit text have been published and translated by F. W. *Thomas* in Hoernle, MS. Remains, p. 108 ff. An Uiguric translation appeared in Bibl. Buddhica in 1914. For fragments of Uiguric texts, s. F. W. K. *Müller*, Uigurica, in ABA 1908, p. 10 ff.; *Lüders*, SBA 1914, p. 99; in the colophon it is expressly stated that the work was translated from the Indian language into Chinese, and from the Chinese into Turkish.

2. *Bagchi* I, p. 4.

3. *Bagchi* I, 220, 422; *Forke*, Pekinger Tripiṭaka, Nos. 121, 127. In the Tibetan Kanjur, s. AMG II, 315 f. The West Mongolian recension (Altan Geral) has been published by Erich *Haenisch*. Leipzig 1929.

4. Geschichte des Buddhismus in Indien, aus dem Tibetischen übersetzt von A *Schiefner*, St. Petersburg 1869, p. 71.

5. On Nāgārjuna, see A. *Grunwedel* Mythologie des Buddhismus in Tibet und der Mongolei, Leipzig 1900, p. 29 ff., *Eliot*, II, 84 ff., Satis Chandra *Vidyābhūṣaṇa* in Proc. IOC, Vol. II, p. 125 ff.; Max *Walleser*. The life of Nāgārjuna from Tibetan and Chinese Sources (Hirth Anniversary Volume, Asia Major I, 421 ff.) ; P. L. *Vaidya*, E'tudes sur Āryadeva et son Catuḥśataka, Paris1923, p. 46 ff.; *Keith*, Buddhist Philosophy, p. 229 f.

supposed in former days ; for there is no doubt that Mahāyāna-Sūtras were in existence long before his time.[1] According to Hsun-Tasang,[2] Aśvaghoṣa, Nāgārjuna, Āryadeva and Kumāralabdha (=Kumāralāta) were contemporaries, and he calls them "the four suns which illumined the world." According to Kalhaṇa's Rājataraṅgiṇī (I, 173), the Bodhisattva Nāgārjuna was "the only lord of the land" in Kashmir at the period of the kings Huṣka, Juṣka and Kaniṣka. Tāranātha says that he was born in the days of Kaniṣka. It is a good working hypothesis, though nothing more, that he lived in the latter half of the 2nd century A.D.[3] On the other hand, so many legends have been woven about his life, that doubts have even been expressed as to whether he was a historical personage at all.

According to the biography of Nāgārjuna translated into Chinese by Kumārajīva (in about 405 A.D.), Nāgārjuna was born as a Brahmin in Southern India, studied the four Vedas and learned all sciences. He was also, however, said to be a great sorcerer. By his magic art he was able to make himself invisible, and, accompanied by three friends, he secretly entered into the royal palace, where they began to violate the women. They were discovered, Nāgārjuna's three companions were sentenced to death, but he himself escaped after he had first vowed to become a monk. He fulfilled his vow, studied the whole of the three Piṭakas in 90 days, and grasped their meaning ; yet he was not satisfied with this, but began to seek other Sūtras, until at last he received the Mahāyāna-Sūtra from a very aged monk in the Himalaya. With the aid of Nāgarāja, a serpent-king, he also found a commentary on it. He zealously propagated Buddhism in Southern India. He directed the religion, says the biographer, for over

1. In the Prajñā-Pāramitā-Sūtra-Śāstra and Daśabhūmi-Vibhāṣā-Śāstra (both translated into Chinese by Kumārajīva in about 405 A.D.), Nāgārjuna quotes numerous Mahāyāna-Sūtras; s. R. *Kimura* in Ind. Hist. Qu. III. 1927, p. 412 ff.

2. Si-yu-ki, Buddhist Records of the Western World transl. by S. *Beal*, II, 97 ff., 302 f.; Hwui Li, The life of Hiuen-Tsiang, translation by S. *Beal*, 1911, p. 199.

3. Cf. *Kern*, Manual of Indian Buddhism, p. 122 f.; *Keith*, Buddhist Philosophy, p. 229; *Walleser* in *ZB* VI, 1924-25, p. 95 ff., 237 ff.

300 years.[1] The Tibetans even go as far as to let him attain the age of 600 years.

Kumārajīva describes Nāgārjuna not only as a great magician, but also as well-versed in astronomy, medicine, the production of precious stones, and other worldly things. The poet Bāṇa (7th century A.D.) relates in the Harṣacarita, that Nāgārjuna received a necklace of pearls from a snake-king, which served as a remedy for snake-bite and in fact all pains. In the Tibetan chronicles Nāgārjuna appears almost exclusively as a mighty magician.[2] In spite of all this, we may safely assume that he came from Vidarbha (Berar) and was born as a Brahmin, for his writings give evidence of an intimate acquaintance with Brahminical learning. So great was the reputation which he enjoyed, that even after the lapse of centuries, numerous works for which people desired to assure special authority, were ascribed to him.[3] The fact of his being the founder of one of the most important schools of the Mahāyāna, namely the Mādhyamika school, accounts for this high degree of veneration : for there is not a shadow of a doubt that he is the author of the Mādhyamika-Kārikās or Mādhyamika-

---

1. *Wassiljew*, Der Buddhismus, p. 232 ff. According to *Walleser* (Hirth Anniversary Volume, p. 443 ff.) it is not certain whether we possess the authentic text of Kumārajiva's biography.

2. Thus especially in No. 16 of the "Stories of the 84 Magicians," translated by A. *Grunwedel* (Baessler-Archiv, V, 1916, 161ff.). A medical writer Nāgārjuna is named as the author of the Uttara-Tantra on the Suśruta; s. J. *Jolly*, Medizin (Grundriss), pp. 16, 125, and in ZDMG 53, 1899, 378. About Nāgārjuna, the author of Tantras, who lived in the 7th century, see below. Alberūni says of the alchemist Nāgārjuna; the author of the Rasaratnākara, that he lived a hundred years before his time, P. C. *Ray* places him in the 7th or 8th century A.D. In the Rasaratnākara we find dialogues between Nāgārjuna and King Śalivāhana (for Śālivāhana or Sātavāhana as a friend of Nāgārjuna, see below), and at the beginning of Chapter III, which deals with quicksilver, we read that the goddess Prajñā-Pāramitā appeared to Nāgārjuna in a dream, and revealed to him the ingredients for a recipe. *Cf.* P. C. *Ray*, A History of Indian Chemistry, I, Calcutta 1903, pp. xxiv. xcii ff.; II, 1909, pp. xx, xxiii ff., xxxviii ff., 6ff. Most likely the Buddhist philosopher, the Tantric writer, the medical writer and the alchemist were four different men, who were confused owing to the identity of the names.

3. For the works ascribed to Nāgārjuna. s. *Nanjio*, col, 369 ff.

Sūtras[1] which present in a *systematic* manner the Śūnyavāda which is taught in the Mahāyāna-Sūtras.

The work consists of 400 memorial verses (Kārikās) in 27 chapters, on which the author himself has written a commentary, the Akutobhayā "The Safe One." Nāgārjuna was perhaps the first, or at all events one of the first, to make use of this style of presentation which is so greatly favoured in the scientific literature of the Indians, to wit—memorial verses with a commentary by the author himself. The Akutobhayā has not come down in Sanskrit, and our knowledge of it rests upon the Tibetan translation. The commentaries by Buddhapālita and Bhāvaviveka have also come down in Tibetan translations only. The commentary entitled Prasannapadā, "The Clear-Worded,"[2] by Candrakīrti, who on several occasions argues against his two predecessors, is the only one which we possess in Sanskrit. The Mādhyamika system, which is taught by Nāgārjuna and his pupil Āryadeva, and which found one of its chief exponents in Candrakīrti derives its name "the middle

1. Mūamadhyamika-Kārikās (Mādhyamika-Sūtras) de Nāgārjuna avec la Prasannapadā, commentaire de Candrakīrti, publie par L. *de La Vallee Poussin*, St. Petersbourg (Bibliotheca Buddhica IV), 1903 ff. *La Vallee Poussin* has translated Chapt. 24 of the Commentary, in Melanges Charles de Harlez, Leiden 1896, p. 313 ff. Chapt. I (on Causality) and Chapt. XXV on Nirvāṇa) with the Commentary of Candrakīrti, transl. by Th. *Stcherbatsky*, The Conception of Buddhist Nirvāṇa, Leningrad 1927, pp. 63-212. A summary of the contents of Candrakīrti's Commentary, the text of Chapt. I, and a translation of Chapts. II, V and VII, are given by Satis Chandra *Vidyābhūṣaṇa* in JBTS V, 1897. part 4. p. 7 ff.; II, 1894 and 1896, part I, p. 13 ff; 1897, part I, 23 ff.; part III, p. 21 ff. The Kārikās with the Akutobhayā have been transl. from Tibetan by Max *Walleser*, Die mittlere Lehre (Mādhyamikaśāstra) des Nāgārjuna, Heidelberg 1911. The same scholar has also translated the Chinese version of the Mādhyamika-Śāstra, the Cuṅ-lun, by Kumārajīva, Heidelberg 1912, and edited the Tibetan version of the Akutobhayā in photographic reproduction according to the Peking edition of the Tanjur, in "Materialien zur Kunde des Buddhismus," Heft 2, Heidelberg 1923.

2. In the opinion of *Stcherbatsky* (Nirvāṇa, p. 67, note 1), it is so entitled "not without some dose of irony, since . . . its extreme dialectical subtlety is equalled by no other work in the whole domain of Northern Buddhist literature." Buddhapālita's commentary is edited in Tibetan by M. *Walleser* in Bibl. Buddhica XVI.

doctrine"[1] from the fact that it declares nothing either positive, or negative, but merely relativity. The work begins with the famous eight negations, but it is here expressly stated that they mean the same as the doctrine of causally dependent origination :[2]

"No passing away and no origination, no destruction and no everlasting continuance, no unity and no multiplicity, no coming and no going: I revere the Completely Enlightened One, the best teachers, him who has thus taught the causally dependent origination, the salutary cessation of the world of phenomena."

There was an obvious objection to this and Nāgārjuna himself makes his opponent voice it in Chapter XXIV: If everything is "empty," and there is neither origination nor passing away, then there can also be no "four noble truths" and no rule of life based on the knowledge of these truths, no fruit of good and evil deeds, no Buddha doctrine (Dharma), no monastic community, and finally also no Buddha. Thus the entire religion of the Buddha collapses into nothingness. Thereupon Nāgārjuna replies : The doctrine of the Buddha rests on two truths, one conventional truth, in which the deeper meaning remains hidden, and one truth in the highest sense. He who does not know the distinction between these two truths, does not understand the profound substance of the Buddha doctrine. The highest truth can be taught only when based on the truth of every-day life, and without the assistance of this highest truth, it is not possible to understand Nirvāṇa.

---

1. Whilst in the "Sermon of Benares" the "middle way" is understood in the ethical sense (avoidance of the extremes of worldly life and exaggerated asceticism), the expression has a metaphysical meaning in this case : the avoidance of extreme statements regarding existence and non-existence.

2. The reproach that the Mādhyamikas are nothing but Nāstikas or 'Nihilists,' is firmly rejected by Candrakīrti (Madhyamika-Vṛtti, p. 368). On the system of the Mādhyamikas, *cf. La Vallée Paussin*, Bouddhisme, pp. 189 ff., 290 ff., and ERE VIII, 235 ff., *Anesaki* in ERE IV. 838; Y. *Sogen*, Systems of Buddhistic Thought, p. 194 ff.; P. L. *Vaidya*, Etudes sur Āryadeva, p. 34 ff.

The same doctrines are expounded by Nāgārjuna in more concise form in two shorter works, Yuktiṣaśṭikā, "Sixty Arguments,"[1] and Śūnyatā-Saptati, "Seventy Verses on Unreality."[2] The Pratītya-Samutpādahṛdaya treats of the "Secret of the causally dependent origination" in 7 Āryā stanzas.[3] The Mahāyāna Viṃ. śaka[4] is a short philosophical treatise in which it is taught that, from the standpoint of absolute truth, there is neither Saṃsāra nor Nirvāṇa and that everything is mere illusion and dream. The Vigraha-vyāvartanī, which is frequently quoted by Candrakīrti, is a work on logic. In the case of other works which are attributed to Nāgārjuna, it is more or less doubtful whether they are really his. This applies, for instance, to the Dharma-Saṃgraha, which is ascribed to him, and which has come down in Sanskrit.[5]This is a short and very useful glossary of Buddhist technical terms, but it is one which any monk might have compiled.[6]

The Suhṛllekha or "Letter to a Friend,"[7] has a more right-

---

1. Yukti-ṣaṣṭikā, die sechzig Sātze des Negativismus nach der chinesischen Version übersetzt von Phil. *Schaeffer*, Heidelberg 1923 (Materialien zum Buddhismus, 3. Heft). It is extant in Tibetan also.

2. Extant in Tibetan in the Tanjur. The work seems to have been the prototype for Vasubandhu's Paramārtha-Saptati and Īśvarakṛṣṇa's Sāṃkhya-Saptati.

3. Tibetan text with French translation by *La Vallée Poussin* in Boud-dhisme, E'tudes et Materiaux, Theorie des douze causes, Gand 1913, p. 1 22ff.

4. Tibetan and Chinese with English translation, edited by Susumu *Yamaguchi* in EB IV, 56 ff., 160 ff.

5. Edited by Kenjin *Kasawara*, *Max Müller* and H. *Wenzel* (Anecdota Oxoniensia, Aryan Series. Vol. I. Part 5), Oxford 1885. Half the termini of the Dharma-Saṃgraha are also to be found in the *Dharma-Śarīra-Sūtra*, a block-print of which was brought from Idiku by *Grunwdel* and published by H. *Stonner* (SBA 1904, p. 1282 ff.). The Dharma-Saṃgraha has much in common with the Buddhist lexicon Mahā-Vyutpatti (edited by J. P. *Minayeff* in Bibl. Buddhica XIII, 1911), the period and author of which are entirely unknown. As Kaniṣka and Aśvaghoṣa are mentioned, and as allusions to Greek astrology occur in the Mahā-Vyutpatti, the work cannot be earlier than the 3rd or 4th century A. D.; s. F. W. *Thomas* in Ind. Hist. Qu. II, 1926, 501 ff.

6. In the Chinese version the name of the author is not mentioned. *Cf. Kasawara*, Dharma-Saṃgraha Edition, p. 68.

7. The complete title is Ārya-Nāgārjuna-bodhisattva-suhṛllekha. Translated into English, after the Chinese translation of Guṇavarman (424-431

ful claim to be regarded as a work of the great master, though it contains no Mâdhyamika doctrines whatsoever. As a matter of fact, there is nothing in the epistle which could not just as well be in the Pāli Canon, and certain verses coincide word for word with the Dhammapada and similar texts, other verses agreeing with Brahminical sayings. The Chinese piligrim I-tsing praises this work of Nâgârjuna very highly, and reports that in his day it was widely read and memorised in India.[1] The Chinese mention Sātavāhana as the friend, to whom the letter is addressed.[2] Now Sātavāhana is not the name of a king, but the title adopted by the rulers of the Āndhra dynasty, which held sway in Southern India from the middle of the 3rd century B.C. until the beginning of the 3rd century A.D. The first prominent Āndhra sovereign, who called himself Sātavāhana, and who favoured both Brahmins and Buddhists, was Gautamīputra (119-128 A.D.) His successor was Rājā Vāsiṣṭhīputra Śrī Pulumāyi, who reigned over 30 years. In the period which we have assumed for Nāgārjuna, Gautamīputra Yajñaśrī, who reigned in 166-196 A.D., would come into question.[3]

There are no grounds for denying Nāgārjuna the authorship of the commentaries Prajñā-Pāramitā-Sūtra-Śāstra and Daśa-Bhūmi Vībhāṣā-Śāstra.[4] The short treatise Eka-Śloka Śāstra, which has

A.D.), by S. *Bedi* in Ind. Ant. 16, 1887, 169 ff. Other Chinese translations by Saṅghavarman (about 433 A.D.) and by I-tsing (about 700 A.D.); s. *Nanjio* Nos. 1440, 1441; *Bagchi*, I, 375, 377. Translated into English, after the Tibetan verse by H. *Wenzel* in JPTS 1886. p. 1 ff., and into German, Leipzig 1886. The Sanskrit original has not come down.

1. *Cf.* I-tsing, transl. *Takakusu*, p. 158 ff.

2. *Cf.* Hwui Li, The Life of Hiuen-Tasiang, tr. by S. *Beal*, p. 135; Th. *Watters*, on Yuan Chwang's Travels in India, II, 200 f., 206. A legend related by Bāṇa (Harṣacarita, transl. by E. B. *Cowell* and F. W. *Thomas*, London 1897, p. 252) also mentions Sātavāhana as the friend of Nāgārjuna.

3. *Cf.* *Smith*, Early History, p. 221 ff. Max *Walleser* (ZB VI, 96 ff.) makes it seem probable that the statement, according to which in the Tibetan version, Udayana is the king to whom the letter is addressed, is based upon an error. He assumcs (l. c., p. 103) that Vijaya Śri Sātakarṇi, who ascended the throne in 213 A.D., was Nāgārjuna's friend.

4. Both commentaries, as well as the Madhyamika-Śāstra, were translated into Chinesc by Kumārajiva; s. *Bagchi* I, 197 f., 423.

come down only in Chinese, and which sets out to prove that true existence (svabhāva) is non-existence (abhāva), is perhaps rightly ascribed to Nāgārjuna. On the other hand, it is not very likely that the Prajñādaṇḍa,[1] which has come down in Tibetan, a book of 260 sayings, only very few of which are Buddhist at all. and the majority of which merely teach general morality and wisdom, with many an allusion to the fables in the Pañcatantra, was the work of Nāgārjuna.[2]

One of Nāgārjuna's pupils was Deva or Āryadeva also known as Kāṇadeva, "the one-eyed Deva" and Nīlanetra, "the blue-eyed."[3] Hsuan-Tsang relates the following of him : The Bodhisattva Deva came from the land of Siṃhala (Ceylon), in order to discuss the difficulties of the doctrine with Nāgārjuna. He asked a pupil to announce him to the Master. Nāgārjuna sends his begging-bowl out, filled with pure water. Deva throws a needle into it. The pupil takes the bowl back, and Nāgārjuna is much delighted at this "eloquent silence." In reply to the question of his astonished pupil, the master says, that the bowl with the water signified his own pure knowledge ; by throwing the needle in, Deva wanted to say that he has reached the very bottom of this knowledge. Deva is shown in, and approaches the Master very modestly. Nāgārjuna was very well satisfied with the discussion he had with Deva, and as he himself was already old and feeble he appointed him as his successor.[4] Deva's biography was

1. Translated from the Chinese by H. R. Rangaswamy *Iyengar* in the Mysore University Journal for Arts and Science I, 1927, No. 2. A short treatise consisting of 9 Kārikās, entitled Yogāvatāra, is ascribed to Nāgārjuna only in one Sanskrit manuscript, and in the Tibetan version is ascribed to Dignāga;. Vidhushekhara *Bhattacharya* in Ind. Hist. Qu. IV. 1928, 775 ff.

2. Shc-rab Dong-bu or Prajña Daṇḍa by Lu-Trub (Nāgārjuna) edited and translated by Major W. L. *Campbell*, Calcutta 1919.

3. He is said to have been named thus, owing to two blue spots, resembling eyes, on his cheeks. According to the legend, he became one-eyed in the following manner : In order to demonstrate that a golden statue of Maheśvara is not the god himself, he tore out the left eye of the statue; but, in order to show that he had not done this out of pride, he tore out one of his own eyes, when Maheśvara paid him a visit the next day.

4. *Cf.* Hwui Li, The Life of Hiuen-Tsiang, tr. by S. *Beal*, p. 135; Th. *Watters*. On Yuan Chwang's Travels in India, II, 200 ff.

translated into Chinese by Kumārajīva (in about 405 A.D.) together with those of Aśvaghoṣa and Nāgārjuna, and is just as legendary as these last named. Legend has it that he died at the hands of a murderer. The pupil of one of the heretical teachers whom Deva had defeated in disputation, waylaid him and pierced him through with a sword, as he sat in the forest absorbed in meditation. Before his death he instructed the murderer, and restrained his pupils who were about to pursue the murderer, with these words : "Everything is unreal. Reflect upon the true meaning of all things in the world of phenomena. Where is the oppression or cruelty? Who is pierced or murdered ? If you recognise the true nature of all things then there is neither murdered nor murderer. Who is a friend and who is a foe? Who is the murderer and who is the murdered ? "[1] Both Hsuan-Tsang and I-tsing mention Āryadeva along with Aśvaghoṣa and Nāgārjuna, as one of the great men who lived "in ancient times." Most probably he lived at about the turning-point of the second and third centuries A.D.[2]

Many works are ascribed to Āryadeva,[3] His most famous work is Catuḥ-Śataka,[4] which, like the Mādhyamika-Sūtra consists of

---

1. *Cf. Wassiljew,* Der Buddhismus, p. 234 f.; Y. *Sogen,* Systems of Buddhist Thought, p. 187 ff.

2. See above, p. 247. According to Kumārajiva's statements H. Ui, The Vaiśeṣika Philosophy, London, 1917, p. 43, calculates the time of Nāgārjuna between 113 and 213, and that of Deva between 163 and 263, whilst Harivarman, the pupil of Kumāralāta and author of the Satyasiddhi-Śāstra (which has come down only in Chinese) is said to have lived about 260 or 270 A.D.

3. See *Nanjio,* Col. 369 ff.

4. It is often quoted by Candrakīrti, under the title Śataka or Śataka-Śāstra, in the Madhyamaka-Vṛtti. *Cf. La Vallée Poussin* in Le Muséon, N. S. I., 1900, 236 ff. The Catuḥśataka has come down in its entirety in the Tibetan version. Fragments of the Sanskrit original of the text and commentary have been discovered and edited by Haraprasāda *Śāstrī* in Memoirs of the Asiatic Society of Bengal, Vol. III, No. 8, pp. 449-514, Calcutta 1914. Chapter VII with Extracts from the Commentary of Candrakirti, reconstructed from the Tibetan Version, with an English Translation, by Vidhushekhara *Bhattacharya,* in Proc. IV OC, Vol. II, pp. 831-871. L. P. *Vaidya,* Etudes sur Āryadeva et son Catuḥśataka, Paris 1923, p. 69 ff., has reconstructed the Sanskrit text of the last 9 chapters (VIII-XVI), on the basis of the Tibetan version, inasfar as the Sanskrit text was

400 Kārikās. With Candrakīrti's commentary, it belongs to the fundamental works of the Mādhyamika school. Deva defends Nāgārjuna's doctrines not only as against other Buddhist schools, but also against Brahmanical systems, especially the Vaiśeṣikas. The importance of distinguishing between the two kinds of knowledge, is very emphatically brought out by Āryadeva in these verses :

"Love for the religion is prescribed by the Tathāgatas for such as long for heaven ; on the other hand, the highest truth is prescribed for such as seek deliverance.

He who desires to acquire religious merit, cannot always talk of unreality (śūnyatā). Does not a medicine, wrongly used, become a poison ?

Just as one can make a thing clear to a barbarian (mleccha) only if one uses his language, even so one cannot explain anything to the common people unless one uses the common language."[1]

Down to the present day, Nāgārjuna's Mādhyamika-Śāstra together with Āryadeva's Catuḥ-Śataka or Śata-Śāstra and the Dvādaśa-Nikāya-Śāstra, form the ground-work of the faith of the Sanron sect in Japan.[2]

Only fragments have come down to us of the Cittaviśuddhi-Prakaraṇa,[3] "Section of the Purification of the Mind," a didactic poem containing among other things controversial arguments against the Brahmanical ceremonial system. The following is declared against the belief that bathing in the Ganges washes away sins : If salvation could be attained by means of Ganges water,

---

not extant, and has added a French translation (p. 129 ff.). Hsuan-Tsang translated the work into Chinese. A complete Italian translation of the text and commentary, from the Chinese, has been published by G. *Tucci* in Studie materiali di storia delle religioni, 1925. For a comparison of the Chinese text with the Sanskrit original and the Tibetan version, s. *Tucci* in RSO X, 1923, 521 ff.

1. Verses 192-194 in P. L. *Vaidya's* Text.

2. *Cf Nanjio*, Twelve Japanese Buddhist Sects, p. 44 ff.: W. M. *McGovern*, Introduction to Mahāyāna Buddhism. p. 205 ff.

3. Haraprasāda *Śāstrī* has also discovered these fragments, s. JASB 67, 1898, 175 ff.

then fishermen would all attain salvation, and more particularly the fishes, which are in the Ganges day and night. It is doubtful, however, whether this work in its present form, in which Tantric ideas, and expressions for the days of the week (vāra) and the zodiac (rāśi) which were borrowed from Greek astronomy, occur, can be ascribed to the ancient Āryadeva.[1]

There are in the Chinese Tripiṭaka two short treatises translated by Bodhiruci (508-535), which are ascribed to Āryadeva, and which constitute a kind of commentary on those sections of the Laṅkāvatāra which deal with heretical doctrines of Nirvāṇa.[2] There is another short treatise by Āryadeva the Hastavāla-Prakaraṇa or Muṣṭi-Prakaraṇa, the Sanskrit text of which W. F. Thomas has endeavoured to reconstruct on the basis of the Chinese and Tibetan translations.[3] In this work it is taught, in 5 memorial verses, that all phenomena are mere illusion, and a sixth verse explains the distinction between the two truths.

Hitherto it has usually been thought that the founder of the Yogācāra school of Mahāyāna Buddhism was Asaṅga or Āryasaṅga. It is now, however, probable that the tradition according to which several of his works are supposed to have been revealed to Asaṅga by the future Buddha Maitreya in the Tuṣita heaven, rests upon the fact that Maitreyanātha, briefly called Maitreya, was a historical personage, the teacher of Asaṅga, and the real founder of the Yogācāra school.[4] This

---

1. *Cf. La Vallée Poussin*, Bouddhisme. p. 383, note I and Haraprasāda *Śāstri* in Ind. Hist. Qu. 1, 1925, p. 464 : "The book has been revised by another Āryadeva in later times, for at the end are mentioned images not known in the great Āryadeva's time, and there was one Āryadeva in Bengal who wrote also in Bengali." For this reason it is impossible to deduce from this work the chronological data, which were deduced by H. *Jacobi*. JAOS 31, 1910, p. 2. See also La Vallée Poussin in BSOS VI, 2 (1931), p. 411 ff.

2. Nanjio, Nos. 1259, 1260. *Cf.* G. *Tucci* in Toung Pao, 2 série, Vol. XXIV, 1926, p. 16 ff.

3. JRAS, 1918, 267 ff. The Chinese translations, which were used by *Thomas*, of Paramārtha and I-tsing (*Nanjio*, Nos. 1255, 1256) are here published by H. *Ui*. Dignāga seems to be the author of the commentary on the Kārikās, for which reason the whole work appears among the works of Dignāga.

4. The Tibetan Bu-ston, in his "History of Religion," ascribes 5 Śāstras to Maitreya : (1) Sūtrālaṃkāra in 7 chapters, (2) Madhyānta-Vibhaṅga,

school teaches the Vijñānavāda, *i.e.* that nothing exists outside consciousness. Thus, like the Śūnyavāda, it denies the reality of the world of phenomena, but yet, in a certain sense, recognises an existence contained in thought and consciousness. The sole Absolute, however, which embraces this consciousness which in its turn includes in itself all psychic processes (ālayavijñāna), is Bodhi. the one and only truth, which is *one*, though revealed in the endless multiplicity of the Buddhas. But this Bodhi is only attainable to the Yogācāra, *i.e.* to him who practises Yoga, and even to him only in stages, after he has gone through all the ten stages (daśabhūmi) of the career of a Bodhisattva. The practice of Yoga which, in Hīnayāna Buddhism also, plays no unimportant part,[1] is here associated systematically with Mahāyāna Buddhism.[2]

At all events, the Abhisamayālaṃkāra-Kārikās, also known as the Prajñā-Pāramitopadeśa-Śāstra, are certainly the work of Maitreyanātha. The text is usually to be found at the beginning of the manuscripts of the Pañcaviṃśatisāhasrikā-

---

(3) Dharma-Dharmatā-Vibhaṅga, (4) Mahāyāna-Uttaratantra-Śāstra, and (5) Abhisamayālaṃkāra-Kārikā. He ascribes to Asaṅga the three works Pañcabhūmi, Abhidharma-Samuccaya and Mahāyāna-Saṃgraha s. *Stcherbatsky* in Le Muséon, N. S., VI, 1905, 144 f. In the Chinese Tripiṭaka a whole series of works is ascribed to Maitreya, s. *Nanjio,* col. 368. It is true that the tradition that Asaṅga received the revelation from Maitreya in the Tuṣita heaven, was already taken to China by Paramārtha (499-569), and was believed by Dharmapāla (528-560), Prabhākaramitra (630-632), who translated the Mahāyāna-Sūtrālaṃkāra-Śāstra into Chinese, as well as by Hsuan-Tsang and I-tsing. However, see below, p. 341, note 2.

1. For instance, the Manual of a Mystic being a Translation from the Pāli and Sinhalese work entitled the Yogācāra's Manual, by F. L. *Woodward,* ed. by Mrs. *Rhys Davids,* London, PTS 1916, is a Hīnayāna manual of Yoga.

2. On the teachings of the Yogācāra school or the school of the Yogācāryas, *cf. La Vallée Poussin,* Boddhisme, p. 200 ff. D. T. *Suzuki,* Outlines of Mahāyāna Buddhism, London 1907, pp. 60 ff., 125 ff.; S. *Lévi* in the introduction to his translation of the Mahāyāna-Sūtrālaṃkāra; Y. *Sogen,* Systems of Buddhistic Thought, p. 210 ff.; Otto *Rosenberg,* Die Probleme der buddhistischen Philosophie, Heidelberg 1924 (Materialien zur Kunde des Buddhismus 8), p. 235 f.; J. *Masuda,* Der individualistische Idealismus der Yogācāra Schule (matrialien zur Kunde des Buddhismus 10), Heidelberg 1928. Th. *Stcherbatsky,* The Conception of Buddhist Nirvāṇa, p. 31 ff.

Prajñā-Pāramitā, which was translated into Chinese between 261 and 316 A.D.[1] In all probability, the text of the Mahāyāna-Sūtrālaṃkāra, which is composed of memorial verses (Kārikās), which was discovered by S. Levi and attributed to Asaṅga by the same scholar, is also the work of Maitreyanātha.[2] Without being a great poet, the author of these memorial verses certainly has the art of writing Buddhist Sanskrit skilfully, and also of utilising elaborate metres side by side with Ślokas and Āryā stanzas. However, he is decidedly more of a philosopher than a poet. Even when, in the last two chapters he glorifies the perfections of the Buddhas, and concludes with a hymn (verses 43-61) there is more erudition than enthusiastic worship in the enumeration of all the perfections of the Buddhas. Only in Chapter IX, in which Maitreyanātha expends all his mental energy in elucidating the conception of Bodhi and Buddhahood, is the dry-as-dust tone occasionally enlivened and elevated by more imaginative and picturesque language. Thus, for instance, Bodhi, by

---

1. *Cf.* Haraprasāda *Śāstrī* in JASB 1910, p. 425 ff., and Descriptive Catalogue of Sanskrit MSS . . . Asiatic Society of Bengal 1, 1917, p. 7 ff. The section on Trikāya in Chapt. VI of the Abhisamayālaṃkāra with commentary, translated into French by P. *Masson Oursel* in JA, II ser., I, 1913, p. 598 ff. S. *Levi* (Rapport sur la mission dans l'Inde et au Japon en Comptes Rendus de l'Academic des inscr. et belles lettres, Paris 1899. p. 83) mentions a commentary by Haribhadra (10th century) on the Abhisamayālaṃkāra. However, according to Haraprasāda *Śāstrī* (JBORS 5, 1919, 176 f.), the monk Haribhadra, who lived under Dharmapāla, the second king of the Pāla dynasty, is the author of the commentary Abhisamayālaṃkārāvaloka on the Aṣṭasāhasrikā-Prajñā-Pāramitā.

2. Asaṅga, Mahāyāna-Sūtrālaṃkāra, Expose de la doctrine du grand vehicule selon le systéme Yogācāra, Edité et traduit par Sylvain *Lévi* t. II (Bibliothequc de l'Ecole des hautes études, t, 159, 190), Paris 1907, 1911. On the style and contents of the work, *cf.* St. *Schayer* in ZII 2, 1923, 99 ff. H. *Ui* (ZII 6, 1928, 215 ff.) has made it seem very probable that Maitreyanātha, and not Asaṅga, was the author of the Mahāyāna-Sūtrālaṃkāra; even previously, Haraprasāda *Śāsirī* (Ind. Hist. Qu. I, 1925, 465 f.) had declared Maitreyanātha to be the founder of the Yogācāra school, and placed him between 150 and 265 A.D. In the work itself Asaṅga is not mentioned as the author, but it is described as being "proclaimed by the Bodhisattva Vyavadātasamaya ('Purifier of the doctrine'). This might be an epithet of Asaṅga just as well as of Maitreyanātha. According to S. *Levi* both the Kārikās and the commentary are the work of Asaṅga. H. *Ui* (l. c., 220 ff.) shows that Vasubandhu is the author of the commentary.

which the Buddhas enlighten the world, is compared with the sun, in a series of metaphors (IX, 20 ff.).

The Yogācāra-Bhūmi-Śāstra or Saptadaśa-Bhūmi-Śāstra, too, of which only a portion, the Bodhisattva-Bhūmi,[1] has come down in Sanskrit, is among the works which are supposed to have been revealed to Asaṅga by the mythical Maitreya : probably, however, it is one of Maitreyanātha's works. It is a prose work after the style of the Abhidharma texts. The Bodhisattva-Bhūmi "The Bodhisattva step," is the fifteenth of the seventeen steps taught in this large work: the last step is that in which no trace of the Karman remains.[2]

The Tibetans attribute the Yogācāra-Bhūmi-Śāstra to Asaṅga Hsuan-Tsang, too, who took Asaṅga's work to China, appears to have regarded it as a work of this master. At all events the name of Asaṅga[3] as the teacher of the YogācāraVijñānavāda has become more famous than that of his teacher Maitreyanātha. It is true that his works have only come down in Chinese translations : Mahāyāna-Samparigraha, translated by Paramārtha (563 A.D.),[4] Prakaraṇa-Āryavācā, Mahāyānā bhidharma-Saṃgīti-Śāstra, translated by Hsuan-Tsang (625 A.D.),[5] and a commentary on the Vajracchedikā translated by Dharmagupta 590-616 (A.D.).[6]

---

1. Bodhisattvabhūmi, a text-Book of the Yogācāra School; an English Summary with Notes etc., by C. *Bendall* and L. *de La Vallée Poussin*, Le Muséon, N. S. VI, 1905, p. 38 ff., VII, 1906, p. 213 ff.; XII, 1911, p. 155 ff.; Unrai *Wogihara*, Asaṅga's Bodhisattvabhūmi, Strassburger Diss. Leipzig 1908. The text of the Bodhisattvabhūmi is also edited by J. *Rahder* in the Appendix to the edition of the Daśabhūmi-Sūtra (1926). *Cf.* also U. *Wogihara* in ZDMG 58, 1904, 451 ff. On Yogācārya and Yogācāra-Bhūmi's. *Ui*, l..c., p. 224 f.

2. *Cf.* E. *Leumann* in ZDMG 62, 1908, p. 89 ff.

3. About him, *cf.* M. *Anesaki* in ERE II, 62; *Wogihara*, l, c.; *Levi* in the introduction to the Mahāyāna-Sūtrālaṃkāra; N. *Péri*, A propos de la date de Vasubandhu, p. 31 ff.; *Winternitz* in WZKM 27, 1913, 33 ff.

4. It is the principal work of the Shōron sect in Japan; s. *McGovern*, Introduction to Mahāyāna Buddhism, p. 209.

5. *Nanjio*, No. 1199.

6. *Nanjio*, No. 1168; *Bagchi* I, 258.

Asaṅga,more properly Vasubandhu Asaṅga, is the eldest of three brothers, who were born as the sons of a Brahmin of the Kauśika family in Puruṣapura (the present-day Peshawar) in the extreme North-West of India. They probably lived in the 4th century[1] and were all three originally adherents of the Sarvāstivāda school. The youngest, Vasubandhu Virincivatsa was not prominent in literature. So much the more important was the middle one of the three brothers, Vasubandhu, one of the most prominent figures in the history of Buddhist literature.[2]

1. N. *Péri*, A propos de la date de Vasubandhu (BEFEO XI, 1911, Nos. 3-4) has adduced sound arguments in favour of Vasubandhu's having lived in the 4th century A.D.
J. *Takakusu* (JRAS 1905, 33 ff.) had placed Vasubandhu between 420 and 500 A.D., but stated later (JRAS 1914, p. 1013 ff.)' without definitely going over to *Péri's* side, that he was inclined to assume that Vasubandhu lived earlier. *Wogihara* (Asaṅga's Bodhisattva bhūmi, p. 16) places Vasubandhu between 390 and 470, and Asaṅga between 375 and 450, but in ERE XII, 1921, 595f., he states 420-500 as the period of Vasubandhu's life. *Lèvi* places Asaṅga's activity in the first half of the 5th century. It appears, however, that there were two Vasubandhus, both of whom dealt with Abhidharma and the elder of whom was the teacher and the younger the pupil of Manoratha. This view was supported by sound arguments in great detail, as early as the year 1922, by the Japanese scholar T. *Kimura* when he visited Prague, and also in a long letter. However, one cannot be fully in agreement with his grounds for assigning the dates 420-500 A.D., to the later Vasubandhu, the author of the Abhidharmakośa. Cf. *Watters*, On Yuan Chwang's Travels in India, I, 211 ff.; *La Vallée Poussin*, Bouddhisme, Etudes et Materiaux, Cosmologie, p. viii ff. and Abhidharmakośa, traduit et annoté, I, p. 26 (note to I, 13), II, p. 70 (note to III, 27), III, p. 7 (note to IV, 3); *Stcherbatsky*. The Central Conception of Buddhism, p. 2, note 2. According to K. B. *Pathak* (Ind. Ant. 41, 1912, 244) Vasubandhu lived under Kumāragupta; and Skandagupta; the monk Buddhamitra, who is mentioned in an inscription, is identified by him with Vasubandhu's teacher, who, according to Paramārtha, was called Buddhamitra. *Smith*, Early History, pp. 320, note 2, 325, 346 f., agrees with N. *Péri*, and places the life-time of Vasubandhu, the author of the Kośa, in the period of the reign of Candragupta I and Samudra gupta (about 280-360 A.D.). Hsüan-Tsang says that the Abhidharmakośa was written during the reign of Vikramāditya or his son Bālāditya s. *Watters* 1, 210.

2. *I-tsing* (transl. *Takakusu*, p. 181) classes Asaṅga and Vasubandhu among the celebrated men of the "middle ages," *i.e.* the period between the time of Aśvaghoṣa, Nāgārjuna and Āryadeva on the one hand, and his own

He combined great independence of thought with astonishing erudition. His chief work, the Abhidharmakośa has unfortunately not come down in the Sanskrit original. We only know the Abhidharmakośa-Vyākhyā, Yaśomitra's commentary on the work,[1] and on the other hand the Chinese and Tibetan versions. The earliest Chinese translation is that of Paramārtha, written between 563 and 567 A.D. A second translation (651-654 A.D.) is by the celebrated Hsuan-Tsang. The Abhidharmakośa treats, in 600 memorial verses (Kārikās) together with the author's own commentary (Bhāṣya), of the entire field of ontology, psychology, cosmology,[2] ethics and the doctrine of salvation. The last chapter, which is given either as Chapter IX or as an appendix to Chapter VIII, and which is not composed of memorial verses, treats of the Buddhist doctrine of the soul (denial

time on the other. The Indian monk *Paramārtha* (499-569 A. D.) compiled a biography of Vasubandhu, in which that of his brother Asaṅga is also included. It has been translated from the Chinese by J. *Takakusu* in T'oung Pao V, 1904, pp. 1 ff.; given in extracts by W. *Wassiljew*, Der Buddhismus, p. 235 ff. Still more fabulous than the Chinese is the Tibetan biography in *Tāranātha's* History of Buddhism, p. 107 ff. Paramārtha took the works of Asaṅga and Vasubandhu from Magadha to China in the year 539. Hsūan-Hūsan-Tsang, too (s. *Watters* I, 354 ff.), relates legends of Asaṅga and Vasubandhu.

1. Sphuṭārthā Abhidharmakośavyākhyā, the Work of Yaśomitra First Kośasthāna, ed. by S. *Levi* and Th. *Stcherbatsky*, Bibl. Buddhica XXI, 1918. L. *de La Vallée Poussin* has translated the Sanskrit text of Yaśomitr's Vyākhyā making use of the Tibetan version of. Vasubandhu's own commentary and the Chinese versions by Paramārtha and Hsūan-Tsang, into French : L Abhidharmakośa de Vasubandhu traduit et annoté, hitherto 5 vols., Par' 1923-1926. *Cf.* also *Burnouf*, Introduction, pp. 397 ff., 502ff.; Rāj. *Mitra* Nep. Buddh. Lit., p. 3ff.; *Bendall*, Catalogue. p. 25 ff.; S. *Lévi* in ERE I, p. 20; *La Vallée Poussin* in ERE IV, p. 129 ff.

2. Chapter III, which deals with cosmology, has already been rconstructed in Sanskrit, and translated into French, by *La Vallee Poussin* in Bouddhisme Etudes et Matériaux, Cosmologie : Le Monde des Etres et le Monde-Réceptacle (Memoires del' Academie Roy. de Belgique, classe de lettres, etc., II serie, t. VI, 1914-1919) according to the Tibetan version. In the appendix to this work, *La Vallée Poussin* gives an analysis of the extant fragments of the Prajñapti-Śāstra (Lokaprajñapti and Kāraṇaprajñapti) by Maudgalyāyana, belonging to the Abhidharma of the Sarvāstivādins. *Cf.* also *La Vallee Poussin* in ERE IV. 129 ff.

of a permanent soul), and is directed against the Pudgalavādins, those who believe in a permanent soul.[1] Though the Abhidharmakoṣa is written from the standpoint of the Sarvāstivāda school of the Hīnayāna, it is nevertheless an authority for *all* schools of Buddhism. We can learn far more from the Kośa with its commentary, about the dogmatics of the ancient Buddhist schools, than from any other work, and it affords us a sidelight upon the debates between the Vaibhāṣikas and the Sautrāntikas. Moreover, the work is rich in quotations from the earlier literature.[2] In the 7th century the Abhidharmakośa was so widely read in India that, in a description of a hermitage of Buddhist monks, Bāṇa says that the parrots explained the Kośa to one another.[3] This work gave rise to an extensive literature of commentaries, and in China and Japan it is largely used as a text-book. It is also the final authority, when controversies regarding points of dogma arise.[4]

There is a book of sayings, thoroughly Hīnayānist in character, extant only in Tibetan and ascribed to Vasubandhu, called the Gāthā-Saṃgraha, with a brilliant commentary, from which

---

1. It has been translated from the Tibetan by Th. *Stcherbatsky*, The Soul Theory of the Buddhists, in Bulletin de l'Academie des Sciences de Russie, Petrograd 1919, pp 824ff., 937 ff. The Pudgalavādins are here called Vātsīputrīyas

2. Some passages from the Abhidharmakośa-Vyākhyā have been compared with corresponding passages in the Pāli Canon, by *La Vallée Poussin* (JRAS 1906, p. 443 ff.) *La Valle Poussin's* book, La moral bouddhique, Paris 1927, is based largely upon the Abhidharmakośa. *Cf.* also Y. *Sogen*, Systems of Buddhistic Thought, pp. 109 ff.

3. Harṣacarita VIII; s. Harṣacarita transl. by E. B, *Cowell* and F.W. *Thomas*, p. 236.

4. *Cf. O. Rosenberg*, Die Probleme der buddhistischen Philosophie, pp. xv, 37 ff., 41. 93. Hwui Li (The Life of Hiuen-Tsiang, transl. by S. *Beal*, p. 80) says of Vasubandhu : "His deep reasoning and ornate style were the admiration of all Western students. The very spirits and demons also studied and followed his teaching." Hwui Li (loc. cit., p. 79f.) also reports : The Kashmiri Saṅghabhadra wrote a Kośa-Kārikā-Śāstra in 25,000 Ślokas and 80 myriads of words. He died before he could) have the meeting with Vasubandhu which he had desired. However, when later on, Vasubandhu became acquainted with Saṅghabhadra's work, he praised it highly, and said it should be called the Nyāyānusāra-Śāstra, because it was in such close agreement with his own teachings.

A. Schiefner[1] has given a few specimens. The 24 Gāthās are sayings in the true manner of the Dhammapada. Provided that the work is correctly ascribed to him, the commentary shows us the philosopher Vasubandhu also as a humorous preacher. Merely a short specimen of this :

"A jackal followed a lion, because he desired the remains of the meat which the lion had devoured. As the lion had once, when he was hungry, slain a great boar, he told the jackal to carry this load. Now as the jackal was too feeble, and could not carry this load, but was afraid that the lion might in wrath, kill him, he had no pleasure in complying with the lion's request But as he knew the lion was proud, he said : 'It is needful to do two things in carrying this load, to groan and to bear the burden; I cannot do both at the same time, you will have to undertake one of them.' As the lion was proud and did not want to groan, he asked the jackal to groan, while he could carry the load himself. So the lion carried the load, but the jackal followed the lion, groaning. In the same way I also bear the burden of presenting the doctrine, but you are not able to say, in agreement with me, 'It is so.' "[2]

In the Abhidharmakośa already, Vasubandhu adduces many arguments against the teachings of Brahmanical philosophy, and he attacks the Vaiśeṣikas in particular. He wrote an especial work in order to refute the Sāṃkhya philosophy, the Paramārtha-Saptati, "Seventy (verses) on the Highest Truth," This work, the Sanskrit original of which is lost also, seems to be a confutation of Īśvarakṛṣṇa's Sāṃkhya-Saptati, though Paramārtha speaks of a heretic Vindhyavāsa as the author of the Sāṃkhya work attacked by Vasubandhu. Strange to say, the Chinese also ascribe a commentary on Īśvarakṛṣṇa's work to Vasubandhu.[3]

---

1. Über Vasubandhu's Gāthā-Saṃgraha, Mélanges asiatiques VIII (Bulletin, t XXV, St. Petersburg 1878), p. 559 ff.

2. *Schiefner, loc. cit.*, p. 582.

3. See *Takakusu* in Toung Pao 1904, pp. 15 ff., 461 ff., BEFEO. t. IV, 1904, p. 1 ff.: JRAS 1905, p. 16 ff *Takakusu's* assumption that Vindhyavāsa is another name for Īśvarakṛṣṇa is not tenable, see S. N. *Dasgupta,* History of Indian Philosophy, I, Cambridge 1922, p. 218, note 3.

It was not until the latter part of his life that Vasubandhu was converted to the Mahāyāna by his brother Asaṅga. Now, as his biographer relates, he regretted his former calumniation of the Mahāyāna so deeply that he wanted to cut off his tongue. But his brother demonstrated to him that it would be a much better penance if he would now employ his tongue, which he had formerly employed in attacking the Mahāyāna doctrine, with equal skill in expounding the Mahāyāna. Vasubandhu did this, and after the death of Asaṅga, wrote a large number of commentaries on Mahāyāna-Sūtras, on the Saddharma-Puṇḍarīka,[1] the Mahā-Parinirvāṇa-Sūtra[2] and the Vajracchedikā-Prajñā-Pāramitā.[3] It was at this time that he also wrote the two classical treatises on idealism, the Viṃśatikā and Triṃśikā,[4] in which in a subtle manner he refutes the belief in the reality of the objective world, but defends the doctrine of the reality of pure consciousness (Vijñānamātra). The Tibetan-Bu-ston also mentions the following works of Vasubandhu: Pañcaskandha-Prakaraṇa, Vyākhyāyukti, Karma-Siddhi-Prakaraṇa and commentaries on Maitreya's Mahāyāna-Sūtrālaṃkāra, on the Pratītya

1. Translated into Chinese between 508 and 535, s. *Nanjio*, Nos. 1232; 1233; *Bagchi* I, 250, 258.

2. Translated between 386 and 550, s. *Nanjio* Nos. 1206, 1207.

3. Translated between 386 and 534s. *Nanjio*, No. 1231.

4. The Sanskrit originals of these two treatises the Viṃśatikā with the author's commentary, and the Triṃśikā with Sthiramati's commentary, were discovered by S. *Lévi* and edited by him for the first time : Vijñaptimātratā siddhi, deux traités de Vasubandhu, Viṃśatikā et Triṃśikā, Paris 1925 (Bibliotheque de l' Ecole des hautes etudes, sc. hist. et phil. 245). The Viṃśatikā with the author's commentary has been translated into French from the Tibetan, by *La Vallée Poussin* (Le Muséon 1912, pp. 53-90). A good idea of the subject-matter of these two important philosophical treatises, is given by Surendra Nath *Dasgupta* in Ind. Hist. Qu. IV, 1928, p. 36ff. There were as many as ten different commentaries on the Vijñapti-matratā-triṃśat-kārikā in India : these were translated by Hsūan-Tsang, who afterwards melted them down to *one* work with Dharmapāla's commentary Vijñapti-mātratā-siddhi-Śāstra. Dharmapāla was the teacher of Hsüan-Tsang's teacher. *Cf.* H. Ui, The Vaiśeṣika Philosophy, London, OTF, 1917, p. 2, and L. de *La Vallée Poussin*, Vijñapti. mātratāsiddhi La Siddhi de Hiuan Tsang, Paris, 1928.

Samutpāda-Sūt~a and the Madhyanta-Vibhāga. Towards[1] the end of his life he said to have become a devotee of Amitābha and to have written a work entitled Aparimitāyus-Sūtropadeśa, in which he gave expression to the longing for Sukhāvatī.[2] Paramārtha concludes his biography of Vasubandhu with these words :

"The sense conveyed in his compositions is fine and excellent; there is no one who, on hearing or seeing it, does not believe and pursue it. Therefore all those who study the Mahāyāna and Hīnayāna in India and in all the frontier countries use the works of Vasubandhu as their text-books. There are no teachers of any other schools (of Buddhism) or of the heretical sects who, on hearing his name, will not become quite nervous and timid. He died in A-yu-ja (Ayodhyā) at the age of eighty. Though he lived an earthly life, his real nature is indeed difficult to be understood."[3]

A work which attempted a synthesis of the teachings of the Mādhyamika and Vijñānavāda schools, is the Mahāyāna-Śraddhotpāda, "The Origin of the Mahāyāna Faith." It is attributed to Aśvaghoṣa, but cannot possibly have been written by the poet of the Buddhacarita. It must remain an open question whether it was attributed to the great poet with a view to securing a greater reputation for the book, or whether there was an Aśvaghoṣa II in about the 5th century A.D., who wrote this philosophical work, which gives evidence of an advanced stage of development of Mahāyāna philosophy.[4] The work has come down only in two

1. See *Stcherbatsky* in Le Musśon, N.S. VI, 1905, 144 ff. According to G. *Tucci* (Ind. Hist. Qu. IV, 1928, 630 ff.) the Vādavidhi, which others ascribe to Dignāga, is also a work of Vasubandhu.

2. *Cf.* U. *Wogihara* in ERE, XII, 596.

3. J. *Takakusu*, The Life of Vasubandhu by Paramārtha (A.D. 499-569). Extrait du "T'oung-pao," 1904, p. 27.

4. In the year 1912 Prof. *Takakusu* said : "Either the poet Aśvaghoṣa is different from the philosopher Aśvaghoṣa (for Buddhists generally believe there were more than one Aśvaghoṣa) or that Śāstra of a different origin has been attributed to him simply because of his great renown. I think the latter is the

Chinese versions, one by Paramārtha (about 553 A.D.) and one by Śikṣānanda (about 700 A.D.).[1] It is entirely unknown in Sanskrit, and is not quoted either by the great masters of the Mahāyāna or their commentators. In a biography of Hsüan-Tsang, the Mahāyāna-Śraddhotpāda is ascribed to the celebrated Aśvaghoṣa, but it is said that Hsüan-Tsang translated it *from Chinese into Sanskrit*, and thus propagated it throughout the five empires of India.[2] Even at the present day the work is much studied in the schools and monasteries of Japan and it is a favourite work of reference.

Buddhapālita and Bhāvaviveka (or Bhavya).[3] who belong to the school of Nāgarjuna and Āryadeva and wrote commentaries on their works, lived and worked at the beginning of the 5th century A.D. Buddhapālita is the founder of the Prāsaṅgika school, which followed the method of leading an opponent *ad absurdum*, whilst Bhāvaviveka founded the Svātantra school, which seeks to prove the correctness of the Mādhyamika doctrines by means

---

case, *for an earlier Catalogue of Chinese texts omits the name Aśvaghoṣa.* In any case the Mahāyāna-Śraddhotpāda does not belong to him. Nor do the contents show any probability of his authorship. It is later than Laṅkāvatāra in which Nāgārjuna's appearance is prophesied by Buddha, and only a step earlier than Vijñānamātravāda." R. *Kimura,* Hīnayāna and Mahāyāna, Calcutta, 1927, pp. 41, 180 ff., is inclined to attribute the work to the beginning of the 5th century A.D. On the doctrines of the Mahāyāna-Śraddhotpāda, cf. Y. *Sogen,* Systems of Buddhistic Thought, p. 252 ff.: S. N. *Dasgupta* History of Indian Philosophy, I, 129ff.; K. J. *Saunders,* Epochs in Buddhist History, p. 97 ff.; *Stcherbatsky,* Nirvāṇa, p. 32; *McGovern,* Introduction to Mahāyāna Buddhism p. 60 ff.

1. It has been translated into English, after the second Chinese version, by *Teitaro Suzuki,* Aśvagoṣa's Discourse on the Awakening of Faith in the Mahāyāna, Chicago, 1900. *Suzuki* regards the poet Aśvaghoṣa as the author. It has been translated into English. after Paramārtha's Chinese version, by Timothy *Richard,* The New Testament of Higher Buddhism, pp. 37-125. On the Chinese translations. s. *Suzuki* l.c., p. 38ff., and *Bagchi,* I, 423.

2. *Cf.* JN. *nobel,* Kumārajīva, in SBA, 1927, p. 231, note. This account would speak in favour of the view, held by a few Japanese scholars, especially *Senshoi Murakami,* that the Mahāyāna-Śraddhotpāda is a Chinese, and not a Sanskrit work. There was a heated controversy on this question in Japan's EB I, 1921, pp. 88, 103 ff.

3. *Cf.* P. L. *Vaidya,* Etudes sur Āryadeva, p. 26 ff.; *Stcherbatsky,* Nirvāṇa, p. 66 f.

of independent (svatantra) arguments. Their works have come down only in Tibetan translations.

In the 5th century A.D. there lived Sthiramati[1] Dignāga (or Diṅnāga), and somewhat younger Dharmapāla, teachers who arose from Vasubandhu's school. Sthiramati wrote a commentary on the Kāśyapa-Parivarta, or Ratnakūṭa,[2] and on Vasubandhu's Triṃśikā. Dharmapāla wrote a commentary on the Vijñaptimātratā-Siddhi. The greatest and most independent thinker among the successors of Vasubandhu is Dignāga, the founder of Buddhist logic, and one of the foremost figures in the history of Indian Philosophy.[3] Only *a single one* of Dignāga's works, the Nyāyapraveśa, has come down in Sanskrit ; we know the others only from the Tibetan translations.[4] The principal works of his successor Dharmakīrti,[5] the Nyāyabindu, has come down to us in Sanskrit.

---

1. The question of the date of Sthiramati is very complicated, and it is probable that there was more than one author of this name. One Sthiramati was a pupil of Guṇamati, and lived before 425 A.D. *Cf.* N. *Péri*, La date de Vasubandhu, Extrait du BEFEO 1911, p. 46ff.; H Uite In ZII 6, 1928, p. 218f.; and A. V. *Stael-Holstein*, The Kāśyapaparivarta, p. xvif.

2. Extant in Chinese and Tibetan translations, s. A. V. *Staël-Holstein*, l.c., p. xiv f.

3. According to Tāranātha, Dignāga was a pupil of Vasubandhu. Works by him were translated into Chinese in 557 and 569 A.D. *Randle*, Fragments from Diṅnāga, p. 3, says : "All that can be said with eertainty is that he lived somewhere between 350 A.D. and 500 A.D." *Cf.* Th. *Waters*. On Yuan Chwang's Travels in India, 11, 209ff.; *Keith*, Buddhist Philosophy, p. 305ff. and *Stcherbatsky*, Nirvāṇa, p. 35. Translations of Dignāga's works on logic are to appear shortly, by Prof. *Stcherbatsky*, who wrote about it on 26th April, 1929 : "You will be astonished to find among the Indians, especially Dignāga, a comprehensive system of critical philosophy. It has long been my conviction that we have before us a most excellent achievement of the Indian mind, this conviction has now grown stronger than ever before, and I hope to be in a position to present it clearly.'

4. The Tibetan text of the Nyāyapraveśa is edited by Vidhusekhara *Bhattāchārya* in GOS No. XXXIX, Baroda, 1927. The Sanskrit text is to be edited by A.B. *Dhruva* in GOS. The Sanskrit fragments which aɹe available in quotations have been collected and translated by H. N. *Randle*, Fragments from Diṅnāga, London 1926. The Nyāya praveśa has also been edited by N.D. Mironov in T'oung Pao, 1931, pp. 1-24.

5. *Cf. Keith*, Buddhist Philosophy, p. 308ff. The trio Nāgārjuna, Āryadeva and Asaṅga, together with the trio Vasubandhu, Dignāga and Dharmakīrti, are called by the Tibetans "the six ornaments of Jambudvīpa,. s.

One of Dharmapāla's pupils is Candrakīrti, who must accordingly have lived in the 6th century, and not, as is usually taken for granted,[1] in the 7th. According to Tāranātha, he was born in Southern India at Samanta, even in childhood showed great intellectual gifts, entered the monastic order, studied all the Piṭakas, and began to study the works of Nāgārjuna under Kamalabuddhi, the pupil of Buddhapālita and Bhavya. After completing his studies, he lived as a Pandit in Nālandā, and wrote numerous works on Mādhyamika philosophy. He is the principal representative of the Prāsaṅgika school, and carried on the work of Nāgārjuna and Āryadeva.[2] His chief work is the Madhyamakāvatāra, "Introduction to the Middle Doctrine," which has come down to us in the Tibetan Tanjur.[3] Candrakīrti frequently refers to this work of his own, in the abovementioned commentary Prasannapadā on the Mūla-Madhyamaka-Kārikās. In this commentary he gives evidence of exceptional erudition, in the numerous quotations, which are very important for us, because many of the texts which he cites, have not come down to us in Sanskrit. Candrakīrti is not only a learned scholastic, but a good writer as well. The numerous verse quotations, which occur especially frequently at the end of a chapter, put life into the narration. His commentary on Āryadeva's Catuḥśatikā is a work of even greater literary merit. In this treatise, the presentation of the dogmas and philosophical doctrines is continually flavoured by means of examples, comparisons and parables.[4]

For instance, the fact that there are more causes for grief than for joy is explained in the following way: "It is just like the wooing of a princess who holds a self-choice of a husband (svayaṁvara).

Grünwedel, Mythologie des Buddhismus in Tibet, p. 36. Dignāga and Dharmakīrti more properly belong to the history of secular philosophy; for further information on them, see Vol. III.

1. *Cf.* P. L. *Vaidya*, Etudes sur Āryadeva, 52. ff

2. *Stcherbatsky*, Nirvāṇa, p. 66, describes him "as a mighty champion of the purely negative method of establishing Monism."

3. The Tibetan text edited in Bibl. Buddhica, IX, 1912, by L. *de La Vallée Poussin*, and translated by the same scholar in Le Museon, N.S. VIII, 1907; XI, 1910; XII, 1911. *Cf.* also Le Muséon, I, 1900, 226 ff.

4. Similarly Book IV of the Sāṃkhya-Sütra contains a whole collection of "little stories" (Ākhyāyikās).

The many who come to woo her, suffer grief; for she is the cause of joy to *one* only, not for all. Though many desire her, they do not win her, hence they are unhappy."

In order to explain that there is nothing which is impure in itself, the following is related: An astrologer declared to a certain king, that rain would fall, and that everyone who used this rain-water, would become mad. Then the king had his own well closed. The rain fell all the people used the water, and became mad. As they were all mad, they all thought that they were all sane, and only the king was considered to be mad. When the king saw how things were, he too used that water, so that the people should not think him mad, laugh at him, or even kill him.

Another example: If only *one* person in the world were to pass urine, he would be avoided as one avoids a leper. But as all people pass urine, it does not occur to anyone to see anything unclean in it.[1]

A contemporary and opponent of Candrakīrti whose teachings he refuted, was Candragomin, who enjoys an immense reputation in the Buddhist world as a grammarian, philosopher and poet. According to Tāranātha,[2] who has much that is legendary to relate of him, he composed an enormous number of hymns and learned works. Of his poetical works we have only a religious poem in the form of a letter to his pupil, the *Siṣyalekhā-Dharma-Kāvya*.[3] Buddhist doctrines are here presented in elegant Kāvya style. His drama Lokānanda has come down to us only in the Tibetan version in the Tanjur.[4]

---

1. Catuḥśatikā by Ārya Deva edited by Haraprasāda *Śāstri*, pp. 458, 459.

2. Geschichte des Buddhismus, p. 156 ff.

3. Edited by I. P. *Minayeff* in Zapiski IV; *cf.* H. *Wanzel*, JRAS, 1889, p. 1133 ff; *Bendall*, Catalogue, p. 31 f.; *Kern*, Manual, p. 11.

4. I-tsing (Record, transl. by J. *Takakusu*, pp. 164, 183) speaks of a Candra or Candradāsa, who was a holy man, a kind of Bodhisattva, who composed a musical play about Prince Viśvāntara (=Pāli Vessantara) to which all people "in the five realms of India" sing and dance, and who was still alive when he came to India (in 673 A.D.). S. *Levi* (BEFEO 3, 1903, p. 41 f.) has identified this Candra with Candragomin. This identification has, however, been refuted on good grounds, by B. Liebich (Das Datum Candragomin's und Kālidāsa's Breslan 1903). *Liebich* (WZKM 13, 1899,

As the most prominent among the later teachers of Mahāyāna Buddhism, who also shone as poets, we have to mention Śāntideva, who probably lived in the 7th century A.D. According to Tāranātha, he was born in Saurāṣṭra (in the present-day Gujarat) as a king's son, but was instigated by the goddess Tārā herself to renounce the throne whilst the Bodhisattva Mañjuśrī, in the form of a Yogin, initiated him into the sciences. He acquired great magic powers, and was for a time the minister of King Pañcasiṃha, but finally he became a monk. He was a pupil of Jayadeva, the successor of Dharmapāla in Nālandā. Tāranātha ascribes to him the works Śikṣā-Samuccaya, Sūtra-Samuccaya and Bodhicaryāvatāra.[1]

The Śikṣā-Samuccaya, "the Sum Total of the Doctrine,"[2] is a manual of Mahāyāna Buddhism, which consists of 27 Kārikās (memorial verses) and an extensive commentary compiled,

---

308 ff. dates Candragomin between 465 and 544 A.D., which would approximately fit in with our dating of his contemporary Candrakīrti. Candragomin was a pupil of Sthiramati. *pery* l.c., (Extrait, p. 50, note, places Candragomin in the beginning or the first half of the 7th century. However, in the first half of the 7th century Candragomin's Grammar is already used by the writers of the Kāśikā. On Candragomin as a grammarian, s. Vol. III.

1. Tāranātha, Geschichte des Buddhismus, übers. von *Schiefner*, p. 162 ff. The biography of Śāntideva, which Haraprasāda *Śāstri* (Ind. Ant. 42, 1913, pp. 49-52) found in a Nepalese manuscript of the 14th century, agrees in the main with Tāranātha. In this MS. Rājā Mañjuvarmā is mentioned as his father. It is said here that he had the additional name "Bhusuka," because he was well versed in the meditation called "Bhusuka." He is also said to have been the author of a Tantra and Haraprasāda found works of the Vajrayāna school and songs in the Old Bengali language, which are attributed to a certain Bhusuka. This biography, too, speaks of *three* works of Śāntideva. The assumption of P. L. *Vaidya* (Etudes sur Āryadeva. p. 54) that by Śikṣā-Samuccaya, the text of the Kārikās is meant, and by Sūtra-Samuccaya the commentary containing the quotations from Sūtras is indeed very tempting : nevertheless, it is far more likely that the statement about the *three* works of Śāntideva is merely based upon an erroneous interpretation of the verses Bodhicaryāvatāra V. 105 f., where Śāntideva recommends the study of his Śikṣā-Samuccaya or the Sūtra-Samuccaya of Nāgārjuna; s. *Winternitz* in WZKM 26, 1912, 246 ff. *Cf.* also P. L. *Vaidya*, l.c., p. 54 ff. and. *Keith*, HSL, pp. 72f., 236.

2. Edited by C. *Bendall* (Bibl. Buddhica I), St. Petersburg 1903. Translated by C. *Bendall* and W. H. D. *Rouse* London 1922 (Indian Texts Series).

together with the Kārikās, by the author himself. We say intentionally that the commentary was "compiled" by Śāntideva, for it consists almost entirely of quotations and extracts from the sacred texts, which he has grouped around his Kārikās and arranged in chapters.

The work betrays an extraordinary degree of erudition and reading, but little originality. Śāntideva himself confesses this modestly in the introductory words to his book : "I have nothing new to say here, neither have I any skill in the writing of literary works. Therefore, my efforts are not for the benefit of others, but my only desire is to perfect my own mind. Nevertheless, the longing for clearness is fostered by this my work, so as to make the good real ; and if another who is of the same mind as myself, should see this longing, then this my work will not have been in vain."[1] The book is, nevertheless, extremely suitable as an introduction, especially to the ethical doctrine of the Mahāyāna, and is also of great value on account of the numerous, often long, extracts from texts which are no longer extant, the more so as Śāntideva, in those cases in which we can judge of his work, proves to be very accurate and very reliable in his quotations.

The fundamental idea of the work and the nucleus of Mahāyāna morality, is expressed in the first two Kārikās :

"If to my neighbour as to myself
Fear and pain are hateful,
In what does my ego differ,
That I should guard it more than another's ?
Do you wish to attain the end of suffering,
And the goal of happiness ?
Then let your faith be as a firmly planted root,
And direct your mind towards enlightenment."

The work was translated into Tibetan between 816 and 838, but was probably written as early as the middle of the 7th century (*Bendall*, Introduction, p. v f.) *Bendall*, Introd., p. xxxi ff. gives a short summary of contents. The edition rests on a single manuscript.

1. The same verses are to be found also in the introduction to the Bodhicaryâvatāra.

By means of numerous extracts from the Mahāyāna-Sūtras, it is shown how salutary *Bodhicittam* is *i.e.*, thought directed towards enlightenment, the Will to Enlightenment, the resolve to embark on the career of a Bodhisattva, in order to become a Buddha in the future. Whoever has formed this resolution, however, must carry self-denial, self-sacrifice for the sake of others, to the extreme. He must be prepared not only to give up his temporal possessions but even his salvation in the Beyond, for his neighbour. He must not shrink from taking the sins and sufferings of the beings in hell upon himself. The Bodhisattva must say :

"I take the sufferings of all beings upon myself, I am firmly resolved to do this, I bear them, I do not turn back, I do not fly, I do not shudder, I do not quake, I do not fear, I do not shrink back and do not despair. And why ? It is necessary that I take the burden of all beings upon myself. It is not my choice. For I have vowed to deliver all beings...I must liberate all beings from the jungle of birth, from the jungle of old age, from the jungle of disease, from the dense jungle of heresy, from the jungle of the loss of good deeds, from the jungle which has grown up through ignorance...I am not concerned with my own liberation only. For, with the boat of resolve of omniscience, I must rescue all beings from the flood of Saṃsāra...I am resolved to spend endless myriads of ages in every single place of torture....And why? Because it is better that I alone suffer, than that all these beings should sink into the places of torture. I give myself as ransom," etc.

But next to active pity, the pure way of life of the Bodhisattva must also include all the other perfections (Pāramitās), above all, meditation, which leads to the highest wisdom, *i.e.*, to insight into the "unreality (Śūnyatā) of all phenomena, and faith, which finds expression in Buddha-worship, in the erection of Stūpas, etc. Yet here, too, his mind should ever strain at the liberation of the beings. "May I lead all beings into the city Nirvāṇa !" Let this be his constant thought.[2]

1. Text, p. 280 ff., quotation from a Vajradhvaja-Sūtra. *Cf. La Vallée Poussin* Bouddhisme, pp. 322 f., 337 f.

2. According to the Ratnamegha-Sūtra.

Of the many texts quoted in the Śikṣā-Samuccaya,[1] we here call attention only to a few, which are represented by a considerable number of quotations or by fairly long extracts. A long passage is quoted from the Ākāśa-Garbha-Sūtra, on the sins (the five principal iniquities of a king, the eight iniquities of an Ādikarmika-Bodhisattva, and so on, p.59 ff.). One short passage and one longer one on sin and confession, are quoted from the Upāli-Paripicchā (pp. 164 f., 168 ff.). Quotations from the Ugra-or Ugradatta-Paripṛcchā[2] are fairly numerous, *e.g.*, on the duties of married life (p.78) and on the life of a hermit in the forest (p. 198 ff.). We find a long passage on the virtues of a Bodhisattva from the Vimala-Kīrtinirdeśa[3] which is quoted several times (p. 324 ff.). The Avalokana-Sūtra, which occurs in the Mahā-Vastu, is quoted by Śāntideva as an independent text (*e.g.* p. 297 ff.). A long passage from the Ratnolkā-Dhāraṇī on the virtues of a Bodhisattva, shows us a "Dhāraṇī" which is not a mere magic formula, but scarcely differs from a Sūtra. The quotation is also interesting owing to the enumeration of vocations and ascetic orders (p. 331 ff.). Other works quoted, are : Tathāgatavyūha-Sūtra, Daśabhūmika-Sūtra, Dharma-Saṃgīti-Sūtra, several recensions of the Prajñā-Pāramitā, Karuṇā-Puṇḍarīka, Gaṇḍavyūha, Candra- Pradīpa-Sūtra, Ratnakūṭa-Sūtra,[5] Ratnamegha, Laṅkāvatāra, Lalita-Vistara, Śālistamba-Sūtra,[6] Saddharma-Puṇḍarīka, Suvarṇa-Prabhāsa, etc.

---

1. They are recorded in the edition by *Bendall*, p. 367 ff.

2. See above, p. 319.

3. The Sūtra has been translated from Chinese, by Karichi *Ohara* in the Japanese monthly publication Hansei Zasschi XIII, 1898, XIV, 1899, and again by *Hokei Izumi* in EB II-IV (1922-1928). It was translated into Chinese by Kumārajīva in 406 A.D., s. *Bagchi* I. 188.

4. P. 327 ff. Cf. *Bendall*, JRAS 1901, p. 122 ff.

5. On these Sūtras, see above, p. 312 ff.

6. This is a principal source for the doctrine of the Pratītya-Samutpāda; it is edited by *La Vallée Poussin*, Theorie des douze causes, Gand 1913. p. 68ff. Cf. also *La Vallée Poussin* in JRAS 1901, p. 307 f. and E. *Hardy* in JRAS 1901, p. 573.

Although the Śikṣā-Samuccaya is the work of a not very original scholar, and the Bodhicaryāvatāra[1] that of a prominent poet, yet there can scarcely be a doubt that they are both by the same author. Apart from external reasons,[2] these two works, which are so fundamentally different from each other in character, are nevertheless both on exactly the same doctrinal standpoint. In both, the ethical ideal is the Bodhisattva, who has formed the resolve one day to attain enlightenment, who strives to reach this, the highest goal, firstly by infinite pity for the beings and secondly by worshipping the Buddhas, and who sees the highest wisdom in the conviction of the unreality of the world of phenomena (Śūnyatā).

But while in the Śikṣā-Samuccaya there is often only a loquacious learnedness which shows itself in a flood of quotations, the Bodhicaryāvatāra ("the Entrance into the Bodhi-Life," *i.e.*, "into the way of life leading to enlightenment") not infrequently rises to the loftiest flights of religious poetry.

---

1. Edited by I. P. *Minayeff* in Zapiski IV, 1889, reprinted in JBTS 1894. Prajñākaramati's commentary (including text) edited by *La Vallée Poussin*, Bibl. Ind. 1901-1914, Chapt, IX also in Bouddhisme, Etudes et Materiaux, Memoires de l'Acad. Belgique, t. 55, 1898, pp. 253-388. Translations : Into French by *La Vallée Poussin*, Paris 1907 (Extrait de la RHR X-XII, 1905-1907; and by La *Finot*, Paris 1920 (Les classiques de l'Orient II); into English (abridged) by L. D. *Barnett*, London. 1909 (Wisdom of the East); into German by Rich. *Schmidt*, Parderborn 1923 (Dokumente der Religion V); into Italian by G. *Tucci*, Torinto 1925. In the Chinese Tripiṭaka the Bodhicaryāvatāra is erroneously attributed to Nāgārjuna, s. *Lévi* in BEFEO II, 253 ff.

2. *Cf. Bendall*, Introduction to the edition of the Śikṣā Samuccaya, p. iii ff. Śāntideva included in the Bodhicaryāvatāra a few passages occurring in the Śikṣā-Samuccaya as quotations, *e.g.*, Śikṣās, p. 155 ff. in Bodhic. VI, 120 ff. In the Bodhic. V. 105, Śāntideva recommends the study of the Śikṣā-Samuccaya.

3. *Barth* (RHR 42, 1900, p. 55=Oeuvres II, 338) terms the Śikṣā-Samuccaya "la scholastiquc verbeuse et delayee usque ad nauscam," whilst he values the Bodhicaryāvatāra very highly as a counterpart to the "Imitatio Christi" of Thomas à Kempis (RHR 1893, p. 259 f.=Oeuvres II, 172). The Bodhicaryāvatāra does not, it is true, teach how to imitate Buddha, but teaches how to become a Buddha. Cf. *La Vallée Poussin*, Bouddhisme, p. 297 ff. C. H. *Tawney* in JRAS 1908, 583 ff; *Foucher* in RHR 1908, t. 57. p. 241 ff.

It is certain that, here too, Śāntideva refrains from pursuing any literary aims in his work : but he gives such fervent and inspired expression to his religious feelings, that he becomes a poet almost in spite of himself.

The work begins with a glorification of bodhicittam, the Will to Enlightenment, the determination to become a Buddha for the sake of the salvation of the beings. Thus it reads, I, 8 :

> "If you would overcome the many hundreds of sufferings of existence,
> If you would deliver all beings from their sufferings,
> If you would enjoy many hundreds of delights,
> Then never, never cease to direct your minds to Bodhi."

In inspired words, the poet describes his feelings after he has thus directed his mind towards enlightenment. He expresses his fervent joy at the good deeds of all beings and at their liberation, he prays to the Buddhas of all parts of the world, that they may light the lamp of religion for all those who are in ignorance, he beseeches all Bodhisattvas to defer their Nirvāṇa, he prays for the salvation of all beings, and finally offers himself for all beings :

> "By the merit which I have ever acquired
> By good deeds, may I bring to all beings
> Relief from all their sufferings !
> I desire to serve as medicine, doctor and nurse
> To all the sick as long as their sickness lasts."

> "I desire to be a protector to those who need protection,
> A guide to those who wander in the desert,
> And a ship, a landing-stage and a bridge
> To those who seek the shore.
> A lamp to those who need a lamp,
> A couch to those who need a couch,
> A slave to all beings who need a slave."[1]

1. III, 6; 7; 17; 18.

Chapters IV-VIII deal with the duties which the Bodhisattva takes upon himself. Whoever has vowed to strive for Bodhi, on him are the hopes of all beings, and he is responsible for the welfare of all beings. He must be diligent in all the perfections (Pāramitās). Above all, he must be prepared to sacrifice himself entirely. He must, however, also obey all the commandments of the religion, and fulfil all the rules of good conduct, as they are laid down in the sacred texts, which he must therefore study diligently.[1]

Our worst enemies are wrath and hatred and passion. These must be overcome. They harm us, not our enemies. We must love our enemies like all other creatures. For if we love the creatures, we delight the Buddhas, but if we injure them, we injure the Buddhas. If others wrong me, it is only the fruit of some action (Karman)—then why should I be angry with them ? One must not hate even those who destroy or despise Buddha-pictures, Stūpas, or even the good religion itself. He who does good to the beings, does good to the Buddhas and Bodhisattvas, who have so often annihilated their bodies and have gone to hell for the sake of the beings. Therefore, one should do good only, even to those who have done much evil to us.[2] From the outset the Bodhisattva aims at making no difference between his ego and his neighbour : to identify his ego absolutely and entirely with that of others, is a kind of spiritual exercise in which the Bodhisattva is particularly active.

> "I must destroy others' suffering, for it hurts like one's own pain :
> I must do good to others, as they are beings like myself."

In the same way as a man loves his hands and feet, because they are limbs of his body, so all other living beings have a right to his love, as they are all members of the same world of the living. It is only a habit to regard our body, which does not

1. Here (V. 103 ff.) some texts are specially recommended for study.
2. See particularly VI, 19; 33; 68; 120; 124; 126.

really exist at all, as our ego; in exactly the same way we can form the habit of regarding our neighbour as our ego.[1]

With admirable eloquence, which can only spring from the most sincere conviction, Śāntideva succeeds in representing it as a matter of course, that for the pious disciple of Bodhi, there is complete "equality between one's neighbour and one's ego" (Parātmasamatā), and that he finally reaches the "transformation of one's neighbour into one's ego" (Parātmaparivartana).[2]

Chapter IX is less attractive, and is purely erudite in its content : here the philosophical doctrine of the unreality of the world of phenomena (Śūnyatā) is developed according to the Mādhyamika system, incompatible though the negativism of this system appears to us with the devotion and self-sacrifice for other beings, as taught in the earlier chapters of the work, yet Śāntideva, too, utilises the doctrine, already familiar to us, of the differentiation between the two truths as a means of bridging the contradiction. Everything in the world is indeed vain and transitory, but only the delusion concerning the ego (ātmamoha) is harmful, whilst the delusion concerning the duties (Kāryamoha) is beneficent.[3] Nevertheless, it is strange enough that, after all the doctrines of active pity, the only conclusion at which the poet can arrive, is (IX, 152 f.) :

> As all existence is so empty and transitory,
> What can be gained, what can be taken away ?
> Who can be honoured, who blamed ?
> How can there be joy and sorrow, beloved objects
> Or objects of hatred ? And greed, and non-greed,
> Seek where you will, you will never find them.

After this excursion into the metaphysics of silence,—for that is really the true essence of the doctrine of unreality—namely that the answer to any question can only be a silence—the

1. See VIII, 90 ff.
2. *Cf. La Vallée Poussin,* ERE II, 749. 752 f.
3. *Cf. La Vallée Paussin,* Bouddhisme, Etudes et Matériaux, Mém. Ac. Belg. 1898, p. 109 ff.

poet comes back to the earth in the concluding chapter (X), and the work ends with an earnest prayer for the welfare of all beings, even for the beings in the hells, and with entreaties to the Bodhisattva Mañjuśrī.[1]

The fact that there are no less than eleven commentaries on the Bodhicaryāvatāra, speaks eloquently for the popularity of the work, though these commentaries have come down only in Tibetan translations.[2]

In the 8th century Śāntarakṣita wrote a large philosophical work Tattva-Saṃgraha,[3] in which, from the standpoint of the Svātantrika Yogācāra school, he criticises numerous other philosophical systems of his day, both Buddhist and non-Buddhist. He himself does not mention the names of the teachers whom he attacks, but we learn them from the commentary which his pupil Kamalaśīla wrote on the work. Among Buddhist teachers we find there Vasumitra, Dharmatrāta, Ghoṣaka, Buddhadeva, Saṅghabhadra, Vasubandhu, Dignāga and Dharmakīrti. Besides these, teachers of the Lokāyata, the Jain philosophy, and of Sāṃkhya, Nyāya and Mīmāṃsā are also named. The Madhyamakālaṃkāra-Kārikās, with the author's own commentary, are a shorter work of Śāntarakṣita. The work has come down only in the Tibetan translation.[4] Tibetan sources also allow us to glean something as to the life of Śāntarakṣita. He came from Nālandā to Tibet, where he

1. In the days of Tāranātha there were doubts as to the authenticity of this chapter, and the commentator Prajñākaramati did not explain the chapter, though it was known to him. However, all the MSS. and the other commentaries have it, and it certainly seems to be a far better conclusion to the work, than if it ended with Chapter IX. *Cf. La Vallée Poussin,* Bodhicaryāvatāra traduit p. 143 f.

2. The titles of the commentaries are given by P. L. *Vaidya*, Etudes sur Āryadeva, p. 56 f.

3. Tattvasaṅgraha of Śāntarakṣita with the Commentary of Kamalaśīla. Edited by *Embar Krishnamacharya* in GOS Nos. XXX, XXXI, Baroda 1926. The General Editor Dr. Benoytosh *Bhattacharyya* deals in detail, in the Foreword, with the life and works of Śāntarakṣita and Kamalaśīla and the authors cited in the commentary; *cf. Winternitz* in Indologica Pragensia I, 1929, p. 73 ff.

4. See P. L. *Vaidya*, l. c., p. 57 f.

founded the monastery of Sam-ye in the year 749 A.D., the first proper Buddhist monastery in Tibet. He lived there for thirteen years, and died in 762 A. D. Padmasambhava, who is usually mentioned as the founder of Lamaism, is said to have been the brother-in-law and collaborator of Śāntarakṣita.[1]

Lastly, among the later Buddhist writers, we may mention Advayavajra, who lived in the 11th or at the beginning of the 12th century, and wrote a large number of short didactic poems on the Mahāyāna and Vajrayāna.[2]

Māhātmyas, Stotras, Dhāraṇīs and Tantras

Repeated reference has already been made to the great similarity between the Mahāyāna-Sūtras and the Purāṇas. We have seen that in the ancient Purāṇas, many texts which were connected with the cult of the Hindu gods, were included or appended, such as Māhātmyas, Stotras and Kalpas.[3] In the same way there is also a Buddhistic "Purāṇa," the Svayambhū Purāṇa, which is not really a Purāṇa, but a Māhātmya. It is a glorification of the holy places in Nepal, especially the Svayambhū-Caitya near Kāṭhmaṇḍu. The work is a manual for pilgrims, and therefore also contains descriptions of ceremonies (*e.g.*, for the worship of Nāgas so as to obtain rain) and many a legend attaching to the various holy places. Thus, for instance, in Chapter IV the Maṇicūḍāvadāna[4] is told by way of glorifying the river Maṇirohiṇī. In the Svayambhū-Purāṇa, Svayambhū, "the Self-Existent," which is in Hinduism one of the names of the god Brahman, appears as the king and teacher of the world, seated on a wondrous lotus, the root of which had been planted in bygone ages by an earlier Buddha. There are five

1. See B. *Bhattacharyya*, GOS No. XXX, pp, x ff., xvi ff.
2. Advayavajrasaṃgraha, edited with an Introduction by Haraprasāda *Śāstrī* in GOS No. XL, Baroda, 1927. cf. Vidhuśekhara Bhattacarya in Ind. Hist. Qu. 6, 1930, 757 ff.
3. See above, Vol. 1, p. 510.
4. Translated by D. *de La Vallée Poussin* in JRAS 1894, p. 297 ff. This self-sacrifice-legend is also to be found in one manuscript as an independent Avadāna, as well as in one manuscript of the Divyāvadānamālā (s. Rajendralala *Mitra*, Nep. Buddh. Lit., pp. 162 ff., 314) and in Kṣemendra's Avadāna Kalpalatā (s. JBTS, Vol. I, part 3, 1893).

different recensions of the work, which differ from one another more in their external form than in contents.[1] None of the recensions can, however, lay claim to very great antiquity. Perhaps the work was not written earlier than the 16th century.

Just as this Māhātmya is composed in the true manner of the Viṣṇuite and Śivaite Māhātmyas, similarly the sole difference between the Buddhistic Stotras or hymns, and those which are dedicated to the worship of Viṣṇu or Śiva, lies in the names of the divine beings which are the objects of adoration. Some of these Stotras are the works of well known poets in the ornate style of poetry and in elaborate metres, others are litanies after the manner of those which we find in the Purāṇas. A few of such Stotras also gained admittance to earlier texts, such as the Mahāvastu, Lalita-Vistara and others. The hymns of Mātṛceṭa have already been mentioned. We have a collection of four hymns (Catuḥstava) of Nāgārjuna in the Tibetan translation.[2] King Harṣavardhana (600-647 A.D.), who, under the influence of the Chinese pilgrim Hsüan-Tsang, leaned more and more strongly towards Buddhism during the last years of his life, composed a Suprabhāta-Stotra,[3] a morning hymn in praise of Buddha, in 24 verses, and an Aṣṭa-Mahā-Śrīcaitya-Stotra,[4] a "hymn in praise of the eight great shrines," in 5 stanzas. The

1. According to S. *Lévi*, the "Svāyambhuva-Mahā-Purāṇa" which has come down in a Paris MS., contains the best recension. It is written in prose and verse in various metres. S. *Lévi* gives a detailed analysis of the work in Vol. I, p. 208 ff., of his book Le Nepal (AMG, Bibliotheque d'études, 17-19, Paris 1905). The "Bṛhat-Svayambhū-Purāṇa" edited by Haraprasāda *Śāstrī* in Bibl. Ind. (1894-1900) is written entirely in Ślokas and in execrable Sanskrit. Book X has been édited by *La Vallée Poussin*, (Universite de Gand, Recueil do Travaux publiés par la faculte de phil. et lett. 9e fasc., Gand and Louvain 1893). Cf. also Raj. *Mitra*, Nep. Buddh. Lit., p. 249 ff.; Haraprasāda *Śāstrī* in JBTS II, 1894, part 2, p, 33 ff.; and *Hodgson*, Essays, p. 115 ff.

2. The French translation by *La Vallée Poussin* was printed in Lé Museon in 1914, but all the copies were destroyed at the time of the burning of Louvain; s. P. L. *Vaidya*, Etudes sur Āryadeva, p. 49.

3. Edited by *Minayeff* in Sapiski de la Societe Archéologique, t. II, fasc. III, 236 f.

4. Translated into Sanskrit by S. *Lévi* (OC, Genéve, 1894, II, 189 ff.) on the basis of a Chinese transcription.

poet Vajradatta, who lived under King Devapāla in the 9th century, is the author of the Lokeśvara-Śataka, the "Hundred (stanzas) in praise of Lokeśvara."[1] Legend has it, that the poet became a leper owing to a curse. He implored Lokeśvara, *i.e.*, Avalokiteśvara, to help him, and each day he composed an elaborate Sragdharā stanza in praise of him. When three months had gone by, and he had completed the hundredth stanza, the Bodhisattva appeared to him, and he was healed.[2] In this very elaborate poem Avalokiteśvara is described in the greatest detail from his fingers to his toes, his fifty names are enumerated, and his qualities, his love and his mercy glorified.

The Paramārthanāma-Saṃgīti[3] is a hymn of the type which occurs as early as in the Yajurveda, the Mahābhārata and very frequently in the Purāṇas,[4] that is to say, a litany consisting of an enumeration of names and laudatory epithets of the deity. Another work which is composed mainly for devotional purposes, is a poem in 9 stanzas, the Sapta-Buddha-Stotra, "Praise of the Seven Buddhas," in which the six Buddhas of previous ages, from Vipaśyin down to Kāśyapa, and then Śākyamuni and the future Buddha Maitreya are worshipped and invoked one after the other; likewise the Naipālīya-Devatā-Kalyāṇa-Pañcaviṃśatikā, by an otherwise unknown "poet" Amṛtānanda, a litany of 25 stanzas, in which the "Nepalese deities," *i.e.*, a motley list of Buddhas, beginning with Svayambhū, Bodhisattvas, Hindu gods and goddesses, Buddhist personifications, Tīrthas and Caityas, are invoked, amid praises, to send down blessings (kalyāṇa).[5]

A large number of Stotras are dedicated to the Buddhist goddess Tārā, "the Rescuer," the female counterpart of

---

1. Edited and translated into French by Suzanne *Karpelès* in JA, 1919. s, II, t. XIV, pp. 357-465.
2. A similar legend is told about Mayūra, the poet of the Sūryaśataka.
3. Raj. *Mitra*, Nep. Buddh. Lit., p. 175.
4. *Cf.* above, Vol I, pp. 172, 381, note 2, 397, note 1.
5. The two Stotras have been translated by H. H. *Wilson*, Works, II, pp. 5 ff., 11 ff. *Cf.* *Winternitz* and *Keith*, Catalogue of Sanskrit Manuscripts in the Bodleian Library, Vol. II, p. 257; Raj. *Mitra*, Nep. Buddh. Lit., p. 99.

Avalokiteśvara. A poem in praise of Tārā, composed in polished Kāvya style by the Kashmiri poet Sarvajñamitra is the Sragdharā-Stotra or Ārya-Tārā-Sragdharā-Stotra in 37 verses. Sragdharā, "(female) wearer of the wreath," is an epithet of Tārā as well as the name of the metre in which the poem is written. The poet lived in the first half of the 8th century. According to the legend, he was a man widely famed for his generosity (according to Tāranātha,[1] a son-in-law of the King of Kashmir), who finally, after he had given away all his treasures, went forth into the world as a mendicant monk. Once he met an old Brahmin on the way, who complained to him that he was poor and needed money for his daughter's marriage. In order to procure the money for this man, Sarvajñamitra sold himself to a king who was just preparing a great human sacrifice for which he needed a hundred persons. When the poet heard the lamentations of his fellow-sufferers with whom he was to be sacrificed, he sang the hymn to Tārā, and the goddess came and rescued the hundred victims. Whilst the Sragdharā-Stotra has some poetical value, the Ārya-Tārā-Nāmāṣṭottaraśataka-Stotra, "the Song of praise consisting of 108 names of the noble Tārā," is a mere litany of names and titles of the goddess and the Ekaviṃśati-Stotra, "the song of praise in 21 verses," is only a loose stringing together of invocations to the goddess Tārā.[2]

---

1. Geschichte des Buddhismus, P. 168 ff. In Rājataraṅgiṇī IV, 210, there is mention of the monk Sarvajñamitra, who appeared as a second Jina, and lived in the Kayya-Vihāra built by Kayya. Kayya was a king of Lāṭa, and was subject to King Lalitāditya, who reigned in Kashmir in the 8th century. *Cf.* S. Ch. *Vidyābhūṣaṇa* in JASB 1, 1905, p. 156 ff.

2. These three Stotras have been edited and translated by G. *de Blonay*, Matériaux pour servir à l'histoire de la déesse Buddhique Tārā (Bibl. de l'ecole des hautes etudes, fasc. 107), Paris, 1895. The Sragdharā-Stotra (with commentary and two Tibetan versions), is also edited in Bauddha-Stotra-Saṃgraha, Vol. I. edited by Satis Chandra *Vidyābhūṣaṇa*, Bibl. Ind., 1908. In the introduction, the editor enumerates no fewer than 96 texts relating to Tārā. 62 of these have come down only in Tibetan translations. A great devotee of this goddess was Candragomin who has been mentioned above (p. 352), and to whom a Tārā-Sādhana-Śataka is ascribed (*Blonay*, l.c., p.17f.). The cult of Tārā was introduced in about the 6th century A.D. Hsüan-

The Bhakti-Śataka, "the Hundred (stanzas) on Bhakti,"[1] by Rāmacandra Kavibhāratī, a Brahmin of Bengal, who came to Ceylon under King Parākramabāhu (about 1245 A.D.) and was converted to Buddhism, affords an example of how the Brahminical-Indian idea of Bhakti or the love for God, was transferred to Buddha. In this work the Buddha is worshipped and praised, in the ornate style of poetry and in elaborate metres, as the only teacher, redeemer and dispenser of mercies, in precisely the same fashion as Rāma, Kṛṣṇa or Śiva in Brahminical Bhakti poems. The work might just as well belong to the Mahāyāna as to the Hīnayāna, for it is essentially a Hindu poem as far as ideas are concerned. By way of example, here are a few verses (31-34) in translation :

"Be gracious, O Lord, ruler of the gods, ruler of the world, conqueror, O Buddha, who deservest to be worshipped by the world, to be worshipped by me, to be worshipped by the good, O enemy of sin, enemy of mundane existence, enemy of lust, enemy of darkness ! To thee verily am I devoted (bhakta) with body, speech, and thought.

He is a son of thy family, he is devoted to thee, he bears the burden of thy teaching, he is a disciple, he takes refuge with thee, he is thy slave,—he who never on any account swerves from thy command.

Doing good to the world, O Buddha, is worship to thee, doing evil to it, O Lord of the world, is pain to thee. O Jina, how should I, when doing evil to the world, not be ashamed of saying that I am devoted to thy lotus-feet !

Where is my mercy, where my sympathy, where my love, as I am doing evil, and not good, to that very world for whose

---

Tsang mentions statues of "Tārā-Bodhisattva," which he had seen in India. In the year 778 A.D. Ārya-Tārā was already worshipped in Java, where she has a gorgeous shrine. *Cf. Waddell* in JRAS, 1894, p. 63 ff. and OZ I, 178 ff.; *Blonay*, l' c., pp. 3, 5, 17; H. *Kern* in OZ II, 1914, p. 481, note 1.

1. Edited by *Sīlaskandha* in Ceylon in 1885, and published by the Buddhist Text Society of India, Darjeeling 1896, and by Haraprasāda *Śāstrī* with an English translation in JBTS I, 1893, part 2, pp. 21-43; translated into German by Rudolf *Otto*, Texte zur indischen Gottesmystik II, Jena 1917, pp. 141-160.. *Cf.* Haraprasāda *Śāstrī* in JASB Proceedings, 1890, p. 125 ff. and JBTS I, 1893, part III, p. iv ff.

benefit thou hast, in a hundred ways, given away wealth, men, power, life, body and kingdom ?"

The Dhāraṇīs[1] or "Protective Spells"[2] constitute a large and important part of Mahāyānist literature. The need for incantations, benedictions, and magic spells, which was supplied in the very earliest times by the Vedic mantras, especially those of the Atharvaveda,[3] played far too great a part in the mind of the Indian people, for Buddhism to have been able to dispense with them. We have already seen how the Buddhists of Ceylon used some of their most beautiful Suttas as Parittās or Pirits.[4] In a similar manner the Mahāyāna Buddhists in India also transformed some of the Sūtras themselves into magic formulas. In addition to these, there were also endless invocations to the divine beings of Buddhist and Hindu origin, so numerous in the Mahāyāna, and—last, but not least—the mysterious words and syllables already so popular in the sacrificial mysticism of the Yajurveda.[5] The protective and salutary magical power of a Dhāraṇī is primarily due to its containing some piece of wisdom *in nunce*, and not to any occult mystical significance of the words and syllables, though it is true that the Dhāraṇīs do also include "magic words" (mantrapadāni) of this kind.

For instance, the Prajñā-Pāramitā-Sūtras in their shortest form were used as Dhāraṇīs : thus the Alpākṣarā Prajñā-Pāramitā, etc.[6] Special mention should here be made of the Prajñā-

---

1. *Cf. Burnouf*, Introduction, pp. 466, 482 ff.; *Wassiljew*, Der Buddhismus pp. 153 ff., 193 ff., 217: LA *Vallee Poussin*, Bouddhisme, Etudes et Matériaux, Memoires Acad. Belg. 1898, p. 119 ff.; L. A. *Waddell* in OZI, 1912, 155 ff.; Ind. Ant. 43, 1914, 37 ff., 49 ff,, 92 ff.; J. *Hauer*, Die Dhāraṇī im nordlichen Buddhismus, Tübingen 1927, and G. *Tucci* in Ind. Hist. Q. IV, 1928, 553 ff.

2. Dhāraṇī is a synonym of rakṣā and the Pāli parittā, "protecting magic formula," "talisman." *Cf. Kern* in OZ II, p. 481, note 2. According to the Saddharma-Puṇḍarika, p. 399, the Dhāraṇīs are taught "for the protection, safety and shelter of the preachers." Dhāraṇis are also used as amulets.

3. Above, Vol. I pp. 99 ff., 109 ff. The tale in the Śārdūlakarṇāvadāna (Divyāvadāna, p. 613) is characteristic of the need for magic formulas, s. above, p. 275 f.

4. See above, p. 77f.

5. See above, Vol. I, p. 172 ff.

6. See above, p. 303.

Pāramitā-hṛdaya-Sūtras, the shorter text of which we have in the ancient palm leaves, which have been kept since the year 609 A. D. in the monastery of Horiuzi in Japan. These Sūtras teach the "heart" (hṛdaya) of the Prajñā-Pāramitā, *i.e.*, the "Mantra which alleviates all pain," which contains the perfection of wisdom, and says : "O Enlightenment, which hast gone, gone, to the other shore, completely gone to the other shore, gone[1] hail !" Even though this saying is, to a certain extent, supposed to present the essence of the negativist doctrine of the Prajñā-Pāramitā-Sūtras, its spiritual level is no higher than that of the UṣṇīṣaVijaya-Dhāraṇī, which has also come down on the palm leaves of Horiuzi, and only consists of a series of senseless invocations.[2] Many Prajñā-Pāramitā texts appear amongst the Dhāraṇīs in the Tibetan Kanjur.[3] There are also Dhāraṇīs in the Kanjur, whose function is to help people to understand the Śatasāhasrī Prajñā-Pāramitā and other long Prajñā-Pāramitās.[4]

There is not always a clear line of demarcation between Dhāraṇīs and Sūtras. There are Mahāyāna-Sūtras which are nothing but recommendations of Dhāraṇīs. Thus the Aparimitāyuḥ-Sūtra,[5] which we have not only in Sanskrit and Old

1. This is nothing but a false etymology of *pāramitā*.

2. *Cf.* The Ancient Palm Leaves containing the Prajñāpāramitā-hṛdaya-sūtra and the Uṣṇīṣa-vijayadhāraṇī edited by F. *Max Muller* and Bunyiu *Nanjio* (Anecdota Oxoniensia, Aryan Series, Vol. 1, Part III), Oxford 1884 and SBE, Vol. 49, part II, p. 145 ff. Prajñā-Pāramitā-Hṛdaya-Sūtra translated from the Tibetan into French by L. *Feer* in AMG V, 176 ff. *Cf.* Haraprasāda *Śāstrī* in Ind. Hist. Q. 1, 1925, p. 469.

3. *Cf. Koros* in AMG II, 305, 307, 312, 314.

4. In a MS. of Dhāraṇīs (Rāj. *Mitra*, Nep. Buddh. Lit., p. 292) there is also a Pañcaviṃśatikā-Prajñā-Pāramitā-hṛdaya. Another Dhāraṇī of this kind, is the Prajñā-Pāramitā-naya-Śata-Pañcāśatikā (or Adhyardha-Śatikā Prajñā-Pāramitā) fragments of which have been found in the neighbourhood of Khotan, in Sanskrit, interspersed with sections in Khotanese. These fragments have been edited by E. *Leumann*, Zur nordarischen Sprache und Litteratur, Strassburg 1912, p. 84 ff.; reprinted and compared with the Tibetan and Chinese texts, by *Shoun Toganoo*, Kyoto 1917. There is also a Pratītya-Samutpāda-Dhāraṇī (*Kōros*, AMG II, p. 321) which is intended to help one to understand the doctrine of causally dependent origination.

5. The Old Khotanese Version together with the Sanskrit Text and the Tibetan Translation ed. by *Sten Konow* in Hoernle, Manuscript Remains, 1,

Khotanese, but also in Chinese and Tibetan translations, is nothing more than the glorification of a Dhāraṇī. The Ratnolkā-Dhāraṇī, which is quoted in the Śikṣā-Samuccaya, might just as well be classed as a Mahāyāna-Sūtra. It is a long work, in which Mahāyāna doctrines are expounded, among other things the doctrine that a Bodhisattva should not aspire to salvation immediately, but is to be reborn again and again in various professions and sects, for the sake of the welfare of the beings : a long list of these professions and sects is enumerated.[1]

The Megha-Sūtra[2] is a good example of a Sūtra with Dhāraṇīs, written for the purposes of magic. It begins, like other Mahāyāna-Sūtras, with the words : "Thus have I heard; once the Lord sojourned in the palace of the serpent princes Nanda and Upananda," ete. It then relates how the snake deities offer adoration to the Buddha and the Bodhisattvas, whereupon one of the snake princes asks the Exalted One the following question :—

"How, Lord, can all the pains of all snakes be alleviated, and how can the snakes be so pleased and delighted, that they may send down torrents of rain over India in due season and may thereby cause all grasses, shrubs, herbs and trees to grow,

---

pp. 289-329 (with English translation); Aparimitāyur-Jñāna-Nāma-Mahāyāna-Sūtram nach einer nepalesischen Sanskrit HS. mit der tibetischen und chinesischen Version herausgegeben und ubersetzt von *Max Walleser* Heidelberg (Sitzungsber. der Akademie) 1916. According to the Chinese Version, the title reads : Ārya-Aparimitāyuḥsuviniścita-tejo-rāja-dhāraṇī-sūtra. Cf. *Hoernle* in JRAS 1910, 834 ff., 1293; 1911, 468 ff., and E. *Leumann*, Zur nordarischen Sprache und Litteratur, pp. 75, 82 f.

1. See C. *Bendall* in JRAS 1901, p. 122 ff. The Nārāyaṇa-Paripṛcchā, too, which is several times quoted in the Śikṣā-Samuccaya, is described as a Dhāraṇī in the colophon of a MS. (Haraprasāda *Śāstrī*, Descriptive Catalogue of Sansk. MSS. in Asiat. Soc. of Bengal, 1, p. 16 f.) On an Āryācala-Mahākrodharāja-Guhya-Dhāraṇī-Sūtra in Sanskrit, Tibetan, Chinese and Japanese, s. C. *Puini* in GSAI 3, 1889, p. 38 ff.

2. *Cf.* C. *Bendall*, JRAS 1880, p. 286 ff. A Mahā-Megha-Sūtra was translated into Chinese as early as between 397 and 439 A. D., other translations were made between 589 and 618, and 746-771. *Cf.* B. *Nanjio*, Catalogue, Nos. 186-188, 244, 970. In the Tibetan Kanjur it is translated among the Sūtras (Mdo), s. *Köros*, AMG II, 264 ff.

all seeds to sprout and all juices to flow forth, so that the people of India be blessed with happiness ?" Pleased with the question, the Buddha replies : "By *one* religious exercise (Dharma), O snake-prince, all the pains of all snakes can be alleviated altogether, and they be blessed with happiness." "Which is this one religious exercise ?" "It is friendliness (maitrī). The gods and men, O snake-prince, who thus live in friendliness, are not burnt by fire, not injured by the sword, not carried away by water, not killed by poison, not overcome by the enemy's host. They sleep calmly and calmly they waken, they are protected by their own virtue.... Therefore, O snake-prince, you must act in friendliness with your body, in friendliness in your speech, in friendliness with your mind. And further O snake-prince, you must use the Dhāraṇi called Sarvasukhānandalā ('the all-hail-bringing'). This alleviates all the pains of all the snakes, brings all salvation, then brings the torrents of rain down over India here in due season, and causes all grasses, shrubs, herbs and trees to grow, all seeds to sprout and all juices to flow forth. And how goes this Dhāraṇī ?

Then follow the actual Dhāraṇīs, which consist of numerous invocations to female deities (as "holder," "supporter," etc.), to Buddhas and Bodhisattvas, between which sentences (such as "Shake off the evil," "Cleanse the paths") and exorcisms against snakes (such as "Come, O great snakes rain in India") are inserted, and lastly, of syllables scattered here and there (such as "sara sire sire suru suru nāgānāṃ java java jivi jivi juvu juvu," etc.). A description of the magic rites which are performed with these Dhāraṇīs is added, and it ends with the assurance that, in times of drought, there are no better means of inducing rain to fall, than the use of this Sūtra.[1]

1. A much simpler form of a snake charm which, however, is to serve as a means of warding off snake-bite, is already to be found in the Vinaya-Piṭaka, Culla-Vagga V, 6, where the snakes are appeased by the Buddhist friendliness (metta, maitrī). *Cf.* also Jātaka 203, Digha-Nikāya 32, and Aṅguttara-Nikāya IV, 67 (Vol. II, p. 72). A Sūtra, similar to the Megha-Sūtra, is the Diśa-Svāstika-Sūtra, which has come down to us in the Uiguric language in a fragment from Turfan (Tiśastvustik by W. *Radloff* and Baron A. von *Staēl-Holstein*, Bibl. Buddhica XII, St. Petersburg, 1910).

Similarly, the Dhāraṇīs often appear as parts of Sūtras which relate the circumstances under which they were proclaimed. There are, however, also numerous Dhāraṇīs which have come down singly in manuscripts, and on the other hand, large collections of Dhāraṇīs.[1] We find there exorcism formulas against the influence of ill-omened constellations, against poison snakes and demons, spells for the healing of diseases and the lengthening of life, magic spells for bringing luck in war, others which cause a person to be reborn in the Sukhāvatī paradise, to ensure against a bad rebirth, and to secure release from sin; there are also such by which a person can conjure up a Bodhisattva or protect himself from unbelief. It is not only the elements which can be influenced by Dhāraṇīs, but they bring about the birth of a son or a daughter according to the wish of the expectant mother. The collection of five Dhāraṇīs entitled '*Pañcarakṣā*' is extremely popular in Nepal. These "Five Protecting Spells" are as follows : (1) Mahā-Pratisarā, for protection against sin, disease and other evils, (2) Mahā-Sahasrapramardinī, against evil spirits, (3) Mahā-Māyūrī, against snake-poison, (4) Mahā-Śītavatī, against hostile planets, wild animals and poisonous insects, and (5) Mahā-(rakṣā) mantrānusāriṇī against diseases.[2] The Mahā-Māyūrī, frequently entitled Vidyārājñī, "Queen of Secret Sciences,"[3] takes its name from the notorious hostility of the peacocks (mayūra) towards the snakes, but it was also used as a general remedy for diseases. In Chapter V of the Harṣacarita, Bāṇa tells us how Harṣavardhana entered the palace of his father

1. *E.g.* Dhāraṇī- (mantra) - saṃgraha, Raj. *Mitra*, Nep. Buddh. Lit., p. 80 f. Other single Dhāraṇis and collections of Dhāraṇis, l. c., pp. 93 f., 174, 176, 267 f., 283, 291 f. Numerous MSS. of Dhāraṇis are also included in *Bendall's* Catalogue, *La Vallée Poussin*, JRAS 1895, p. 433 f., assumes that a "Vidyādhara-Piṭaka" quoted in the Ādikarma-Pradipa and in the Śikṣā-Samuccaya, p. 142, is the same as a Dhāraṇi-Piṭaka. According to Hsüan-Tsang, a Dhāraṇi-Piṭaka of this kind was contained in the Canon of the Mahā-Sāṅghikas (*Kern*, Manual, p. 4).

2. *Cf.* Rāj. *Mitra*, Nep. Buddh. Lit., pp. 164 ff., 173 f. *Winternitz* and *Keith*, Catalogue of Sanskrit MSS. in the Bodleian Library, Vol. II, p 257 ff. In the Nepalese courts of justice, the Buddhists are sworn on the Pañcarakṣā (*Hodgson*, Essays, p. 18).

3. *Cf.* J. *Przyluski* in BEFEO 23, 1923, p. 308 f.

who was lying sick unto death, and that all kinds of sacrifices and ceremonies were performed, and that among other things, the Mahā-Māyūrī was recited.[1] Most probably this Dhāraṇī can be traced back to the same sources as the verses in the Mora-Jātaka (No. 159) and the similar incantations in the snake-charms which we have in the Bower manuscript.[2]

Moreover, the Dhāraṇīs penetrated to a great extent into the ancient Mahāyāna-Sūtras. We have found them in Chapters XXI and XXVI, *i.e.* those chapters which were added at a later time, of the Saddharma-Puṇḍarīka, and also in the last two chapters of the Laṅkāvatāra, chapters which are missing in the earliest Chinese translation of 443 A.D. Thus we see that they are a later element in the Mahāyāna-Sūtras. Nevertheless we should not regard them as a very modern product of Buddhist literature, for we already find them in Chinese translations made as early as in the 4th century A.D.[3] And if the passage in the longer Sukhāvatī-Vyūha (VIII, 33) where it says that the beings in Sukhāvatī receive Dhāraṇīs, was already included in the text which was translated into Chinese in the 2nd century A.D., we should be compelled to assume that there were Dhāraṇīs as early as that period. It is not possible, however, to trace the Dhāraṇīs back to the early days of

---

1. Horṣacarita transl. by E. B. *Cowell* and F. W. *Thomas*, p. 137 Furthermore, a verse by Rājaśekhara in Jalhaṇa's Sūktimuktāvalī contains an allusion to the Māyūrī vidyā :

darpaṃ kavibhujaṅgānāṃ gatā śravaṇagocaram /
viṣavidyeva māyūrī Māyūrī vāg nikṛntati //

"The speech of (the poet) Mayūra destroys the pride of the poets, when it comes within reach of their ears, just as the peacock science against poison (destroys the pride) of the snakes (when it comes within reach of their ears)": Cf. G. P. *Quackenbos*, The Sanskrit Poems of Mayūra, CUIS 1917, Intron ., p. 5.

2. *Cf. Waddell* in OZ I, 166 ff. The Mahā-Māyūrī (in a longer and a shorter form) has been translated into Chinese repeatedly, by Śrīmitra (307-342 A. D.), by Saṅghapāla (516 A.D.), I-tsing (705 A.D.) and Amoghavajra (746-771 A.D.). *Cf.* K. *Watanabe* in JRAS 1907, p. 261 ff., *Lévi* in JA 1915, s. 11, t. V, pp. 19 ff., 26; and *Bagchi*, 1, pp. 320, 417.

3. Śrimitra (307-342 A.D.) translated more Dhāraṇīs than anything else. s. *Bagchi*, I, 319 f.

Buddhism, much less to Buddha himself.[1] It is true that Buddha lived in an environment of people who believed in the power of magic spells : but if there is one thing which we do know of Buddha, it is that he desired to bear a new message to his compatriots, a message which was at variance with the old Brahmanical cult of sacrifices and magic. The Dhāraṇīs belong to a period at which Buddhism in India began to be more and more assimilated to Hinduism,[2] while outside India it tended to make compromises and to become contaminated by the popular religions of the countries in question. In the course of time the difference between the Dhāraṇīs, and the Mantras belonging to the Tantras, became more and more obliterated, and finally the Dhāraṇīs were completely supplanted by the Mantras. In the Tibetan Kanjur the Dhāraṇīs are to be found both among the Sūtras (Mdo) and the Tantras (Rgyut).[3] The numerous fragments of Dhāraṇīs in various languages of Central Asia, which have been found in Eastern Turkestan,[4] and also

1. Thus *Waddell* in OZ I, 155 ff. The expression Dhāraṇī first occurs in the Lalita Vistara and Saddharma Puṇḍarīka. *Waddell* (Asiatic Quart. Review N. S. 1,1913, p. 293 ff.) compares the Dhāraṇīs with the magic formulas of the Nestorian Christians, and is of opinion that these formulas are derived from Chaldean ones, and that even the Buddhist magic formulas came to India from Chaldea and Iran. This is very unlikely, when we take the universality of protecting magic formulas into consideration; we need only compare, for instance, ERE III, 392-472, and VIII, 245-321. J. W. *Hauer* (Die Dhāraṇī, etc. 1927) has pointed out the similarity between the Dhāraṇīs and the Mithras liturgy, but he is right in not assuming anything beyond a parallel development.

2. It is significant that there is a Gaṇapati-Dhāraṇī, addressed to the Śivaite god Gaṇapati, in spite of the fact that it is "proclaimed by Buddha"; s. Rāj. *Mitra*, Nep. Buddh. Lit., pp. 89 f., 292.

3. *Köros* in AMG II, 249, 318 ff., 561 ff.

4. A fragment of a Nīlakaṇṭha-Dhāraṇī, brought from Central Asia by M. A. *Stein*, Sanskrit text in Brāhmī script and in Sogdienne transcription, has been edited by *La Vallée Poussin* and R. *Gauthiot* in JRAS 1912, 629 ff. This Dhāraṇī was already very popular in China between 650 and 750 A.D., s. *Lévi* in JRAS 1912, 1063 ff. Dhāraṇīs in Uiguric language (Uṣṇīṣa Vijayā, Sitātapatrā) have been edited from Central Asian block prints, by F. W. K. *Müller*, Uigurica II, in ABA 1911, pp. 27 ff., 50 ff. A Jñānolka-Dhāraṇī in the Khotanese language, has been edited by E. *Leumann*, Buddhistische Literatur Nordarisch und Deutsch, Leipzig 1920 (AKM XV, 2)

the large amount of space which the Dhāraṇīs occupy in the Tibetan Kanjur and the Chinese Tripiṭaka, are evidence of the great popularity and wide propagation of this literature in all Buddhist countries.

Mantrayāna and Vajrayāna are branches of the Mahāyāna, from which they are not separated by any hard and fast line of demarcation. Mantrayāna is the 'vehicle' in which the Mantras, words and syllables of mysterious power, are the chief means of attaining salvation. Vajrayāna is the 'vehicle' which leads men to salvation not only by using Mantras, but by means of all things which are denoted by the word vajra. Now vajra is a word with many meanings. It means 'diamond,' and denotes everything which is hard and impermeable. which cannot be cleft, nor burnt, nor destroyed. Vajra also means the 'thunderbolt,' the weapon of the god Indra, who appears in Buddhist mythology as Vajrapāṇi, "he who holds the Vajra in his hand." It is also the name for the weapon of the ascetics and monks when fighting against hostile powers. Then again, the Śūnya, the indescribable absolute: which is taught by the Mādhyamikas to be the sole realily, and also the Vijñāna or consciousness, which according to the Yogācāryas is the sole reality,—both of these are described as being indestructible as a Vajra. Lastly, in the mystic language of some of the adherents of the Vajrayāna, and that of the Śāktas, Vajra also means the male organ, just as Padma, "the lotus," serves as a term to describe the female sexual organ. Furthermore, the Vajrayāna teaches a monistic (Advaita) philosophy. All beings are Vajra beings (vajrasattva), and the one and only Vajrasattva is immanent in all beings. In addition to the "three bodies" (Trikāya) of a Buddha, the Śāktas have a fourth body, the "body of happiness" (sukhakāya), with which the eternal Buddha embraces his Śakti, Tārā or Bhagavatī. This "highest bliss" (mahāsukha) is attained by the adepts of the Buddhist Śākta religion, in like manner as the non-Buddhist Śāktas,[1] by

p. 151 ff. A Central Asian fragment of a Mahā-Pratyaṅgirā-Dhāraṇī in Sanskrit, containing invocations to Tārā, has been edited by *Hoernle*, in Hoernle Manuscript Remains, I. p. 52 ff.

1. See above, Vol. 1, 564.

a ritual connected with the enjoyment of meat, intoxicating liquors and sexual intercourse. Thus the Vajrayāna is a queer mixture of monistic philosophy, magic and erotics, with a small admixture of Buddhist ideas.

We have seen that there is no rigid boundary-line between the Mahāyāna and the Mantrayāna-Vajrayāna : and the same may be said of the Mahāyāna-Sūtras and the Tantras,[1] the literature of the Mantrayāna and Vajrayāna. As we have already seen, there are some Mahāyāna-Sūtras which contain Tantric sections,[2] and the Tantras treat not only of the rites of the Vajrayāna, but also of the ritual of the Mahāyānist cult (the erection of Stupas, construction and setting up of images, Stotras and daily sacrifices), as well as sections on the philosophical doctrines of the Mahāyāna. The only thing which distinguishes the Buddhist Tantras from the Tantras of the Śāktas,[3] is the sparse element of Buddhism which is still to be found in them. There are four classes of Buddhist Tantras : Kriyā-Tantras, which treat of ceremonies at the building of temples, erection of images of gods, etc.; Caryā-Tantras, which teach the practical cult; Yoga-Tantras, which deal with the practice of Yoga, and Anuttarayoga-Tantras, which deal with higher mysticism.[4]

Among the first class of Tantras we have the Ādikarma-Pradīpa.[5] This is a work which, in the style of the Brahmanical

1. Cf. *Burnouf*, Introduction, pp. 465 ff., 486 ff., 578 f.; *Wassiljew* Der Buddhismus, p. 201 ff.; *La Vallée Poussin*, Bouddhisme, Etudes et Materiaux. Mém. Acid. Belg., t. 55, 1898, pp. 72 ff., 130 ff.. 162 ff.; Bouddhisme, pp. 343 ff., 378 ff.; OC Paris 1899, 1, 241 ff.; ERE XII, 193 ff.; J. *Woodroffe*, Shakti and Shākta, 2nd Ed., Madras, 1920, pp. 30, 116 ff; J. N. *Farquhar*, Outline of the Religious Literature of India, pp. 209 ff., 272 f·; Benoytosh *Bhattacharyya* in Ind. Hist. Qu. III, 1927, p. 733 ff., and Sādhanamālā, II, Introduction. Extracts from texts of Tantras are contained in the anthology Subhāṣita-Saṃgraha, edited by C. *Bendall* in La Muséon, N. S. IV, 1903, and V, 1904.

2. See above, pp. 296, 327.

3. See above. Vol. I, 564 ff.

4. *Cf. La Vallée Poussin* in IRAS, 1901, p. 900 f.

5. Edited with Introduction and analysis of contents, by *La Vallee Poussin* Bouddhisme. Etudes et Matériaux, Mém. Acad, Belg. 1898, pp. 177-232. The Kriyā-Saṃgraha-Pañjikā by Kuladatta, in which detailed prescriptoins

manuals of rituals (Gṛhya-Sūtras, Karma-Pradīpas) describes the ceremonies and religious acts which the "Ādikarmika-Bodhisattva," *i.e.* the adherent of the Mahāyāna and candidate for enlightenment, has to perform. The work consists of a Sūtra text (Mūla-Sūtra) with a running commentary, and contains precepts on the initiation ceremonies for the disciple (who can be a layman or a monk), sprinklings, washings and prayers, rules for rinsing the mouth, cleaning the teeth, morning and evening devotions, offerings of water for the departed (Pretas), almsgiving, meals, worshipping of the Buddhas and other sacred beings, reading of the Prajñā-Pāramitā, meditations, and so on, as they are to be performed at the various times of the day by the candidate (the beginner as opposed to the accomplished Yogin).

The Aṣṭamīvrata-Vidhāna, too, which contains the rules for the ceremonies to be performed on every eighth day of every half month, belongs to the Kriyā-Tantra texts. Mystical diagrams and intertwinings of the fingers are employed, and sacrificial gifts and prayers (with mysterious syllables such as "hrum hrum hrum phaṭ phaṭ phaṭ svāhā") are addressed not only to Buddhas and Bodhisattvas, but to Śivaite deities also.[1]

In the Tantric ritual literature we have also the Sādhanas or works on magic ritual. These teach the methods by which a person can attain to Siddhi, *i.e.* "perfection" or mysterious powers, and become a Siddha, "an accomplished one." The virtue of these Siddhis is that the Siddha has the power of making himself small, large or light, at his own will, can penetrate into other bodies, can rise and move about in the air, can converse with heavenly beings, can obtain everything he desires, can have gods and goddesses, men and women in his power, has the power of healing diseases by merely looking at the sufferer, and also of attaining omniscience and Nirvāṇa at will. The methods taught in the Sādhanas consist of using the

---

are given for the erection of monasteries (Vihāras) is most probably also a ritual work of similar nature. (Rāj. *Mitra*, Nep. Buddh. Lit., p. 105.), and Haraprasāda *Śāstrī*, Descriptive Catalogue of Sanskrit MSS. in As. Soc. of Bengal, I, 119 ff.

1. *Cf.* H. H. *Wilson*. Works. II, p. 31 ff.

Mantras according to very detailed instructions, the use of certain positions of the fingers (Mudrās); and most specially is it emphasized that the Sādhaka is to become absorbed in meditation (Dhyāna) on some deity, and is to bring that deity before his mind in so intensive a fashion that he becomes entirely identified with it.[1] For the purposes of this identification it is essential that the deity be accurately described in every detail. These descriptions were utilised by the sculptors and painters in the construction of images of the gods. It is for this reason that the Sādhanas, which are collected in such works as the Sādhanamālā or Sādhana-Samuccaya,[2] are of the very greatest importance from the point of view of Buddhist iconography. The deities which are worshipped in these Sādhanas, are the Dhyāni-Buddhas and their 'families,' and also numerous forms of Tārā and other female deities. There is also a Buddhist god of love, Vajrānaṅga, an incarnation of Mañjuśrī, who is invoked in Sādhanas (Nos. 59 and 60) where it is taught how a man can get a woman into his power. The essential content of the Sādhanas is magic. It is true that the preparations for the magic ritual also include Yoga exercises, meditations, devotion (pūjā), confession of sins, love (maitrī) and mercy (karuṇā). For this reason we find, for instance, in the very long Tārā-Sādhana,[3] not only meditations and Mantras, but also a confession of sins, the confession of faith in the "three jewels" the vow to walk in the path of the Buddhas, the Brahmavihāra absorptions, *i.e.* the yielding to the feelings of love, pity, sympathy in joy, and equanimity,

1. *Cf. La Vallée Poussin* in ERE VIII, 406.

2. Sādhanamālā. ed. by Benoytosh *Bhattacharyya* in GOS, Nos. XXVI, XLI, Baroda 1925, 1928. *Cf.* F. W. *Thomas*, Deux collections Sanscrites et Tibétaines de Sādhanas, Muséon IV. 1903, No. 1; Vidhushekhara *Bhattacharyya* and K. S. Ramaswami *Sastri* in Ind. Hist. Qu. II, 1926, 626 ff. and III, 161 ff.; A *Foucher*, Etude sur l'iconographie bouddhique (Bibl. de l'ecole des hautes etudes 13, II, 1905); Benoytosh *Bhattacharyya*, The Indian Buddhist Iconography mainly based on the Sādhanamālā and other cognate Tantric Texts and Rituals, Oxford, 1924. See also P. C. Bagchi in Ind. Hist. Qu. 6. 1930, 576 ff.

3. No. 98. Text and English translation by B. *Bhattacharyya*, The Indian Buddhist Iconography, p. 169 ff.

together with detailed definitions of these qualities. The language of the Sādhanas is a very frequently defective Sanskrit, and the metre of the verses is very irregular. Of the 312 Sādhanas contained in the Sādhanamālā, some are in prose and are quite short, others are longer, with verse Mantras, and a few are entirely in verse. Every single Sādhana is an independent work. Most of them are anonymous, whilst in a number of cases, the name of the author of the Sādhana is mentioned. The authors mentioned in them belong to the 7th-11th centuries A.D., as far as their period can be determined. As a manuscript of the Sādhanamālā was written in the year 1165, the collection must have been compiled in the 11th century.

The authors mentioned in the Sādhanamālā also appear in other places as authors of Tantras. One Sādhana (No. 159 which is dedicated to the worship of the Prajñā-Pāramitā, is attributed to Asaṅga. It is scarcely feasible, however, that Asaṅga himself should already have written Tantric works, though there seems to be a historical connection between the Yogācāra school and the rise of the Vajrayāna.[1] The Nāgārjuna who is mentioned as the author of Sādhanas and numerous Tantric works, is not the founder of the Mādhyamika system, but a teacher, who probably lived about the middle of the 7th century. It is said of him that he brought a Sādhana from the land of Bhoṭa (Tibet ?). Many of his Tantric works are to be found in the Tanjur.[2] A great Tantra teacher, to whom a Sādhana is also attributed, is Indrabhūti (about 687-717 A.D.), the author of Jñānasiddhi and numerous other

---

1. Tāranātha (Geschichte des Buddhismus, p. 201) says that Tantrism was handed down by secret means from the time of Asaṅga until the time of Dharmakīrti, and Benoytosh *Bhattacharyya* Ind. Hist. Q. III, 736 f. and Sādhanamālā, II, pp. xxiii ff. xxvii f.) believes that Asaṅga actually had something to do with the rise of the Vajrayāna. It seems that Tāranātha's statement is accounted for by the mere fact that the adherents of the Vajrayāna had an interest in ascribing a greater antiquity to their doctrines. S. *Lévi* thought he could detect an allusion to Tantric rites in Mahāyāna-Sūtrālaṃkāra IX, 46 (which he attributed to Asaṅga). We are unable to see this allusion.

2. *Cf.* B. *Bhattacharyya*, Sādhanamālā II, pp. xlvi, cvi ff.

Tantric works.[1] He was a king of Uḍḍiyāna (Orissa ?) and father of Padmasambhava, the founder of Lamaism. Padmavajra,[2] whose Guhyasiddhi has come down to us in Sanskrit, was a contemporary of Indrabhūti. In this work, which is written in the "Sandhyā-language,"[3] all the secret rites of the Vajrayāna are described and recommended. Lakṣmīṃkarā, who, in her Advayasiddhi, proclaimed novel, monistic doctrines, which were called Sahajayāna, and which are even at the present day prevalent among the Bāuls in Bengal, was a sister of Indrabhūti. She refutes asceticism, ceremonies and the worship of images, and recommends only meditation on the body in which all the gods dwell.[4] Another prominent Tantra authoress is Sahajayoginī Cintā (about 761 A.D.), and indeed it is no rare thing to find women among the writers of Tantric works.[5]

The earliest Tantras are difficult to distinguish from the Mahāyāna-Sūtras. It may be that Mahāyāna doctrines mingled with Tantric rites, or perhaps works which were originally Sūtras, were remodelled into Tantras. Among the earlier Tantras we have the Tathāgata-Guhyaka or Guhyasamāja, which was a very authoritative work as early as in the 7th century. It was an authority for Indrabhūti,[6] and even in the Śikṣā-Samuccaya a Tathāgata-Guhya-Sūtra is quoted several

1. B. *Bhattacharyya,* l.c., pp. xli ff., li ff xcviii f. 23 of his works are translated in the Tanjur. In Sanskrit only the Kurukullā-Sādhana (Sādhanamālā No. 174) and the Jñānasiddhi have come down. On the latter (an edition is to appear in GOS) s. *Bhattacharyya,* l. c., p. lii f.

2. B. *Bhattacharyya,* l. c., pp. xxvii, xlvii ff.

3. Haraprasāda *Śāstrī* called this language Sandhyā-bhāṣā or "twilight-language." Panchcowrie *Banerjee* (Visva Bharati Quarterly, 1924, p. 265) called it the language of the borderland between the ancient Āryāvarta and the actual Bengal. Vidhushekhara *Bhattacharya* (Ind. Hist. Q. IV, 1928, p. 287 ff.) has, however, shown that the correct name is Sandhyā-bhāṣā, and means "intentional speech, "*i.e.,* enigmatical speech in which a secret meaning is intended.

4. B. *Bhattacharyya* l. c., p. liv f.

5. B. *Bhattacharyya,* l. c., pp. liv ff., lviii f.

6. According to one tradition, Asaṅga is even supposed to have written an introduction to the work. *Cf.* B. *Bhattacharyya,* l. c., pp. xxvii f., xxxv.

times.[1] The passages quoted, however, teach a pure Mahāyāna morality, and appear to have been culled from a Mahāyāna-Sūtra rather than from a Tantra, for instance :

"In whom does the Will to Enlightenment arise, O Lord ?" He said : "In that one, O great king, who has formed the immutable resolve to obtain it." He said : "O Lord, and who has this immutable resolve ?" He said : "He, O great king, in whom the great pity has arisen." He said : "In whom, O Lord, has the great pity arisen ? " He said : "In him, O great king who does not desert any living being." He said : "In what way, Lord, is no living being deserted ?" He said : "O great king, it is by renouncing one's own welfare."

In another passage it is explained : All beings are released from everything evil and from all ills by the contact of a Bodhisattva who is permeated with the Dharmakāya. This is illustrated by the parable of the "medicine girl :"[2]. Jīvaka the king of physicians, had taken all the medicaments and formed them into a girl. All the sick people who came to him, were then united with this girl, after which they were immediately healed.

Then, in another quotation, the ten things are enumerated, by means of which a Bodhisattva acquires power : "Here, O great king, a Bodhisattva gives up his body and his life, but he does not give up the good religion. He bows his head before all beings, and does not allow his pride to rise. He has patience with the feeble beings and does not put any difficulties in their way. He gives the best, excellent food to those beings who are suffering from hunger. He gives security to those beings

1. According to *Watters* (s. Śikṣāsamuccaya, ed. *C. Bendall*, p. 274, note), the work cited by Śāntideva corresponds to the Chinese translation made in about the year 1000 A.D. [*Nanjio*, Nos. 23 (3),1043], in which the title corresponds to a Tathāgatacintya-guhyanirdeśa, and which is a Mahāyāna-Sūtra entirely different from the Tantra described by Rāj. *Mitra*. K. *Watanabe* (JRAS 1907, p. 664) says that Nanjio No. 1027 corresponds to the Śriguhyasamāja-Tantrarāja, and adds : "Some parts of the original text which are not fit for publication as Dr. Rājendralāla Mitra indicates... are omitted in the Chinese."

2. A counterpart to the "poison girl" well known in narrative literature.

who fear. He is full of zeal for the complete healing of the sick. He satisfies the poor with riches. He repairs the shrines of the Tathāgata by lumps of plaster. He brings glad tidings to the beings. He shares his possessions with the poor and the unfortunate. He bears the burden of those who are weary and exhausted."[1]

It is true that the Tantra described by Rājendralāla Mitra[2] also begins with instructions as to various kinds of meditation, but, for the most part, it merely teaches Mantras and Yantras, and as a means to the highest perfection the enjoyment of meat, as well as daily sexual intercourse with young and beautiful Caṇḍāla girls. Whether this Tantra is a later variant of an earlier Mahāyāna-Sūtra, or whether it is entirely different from the work cited in the Śikṣā-Samuccaya, can only be decided by a comparison of the Chinese translation with the Sanskrit manuscripts.[3]

The Pañcakrama[4] is said to be an extract from the Guhyasamāja. It is an Anuttarayoga-Tantra, and deals more with Yoga than with the actual Tantric usages. As the name implies, the Pañcakrama is a presentation of the "five stages," the last of which is the final possession of the highest Yoga. The preliminary stages consist of the purification of body, speech and mind, so that these receive the "diamond nature',[5] of the

1. Śikṣā-Samuccaya, pp. 7 f., 158 f., 274.

2. Nep. Buddh. Lit., p. 261 ff.

3. Haraprasāda *Śāstrī* (Descriptive Catalogue of Sanskrit MSS. in the As. Soc. of Bengal, I, 1917; pp. 17-21 and 72) describes 3 MSS. of the work, in which the Vajrapāṇi-Guhyakādhipati and the Bodhisattva Śāntimati appear in conversation. Śāntimatī is also addressed in a quotation in Śikṣā-Samuccaya, p. 242. H. *Śāstri* assumes that the earliest of the three parts of the work is a Mahāyāna-Vaipulya-Sūtra, whilst the later parts belong to the Vajrayāna. *Cf.* also B. *Bhattacharyya* in Ind. Hist. Q. III, pp. 737, 742 f. and Sādhanamālā II, pp. xxvii f., xxxv.

4. Edited, with an Introduction, by *La Vallée Poussin*, Etudes et Textes Tantriques (Recueil de Travaux publiés par la faculte de philosophie et lettres, Université de Gand, fasc. 16), Gand et Louvain 1896. *Cf. Burnouf*, Introduction, p. 497 ff. *La Vallée Poussin* in OC Genéve 1894, I, pp. 137-146· and Bouddhisme, Etudes et Materiaux, Mem. Ac. Belg. 1898, p. 146 : "manuel qui se presente comme un extrait ou résumé du Guhya samāja-Tantra."

5. For the nature of Vajra, see above p. 374.

body, the speech and the mind of the Buddhas. However, the means for attaining the five stages are magic circles, magic formulas, mysterious syllables and the worshipping of Mahāyānist and Tantric deities. In this manner, the Yogin reaches the highest stage of all, where all differences cease and where no duality of any kind exists. Of this Yogin it is said (VI, 30 ff.) :

"He feels towards his enemy as towards himself; his mother is to him as his wife; a harlot is to him as his mother; a Brahmin woman is to him as a Dombī (a female musician of the lowest caste) ; the skin of an animal is to him as a garment; a blade of straw is like a precious stone, wine is like urine, food is like mud, an insult like a hymn of praise, Indra like Rudra, day like night, what he has seen is like a dream, things which exist are like things which have been destroyed, pain is like pleasure, his son is like a rascal, heaven is like hell-and thus even good and evil are one and the same to him."

Śākyamitra is mentioned as the author of Section III of the work, which consists of five sections : the other four sections are attributed to Nāgārjuna, which probably means the tantra writer of this name (see above, pp. 378 f.). Śākyamitra is mentioned by Tāranātha as a contemporary of Devapāla of Bengal (about 850 A.D.).[1]

A work which describes itself as a Mahā-Vaipulya-Mahāyāna-Sūtra and as belonging to the Avataṃsaka, is the Mañjuśrī-Mūla-Kalpa.[2] Nevertheless, as far as its contents are concerned, the work is entirely in the spirit of the Mantrayāna. In the major portion of the work, Śākyamuni speaks in a large assembly, but addresses himself only to Mañjuśrī. In the first three chapters Mañjusrī himself speaks, and in the last two chapters the goddess Vijayā. Śākyamuni gives Mañjuśrī instructions as to magic rites with Mantras, Mudrās, Maṇḍalas,

1. A Pañcakramopadeśa Śrighaṇṭa is mentioned in the Catalogue of Buddhist Sanskrit MSS. in the Royal Asiatic Society, by E. B. *Cowell* and J. *Eggeling* (JRAS, 1876, reprint p. 28).

2. Edited by T. Gaṇapati *Śāstrī* in TSS, Nos. LXX and LXXVI, 1920, 1922. *Cf.* J. *Przyluski* in BEFEO, t. XXIII, 1923, p. 301 ff. and B. *Bhattacharyya*, Sādhanamālā II, p. xxxivf.

etc. In Chap. IX, for instance, the "great king of sciences," the Mantra of Mañjuśrī, is taught, which includes all sciences within itself, by means of which one can attain all things, which destroys all the Mantras of evil-doers, blots out all sins, etc.—this is the "kllhuṃ" Mantra. In Chapter XIV the same powers are claimed for the "bhrūṃ" Mantra. There is very little trace of Buddhism in this manual of magic, though the worship of the "three jewels" is mentioned in Chap. 47. The work was translated into Chinese as a Mahā-Vaipulya-Sūtra between 980 and 1000 A.D. and into Tibetan as a Tantra in the 11th century A.D.[1]

The (Ekallavīra-) Caṇḍa-Mahāroṣaṇa-Tantra[2] explains on the one hand (in Chapt. XVI) the Pratītya-Samutpāda according to the philosophical doctrines of the Mahāyāna,[3] whilst on the other hand, the cult of Yoginīs, such as Mohavajrī, Piśunavajrī, Rājavajrī, etc., and that of female deities with sexual actions, are recommended.

It is shown how the six perfections can be attained by means of sexual union. In one passage Bhagavatī asks :[4] "O Lord, can the dwelling of Caṇḍamahāroṣaṇa be attained without a woman, or is that not possible ?" The Lord said : "That is not possible, O goddess."... "Enlightenment is attained by means of bliss, and there is no bliss without a woman".... "I am the son of Māyā, and I have assumed the form of

---

1. *Körös* in AMG II, 313 f. It is frequently cited by Tibetan scholars. The Bodhisattva Mañjuśri also occurs in the titles of other Tantra works. The Mañjuśrināma-saṃgīti (edited by *Minayeff* in his Russian work on Buddhism, Petrograd 1887) admits of a double interpretation, one purely philosophical and the other Tantric with allusions to Śākta rites. Thus according to *La Vallée Poussin* in ERE XII, 194.

2. Considerable extracts from MSS. of the work, are given by Haraprasāda *Śāstrī*. Descriptive Cat. of Sanskrit MSS. in the As. Soc. of Bengal, I, pp. 131-141. Caṇḍaroṣaṇa is an emanation of Akṣobhya. On his secret cult see B. *Bhattacharyya*, Indian Buddhist Iconography, p. 60 ff.

3. See *La Vallée Poussin*, Théorie des douze causes, 1913. p. 125 ff.; JRAS 1897, 466 ff.; OC XI, Paris, I. 244; ERE XII, 196.

4. "The Exalted One (feminine)" is the personified Prajñā-Pāramitā, wisdom conceived as a goddess. On strīpūjā, *Cf.* Haraprasāda *Śāstrī* in JASB, Vol. 67, 1898, p. 175.

Caṇḍamahāroṣaṇa; you are the exalted Gopā,[1]) who are one with the Prajñā-Pāramitā. And all women in the universe, are regarded as incarnations of her, and all men as incarnations of myself."

The ritual of the "great bliss" (mahāsukha) is described in the Śrīcakrasambhāra-Tantra,[2] which we have only in Tibetan. The book teaches the Mantras, the meditations, the pictures of the divine couples which one has to present to one's mind, the sacrificial ritual and the symbolical significance of the Mantras connected with the Mahāsukha.

As regards the immoral character of this literature and these cults, we should neither exaggerate it, nor should we seek to deny it. There is no doubt that the ritual of the Vajrayāna has led to gross abuses; on the other hand, we must admit that it has a mystic, philosophical background. The Vajrayāna teaches a monistic philosophy. Just as Śiva and Pārvatī are one, Buddha and his Śakti, Tārā or Bhagavatī or Prajñā-Pāramitā, are one. This unity is symbolised figuratively by the intimate embrace (yuganaddha, Tibetan vabyum) of the gods and goddesses, who, for the most part, are merely male and female personifications of abstract ideas. The sexual union, in which the man is regarded as the incarnation of Buddha, and the woman as that of Bhagavatī, in reality serves the same symbolical purpose as those pictures in the cult.[3]

In his "History of Buddhism in India," Tāranātha[4] gives us a good idea of the spirit of the Tantra Buddhism. Though he

---

1. Gopā is the consort of Gotama, Because the accomplished Buddha, before he withdrew from the world in order to attain to Bodhi, was happy in the harem united to Gopā. Sexual union is also recommended to his adherents as a means of attaining to Bodhi.

2. Ed. by *Kazi Dawa-Samdup* in Tantrik Texts, Vol. VII (Introduction and English translation) and XI (Tibetan text). *Cf.* H. *Zimmer*, Kunstform und Yoga im indischen Kultbild, Berlin 1926, 67 f., 74 ff.

3. *Cf. La Vallée Poussin*, Bouddhisme, Etudes et Matériaux, Mem. 1898, p. 141 ff.

4. Tāranātha was born in 1573, and completed his work, which was written on the basis of Indian and Tibetan sources, in the year 1608. Translated into German by A. *Schiefner*. He describes regular competitions in magic (*e.g.*, on p. 189 ff.).

also speaks of Mahāyāna and Tripiṭaka, of Buddhist science and Buddhist self-sacrifice, it is nevertheless Siddhi, the magic art acquired by means of Mantras and Tantra rites, which plays by far the more prominent part. Just as the contents of the Tantras present a medley of Buddhism and Hinduism, of religion, philosophy, occultism and magic, popular belief and hair-splitting, erudite argumentation, truly Indian cults and cults savouring of foreign influence, thus, the history of Buddhist Tantra literature too, is a very complex one. When Tāranātha says that at the time of the Pāla dynasty of Bengal, that is to say, from the 9th to the 11th century, Yoga and magic were paramount in Buddhism, his statement is probably not far from the truth. Most likely the Buddhist Tantras did not come into being until the 7th or 8th century under the influence of the Śivaite Tantras, and belong to the period at which Buddhism was almost entirely assimilated to Hinduism. The very names of the deities in the Buddhist Tantras betray their dependence upon the Śivaite Tantras. The Mahākāla-Tantra is in the form of a dialogue between Śākyamuni and a goddess, and it is said that it was "proclaimed by Buddha." However, it contains explanations as to the Mystical significance of the letters of which the name Mahākāla, *i.e.*, Śiva, is composed, and on the means of finding hidden treasures, gaining a kingdom, obtaining the desired wife, and even Mantras and magic rites, by which one can make people insane, enslave them, and kill them.[1] The Saṃvarodaya-Tantra, again, in spite of the form of a dialogue between Buddha and the Bodhisattva Vajrapāṇi, is more of a Śivaite than a Buddhist work. The Liṅga cult and the worshipping of Śivaite gods are expressly recommended in it.[2]

The lands where tantrism was the most widespread, and perhaps where it originated, are Assam and Bengal.[3] From the

---

1. *Burnouf*, Introduction, p. 480; Rāj. *Mitra*, Nep. Buddh. Lit., p. 172. ff: E. B. *Cowell* and J. *Eggeling*, Catalogue of Buddhist Sanskrit MSS., p. 37 f.

2. *Burnouf*, Introduction, p. 479 ff.

3. *Cf.* B. *Bhattacharyya* in Ind. Hist. Q. III, 744; Buddhist Iconography, p. xxvii; Proceedings of Madras Or. Conf. p. 133: Sādhanamālā II, p. xxxvi ff.

8th century onwards it proceeded from this territory in a veritable triumph to Tibet and China, where it mingled with native cults. Vajrabodhi and Amoghavajra went to China in about 720 A.D., and contributed largely towards the propagation of the Tantras.[1] In Japan, where only the Mantrayāna, and not the Vajrayāna, obtained a footing, the Shin-go sect takes its stand upon the Tantras.[2] In the later Tantras we again find traces of Tibetan and Chinese influences, and in the case of some cults, it is expressly stated that they were brought from Cīna (China) or Mahācīna (Tibet). In the Tārā-Tantra Buddha and Vasiṣṭha are described as great Bhairavas. Buddha was a form of Viṣṇu, and obtained the position of a creator, after his initiation into the Mantras of Ugra-Tārā. Tārā is Buddha's Śakti, and a form of wisdom (Prajñā). Vasiṣṭha, however, is said to have learned the knowledge of Tārā in Cīna from the lips of Buddha. The Tantric manual Tārā-rahasya by Brahmānanda also teaches the cult of Tārā in agreement with the usages of Mahācīna.[3] At this late period it also occasionally happened that the Hindu Tantras were influenced by the Buddhist ones.[4] It is related in the Hindu Tantras Rudrayāmala and Brahmayāmala that Vasiṣṭha, in spite of all his ascetic endeavours, did not succeed in causing the goddess

1. *Cf.* L. *Wieger*, 'Histoire des croyances religieuses et des opinions philosophiqes en Chine, 1922, p. 535 ff. The most important text of Mantra Buddhism in China, namely the Mahā-Vairocana-Abhi-Sambodhi, was brought to China by Śubhakarasiṃha (died in 735 A.D.; s. *Anesaki* in ERE IV, 840.) On foreign elements in the Tantra, see also P. C. Bagchi in Ind. Hist. Qu, 7, 1931, 1 ff.

2. B. *Nanjio*, Twelve Japanese Buddhist Sects, p. 78 ff.

3. On Tārā-Tantra and Tārā-Rahasya, s. Haraprasāda *Śāstrī*, Notes of Sanskrit MSS., 2nd Series, I, 1900, pp. xxxii f. Thus the cult of Mañjuśri was taken from India to China, but became so popular there, that people in India said Mañjuśrī lived in China, and his cult was then again taken from China to Nepal. I-tsing (Record, translation by J. *Takakusu*, p. 169) calls attention to an Indian book, probably a Tantra, in which China is praised because it is the home of Mañjuśri. Cf. *La Vallée Poussin* in ERE VIII, 405 f.

4. It is, however, quite contrary to the facts, when B. *Bhattacharya* (Sādhanamālā II, pp. lxvi ff., lxxviii) assumes that the Tantras first came into existence in Buddhism, and went over into Hinduism afterwards.

Pārvatī to appear to him. In the end his Guru tells him that he should go to Mahācīna, the land of the Buddhas. He follows this advice, and seeks the help of Mahādeva Buddharūpa, who teaches him the Pañcatattva ritual.[1] Tantras still continued to be written even in very late times. Thus, for instance there is a Kālacakra,[2] which already mentions Mecca and Islam.

The Sanskrit in which the Tantras are written, is, as a rule, just as barbarous as their contents. Inferior as they may be from the literary point of view, they are nevertheless extremely important owing to their great popularity over a wide area, and the great influence which they exerted over the spiritual life of Western India and of considerable portions of Asia.

Buddhist Literature and Universal Literature

Just as Buddhism became one of the great religions of the world, a great part of Buddhist literature belongs to universal literature. We have already seen, on various occasions, that Buddhist fables, anecdotes, fairy tales and legends not only migrated to the Far East with Buddhism, but also frequently have their parallels in European literatures, though it is not always certain that the Buddhist narratives migrated to Europe, for the reverse may sometimes have been the case.[3] We have also seen that the Buddha legend has some features in common with the legend of Christ,[4] and that certain speeches and parables in the Suttas of the Tipiṭaka and the Mahāyāna Sūtras are, more or less strikingly, reminiscent of passages in the Christian gospels.[5]

The question as to how far these points of agreement between Buddhist and Christian literature actually exist, and what significance is due to them, is sufficiently important to warrant our treating of them once more as a whole. Are they more or

---

1. Cf. *Woodroffe*, Shakti and Śhākta, p. 104 ff.
2. Only extant in Tibetan, s. *Burnouf*, Introduction, p. 480 f.
3. See above, pp. 62, note 1, 105, note 1, 122 f., 126 128, note 1. 129ff., 145, notes 2, 3, 146, note 1, 187 f., 193 f. 207f.
4. See above, pp. 94, notes 1 and 2, 242 note 1, 275, note 3.
5. See above, pp. 29, note 1, 72, note 1, 287 note 1.

less accidental similarities, resemblances which may be explained by the fact that the respective legends, similes and utterances have arisen out of the same situations and religious moods, or is it a question of the actual dependence of the one literature upon the other? Were the Christian gospels influenced by the Buddhist sacred texts, which date from pre-Christian times? Or were later Buddhist texts, like the Lalita-Vistara and the Saddharma-Puṇḍarīka, influenced by the Christian gospels? These questions have repeatedly been the subject of research and have been answered in most varying ways.

Rudolf Seydel,[1] in particular, thought he could prove such numerous coincidences between the Buddha legend and the life of Jesus according to the gospels that he framed the hypothesis that the Evangelists, besides using an "original text" of St. Matthew and an "original text" of St. Mark, had also made use of a poetical gospel, Christian though influenced by Buddhism, and had taken from this all those legends, parables and utterances which have parallels in the Buddhist texts. He considered this hypothesis to be necessary, because the points of agreement (in his opinion) do not appear singly but massed together, and actually form groups, indeed, a connected whole. A single stick, he says, can easily be broken, but it is more difficult to break a bundle, or indeed a bundle of bundles. This is well said! But if the stick is no stick, but only the phantom of a stick, then even a bundle, or a bundle of bundles of such "sticks" is of no use to us. In reality it is not difficult to show, and has repeatedly been shown, that the majority of the "parallels" indicated by Seydel will not bear closer examination.

The Dutch scholar *G. A. van den Bergh van Eysinga*[2] has approached the problem of the Indian influences on the Christian

1. Das Evangelium von Jesu in seinen Verhältnissen zu Buddha-Sage und Buddha-Lehre, Leipzig 1882; Die Buddha-Legende und das Leben Jesu nach den Evangelien, erneute Prufung ihres gegenseitigen Verhültnisses, 2. Aufl. mit ergänzenden Anmerkungen von Martin Seydel, Weimar 1897.

2. Indische Einffüsse auf evangelische Erzählungen, Gottingen 1904, 2. Aufl. 1909.

gospels far more cautiously than Seydel. He begins by eliminating everything which could easily be explained by the similarity of circumstances under which the texts originated, similarity of religious development, and finally on general human grounds. Nevertheless, even according to this scholar there still remain actual parallels which can only be explained as loans. He is, however, of opinion that we are not justified in assuming that there was any dependence upon written texts, but by mere oral transmission at the time of the Roman Empire, Indian subjects, themes and ideas reached the West, and certain of these features were borrowed in the formation of the legends of the earliest Christianity. Of the 51 parallels which Seydel believed to have found, Bergh van Eysinga regards only nine as worthy of discussion, and only six as more or less important.

What Seydel undertook to produce with inadequate material, for Buddhist literature was but very incompletely known in his day, namely, a "Buddhist-Christian Gospel Concordance," was once again attempted later, on the basis of a far more accurate knowledge of the Pāli and Sanskrit texts, by the American scholar *Albert J. Edmunds*.[1] He expressly states that he is not out to prove the dependence of the Christian sacred scriptures upon the Buddhist texts, but only to compare the two religions, "as such a comparison will finally have the effect of making them respect each other." Nevertheless he inclines to the view that Christianity, as the more eclectic religion, borrowed from Buddhism, and that St. Luke, in particular, was acquainted with a Buddha-epic. On the other hand, it is precisely Edmund's comprehensive collection of all the passages in both literatures which can possibly be dragged in, as it were, for comparison, which shows most clearly, firstly, that there is no instance in which a loan on the part of the four gospels must necessarily be assumed, secondly, that in most instances there is only a similarity of ideas, which does not presuppose a literary connection,

1. Buddhist and Christian Gospels now first compared from the Originals by A. J. *Edmunds*, edited by M. *Anesaki*, 4th Ed., Philadelphia 1908-9; A. J. *Edmunds* Buddhist Texts quoted as Scripture by the Gospel of John, 2nd Ed.; Philadelphia-London 1911; and Buddhist Loans to Christianity in The Monist, January 1912, p. 129 ff.

and thirdly, that in the best cases, only a possibility of mutual influence can be admitted, and that this *possibility* amounts to *probability* only in very few cases. Very frequently, indeed. Edmunds' comparison of the texts shows how very much greater the differences are than the points of contact.

We need only to read the texts, compared by Edmunds,[1] on the miraculous conception and birth of Christ and of Buddha, and the differences become obvious. It is true that there are miracles in both cases; but as the history of religion, mythology and folk-lore teach us, the birth of great men is attended by miracles everywhere. Greek mythology affords far closer parallels to the virgin birth than does the Buddhist legend.[2] As a matter of fact, Buddha is conceived and born of a married queen and not of a virgin at all. Again, the texts about the temptation of Buddha by Māra and of Christ by Satan[3] show more differences than points of agreement, and the temptation of Zoroaster by Ahriman proves that it cannot be a question of the mere borrowing of texts but at most a matter of connections in religious history, harking back to far earlier times. Likewise in the legend of the transfiguration of Jesus, as compared with the account in the Mahā-Parinibbāna-Sutta of the radiance of the Buddha's body, we can see only a striking parallel, of great

1. 1, 107 f., 167 ff.: St. Luke I, 35; Majjhimanikāya 38 and 123.

2. *Cf.* H. *Gunkel*, Zum religionsgeschichtlichen Verständnis des Neuen Testaments, Gőttingen 1903, p. 65 ff.; *Garbe*, Indien und das Christentum. p. 31 f.; *Günter*, Buddha in der abendländischen Legende? 194 ff.; *Haas*, Buddha in der abendländischen Legende? 17 ff.; W. *Printz* in ZDMG 78, 1925, 119 ff.

3. *Edmunds*, 1, 198 ff.; also *Pischel*, Leben und Lehre des Buddha, p. 26 f., denies the connection in this instance. Similarly *Gotz*, "Der Katholik" 1912 (IV, 9), 435 ff.; *Beth*, Theolog. Studien und Kritiken 1916, 202 ff.; *Carpenter*, Buddhism and Christianity, p. 180; and E. *Leumann*, Buddha und Mahāvira, reprinted from ZB 1921, p. 60 ff. On the other hand, *Görbe*, loc. cit., 50 ff., regards the points of agreement as so striking, that he deems it necessary to trace the Gospel narrative back to the Buddhist temptation stories, "for a devil in the flesh does not appear anywhere else in the Bible, but occurs constantly in the Buddhist Canon." *Cf.* 7. *Charpentier* in ZDMG 69, 1915, 441 f.

interest from the point of view of the history of religion, but not a loan from Buddhist literature.[1]

In his comprehensive work[2] on Indian influences on Christianity and Christian influences on the Indian religions, *Richard Garbe* assumes a loan from Buddhist tradition on the part of Gospel narratives, in four cases only : the story of Simeon in the temple, the legend of the temptation, St. Peter walking on the sea, and the miracle of the loaves. With regard to the parallel to the "widow's mite," Garbe assumes that the Christian legend is the original one, and that it was taken over by the Buddhists.

It will never be possible to give a conclusive answer to these questions. Any decision in this matter is more or less subjective, for parallels are never equations. In each instance there are both resemblances and divergences. In the vast mass of literature which has accumulated on this problem and which is well-nigh[3] overwhelming, some scholars emphasize above all, the

---

1. *Edmunds,* II, 123 ff.; Mark IX, 2 ff.; Luke IX. 30 f.; *Rhys Davids,* Dialogues of the Buddha, II, p. 146; *Dutoit,* Leben des Buddha, p. 283 f. *Bergh van Eysinga.* p. 73, alludes to the transfiguration of Moses (Exodus XXXIV, 29 ff.).

2. Indien und das Christentum, Tübingen 1914. In his earlier studies (Deutsche Rundschau, Vol. 144, 1910, 73 ff., Vol. 149, 1911, 122 ff., and Contributions of Buddhism to Christianity. Chicago 1911), *Garbe* had taken up a more sceptical attitude. Joh. B. *Aufhauser,* Buddha und Jesus in ihren Paralleltexten, Bonn 1926, has confronted the parallel texts, giving the Gospel legends in the Greek text and the Indian legends in German translations, for the cases treated by *Garbe.*

3. *Cf,* Hans *Haas,* Bibliographie zur Frage nach den Wechselbeziehungen zwischen Buddhismus und Christentum (Veroffentlichungen des Forschungsinst. f. vergl. Religionsgeschichte an der Universität Leipzig No. 6) and *Aufhauser,* Buddha und Jesus, Introduction. Besides *Seydel, Bergh van Eysinga, Edmunds* and *Garbe,* other supporters of the theory of the dependence of the canonical Gospels upon the Buddhist texts or traditions, are H. *Kern* (DLZ 1882, col. 1276) and R. O. *Franke* (DLZ 1901. col. 2757 ff.), who have a prehistoric ("Aryan") connection in mind; also : O. *Pfleiderer,* Dic Entstchung des Christentums, 2 Aufl., Munchen 1907, p. 198 f., Ernst *Kuhn* in the Appendix to Bergh van Eysinga's work (p. 102 ff.) and R. *Pischel* (DLZ 1904, col. 2938 ff.) who confidently asserts : "The question as to whether Indian influences are at all to be found in the narrative literature of the Gospels can no longer be denied at the present day"; also K. E. *Neumann,*

divergences, whilst others lay stress upon the resemblances. The question of chronology, moreover, can rarely be decided in such a way as to exclude all doubt. All that can be said with certainty[1] is that, centuries before the birth of Christ, numerous

Reden Gotamo Buddho's III, 112, 256 note, 258 note, 259 note, 260 note 334 note and elsewhere (cf. the criticism of *Günter*, Buddha, 259 ff.); K. *Seidenstücker* in his German translation of Udāna II, 8; VII, 9; VIII 5; 9; 10 and introduct:on p. xxii; in a few cases also H. *Haas*, "Das Scherflein der Witwe" and seine Entsprechung in Tripiṭaka, Leipzing 1922 (Verffentli-chungen etc. No. 5) and Buddha in der abanländischen Legende ? Leipziendg 1923 (Veroffentlichungen etc. No. 9). A. *Weber* (Griechen in Indien, SBA 1890, p. 928 f.) and H. *Oldenberg* (Theolog. Litztg. 1905, Col. 65 ff., Aus dem alten Indien, p. 47 f.) regard it as an open question. An entirely or almost entirely negative attitude is taken up by T. W. *Rhys Davids*, SBE XI, 165 f.; J. Estlin *Carpenters*. The first three Gospels, their Origin and Relations, 2nd Ed., London 1890, pp. 136 ff., 161 ff., 174 ff., 203 ff-, 237 f.: "Buddhist and Christian Parallels" in "Studies in the History of Religions" presented to Crawford Howell Toy, New York, 1912 and Buddhism and Christianity (London 1923), p. 179 f.; E. *Hardy*, Der Buddhismus, new ed. by Rich. *Schmidt*, Munster i. W. 1919, p. 175 ff.; E. W. *Hopkins*, India Old and New, New York and London 1902, p. 120 ff.; E. *Windisch*, Māra und Buddha, pp. 60 ff., 214 ff.' 312 and Buddha's Geburt, p. 195 ff.; *La Vallée Poussin*, Revuc biblique 1906, p. 353 ff., Bouddhisme, p. 5. ff.; L'histoire des religions de l'Inde et l'Apologetique, London 1912 S. *Levi* in Revue critique 1908, N. S, 65, p 382; A. B. *Keith* in JRAS 1910, 213 f.; History of Sanskrit Lit., 501 ff.; Edv. *Lehmann* Der Buddhismus als indische Sekte als Weltreligion, Tubingen 1911, p. 78 ff.; *Faber*, Buddhistische und Neutestamentliche, Erzählungen, Leipzig 1913; A. *Gotz* in "Der Katholik" 1912 (IV, 9), 74 ff.; 254 ff.; (IV 10), 16 ff.; 1915, 363 ff.; Karl *Beth* in DLZ 1915, 893 ff., 957 ff. and Thelogische Studien und Kritiken 1916, 169 ff.; Carl *Clemen* in Zeitschrift für die Neutestamentliche Wiss. 1916, 128 ff.; DLZ 1917, 668 ff.; OZ IX, 185 ff. and RGG I, 1332 ff.; Joh. B. *Aufhauser*, Christentum und Buddhismus im Ringen im Fernasien, Bonn and Leipzing 1922, p. 349 ff.; Edward J. *Thomas*, The Life of Buddha. 1927, p. 237 ff. J. *Kenmedy* (JRAS 1917, 209 ff., 469 ff.) seeks the origin of all legends in the West. H. *Günter* (Buddha in der abendländischen Legende ? Leipzig 1922) is inclined to explain all the Buddhist-Christian parallels on the grounds of the "relationship of life," *i.e.* the similarity of religious moods and experiences is the two religions; R. *Fick* in GGA 1924, p. 172 ff. agrees with him, but in more in favour of a "non liquet."

1. *Cf. Bergh van Eysinga*, loc. cit., 88 ff.; *Edmunds*, Buddhist and Christian Gospels, I, pp. 111-164, and R. *Stübe* "Indien und der Westen," in M. Kern' "Das Licht des Ostens," p. 242 ff.

trade connections and manifold intellectual relations were already in existence between India and the West, and that there is a possibility of Christianity's having been influenced by Buddhism. We also know that, from the 2nd and 3rd centuries A.D., representatives of various religions, Syrian Christians, Zoroastrians and Buddhists, met one another, especially in Eastern Turkestan. At this period it was just as much possible for Christian themes to find their way into Buddhist tales, as for Buddhist ideas to be incorporated in Christian legends. On the other hand, it is very improbable that Christian ideas penetrated to India as early as in the 1st century A.D. It is true that J. *Dahlmann*[1] was at pains to prove that there is a historical basis for the Acts of St. Thomas, that a Christian mission was at work in Northern India as early as the first century A.D., and that Mahāyāna Buddhism developed under Christian influence—but his arguments are by no means convincing. The mention of historical names, such as Gundaphorus and Gad only proves that the background of the legend is historical, but not that the nucleus of the legend itself is necessarily so. There is not the least proof of Christian missions in India in the 1st century, and it is highly improbable that Christianity influenced the origin of the Mahāyāna.[2] It is not likely that anything much about Christians was known in India prior to the 3rd century.[3] It must be admitted, however, that the Buddhist texts can scarcely ever be dated with any degree of certainty. Moreover we have always to reckon with the possibility that a legend might have originated at an early period, even though it was not written down until later. We see, then, that these are very complex questions, and each case must be decided on its own merits. It is only such elaborate monographs as those of *Hans*

1. Indische Fahrten, Freiburg i. B. 1901, II, 100, 129 ff., 152 ff.; Die Thomas-Legende, Freiburg i. B. 1912; cf. Alfons *Vāth*, Der hl. Thomas der Apostel Indiens, Aachen 1925, and J. *Charpentier*, The Apostle of India, in Kyrko-historisk Arsskrift 1927, 21 ff.

2. *Cf. Winternitz* in DLZ 1913, 1750 ff. and *Garbe*, Indien und das Christentum, 128 ff., 159 ff.

3. *Cf.* A. *Harnack*, Die Mission und Ausbreitung des Christentums in den ersten drei Jahrhunderten, 4. Aufl. Leipzig 1924, p. 698.

Haas[1] on the "widow's mite" and *William Norman Brown*[2] on the miracle of walking on the sea, which can pave the way for a tolerably satisfactory result.

The Buddhist parallel to the story of the "widow's mite" is the legend of the poor girl who gives the monks the whole of her possessions, two copper coins which she has found in the dust-heap, and is praised for it by Buddha, her gift being valued as highly as that of the rich man who gives all his estates and treasures as alms. She does not go without a reward for her good deed, for soon afterwards she is discovered by a passing king, who immediately falls in love with her and makes her his queen. There is no doubt that the Buddhist narrative, in the form in which we know it from the Chinese translation of the Kalpanāmaṇḍitikā,[3] is far inferior to the Gospel story, so beautiful in its simplicity, of the widow's two mites. As the Buddhist tale is first attested by the Chinese translation of 402 A.D., and can scarcely be earlier than 200 A.D., it is not impossible that the Buddhists learned it from Christians, and made it end like a fairy tale. It is also possible, however, that an earlier and better form of the Buddhist legend has been lost. The agreement with regard to so small a detail as the "*two* mites" makes it highly probable nevertheless, that the Buddhist and Christian stories did not originate independently of each other.

Similarly, the parallel to St. Peter's walking on the sea, is not found until the time of the later Buddhist literature : we have it in the Jātaka commentary. Just as in Matth. XIV, 28 ff. St. Peter walks on the sea, and begins to sink as soon as his faith wavers, similarly, in the "Story of the present" of Jātaka No. 190, a believing layman walks across the river as long as he thinks joyfully of Buddha, and begins to sink as soon as this joyful mindfulness of Buddha diminishes at the sight of the

1. "Das Scherflein der Witwe" (s. above p. 391 note 3).

2. The Indian and Christian Miracles of Walking on the Water, The Open Court Company, Chicago, London 1928.

3. Sūtrālaṃkāra. trad, Huber, p. 119, ff.; Mark XII, 41 ff.; Luke XXI, I ff.; *Bergh van Eysinga*, p. 50ff.; *Lehmann*, loc, cit., p, 88 ff.; *Götz* in "Der Katholik" 1912 (IV; 10), 18f. *Clemen* in OZ IX, 186f. 199f.; *Garbe*, Indien und das Christentum 33 f.; *Haas*, l. c.

waves. In this instance the details coincide so strikingly, that it is highly improbable that the two legends originated independently of each other. As the Indian legend is not an isolated one, whilst as far as the New Testament is concerned, it occurs only in St. Matthew, it is very likely that the Christian legend was derived from an Indian source. We must assume, it is true, that the narrative which has come down to us in the Jātaka commentary, is based upon a much earlier tradition.[1]

Again, the parallel to the miracle of the feeding of the multitude, does not occur earlier than in the Jātaka commentary. Just as Jesus feeds 5,000 people with five loaves and two fishes, the Buddhist narrative tells us that 500 monks were fed with a cake which increased of itself. There is, however, a considerable difference between the two. In the Gospel we have a miracle which Jesus performs in order to feed a multitude of poor people, and in which he raises his eyes to heaven, and blesses, whilst in the Jātaka commentary we have a comical, not to say silly, fairy-tale, in which the miracle is performed by a saint in order to convert a miser. Indeed, the miracle of Jesus has more in common with the miraculous feeding of the children of Israel with quails and manna (Exodus XVI, cf. Numbers XI, 31 f.) than with the Buddhist fairytale.[2] There is also an account of a miracle of feeding in the Mahāyāna-Sūtra, Vimala-

1. *Cf.* W. N. *Brown*, loc. cit.; *Edmunds* II, 257 f.; *Bergh van Eysinga*, p. 52 ff.; *Carpenter*, First Three Gospels, p. 203 ff.; Buddhism and Christianity, p. 180; *Garbe*, Contributions, p. 12 f.; Indien und das Christentum, 56 ff.; *Götz*, l. c., 19 ff.; *Beth* in DLZ 1915. col. 1900; Theolog. Studien 1916, 214 ff.; *Clemen* in Zeitschr. für die neutes tamentliche Forschung 1916, 137; *Charpentier* in ZDMG 69, 441; *Günter*, Buddha in der abendländischen Legende ? 218 f.; *Haas*, Buddha inder abendländ. Legende ? 25 f.

2. Matth. XIV, 16 ff.; XV, 32 ff.; Jātaka, No. 78. *Cf. Edmunds* II, 253 ff.; *Garbe*, Indien und das Christentum, 59f.; *Charpentier* in ZDMG 69, 441; *Carpenter*, Buddhism and Christianity, p. 180; *Clemen* in OZ IX, 185 f.; Zeitschr. f. d. neutest. Wiss. 1916, 137 f.; *Beth* in DLZ 1915, 900 f.; Theolog. Studien 1916, 219 ff.; *Günter*, l. c., p. 214; *Haas*, "Scherflein der Witwe," 37 f. The Rasavāhini, in which similar legends occur (*Lehmann*, l.c., p. 90 ff.) is quite a late work (see above, p. 216 f.). In his book "Unter Brahmanen und Pariaś," Leipzig 1923, p. 68 f., J. A. *Sauter* tells of a miracle of feeding which he says he witnessed himself, on the part of Dayanandi Svami, who fed and satisfied twenty guests with two handfuls of rice.

Kīrti-Nirdeśa.[1] Many Bodhisattvas have assembled for a pious conversation. It is time for the meal, and by his miraculous power, Vimalakīrti causes a being from the world of sweet perfumes to produce a tiny fragment of food, which satisfies the whole assembly, and yet does not grow smaller. This miraculous feeding differs as widely from that of the Jātaka as it does from that of the Gospel. Finally, if we remind ourselves of the fairy-tale motif of "Table, fill thyself", which has its counterpart even in the Mahābhārata[2] in the self-filling pot which was the gift of the sun-god, we shall come to the conclusion that all these miracles of feeding are but variations of a motif which could quite well crop up afresh as a new invention at different times and in different places.

There is a far more striking similarity between the legend of Asita and that of Simeon in St. Luke. In spite of some differences, which, here too, are undeniable, we can regard it as fairly probable that the author of the Christian narrative was acquainted with the Buddhist legend.[3] It is possible, too, that there is a connection between the legend of Buddha who, as a boy, goes apart from his companions, and after being missed by his family, is found absorbed in deep meditation, and the story of the twelve-year old Jesus who, instead of returning to Nazareth with his parents, remains behind in the temple in Jerusalem and converses with the teachers.[4] We can also consider it within the realm of possibility that the beatification of the mother of the

---

1. Communicated by *Haas*, "Das Scherflein der Witwe," p. 89 ff.

2. See above, Vol. I, p. 327 f.

3. See above, p. 93 f. *Cf. Bergh van Eysinga*, 28 ff.; *Edmunds* I, 181 ff.; *Pischel* in DLZ 1904, 2938 ff.; *Garbe*. l. c., 48 ff.; *Charpentier* in ZDMG 69, 441. The divergences between the two legends are emphasized by *Götz* in "Der Katholik" 1912 (IV, 9), 429 ff.; *Beth* in DLZ 1915, 898 f.; Theolog. Studien 1916, 192 ff.; *Clemen* in Zeitschr. f. d. neutest. Wiss. 1916, 134 f.; *Carpenter*, Buddhism and Christianity, 179 f.; and by *Günter*. l. c., p. 203 f. (on the other hand, cf, *Haas*, Buddha in der abendländischen Legende? 24).

4. St. Luke II, 41 ff.; Lalita-Vistara XI; Nidāna-Kathā, Jātaka Ed., p. 58; *Rhys Davids*. Buddhist Birth Stories, p. 75; *Kern*, Der Buddhismus I, 39 f. *Cf. Bergh van Eysinga*, p. 33 f.

Lord by a woman in St. Luke XI, 27 f. is connected with that in the Nidāna-Kathā.[1]

It is less probable that the parable of the "prodigal son" in the Saddharma-Puṇḍarīka is connected with that in St. Luke. Even Seydel[2] says : "The parable of the 'Lotus' has in reality nothing in common with the Christian parable, except that a wandering son returns in poverty, and above all the tendency of the comparison is entirely different in the two parallels." Also the similarity between the legend of Jesus and the woman of Samaria in the Gospel of St. John, and that of Ānanda and the pariah girl in the Divyāvadāna is none too great.[3] Besides, in both cases they are Buddhist texts of post-Christian times.

Even the death of Christ has been compared with Buddha's entrance into Nirvāṇa. Seydel has pointed out that both events are accompanied by an earthquake, while Edmunds goes so far as to emphasize the fact that Jesus and Buddha both die in the open-air ![4] And yet the difference between the two religious texts is nowhere shown so clearly as here. What a vast difference between the Mahā-Parinibbāna-Sutta and the 27th chapter of St. Matthew ! Here the heart-rending tragedy of a martyr and a victim of fanaticism, there the calm passing of a sage—a glorious Euthanasia. In the Gospel of St. Matthew, the earth opens and quakes, and the graves yawn in horror at the crime

---

1. Jātaka I, p. 60; *Rhys Davids*, Buddhist Birth Stories, p. 79 f.; *Seydel*, die Buddhalegende, p. 26 f.; *Bergh van Eysinga*, p. 48 ff. It is true enough that such beatitudes also occur elsewhere in poetry (*Neumann*, Lieder der Mönche und Nonnen, p. 309 note; *Lehmann*, Der Buddhismus, p. 85); nevertheless, it is a remarkable coincidence that both Buddha and Jesus append to the benedictions a remark concerning that whereof true blessedness consists. The connection is denied by *Götz* in "Der Katholik" 1912 (IV, 10), 16 f., and doubted by *Garbe*, l. c., p. 32 f.

2. Das Evangelium von Jesu, p. 230; cf. above, p. 286 f.; J. M. *Carter*, JRAS 1893, p. 393 f.; *Bergh van Eysinga*, p. 67 ff.; *Edmunds* II, 260 f. *Seydel*, l. c., p. 232 f., has, however, compared the allegory of the man who was born blind (John IX) with Saddharma P. V. (see above, p. 287), though the Indian *parable* has nothing in common with the Christian *legend*, except that a man who was born blind occurs in both.

3. See above, p. 275 f.; *Bergh van Eysinga*, p. 57 ff.

4. *Seydel*, l. c., p. 280 ff.; *Edmunds* II, 169 f.; cf. *Windisch*, Māra und Buddha, p. 60 ff.

which was being committed ; in the Mahā-Parinibbāna-Sutta the earth quakes in token of her jubilation that the complete Nirvāṇa of the Lord, a beautiful event, has taken place.

When we come to the single utterances and parables of Jesus and Buddha, it is still more difficult to prove a probable connection than it is in the instance of the legends. It is mostly only a question of resemblances[1], or of such general ideas that they could easily occur and actually do occur, in the sacred books of all religions ; when, for instance, Majjhimanikāya 110, where there is talk of the sowing and reaping of good works, is compared with the parable of the sower (St. Matth. XIII, 18 ff.), or when, in the Sutta of the "real treasure,"[2] a similar idea is expressed as in Matth. VI, 19f. : "Lay not up for yourselves treasures upon earth, where moth and rust doth corrupt," etc.

When we sum up all that has been brought to light by the comparison of the four gospels with the Buddhist texts, it is seen that the differences greatly outweigh the points of agreement. There is a great difference to be seen in the whole character of even those legends which bear comparison. Whilst in Buddhism all the miracles are explained by the Karman, the act working through the rebirths, the Christian miracles are only the outcome of God's mercy and onnipotence. Edv. Lehmann[3] says very aptly : "For the taste of Indians the events in the Christian narratives will always seem to be insufficiently justified by reason and for us Christians the Indian narratives, even from the purely aesthetic points of view, will appear to have an almost unbearably efficient sequence of cause and effect."

Whilst we have thus seen that doubts as to an historical connection on the strength of any of the parallels cited from the

---

1. For instance, above, pp. 29 note 1, 72 note 1, 105 note 1 ; *cf. Neumann*, Lieder der Mönche und Nonnen, p. 359 note. There is greater similarity between St. Matth. XVII, 19, where there is talk of removing the mountain by faith, and Aṅguttaranikāya VI, 24, where it is said that the monk could cleave the Himalaya by meditation (*Edmunds* II, 40). Nevertheless, even this agreement is most probably only an accidental one. Cf. also *Garbe*, Indien und das Christentum, p. 39 ff.

2. Khuddakapāṭha VIII, translated by *Winternitz*, Der ältere Buddhismus (Religiousgesch. Lesebuch, 2, Aufl.) 1929, p. 105 f. *Cf.* Edmunds I, 222.

3. Der Buddhismus, p. 92.

canonical gospels are more than justifiable, and whilst we can at the very most speak of the possibility of such a connection, we find in the apocryphal gospels which originated in the 2nd and 3rd centuries A.D., a whole series of legends, the loan of which from Buddhist literature may be asserted with as great a degree of probability as is at all possible in questions of this kind. The tales of the Bodhisattva, who is taken to the temple in his boyhood, and before whom the statues of the gods arise, so as to fall down at his feet, and that of the Bodhisattva's first day at school, coincide so exactly with the stories of the childhood of Jesus as related in the pseudo-St. Matthew's gospel, Chapter XXIII and in St. Thomas's gospel, Chapts. VI-VIII and XIV, that the dependence of the Christian legend upon the Buddhist one, could only be doubted by persons who refute any such dependence on principle. Or take such legends as the following : in Pseudo-Matth., Chapt. XIII, it is said of the child Jesus that, while still in his mother's womb, a light shone forth from him, so that the dark cavern into which Mary entered, was illuminated and became bright as day, and that the Saviour's mother was in no wise stained with blood through the birth of the child, and felt no pain : in the proto-gospel of St. James chapt. VI, it is told of the six-months old Mary, that she walked towards her mother with seven steps ; in the same gospel, Chapt. XVIII, it is related that the forces of nature and the activities of mankind came to a sudden standstill at the birth of Jesus ; in Pseudo- Matth., Chapt. XX, a palm-tree inclines its branches down to the ground at the command of the infant Jesus, in order to offer its fruits to Mary, who is thirsty and exhausted. It is so very obvious to anyone acquainted with the legend of Buddha, that these wonder-tales must be assumed to be of Indian origin, that even among Christian theologians, there are only few who doubt an historical connection.[1]

---

1. See above, p. 241; *Bergh van Eysinga*, p. 75 ff.; *Garbe*, Contributions, p. 19 ff.; Indien und das Christentum, p. 70 ff.; *Charpentier* in ZDMG 69, 442; E. *Hennecke*, Neutestamentliche Apokryphen, 2. Aufl., Tubingen 1924, p. 95 f. Even *Götz* in "Der Katholik," 1912 (IV, 9), 271, says : "An influence on the part of Indian and presumably also Buddhist traditions on the apocryphal writings of semi-Christian elements of the West is, then, an

It has also been attempted to trace some of the mediaeval legends of the Christian saints back to Indian sources. Māra appears in the form of Buddha in two different Buddhist legends, on one occasion it is in order to seduce a pious man, in which he does not succeed ; and the other time, Upagupta causes Māra, whom he has converted, to appear in the form of Buddha.[1] Christian legends tell of several monks to whom the devil appeared in the guise of the Saviour. The Christian legend of the presumptuous monk Valens, to whom the devil appeared in the shape of Christ, whereupon the monk worshipped the devil and related that Christ had appeared to him, is traced by Garbe[2] to the Buddhist narratives, especially as "the monstrous idea of the apparition of the devil in the shape of the Saviour is not to be found anywhere in Christian literature except in this one isolated instance." Gunter[3] has shown, however, that "the monstrous idea" occurs frequently enough in Christian legendary literature. For this reason it is just as much possible for the legends to have originated independently of each other in Christianity and in Buddhism, as for the theme to have migrated to the West from India, where a legend of this nature was translated into Chinese as early as in the year 401 A.D.[4]

historical fact." J. *Kennedy* in JRAS 1917, 508 ff., explains the undeniable resemblances between the apocryphal stories of the childhood of Jesus and the Buddhist legends, by the hypothesis of Christian-Gnostic influences on Buddhism. Among those who make it their principle to deny any connection whatsoever, even in this case, we may mention *Clemen* in Zeitschr. f, neutestament. Wiss. 1916, 131 ff. and *Günter*, l. c., 74 ff., 78 f., 91 f.; see, however, *Haas*, Buddha etc., pp., 12 f., 22 f. As early as in 1762 the Augustine hermit Georgius pointed out that a similar story to that told of the five-year old Jesus and Zakchaios in the Gospel of St. Thomas, was told in Tibet about Buddha, see L. *Conrady*, Das Thomasevangelium (Thelog. Studien und Kritiken, Gotha 1903), p. 403 ff.

1. See above, pp. 195 and 277.
2. Indien und das Christentum, p. 111 ff.
3. Loc. cit., p. 234 ff.; cf. *Haas*, Buddha in der abendländischen Legende p. 32.
4. *Chavannes*, Cinq cents contes et apologues, t. II, p. 86 (No. 206).
5. *Cf.* above, pp. 132 note 2, 150 note 2, and *Garbe*, Indien und das Christentum, p. 86 ff.: 101 ff.; *Haas*, l. c., p. 9.; *Günier*, l. c., p. 7 ff.; *Charpentier* in ZDMG 69, 442 f.; *Beth*, Theolog Studien 1916, 197 f.

Garbe and others before him have also traced the legends of St. Eustace and St. Christopher back to Buddhist Jātakas. Nevertheless, in spite of Garbe's arguments we cannot believe that this is a case of an actual connection.

On the other hand, it is a fully established fact that one of the favourite books of the whole of Christendom in the Middle Ages, the story of Barlam and Josaphat, was composed by a devout Christian on the basis of the Buddha legend, with which he might have become acquainted from the Lalita-Vistara.[1] This story, which is otherwise entirely imbued with the spirit of Christianity, has a Buddhist setting : the main features of the Buddha legend, the three excursions, at which the Bodhisattva becomes acquainted with age, disease and death, recur in it, a few of the interpolated parables (*e.g.* that of the "man in the well") are familiar from Indian literature, and references to India occur in the story itself.[2] In Eastern Iran or in Central Asia, where, as we know through the finds of Sir Aurel Stein, Grunwedel and v. Le Coq in Khotan and Turfan, Zoroastrians,

1. *Max Müller*, Essays III, p. 538 f. (cf. *Foucaux*, Lalita Vistara trad. II, 43 ff.) quotes a few passages from which it seems evident that the author "heard the story not only, as he says, from the lips of people who had brought it to him from India, but that he even had the text of the Lalita-Vistara before him."

2. As early as in the year 1612 the Portuguese Diogodo Conto compared the Barlaam-Josaphat legend with that of Buddha (Ind. Ant. XII, p. 288 f.). It was, however, Laboulaye who first asserted the Buddhist origin of the legend, in Journal des Debats of the 26th July 1859. The proof was then furnished by Felix Liebrecht (in Jahrbuch fur romanische und englishe Literatur II, 1860, p. 314 ff. and in his book "Zur Volkskunde", Heilbronn 1879, p. 441 ff.). The whole history of the story has been traced throughout universal literature, by E. *Kuhn* ("Barlaam und Joasaph, eine bibliographisch litterargeschichtliche Studie," A BayA XX, Munchen 1897). Kuhn (p. 39) believes, however, that the author "made very free use of the entire Buddhist tradition, and not of one particular text like the Lalita Vistara." Cf. also the literature cited in V. *Chauvin*, Bibliographie des ouvrages Arabes III. 1898, p, 83 ff,, and H. G. *Rawlinson* in JBRAS 24, 1915, p. 96 ff. Even *Gunter*, l. c., p. 92 ff., cannot but admit that Josaphat is the Bodhisattva, though he is very anxious to minimize the influence of the Buddhist legend over the Christian one, and prefers to assume nothing more than a "distant indirect influence" (p. 41).

Buddhists, Christians and Manicheans lived together in closest proximity, a Christian monk[1] could easily become acquainted with the Buddha legend, and be stimulated by it to compose a work which was to impart Christian doctrines. This work was presumably written in the 6th or 7th century, first in the Pahlavi language and afterwards translated into Arabic and Syriac. The Georgian and Greek translation might be traced back to the Syriac text. The Greek text gave rise to Arabian, Hebrew, Aethiopian, Armenian, Ecclesiastical-Russian and Rumanian versions, which came into being in later times. The numerous European translations and recensions (Lope de Vega has even dramatised the story) can be traced back to the Latin text translated from the Greek. German recensions have been in existencc since 1220 A.D. In course of centuries the characters in this work had grown so familiar to the Christian peoples, that they were regarded as pious Christian men who had really lived and taught, so that the Catholic Church finally made the two heroes of the story, Barlaam and Josaphat into saints. Josaphat, however, is none other than the Bodhisattva.[2]

It is not only pious narratives such as that of Kisā-Gotamī[3] which wandered from India to the West, but also many secular fables, and narrative motifs as are to be found in the Jātaka,

---

1. It has been supposed by A. v. *Le Coq* (SBA 1909, p. 1205) that the Buddha legend was first brought to Europe, not by Christians, but by Manicheans. The actual author of the story, however, can only have been a Christian, as the doctrines contained in the book are specially Christian. It was just as possible for Christians to become acquainted with the subject as it was for Manicheans.

2. In Greek the prince is called Joasaph, the Arabic Jūdāsaf, which is derived from Būdāsaf, *i.e.* Bodhisattva, In Arabic, Syriac and Pahlavi, "f" and "b" are easily confused in the script. The sage Barlaam is called Balauhar in Arabic, which might be derived from Bhagavān. (Kuhn, loc. cit., pp. 17, 19, 34 f.) Barlaam and Josaphat already appear as saints in the "Catalogus Sanctorum" of Petrus de Natalibus, who died in about 1370. Even in more recent times, the legend of Barlaam and Josaphat has been made the subject of a romance for children and also of a drama in Germany; s, *Slepcevic,* Buddhismus in der deutschen Litteratur; p. 33 ff.

3. See above, p. 56 f.

the Dhammapada commentary and Buddhaghosa's commentaries.[1] Even down to our own day, the Indian legend of Buddha has so well preserved its ever youthful freshness and vitality, that again and again it has inspired poets, including Western poets, to compose epic and dramatic rendering of this immortal theme.[2] Thus *Edwin Arnold's* epic "The Light of Asia" was in the 19th century, still capable of inspiring such enthusiasm that it saw over sixty editions in England and over a hundred in America, and really laid the foundation for this poet's fame.[3] Whilst Edwin Arnold kept closely to the Indian legend the German poet *Jaseph Viktor Widmann*, in his "Buddha,"[4] has left little of the ancient Indian legend. On the other hand, much of the spirit and mentality of Buddhism is embodied in the beautiful epic poem "The Saint and the Animals" by the same poet. The Buddha legend was made the theme of a drama in Germany by *Ferdinand Hornstein*, whose "Buddha"[5] was produced at the Hoftheater in Munich in 1900.

Under the influence of the philosophy of Schopenhauer, Richard Wagner felt strongly attracted towards the Buddhist doctrine of salvation and morality of pity. "You know that I have become a Buddhist in spite of myself," he wrote to Mathilde Wesendonk on the 22nd February, 1859 ; and on

---

1. See above, p. 193 f.; also *Günter*, l. c., 107 ff., admits that a steady stream of Indian motifs, including such as we find in the Jâtaka-Book, poured into the European literatures from the 12th century onwards.

2. On the influence of Buddhism on German literature, see Pero *Slepcevic* Buddhismus in der deutschen Litterature (Diss. der Universität Freiburg in der Schweiz), Wien 1920.

3. *Cf.* E. F. *Oaten*, Sketch of Anglo-Indian Literature, London, 1908, p. 84 ff.; Leon *Kellner*, Die englische Literature im Zeitalter der Konigin Viktoria Leipzig 1909, p, 404 ff., and Beil. Allg. Zeitung 1889, Nos. 30 ff.; Artur *Pfungst* translated "The Light of Asia" into German (Leipzig 1887).

4. Epische Dichtung in 20 Gesängen, Bern 1869. As the poet himself wrote (in a letter of the 27th August 1905), this poem of Buddha was "really only modern free thinking views disguised in that Oriental garb." *Cf.* also *Slepcevic*, l. c, p. 55 ff.

5. Legende in 3 Akten, Musik von Robert v. Hornstein, München 1899. See *Slepcevic*, l. c., p. 69 ff. Angelo de *Gubernatis* and A. *Obolonsky* (Le Prince-Siddhartha, drama en 5 actes et 22 tableaux, Tours 1899) have also dramatised on the life of Buddha.

the 9th July of the same year, he wrote to the same friend, full of enthusiasm about Buddhism : "Yes, child, this is a philosophy compared with which all other dogmas must appear petty, narrow and inadequate !"[1] Three years prior to that, he had already sketched out a Buddhist musical drama "The Victors," in which he intended to dramatise the legend of Ānanda and the Caṇḍāla girl Prakṛti. A year later he embodied the ideas of this sketch, which was never completed, in "Parsifal." Not only here, but in others of Wagner's works, too, we have sufficiently frequent instances of a perfectly clear expression of the Buddhist view of life. In the "Gotterdämmerung" ("The Twilight of the Gods,") Brunhilde says :

"Wisst ihr, wohin ich fahre ?
Aus Wunschheim zieh'ich fort,
Wahnheim flieh'ich auf immer ;
Des ew'gn Werdens offne Thore
Schliess ich hinter mir zu...
Von Wiedergeburt erlöst,
Zieht nun die Wissende hin."[2]

These thoughts are Buddhist through and through.

During the last years of his life, Wagner's mind was occupied with the personality of the Buddha, though there is no sufficient evidence to justify the rumour, spread abroad after his death, that he had worked at a musical drama "Buddha."[3]

Like Richard Wagner, the Danish poet Karl Gjellerup found Buddha by way of the philosophy of Schopenhauer. He drew

1. See Richard Wagner und Mathilde Wesendonk, 21. Aufl., Berlin 1904, p. 59 f., 77 f., 105, 161 f.

2. "Do you know whither I go ?
I bid farewell to the land of desires.
I flee for ever from the land of illusions;
I close behind me the open portals
Of never-ending existence . . .
Released from re-birth,
She who has gained knowledge now departs."

3. See above, p. 276, note 1; H. *Lichtenberger*, Richard Wagner, Dresden und Leipzig 1899, pp. 357 f.; 499 f.; Max *Koch* in Studien zur vergleichenden Literaturgeschichte 3. 1903, 412 ff.; *Slepcevic*, l. c., p. 40 ff,

upon K. E. Neumann's translations, but also made himself acquainted with Buddhism through his own independent study. Though his beautiful prose poem "The Pilgrim Kamanita"[1] is entirely an invention of the poet's own, the figure of Buddha himself has been sketched lovingly according to the sources, and what is more important, the whole poem is instinct with the true spirit of Buddhism. The delicate poetical description of the Buddhist paradise Sukhāvatī is full of charm, and there is no harm in the poet's having woven this picture, which is a part of the Mahāyāna, into his poem, which is mainly based upon the Pāli sources. In the drama "The Wife of the Perfect One,"[2] Gjellerrup has endowed Buddha, who first appears in the play as Prince Siddhārtha, but later on as the Enlightened One, with more worldly traits, and above all more attachment to his family, than the Buddha of the legend really possessed. It would scarcely be possible to find in Buddhist texts a counterpart to the scene in which Buddha yields the sovereignty to his half brother Nanda. The Buddha of the texts never troubled about such matters. Neither could we find in any Buddhist text such words as Buddha is made to speak, in the last scene in the drama, when he hands his weapons to Nanda, and passes him the swords, with the words :

> "Draw it in a just cause only ! But then
> Wield it well, and win, so that wrong may not triumph !"

The true Buddha had no dealings with the sword. For him there is no "just cause," for the sake of which we are justified in doing violence, for he knew, what we have learned but yesterday, that the "just cause" is always merely another name for our own cause, however unjust that cause may be.

---

1. "Pilgrimen Kamanita," Kopenhagen 1906; Der Pilger Kamanita, ein Legendenroman, 7-10. Tausend, Frankfurt a. M. 1917. Also translated into English.

2. "Den fuldendtes Husfru," Kopenhagen 1907; 'Das Weib des Vollendeten, ein Legendendrama, Quelle & Meyer, Leipzig. This drama was also staged in Germany.

Fritz Mauthner, too, in his prose work "The Last Death of Gautama Buddha,"[1] has made Buddha utter many a very un-Buddhistic speech.

Among the works which serve Buddhist propaganda, "The Gospel of Buddha" by *Paul Carus* may be mentioned. In this work, edifying passages from the most varied sources, from earlier and later Pāli texts, from the various biographies of Buddha and European works on Buddhism have been combined to form a mosaic which, from a scholarly point of view, is not always faultless, but is eminently suited to affect people's minds in the religious sense. Since its publication in the English language in America in 1894, this work has seen numerous editions, and it has been translated into many languages. In Ceylon and Japan the work is read in Buddhist schools and temples for purposes of edification.[2]

Whilst Paul Carus lays no claim to erudition, the Italian indologist *Luigi Suali* has recently (1924) retold the Buddha legend in beautiful, poetical language, in his book "Il Illuminato,"[3] on the basis of an accurate knowledge of the original sources. Without the slightest thought of propaganda, he has allowed himself to become absorbed in the very spirit of the legend, and with a loving hand, has portrayed the Buddha with all his human, super-human and super-divine qualities, such as he has lived for over two thousand years, and still lives to-day, in the faith of devout Buddhists.

We may also mention *Lafcadio Hearn*,[4] who has brought us into closer contact with Japanese Buddhism, in many of his

1. "Der letzte Tod des Gautama Buddha," München und Leipzig 1913. The poem is based upon the Mahā-Parinibbāna-Sutta in K. E. *Neumann's* translation.

2. See Das Evangelium des Buddha nach alten Quellen erzählt von Paul *Carus*, illustriert von O. *Kopetzky*, 2. deutsche Auflage von Karl *Seideastücker*, Chicago und London, The Open Court Publishing Company, 1919. The translation was made according to the 13th English edition. Paul *Carus* died on 2nd Febr. 1919.

3. We only know the German translation : "Der Erleuchtete, das Leben des Buddha" (aus dem Italienischen übersetzt von Dora *Mitzky*), Frankfurt a. M. 1928. The Italian original was published in Milan in 1925.

4. "Gleanings in Buddha Fields" "Out of the East," and others, which are well known in German translations also.

sketches and tales. Free from any propagandist intentions, he has with love and sympathy, and with consummate art, given us an insight into Buddhist thought and sentiment as they still exist, even to-day, in the hearts of the devout Buddhists of Japan.

There is not much of importance to be found in the propaganda literature which serves the Neo-Buddhist movement. Translations of Pāli texts are the best thing which we owe to it. *Paul Dahlke's* "Buddhist Stories"[1] may be mentioned, and also the lyric poems of *Hans Much.*[2] But though the latter are Buddhist in sentiment, this European monastic poetry is very feeble when compared to the Thera-Gāthās and Therī-Gāthās, the songs of the ancient Buddhist monks and nuns.

Nevertheless, whatever our views of the new Buddhist movement may be, we cannot but admire the vitality of Buddhism and of the works of Buddhist literature, which have ever and again inspired the minds of thinkers and poets of all nations, and still continue to do so. We hope, too, that we have succeeded in showing in the above chapters, that there is still much in Buddhist literature which well merits being introduced into European literatures and made the common property of universal literature.

---

1. "Buddhistische Erzählungen," Dresden 1904.

2. "Ich nahm meine Zuflucht... Flugsamen aus einem abendländischen Buddhagarten," Leipzig 1920; "An Buddhas Hand, Leider der Erweekung im Felde," 1917, in "Buddhistische Weisheit" von Georg *Grimm* und Hans *Much*, 1920.

SECTION IV

JAINA LITERATURE

JINISM AND ITS LITERATURE

Buddhist texts frequently mention Nigaṇṭha Nātaputta as a rival and opponent of Gotama Buddha. This is none other than the saint known and venerated by the name of Mahāvīra, *i.e.*, "the great hero," the founder or reformer of the sect of the Jainas, which had developed out of the far older sect of the Nigaṇṭhas (*i.e.*, the Fetter-less), under the leadership of Vardhamāna Mahāvīra, probably not long before the appearance of Gotama.[1] The religion of the Jainas, Jinism,[2] has so much in common with Buddhism that, for a long time, it was considered merely as a Buddhist sect. Nevertheless, it presents a marked divergence from the Buddhist religion in such essential points,

---

1. On the strength of the unanimous tradition of both Buddhists and Jainas, we may take it as certain that Mahāvīra was a senior contemporary of Buddha, and that both were contemporaries of Kings Bimbisāra and Ajātaśatru of Magadha. The year of Mahāvīra's death is, however, at least as uncertain as that of Buddha's. Appendix VI. H. *Jacobi* (Ind. Ant. 9, 1880. 158 ff.; SBE 45, p. xx ff.) has made it seem very probable that Mahāvīra was not the founder but only the reformer of an earlier sect of the Nigaṇṭhas founded by Pārśva. Nevertheless, when the tradition says that Pārśva lived exactly 250 years before Mahāvīra, we are not by any means justified in taking this as a certain historical fact.

2. The epithets "Enlightened One" (Buddha) and "Victor" Jina) were applied to Gotama as well as to Mahāvīra (and other founders of religions). However, whilst "Buddha" came to be the name of Gotama, "Jina" came to be the usual name of Mahāvīra, and his adherents called themselves "Jainas" *i.e.*, disciples of the Jina." It has grown customary to use the expressions "Jainism" and "Jainistic." However, as we never say "Bauddhism" and "Bauddhistic," we ought by rights to say "Jinism" and "Jinistic" just as we say "Buddhism" and "Buddhistic." Scholars like A. *Weber* and Th. *Benfey* still considered the Jainas as a Buddhist sect. It has been proved by *Jacobi* (SBE 22, Introd., and in the introduction to his edition of the Kalpa-Sūtra) that this view is erroneous.

that it must be regarded as an independent creed. Jinism[1] lays far more stress than Buddhism on asceticism and all manner of cult exercises, and in contrast to the Buddha, Mahāvīra taught a very elaborate belief in the soul. All that the two religions have in common, is the ancient Indian "ascetic-morality" which we have already characterised more than once; the points of contact, too, between Buddhist and Jaina literature, are precisely those which they both share with the whole of Indian ascetic poetry. It is the Jainas, however, who far more than any other Indian religion, emphasize the commandment of Ahiṃsā, non-violence.

An essential difference between the two religions is, however, that Jinism has always remained a national Indian religion, whilst Buddhism developed into a world religion. It is true that, according to the belief of the Jainas, their religion is a "world religion" in the sense that it is a religion not only for human beings of all races and classes, but even for animals, gods and denizens of hell. Notwithstanding, the Jainas have retained the Indian system of castes and classes in its entirety,[2] and Jinism has a much stronger tendency than Buddhism to adapt itself to Brahmanism and Hinduism, and also it is confined within the frontiers of India. The Jainas themselves explain the close relations of their religion with Brahmanism by asserting that their religion is the oldest of all religions, and the religion of the

1. *Cf.* G. *Buhler,* Ueber die indische Sekte der Jainas (Almanach der k. Akademie der Wissonschaften, Wien 1887); translated into English by J. *Burgess,* On the Indian Sect of the Jainas, with an Outline of Jaina Mythology, London 1903; H. *Jacobi* in ERE VII. 1914, 465 ff.; Mrs. Sinclair *Stevenson,* The Heart of Jainism, Oxford and London 1915; Puran Chand *Nahar* and Krishnachandra *Ghosh,* An Epitome of Jainism, Calcutta 1917; Helmuth v. *Glasenapp,* Der Jainismus, Berlin 1925. A. *Guerinot,* La religion Djaina, histoire, doctrine, culte, costumes, institutions, Paris 1926. A presentation of the Jaina religion from the view-point of an enthusiastic European is given by Herbert *Warren,* Jainism in Western Garb as a Solution to Life's Great Problems, Arrah 1912, second ed. 1916. On the history of the Jainas, see also A. *Guerinot,* Repertoire d'Epigraphie Jaina precede d'une esquisse de l'historie du Jainisme d'apres les inscriptions, Paris (Publ. de l'Ecole francaise d'Extreme-Orient) 1908, and J. *Charpentier* in Cambridge History I, 150 ff.

2. H. v. *Glasenapp,* Der Jainismus, pp. 314 ff, 316 ff.

Brahmins is merely a degenerate form of it. Although, as has already been mentioned, Jinism is older than Buddhism, the canonical literature of the Jainas has not come down to us in its earliest form. Unfortunately, only parts of it have been preserved, and in its present form it only dates back to a comparatively recent period. It is solely for this reason that we deal with it here *after* Buddhist literature.

With rare exceptions, the sacred books of the Jainas are written in a dry-as-dust, matter of fact, didactic tone, and as far as we know them hitherto, are seldom instinct with that general human interest which so many Buddhist texts possess. Hence, important as they are for the specialist, they cannot claim the interest of the general reader to anything approaching so great an extent. If, for these reasons, the following treatment of Jinist literature[1] occupies a comparatively small space, we shall be giving only a faint idea of the exceedingly wide range of literary activity of the Jaina monks, to which the catalogues of Jaina manuscripts[2] and the very numerous editions

---

1. The first to open up the rich treasures of the Jaina libraries was G. *Bühler*, who in the years 1873-1878 acquired a large collection of Jaina manuscripts for the royal library at Berlin. This collection formed the basis of the first comprehensive and epoch-making accounts of the literature of the Jainas, by Albrecht *Weber*, Ind. Stud. 16, 1883, pp. 211-479; 17, 1885, pp. 1-90 (translated into English by H. W. *Smyth* in Ind. Ant., vols. 17-21, 1888-1892) and HSS. Verz. II, 1888-1891. *Cf.* E. *Windisch*, Geschichte der Sanskrit-Philologie (Grundriss I, 1 B), p. 346 ff; A. *Guerinot*, Essai de bibliographie Jaina, Paris 1906 (AMG, bibl. d'etudes, t. 22); Addenda to it JA 1909, s. 10, t. XIV, 47-148; 1912, s. 10, t. XIX, 373 ff., and B. *Geiger* in GGA 1908, 124 ff.; *Guerinot*, La religion Djaina, pp. 69-90; H. v. *Glasenapp*, Der Jainismus, pp. 81-134 and Die Literaturen Indiens (in "Handbuch der Literaturwissenschaft"), p. 118 ff For important data on Jain authors, see J. *Klatt* in Ind. Ant. 11, 1882, pp. 245-256 and Specimen of a Literary-Bibliographical Jaina-Onomasticon, Leipzig 1892. The little book by U. D. *Barodia*, History and Literature of Jainism, Bombay 1909, has no scientific value.

2. The following accounts of Jaina MSS, are of great importance :— those by R. G. *Bhandarkar*, Report 1883-4; P. *Peterson*, 3 Reports, Report IV and Rep. V; by *Jacobi. Klatt* and *Leumann*, ZDMG 33, 693 ff., 478 ff.; 45. 454 ff.; 47, 308 ff.; WZKM 11, 1897, 297 ff. F. L. *Pulle*, Catalogo dei manoscritti giainici della Bibliotheca n. c. di Firence 1894 and OC X, 1894,

of texts that have appeared during the last decades in various collections, bear testimony.[1]

The literature of the Jainas is also very important from the point of view of the history of the Indian languages : for the Jainas always took care that their writings were accessible to considerable masses of the people. Hence the canonical writings and the earliest commentaries are written in Prākrit dialects (Māgadhī and Māhārāṣṭrī).[2] It was not until a later period that the Jainas—the Śvetāmbaras from the 8th century, and the Digambaras somewhat earlier—used Sanskrit for commentaries and learned works as well as for poetry. Some of these authors write a simple, lucid Sanskrit, others compete with the classical Sanskrit poets in their use of an elaborate Sanskrit in the Kāvya style, whilst yet others affect a Sanskrit shot with Prākritisms, approaching the vernacular.[3] At a later time, from the 10th to

II, p. 15 ff.; A. B. *Keith,* Catalogue of Prākrit Manuscripts in the Bodleian Library, Oxford 1911, col. 1-45; *Rai Bahadur Hiralal,* Catalogue of Sanskrit and Prakrit MSS. published under the Orders of the Government of the Central Provinces and Berar, Nagpur 1926; H. D. *Velankar,* A Descriptive Catalogue of Saṁskṛta and Prākṛta Manuscripts in the Library of the Bombay Branch of the Royal Asiatic Society, Vols. III-IV, Jain and Varnacular Literatures, Bombay 1930.

1. A collection of the canonical writings, "Āgama-Saṃgraha," was printed between 1875 and 1885 in Calcutta, Bombay, Benares and Ahmedabad in 45 volumes. Numerous texts have appeared in the Śrī-Jaina-Jaso-Vijaya-Granthamālā published by the great Jainācārya Vijaya Dharma Sūri; learned societies, such as the Jaina Dharma Prasāraka Sabhā in Bhavnagar, the Jaina Vidyā Prasāraka Varga in Palitana, the Jaina Jñāna Prasāraka Varga in Bombay, the Jaina Vidyā Śālā in Ahmedabad, the Āgamodaya Samiti in Mehsana, and others, and wealthy patrons such as Sheṭh Devchand Lalbhai Jhaveri in Bombay, Sheṭh Bhagabāi Mansukhbhāi in Ahmedabad, and others, have assisted towards the publication of Jain texts. See E. *Hultzsch* in Ind. Ant., Vol. 39, 1910. p. 228; *Jacobi* in AR 13, 1910, 615 ff., and 18, 1915, 275 f. We are indebted to the Digambara Jainas also, for such valuable publications as the "Sacred Books of the Jainas" and "The Library of Jaina Literature," both of which are appearing in Arrah.

2. See above I, p. 41, and W. *Denecke,* in Festgable Jacobi, p. 160 ff. Also Franklin Edgerton, "Notes on Jaina Mahārāṣṭrī" in Lamman studies, p. 27 ff.

3. See M. *Bloomfield,* Some Aspects of Jaina Sanskrit, in Festschrift Wackernagel, I923, p. 220 ff,; also Bloomfield, "on Dimunitice Pronouns in Jaina Sanskrit", in Lamman Studies, p. 7ff.

the 12th century, there is a return of poetry to the Apabhraṃśa dialects adapted to the vernacular.[1] Lastly, in quite recent times, the Jainas also use various modern Indian languages, and they have enriched more especially Gujarati and Hindi literatures, as well as Tamil and Kanarese literatures in the south.

The Canon (Siddhānta) of the Jainas[2]

The most important schism within the Jaina religion, namely, into the two great sects of the Śvetāmbaras, *i.e.*, "those clad in white", and the Digambaras, *i.e.*, "those clad in air" or "naked", occurred as early as in the first century A.D. The collective term given by the Jainas to their sacred books, is Siddhānta or Āgama. Both sects are unanimous in calling the twelve Aṅgas, *i.e.*, "limbs" (of the body of the religion) the first and most important part of their Canon. Hitherto, however we have a detailed knowledge only of the Siddhānta of the Śvetāmbaras. It consists of the following texts :—

I. The twelve Aṅgas : 1. Āyāraṃga-Sutta[3] (Ācārāṅga-Sūtra); 2. Sūyagaḍaṃga (Sūtrakṛtāṅga) ; 3. Ṭhāṇaṃga (Sthānāṅga); 4. Samavāyaṃga; 5. Bhagavatī Viyāhapannatti (Vyākhyā-

1. See above I, p. 42, and *Jacobi*, Zur Frage nach dem Ursprung des Apabhraṃśa, in Festschrift Wackernagel, p. 124 ff.

2. On the Canon and its history see *Jacobi* in the introductions to his edition of the Kalpa-Sūtra, p. 14 ff, and to SBE, Vols, 22 and 45, and ZDMG 28, 1 ff.; *Hoernle* in the introduction to his translation of the Uvāsagadasāo, p. vii ff. and Proceedings ASB 1898, p. 39 ff. (French Le Museon, N. S., VII. 1906, 109 ff.) ; G. *Buhler*, WZKM I, 1887, 165 ff.; 2, 1888, 141 ff.; 3, 1889, 233 ff.; 4, 1890, 313 ff; A. *Barth*. RHR 3, 1881, 89 ff.; 11, 1885, 185; 19, 1889, 280 ff.; 20, 332; 29, 1894, 25 ff.; 45, 1902, 178; Oeuvres I, 306 ff., 344 ff., 397; II, 59 ff., 192 ff., 378 ff,; P. C. *Nahar* and K. C. *Ghosh*, An Epitome of Jainism, Calcutta 1917, Appendix C; J. *Charpentier* in the introduction to his edition of the Uttarādhyayana-Sūtra (Upsala 1921) and W. *Schubring*, Worte Mahāvīras, Göttingen 1927, p. VIII f. and ff. Selected passages from canonical texts translated into German by W. *Schubring*, Die Jainas (in Religionsgeschichtliches Lesebuch von. A, Bertholet, 2. Aufl., Nr. 7) Tubīngen 1927,

3. The titles are given in their Prākrit form, with the traditional Sanskrit translation beside them in brackets.

Prajñapti); 6. Nāyādhammakahāo (Jñātādharmakathāḥ); 7. Uvāsagadasāo (Upāsakadaśāḥ); 8. Aṃtagaḍadasāo (Antakṛd-daśāḥ); 9. Aṇuttarovavāiyadasāo (Anuttaraupapātikadaśāḥ); 10. Paṇhāvāgaraṇāiṃ (Praśna-Vyākaraṇāni); 11. Vivāgasuyaṃ (Vipāka-Śrutam); 12. Diṭṭhivāya (Dṛṣṭivāda).

II. The twelve Uvaṃgas (Upāṅgas) or "secondary limbs" : 1. Uvavāiya (Aupapātika); 2. Rāyapaseṇaijja or Rāyapasenaiya (Rājapraśnīya); 3. Jīvābhigama; 4. Pannavaṇā (Prajñāpanā); 5. Sūrapannatti or Sūriyapannatti; 6. Jaṃbuddīvapannatti (Jambūdvīpa-Prajñapti); 7 Caṃdapannatti (Candraprajñapti) 8. Nirayāvalī; 9. Kappāvadaṃsiāo (Kalpāvataṃsikāḥ); 10. Pupphiāo (Puṣpikāḥ); 11. Pupphacūliāo (Puṣpacūlikāḥ); 12. Vaṇhidasāo (Vṛṣṇidaśāḥ).

III. The ten Paiṇṇas, Prakīrṇas *i.e.*, "scattered pieces") : 1. Caüsaraṇa (Catuḥśaraṇa) by Vīrabhadra; 2. Āurapaccakkhāṇa) (Āturapratyākhyāna); 3. Bhattaparinnā (Bhākta-Parijñā); 4. Saṃthāra (Saṃstāra); 5. Taṃdulaveyāliya (Tandulavaitālika); 6. Caṃdāvijjhaya; 7. Deviṃdatthaa (Devendrastava); 8. Gaṇivijjā (Gaṇi-Vidyā); 9. Mahāpaccakkhāṇa (Mahā-Pratyākhyāna); 10. Vīratthaa (Vīrastava).

IV. The six Cheya-Suttas (Cheda-Sūtras); 1. Nisīha (Niśītha); 2. Mahānisīha (Mahā-Niśītha); 3. Vavahāra (Vyavahāra); 4. Āyāradasāo (Ācāradaśāḥ) or Dasāsuyakkhandha (Daśāśrutaskandha), also called briefly Dasāo (Daśāḥ); 5. Kappa (Bṛhat-Kalpa); and 6. Paṃcakappa (Pañca-Kalpa). Instead of the last-named the Jīyakappa (Jita-Kalpa) by Jinabhadra is also mentioned.

V. Individual texts : 1. Nandī or Nandī-Sutta (Nāndī-Sūtra); 2. Aṇuogadāra (Anuyogadvāra).

VI. The four Mūla-Suttas (Mūla-Sūtras) : 1. Uttarajjhāyā (Uttarādhyāyāḥ) or Uttarajjhayaṇa (Uttarādhyayana); 2. Āvassaya (Āvaśyaka); 3 Dasaveyāliya (Daśavaikālika); 4. Piṃḍanijjutti (Piṇḍa-Niryukti). The third and fourth Mūla-Suttas are also sometimes given as Ohanijjutti (Ogha-Niryukti) and Pakkhi (Pākṣika-Sūtra), and sometimes the Piṃḍanijjutti and Ohanijjuti appear in the list of the Cheya-Suttas.[1]

---

1. See *Weber*, Ind. Stud. 17, 85.

Indeed, with the exception of the Aṅgas, the lists and titles of the canonical texts are not always mentioned in the same way. The list of the Paīṇṇas, in particular, is very indefinite. Sometimes Nandī, Aṇuogadāra and Paṃcakappa are placed at the head of the Paīṇṇas. The traditional number of books in the Siddhānta is 45, but the number of texts mentioned in various places varies between 45 and 50. In the Canon itself, *viz.*, in the Ṭhāṇaṃga, in the Nandī and in the Pakkhi-Sutta, we find lists of canonical works, in which the only distinction made is either between Aṅgas and Aṅgabāhiriyas ("texts standing outside the Aṅgas") or between Aṅgapaviṭṭha ("belonging to the Aṅgas") and Aṇaṅgapaviṭṭha ("not belonging to the Aṅgas"). The last-mentioned include the names of works which occur in the Siddhānta either as independent texts or as sections of well-known texts, but also works which no longer exist in the Siddhānta.[1]

The language of this Canon is a Prākrit which is known as Ārṣa (*i.e.*, "the language of the Ṛṣis") or Ardha-Māgadhī (*i.e.*, "half-Māgadhī"). Mahāvīra himself is said to have preached in this language. There is, however, a difference between the language of prose and that of verses. As was the case with the Pāli verses in the Buddhist Canon, here too, the verses present more archaic forms. The most archaic language is to be found in the Āyāraṃga-Sutta, and next to this, in the Sūyagaḍaṃga-Sutta and the Uttarajjhayaṇa. Ardha-Māgadhī is quite different from Jaina-Māhārāṣṭrī, the dialect of the non-canonical Jaina texts.[2]

---

1. See *Weber*, Ind. Stud. 16, 222 ff., 369 f., 372 f.; 17, 10 ff. Some texts which *Weber* still thought were lost, have come to light since. In a few cases, too, gaps have been filled by other texts. *Cf.* *Schubring*, Worte Mahāvīras, p. 13. A list which is strikingly different from the traditional one, is that by Rajendralala *Mitra*, Notices of Sanskrit Manuscripts III, Calcutta 1874, p. 67. *Nahar* and *Ghosh*, Epitome of Jainism, Appendix C, p. xxxvii, describe the Nandī and the Anuogadāra as "Cūlikā Sūtras," and enumerate, in addition to the 45 "Āgamas" another 36 works, otherwise unknown, as "Jain Nigamas or Upaniṣads."

2. R. *Pischel*, Grammatik der Prākrit-Sprachen (Grundriss I, 8) paragraphs 16-21. *Cf.* *Jacobi*. Kalpasūtra, p. 17 ff; *Weber*, Ind. Stud. 16, 232 ff According to the belief of pious Jainas, Mahāvīra was understood by all creatures, whatever their language was.

Regarding the antiquity and the authority of the Canon, the Śvetāmbara Jainas themselves have the following tradition :

The original doctrine was contained in the 14 Puvvas (Sansk. Pūrvas, *i.e.*, "old texts"), which Mahāvīra himself had taught to his disciples, the Gaṇadharas or "heads of schools." The knowledge of the "old texts" was, however, soon lost. Only one of Mahāvīra's disciples handed them down, and they were only preserved during six generations more. Now in the second century after Mahāvīra's death, there was a terrible famine in the land of Magadha, which lasted for twelve years. At that time the Maurya Candragupta was king of Magadha, and the Thera Bhadrabāhu was the head of the Jaina community. Owing to the famine Bhadrabāhu emigrated with a host of his adherents to Karṇāṭa in South India, and Sthūlabhadra—the last one who had a knowledge of all the 14 Puvvas became head of the community which remained behind in Magadha. During the absence of Bhadrabāhu it was evident that the knowledge of the sacred texts was threatening to lapse into oblivion. A Council was therefore convened at Pāṭaliputra,[1] at which the 11 Aṅgas were compiled, and the remnants of the 14 Puvvas were united to form a twelfth Aṅga, the Diṭṭhivāya. When the adherents of Bhadrabāhu returned to Magadha, there was a great gulf fixed between those who had emigrated and those who had stayed at home. The latter had grown accustomed to wearing white garments, whereas the former, in pursuance of the strict requirement of Mahāvīra, still persisted in going naked. And this is how the great schism between the Digambaras and the Śvetāmbaras came about.[2] Consequently the Digambaras also refused to acknowledge the Canon, as they declared that, in their eyes, the Puvvas and the Aṅgas were lost. In the course of time the

1. If *Sten Konow* (Acta Or. 1, 1922, p. 20 ff.) is right in his explanation of the Hāthīgumphā inscription of Khāravela, then this inscription would furnish a confirmation of the Jaina tradition regarding the Council of Pāṭaliputra and the Diṭṭhivāya, and King Khāravela (170 B.C. ?) would in that case have compiled a recension of the Aṅgas in 64 sections. Konow's explanation is ingenious, but very much open to doubt.

2. The Digambaras relate a legend about the origin of the schism, which differs from the legend told by the Śvetāmbaras. *Cf.* H. v. *Glasenapp*, Der Jainismus, p. 347 ff.

Canon of the Śvetāmbaras was reduced to a state of disorder, and was even in danger of being lost altogether. Hence, in the year 980 (or 993) after the death of Mahāvīra (*i.e.*, about the middle of the 5th or the beginning of the 6th century A.D.) a Council was held at Vallabhi in Gujarat, presided over by Devarddhi Kṣamāśramaṇa, the head of a school, for the purpose of collecting the sacred texts and writing them down. The twelfth Aṅga, containing the remnants of the Puvvas, had already gone astray at that time. This is why we find only eleven Aṅgas in the recension which has come down to us, and which is supposed to be identical with that of Devarddhi.

Thus we see that, according to the tradition of the Śvetāmbara Jainas themselves, the authority of their sacred texts does not go beyond the 5th century A.D. It is true that they assume that the texts which were written down at the Council of Vallabhi, are based on those old texts that had been compiled at the Council of Pāṭaliputra, and which can be traced back to Mahāvīra and his disciples. The Gaṇadharas or heads of schools who were still pupils of Mahāvīra, especially Ajja Suhamma (Ārya Sudharman), are said to have compiled the Master's words in the Aṅgas and Upāṅgas. Certain individual texts are, however, ascribed to later authors even by tradition, for instance the fourth Upāṅga is ascribed to Ajja Sāma (Ārya Śyāma), who is said to have lived 376 or 386 years after Mahāvīra's death,[1] the fourth Cheda-Sūtra, the Piṇḍanjjutti and the Ohanijjutti to Bhadrabāhu (2nd century after Mahāvīra's death), the third Mūla-Sūtra to Sejjaṃbhava, (Śayyambhava), who counts as the fourth head of the school after Mahāvīra,[2] and the Nandī, which is actually attributed to so late a writer as Devarddhi, the president of the

1. He is reckoned as the 23rd head of a school after Mahāvīra, and is said to be identical with the teacher Kālaka famous in legend, who lived at the time of Gardabhila (74-61 B.C.). *Cf. Weber*, Ind. Stud. 16, 392 f. and. J. *Charpentier*, Uttarādhyayanasūtra, Introd., p. 27, and Cambridge History I, 167 f. In the Commentary on the Kalpa-Sūtra, however, a distinction is made between 3 Kālakācāryas; s. *Jacobi* in ZDMG 34, 1880, 250 ff.

2. The year 98 after the death of Mahāvīra is mentioned as the date when the Dasaveyāliya was written. *Cf. Weber*, Ind. Stud. 17, 77.

Council of Vallabhi, in the 10th century after the death of Mahāvīra.[1] Even the Digambaras admit that the first disciples of Mahāvīra knew 14 Puvvas and 11 Aṅgas. They relate, however, that not only was the knowledge of the 14 Puvvas lost at an early period, but that, as early as 436 years after Mahāvīra's Nirvāṇa, the last who knew all the 11 Aṅgas died, and the teachers who succeeded him knew less and less Aṅgas as time went on, until the knowledge of these works was completely lost 683 years after Mahāvīra's Nirvāṇa.

Even though the tradition of the Jainas themselves would not appear to be in favour of investing their sacred texts with a very great antiquity, there are nevertheless good reasons for attributing their first origin, at least in part, to an earlier age, and for assuming that Devarddhi's labours consisted merely of compiling a Canon of sacred writings partly with the help of old manuscripts, and partly on the basis of oral tradition. As a matter of fact, there are inscriptions of the 1st and 2nd centuries A.D. which prove that, even at that early period, the Jainas were split into Śvetāmbaras and Digambaras, and that there were schools (gaṇa) where the successive teachers were enumerated just as in our texts. As the same inscriptions also mention monks with the title of Vācaka, *i.e.*, "reader," there must have been sacred texts at any rate in those days. Inscriptions and bas-reliefs prove that the legend of Mahāvīra as known in the first century A.D. was very similar to that found in our texts. The fact that the Śvetāmbaras did not alter in their Siddhānta those rules which require that Jaina monks shall go naked, shows that they did not venture to make any arbitrary alterations in the texts, but handed them down as faithfully as they could.[2] Lastly, it is also an eloquent argument in favour of the trustworthiness of the Jaina tradition, that it should coincide exactly with the Buddhist tradition in many remarkable details.[3]

---

1. *Cf.* also *Glasenapp,* Der Jainismus, p. 99 f.

2. *Jacobi,* ZDMG 40, 97; SBE 22 xxxvii ff.; *Charpentier.* Uttarādhyayanasūtra, Introd., 25 ff.

3. *Jacobi,* SBE 45, XV ff.; *Oldenberg,* Buddha, 5. Aufl. p. 95 f. *Bhandarkar* (Report 1883-4, 124 ff.), relying on the tradition of the Digambaras, believes that the Jainas did not receive any written sacred books until 683 years after

So much is certain : the works of the Siddhānta cannot have originated at one period. The Canon which Devarddhi compiled, and which has come down to us, is the final result of a literary activity that must have begun as soon as the organisation of the Order and the monastic life were firmly established. This was in all probability the case not long after the death of Mahāvīra. The earliest portions of the Canon may therefore quite possibly belong to the period of the first disciples of Mahāvīra himself, or at the latest to the 2nd century after Mahāvīra's death—the period of the Maurya Candragupta, in which tradition places the Council of Pāṭaliputra—whilst the latest portions should probably be dated nearer the time of Devarddhi.[1] Scholars have only just begun to distinguish between the earlier and the later strata of the Canon.[2]

As is usual in India in the compilation of collections of texts, here also the principle followed in the compilation and arrangement of the Canon is often, not the contents, but something purely external. It is numbers which play a particularly prominent part. Thus, to correspond to the 12 Aṅgas there had to be 12 Upāṅgas,[3] or texts were grouped according to the number of sections they contained. Groups of ten (Dasāo, "decades") are special favourites, and the compilers of the Canon tried all possible methods of achieving the number ten.

We now proceed to examine the individual works n the Canon, and shall deal more fully with those which are of greater importance from a *literary* point of view.

---

the death of Mahāvīra (that would be 216 A.D., but according to Bhandarkar 139 A.D.), when the last of the teachers who knew any portion of the sacred writings from memory, was dead. On the other hand, *Jacobi* (SBE 22, xxxvii ff.) thinks that we might place the writing of the works of the Jaina Canon towards the end of the 4th or beginning of the 3rd century B.C.

1. As the commentaries mention variants and books which have got lost, not even the redaction of Devarddhigaṇi has come down to us unchanged, and some additions were surely made later. *Cf. Weber*, Ind Stud. 16, 229 ff.

2. In this connection the investigations of W. *Schubring* (Ācārāṅga-Sūtra Erster Śrutaskandha 1910, and Worte Mahāvīras, 1926, p. 2 ff.) are valuable.

3. *Schubring*, Worte Mahāvīras, p. 8, assumes that there were originally only 5 Upāṅgas.

The first Aṅga is the Āyāraṃga-Sutta.[1] In two lengthy sections (śruta-skandha) it treats of the way of life (āyāra, Sansk. ācāra) of a monk. The first section, which makes a very archaic impression, is most decidedly earlier than the second and yet even the first is a mosaic pieced together from heterogeneous elements. Here again we meet with the mixture of prose and verse which we so frequently encountered in Buddhist literature. Now we have long series of stanzas, now long prose passages without verse, then again a rapid change between prose and verse, and often it is only fragments of verses, some long, some short, which are inserted into the prose passages.[2]

These sermons consist mainly of exhortations and warnings, *e.g.*, the warning against any kind or killing or injury of living creatures, for instance :

"I speak thus. All Saints (Arhats) and Lords (Bhagavats) in the past, in the present and in the future, they all say thus, speak thus, announce thus and declare thus : One may not kill nor ill-use nor insult nor torment nor persecute any kind of living being, any kind of creature, any kind of thing having a soul, any kind of beings. That is the pure, eternal, enduring commandment of religion, which has been proclaimed by the sages who comprehend the world."

"You yourself are the (being) which you intend to kill; you yourself are the (being) which you intend to ill-use; you yourself are the (being) which you intend to insult; you yourself are the (being) which you intend to torment; you yourself are the (being) which you intend to persecute.[3] Therefore the righteous

---

1. Edited by H. *Jacobi*, London PTS 1882 and translated by the same scholar in SBE, Vol. 22. The first Śrutaskandha, the Bambhacerāiṃ (brahmacaryāṇi "Rules for the holy life") has been newly edited by W. *Schubring* in AKM XII; 4, Leipzig 1910, and translated into German by him in Worte Mahāviras," pp. 66-121. Edition with commentary in the AUS series.

2. *Schubring* in his edition and his translation of the Bambhacerāiṃ, has made an attempt to separate out the mosaic-life portions of the work, metrical and prose passages, and to throw light on the very entangled assortment of texts. Though he has brought much ingeniousness to bear on his task, he has only succeeded in part. *Cf*. *Jacobi* in AR 18, 1915, 283 ff.

3. The intended meaning is : The consequences of the action return to yourself.

one, who has awakened to this knowledge, and lives according to it, will neither kill nor cause to kill."[1]

The essential difference between the monastic rules of the Jainas and the Buddhists is, that those of the Jainas lay much more stress on severe asceticism, and even go as far as to recommend religious suicide. If a monk suffers from cold, he should rather freeze to death than break his vow. However ill and weak he may be, he should rather die than break his vow of fasting. He is to go naked, so as to expose himself to the pricking of the blades of grass, to the inclemency of the weather and the bites of the flies and mosquitoes. A long verse passage (I. 7, 8) includes, it is true, the famous ascetic rule which is known to the Brahmins and Buddhists also, *viz.*, "He should not desire life, he should not long for death" : this is, however, immediately followed by the characteristic rules on the various methods by which the accomplished sage is to starve himself to death by slow degrees. This passage is followed by a long narrative poem—really a mosaic of verses, in which it is often doubtful whether they *are* verses—the Ohāṇasuyaṃ (I, 8),[2] describing in a very graphic manner the ascetic life of the "Great Hero :"

He wandered naked and homeless. People struck him and mocked at him—unconcerned, he continued in his meditations. In Lāḍha the inhabitants persecuted him and set dogs on him. They beat him with sticks and with their fists, and threw fruits, clods of earth and potsherds at him. They disturbed him in his meditations by all sorts of torments. But "like a hero in the forefront of the battle," Mahāvīra withstood it all. Whether he was wounded or not, he never sought medical aid. He took no kind of medicaments, he never washed, did not bathe and never cleaned his teeth. In winter he meditated in the shade, in the heat of summer he seated himself in the scorching sun. Often he drank no water for months. Sometimes he took only every sixth,

1. I, 4, 11; 5, 5, 4. This kind of repetition and accumulation of synonymous or almost synonymous expressions is just as popular in the Jinistic sermons as in the Buddhist ones.

2. Translated in its entirety by *Jacobi* in SBE, Vol. 22, p. 79 ff.; and *Schubring*, Worte Mahāvīras, p. 115 ff.

eighth, tenth or twelfth meal, and pursued his meditations without craving.

Section II of the Āyāraṃga is a much later work, as can be seen by the mere fact of the sub-divisions being described as Cūlas, *i.e.*, "appendices." The subject-matter of the first two Cūlas is dry rules for begging and wandering, and the daily life of the monks and nuns. In the rules as regards begging, and in the dietary regulations, the main point is that only such food is to be taken as does not in any way entail the destruction of life. In the rules for speaking (II, 4) the essential point is that the monk shall utter no falsehood, nor anything which may hurt. The third Cūla contains the materials for a biography of Mahāvīra, which have been utilised in Bhadrabāhu's Kalpa-Sūtra, and which recur there in part. The book ends with twelve verses, the contents of which are somewhat reminiscent of the Buddhist Theragāthās.

The second Aṅga, the Sūyagaḍaṃga,[1] treats of the pious life of monks. and is mainly devoted to the confutation of heretical opinions. This Aṅga, too, consists of two books, the second of which is probably only an appendix, added later, to the old Aṅga which we have in the first book. This is composed in verses, Ślokas and also more artificial metres;[2] the similes, too, show that the author was desirous of proving himself to be a poet. Some of these similes are turned quite prettily, as for

1. Published with various commentaries in the Āgama-Saṃgraha, Vol. 2, Bombay 1880; with Śīlāṅkācārya's commentary, Bombay 1917 for AUS. Translated into English by *Jacobi* in SBE, Vol. 45, and selected sections into German by *Schubring*, Worte Mahāvīras. Sūtrakṛtāṅga is a false Sanskritisation, for, as *Schubring* (Worte Mahāvīras, p. 12) has rightly observed, *sūtra*, "text," is *sutta* in Prākrit, and not *sūya*. He therefore explains sūyagadaṅga as the Aṅga of the Sūcākṛt or "philosophers," and is thinking of the meaning *dṛṣṭi* which is given by lexicographers both for *sūcā* and *sūci*. It is true that neither *sūcikṛt* nor *dṛṣṭikṛt* occurs anywhere else in the sense of "philoshpher." The Nijjutti says that there are three names of the Aṅga : sūtagadaṃ, suttakaḍam. and sūyagaḍam The last is explained thus by Śīlāṅka: *sūcākṛtam iti svaparasamayārthasūcanaṃ sūcā sāsmin kṛteti.* This is right. The title means: "The Aṅga in which the distinction (between the true and the false doctrines) is made."

2. Vaitālīya stanzas and Yamakas occur, cf. *Jacobi*, ZDMG 38, 593; 40 101.

instance, when it says : As birds of prey swoop down upon young, unfledged birds and carry them off, thus unscrupulous people seek to entice young monks (I, 14, 2ff.). The explicit purpose of the book is to keep young monks away from the heretical doctrines of other teachers, to warn them of all dangers and temptations, to confirm them in their faith and thus lead them to the highest goal. The work begins with a condemnation of the doctrines of the Buddhists and heretics, and the principal teachings of Mahāvīra are set forth in opposition to these. It is true, nevertheless, that what is here said about Karman and Saṃsāra does not differ greatly from the "heretical" doctrines. For instance, such sentences as the following (I, 2, 1, 13) might be found equally well in a Buddhist text :

"It is not myself alone who suffers, all creatures in the world suffer; this a wise man should consider, and he should patiently bear (such calamities) as befall him, without giving way to his passions."[1]

There is a graphic description of the cares and dangers with which the monastic life is fraught, but by which the novice should not allow himself to be repelled. His friends and relatives seek to hold him back, and paint the joys of family life to him in attractive colours. Kings and ministers, Brahmins and warriors endeavour to entice him to return to the world, but he is to withstand all these temptations. Critics and heretics attack him, and he should stand up to them courageously. Most especially, however, the young monk should beware of the blandishments of women, who use their utmost endeavours to fascinate him in every manner imaginable. By way of warning, there is a description, not devoid of humour, of the plight of men who have been caught in the web of women.

"And then they make him do what they like, even as a wheelwright gradually turns the felly of a wheel. As an antelope caught in a snare, so he does not get out of it, however he struggles."

"Afterwards he will feel remorse like one who has drunk milk mixed with poison; considering the consequences a worthy monk should have no intercourse with women."

1. I, 2, 1, 13, translated by *Jacobi* in SBE. Vol. 45, p. 251.

..."Now hear the pleasures of Śramaṇas which some monks enjoy."

"When a monk breaks the law, dotes (on a woman), and is absorbed by that passion, she afterwards scolds him, lifts her foot, and tramples on his head...."

"But when they have captured him, they send him on all sorts of errands : 'Look (for the bodkin to) carve the bottle-gourd, fetch some nice fruit."

"(Bring) wood to cook the vegetables, or that we may light a fire at night; paint my feet, come and meanwhile rub my back !..."

"Reach me the lip-salve, fetch the umbrella and slippers, the knife to cut the string, have my robe dyed bluish !..."

"Fetch me the pincers, the comb, the ribbon to bind up the hair, reach me the looking-glass, put the tooth-brush near me"...

..."Pregnant women order their husbands about like slaves to fulfil their craving.

"When a son, the reward (of their wedded life), is born, (the mother bids the father) to hold the baby, or to give it to her. Thus some supporters of their sons have to carry burdens like camels."

"Getting up in the night they lull the baby asleep like nurses; and though they are ashamed of themselves, they wash the clothes like washermen."[1]

Like the authors of so many of the texts of the Purāṇas and Buddhist Suttas, a section of this Jaina Aṅga, too, dwells with truly Sadistic complacency on the fantastic description of the hells and the most gruesome torments of hell (I, 5, 1 f.). However, the author invariably reverts to polemics. Thus, for instance, he assails Brahmanical ritual, in the following terms (I, 7) : If it were true that perfection can be attained by ablutions with cold water, then fishes, tortoises and snakes would attain the highest perfection; and if water really washed away the evil deed, then it must needs wash away the good deed also. Brahmins assert that perfection is to be attained by

---

1. I, 4, 1, 9 f.; 2, 1 ff., translated by *Jacobi* in SBE, Vol. 45, pp. 272 f., 275 ff.

the daily lighting of the fire; if this were true, smiths and artisans of a similar nature would attain the highest sanctity.

It is possible that this book is the work of a single author. It is more probable, however, that a compiler united various poems and sermons on the same theme. to form one book. On the other hand, Book II, written in prose, is merely a somewhat clumsy conglomeration of appendices. These, too, are for the most part polemical in content and have only been appended because they deal with the same kind of themes as the old Aṅga. Nevertheless, even this book is of importance as contributing to our knowledge of the life of religious sects in India.[1]

In the third Aṅga, the Ṭhāṇaṃga,[2] as in the Aṅguttara-Nikāya of the Buddhists, various themes of the religion are dealt with in numerical order from 1 to 10. These enumerations sometimes contain parables in a nutshell, as for instance : There are four kinds of baskets, and also of teachers; there are four kinds of fishes, and also of mendicants; there are four kinds of balls, and also of men, etc. Occasionally, too, enumerations occur which are not directly connected with religion, *e.g.*, the ten themes of mathematics (in Sūtra 747). This Aṅga also contains important literary data regarding the Siddhānta, especially a table of contents of the Diṭṭhivāya which has gone astray.[3]

The fourth Aṅga, the Samavāyaṃga,[4] is in a way a continuation of the third, the subject-matter of the first twothirds of the work being arranged in numerical groups,[5] just like the Ṭhāṇaṃga, except that in this case the numbers do not stop at 10, but go a long way beyond 100, as far as a million.

1. On the heretical doctrines dealt with in the Sūyagaḍaṃga, s. *Jacobi*, SBE 45, p. xxiii ff. Sūyagaḍa II, 1, as has been shown by *Schubring* (Worte Mahāvīras, p. 17 f.) is closely related to Āyāra I (Bambhacerāiṃ) both in wording and mode of expression.

2. Edited in the Āgama-Saṃgraha, Vol. 3, Benares 1880, with a Sanskrit and a Prākrit commentary; with Abhayadeva Sūri's commentary, Bombay 1918-1920. The title means "The Aṅga of the items," *i.e.* of the subjects enumerated under numbers 1-10. *Cf.* E. *Leumann*, GGA 1899, 588, 592.

3. *Cf. Weber*, Ind. Stud. 16, 267 ff.

4. Edited with commentary in the Āgama-Saṃgraha, Vol. 4, Benares 1880; with Abhayadeva Sūri's commentary, by the AUS, Bombay 1918.

5. Hence the title samavāya, *i.e.*, "group," "aggregate."

The work begins with an enumeration of the twelve Aṅgas and a table of contents of the fourteen Puvvas. At the conclusion, however, we find very exact data regarding not only the contents but also the extent of all the twelve Aṅgas, including the Samavāya itself. There is evidence of the fact that the Aṅga in its present form is either a late work or that it contains portions of later date, in such things as the enumeration, under the number 18, of the eighteen kinds of Brāhmī script, the enumeration, under number 36, of the thirty-six sections of the Uttarajjhayaṇa, and the mention of so recent a work as the Nandī. The data in regard to the extent of the Aṅgas do not tally with their present extent, and some of the figures given are very fantastic.[1]

The fifth Aṅga, the Bhagavatī Viyāha-Pannati, "the holy teaching of explanations," usually entitled briefly "Bhagavatī,"[2] contains a bulky, circumstantial presentation of the dogmatics of Jainism, partly in the form of questions and answers, Mahāvīra replying to the questions of his principal disciple Goyama Indabhūti, and partly in the form of dialogue-legends (itihāsa-saṃvāda). The contents are a motley mixture of ancient doctrines and traditions, with numerous later additions containing frequent allusions to other works, more especially to the Pannavaṇā, the Jīvābhigama, the Uvavāiya, the Rāya-Paseṇaijja, the Nandī and the Āyāradasāo. This work gives a more vivid picture than any other work, of the life and work of Mahāvīra, his relationship to his disciples and contemporaries, and his whole personality. Side by side with reports concerning apparitions of deities and the miraculous powers of Mahāvīra, we also find purely human traits, such as in the following account of the meeting of Mahāvīra with his mother :

---

1. *Cf. Weber*, Ind. Stud. 16, 285 ff.

2. Vivāha-Pannatti is only a corrupt form of Viyāha-P. Edition with Abhayadeva's commentary by the AUS, Bombay 1918-1921, 3 Vols, *Cf.* A. *Weber*, Ein Fragment der Bhagavatī, in ABA 1865, 367-444; 1866, 155-352; and W. *Schubring*, Worte Mahāvīras, p. 10, 18 ff. Portions of the Viyāha-Pannatti have been translated into German by *Schubring*, Die Jainas (Religionsgesch. Lesebuch).

(The Brahman Usabhadatta and his wife Devāṇandā went on pilgrimage to Mahāvīra.) "Then milk began to flow from the breast of the Brahman woman Devāṇandā, her eyes filled with tears, her arms swelled beside her bangles, her jacket stretched, the hairs of her body stood erect, as when a Kadamba unfolds itself in response to a shower of rain; thus she gazed at the holy monk Mahāvīra without averting her eyes. "Why, Master," said the venerable Goyama to the holy monk Mahāvīra, "does the Brahman woman Devānandā gaze...(thus)...without averting her eyes?" "Hear, Goyama," said Mahāvīra, "the Brahman woman Devāṇandā, is my mother, I am the son of the Brahman woman Devāṇandā. That is why the Brahman woman Devāṇandā gazes at me with tender love, the cause of which is that I first originated in her." (It is then related how Devāṇandā was received into the Order by Mahāvīra himself).[1]

We are probably also justified in regarding many of the doctrines, and particularly the similes and parables contained in this book as traces of the founder's own peculiar manner of expression.

'Numerous parables', which have been handed down faithfully as such, show Mahāvīra endeavouring to make his meaning comprehensible to his hearers. He must condescend very low to the level of their intelligence, and draw on incidents familiar to them from their daily lives. Thus, for instance, the old man, to whom a blow from an axe causes the same pain as grief causes to an elemental being (19, 3); the immense number of glances fixed upon a dancing girl, the crowdedness and yet isolation of which corresponds to the kindred qualities of the single points of space (11, 10); the goat-shed which is as full of the excrements of the goats, as origination and decay are taking place at every point of space (12, 7). Souls and substances permeate one another, as water permeates a sunken ship (1, 6)" etc.[2]

It is quite likely that Mahāvīra delivered the speeches about Saṃsāra and Kamma as they are written down here, *e.g.* :

1. 9, 33, after the translation by *Schubring*, Die Jainas (Rel. Leseb.), p. 4.
2. *Schubring*, Worte Mahāviras, p. 21 f.

"As each mesh in a piece of netting, which is set in a row of meshes, without a gap, occupying a regular and co-ordinated position in contact with the other meshes, reacts on the next mesh in regard to heaviness, drag, full-weight and closeness, even so in every single soul in many thousands of reincarnations, each one of many thousands of forms of life reacts in regard to heaviness, drag, full-weight and closeness on the life next to it" (5, 3).

"This soul of yours, Goyama, has already been incarnated as a mother, father, brother, sister, wife, son, daughter-in-law as a foe, adversary, murderer, injurer and opponent, as a prince, royal heir, governor, mayor, magistrate, millionaire, master of guild, commander and merchant,—as a slave, messenger, servant, serf, pupil and domestic, in relation to all souls, and all souls have already been incarnated...(as the same)...in relation to your soul and that more than once or an endless number of times" (12, 7).

"Just as if a man should eat food which tastes delicious, well cooked in a saucepan, and containing the desired quantity of each of the eighteen principal ingredients, but nevertheless mixed with poison, and after having consumed it, though he is in good health, yet changes... (to a condition which is bad in every respect) even thus, Kālodāī, souls change... (to a condition which is bad in every respect)...if they take unto themselves the hurting of beings, untrue speech, misappropriation, sexual stimulation, possession, anger, pride, deceit and greed, love and hate, strife, slander, gossip and back-biting, dislike, and lking, lying and deception, and that thorn of false belief. Thus it comes about, Kālodāī, that souls perform evil deeds, from which evil fruits ripen. But if a man eats delicious food...mixed with wholesome substance, and though he is not in good health when he consumes it, but yet changes afterwards... (to a condition which is good in every respect), even so, Kālodāī, souls change, when they incorporate abstinence from hurting...from false belief, that thorn...(to a condition which is good in every respect)...Thus it comes about Kālodāī, that souls perform good deeds, from which good fruits ripen" (7, 10).[1]

1. After the translation by *Schubring*, Die Jainas (Rel. Leseb.), p. 15 f., 19f.

The legendary portion of the work also gives an account of the predecessors of Mahāvīra, and of pious ascetics who attained great divine dignity through their severe castigations. Considerable space is also devoted to the descriptions of the heavenly worlds of the gods, which are granted as a reward to the pious and the hells with their torments, to which the wicked are doomed. Among the legends, those dealing with the predecessors and contemporaries of Mahāvīra are specially important, namely those of the disciples of Pārśva and of Jāmāli and Gosāla Makkhaliputta, the founders of sects, to which Book XV of the Bhagavatī is devoted. This section is a good example of the way in which one sect presents the life of the founder of a hostile sect : The nucleus of history in the background of this presentation, appears to be the fact that the two hostile sects, the Nigaṇṭhas, *i.e.*, the adherents of Pārśva and Mahāvīra, and the Ājīvikas, *i.e.*, the adherents of Gosāla, were originally very closely connected, before they came to a parting of the ways.[1] It would seem that this Book XV of the Bhagavatī was orginally an independent text, and indeed the whole of the fifth Aṅga has the appearance of a mosaic, into which various texts were inserted little by little.

The sixth Aṅga is entitled Nāyā-Dhammakahāo,[2] which probably means "Examples and religious narratives."[3] Book I

---

1. In the Appendix to his translation of the Uvāsagadasāo *Hoernle* has translated the story of Gosāla Makkhaliputta from Bhagavatī XV. *Cf.* also *Hoernle,* ERE 1, 261, and B. M. *Barua* in Calcutta Review, June 1927, p. 355 ff.

2. Edited with Abhayadeva Sūri's Commentary, Bombay 1916 by the AUS. *Cf.* P. *Steinthal,* Specimen der Nāyādhammakahā, Diss. Leipzig 1881; W. *Hottemann,* Die Jñāta-Erzählungen im sechsten Aṅga des Kanons der Jinisten, Strassburg 1907.

3. This is how the Jainas themselves explain the title. The nāyas (Sansk. jñāta) are a certain kind of stories, "they are to lay such emphasis upon either a certain definite *subject of their action* or a definite *passage in the narrative* that the hearer will recognise that *everything* depends on *this* point of narrative" (Hüttemann, loc. cit., p. 47 f.). There is already a classification of the nāyas to be found in the Thāṇaṃga 4, 3 (s. *Leumann* in ZDMG 46, 1892, 602 f.). *Weber* explains the title otherwise : "Stories for the Dharma of Nāya," *i.e.*, of Jñātṛ; according to his descent, Mahāvira is also called Jñātṛputra or Nāyaputta (in the Buddhist Pāli texts Nātaputta).

of this Aṅga consists of 21 chapters, each one of which as a rule presents a complete, independent narrative. Most of these tales are of the type which lays more stress on some parable incorporated in them than on the tale itself; some are, indeed, nothing but parables spun out and enlarged to form narratives. As an instance of this type, there is Chapter 7, in which the following is related:

A merchant had four daughters-in-law. In order to put them to the test, he gives each of them five grains of rice with orders to preserve them carefully until he shall ask for them back again. The first daughter-in-law throws the grains away, and thinks to herself: "There are plenty of grains of rice in the larder, I shall give him others instead." The second thinks in the same way, and eats the grains. The third daughter-in-law preserves them carefully in her jewel-casket. But the fourth one plants the grains, and reaps; she again sows the harvest and reaps again, until at the end of five years she has accumulated a large store of rice. Then the merchant returns and punishes the first two daughters-in law, assigning them the meanest tasks in the household ; he entrusts the third one with the guarding of the entire property; but he gives the entire management of the large household into the hands of the fourth daughter-in-law.—These four women represent the monks some of whom do not keep the five great vows at all, others neglect them, the better ones observe them conscientiously, but the best of whom are not content with observing them, but propagate them also.[1]

Side by side with legends and parables of this nature, we also encounter regular novels, tales of travellers' adventures, mariners' fairy-tales, robber tales and the like, in which the parable only appears in the form of a moral clumsily tacked

1. E. *Leumann* (WZKM 3, 1889, 331 f.; GGA 1899, 588) has compared the parable of the talents in St. Matth. 25 and St. Luke 19, 12 ff. It is, however, scarcely feasible to assume any historical connection between the Jinistic and the Christian parable. Thus also *Garbe*, Indien und das Christentum. p. 43 f. Note; and now also *Leumann*, Buddha und Mahāvīra, ZB 1921- p. 55 ff.

on to the end.[1] In Chapter 8 the legend of Mallī, the only female Tīrthaṅkara[2] is told, with that morality which, though sickly to our taste, is so characteristic of the monastic conception of life:

Mallī, the daughter of the king of Mithilā, is of wondrous, incomparable beauty. Six princes learn of her beauty, each in a different way, and woo her. One of them, the king of the Kuru land, gets to know of Mallī through a portrait which an artist has painted of her, after he had seen only the princess' great toe.[3] Mallī's father refuses all the six princes. They are infuriated, and combine to wage war against the king. Mithilā is besieged, and the king is helpless. Then Mallī advises the king to invite each one of the princes into the city, promising each one her hand. Owing to her power of clairvoyance, she had already foreseen everything long before, and had a "puzzling house"[4] constructed ; then she made a figure which bore exact resemblance to herself, and put it into this house. This figure had an opening on the head, into which she put remnants of her meals every day. She took care to conceal the opening carefully with lotus blossoms. The princes were conducted into this "puzzling house." While they are admiring the figure of the princess through a wall of netting, Mallī herself appears.

1. In the mariner's fairy tale in the ninth Jñāta story, the winged horse also occurs, as in the Valāhassa-Jātaka (No. 196). See above, p. 127 f,. and *Charpentier*, WZKM 27, 1913, 93.

2. According to the hagiology of the Jainas, there are 24 Tīrthaṅkaras, "preparers of the path," also called Jinas, "victors" of whom Ṛṣabha was the first and Mahāvīra the last. All of them possessed perfect knowledge (kevalajñāna), and ever again proclaimed anew the religion which had sunk into corruption. With the Digambaras, the 19th Tīrthaṅkara is a man, Malli, like all the others, but according to the Śvetāmbaras, a woman, Mallī. *Cf.* Mrs. *Stevenson.* Heart of Jainism, p. 50 ff., 56 f.; H. v. *Glasenapp*, Der Jainismus, p. 247 ff., 284 and in Festgabe Jacobi, p. 337.

3. This episode reminds us of the Buddhist stories of famous artists, above, p. 131 f., and the entire narrative betrays a highly cultivated art.

4. Mohanaghara, "a house intended for confusion," namely a house in which a second house, and in the latter a third house stands, with net-work walls, so that the princes could be led into the house, without knowing of one another, and yet could all see the same figure.

She opens the figure, and a terrible stench is spread about, so that the princes hastily cover their faces and turn away, whereupon the beautiful princess moralises on the fact that the inside of her lovely body is even much more loathsome than the inside of this figure. They should therefore not set any store on the enjoyment of love. She then tells the story of her former births, in which the six princes also played a part, and announces that she has decided to become a nun, whereupon the six princes also renounce the world.

It is a favourite theme in Jinist legends in general, as in this particular instance, to follow up the fate of persons through various rebirths. In Chapter 13, a pious layman who had lapsed into heresy for lack of a suitable teacher, was reborn as a frog, in spite of his many good works. In this existence he is crushed by a horse's hoof, but is just able to summon his remaining strength sufficiently to repeat the formula of worship to Mahāvīra, and is consequently reborn immediately as a god in heaven.[1] Chapter 16 contains the legend of Dovaī, *i.e.*, Draupadī, in the form of a story of rebirth. This is a monkish corruption of the legend from the Mahābhārata of Draupadī's marriage to the five brothers.[2]

Book II of this Aṅga is a complete contrast to Book both in form and contents, and is more closely associated with the seventh and the ninth Aṅgas. Curiously enough, the story of the goddess Kālī is here told as a Dhammakhā, "sermon,"[3] though it is eminently unsuitable for this purpose.

---

1. The same legend is also told in the Painna Bhattaparinnā (cf. K. v. *Kamptz*, Uber die vom Sterbefasten handelnden älteren Paīnna des Jaina-Kanons, p. 31); similarly in the Visuddhi-Magga, above, p. 197.

2. E. *Leumann*, OC VI Leiden 1883, 3, 539 ff., believes that an archaic tradition is embodied in the Jinistic form of the legend. That is certainly not the case. See also *Weber*, HSS. Verz. II, 2, 473 f. Leumann (loc. cit. 551 f.) discusses Chapter 14 of the Aṅga, which he compares, as the Indian "Herod legend," with that part of the Kṛṣṇa legend which is told in the Bhāgavata-Purāṇa 10, 2-4. There is, however, only a very slight connection between the legend of the massacre of the innocents and the pious Jinistic legend.

3, See *Schubring*, Worte Mahāvīras, p. 6, 13.

The seventh Aṅga Uvāsagadasāo,[1] *i.e.*, "the ten (chapters on the duties) of the lay adherent" also contains narratives for the most part. Legends are told of ten pious householders, most of whom are wealthy merchants, who impose on themselves certain forms of self-denial, take the vows enumerated by Mahāvīra, and become pious lay adherents. By dint of their asceticism they actually attain to miraculous powers while they are still lay adherents : finally they die a voluntary death by starvation as genuine Jaina saints, and are reborn as gods in the heaven of the pious. Just as in the Purāṇas and the Buddhist Mahāyāna-Sūtras, ten stories of this kind are included in one and the same frame, being told by the venerable, Suhamma to Jambū. The legends are all told after a stereotyped pattern in the most monotonous manner imaginable, so much so that in the later stories there is often only a catch word given by way of allusion to the earlier stories. The part that has the greatest claim upon our interest, is Chapter VII, in which the story is told of the wealthy potter Saddālaputta, who had been an adherent of Gosāla Makkhaliputta, but seceded from him and went over to Mahāvīra. The description of how Mahāvīra convinces the potter of the truth of his doctrine, is in places reminiscent of the best Buddhist dialogues. It is obvious, however, that the whole work was only compiled for devotional purposes.[2]

The next two Aṅgas, composed on the same plan, can lay just as little claim to literary merit. The eighth Aṅga, Aṃtaga-

---

1. Ed. in the original Prākṛta with the Sanskrit Commentary of Abhayadeva and an English Translation with notes by A. F. R. *Hoernle*, Calcutta, Bibl. Ind. 1885-1888. Edited with the Commentary of Abhayadeva Sūri by the AUS, Bombay 1920. *Cf. Leumann*, WZKM 3, 1889, 328 ff.; *Barth*, RHR 19, 1889, 284=Oeuvres II, 61 f. There is a metrical, elaborated version of the contents of this Aṅga, namely the Vardhamānadeśanā in Prakrit-Gāthās (with interlinear version in Sanskrit) ; s. *Weber*, HSS. Verz. II, 2, 492. A new edition of the Uvāsagadasāo by P. L. Vaidya has been published at Poona in 1930.

2. This is also expressly stated at the conclusion of the book; "The seventh Aṅga, Uvāsagadasāo, forms a book of the sacred scripture. Its ten chapters are recited in exactly ten days. Thus the whole book is read completely. It is however, permitted to do this with the Aṅga in two days."

ḍadasāo,[1] *i.e.*, "the ten (chapters) on the (pious ascetics) who have made an end," originally consisted of ten chapters, but is now divided into eight sections. The ninth Aṅga, too, Aṇuttarovavāiyadasāo, *i.e.*, "the ten (chapters) on the (pious ascetics) who have attained to the very highest (regions of heaven)," is now divided into three sections with thirty-three lessons, instead of the original ten lessons. As we learn from Ṭhāṇaṃga 10, the original contents of these two Aṅgas were totally different from the present contents.[2] On the ground of their form, if for no other reason, these works must be denied any claim to literary excellence. Not only are the legends related after a stereotyped pattern, but they often present merely a skeleton, which the reciter is left to fill in with set words and phrases like cliches. For instance, one passage reads : "There was once a city named Campā, a shrine Puṇṇabhadda, a forest. Description."[3] What is, meant is, that a complete description of the city, the shrine and. the forest is to be inserted here, as it stands in the first Upāṅga. Another instance is the part about the Thera Suhamma, one of Mahāvīra's disciples, where there is a mere indication that a detailed description of this holy man is to be given, which can be found in the sixth Aṅga. In those cases where they are given in full, these "descriptions" (vannaa, varṇaka) are composed in an ornate style characterised by the conglomeration of long compound words. In all probability they belong to the earlier poetical portions of the Canon. Even the earliest commentaries read these descriptions as ornate prose. Prof. Jacobi[4] attempted

1. The 8th, 9th and 11th Aṅgas with Abhayadeva Sūri's Commentary are edited in one volume by the AUS, Bombay 1920. The Antagaḍa-dasāo and Aṇuttarovavāiyadasāo translated from the Prākrit by L. D. *Barnett*, London OTF 1907.

2. See *Schubring*, Worte Mahāvīras, p. 6 ff.

3. We find something similar in the Canon of the Sarvāstivādins; s. above II, 280f., 268f., 273 and *Speyer*, Avadānaśataka II, p. xvi f. The "Varṇakas" occur in all the texts of the Canon.

4. Ind. Stud. 17, 389 ff.; *cf. Schubring*, ZII 2, 178 ff. and Worte Mahāvīras, p. 3 ff., who regards this metre (veḍha, veṣṭaka) as a forerunner of the āryā. He too observes : "The absence of a division into stanzas which is caused by the varying lengths of the Veḍhas, gives a Veḍha text the character of rhythmic prose." It is true that in the Anuogadāra (p. 233 f. of the

to find in them traces of a long metre not arranged to form stanzas, but himself remarks that, though they are metrical, they are more closely akin to prose than to actual poems. However, even where the descriptions are given in the text itself, *e.g.*, that of the marriage of Prince Goyama, they are very tedious, and mostly consist of nothing but endless enumerations. The only time when the narrative becomes more poetical is, when the prince announces his resolve to become a monk, and his parents endeavour to dissuade him from this course. The words in which Goyama begs for admittance into the monastic order, in the eighth Aṅga—"The world is in flames, the world is being burnt by old-age and death"—put us in mind of the famous "Fire Sermon" of Buddha. This Aṅga is of importance from the point of view of Indian mythology and history of religion, because it embodies the Kṛṣṇa-legend in a corrupted Jaina version, related so as to suit Jaina requirements. The story of the downfall of the city of Dvāravatī and the death of Kṛṣṇa is told as in the Mahābhārata, only Kṛṣṇa is made into a pious Jaina.

The ninth Aṅga gives a hopelessly monotonous account of how the saints again and again attain to the highest perfection by starving themselves to death. To our minds at least, it is not very edifying to have the "beauty of asceticism" illustrated by a minute description of every single part of the body, accompanied by a series of drastic comparisons, in order to show how lean and emaciated it had grown. It is a remarkable contradiction : this exaggerated love of death on the part of the Jaina saint, and on the other hand, the equally exaggerated fear of killing any living thing, even though it might be only a worm or a green herb.

The tenth Aṅga, the Paṇhā-Vāgaraṇāiṃ, "Questions and Explanations,"[1] treats in ten "Gates" (dāra) firstly of the five

---

1924 Bombay edition) veḍha is mentioned after gāhā (gāthā) and siloga (śloka), but it is not certain whether it here means a metre, because, after veḍhasaṃkhā we find nijjuttisaṃkhā, etc. *Cf. Leumann*, Jitakalpa in SBA 1892, p. 1196. We must bear in mind that, from the Indian point of view, the metre is no criterion of poetry, as prose can just as well be poetry as can verses so that it really does not make much difference whether we read these passages as verses or rhythmic prose.

1. Edited with Abhayadeva Sūri's Commentary, by the AUS, Bombay, 1919.

"great vows" (not to hurt any living being, not to lie, not to steal, not to be unchaste, not to be attached to possessions), and then of the five virtues corresponding to these. It is a purely dogmatic presentation, which does not correspond either to the title of the work or to the table of contents in the Ṭhāṇaṃga 10 and in the Nandī. Thus a later work took the place of the old Aṅga. which had got lost.[1]

The eleventh Aṅga, Vivāgasuyam, *i.e.*, "the text of the ripening (of actions),"[2] contains legends on the retribution of good and evil deeds after the manner of the Buddhist Karman stories in the Avadāna-Śataka and Karma-Śataka. Goyama Indabhūti, the oldest pupil of Mahāvīra, sees various unhappy people, and at his request Mahāvīra explains by what actions in a former birth the person has deserved such misfortune, through what bad rebirths the person has already passed, what is still in store for him, and by what means he may finally attain to a good rebirth again. There is, for instance, a certain Umbaradatta, who is afflicted with all manner of horrible diseases. Why? Because when he was a doctor, in a previous existence, he had prescribed meat diet to a patient, thus causing the killing of numerous living creatures. He will still be born again in worse incarnations, as a dog etc., but finally he will nevertheless be born again as a merchant.

In regard to the contents of the twelfth Aṅga, the Diṭṭhivāya ("Doctrine of the various views"), which went astray, there is nothing beyond all kinds of information given in other texts.[3]

---

1. *Cf. Weber*, Ind. Stud. 16, 326 ff.; *Schubring*, Worte Mahāvīras, p. 13.

2. For edition (together with Aṅgas 8 and 9) s. above, p. 433, note 1. According to Ṭhāṇaṃga 10, where this Aṅga is called Kamma-Vivāga-Dasāo, it originally contained only 10 chapters, whilst it contains 20 to-day. "This extension is made for the purpose of setting the reward for previous merits beside the evil consequences of previous guilt" (*Schubring*, Worte Mahāvīras, p. 6).

3. Thus in the fourth Aṅga, in the Nandī and the Cheda-Sūtras. A short text, after the manner of a Tantra, seems to have stood at the beginning of this Aṅga; s. *Leumann* OC VI, Leiden 1883, III, 2, 558 ff. A Karma-Grantha by Candrarṣi and a work by Śivaśarmasūri called Karma-Prakṛti, old texts in Prākrit Gāthās on the doctrine of Karman, are said to have been taken

Five divisions of the Diṭṭhivāya are distinguished: (1) Parikammaṃ (Parikarmāṇi); these are said to be 16 "Preparations" for the right understanding of the Sūtras, after the analogy of the 16 arithmetical operations; (2) Suttāi (Sūtrāṇi), 88 (4×22) Sūtras, in which the heretical doctrines are confuted; (3) Puvvagae (Pūrvagatam), the 14 Puvvas; (4) Anuyoga, legends of the Tīrthakaras and other great men; and (5) Cūliyā (Cūlikāḥ or "Addenda."[1] The existence of twelve Upāṅgas is additional evidence of the fact that twelve Aṅgas once existed.

There is an Upāṅga to every Aṅga. Nevertheless the connection is merely external. The subject-matter of the twelve Upāṅgas is purely dogmatic and mythological, and they are not very interesting from a literary point of view.

The first Upāṅga is the Uvavāiya.[2] The first part describes the departure of Mahāvīra for the Puṇṇabhadda shrine, and the pilgrimage of King Kuṇiya Bhiṃbhasāraputta to the same place in order to hear Mahāvīra's sermon.[3] The sermon deals with the retribution ofgood and evil deeds in the four forms of existence (as denizens of hell, animals, human beings and gods), and also with the duties of monks and laymen. In the second part which has no connection whatsoever with the first, Goyama Indabhūti journeys to the Master, in order to question him regarding the various re-births. It is then taught in the form of questions and answers, how every being which has done evil, has to bear the consequences, and the beings which have not

---

from the Diṭṭhivāya; s.H.v. *Glasenapp*, Die Lehre vom Karman in der Philosophie der Jains nach den Karmagranthas dargestellt, Leipzig 1915. p. 9 f. The Siddhapañcāśikā by Devendra Sūri, is an extract from the Diṭṭhivāya in 50 Gāthās; see *Weber*, HSS. Verz. II, 2, 534 ff.

1. *Cf. Weber*, Ind. Stud. 16. 349 ff.; *Guerinot*, La Religion Djaina, p. 71, and H. v. *Glasenapp*, Der Jainismus, p. 93 ff.

2. Das Aupapātika-Sūtra, erstes Upāṅga der Jaina, 1. Teil. Einleitung, Text und Glossar von E. *Leumann*, AKM VIII, 2. Leipzig 1883. Complete edition in the AUS series. The Sanskritised form "Aupapātika" given by the commentaries is erroneous. Uvavāiya stands for upapādika, "dealing with the upapāda (uvavāya)"; uvavāya means "the attainment of an existence." *Cf.* S. *Levi* in JA, 1912, ser. 10, t. XX, 502 f. The Digambaras call the 9th Aṅga Anuttaraupapādikāṅga, s. *Bhandarkar*, Report 1883-4, p. 107.

3. The descriptions (varṇaka) are given completely in the first two Upāṅgas.

sinned so grievously, reappear in a world of the gods under certain circumstances. The various circumstances which lead to the "attainment of an existence" (uvavāya) in one of the twelve worlds of the gods, are enumerated in 16 categories. The last site lies beyond the borders of the universe, and is destined for those who have attained to complete knowledge. These mansions of the blessed are described in great detail :

"The same form which the enlightened one had at the last moment, when leaving this earthly existence, that same form he has yonder, only that it is intensified in its soul-atoms. From the form which was large or small in the last existence, one-third will be lacking in the size and bulk of the enlightened one...They are without a body, densely compact of soul-atoms, they cherish a right belief and a right knowledge as regards objects in particular as well as in general. By reason of their being able to exercise omniscience, they recognise the nature of all things and their temporal qualities; with a never-ending, penetrating, keen glance of their intellect, they look in every place. Neither among human beings nor among all the gods is there such illimitable bliss as has begun for the enlightened one. The bliss of the gods, multiplied in duration to eternity, even though it were endlessly augmented in its fulness, is not so great as the blissfulness of liberation...As a savage, who becomes acquainted with the manifold beauties of a city, cannot describe them, because he lacks something with which to compare them, so, too, the blissfulness of the enlightened ones is incomparable, there is no comparison, and yet I shall mention something which can be compared with it in a certain sense. As a man, when he has eaten food containing all desirable ingredients, no longer experiences thirst and hunger, as though he had sated himself with the celestial beverage, so the enlightened ones who have come to the unique extinguishing, dwell sated for all time, rapturous in the possession of illimitable blissfulness without end."[1]

As a work of literature, the second Upāṅga, the Rāyapaseṇaijja[2], is of greater importance. It is true that it begins with

1. 170 f., 178 ff. After the translation of W. *Schubring*, Die Jainas (Rel. Leseb.), p. 29 f.

2. Rājapraśnīyasūtram, edited with Malayagiri's Commentary by the AUS, Bombay 1925. On the contents s. *Leumann* OC VI, Leiden 1883, III,

a long and tedious story, in the style of the Purāṇas, of the pilgrimage of the god Sūriyābha to Mahāvīra, but the nucleus of the work is really the dialogue, included in this tale, between King Paesi and the monk Kesi, concluding with the conversion of the free-thinking king. This is a splendid lively dialogue, in which Kesi endeavours to prove to Paësi that there is a soul independent of the body, whilst Paësi thinks that he has established the contrary by means of experiments. He says, for instance, that he has had a thief sentenced to death, cut up, and hacked to pieces, and found no trace of any soul: whereupon Kesi retorts that he is even simpler than certain people who wanted to make a fire and chopped up the fire-sticks.

The next two Upāṅgas again take the form of questions (by Goyama) and answers (by Mahāvīra). The third Upāṅga Jīvājīvābhigama, the doctrine of the living and the lifeless things,"[1] gives in 20 sections a comprehensive classification of living creatures and a description of the universe in all its details (oceans, islands, palaces of gods, etc.). The section dealing with the continents (dīva) and the oceans (sāgara) is connected with the Jambuddīva-Pannatti, and is an interpolation.[2]

The fourth Upāṅga, Pannavaṇā,[3] which describes itself as a work of Ayya Sāma,[4] also gives in 36 chapters a classification of

---

2, 490 ff. The Sanskrit translation of the title, Rājapraśnīya, is probably erroneous. Presumably the work originally treated of a king Prasenajit, in whose place Paesa was inserted; see *Weber*, Ind. Stud, 16, 382 ff. On a Buddhist version of the Paesi dialogue in the Dīgha Nikāya see above II, 42.

1. Jīvājīvābhigamopāṅga with Malayagiri's Commentary edited in JPU 50, Bombay 1919. See *Weber*, Ind. Stud. 16, 388 ff. The title is usually given as Jīvābhigama, but Jīvājīvābhigama seems to be more in keeping with the contents of the work.

2. *Cf.* W. *Kirfel* in ZII 3. 1925, p. 50 ff. According to the data in the Ṭhāṇaṃga and in the Nandi, there was an independent text Dīvasāgara-Pannatti in the Canon.

3. Pannavaṇā Bhagavatī with Malayagiri's Commentary and Sanskrit translation by Nārakacandra, publ. Benares 1884 : Śyāmācārya-dṛbdhaṃ śrīman-Malayagiryācārya-vihita-vivaraṇa-yutaṃ śrī-Prajñāpanopāṅgam, Bombay 1918, AUS.

4. See above, p. 416, note 1.

the living beings, containing under "human being" geographical-ethnographic outline, in which the Aryans (ariya, ārya) and the barbarians (milikkha, mleccha) are enumerated with their habitations.

The fifth, sixth and seventh Upāṅgas are "scientific" works dealing with astronomy, geography, cosmology and the division of time. Curiouly enough, the Canda-Pannatti, which is counted as the seventh Upāṅga, according to its title an astronomical theory of the heavens based upon the moon, is completely identical in all available manuscripts with the Sūtra-Pannatti,[1] the description of the heavens based upon the sun. Originally it was most probably a text preceding the Sūra-Pannatti and a work separate from this text. The Sūra-Pannatti contains a systematic presentation of the astronomical views of the Jainas. It deals with the orbits which the sun describes during the years, with the rising and setting of the sun, with the speed of the course of the sun through each of its 184 circuits, the light of the sun and moon, the measure of the shadow at various seasons of the year, the connection of the moon with the lunar mansions (Nakṣatras), the waxing and waning of the moon, the velocity of the five kinds of heavenly bodies (the sun, the moon, planets, Nakṣatras and Tārās), the qualities of the moonlight, the number of suns in Jambudvīpa, etc. As the work deals with the sun as well as with the moon, it almost looks as though the original Canda-Pannatti had been worked into the Sūra-Pannatti.

The sixth Upāṅga, the Jaṃbuddīva-Pannatti, "the description of Jambudvīpa,"[2] the central continent, contains the mythical geography of the Jainas. In the description of Bhāratavarṣa

---

1. Sūryaprajñapti-Upāṅgam with Malayagiri's Commentary, edited by the AUS, Bombay 1919, *Cf. Webtr*, Ind, Stud. 10, 254 ff.; 16, 401 ff.: HSS. Verz, II, 2, 573 ff.; G. *Thibaut* in JASB 1880, 49, 107 ff., 181 ff.: *Leumann* in OC VI, Leiden 1883, III, 2. 490 ff. and *Schubring*, Worte Mahāviras, p. 13. In Ṭhāṇaṃga 4, 1 Canda-Pannatti, Sūra-Pannatti, Jaṃbūddiva-Pannatti and Divasāgara-Pannatti are enumerated as Aṅgabahiriyas.

2. Jambūdvipa-Prajñapti with Śānticandra's Commentary in JPU, Nos. 52 and 54. *Cf.* on the mythical geography of the Jainas, W. *Kirfel*, Kosmo-, graphie der Inder, Bonn und Leipzig 1920, p. 208 ff. add H. v. *Glasenapp* Der Jainismus, p. 225 ff.

(India), however, the legends of King Bharata occupy much space.[1]

Upāṅgas 8-12 are sometimes also comprised as five sections of one text entitled Nirayāvalī-Suttam. Probably, they originally formed one text, the five sections of which were then counted as five different texts, in order to bring the number of Upāṇgas up to twelve. They are all of legendary contents, and deal with life in the beyond. The eighth Upāṅga, Nirayāvaliyāo,[2] the "series of hells", relates how the ten half-brothers of the king of Campā, Kuṇiya or Ajātaśatru, were killed by their grandfather Ceḍaga of Vesāli in the battle against him, and after their death were re-born in the various hells (niraya). The Buddhists relate that Ajātaśatru killed his father Bimbisāra, the contemporary of Buddha, and that he was altogether a bad, cruel ruler. The Jainas endeavour to show him in a better light, obviously because he favoured their order. The ninth Upāṅga, Kappāvaḍaṁsiāu, gives an account of the ten sons of the same princes whose story was told in the eighth Aṅga : like their grandmothers they were converted to the ascetic life, and each one reached a different heaven. The tenth Upāṅga, Pupphiāo, gives an account of ten gods and goddesses, who drove earthwards in their heavenly chariots (puṣpakāḥ) from their heavenly world, in order to pay homage to Mahāvīra, whereupon the latter tells Goyama Indabhūti their previous history. In the eleventh Upāṅga, Pupphacūliāo, ten similar stories are told, or rather they are indicated merely by catch-words. The twelfth Upāṅga, Vaṇhidasāo, deals with the conversion of the twelve princes of the Vṛṣṇi dynasty by the saint Ariṭṭhanemi. The first of the legends deals with Nisaḍha, son of Baladeva and nephew of Kaṇha (Kṛṣṇa) Vāsudeva, and is thus connected with Kṛṣṇa legend.

The ten Paiṇṇas or "scattered pieces" correspond to the Vedic Pariśiṣṭas, and are, like the latter, mostly metrical,

1. According to *Leumann* (ZDMG 48, 82) these legends "can be called an exactly parallel text to Viṣṇu-Purāṇa II and Bhāgavata-Purāṇa V."

2. Nirayāvaliyāsuttam. een Upāṅga der Jaina's. Met inleading. . . . van S. *Warren*, Amsterdam 1879. Nirayāvalikasūtram with Candrasūri's Commentary, publ. by the AUS, Ahmedabad 1922.

and deal with all kinds of subjects pertaining to the Jaina religion. The Causaraṇa 'deals in 63 verses with the prayers by means of which one may take the "fourfold refuge" namely, that of the saints (Arhat), the perfected (Siddha), the living pious (Sādhu) and of religion (Dharma). The first verses, however, prescribe the six daily duties (ṣaḍāvaśyakam) essential for the purification of one's mode of life.[1] Vīrabhadda (Vīrabhadra) is mentioned as the author of the Causaraṇa. There is a whole series of Paiṇṇas which deal with the voluntary death of the sage :[2] Bhattaparinnā, the "dispensing with food", in 172 verses Saṃthāra, "the pallet of straw," upon which the sage, sick unto death, stretches himself in order to meditate, in 122 verses; Āura-Paccakhāna, "the sick one's refusal" (of the pleasures of life), and Mahā-Paccakkhāna, "the great refusal," a formula of confession and renunciation in 143 verses. "The death of the fool" (bālamaraṇa) is the involuntary death from various causes of ordinary people who are strangers to the Jaina doctrine, and also the suicide of such people. The "death of the semisage" is that of the lay adherent who, though he does not die by voluntary fasting, dies after making a confession, on a bed known to be his death bed. In contrast to these the "death of the sage" is the solemn passing of the man who is sick unto death, by means of voluntary fasting, after he has completed his confession and all vows and penances. Though the texts mentioned really contain nothing but the rules for attaining death by fasting, they are nevertheless in the form of didactic poems, and mostly in verse, and make use of plays on numbers and all kinds of figures of ornate poetry. They also contain sermons which are adorned with poetical comparisons, as for instance the following :

1. These are : (1) sāmāiaṃ (sāmāyikam), "equanimity," obtained by desisting from all evil, (2) cauvisaīthaa (caturviṃśatistava), "the glorification of the twenty-four" (Tīrthaṅkaras), (3) vaṃdana, "the veneration" (of the Guru), (4) padikkamaṇaṃ (pratikramaṇa), "confession," (5) kāussagga (kāyotsarga), penance through certain postures of the body, and (6) paccakkhāṇaṃ (pratyākhyāna), "the refusal" (of certain pleasures), *i.e.*, the vow to renounce certain pleasures.

2. *Cf.* Kurt von *Kamptz*, Uber die vom Sterbefasten handelnden älteren Painna des Jaina-Kanons, Diss. Hamburg 1929, The "death of the fool" and the "death of the sage" are also dealt with in Bhagavatī II, 1, 48 in detail; s. *Weber*, Bhagavatī, in ABA 1866, p. 266 f.

"Even as a needle through which a thread has been drawn, cannot get lost in the rubbish heap, so also a soul does not disappear in Saṃsāra. Souls which do not renounce the world, and which are lacking in character and good qualities, plunge into Saṃsāra, just as birds with a broken wing and without tail-feathers fall into the ocean. A dog which licks a bone, does not reach the marrow, and persuades himself that he is happy, whilst in reality he is only keeping his throat dry. Similarly, a man takes for bliss intercourse with women, which in reality, serves to exhaust him. A sinner who makes a sincere confession is like the bearer of a burden, whose burden is taken from him."[1]

In the Bhattaparinnā and the Saṃthāra there are also numerous legends of grievous sinners who did penance and became saints, of martyrs, of strange destinies in the cycle of re-births, etc.[3]

The other Paiṇṇas deal with very varied themes : the Taṃdula-Veyāliya,[3] in mixed verse and prose, is a dialogue between Mahāvīra and Goyama on physiology and anatomy, the life of the embryo, the ten ages of man, the measure of length and that of time, the number of bones and sinews, etc. The Caṃdā-Vijjhaya) or caṃdā-vejjhagā)[4] deals in 174 verses with teachers and pupil, and with discipline in general. The Devindatthaa in 300 verses contains a classification of the kings of gods according to their groups, residences, etc. The contents of the Gaṇivijjā,

---

1. Bhattaparinnā 86, 141 ff., Mahāpaccākhāṇa 30, according to the translation of *Kamptz*, loc. cit., p. 23 f.

2. K. v. *Kamptz*, loc. cit., p. 24 ff.

3. Usually written Taṃdula, Tandula, sometimes also Taṇḍula. The explanation of the title (in Sanskrit it is both Tandulavaikālika and Tandulavaicārika) is doubtful. Vijaya Vimala explains it as follows: tandulānāṃ varṣaśatāyuṣkapuruṣapratidinabhogyānāṃ saṃkhyāvicāreṇopalakṣitaṃ tandula vaicārikaṃ nāmeti, "an examination of rice grains (tandula=taṇḍula), characterised by the number of rice grains, to be eaten day by day, by a man who lives for a hundred years." Does the title refer to the great number of details, dealt with in the work ? Editions in the AUS, and Pratnapūrvadharanirmitaṃ śrī-Tandulavaicārikaṃ śrīmad-Vijaya-Vimalagaṇi-dṛbdhavṛtti-yutaṃ sāvacūrikaṃ ca Catuḥśaraṇam, Bombay 1922, JPU 59.

4. After *Schubring*, Worte Mahāvīras, p. 2. note 2 : candrakavedhyaka, "the apple of the eye which is to be bored through" = "hitting the mark." (?)

in 86 verses, are astrological. The Vīrathaa contains an enumeration in 43 verses of the names of Mahāvīra.

In reality, however, as has already been observed above, the list of the Paiṇṇas is quite indefinite. A Gacchāyāra (Gacchācāra), "School rules,"[1] is also enumerated as a seventh or eighth Paiṇṇa, and a Maraṇa-Samāhī (Maraṇa-Samādhi), "Death-Meditation," as a tenth Paiṇṇa. The Gacchāyāra contains rules of life for teachers, monks and nuns, and is an extract from the Cheya-Suttas Mahā-Nisīha and Vavahāra. The Maraṇa-Samāhī, of course, also belongs to the texts which deal with the "death of the sage." Sometimes, however, also 20 or more texts are counted among the Paiṇṇas.[2]

The six Cheda-Sūtras[3] did not, perhaps, form a group in the Canon until a late period, as it is not always the same texts which are placed in this group. The nucleus of this group, however, Cheda-Sūtras 3-5, belongs to the earliest portion of the Canon. These three texts are treated by tradition as one book (śrutaskandha) and called Dasā-Kappa-Vavahāra. Side by side with an assortment of legendary material, the contents of the Cheda-Sūtras are what we have met with under the name of

---

1. Gacchācāraprakīrṇakam with Vānararṣi's Commentary, publ. by the AUS, Bombay 1923. *Cf. Weber*, Ind. Stud. 16, 445 f.; *Schubring*, Das Mahānisīha-Sutta, p. 50 f.

2. According to tradition (*cf.* Nandīsūtra 44 and Vijaya Vimala Gaṇi in the Commentary on the Tandulavaicārika) there were no less than 84,000 Prakīrṇakas of each one of the pupils of Ṛṣabha and 14,000 of each one of the 14,000 Sādhus who had still been taught by Mahāvīra himself. One of them is said to have been Virabhadra, the author of the Caüsaraṇa. The edition, Catuḥśaraṇādi-Maraṇasamādhy-antaṃ Prakīrṇakadaśakaṃ chāyāyutam, Bombay, saṃvat 1983, AUS 46, contains : Caüsaraṇa, Āurapaccakkhāṇa, Mahāpaccakkhāṇa, Bhattaparinnā, Tandulaveyāliya, Saṃthāra, Gacchāyāra, Gaṇivijjā, Devindatthya and Maraṇasamāhī. An older edition Bhavnagar, saṃvat 1966, contains : Caüsaraṇa, Āurapaccakkhāṇa, Bhatt aparinnā and Saṃthāraga. *Cf. Weber*, Ind. Stud. 16, 426 ff.; *Schubring*, Worte Mahāvīras, p. 2 f.; K. v. *Kamptz*, loc. cit., pp. 5-8.

3. The meaning of the word is not clear. Cheda means "cut." As *cheda* and *mūla* in Jaina discipline mean two kinds of penances, *Schubring* (Kalpasūtra, p. 8, and OLZ 1921, 481) assumes that the expressions Cheda-Sūtra and Mūla-Sūtra are derived from these. Nevertheless, the Mūla-Sūtras, at least in their present form, have nothing to do with penances.

Vinaya in Buddhist literature, namely, the rules of life for the monks and nuns and the prescriptions as regards atonements and penances, and in fact the entire discipline of the Order. The fourth Cheda-Sūtra, entitled Āyāradasāo ("the ten sections of behaviour"), also known as Dasāo or Daśāśrutaskandha, is ascribed by tradition to Bhadrabāhu and the eighth section of this Dasāo has long been known by the title "Kalpa-Sūtra of Bhadrabāhu."[1]

Bhadrabāhu is reckoned as one of the earliest teachers and most prominent authors among the Jainas. He is said to have been the sixth Thera after Mahāvīra, and to have died 170 years after Mahāvīra's Nirvāṇa. Tradition has it that he was the last who knew the Puvvas that had gone astray, and he is said to have extracted the third and fourth Cheda-Sūtras from the ninth Puvva. Besides the Dasāo, the Nijjutis (Niryuktis), concise metrical explanations of certain parts of the Canon, are also attributed to him.

Three different texts are united to form a whole in the Kalpa-Sūtra, and it does not seem feasible that Bhadrabāhu was the author of all three. Section I contains the Jinacaritra, the biographies of the Jinas."[2] The main portion of this section is the biography of Mahāvīra, which is told in great detail, with great differences, with descriptions in the Kāvya style and with exaggerations beyond all measure, reminding us of the Lalita-Vistara. The conception, transference of the

---

1. A very faulty translation by J. *Stevenson* appeared as early as 1848, a critical edition by H. *Jacobi*, AKM VII, 1, Leipzig 1879, an English translation by the same scholar in SBE, Vol. 22. Edition with the Commentary Subodhikā of Vinayavijaya Gaṇi, pupil of Kirtivijaya Gaṇi, Bombay 1911, JPU 7.

2. A manuscript of this Jinacaritra preserved in the Museum fur Volkerkunde at Berlin, contains very interesting miniatures representing the principal events in the life of Mahāvīra. They have been described by W. *Huttemann* in Baessler-Archiv; Vol. 4, 1914, p. 47 ff. For the life of Mahāvīra, *cf.* Mrs. *Stevenson*, Heart of Jainism, p. 21 ff.; H. v. *Glasenapp*, Der Jainismus, p. 296 ff.; Harisatya *Bhattacharyya*, Lord Mahavira, a short sketch of the Life of Bhagwan Mahavira, and Kamta Prasad *Jain*, Lord Mahavira and some Other Teachers of His Time : Jain Mittra Mandal Tracts, Nos. 43 and 47, Delhi 1926 and 1927.

embryo,[1] and birth of Mahāvīra are presented in the same way as in the Āyāraṃga-Sutta. Then come the 14 dreams of Devānandā, the mother of Mahāvīra, and the interpretation of them, Mahāvīra's life at home, his twelve years' ascetic life, and the activity which he displayed during nearly thirty years as an accomplished sage (Kevalin). The biographies of Mahāvīra's predecessors, the remaining Jinas down to Pārśva, which follow after the biography of Mahāvīra, are composed absolutely after the pattern of the last-mentioned, and were intended for liturgical purposes.[2]

Section II of the Kalpa-Sūtra consists of the Therāvali a list of school (gaṇa), their branches (śākhā) and heads of schools (gaṇadhara). This list goes far beyond Bhadrabāhu, hence could not possibly have been written by him. Inscriptions from the 1st century A.D. prove, however, that the names in this list are historical, and not mere inventions.

Section III is probably the oldest nucleus of the Kalpa-Sūtra. It contains the Sāmācārī or "Rules for the ascetics," namely, the rules for the rainy season (Pajjusan). Another point in favour of the assumption that this is the oldest portion of the work, is the fact that the complete title of the "Kalpa-Sūtra' is Pajjosavaṇākappa (Sanskrit Paryūṣaṇā-Kalpa), though in reality it only fits this third part. Even at the present day the Kalpa-Sūtra is read aloud to the laymen every year during the Pajjusan days. The tradition which maintains that the Jinacaritra, Therāvalī and Sāmācārī were not contained in the original Canon under the title "Kalpa-Sūtra," but were added to the Siddhānta later by Devarddhi, is most probably right.[3]

---

1. This transference of the embryo is borrowed from the Kṛṣṇa legend, but is already presented on sculptures of the Jainas in Mathurā as early as in the 1st century B.C.

2. When the images of the Jinas or Tīrthaṅkaras are worshipped in the Jaīna temples, hymns are sung to them, one of which summarises the happy moments of their lives, and it is precisely of these that the biographies of the Jinas treat.

3. According to one tradition, all three Cheda-Sūtras 3-5 are the work of Bhadrabāhu. *Weber* (Ind. Stud. 16, 472 ff.) adduces sound reasons for the theory that the whole of this "Kalpa-Sūtra" is erroneously ascribed to Bhadrabāhu. *Cf.* also *Oldenberg*, ZDMG 34, 1880, 755. At any rate it is

The old, genuine Kalpa-Sūtra is the fifth Cheda-Sūtra, which is also called Bṛhat-Kalpa-Sūtra or Bṛhat-Sādhu-Kalpa-Sūtra.[1] It is the principal work on the rules and regulations for the monks and nuns. A necessary supplement to it is the Vavahāra, the third Cheda-Sūtra. The Kalpa-Sūtra teaches the liability for punishment, and the Vavahāra the meting out of the punishment. The Nisīha, the first Cheda-Sūtra, containing regulations for punishment for various transgressions against the rules of daily life, is a later work.[2] It has embodied the major portion of the Vavahāra in its last sections, and has numerous similar Sūtras in common with Cūlas I and II of the Āyāraṃga. Probably both these works originated in one and the same earlier source. The Paṃcakappa does not appear to be in existence any longer. Sometimes, however, the Jīyakappa by Jinabhadra,[3] a detailed, metrical compilation of the cases in which the individual transgressions are valid is called the sixth Cheda-Sūtra, though it is a later work on monastic discipline. The Piṇḍa-Nijjutti and Oha-Nijjutti, which also deal with discipline, are also occasionally classed among the Cheda-Sūtras. A still later work than these two Nijjuttis is the Mahā-Nisīha-Sutta, which appears as the second, and sometimes as the sixth Cheda-Sutta, but which in reality can scarcely be attributed to the Canon with correctness. The principal contents of the text which we have before us and which perhaps took the place of an earlier canonical Mahā-

worth noticing that biographical passages are inserted in the Chedas just as is the case in the Buddhist Vinaya-Piṭaka. It is possible that there was an earlier Mahāvira biography which was supplanted by this "Kalpa-Sūtra." B. M. *Barua*, Calcutta Review, Oct. 1924, p. 52, is of opinion that "the original purpose of the Jinakalpa was rather biographical or historical than liturgical.

1. Das Kalpasūtra, die alte Sammlung jinistischer Monchsvorschriften, Einleitung, Text, Anmerkungen, Ubersetzung, Glossar von W. *Schubring* (Indica ; herausg. von E. *Leumann*, Heft 2), Leipzig 1905.

2. Vavahāra und Nisīha-Sutta, edited by W. *Schubring*, Leipzig 1918, AKM XV, 1. The title Niśītha is a false Sanskritisation of Nisīha, which probably corresponds to Sanskrit niṣedha, "prohibition."

3. Jinabhadra's Jītakalpa, edited with extracts from Siddhasena's Cūrṇi, by E. *Leumann*, SBA 1892, 1195 ff. It is often called Yati-Jītakalpa, to distinguish it from the Śrāddha-Jītakalpa, dealing with the penances for laymen.

Nisīha that went astray, are rules regarding confession and penance, which are emphasized as the most important steps towards liberation. Ethical sections deal with the suffering of the beings in connection with the doctrine of Karman, with the sin of breaking the vows, especially the vow of chastity, with good and bad monks, etc. Legends, some of which are original inventions and others taken from earlier sources, are also inserted. Both language and subject-matter, *e.g.*, the occurrence of Tantric sayings, the mention of non-canonical writings, etc., seem to indicate a late origin of this work.[1]

Four canonical texts, the first three of which are not unimportant even from the literary point of view, are described as Mūla-Sūtras.[2] Above all, the first Mūla-Sūtra, the Uttarajjhayaṇa or Uttarādhyana-Sūtra[3] as a religious poem, is one of the

---

1. W. *Schubring*, Das Mahānisīha-sutta, Berlin 1918 (ABA 1918 Nr. 5). According to one tradition, Haribhadra is supposed to have taken part in the compilation of the Mahā-Nisiha, which is not likely, although he occupied himself with the text; s. *Schubring*, loc. cit., p. 5f. Chapter 8 of the Mahā-Nisiha has been worked up by Devendra Sūri in 519 Āryā stanzas with the title Susaḍhakahā; s. *Schubring*, loc, cit., p. 48 ff.

2. Why these texts are called "root-Sūtras" is not quite clear. Generally the word mūla is used in the sense of "fundamental text" in contradistinction to the commentary. Now as there are old and important commentaries in existence precisely in the case of these texts, they were probably termed "Mūla texts." The explanation given by *Charpentier* (Uttarādhyayana-Sūtra, Introduction, p. 32). "Mahāvīra's own words," does not seem to me to be justified in any way. *Schubring* (Worte Mahāvīras, p. 1, cf. also OLZ 1924, 484 and above, II, p. 443, note 3) is of opinion that "the Mūla Sūtras are," as their name indicates, "intended for those who are still at the beginning (mūla) of their spiritual career." *Guérinot* (La Religion Djaina, p. 79) translates Mūla-Sūtra by "traitês originaux."

2. Edited with an Introduction, Critical Notes and a Commentary by Jarl *Charpentier*, in Archives d' Etudes Orientales, Vol. 18, Uppsala 1922. Indian editions appeared with Śānti Ācārya's Commentary in JPU Nos. 33, 36 and 41, in the AUS series, and recently again by Muni Śrī Jayanta Vijaya, a pupil of Vijaya Dharma Sūri, with a Commentary by Upādhyāya Kamalasaṃyama from the Kharatara Gaccha, Agra, 1923-1927, 3 vols. English translation by *Jacobi* in SBE, Vol. 45. *Leumann* (WZKM 5, 1891, p. 112, n. 1) assumes that the title "The later (uttara) readings" should be explained with reference to the sixth Aṅga, to which the work is closely related in contents. However, uttara can also mean "answer," and perhaps the title means "answer readings" having reference to a tradition according

most valuable portions of the Canon. The work, consisting 36 sections, is a compilation of various texts, which belong to various periods. The oldest nucleus[1] consists of valuable poems—series of gnomic aphorisms, parables and similes, dialogues and ballads—which belong to the ascetic poetry of ancient India, and also have their parallels in Buddhist literature in part. These poems remind us most forcibly of the Sutta-Nipāta. Several sections are sermons in series of aphorisms, admonitions to the pupils, elaborations on the cares which the monk must endure with patience, on the four most precious things (birth as a human being, instruction in the religion, faith in the religion, strength in self-control), on Karman and sin, on the voluntary death of the sage and the involuntary death of the fool, on true and false ascetics, etc. We find here many sayings which excel in aptitude of comparison or pithiness of language. As in the Sutta-Nipāta and the Dhammapada, some of these series of sayings are bound together by a common refrain. A few instances are given here :

"As the burglar caught in the breach of the wall, perishes by the work the sinner himself had executed, thus people in this life and the next cannot escape the effect of their own actions."

"As a charioteer, who against his better judgment leaves the smooth highway and gets on a rugged road, repents when the axle breaks; so the fool, who transgresses the Law and embraces unrighteousness, repents in the hour of death, like (the charioteer) over the broken axle."[2]

Section VII consists mainly of parables. Here we meet with the parable of the three merchants, which reminds us of the Biblical parable of the talents:

"Three merchants set out on their travels, each with his capital; one of them gained there much, the second returned

to which, during the last rainy season before his death, Mahāvīra recited, "the 36 explanations of questions not asked," which, according to the commentary, is supposed to be an allusion to the Uttarajjhayaṇa. *Cf.* also *Charpentier*, l. c., Introduction, p. 33f.

1. The earlier sections contain "an abundance of archaic and curious forms" of Prākrit, s. R. *Pischel*, Grammatik der Prākrit-Sprachen, in "Grundriss 1, 8, para. 19.

3. IV, 3; V, 14f. Translated by *Jacobi* in SBE, Vol. 45, pp. 18, 22.

with his capital, and the third merchant came home after having lost his capital. This parable is taken from common life; learn (to apply it) to the Law.

"The capital is human life, the gain is heaven ; through the loss of that capital man must be born as a denizen of hell or a brute animal.[1]

Whilst all the other sections are reckoned as a matter of course to be the words of Mahāvīra, Adhyāya VIII is expressly ascribed to Kapila, and forms an independent poetical discourse entitled "Kāvilīyaṃ."[2] It contains admonitions to the monks to cast off all things which fetter the soul, to give up all hate, to renounce all the joys of life, and not to kill any living thing. There are sayings to be found there, such as are familiar to us in other branches of ascetic literature, e.g. :

"And if somebody should give the whole earth to one man, he would not have enough; so difficult is it to satisfy anybody.

"The more you get, the more you want; your desires increase with your means. Though two māṣas[3] would do to supply your want, still you would scarcely think ten millions sufficient.

"Do not desire (women), those female demons, on whose breasts grow two lumps of flesh, who continually change their mind, who entice men, and then make a sport of them as of slaves.

"A houseless (monk) should not desire women, he should turn aways from females ; learning thoroughly the Law, a monk should strictly keep its rules."[4]

---

1. VII, 14-16. Translated by *Jacobi* in SBE, Vol. 45, p. 29. *Cf.* Matth. 25, 14; Luke 19, 11; *Jacobi*, l. c., p. xlii, who calls attention to the fact that the agreement with the Hebrew gospel (s. Neutestamentliche Apokryphen, published by E. *Hennecke*, p. 20) is still more striking; *Edmunds*, Buddhist and Christian Gospels, 11, 268 ff.; *Garbe*, Indien und das Christentum, p. 42 ff.; and *Hertel* in "Geist des Ostens" 1, 1913, 247 f.

2. An interesting legend of Kapila Muni, the son of the Brahmin Kāśyapa and of Yaśā, is told by Śānti Sūri in the Commentary (reproduced by *Jacobi* in SBE, Vol. 45, p. 31, note 1). This Kapila does not appear to have any connection with the Kapila of the Sāṃkhya system.

3. Small coins. *Cf.* Yayāti's saying, above, I, 364.

4. Uttar. VIII, 16-19, translated by *Jacobi* in SBE, Vol. 45, p. 34 f.

The whole of Chapter XVI, too, is devoted to the commandment of chastity.

Just as in the Sutta-Nipāta, so, too, in the Uttarajjhayaṇa we meet with a number of beautiful old Itihāsa dialogues and ballads of ascetic poetry. Here again we come across one of the Buddhist Pratyeka-Buddha legends in the beautiful ballad of King Nami, in which the ideal of asceticism is put forward as against that of the warrior and ruler.[1] Likewise in the ballad Harikeśa, in a vivacious dialogue between a proud Brahmin and a despised ascetic of low-caste origin, the contrast is set forth between the formalism and ceremonialism of the priestly religion on the one hand, and the self- control and the virtuous life of the pious monks on the other.[2] In the splendid dialogue too, between the Purohita and his sons, the ascetic ideal is set forth against the Brahmanic ideal as the better and higher one. The fact that we find this conversation also in the Mahābhārata, the Purāṇas and in the Jātaka,[3] in part even literally, proves that it belongs to general Indian ascetic poetry. The dialogue in Adhyāya XXIII, in which a pupil of Pārśva and a pupil of Mahāvīra converse regarding the advantages and differences of their respective creeds which are so closely related, is of interest from the point of view of the history of Jinism. In this instance the dialogue is carried on in part in the form of riddles, which remind us of the Brahmodyas. In the majority of these ballads, the dialogues are the principal part. Only in Adhyāya XXII the narrative portion of the ballad is the more interesting, firstly because the tale is connected with the Kṛṣṇa legend by the names that occur in the legend, and secondly on the strength of the content itself, which is as follows:

In the city of Śauryapura there lived two mighty princes. The first, Vasudeva by name, had two wives, Rohiṇī and Devakī,

---

1. Adhyāya IX. The legend of Citta and Sambūta, well-known from the Jātaka, is to be found in Adhyāya XIII. See above, II, 140.

2. Adhyāya XII, compared by *Charpentier* (ZDMG 63, 1909, 171 ff.) with its Buddhist counterpart (Jātaka No. 497).

3. Adhyāya XIV; see above, I, 403 ff., 561; Jātaka 509 and *Charpentier*, ZDMG 62, 1908, 725 ff.

each of whom bore him a son, Rāma and Keśava. The second, Samudravijaya by name, had a son Ariṣṭanemi by his wife Śivā. Keśava sought Rājimatī, the daughter of a mighty king, as a wife for Ariṣṭanemi, and she is granted him. Ariṣṭanemi sets forth with great pomp to fetch his bride ; but on the way he sees many animals confined in cages and enclosures, and learns, in answer to his question, that these animals are all to be slaughtered for his marriage-feast. He is so deeply shocked by this, that he resolves to take the vow of an ascetic. When Princess Rājīmatī hears of it, she breaks forth into lamentations but then resolves, in her turn, to become a nun. In her wanderings as nun, she one day takes refuge in a cave during a torrent of rain. She believes herself to be alone, and undresses herself in order to dry her garment. Now the ascetic Rathanemi, Ariṣṭanemi's elder brother, had previously taken refuge in the same cave. Now when he sees Rājīmatī in her nude beauty, he is seized by passion and makes advances to her. However, she reproves him, and admonishes him not to wish to "drink that which another has spat out." Reminded of his vow by her forcible words, "he returned to religion, like an elephant spurred on by the goad."[1]

As a contrast to these poetical passages, the last Adhyāyas (XXIV and XXVI-XXXVI) contain only dry sermons, partly catechistical enumerations, partly erudite elucidations of various points of Jaina dogmatics, and partly regulations for the life of the monks.

The second Mūla-Sūtra is the Āvassaya or Āvassaga (Saḍāvaśyaka-Sūtra) which has come down only in conjunction with the Nijjutti.[2] The Sūtra consists of six sections (Adhyāyas), which correspond to the six Āvassayas, *i.e.*, the six "essential" (āvaśyaka) daily duties of a Jaina (desisting from all evil, glorification of the Tīrthaṅkaras, veneration of the teacher,

1. The extended form of this legend in the Commentary of Devendra, has been edited and translated by *Charpentier* (ZDMG 64, 1910, 397 ff.).

2. Śrī Āvaśyaka Sūtra, Part 1, with Niryukti (gloss) by Śrutakevalin Śrī Bhadrabāhu Svāmin, along with the Commentary by Śrī Malayagiri Sūri, Bombay 1928, AVS No. 56.

confession, asceticism and renunciation of sensual pleasures).[1] Attached to the formulas with which these duties are performed there are stories which have come down in the old commentaries.[2]

The third Mūla-Sūtra, Dasaveyāliya,[3] is said to have been written by a certain Sejjaṃbhava. Legend tells that this man was enlightened by the apparition of a picture of the Jina, and left his house when his wife became pregnant. She bore a son, whom she named Mānaka. When the boy was eight years old, he asked after his father, and when he heard that the latter had become an ascetic, he went forth to seek him and become his pupil. As the father knew that his son had only six months more to live, he taught him the Dasaveyāliya within that period, whereupon he gave up the ghost by means of deep meditation.[4] The Sūtra consists of sayings pertaining to the monastic life, some of which remind us of the sayings in the Dhammapada, whilst others contain only rules for monastic discipline. Section II is connected with the ballad of Rājīmatī in the Uttarajhayaṇa; they are verses in which she admonishes Rathanemi who wishes to seduce her. This Sūtra, too, is connected with an abundant narrative literature which is contained in the commentaries.

As the fourth Mūla-Sūtra the Piṃḍa-Nijjutti[5] is usually

---

1. See above, p. 441, note 1, *Cf.* B. L. *Garr*, Sāmāyika or A Way to Equanimity, Arrah, 1918.

2. *Cf.* E. *Leumann* in OC X, Genéve 1894, I, 125 and "Die Āvaśyaka-Erzählungen" (herausgegeben), erste Hälfte, Leipzig 1897 (AKM X, 1). There are, belonging to the text of the Āvaśyakas, besides the Nijjutti, two old commentaries, the Cūrṇi and Haribhadra's Ṭīkā. Haribhadra's Commentary (Hāribhadrīyāvaśyaka-Vṛtti) has been published with elucidations, by Hemacandra Sūri, a pupil of Abhayadeva Sūri, Bombay 1920, JPU 53. *Cf.* also *Weber*, Ind. Stud. 17, 50 ff.

3. E. *Leumann* (ZDMG 46, 1892, 581-663) has not only translated the Sūtra, but has also edited the Niryukti and examined the contents of its narrative portions.

4. He is said to have died 98 years after the Nirvāṇa of Mahāvīra. The legend is told at the end of the edition of the Daśavaikālika-Sūtram (Bombay 1919). *Cf.* also *Peterson*, Report IV, p. cxviii.

5. Bhadrabāhusvāmi-praṇītā Piṇḍaniryuktiḥ, Malayagiryācārya-vivṛtā, publ. in JPU, Bombay 1918.

mentioned, sometimes also the Oha-Nijjutti,[1] and occasionally the Pakkhi.[2] The Piṃḍa-Nijjutti and the Oha-Nijjutti are ascribed to Bhadrabāhu, and are sometimes counted among the Cheda-Sūtras. They treat of the pious life, and of subjects of discipline. The Pakkhi or the Pākṣika-Sūtra is a liturgy in verse for the Pakkhi-Paḍīkamaṇaṃ (Pakṣi-Pratikramaṇa), i.e., the fourteen days' confession.[3] The confession of the "five great vows" (mahāvrata), with which the work begins, also includes the worship of the "patient ascetics" (khamāsamaṇa), who are accounted the authors of the "sacred scriptures which stand outside the Aṅgas" (aṅgabāhiram), and of the twelve Aṅgas, which gives rise to a solemn enumeration of all the sacred writings (suttakittanam).[4]

The Nandī and the Aṇuogadāra[5] are sometimes counted among the Paiṇṇas, but they are usually mentioned either before or after the Mūla-Sūtras as independent texts standing outside the groups. They are in prose with occasional verses. The Aṇuogadāra is in the form of questions and answers. The Nandī (probably "auspicious introduction") which, according to tradition, was written by Devarddhi, the redactor of the

1. Oghaniryuktiḥ, Bhadrabāhusvāmi-viracita-niryukti-śrīmat-pūrvācāryaviracita-bhāṣya-yutā..śrīmad-Droṇācāryasūtrita-vṛtti-bhūṣitā, publ. by the AUS, Bombay 1919. *Cf. Weber*, Ind. Stud. 17, 61, 82 ff.

2. Pākṣikasūtram with Yaśodeva Sūri's Commentary, publ. in JPU No. 4, Bombay 1911, *Cf. Weber* in HSS. Verz. II, 819 ff.; Ind. Stud. 17, 85.

3. *Cf.* Mrs. *Stevenson*, Heart of Jainism, p. 166; H. v. *Glasenapp*, Der Jainismus, p. 374 f.

4. Ritual books such as Śrāddha-Pratikramaṇa-Sūtra (publ. with Devendra Sūri's Commentary, Bombay 1912, JPU 8), and Śramaṇa-Pratikramaṇa-Sūtra (publ. with Commentary, Bombay 1911, JPU 2), and Sāmācāri-Prakaraṇam (pūrvācāryavihitam..Yogaviśeṣavākyayutam, ed. Bombay 1911, JPU) may also be described as semi-canonical. *Cf. Weber*, Ind. Stud. 16, 369 ff.; 17, 71 ff.

5. Nandisūtram, śrīman-Malayagiryācārya-praṇita-vṛtti-yutaṃ, śrīmad-Deva-vācaka-kṣamāśramaṇa-nirmitam, ed. AUS, Bombay 1924. Anuyogadvārāṇi.. Hemacandrasūri-nirmita-vṛtti-yutāni, ed. AUS, Bombay 1924. *Cf. Weber* HSS. Verz. II, 672 ff.; 692 ff. Ind. Stud. 17, 1 ff. A specimen of Malayagiri's Commentary to the Nandī (the refutation of Theism) is given by F. C. *Schrader*, Über den Stand der indischen Philosophie zur Zeit Mahāvīras und Buddhas, p. 62 ff.

Siddhānta, in person,[1] begins with a hymn of praise to Mahāvīra, and is followed by an enumeration of the twentyfour Tīrthaṅkaras and the eleven Gaṇadharas (heads of schools) and a Therāvalī (list of teachers) which ends with Dūsagaṇi, the teacher of Devarddhi. Both works are huge encyclopaedias, dealing with everything which should be known by a Jaina monk. The survey of the Canon which they give, is of great importance. They do not, however, deal exclusively with themes pertaining to religion, but treat also of profane branches of knowledge. Both texts contain an interesting enumeration of the "false tradition" (micchāsuaṃ, mithyā-śrutam) or "worldly" (loie, laukika) sciences, which begins with Bhārahaṃ (Mahābhārata) and Rāmāyaṇam, but mentions, besides some hitherto unexplained titles, among others Koḍillayaṃ (Kauṭilīya Arthaśāstra), Ghoḍayamuhaṃ (the Kāma-Sūtra of Ghoṭakamukha, a predecessor of Vātsyāyana), Vaīsesiyam (the (Vaiśeṣika system of philosophy), Buddha-Sāsaṇaṃ (the doctrine of Buddha), Kāvilaṃ (the system of Kapila), Logāyataṃ (Lokāyata, system of materialism), Purāṇa, grammar (vāgaraṇaṃ), Bhāgavayaṁ (Bhāgavata-Purāṇa), Pāaṃjali (Patañjali), mathematics (gaṇiaṃ) and drama (nāḍayāī, nāṭakāni) and lastly "the four Vedas together with the Aṅgas and Upāṅgas."[2] There are entire sections dealing with moods in poetry (kāvyarasa), including love lyrics in illustration of the subject, with grammar (compound words, word-formation), the division of time, etc.

So much for the Canon of the Śvetāmbara Jainas. Hitherto little is known about the Siddhānta of the Digambaras.[3]

1. Against the authorship of Devarddhi, the argument is brought forward that the Nandī contains data on the Canon which do not agree with its present form. But, then, do we possess the Canon in exactly the form in which Devarddhi edited it. *Cf. Weber*, Ind. Stud. 17, 2, 17 ff.: *Charpentier*, The Uttarādhyayanasūtra, Introd., p. 18.

2. Nandī, p. 194, sūtra 41, Aṇuogadāra, p. 36, sūtra 41. *Cf.* with this list *Weber*, Ind. Stud. 17, 9 and Bhagavatī, ABA 1866, 248; *Charpentier*, l. c., p. 29 f.

3. A complete survey of the Canon of the Digambaras is given by *Bhandarkar*, Report, 1883-4, p. 106 ff., according to Sakalakīrti's Tattvārthasāradīpaka. *Cf.* also *Weber*, HSS. Verz. 11, 3, 823 f. and *Guérinot*, p. xxx f.; J. L. *Jaini* tn SBJ, Vol. V, Preface, p. 12 ff.

They, too, recognise the twelve Aṅgas. The title of the sixth Aṅga reads Jñātṛ-Dharma-Kathāṅga. They, too, include in the twelfth Aṅga the fourteen Pūrvas, which form one of the five sections of this Aṅga. Section I of the Dṛṣṭivāda, the Parikarmāṇi, includes among others Candraprajñapti, Sūryaprajñapti and Jambūdvīpaprajñapti. Those texts which do not belong to the Aṅgas are called the fourteen Aṅgabāhyas ("standing outside the Aṅgas") or Prakīrṇakas ("Miscellanea"), and are said to have been written "for the benefit of the simple-minded." The first four Aṅgabāhyas, according to their titles : Sāmāyika, Caturviṃśatistava, Vandana and Pratikramaṇa, correspond to sections of the second Mūla-Sūtra. Besides these, the only texts to be found among the Aṅgabāhyas which also occur in the Canon of the Śvetāmbaras, are the Daśavaikālika, Uttarādhyayana and Kalpa-Vyavahāra (probably corresponding to the Dasākappa-Vavahāra of the Śvetāmbaras). It is feasible to assume that those texts which are common to both sects, present the earliest portions of the sacred writings of the Jainas. Nevertheless, the question of how far the subject-matter of texts bearing the same titles is correspondingly similar, remains to be investigated.

The Digambaras of the present day have, in addition, a "secondary Canon," which might perhaps be more correctly termed a "substitute Canon," and which they also describe as "the four Vedas." "This "Canon" consists of a number of important texts of later times, which are classified into four groups: (1) Prathamānuyoga, legendary works, to which belong the "Purāṇas" (Padma-, Harivaṃśa-, Triṣaṣṭilakṣaṇa-, Mahā- and Uttara-Purāṇa) which will be mentioned below; (2) Karaṇānuyoga, cosmological works : Sūrya-Prajñapti, Candra-Prajñapti and Jayadhavalā; (3) Dravyānuyoga, philosophical works of Kundakunda, Umāsvāti's Tattvārthādhigama-Sūtra with the commentaries and Samantabhadra's Āptamīmāṃsā with the commentaries; (4) Caraṇānuyoga, ritual works : Vaṭṭakera's Mūlācāra and Trivarṇācāra and Samantabhadra's Ratnakaraṇḍa-Śrāvakācāra.[1]

1. Cf. G. *Bühler*, in Ind. Ant. 7, 1878, p. 28 f.; *Farquhar*, Outline, 218 f. *Guérinot*, La religion Djaina, p. 81 ff., 85 f. A somewhat divergent division of the Anuyogas is given by S. C. *Ghoshal* in SBJ, I, p. xi.

The Non-canonical Jaina Literature

As the Jaina Canon was written down at so late a period, it is not possible to fix a definite line of demarcation between the canonical and the non-canonical literature. At all events the non-canonical literature already begins before the completion of the Canon, and it has continued through all the centuries down to the present day.

The language of the post-canonical Jaina works is partly Prākrit—the so-called Jaina-Māhārāṣṭrī—and partly Sanskrit. In general it may be said that the earlier works were in Prākrit, and that later, certainly not until the centuries of the Christian era, Sanskrit was also used. Side by side with Sanskrit, however, in which language some Jaina authors reached a great perfection, though others wrote it rather clumsily, Prākrit and the Apabhraṃśa dialects were still used, even in the later centuries, and lastly the modern Indian languages too: for the Jainas, more than any other sect, have in their writings, and especially in their exceptionally comprehensive narrative literature, never addressed themselves exclusively to the learned classes, but made an appeal to other strata of the people also. As is still the case at the present day, it was among the merchant classes in particular that they found their most loyal lay adherents.

It is extremely difficult to establish a chronology of the earlier non-canonical Jaina literature from the 1st to the 8th century A.D. It is true that we possess a large number of so-called Paṭṭāvalīs, Therāvalīs, genealogical lists of the teachers and heads of schools, which frequently contain very exact chronological data. On the other hand, these lists often contradict one another : sometimes there are external reasons why credence should not be given to them, and yet it is scarcely feasible to regard them as pure invention. A further difficulty is that frequently the same names occur several times, so that it would be necessary to devote a separate investigation to each single author and each individual work.

It may be assumed as certain that, long before the final compilation of the Canon under Devarddhi, the Jaina monks began to write explanations of the sacred texts. The earliest commentaries, the Nijjuttis or Niryuktis, are in some instances very closely interwoven with the Sūtras, or they even supplanted the latter. The Piṇḍa-Nijjutti and the Ogha-Nijjutti appear in the Canon itself, and the Ogha-Nijjutti is even supposed to have been taken from one of the Pūrvas.[1]

Bhadrabāhu, who is said to have died 170 years after the death of Mahāvīra, has already been introduced to us above, as the author of a Kalpa-Sūtra, and tradition is unanimous in naming him as the author of Nijjuttis on 10 works of the Canon.[2] The Digambaras tell us, however, that there were two Bhadrabāhus, the first of whom died 162 years after the Nirvāṇa of Mahāvīra (*i.e.* 365 B.C.) and the second 515 years after the Nirvāṇa (*i.e.*, 12 B.C.).[3]

Kundakunda,[4] who according to the Paṭṭāvalīs of the Digambaras, lived in the 1st century A.D., calls himself a pupil of

---

1. See above, pp. 444, 446, and *Charpentier* in ZDMG 70, 1916, 219 f.

2. On Āyāraṃga, Sūyagaḍaṃga, Sūriyapannatti, Uttarajjhayaṇa, Āvassaya, Dasaveyāliya, Dasāsuyakkandha, Kalpa-Sūtra, Vavahāra and Ṛṣibhāṣita-Sūtra. Cf. *Bhandarkar*, Report, 1883-4, p. 131 f.; *Peterson*, Report IV, p. lxxxiv.

3. *Cf.* H. *Jacobi* in the Introduction to the Bhadrakalpa-Sūtra, p. 10 ff.; J. *Klatt* in Ind. Ant. 11, 1882, p. 245; Satis Chandra *Vidyābhūṣaṇa*, History of Indian Logic, Calcutta 1921, p. 164 ff If a recent Śvetāmbara tradition makes him a brother of Varāha-mihira, it refers to the author of Bhādrabāhavī Saṃhitā, a work on astronomy which is later than Varāhamihira. *Cf. Jacobi*, loc. cit., p. 13 f. It is yet an entirely different Bhadrabāhu who wrote the Bhadrabāhu-Saṃhitā, a work on the right of succession: text and Engl. translation by J. L. *Jaina*, Jaina Law, in the Library of Jaina Literature, Vol. IV, Arrah, 1916.

4. He belongs to the Draviḍa-Saṃgha, *i.e.*, the Jaina community of the South. He has also the epithets Vakragrīva, Elācārya, Gṛdhrapiccha, and his original name is said to have been Padmanandin. According to a Digambara-Paṭṭāvali, he is the fifth in the genealogical tree of teachers beginning with Bhadrabāhu. The school which he founded is first mentioned in an inscription of 797 A.D. *Cf.* A. *Guérinot*, Répertoire d'Epigraphie Jaina, Paris 1908, p. 42 ff.; *Peterson*, Report II, 80 ff., 153, ff.; Report, IV, p. xix f., *Hiralal*, Catalogue, p. vi f. It is not so likely that he is also the author of the famous Tamil book of sayings Kurral, as is believed by *Chakravartinayanar* (SBJ, III, p. ix f.). He wrote three of his works for his royal pupil Śivakumāra Mahārāja. This prince is identified by K. B. *Pathak* (Ind. Ant. 14, 1885, p. 15) with the Kadamba king Śiva Mṛgeśa Mahārāja

Bhadrabhāu, perhaps referring thereby to Bhadrabahu II.[1] He wrote his learned works only in Prākrit. Umāsvāmin, who is called Umāsvāti by the Śvetāmbaras, and who is recognised by both sects as a great authority in matters pertaining to the faith, is according to the Digambaras, a pupil of Kundakunda. Vaṭṭakera and Kārttikeya Svāmin, too, probably belong to the first centuries of the Christian era. Siddhasena Divākara, who is by some also ascribed to the earlier centuries of the Christian era, and by others to a period as late as the 7th century A.D., is celebrated both as a logician and a lyrical poet.[2] Vimala Sūri, who accordtng to his own statements, composed his Rāma-epic Paumacariya in Prākrit 530 years after the Nirvāṇa,[3] is certainly

(5th century A.D.), by *Chakravartinayanar* (SBJ, III, p. xii ff.) with Śiva-skandavarman of the Pallava dynasty.

1. *Cf.* W. *Denecke* in Festgable Jacobi, p. 163 f.

2. According to a Śvetāmbara tradition he is said to have converted King Vikramāditya in the year 470 after Mahāvīra (57 B.C.) (*Klatt* in Ind. Ant. 11, 1882, p. 247), whereas the Digambaras state 714 to 798 after Mahāvīra (187-271 A.D.) as his time. Vṛddhavādī Sūri is named as his teacher. He is supposed to be a contemporary of Siṃhagiri (who is 15th in the Kharatara-Gaccha-Paṭṭāvali, in which Samantabhadra is the 19th) and of Pālitta. For the legends about Siddhasena and King Vikramāditya, s. *Weber*, Ind. Stud. 15, 278 ff. He is said to have received the name Kumuda-candra at his consecration. See *Peterson*, Report IV, p. cxxxi f. *Jacobi* (Ind. Stud. 14, 376) thinks that this may be merely an invention on the part of the commentator, who was anxious to interpret the concluding verse of the Kalyāṇamandira-Stotra as alluding to the name of the author. *Jacobi* (Samarāicca Kahā, Ed., Introduction, p. iii) considers 670 A.D. as his probable date. The arguments adduced by S. Ch. *Vidyābhūṣaṇa,* History of Indian Logic, p. 173 f., for placing him in about 480-550 A.D. are not convincing. L. *Suali*, Introducione allo studio della Filosofia Indiana, Pavia 1913, p. 38 f., agrees with Vidyābhūṣaṇa, who already previously (Mediaeval School of Indian Logic, p. 14 f., and Nyāyāvatāra, Introduction, p. iv) gave the date as 533 or as 550 A.D. See also *Hiralal*, Catalogue, p. xii ff.

3. That is, according to the usual calculation, in the year 4 A.D. As in the work itself the terms dīnāra and lagna occur, and there is mention of Yavanas and Śakas, *Jacobi* (Bhavisatta Kahā, p. 59,* Upamitibhavaprapañca-Kathā Ed., Preface, p. x) thinks that the work can have originated "in the 2nd or 3rd century A.D. at the earliest." In this case we should have to assume that, in Vimala's days a later date was assumed as the date of Mahāvir's death, than that now usually assumed, *i.e.*, 527 B.C. *Leumann* regards the Mahāvīra's date 4 A.D. to be incontestable, See above letter. Vol. 1, 492.

a very early Prākrit poet. During the first centuries, at all events prior to the 5th century A.D., Pālitta (Pādalipta)[1] wrote a religious novel in Prākrit. It is possible that the poet Mānatuṅga[2], who, according to some lists of teachers, lived as early as at the beginning of the 3rd century A.D., also belongs to the early period of classical Sanskrit poetry. Devanandin or Jinendrabuddhi, who is usually called by his honorific name Pūjyapāda, and who is famous as a grammarian, poet and erudite writer, lived between the 5th and 7th centuries.[3]

The second half of the 7th and the first half of the 8th century A.D. was a period of lively philosophical disputes. Kumārila, the great Mīmāṃsā philosopher and representative of Brahmanical orthodoxy, attacked the Buddhist and Jinistic logicians, including among the last-named the prominent teachers Samantabhadra and Akalaṅka, whilst Prabhācandra and Vidyānanda defended their co-religionists against Kūmārila.[4]

1. According to the Paṭṭāvalis, Vṛddhavādin, Pādalipta (Pālitta) and Siddhasena Divākara were contemporaries. (*Klatt*, Ind. Ant. 11, 251.)

2. In the chronology of the heads of schools in the Kharataragaccha-Paṭṭāvalī, he appears as the 23rd, immediately before Devarddhi, as whose date 980 after Vīra (453 A.D.) is given, whilst Samantabhadra appears as the 19th (Klat, Ind. Ant. 11,247). In the Tapāgaccha Paṭṭāvalī Samantabhadra is the 16th and Mānatuṅga the 20th in the list (loc. cit. 252).

3. *Bhandarkar*, Early History of the Dekkan, second Ed., p. 59, places him about 678 A.D., B. Lewis *Rice* in JRAS 1890, 245 ff., about the middle of the 5th century A. D. A Digambara Paṭṭāvali gives 251 A.D. as his date. See *Hoernle* in Ind. Ant. 20. 1891, 351; *Klatt*, Specimen of Jaina Onomasticon p. 45 f., and *Jacobi* in ZDMG 60, 290. That he lived before Samantabhadra is shown by K. B. *Pathak* in Ann. Bh. Inst. 11, 1930, pp. 53 f., 153.

4. Akalaṅka lived during the reign of the Rāṣṭrakūṭa-King Sāhasatuṅga Dantidurga, and Prabhācandra until the reign of Amoghavarṣa I. According to S. Ch. *Vidyābhūṣaṇa*, History of Indian Logic, p. 193 f., he lived in the 9th century A. D. See K. B. *Pathak* in JBRAS 18, 219 ff.; OC IX, London 1891, 1, 186 ff., and Ann. Bh. Inst. 11, 1930, p. 149 ff.; 12, 1931, p. 123 ff. There is an inscription, first edited by Lewis *Rice* in 1889, in Śravaṇa Belgola (Mysore) in which it is reported that an Ācārya by the name of Prabhācandra died the voluntary death of an ascetic on the mountain Kaṭavapra. The inscription is not dated, but on palaeographical grounds is said to be not later than 750 A.D., probably earlier. E. *Eeumann* in WZKM 7, 1893, p. 382ff. was the first to express the conjecture that this Prabhācandra and the Digambara author and logician are identical, and J. F. *Fleet* (Ep. Ind. 4,

In the 8th century, probably between 705 and 775 A.D., there also lived one of the most distinguished and prolific writers of the Jainas, Haribhadra,[1] a pupil of Jinabhadra (or Jinabhaṭa) and Jinadatta)[2] from the Vidyādharakula. He was born at Citrakūṭa the present-day Chitore, as the son of a Brahmin, and was instructed in all branches of Brahmanical learning. Proud of his enormous erudition, he declared that he

---

1896-97, p. 22 ff.) agrees with him. A. *Venkatasubbiah* (JBRAS 3, 1928, 144 ff.), however, is right in saying that there is no proof of this identity. In Digambara Paṭṭāvalis one Prabhācandra is mentioned with the date 396 A. D. and another with the date 1250 A.D.; see *Hoernle* in Ind. Ant. 20, 1891, pp. 351, 354. There are 4 or 5 different writers named Prabhācandra, s. *Hiralal*, Cat., p. xxviii.

1. Thus according to the researches of Muni *Jinavijayaji* the Date of Haribhadrasūri, (in Proc. I. OC, Poona, Vol. I. 1920, p. cxxiv ff.), with whom *Jacobi* (Samrāicca Kahā Ed., pp. i-iv) agrees. *Peterson* (3 Reports, p. 3 f. and Appendix II, 284) quotes a Prākrit verse, out of the Gāthāsahasri written in 1630, according to which the famous Haribhadra is said to have died in 535 of the Vikrama era, *i.e.*, in 478 A.D. Another tradition, which can be traced till the 13th century, gives 529 A.D. as Haribhadra's date (*Klatt*, Ind. Ant. II, pp. 247, 253). However, as writers of the 6th and 7th centuries are mentioned in works attributed to Haribhadra, these dates cannot be correct. Perhaps Mahāvīra's Nirvāṇa was reckoned differently in those days. (See above p. 408, note 1, and *Jacobi*, Upamitibhavaprapañcakathā Ed., Preface, p. viii ff.) S. Ch. *Vidyābhūṣaṇa* (History of Indian Logic, p. 208 ff.) has certainly assumed that the younger Haribhadra, who wrote in about 1120 A.D., is the author of the works Ṣaḍdarśanasamuccaya, Daśavaikālika-niryukti-ṭikā, Nyāyapraveśaka-Sūtra and Nyāyāvatāra-vṛtti, but this is in contradiction to the entire tradition. Muni *Jinavijayaji* has established, however, that Uddyotana in his Prākrit poem Kuvalayamālā, completed in 779 A.D., calls Haribhadra his teacher. As he quotes authors who lived in the second half of the 7th century, he must have lived in the 8th century. Śāntarakṣita (8th century A.D.) quotes in Tattvasaṃgraha an Ācārya Sūri, whom Benoytosh *Bhattacharyya* (GOS, Vol. 30, p. lxxv) identifies with Haribhadra Sūri.

2. Haribhadra says of himself in the colophons at the end of some of his works, that he obeys the command of Jinabhaṭa, a teacher of the Śvetāmbaras, and that he is the pupil of Ācārya Jinadatta, the ornament of the Vidyādharakula (gaccha). See *Jacobi*, Samarāicca kahā Ed., p. iv. Besides the famous Haribhadra there are at least 8 other Jaina writers of the same name, s. *Klatt*, Specimen of a Literay Bibliographical Jaina Onomasticon, pp. 5, 8f.; Muni *Kalyāṇavijaya* in the Introduction to his edition of Haribhadra's Dharmasaṃgrahaṇi, Bombay, 1918 (JPU 23) and *Jacobi*, Sanatkumāracaritam, p. VII, Note 3.

would become the pupil of any man who could tell him a sentence the meaning of which he did not understand. This challenge was inscribed on a plate which he wore on his stomach, whilst another legend has it that he laid gold bands aronud his body to prevent his bursting owing to so much learning. One day he heard the Jaina nun Yākinī reciting a verse, the meaning of which he did not understand. He asked her to explain the meaning to him. She referred to a teacher Jinabhaṭa, who promised to instruct him, if he would enter the Jaina Order. So Haribhadra became a monk, and thenceforth called himself the "spiritual son" (dharmaputra) of the nun Yākinī. He soon became so well-versed in the sacred writings of the Jainas, that he received the title Sūri (honorific epithet of learned Jain monks), and his teacher appointed him as his successor. According to an unauthenticated tradition, he wrote no less than 1,444 works. Hitherto 88 of his works have indeed been found in manuscripts, and 20 of these are also printed. In all probability he soon wandered away from his birthplace Citrakūṭa, for his life as a monk was spent for the most part in Rājputāna and Gujarat. A Brahmin by birth, Haribhadra was thoroughly well versed in Brahmanism, but he also had a considerable knowledge of the Buddhist doctrines, which may have given rise to the various legends, according to which he secretly procured a knowledge of Buddhism through his pupils and his nephews Haṃsa and Paramahaṃsa, in order to be able to refute its doctrines thoroughly.[1] Haribhadra wrote both in Sanskrit and Prākrit. He was an eminent composer in verse and in prose, and also wrote systematic scientific treatises (Prakaraṇas) and comprehensive philosophical works. Probably, he was also the first to write commentaries to the Canon in Sanskrit. Among his commentaries, those to the two Mūla-Sūtras Āvassaya and Dasaveyāliya have come down to us. While utilising the ancient Prākrit commentaries, he retained the narratives (Kathānakas) in their original Prākrit form.

1. On the numerous legends and anecdotes which are told regarding the life of Haribhadra, see *Klatt* in Ind. Ant. 11, p. 247; *Hertel,* Jinakirtis "Geschichte von Pāla und Gopālā," p. 141 ff.; *Glasenapp,* Der Jainismus, p. 107 f.; *Jacobi,* Samarāiccakahā Ed., pp. iv-xviii.

Śīlāṅka or Śīlācārya, who lived about a century later, and wrote commentaries on the first two Aṅgas in about 862 or 872 A.D., already translated all the Prākrit sources which he used, including the narratives, into Sanskrit. He also wrote a Mahāpuruṣa-Carita in the year 869 A.D.[1]

In the 9th century Jinasena, the friend of King Amoghavarṣa I (815-877 A.D.) wrote the Ādi-Purāṇa. At the beginning of the 10th century (906 A.D.) the poet Siddha, usually called Siddharṣi, wrote his famous allegorical romance in which the existence of the beings is set forth in symbolical terms. At the end of the 10th and the beginning of the 11th century, the Digambara Amitagati wrote two famous didactic poems and a number of other works. Round about the same time, the Digambara Nemicandra, the teacher of the minister Cāmuṇḍarāya, in Southern India, wrote the Gommaṭasāra and other erudite works on the Jaina religion. In the 11th century Śānti Sūri and Devendragaṇin wrote their exhaustive commentaries on the Uttarajjhayaṇa,[2] and the famous Abhayadeva, pupil of Jineśvara, his commentaries on nine Aṅgas. His commentary on the 6th Aṅga was written in 1064 A.D.[3] Maladhāri—Hemacandra Sūri, who wrote commentaries and didactic poems at the beginning of the 12th century, was a pupil of Abhayadeva.

Somewhat later than the last-named, and far more celebrated, is the great Hemacandra,[4] also called Hemācārya, the pupil of Devacandra. He was one of the most versatile and prolific of writers, and worked in the most varied domains, both as a poet and a scholar. It is due to him that Gujarat became a main stronghold of the Śvetāmbara Jainas and has remained so for centuries, and that Jaina literature flourished so exceed-

---

1. H. *Jacobi*, Sanatkumāracaritam, p. xiii.

2. On this commentary, see *Charpentier*, Uttarādhyayana, Introduction, p. 53 ff.

3. He is said to have died in 1075 or 1082 A.D. See *Klatt* in Ind. Ant. 11, 253. There are, however, no less than 6 Jaina authors by the name of Abhayadeva, s. *Peterson*, Report IV, p. iii ff.

4. See G. *Bühler*, Ueber das Leben des Jaina-Monches Hemchandra, des Schülers des Devachandra aus der Vajraṣākhā : Denkschriften der Kais. Akademie der Wissenschaften in Wien 1889; also *Jacobi*, ERE VI, 591.

ingly there in the 12th and 13th centuries. He was not, however, only the author of Jainistic works, but, in addition, he provided his co-religionists with important text-books on temporal branches of learning (grammar, lexicography, poetics and metrics), so that he was called "the Omniscient of the Kali Age" (Kalikālasarvajña). He was born at Dhundhūka, a town in the neighbourhood of Ahmedabad (Gujarat) in 1089 A.D. as the son of a merchant. His parents were pious Jainas, and in his early childhood he was already destined for the life of a monk. As a Jaina teacher he spent the greater part of his life in the capital of Gujarat. His patron was at first the Caulukya king Jayasiṃha Siddharāja (1094-1143). This king favoured literature and science, and was a devout worshipper of Śiva, but he was so much devoted to philosophy that he called teachers of various sects to his court. Among these teachers was Hemacandra, who, owing to his great erudition, not only attracted the attention of the king, but attempted to win the king's sympathy for the Jaina religion; with a view to achieving this end, he made it his business to emphasize more specially the points of agreement between the Jaina religion and authoritative Brahmanical works. Jayasiṃha's successor was Kumārapāla, who was originally also a devotee of Śiva but was converted to Jinism by Hemacandra. After his conversion, which is said to have taken place in 1159 A.D., he endeavoured to make Gujarat a model Jaina state. He personally renounced the sport of hunting, and prohibited in his entire realm the slaughter of animals, the eating ofmeat and the drinking of intoxicants, dice-playing, animal fights and betting. In addition he erected Jaina temples, and favoured the literary and scientific efforts of the Jainas. During the reign of these two kings Jayasiṃha and Kumārapāla, Hemcandra enjoyed a period of intense literary productivity. He died in the year 1172 A.D. at the age of 83 years.

There is scarcely any province of Indian literature in which the Jainas have not been able to hold their own. Above all, they have developed a voluminous narrative literature, they have written epics and novels, they have composed dramas and hymns; sometimes they have written in the simple language of the people, at other times they have competed, in highly elaborate poems, with the best masters of ornate court poetry, and they have also produced important works of scholarship.

The Nijjuttis, which have already received mention, consist of very concise explanations in Āryā-verses and Jaina-Māhārāṣṭrī. They are probably memorial verses which served as an aid to the memory of the teachers in their oral interpretation of the sacred texts. At a later date, these Nijjuttis were extended to form exhaustive commentaries in Prākrit (Bhāṣyas and Cūrṇis). These in their turn formed the foundation for the Sanskrit commentaries (Ṭikās, Vṛttis, Avacūrṇis), which were compiled between the 11th and 12th centuries A.D. These various strata of commentaries are often so much intermingled that it is difficult to distinguish them from one another.[1]

The value of all these commentaries lies in their serving as a depositary of very many ancient, historical or semi-historical traditions on the one hand, and of a great mass of popular narrative themes on the other. Like the Buddhist monks, the Jaina monks, too, delighted at all times in adorning their sermons with the telling of stories, in converting worldly stories into legends of saints, in elucidating Jinistic doctrines by means of "examples," thus exploiting the inborn Indian love for fables in order to win over and retain as many adherents as possible for their religion. As we have seen, a part of these stories had already found a place in some texts of the Canon in the form of legends and ballads. The majority of them is to be found dispersed in great masses throughout the commentary literature which extends down the centuries. The narratives contained even in the later Sanskrit commentaries hark back to earlier sources : evidence for this is provided by the fact that the writers frequently do not tell them in the Sanskrit which would be their natural medium of narration, but in Prākrit, *i.e.*, the language in which the stories had come down to them from their predecessors.[2]

1. See *Leumann* in ZDMG 46, 1892, 556 ff.

2. An older form of Jaina-Māhārāṣṭrī appears in the Cūrṇis, Kathānakas and Āvaśyaka narratives. Moreover, the language of the verses differs from that of the prose. See H. *Jacobi*, Uber das Prakrit in der Erzählungs-Litteratur der Jainas (RSO, Vol. II, Roma 1909, p. 231 ff.).

As is the case with the Buddhist Jātakas, this narrative literature imbedded in the Commentaries, contains many popular themes, including some which occur also in other Indian and non-Indian literatures, and form part of the common treasury of universal literature. Much of this kind is already to be found in the narratives of the Nijjuttis.

Thus in the Nijjutti to the Dasaveyāliya we find the story of the fatal purse :

Two poor brothers are returning from a business journey with a purse full of money. On the way, each of them plans to kill the other, so as to be the sole possessor of the money. They are, however, ashamed of their intentions, and confess to each other, whereupon they throw the purse into the pond. It is swallowed by a fish, the fish is bought by the sister of the two brothers and the purse found by the maid-servant in the fish's stomach. A quarrel arises between the maid-servant and the woman, in the course of which the woman loses her life.[1]

It is in the same Nijjutti that we find the following humorous dialogue, which also points to the fact that at the period of these old commentaries there must already have been monks of very dubious character.

"O Monk, your cloak has so many folds."
"Yes, it serves me as a net when I catch fish." "You eat fish ?"
"I eat them along with my brandy." "You drink sweet brandy ?"
"Oh yes, with the harlot." "What, you go to harlots ?"
"After I have crushed my enemies." "You have enemies, then?"
"Only those whose houses I rob." "You are a thief, then ?"
"Only because of the game of dice." "How, are you a gambler?"
"Am I not, after all, the son of a slave mother ?"[2]

1. *Leumann* in ZDMG 46, p. 602.

2. *Leumann*, loc. cit., p. 607. The story also occurs in the second narrative of Hemavijaya's Kathā-Ratnākara (German translation by Joh, *Hertel*, I, p. 10). A similar Sinhalese-Buddhist dialogue, in J. E. *Seneviratne*, The Life

The accounts of the schisms, in Haribhadra's commentary on the Āvassaya and Śānti Sūri's commentary on the Uttarajjhayaṇa,[1] are of great interest from the point of view of the history and development of the Indian sects. For instance, when we meet, in one of these accounts, with a wandering monk who has bound a copper wire around his garment, and runs about with the branch of a Jambu-tree, offering as a reason for his behaviour, that his garment might burst owing to the fulness of his erudition, and that he has no equal in the whole of the Jambu-continent (*i.e.*, in the whole of India), we are reminded of similar pictures from the lives of Indian sophists in the Upaniṣads and the Buddhist texts.

The commentaries on the Uttarajjhayaṇa are especially remarkable for their wealth of narrative themes.[2] The Nijjutti ascribed to Bhadrabāhu, consisting of nearly 600 verses, is the earliest commentary. The Cūrṇi by an unknown author, is later. The most important commentaries, however, are those by Śānti Sūri and Devendragaṇin. The earlier of the two is Śānti Sūri, who died in about 1040 A.D. In his commentary, entitled Śiṣyahitā, the narratives are only retold in quite a short form : but this work forms the foundation for the Sukhabodhā, completed in the year 1073 A.D. by Devendragaṇin, who tells the stories in leisurely and ambling fashion. There is

of Kālidasa, Colombo 1901, p. 20 f.; in Vallabhadeva's Subhāṣitāvali 2402; Kṣemendra's Lokaprakāśa (*Weber*, Ind. Stud. 18, 366 f.) ; *Böhtlingk*, Indische Sprüche, 2. Auflage, Nr. 4588. *Cf.* the story "Ein Wort gibt das andere" in J. P. *Hebel*. Schatzkästlein, Stuttgart, 1888, p. 168 f., and Th. *Zachariae*, Kleine Schriften, Bonn, Leipzig 1920, p. 195 ff.

1. E. *Leumann*, Ind. Stud. 17, 91 ff.; *Charpentier*, Uttarādhyayana-Sūtra, Ed., Introduction, p. 48 ff. *Leumann* edited one part of the Āvaśyaka narratives (mainly after Haribhadra's commentary on the Āvassaya) in AKM X, 2, Leipzig 1897.

2. The most interesting tales from these commentaries have been published by H. *Jacobi*, Ausgewählte Erzählungen in Māhārāṣṭrī, Leipzig 1886, and translated into English by J. J. *Meyer*, Hindu Tales, London 1909. See also *Jacobi*, ZDMG 42, 493 ff., and Appendix to Hemacandra's Pariśiṣṭaparvan, pp. 1.28; J. *Charpentier*, ZDMG 64, 397 ff.; 66, 38 ff.; 67, 668 ff. The legend of the saint Pārśva, the 23rd Tīrthakara, has been edited and translated by *Charpentier*, from Devendragaṇin's Commentary, in ZDMG 69, 1915, 321-359.

a Sanskrit recension of the tales from this commentary included in the commentary by Lakṣmīvallabha, the date of whom is not known.

More than the Buddhists, the Jainas were at pains to appropriate to themselves all the favourite popular themes from Brahmanical and general Indian literature, so as to be in a position thus to offer their adherents within the fold of their own religious community, all that they could find elsewhere too. At times they established but a very slight connection between these ancient themes and the Jaina religion : in other cases, however, they completely changed and spoilt them, in order to give them a Jinistic appearance. At all events, many a gem of the narrative art of ancient India has come down to us by way of the Jaina commentary and narrative literature, which would otherwise have been consigned to oblivion, and in other cases the Jainas have preserved interesting versions of numerous legends and tales which are known from other sources also.

For instance, the Jainas incorporated the Kṛṣṇa-cult into their religion at a very early period, and consequently also interwove the Kṛṣṇa-legend with their own treasury of legends. As early as in the eighth Aṅga we met with a Jinistic form of the legend of the destruction of the city of Dvāravatī and the death of Kṛṣṇa. This is told in greater detail in Devendra's commentary on the Uttarajjhayaṇa.[1] It is in the same commentary that we find the ancient legend of the descent of Gaṅgā and the destruction of the sixty thousand sons of Sagara,[2] which is familiar to us from the epics. The great attractiveness of this epic legend for the Jaina narrator lay in the fact that the death of the sons was such a convenient peg on which to hang consolatory speeches, with pious thoughts as to the transitoriness of all earthly things. Moreover, their death is justified by Karman in the Jinistic sense.

1. See above, p. 451, note 1; *Jacobi* in OC VII, Wien, 1886, Berichte, p. 75 ff.; ZDMG 42, 1888, 493 ff., and E. *Hardy*, ZDMG 53, 1899, 44 ff.

2. R. *Fick*, Eine jainistische Bearbeitung der Sagara-Sage. Diss. Kiel 1888. A. *Holtzmänn*, Indische Sagen (Nr. VI : "Dass Meer") has treated the legend according to the Mahābhārata (III, 100-109). On the same legend in the Rāmāyaṇa, see above, Vol. I, 459 I, p. 480.

This is also used as an opportunity to introduce a Consolatory Story, which is but a variant of the Buddhist legend of Kisā-Gotamī and the mustard-seed.[1] The Pacceka-Buddha stories, which Devendra tells as a connected whole in his commentary, show points of contact with Buddhist literature. In the story of the fourth of these royal saints, namely King Naggaī, the story of Kaṇayamañjarī is inserted, who has been regarded as the prototype of Sheherezade.[2] One of the most charming romances which Devendra has preserved for posterity, is that of Mūladeva, the Jack of all trades, and the courtezan Devadattā.[3] Connected with Mūladeva who, by the way, seems really to have lived and to have been the author of a Kāma-Śāstra[4], there is also the interesting robber tale of Maṇḍiyo, who excites the pity of the people as a beggar by day, whilst he reduces the city to a state of terror as a murderous robber and burglar by night. Another robber tale is the prose narrative of Agaladatta, of which, however, a far more beautiful, and undoubtedly earlier poetic setting has come down to us in Devendra's commentary.[5]

Many interesting tales are also to be found in Haribhadra's commentaries. In the Āvaśyaka narratives, for instance, we meet with the pretty legend of Vāsudeva, who sees only the good in all things :

A deity transforms himself into the carcass of a dog, with beautiful teeth, lying by the roadside. All the passers-by draw back, disgusted at the stench of the carcass. Then Vāsudeva

---

1. See above, p. 187 f.

2. See P. E. *Pavolini* in GSAI 12, 159 ff. *Charpentier*, Paccekabuddha-Geschichten, p. 146 ff., and J. J. *Meyer*, Two Twice-Told Tales, Chicago (Decennial Publications), 1903. The text according to Bhāvavijaya's Commentary on the Uttarajjhayaṇa is given by *Charpentier* (JA 1911, s. 10, t. XVIII, 201-255). The story of Kaṇayamañjarī is also translated into German by Hertel, Indische Märchen, Jena 1919, p. 271 ff.

3. Translated by *Charpentier*, Peccekabuddhageschichten, p. 62 ff.

4. See *Charpentier*, loc. cit., p. 57 ff.: P. E. *Pavolini*, GSAI 9, 175 ff. and M. *Bloomfield*, The Character and Adventures of Mūladeva : Proceedings of the American Philosophical Society, Vol. 52, 1913, 616-650.

5. Transl. into German verse by J. J. *Meyer*, Kāvyasaṃgraha, p. 72 ff. Italian transl. by A. Ballini, Agaḍadatta, Firenze 1903.

comes along, gazes calmly at the carcass, and exclaims : "How gloriously this dog's teeth gleam !"[1]

The Jainas did not rest content with adopting popular epic themes such as the Kṛṣṇa-legend, the legend of Draupadī, and others, into their sacred writings and the commentaries on them, but they also created poems of their own, which were to serve their adherents as a complete substitute for the great epics Rāmāyaṇa and Mahābhārata. The earliest poem of this kind is the Prākrit epic Paumacariya (Padma-Carita)[2] by the poet Vimala Sūri, which was written, according to the data given by the poet himself (CXVIII, 103), 330 years after the demise of Mahāvīra. It is written in pure Jaina-Māhārāṣṭrī and in the Āryā metre, which is the real metre of Prākrit poetry. The "Life of Padma"—Padma is the name of Rāma in the poem, though the name Rāma also occurs frequently enough—is told in 118 cantos,[3] which are only in partial agreement with the Rāmāyaṇa. It is no part of the author's intention to follow Vālmīki, whom indeed he puts down as a liar, but he wants to tell the story of Rāma in such a way as to fit in with the "history of the world" according to Jinistic tradition, and as it was communicated by Goyama (Gautama), the principal pupil of Mahāvīra, to King Seṇiya (Bimbisāra) in accordance with Mahā-

---

1. J. J. *Meyer*, Hindu Tales, p. 88, note 1. According to K. *Seidenstücker* ("Der Buddhist." 2, 1910. 456 f., quoted by *Günter*, Buddha, p. 86 f.) the legend of the dog's carcass is Buddhist, as it is told in the Commentary on the Udāna-Varga. The same legend, in which Jesus plays the part of Vāsudeva, has been retold by *Goethe* (in the "Noten und Abhandlungen zum besseren Verständnis des westöstlichen Diwans") after the Persian poet *Nisami*. The story of Śatānika and Pradyota from Haribhadra's Commentary on the Āvaśyakas, is given by *Hertel*, Jinakīrti's "Geschichte von Pāla und Gopāla." p. 98 ff. The text of the stories of the former existences of Jina Ṛṣabha after Haribhadra's Commentary on the Āvaśyaka-Niryukti (AUS. Bombay 1916) reprinted in Jaina Jātakas, ed. by Banarsi das *Jain*, Lahore 1925, p. xixff.

2. Edited by H. *Jacobi*, Bhavnagar 1914. The fact that I am in a position to give more detailed information regarding this work is due to the courtesy of my friend Prof. *Leumann*, who kindly placed the manuscript of his abridged translation of Cantos I-XXXI at my disposal, and also gave me valuable information by letter.

3. In the colophons of I-XXXV they are called uddesa (uddeśa), and after that, pavvaṃ (parvan).

vīra's own instructions. As the author says (CXVIII, 118), there is much that he already found in the Pūrvas. Canto I contains a table of contents. In the Introduction (Canto II) the following is related :

It was in the days when King Seṇiya, *i.e.* Śreṇika Bimbisāra, reigned in the Magadha city of Rājapura. Now in the city of Kuṇḍagrāma the Jina Mahāvīra was born as the son of Prince Siddhārtha and his consort Triśalā; at the age of 30 years he left his home, and attained to perfect knowledge. Once Mahāvīra preached a sermon upon souls and transmigration, on the Vipula hill in the presence of gods, men and animals. Among those present was king Seṇiya. When the latter had returned home, he dreamed about the Jina, and the next morning he made the following reflection :

"How is it possible that the demon heroes in all their mighty strength were defeated by the monkeys? And the demons with Rāvaṇa at their head, who, according to the Jaina faith, were certainly of noble descent, are said to have eaten meat ! Then again it is said that, in spite of all the disturbances, Rāvaṇa's brother Kumbhakarṇa slept for half a year, and then after his awakening, devoured elephants, etc., whereupon he again slumbered for half a year. Then again Indra, though he rules over gods, and men, is said to have been taken captive to Laṅkā by Rāvaṇa ! At that rate we might as well affirm that the lion is overcome by the gazelle, the elephant by the dog. These Rāmāyaṇa stories are most certainly lies."[1]

In order to obtain enlightenment on these matters, the king with his retinue repairs to Goyama, and requests him to instruct him correctly regarding the life of Padma, as it seemed to him that the absurdities which are related regarding Rāma, Rāvaṇa, and others were not worthy of belief. Goyama declares his willingness to impart to the king that which Mahāvīra himself proclaimed, for "that which bad poets relate about Rāvaṇa, is indeed lies, I shall instruct you first as to place and time, and then as to the lives of the great men" (III, 14-17).

1. After *Leumann's* rendering of II, 99-119. In the following extracts, too for the portions given in quotation marks Professor *Leumann's* German translation has been freely used.

The narrative begins (III, 18) as in a Purāṇa,[1] with a description of the universe and the history of Ṛṣabha, the first Jina, who lived in the Kṛta age, when there were only three castes, Kṣatriyas, Vaiśyas and Śūdras. The origin of the Vidyādharas, "holders of spells," a kind of demigods, is related (III, 144ff.; *cf.* V, 13ff.), also the origin of the Brahmins (IV, 64ff.), of the Ikṣvāku dynasty and the dynasty of the moon (V,1 ff.). Then comes the history of the second Jina with all manner of preliminary stories (V,48 ff.).

The story of the "race of monkeys" is told in Canto VI. On the monkey island there is the city of Kiṣkindhāpura. "The "monkeys" are in reality a race of Vidyādharas, which is so-called, because it has monkeys by way of a badge on the arches of gates, banners, and the like. Canto VII treats of Indra, of the guardians of the universe, Soma, Varuṇa, Kubera and Yama, the Asuras, Yakṣas etc., Vaiśramaṇa (who is distinct from Kubera) and the birth of Rāvaṇa, his sister Candramukhā and his brothers Bhānukarṇa and Vibhīṣaṇa. Rāvaṇa and his brothers acquire enormous magic powers by virtue of asceticism. The Rākṣasas, whose prince Rāvaṇa is, are not man-eating demons, however, but adherents of the race of the Vidyādharas. Rāvaṇa's mother hangs around his neck a wondrous string of pearls, in which his face is reflected nine times, hence his epithet of Daśamukha, "the man with ten faces" (VII, 95f.).[2] The succeeding cantos tell of all manner of heroic deeds of Rāvaṇa. This Rāvaṇa is a great devotee of the Jinas; he restores ruined Jina shrines, and establishes the Jina faith (XI, 1 ff.)

In Canto XI Goyama replies to the king's question as to how the sacrifice of animals originated. A Brahmin had a son Parvata and a pupil Nārada. Owing to blameworthy ascetic practices, Parvata was born again as a Rākṣasa, and in the guise of a

1. The work calls itself a "Purāṇa" in the Introduction (1, 32) and at the end (CXVIII, 111).

2. This is obviously a realistic explanation of the epithet of Rāvaṇa, who in Rāmāyaṇa, III, 9 f., is a ten-headed monster, and is therefore called Daśagrīva or Daśānana, See Chintāharan *Chakravarti* in Ind. Hist. Qu. 1,1925, 779ff. G. *Ramadas* (Ind. Hist. Qu. 5, 1929, 281 ff.) has shown that in many passages in the Rāmāyaṇa Rāvaṇa has only *one* head and *one* face. The interpretation of the "monkeys" as Vidyādharas with monkeys on their banner, is also realistic.

Brahmin he introduced animal sacrifices. Nārada, however, who is a pious Jaina, declares that these sacrificial acts should be interpreted in the spiritual sense : "The sacrificial animals which are to be killed, are the passions, the sacrificial fee which is to be paid, is truth, forbearance and non-violence, the blessing (to be expected) is (not heaven, but) Nirvāṇa; those, however, who really slaughter sacrificial animals, go to hell like hunters." (XI,75-81).

Cantos XII and XIII tell of a fight between Rāvaṇa and the god Indra. Indra is defeated and is brought in triumph to Laṅkā, but is then released. The reason for his humiliation is that in a previous incarnation he had molested a monk. Indra places his son on the throne, becomes a monk, and attains to bliss. Rāvaṇa visits shrines on the Meru hill, where the gods are just paying homage to Anantavīrya, who has attained to perfect knowledge, and he hears the sermon of the latter upon Karman, generosity, the duties of monks and the duties of laymen (XIV). This sermon is also responsible for the conversion of Hanumant, whose descent and whose fights as the ally of Rāvaṇa, are related in Cantos XV and XIX. Through Rāvaṇa Hanumant receives a thousand wives. Canto XX treats of the Jinas, the rulers of the world, the Baladevas and the Vasudevas. It is not until Canto XXI that King Janaka is mentioned, and the story of Daśaratha and the actual Rāma epic begins : it is only in its main features that this story agrees with Vālmīki's Rāmāyaṇa : as regards the details there are many divergences.

Daśaratha is presented by each of his wives Aparājitā and Sumitrā with a son, whose birth has been announced by three lucky dreams. The first is named Padma,[1] and the second Lakṣmaṇa : his sons Bharata and Śatrughna are born to him by Kaikeyī (XXV, 1-13).

Whereas the heroes of the Rāmāyaṇa move in an entirely Brahmanical atmosphere, in the Paüma-Cariya the religion of the Jina is everywhere very much to the fore. The kings are generally pious laymen, who retire from the world in their old

1. It is noteworthy that it is only Rāma who has received another name, whilst the other names remain unchanged.

age, and become Jaina monks. As in all narrative poems of the Jainas, the preliminary stories, *i.e.*, the stories of the previous existences of the heroes, are told with a great wealth of detail. Daśaratha takes up the reins of government, because his elder brother Anantaratha has become a monk (XXII, 100-105). A festival in the Jaina temple is described (XXIX, 1-18) at which King Daśaratha with his sons performs the ablution of the Jina images, and after an eight days' fast worships the Jinas. After the ablution he sends the water to his wives, and the young women, the daughters-in-law, pour it over the heads of their mothers-in-law. Now the principal wife did not receive the water which was intended for her, and feels herself slighted, so that she wishes to hang herself. The king, however, surprises her. While she is explaining things to him, the chamberlain comes with the water, and pours it over her head, whereupon she calms down. But the king reproaches the chamberlain with his thoughtlessness, whereupon the latter excuses himself on the ground of old age :

"The body goes slowly like an old cart,
The eyes are short-sighted like bad friends,
The ears are deaf like bad sons,
The teeth have fallen out like spokes out of the wheel,
The hands find it difficult to grasp, like elephants taking a bite,
The legs are unreliable like bad women ;
Only the crutch is like the beloved of the heart."

These words are a warning for the king, intimating that he, too, is ripe to say farewell to worldly things.

There are, however, also many divergences in the epic, which have no connection with the Jaina faith. Sītā does not come forth out of the earth, as in Rāmāyaṇa, but is born in a natural way by Videhā, the wife of King Janaka. Sītā is betrothed by Janaka to Padma (Rāma) because the latter has aided him in the fight against the Mlecchas of Ardhabarbara (the land of the semi-barbarians) and has distinguished himself. The story of the bending of the bow is told differently. The bow is brought by the Vidyādharas, who insist upon Sītā's being given in marriage to the Vidyādhara prince Candragati; but at the self-choice of a husband arranged by Janaka, Rāma is the only man who succeeds in bending the bow.

Daśaratha wishes to become a monk and to entrust Padma-Rāma with the responsibility of governing. Bharata, too, desires to withdraw from the world, but is persuaded by Kaikeyī and Padma to take over the reins of government. He makes a vow, however, in the presence of the Jaina monk Dyuti, to renounce the world as soon as Padma returns home, and he governs as a pious Jaina layman, without giving himself up to pleasure. The main story—the stealing of Sītā, the sending of Hanumant, the fights with Rāvaṇa and his defeat, the bringing home of Sītā, the discontent of the people, the banishment of Sītā, and the lamentations of Padma, the birth of Kuśa and Lava—is ever and again interrupted by incidental stories (upākhyāna). Finally Padma attains to perfect knowledge, and enters Nirvāṇa.

Vimala's work probably served as a model for all the later adaptations of the Rāma legend among the Jainas. In the year 678 A.D. Raviṣeṇa wrote his Padma-Purāṇa,[1] which is merely a slightly extended recension of the Pauma-Cariya in Sanskrit, agreeing with it in all essential points. The Sanskrit epic, too, begins with a description of the world, especially the world of the Vidyādharas, and a glorification of the first Tīrthakara Ṛṣabha. Here, too, the "monkeys" are Vidyādharas, who have the picture of a monkey emblazoned on their banner.[2] As in the Paüma-Cariya, Parvan XX treats of the Tīrthakaras, and the actual story does not begin until Parvan XXI, with Daśaratha. Here, too, Padma is the name given to Rāma, and Kuśa and Lava are called Lavaṇa and Aṅkuśa etc.[3] It goes without saying

1. Edited by Pandit Darbārī Lāla *Nyāyatīrtha Sāhityaratna* in MDJG Nos. 29-31, 1928. See *Bhandarkar*, Report 1883-84, pp. 117f.. 417 ff., and Hiralal, catalogue. p. xxi. Chintaharan *Chakravarti* has given a synopsis of the contents in the Bengali language : on this see Batakrishna *Ghosh* in Ind. Hist. Qu. 5, 1929, 157 ff.

2. VI, 1.215.

3. 123 Parvans in the edition of the Padma-Purāṇa correspond to the 118 sections of the Pauma-Cariya. How exactly Raviṣeṇa follows Vimala is shown. for instance. in Padma-Purāṇa 1, 43 f., where the 7 objects of the

that, in a Jaina poem sermons are also inserted, *e.g.*, XXVI, 54 ff., on the dreadful consequences of killing and of the eating of flesh, with a description of hells appended.

Later adaptations of the Rāma legend are to be found in Parvan 68 of the Uttara-Purāṇa and in Hemacandra's Triṣaṣṭi-śalākā-Puruṣa-Caritra, Parvan 7 of which is also called "Jaina-Rāmāyaṇa."[1] Hemacandra, too, begins with the stories of the Rākṣasas and monkeys, and depicts Rāvaṇa as a great and mighty ascetic. It is not until Sarga IV that the story of Rāma, Lakṣmaṇa and Sītā begins, and this ends in the last Sarga (X) with Rāma's entrance into Nirvāṇa. In the year 1596 A.D. Devavijayagaṇin, a pupil of Rājavijaya Sūri wrote a Rāma-Caritra in prose. The author himself says that he is following Hemacandra's "Rāmāyaṇa."[2]

The Mahābhārata also has repeatedly been adapted by the Jainas. The earliest work of this nature which has come down to us, is the Harivaṁśa-Purāṇa[3] in 66 Sargas by Jinasena, who himself mentions in the concluding verses, that he completed his

---

"Purāṇa" are enumerated in almost literal agreement with Paūma-Cariya 1, 32 f. It is very desirable, however, that a careful comparison of all the Jinistic adaptations of the Rāma legend be made.

1. It has been printed in India as "Hemacandra's Rāmacarita" or "Jaina-Rāmāyaṇa," thus in Poona 1890. On this, see D. Ch. *Sen.* The Bengali Rāmāyanas, Calcutta 1920, p. 26 ff., and above. Vol. I. p. 492, Note 3. For the various versions of the Rāma legend in which Sitā is the daughter of Rāvaṇa, see also W. *Stuttehcim* Rāma-Legenden und Rāma-Reliefs in Indonesien, München 1925, p. 92f.

2. See *Bhandarkar,* Report 1882-83, pp. 94; 229. Rajendralala *Mitra,* Notices of Sanskrit MSS., VI, 1882, p. 70ff. tells of a Puṇyacandrodaya-Purāṇa by Kṛṣṇadāsa, which similarly treats the subject-matter of the Rāmāyaṇa. A Jaina-Rāmāyaṇa in the Kanarese language is said to have been written in the 12th century, see *Guérinot,* p. 270.

3. Edited by Paṇḍit Darbāri Lāla *Nyāyatīrtha Sāhityaratna* in MDJG, 32 and 33. The complete title is Bṛhad-Harivaṃśa-Purāṇa or Ariṣṭanemipurāṇa-saṃgraha-Harivaṁśa. An analysis of the work is given by Rajendralala *Mitra,* Notices of Sanskrit MSS.. Vol VI, 1882, pp. 74-97. See *Peterson.* Report IV, 167ff.; *Leumann* in WZKM 11, 1897, p. 307; *Hiralal,* Catalogue, pp. xxii, 688, 715. On the dates given in the Praśasti, see *Peterson,* Report IV. p. 176; *Bhandarkar,*Early History of the Dekkan, 2nd ed,, p65; *Hoernle* in JRAS 1904, p. 644; K. B. *Pathak* in Ind. Ant. 15, 141ff.; *Fleet* in Ep. Ind., VI., 195ff.

work in the year 705 of the Śaka era, *i.e.*, 783 A.D. In this Purāṇa not only are the legends of Kṛṣṇa and Balarāma told in a Jinistic setting, but Gautama, the pupil of Mahāvīra, is made the narrator of the story, and in many places sermons on the Jaina doctrine are inserted. The legend of Ṛṣabha, the first Jina, is told by way of introduction, and, connected with the story of Kṛṣṇa, we have the legend of Ariṣṭanemi or Nemi, Kṛṣṇa's cousin. Nemi is the 22nd Jina, and wanders around the world preaching. The story of the Kauravas and Pāṇḍavas and the descendants of Kṛṣṇa and Balarāma is also told. The Kauravas and Karṇa are converted to the Jaina religion. Finally the Pāṇḍavas also become ascetics, and like Nemi, attain to Nirvāna.

Another Harivaṃśa in 39 Sargas was written by Sakalakīrti and his pupil Jinadāsa in the 15th century.[1] Among his predecessors Jinadāsa mentions Raviṣeṇa and Jinasena Ācārya, and he honours Bhadrabāhu, Kundakunda along with other Munis and his teacher Sakalakīrti, who is praised in the concluding verses as the "ornament of the Kundakunda race."

In about 1200 A.D. the Maladhārin Devaprabha Sūri wrote a Pāṇḍava-Carita[2] in 18 Sargas, in which the contents of the 18 Parvans of the Mahābhārata are given in a concise form, though remodelled in many of its details. The lengthy Sarga 6 contains the story of the game of dice, and the Nala episode—

---

1. The first 14 Sargas were written by Sakalakīrti, the rest by Jinadāsa. See *Bhandarkar*, Report 1883-84, pp. 123 and 433f.; *Leumann*, in WZKM 11, 1897, 312; Hiralal, Catalogue, p. 715 f. In Bhandarkar's MS. only Jinadāsa is mentioned as the author. Sakalakīrti lived in about 1464 A.D., and Jinadāsa therefore in the second half of the 15th century. *Hiralal*, Catalogue, pp. 715 f. 760ff., 768, also mentions Harivaṃśa-Purāṇas by Raviṣeṇa, Śrībhūṣaṇa, Dharmakīrti and Rāmacandra. Besides these Sanskrit epics, there is a Harivaṃśa-Purāṇa in the Apabhraṃśa language, which was written by the poet Dhavala in the 10th or 11th century. See *Hiralal*, Catalogue, pp. xlviii f., 716 762ff.

2. Published in Km. 93. Bombay 1911. Earlier editions appeared in the Jaina-Śāstra-Kathāsaṃgraha and the Caritra-Saṃgraha in Ahmedabad in 1884. See *Peterson*, 3 Reports, Appendix 1. 131-134. Devaprabha is a pupil of Municandra Sūri, whose teacher was Candra Sūri, who wrote a commentary on the Āvaśyaka-Sūtra in the year 1165 A.D. : s. *Peterson*, Report IV, pp. xxvii f., lii.

it is here called "Story of Nala and Kūbara," the latter being the name of Nala's brother—is related by Vidura as a warning example. Sarga 16 tells the legend of the Jina Ariṣṭanemi in connection with the Pāṇḍava legend, and Sarga 18 relates how Baladeva reaches heaven and Ariṣṭanemi and the Pāṇḍavas enter Nirvāṇa. A Pāṇḍava-Purāṇa,[1] which is also known as "Jaina-Mahābhārata," was written by Śubhacandra in 1551 A.D. In the opening verses the author does honour to the teachers Kundakunda, Samantabhadra, Pūjyapāda, Akalaṅka, Jinasena and Guṇabhadra. Devaprabha's epic was done into prose with inserted verses in 1603 A.D. by Devavijaya Gaṇin, pupil of Rājavijaya Sūri.[2] Among the verse many have been taken literally from Devaprabha's work, whilst many others belong to the gnomic poetry and are known from other sources.[3]

It is, however, the biographies of the 63 "Great Men,"[4] that is to say 24 Tīrthakaras, and their contemporaries, the 12 Cakravartins or rulers of the world, and the 27 heroes (9 Baladevas, 9 Vāsudevas and 9 Prativāsudevas) of antiquity, which constitute the favourite substitute, most popular among the Jainas, both for the heroic epics and for the Brahmanical Purāṇas. These works are usually called "Purāṇas" by the Digambaras, whilst among the Śvetāmbaras they go by the name of "Caritras." Among the earliest of these works is the Triṣaṣṭilakṣaṇa-Mahā-

1. See *Peterson*, Report IV, 1856 ff.; *Leumann* in WZKM 11, 1897, p. 306. There is also a Pāṇḍava-Purāṇa in 18 Sargas by Vādicandra, s. *Leumann* l.c. It would certainly be worth while to compare the various Jaina versions of the Mahābhārata carefully with one another and with the old epic.

2. Edited by Haragovind *Das* and Bechar *Das* in YJG Benares V. E. 2438 (1911).

3. Thus for instance, there is on p. 133 the well-known verse from the Pañcatantra. "One should not act rashly, one should act after mature reflection, otherwise repentance will follow, as in the case of the wife of the Brahmin because of the ichneumon."

4. See *Glasenapp*, Der Jainismus, p. 247 ff. The earlier tradition in the Samavāyāṃga 54 and in Śilācārya knows only 54 "excellent men" (uttamapuriṣa), as it does not count the Prativāsudevas especially. *Cf.* Banarsi Das *Jain*, Jaina Jātakas, p. II.

Purāṇa,[1] "the Great Purāṇa of 63 Excellent Men," also named briefly Mahā-Purāṇa,[2] by Jinasena and Guṇabhadra, containing the biographies of all the 63 men. It consists of the Ādi-Purāṇa in 47 chapters, of which 42 are written by Jinasena and the last 5 by his pupil Guṇabhadra, and the Uttara-Purāṇa, which is exclusively from the pen of Guṇabhadra. The Ādi-Purāṇa, or the "first Purāṇa," contains the story of Ṛṣabha, the first Tīrthakara, and of the first Cakravartin, whilst the Uttara-Purāṇa contains the life-stories of all the remaining "Great Men." The work does not, however, consist only of these life-stories of saints and heroes, and the episodes interwoven with them (stories from former incarnations of the principal personages, the stories about their contemporaries, etc.), but in the true manner of the Brahmanical Purāṇas, this "Great Purāṇa" too, is at the same time an epic poem, which claims to give a "history of the world," and presents at the same time an encyclopaedia of all that is edifying to the pious Jaina and that is worthy of his knowledge. Thus, for instance, in the Ādi-Purāṇa (38-40) the Saṃskāras, the "consecrations," which accompany the life of the individual from his conception until his death, are described in fair agreement with the corresponding Brahmanical rites. Chapter 41 treats of the interpretation of dreams. A short treatise on town planning is to be found in Chapter 16, a treatise on the duties of the warrior and the art of governing (Nīti) in Chapter 42. On the other hand, there are, various places, hymns of considerable poetical value.

Like the Pauma-Cariya, the Mahā-Purāṇa, too, traces its origin back to Mahāvīra himself, who communicated its contents to Gautama, who in his turn imparted them to King Śreṇika. The knowledge of the sacred legends is said to have

1. A survey of the contents and the position of the work in Jaina literature is given by *Glasenapp* in Festgabe Jacobi, p. 331 ff., based on the edition of the text by Pandit Lālārām *Jain* in the Syādvādagranthamālā with a Hindi translation Indore, Vik. S. 1973 and 1975. See *Bhandarkar*, Report 1883-84, pp. 118 ff., 422 ff.; *Hiralal*, Catalogue, p. xxii ff.

2. There is, however, also a "Mahā-Purāṇa" by Malliṣeṇa, written in 1047 A.D.; s. K. B. *Pathak.*, Ind. Ant. 40, 1911, 46 ff.

been transmitted by Gautama to those versed in the Aṅgas and Pūrvas, and in several passages the Aṅgas are cited as an authority. The real source of the work is, however, the Prathamānuyoga, that is, the third part of the Dṛṣṭivāda, which has gone astray, though we do not know how far the legends of the Mahā-Purāṇa agree with those of the original Dṛṣṭivāda.[1]

The authors of the Mahā-Purāṇa took pains to obliterate the difference between Jinism and the older religion as far as possible by retaining the names of the saints and heroes, by the use of Brahmanical terms and even by the adoption of Brahmanical rites. The underlying tendency in all this was to cause Brahmanism and Hinduism to appear as merely a decayed form of the true faith, namely the Jaina religion, which had existed from time immemorial.[2]

We have fairly accurate information regarding the time when the Mahā-Purāṇa was written.[3] It is stated at the end of the work that it was consecrated on the 23rd June, 897 A.D. during the reign of the Rāṣṭrakūṭa-king Kṛṣṇa II Akālavarṣa by Guṇabhadra's pupil Lokasena. Jinasena, the author of the Ādi-Purāṇa, was a pupil of Vīrasena, and was highly honoured by King Amoghavarṣa I, who reigned from 815 to 877 A.D. According to this, then, the work was undoubtedly composed in 9th century. Jinasena, the author of the Ādi-Purāṇa, is not, however, identical with Jinasena, the author of the Harivaṃśa-Purāṇa.[4] An allusion to Guṇāḍhya's Bṛhatkathā in the

1. *Glasenapp*, Festgabe Jacobi, p. 336 ff., points out numerous divergences of the Mahā-Purāṇa both from the tradition of the Śvetāmbaras and from other Digambara traditions.

2. See *Glasenapp, loc. cit.*, p. 339 ff.

3. Through the Praśasti at the end of the Uttara-Purāṇa. See *Bhandarkar, loc. cit.*, and Early History of the Dekkan, p. 69 f.

4. In the Maṅgala of the Harivaṃśa (quoted by *Hiralal*, Catalogue, p. xxii) Raviṣeṇa, Kumārasena, Vīrasena and Jinaseṇa are mentioned with praise. The teacher of this Jinasena is Kīrtisena of Punnāṭa Gaṇa. According to this, Jinasena, the pupil of Vīrasena, and author of the Ādi-Purāṇa, would have lived before the Jinasena of the Harivaṃśa, that means before 783 A.D., which is scarcely possible. Unless there is some mistake, we must assume that there were teachers named Vīrasena and Jinasena both before and after the author of the Harivaṃśa. The name Jinasena frequently occurs as the name of an author; s. *Hiralal*, Catalogue, pp. xxiii, 644, 651, 707.

Ādi-Purāṇa, is worthy of notice.[1]

One of the favourite stories in the Uttara-Purāṇa is that of Jīvandhara, which has also been treated several times by later poets both in Sanskrit and in Tamil. By way of a specimen, we here give the contents of this legend, which is told in Chapter 75.[2]

Queen Vijayā, the consort of King Satyandhara of Rājapura, is warned in dreams that she is about to be visited by both joy and sorrow. Soon afterwards a being from the heavenly world of the gods descends into the womb of the queen, "just as a beautiful flamingo would decend upon a pleasant lake covered with autumnal lotus-flowers." Soon after this, the king is bereft of his throne, and killed by his treacherous minister Kāṣṭhāṅgāraka.[3] The queen, protected by a friendly female elf (Yakṣī) gives birth to a son on a cremation-ground, "as the sky brings forth the moon." The Yakṣī, who places jewel-lamps (*i.e.*, shining jewels used as lamps) around the newly-born child (to protect it from evil demons) consoles the queen in her grief with a speech on the transitoriness of all things and the destinies brought about by deeds in former births. The merchant Gandhotkaṭa, to whom it had been prophesied by an ascetic that he will have a long-lived son if he exposed his newly-born child, who would die just after birth, comes along, and hears the voice of the boy born by Vijayā. He exclaims "Jīva, jīva, ("live, live") for which reason the boy receives the name Jīvandhara. When the queen recognised Gandhotkaṭa, she entrusted her child to him, begging him to take care of the boy. The merchant takes the child to his wife Nandā, who considers it as her own. Vijayā was taken by the Yakṣi to a hermitage of ascetics, and lived there in secret, consoled by the Yakṣī with stories and pious instructions concerning the religion of the Jina. Two younger wives of King Satyandhara, and the wives of the

---

1. I, 115. See A *Venkatasubbiah* in Ind. Hist. Qu. 5. 1929. 31 ff., and Kamta Prasad *Jain*, *ibid*, p. 547 ff.

2. After E. *Hultzsch*, The Story of Jivandhara, in Quarterly Journal of the Mythic Society 12, 1922, 317-348. The text of this Jivandhara-Caritra is edited by T. S. *Kuppusvami Śāstrī*, Tanjore 1907 (Sarasvativilasa Series 11).

3. *I.e.* "charcoal," probably an allusion to the man's former occupation.

four most faithful followers of the king, also bear sons, who are all brought up together by Gandhotkaṭa, and Nandā also bears another son Nandāḍhya, who grows up with the seven boys. As he advances in years, Jīvandhara evinces exceptional wisdom. For instance, he weeps, as children do, because his food was too hot. When the ascetic who is present admonishes him, telling him that a sensible child should not weep, the boy replies, asking him whether he is not aware that weeping has the following advantages : The mucus collected in the body flows out, the eyes become clear, and the food becomes thoroughly cooled. The ascetic who had formerly been a king, becomes the teacher of Jīvandhara and the other boys.

In consequence of his good deeds in previous incarnations, Jīvandhara, after he has attained to manhood, wins eight beautiful women as his wives one after another. The Vidyādhara prince Garuḍavega wishes to marry his charming daughter Gandharvadattā, a pious devotee of the Jinas. He arranges a self-choice. The princess appears in the hall which has been erected for this purpose, with a lute, on which she plays beautifully, accompanying the music by song. Jīvandhara steps into the hall to take part in a musical contest. However, he returns as being unsuitable the lutes which are handed to him, and asks whether he may have the princess's lute. She hands it to him, and he now plays and sings far more beautifully, whereupon she hands him the wreath and selects him as her husband.

Jīvandhara gives further proof of exceptional wisdom and bravery. He decides the quarrel between two maidens, Suramañjarī and Guṇamālā, as to the goodness of their perfumes, by scattering the powders, whereupon it is seen that the bees swarm to the more sweetly scented powder, that of the Suramañjarī. He also tames a furious elephant. On this occasion Suramañjarī falls in love with the prince, and he accepts her as his second wife. He rescues a dog, which is being persecuted by bad boys, from its tormentors. The dog remembers its former incarnation, and transforms itself into a Yakṣa, who thenceforth becomes a faithful friend to the prince; he also gives him a ring; by the aid of which he can assume any kind of form he desires. Padmottamā, the daughter of King Dharmapati, is bitten by a poisonous snake. The king promises his daughter to the man who will cure her of the snake's poison. Jīvandhara alone is able to do this with the help of his Yakṣa friend, and he wins this princess, too, as his wife. A few days later he comes to a lovely grove, where he worships in a Jaina temple. All of a sudden a Campaka tree begins to burst forth in red blossoms, the cuckoos begin to sing charmingly, the pond by the temple fills itself with limpid water, the water-lilies open, bees approach in swarms, and the doors of the Jaina temple fly open of their own accord. Now it had been prophesied that the merchant Subhadra should give his daughter Kṣemasundarī in marriage to the man at whose coming all these miracles should take place. So Kṣemasundarī, too, became the wife of Jivandhara. He wins a fifth wife, Hemābhā, owing to his skill in archery. Princess Śrīcandrā observes a pair of doves enjoying themselves and falls into a swoon, for she remembers that she had been a dove in a previous existence and had lost her husband. After a long search, and with the assistance of Jīvandhara, the former husband of the princess is found in the person of Nandābha, Jīvandhara's half-brother, who is again married to her. Jīvandhara stays away from his family for 16 years, because in a former birth he had separated the young one of a flamingo from its parents for 16 months. At last comes the reunion with his mother, which is described very touchingly. She enlightens him regarding the fact that he is the son of King Satyandhara who was killed, and asks him to seize the reins of government. He promises to do this when the right moment shall have come.

By the aid of his magic ring he comes to Rājapura as a merchant. There the merchant Sāgaradatta gives him his daughter in marriage, as he was her destined husband according to prophesy on the part of the astrologers. Disguised as an old and wandering Brahman ascetic, he comes one day into the audience hall of Kāṣṭhāṅgāraka and is entertained by him. After leaving the hall, he offers the princes a powder which has the power to make people docile to one's wishes. The princes laugh, and say he should make the maiden Guṇamālā, who has become a man-hater since Jīvandhara declared her perfume to be inferior, docile. He boasts that he will win Guṇamālā. He goes to her and announces his arrival. She asks : "Whence have you come, and whither are you going:?" He replies: 'I have come afterwards,

I shall go again before." As the waiting-maids laugh at this reply, he says : "Do not laugh, old age brings perversity in its train; will this not be your lot also ?" Guṇamālạ asks again : "Whither are you going ? " He answers : "I shall go so long, until I reach a worthy maiden." When she heard this, she said jokingly: "He is old in body and in years, but not in his heart," gave him a place of honour, ate with him and said : "Now go quickly where you want to go." He praised her, and said : "You have said well, my dear one," rose with an effort, supported by his stick, and sat down upon her couch, as if she had said that he was to do this. When the waiting-maids saw this, they exclaimed: "Just see this impertinence!"and were about to drive him away. But Guṇamālā has a feeling that this is no ordinary Brahmin, and restrains the maids, saying: "What harm is there? The Brahmin is my guest, let him stay here." At the end of the night he sang sweet melodies, which reminded Guṇamālā of Jīvandhara's singing at Gandharvadattā's self-choice. Finally he discloses his identity, and receives Guṇamālā as a wife from her parents. The merchant Gandhotkaṭa arranges a feast.

Soon after this Jīvandhara wins Ratnavatī, the daughter of King Videha, as his eighth wife, this time again through his skill in drawing the bow. Kāṣṭhāṅgāraka aṇd other persons of evil intent, try to carry away his wife in a fight. Jīvandhara notices this, reveals his identity to the former vassals of Satyandhara as the son of the old king, fights with them against Kāṣṭhāṅgāraka, defeats his army and cuts off his head. After he has duly worshipped the Jinas, he is anointed king, celebrates his marriage with Ratnavatī, crowns Gandharvadattā as first queen, and lives happily as a good sovereign with his mother, his wives and friends, enjoying the reward of his former good deeds. One day he meets a Jaina monk, and takes the monastic vow upon himself. His brothers do likewise. While he is living with them in the forest, he notices a herd of monkeys fighting furiously among themselves, and he is filled with disgust at the world. After a meeting with Mahāvīra, he renounces his kingdom in favour of Prince Vasundhara, son of Gandharvadattā, and becomes a monk. His companions do the same, whereupon his mother and his eight wives become nuns.

The Śatruñjaya-Māhātmya[1] by Dhaneśvara, who, according to his own statement, wrote his work in Valabhī at the desire of Śīlāditya, King of Surāṣṭra,[2] is a work after the style of the Māhātmyas of the Purāṇas. This is an epic, mostly in Ślokas, in 14 Sargas, the theme of which is the glorification of the sacred mountain Śatruñjaya. It begins with a cosmology, then tells of the adventures of a King Mahīpāla, whereupon the story of the first Jina Ṛṣabha follows. It tells of the fights of the two brothers Bharata and Bāhubali and the pilgrimages and pious foundations of Bharata, especially the shrines erected on the Śatruñjaya mountain. In Book IX we come across the Rāma legend, whilst in Book X to XII the story of the Pāṇḍavas, connected with the Kṛṣṇa legend and the legend of the Jina Ariṣṭanemi, is told. The stories told in Book X about Bhīmasena refer, however, to a Bhīma totally different from that of the Mahābhārata. He is a thief and a good-for-nothing, though a keen adventurer, about whom, for instance, the following is told :

A merchantman vessel, on which he is sailing overseas, runs aground in mid-ocean on a coral-reef. A parrot indicates a way of rescue. One of them must be prepared to die, swim to a mountain and there startle up the Bhāraṇḍa birds.[3] Bhīma undertakes

---

1. A. *Weber*, Ueber das Śatruñjaya-Māhātmyam AKM I, Nr. 4 Leipzig 1858; transl., with appendices, by J. Burgess, Ind. Ant. 30, 1901, 239 ff.; 288 ff.

2. The text has Śilāditya. Between 605 and 766 A.D. there were six different rulers of the Valabhī dynasty named Śīlāditya (s. *Duff*, p. 380). Though there are a few quite definite chronological data in the work itself (I, 13 f.; XIV, 101 ff.; 165 ff.; 281 ff.) these contradict one another to such an extent that it is not possible to assign an exact date to the work, See Weber, l.c., p. 8ff., 15, 39ff. According to XIV, 283, Dhaneśvara was "the moon in the ocean of the Moon-Gaccha" (śaśigacchāmbudhiśaśi). A Dhaneśvara of the Candragaccha is mentioned in the list of teachers by Abhayadeva, the teacher of Āsaḍa. The last-named lived in about 1191 A. D.; hence Dhaneśvara, the teacher of Devendra Sūri, the teacher of Bhadreśvara, the teacher of Abhayadeva, would have lived in about 1100 A.D.

3. According to Mahābhārata VI, 7, 13, there live in the northern Kuru-land the Bhāraṇḍa birds, which have sharp teeth and are very strong, and throw the corpses of men who live to the age of thousands of years, into

this, and saves the ship, but remains alone on the mountain. The helpful parrot gives him a means of escape. He is to cast himself into the ocean, allow himself to be swallowed by a fish and thrown ashore. This takes place, and he lands in Ceylon. After manifold adventures he acquires a kingdom, but renounces it after some time, in order to withdraw as a hermit on Raivata, one of the peaks of the sacred Śatruñjaya. Book XIV contains the legend of the Jina Pārśvanātha and at the end a long prophecy of Mahāvira, which contains all manner of historical allusions, the significance of which is, however, not yet explained.

Corresponding to the Purāṇas of the Digambaras, the Śvetāmbaras have the Caritras, some of which describe the lives of individual Jinas, whilst others treat of the lives of all 63 Śalākā-puruṣas[1] or "excellent men." The work of the last-named type which enjoys the greatest reputation among the Śvetāmbara Jainas, is the Triṣaṣṭi-Śalākāpuruṣa-Carita,[2] "The Lives of the 63 Excellent Men" by the famous Jaina monk Hemacandra. This work, which was written at the desire of King Kumārapāla between 1160 and 1172 A.D., the latter being the year of Hemacandra's death, contains in 10 Parvans the legends about the 24 Jinas, the 12 Cakravartins, the 9 Vāsudevas, the 9 Baladevas and the 9 Viṣṇudviṣas (enemies of the 9 incarnations of Viṣṇu). The language of the work, which the author himself describes as a Mahākāvya, "a great ornate epic," and which in bulk if in nothing else, seems to vie with the Mahābhārata,[3] is simple and

mountain caves. According to XII, 169, 10, they have human faces. The Pañcatantra (s. *Benfey.* Das Pantschatantra I, 111 f., 538; II, 360 f., 525) tells of Bhāraṇḍa birds with two beaks.

1. Śalākā (Pāli salākā) means "arrow" or "little stake," also the small bamboo sticks which are used by the Buddhist monks as an identity badge. Śalākāpuruṣa would probably mean "legitimised, characterised men," so that Śalākāpuruṣa and Lakṣaṇapuruṣa are synonymous. The Commentary on Abhidhānacintāmaṇi 111, 364, however, explains : puruṣeṣu jātarekhā ity arthaḥ, "which form aṣ it were lines of demarcation among the monks."

2. The text has been published by the Jaina-Dharma-Prasāraka-Sabhā (in a new edition), Bhavanagar 1906-1913.

3. Even the division into Parvans seems to indicate the proud comparison with the Mahābhārata.

unaffected. The description "Mahākāvya" is justified by many beautiful comparisons, such as when, for instance, the poet (I, 70) compares the buffaloes carrying water, with clouds which have fallen to earth, and many a pretty description of seasons, love-scenes, and so on, in the style of ornate poetry. The main purpose of the work is, however, instruction and edification; for, as the author himself says (I, 29) : "To sing in praise of the pious, leads to liberation." The narrative is often interrupted by long instructive discourses on subjects of religion and morality. There is often mention of the doctrine of Karman, and all the stories of the rebirths of the great men and their destinies, are instance of the effects of good and bad deeds. In the case of each one of the "excellent men," his destinies in his former existences are related. In the main, they are the same legends as are to be found in the earlier Jinistic epics and Purāṇas.[1] It is still a matter for more detailed investigation as to what earlier sources Hemacandra drew upon for his poem.[2]

Parvan I begins, after the usual benedictions, with the life of Ṛṣabha, the first Tīrthakara, in his previous existences.[3] Parvan X, which also occurs as an independent text in manuscripts, entitled Mahāvīra-Caritra, "Life of Mahāvīra" is of

1. See *Glasenapp*, Der Jainismus, p. 259 ff.

2. We are tempted to think of the Triṣaṣṭilakṣaṇamahāpurāṇa, but the Caupannamahāpurisacariya, a work written in Prākrit prose by Śīlācārya in the year 868 A.D. must also be taken into consideration. On this little-known' work which has not yet been published, s. *Peterson*, 3 Reports, p. 38, App. p. 91; Banarsi Das *Jain*, Jaina Jātakas, p. iii ff. and *Jacobi* Sanatkumāra caritam, p. xiii. According to *Jacobi* in ERE VII 466b, the legend-collection Vasudevahiṇḍi would be one of the sources of Hemacandra's work. Vasudevahiṇḍi is the work of Saṅghadāsa Gaṇin (the first part, which also contains the Dhammillahiṇḍi, is published, as No. 80 of the Ātmānanda -Jaina-Grantharatnamālā, Bhavanagar 1930).See also *Peterson*, Report 1882-83 p. 58; 3 Reports, p. 184 f.; *Guerinot*, P. 75 and *Farquhar*, Outline, pp. 278, 280, erroneously state Hemacandra to be the author of the Vasudevahiṇḍa (=Vasudevahiṇḍi).

3. On Parvan I, see L. *Suali* in SIFI VII, 3 ff. An English translation of Canto I of Parvan I has appeared in the Punjab Sanskrit Series No. 8. Jaina Jātakas or Lord Ṛshabha's Pūrvabhavas, translated by Amūlyacharan *Vidyābhuṣaṇa* revised and edited with Notes and Introduction by Banarsi Das *Jain*, Lahore, 1925. The Ādiśvaracaritra, the first book of the Triṣaṣṭiśalākāpuruṣacaritra, has been translated into English by Helen M. Johnson, Baroda, 1931 (GOS No. 51).

greater significance. It contains the life story of Mahāvīra, which agrees on the whole with the accounts in the Kalpa-Sūtra and the Āyāraṃga, but gives far greater detail. We find here also detailed data, which are probably based on earlier traditions and which are for that reason important from the historical point of view, regarding King Śreṇika Bimbisāra, the contemporary of Mahāvīra and Buddha.[1] In the form of a prophecy of Mahāvīra, Hemacandra also describes in a lengthy passage the ideal reign of his pious pupil King Kumārapāla, who ascended the throne 1669 years after the Nirvāṇa of Mahāvīra.[2] Interwoven with the more or less historical accounts of King Śreṇika and his son, Prince Abhaya, there are also many interesting tales, such as the story of the master-thief Rauhiṇeya who by reason of his boldness and artfulness, succeeds in eluding all pursuit but who in the end would almost have been outwitted by Prince Abhaya himself, had he not by a mere chance heard a few words of Mahāvīra, which save his life. This causes him to hear the sermon of the Jina and to become a monk, and he enters into heaven as a sage.[3]

The Pariśiṣṭa-Parvan or Sthavirāvalī Carita,[4] *i.e.* "Appendix-Section" or "Lives of the Series of the Elders," the appendix to the Triṣaṣṭi-Śalākā-puruṣa-Carita, has a still greater wealth of fairy-tales and stories of all kinds. This book treats of the history of the Daśapūrvins, *i.e.*, the earliest teachers of the Jaina religion, who were still knowers of the ten Pūrvas. Whilst with the exception of the last two Tīrthakaras, Pārśvanātha and

1. See Helen M. *Johnson* in JAOS 45, 1925, 301ff.

2. See *Bühler,* Ueber das Leben des Jainamonches Hemachandra, pp. 37 ff., 78ff.

3. See Helen M. *Johnson,* in JAOS 44, 1924, p. 1 ff. The great popularity of this story is shown by the fact that it has again been remodelled in extended form as an independent work by a more recent poet Devamūrti (15th century) in the Rauhiṇeya. caritra (Jamnagar 1908, 2nd Ed. by the Ātmānanda-Sabhā, Bhavangar (1916); translated into English by Helen M, *Johnson* in Studies in Honor of M. Bloomfield, New Haven, 1930, p. 159ff.; cf. JAOS 45, 1924, 73ff.

4. Edited by H. *Jacobi,* Calcutla, Bibl. Ind.. 1891. Extracts translated into German by J. *Hertel,* Erzählungen aus Hemacandras Pariśiṣṭaparvan, Leipzig, 190

Mahāvīra, the personages of the Triṣaṣṭi-Śalākāpuruṣa-Carita belong throughout to mythology or epic poetry, the Sthavirāvali-Carita contains the life-stories of the Elders (Sthaviras, Theras), *i.e.*, the disciples of Mahāvīra, whose names and sequence in accordance with the unanimous tradition of the Śvetāmbaras may be regarded as historical. It is true that the stories by themselves alone seldom contain any historical nucleus. Hemacandra took them from earlier works of legendary lore and commentaries, especially those of Haribhadra. Frequently enlivened by proverbs and colloquialisms of the common people the stories reveal clearly their popular origin. Hemacandra translated them from the Prākrit without making many alterations.

There are many interesting parallels to be found among the stories of the Pariśiṣṭa-Parvan, not only to such stories as are familiar to us from other Indian works, but also to such as form part of universal literature. The story of the twins, Kuberadatta and Kuberadattā, the children of the courtesan Kuberasenā, is a kind of Oedipus tragedy. The time-honoured theme of incest committed unconsciously, is here diluted, even more than in the Christian legend of Saint Gregory, into a pious monastic legend. What appeals to the Indian narrator is, not so much the tragic situation, as the subtlety of the complicated relationship. When a monk writes stories, it is conceivable that the wickedness of womankind will furnish him with inexhaustible material for the most subtle stories of adultery. There is an abundance of such stories in the Pariśiṣṭa-Parvan, including some, the individual motifs of which often recur in universal literature.[1] The tale of Sthūlabhadra and the nun Kośā (VIII, 110-193) is one of the characteristic monastic stories :

Three monks each made a vow in the presence of the master. The first said that he would sit in front of a lion's den throughout the four months of the rainy season; the second said that

1. Thus the motif of the ordeal of the adultress, among others, in the narrative II, 446-640, translated into German by J. J. *Meyer*, Isoldes Gottesurteil, Berlin 1914, p. 130 ff. The Ṛṣyaśṛṅga legend is imitated in the story of Valkalacirin, 1, 90-258.

he would sojourn for the same length of time in front of the hole of a snake, the mere sight of which is fatal; the third declared that he would sit on a well-wheel throughout the rainy season. Then the monk Sthūlabhadra comes along, and says he will spend the four months in the house of the courtesan Kośā (whose lover he had been before he became a monk), without violating his vow of chastity. He not only succeeds in this, but Kośā is also converted to the Jaina faith. At the end of the rainy season the four monks return to the master, who declares that Sthūlabhadra has accomplished the greatest feat. The other monks are jealous at this, and the one who had sat in front of the lion's den, declares that, before the beginning of the next rainy season, he will perform the same feat as Sthūlabhadra. He repairs to Kośā, who sees through him : he falls an easy victim to her, but is at length brought back to repentance and to the monastic life by Kośā herself, who finally becomes a nun.

Side by side with such stories there are also purely Jinistic legends, some of which read like historical or biographical accounts. Thus it is related in Book V, how Śayyambhava wrote the Daśavaikālika-Sūtra, in order to give his son, who, he knows, must die in six months, the chance of grasping the essence of the Jaina doctrine in the shortest possible time, without studying the other sacred texts. The legends told in Books IX and XIII also have reference to the compilation of the Canon. The stories in Book VIII relating to the royal dynasty of the Nandas are of some historical interest, though the legends themselves probably contain but little actual history. At any rate the fact that the last Nanda prince was overthrown by Candragupta, the founder of the Maurya dynasty (*ca.* 317 B.C.) is historical. According to the legend, Candragupta, who was of low descent on the maternal side, only succeeded in pushing his way to power and consolidating his throne, because he had the astute Brahmin Cāṇakya as his minister. There were many popular tales current about this man, and Hemacandra did not fail to make use of them, though Cāṇakya was of all men thoroughly unsuitable as an example for a pious Jaina to imitate. From time immemorial, however, the Jainas have always taken pains to make every hero of the popular stories into one of their own also. Nevertheless, it is so remarkable that they should have done this even in the case of Cāṇakya, that crafty, unscrupulous intriguer and despotic politician, who shrank back from no trick however bad, that we are inclined to believe, with the tradition, that Candragupta really favoured the Jaina faith, and that, for this reason, he and his famous minister were extolled by the Jainas. It is true that Hemacandra succeeded in making a pious Jaina of even this man. Indeed, this out and out worldly man, who shortly before his death, takes his revenge on his enemy, nevertheless retires at the end of his days to the vicinity of a dung-heap, in order to starve himself to death, in the true manner of a Jaina saint. Owing to the rascality of a rival, who sets fire to the dung-heap, he is, however, burnt against his will. After his death, he curiously enough becomes a goddess.

The Caritras which describe the life of individual Jinas, are numerous. Among these, Ṛṣabha, the first, Śāntinātha, the sixteenth, Ariṣṭanemi or Neminātha, the twenty-second, Pārśva, the twenty-third, and of course the last Jina, Mahāvīra himself, are most especially honoured by the Jainas, and their biographies are among the most popular themes of narrative poetry.

Even in the Canon there are already Mahāvīra-Caritas, descriptions of the life of the last Jina. Hemacandra's Mahāvīra-Carita forms Parvan X of his Triṣaṣṭi-Śalākāpuruṣa-Carita. A Mahāvīra-Cariyam in Prākrit was written in the year 1082 A.D. by Guṇacandra Gaṇin,[1] and another in 1085 A.D. by Devendra Gaṇin,[2] also known as Nemicandra.

The life of Ṛṣabha is, as we have seen, told in the introductory sections of the Rāma epics. Kṛṣṇa and the heroes of the Mahābhārata are supposed to be contemporaries of the Jina Neminātha, about whom legends are told in all adaptations of the Mahābhārata. Furthermore it is the legend of Neminātha which has been made the theme of innumerable poetic versions,

1. Edited in AUS Granthoddhāra 1929. Cf. *Peterson*, Report V, p. xiii f.

2. Edited in Jaina-Ātmānanda Granthamālā, No. 59. The work also contains Apabhraṃśa stanzas, s. *Jacobi*, Sanatkumāracaritam, p. xxii. The author is probably the same as that of the commentary on the Uttarādhyayana-Sūtra.

beginning with the early one in the Uttarajjhayaṇa.[1] In later times there are at least a dozen life-stories of Neminātha. Thus in the 11th century we have a Neminātha-Carita in Sanskrit by Sūrācārya and one by Maladhāri-Hemacandra. In the year 1159 A.D. Haribhadra, a pupil of Śrīcandra, who himself was a pupil of Jinacandra, completed his Neminähacariu in Apabhraṃśa.[2] The author was a contemporary of Hemacandra, and completed his work, which he had written at the request of the minister Pṛthivīpāla, on the day of the conversion of King Kumārapāla. The legend of Neminātha is the same in all the presentations. Haribhadra, however, is at pains to depict romantic scenes after the manner of the ornate poetry, to interweave descriptions of nature, etc. He takes such a delight in doing this, that the entire first half of the poem treats only of the previous births of Nemi and Rājīmatī, and insufficient attention is devoted to the actual legend of the Tīrthakara. Interwoven with the story of the second reincarnation, there is a Sanatkumāra-Carita, which relates the legend of the fourth Cakravartin Sanatkumāra,[3] the contemporary of the fifteenth Tīrthakara. The narrative is full of romance, the scene of which is laid partly on earth, and partly in the world of the Vidyādharas and gods. After many amorous adventures and numerous victorious fights, after he had become a ruler of the world (Cakravartin) famed for his incomparable beauty, and after he had lived happily for 300,000 years, old age approached him suddenly. Then he renounced the world, devoted himself to rigorous asceticism, died the voluntary death through fasting and entered into the Sanatkumāra-heaven. The poet evidently wanted to show that he could apply all the subtleties of the Kāvya style in Apabhraṃśa just as well as in Prākrit, for the legend itself had been treated often enough before him.[4]

---

1. See above, p. 450 f.
2. *Cf.* H. *Jacobi*, Sanatkumāracaritam, ein Abschnitt aus Haribhadra Neminātha-caritam, eine Jainalegende in Apabhraṃśa, in A Bay A XXXI, 2 München I921. This Haribhadra is also the author of Mallināth-carita in Prākrit.
3. *Cf. Glasenapp*, Der Jainismus, p. 279.
4. Thus already by Devendra in his commentary on the Uttarajjhayaṇa in the year 1073 A.D., and only one year earlier than Haribhadra

The life-story of Neminātha is also treated by the poet Vāgbhaṭa in his Nemi-Nirvāṇa,[1] a Mahākāvya in 15 cantos. The poem Nemidūta[2] by Vikrama, the son of Sāṅgaṇa, is a most artificial work. The theme of this poem is the lament of Rājīmatī, after her husband had become a monk. The work is an example of the "Completing of verses" :[3] The last line of each verse is taken from Kālidāsa's "Meghadūta," whilst the first three lines are composed by the poet himself. This appears to be a very modern work.

An earlier work of the same kind is the Pārśvābhyudaya,[4] a poetical life-story of Pārśvanātha by Jinasena, who wrote the Ādi-Purāṇa in the 9th century. In this poem the entire "Meghadūta" has been incorporated by inserting one or two lines from Kālidāsa's in each verse, whilst Jinasena composed the rest.

The number of poetical life-stories of Pārśvanātha, the predecessor of Mahāvīra, is very great. The Pārśvanātha-Caritra[5] by Bhavadeva Sūri, who probably wrote it in 1225 A.D.[6] tells with an exceptional wealth of detail, not only the

---

Śrīcandra wrote a Sanatkumāracarita in Prākrit. As there are several writers, named Śrīcandra, it is not certain whether this is the same one who wrote a Kathākośa. Cf. *Hiralal*, Catalogue, p. xlix ff, and *Jacobi*, l. c. p. xiii.

1. Edited in Km., 56, 1896. The poet lived under Jayasiṃha of Gujarat (1093-1154) and is also the author of a work on poetics (Vāgbhaṭālaṃkāra).

2. Edited in Km., Part 11, pp. 85-104. *Cf.* p. *Pavolini* in GSAI 18, 329 ff. ; E. *Hultzch.* Kālidāsa's Meghadūta, Ed. London 1911, p. vi f.

3. Samasyāpūraṇa, a poetical exercise consisting of one or two lines of a stanza being given to which the poet must compose the remaining lines.

4. The Meghadūta as embodied in the Pārśvābhyudaya with the Commentary of Mallinātha, with a literal English Translation Ed. by K. B. *Pathak*, Poona 1894 and edited with a commentary by *Yogirāṭ Paṇḍitācārya*, Bombay NSP 1909. Cf. *Guerinot* in JA, 1909, s. 10, t. XIV, pp. 72, 75; E. *Hultzsch* l.c., p. vii, and T. S. Kuppuswami *Śastri* in Ind. Ant. 36, 1907, 285 ff.; *Hiralal*, Catalogue, p. xxiii.

5. Edited by *Haragovindadāsa* and *Becaradāsa*, Benares 1912, YJG 32. An analysis of the work is given by M. *Bloomfield*, The Life and Stories of the Jaina Saviour Pārśvanātha, Baltimore, 1919. Bloomfield also gives numerous parallels from Indian and worldliterature.

6. At the end of the work the author says that he completed the work in the yeat 1312. The era is not stated. If it is the Saṃvat era, 1255

life-story of this saint in his last incarnation, but also his previous nine existences.

Marubhūti and Kamaṭha are sons of a court priest. Marubhūti hears a pious sermon, and renounces the world and the pleasures of the senses. Kamaṭha commits adultery with the neglected wife of his brother, Marubhūti denounces him to the king, and causes the adulterer to be punished. Kamaṭha kills his brother in revenge. Marubhūti dies with gloomy thoughts, and is therefore reborn as an elephant. As such he is converted by the king, who had withdrawn into solitude, and from that time onwards he lives a pious life. As an elephant he is killed by Kamaṭha who had in the meantime been reborn as a snake.[1] As the elephant is just meditating upon religion, he is reborn in heaven, whilst Kamaṭha descends to hell. In the succeeding incarnations the former Marubhūti is reborn now as a god in some heaven, now as a prince who after ruling justly and piously, retires from the world. Reborn as a snake, as a wild Bhil and as a lion, Kamaṭha ever and again kills the former Marubhūti, and ever and again descends to hell. At length in the tenth reincarnation the former Marubhūti is reborn as a prince in Benares, amidst all manner of miracles and signs proclaiming the future Jina. While his mother was pregnant with him, she saw a snake at her side one night (pārśvataḥ), hence the prince received the name Pārśva. The former Kamaṭha is reborn as Kaṭha, the son of a Brahmin, is very poor and becomes an ascetic. One day Pārśva sees Kaṭha seated between five fires performing ascetic practices, and throwing a large snake into the fire. Pārśva rescues the snake, which then reappears as the Nāga king Dharaṇa, whilst Kaṭha is reborn as an Asura. The sight of a picture of the former Jina Nemi causes Pārśva to give up wealth and power, tear out his hair, and wander forth as an itinerant monk. At the age of 30 years he attains perfec-

---

A.D. would be the corresponding date. If this date is correct, Yaśas, whom he names as his teacher, cannot be identical with Yaśodeva Sūri, who wrote a commentary on the Pākṣika-Sūtra in 1124 A.D.

1. It is one of the favourite themes in Jinistic legend literature to trace the destinies of two sworn enemies through many rebirths. *Bloomfield. loc. cit.*, p. 13ff.

tion. Like Māra in the Buddha legend, the Asura Meghamālin (the former Kaṭha) attacks Pārśva, in order to disturb him in his meditation, but he is protected by the snake king Dharaṇa. At length the Asura repents, and becomes a pious layman. Pārśva becomes a Kevalin (possessor of the perfect knowledge), visits his parents, and finally attains Nirvāṇa. After his passing, he enters the highest heaven, and is much honoured by Śakra. His corpse is cremated by the gods, and Śakra erects a jewelled Stūpa over his ashes.

The legend of Pārśvanātha, however, forms merely the frame, into which numerous stories, fables and fairy-tales are inserted in the manner so familiar in Indian narrative literature. Not a few of these stories are also known from other Jinistic and secular narrative works (such as Pañcatantra, Vetālapañcaviṃśati, and others), *e.g.*, the story of the Goldman, who is killed, and transforms himself into a gold treasure (II, 959 ff.), of the Brahmin who builds castles in the air (II, 1015 ff.), of the patient Hariścandra (III, 556 ff.), the parable of the four daughters-in law[1] (VI, 389 ff.) and others. The story of the emperor Suvarṇabāhu not only contains themes of the Śakuntalā legend, but actually reveals (IV, 41) an acquaintance with the drama of Kālidāsa. One of the most interesting stories is that of King Vikrama as a parrot (III, 105ff.)[2]

The mighty King Vikrama who is endowed with all the virtues, learns from a sage the magic art of penetrating into another body. At the same time with him a Brahmin learns the same art. The latter, a scoundrel, seizes the opportunity when Vikrama leaves his own body and enters that of an elephant, to penetrate into the body of the king, and to give himself out as the king. When the real King Vikrama is aware of this, he enters into the body of a parrot, allows himself to be caught by a hunter, and causes this man to sell him to the queen. As a parrot he becomes the queen's favourite and converses with her; they ask each other riddles, and he recites to

1. Already in Nāyādhammakahāo, Chapt. VII; see above, p. 426.

2, Cf. *Bloomfield loc. cit.*, p. 74ff., and the treatise "On the Art of Entering Another's Body" in Proceedings of the American Philosophical Society, Vol. LVI. 1, 1917.

her all kinds of wise sayings and instructions on the religion of the Jina. The riddles are erudite rather than popular. One of the simpler riddles is that of the queen : "It makes snakes poisonless, the gods powerless, lions motionless, and yet children hold it in their hands, what is it ?" The parrot guesses it at once : "A painter's brush." After so many proofs of sagacity the queen no longer doubts that the wise parrot is none other than the real King Vikrama, her husband. One day Vikrama's soul leaves the parrot's body, and enters into the body of a lizard. When the queen sees the dead body of the bird, she begins to lament, and wishes to burn herself with it. In order to prevent the self-immolation of the queen, the false king enters into the parrot's body, which enables the real king to assume his own body and to appear before the queen in all his splendour.

Like other Indian narrative works, the Pārśvanātha-Caritra also contains many gnomic sayings both on morality and on worldly wisdom. There are more than a thousand of them, many of which are well-known from other sources too. A few examples are given here :

"It is better for a man to be cast into a dungeon, better to wander in strange lands, better to live in hell,—than to have two wives." (II, 833).

"Better is death, better to beg, better to serve one's enemies, if one meets with a misfortune through the visitation of fate,—than to seek help from relatives." (III, 785.)

"The wise ones know how much sand there is in the Ganges and how much water in the ocean, they know the dimensions of great mountains—but the thoughts of a woman they cannot fathom." (VII, 82.)

Other Pārśvanātha-Caritras (or Caritas) are written by Vādirāja (1025 A.D.) the teacher of the Western Calukya King Jayasiṃha II Jagadekamalla,[1] by Māṇikyacandra (1217 A.D.),[2]

---

1. Cf. *Hultzsch*, in ZDMG 68, 1914, p. 698 and Quarterly Journal of the Mythic Society, 12, 1922, p. 319; A. *Venkatasubbiah* in ZII 7, 1929, 179 ff.

2. *Peterson*, 3 Reports, p. 157 ff.; Report IV, p. xci. He also wrote a commentary on Kāvyaprakāśa.

by Sakalakīrti (15th century)[1], by Padmasundara (1565 A.D.)[2] and by Udayavīra Gaṇin.[3]

Māṇikyacandra and Sakalakīrti also wrote Śāntinātha-Caritas, life-stories of the 16th Tīrthakara.[4] A Śāntinātha-Carita in Sanskrit verses was written by Devasūri in 1282 A.D.[5] Devasūri was the teacher of Tilakaprabha, the teacher of Vīraprabha, whose pupil Ajitaprabha wrote a great epic Śāntinātha-Caritra.[6] The date of a Śānti-Purāṇa by *Aśaga*[7] is not known.

The Sumatinātha-Caritra by Somaprabha (second half of the 12th century) in Prākrit treats of the life of the 5th Tīrthakara.[8]

A voluminous Prākrit poem Supārśvanāha-Cariyaṃ[9] by Lakṣmaṇa Gaṇin, deals with the story of the 7th Tīrthakara. This work, composed in the year 1143 A.D., also contains 68 Apabhraṃśa verses. A Vimala-Purāṇa by Kṛṣṇadāsa,[10] deals

1. See above, p. 476 and Note 1; and *Bhandarkar*, Report 1883-84, pp. 122f.; 433. The Ādīśvaracarita, the first book of the Triṣaṣṭiśalākāpuruṣacaritra, has been translated into English by Helen M. *Johnson*, Baroda 1931 (GOS No. 51)

2. Pārśvanāthakāvya, s. *Aufrecht*, Bodl. Cat., p. 392; *Peterson*, 3 Reports, p. 255 ff.; Report IV, p. lxxv.

3. Date not known; s. *Bloomfield, loc cit.*, p. i f. The contents of a Pārśvanātha-Caritra written in the year 1597 A.D. is given by Major James *Delamaine* (Transactions of the Royal Asiatic Society I, 1827, p. 428 ff.). The name "Bṛddha Tapā Gaccha" given by him as the name of the author is probably based on some error.

4. Cf. *Kielhorn* in Ind. Ant. 10, 1881. p. 101. *Bhandarkar*, Report 1883-84, pp. 121 f.. 430 ff.

5. This was corrected by Pradyumna Sūri. It is an abridged translation into Sanskrit, of Śrīśānti-vṛtta, which was written in Prākrit, by an earlier Devasūri, who is said to have written a Stuti on his teacher Municandra in Apabhraṃśa, a Syādvādaratnākara and a Pramāṇagrantha and lived from 1068 to 1169 A.D. Cf. *Klatt* in Ind. Ant. 11, 254; *Peterson*, Report 1882-83, p. 59 f., Report IV, p. lv f.; *Jacobi*, Sanatkumāracaritam, p. xxii.

6. Edited by *Muni Indravijaya* in Bibl. Ind. 1909 f. On Ajitaprabha and his genealogical tree of teachers, s. *Peterson*, Report V, p. i f.

7. *Aufrecht*, Bodl. Cat., p. 372 f.

8. *Cf. Munirāja Jinavijaya*, Kumārapāla-Pratibodha Ed. GOS No. XIV, p. v.

9. Edited by Pandit Haragovind Das *Seth*, Benares 1918. *Cf.* P. D. *Gune* in Proe. IOC Poona 1922, p. 161 f. and *Jacobi*, Sanatkumāracaritam, p, xxii.

10. See *Aufrecht*, Bodl. Cat., p. 372 f.

with the life of the 13th Tīrthakara. The story of Dharmanātha, the 15th Tīrthakara, is treated by the poet Haricandra in the great epic Dharmaśarmābhyudaya.[1] The epic is an imitation of Māgha's Śiśupālavadha. The legend of the 12th Tīrthakara is treated by Vardhamāna Sūri in the Vāsupūjya-Caritra.[2] In this case the biography is quite stereotyped, but it forms the frame for a series of instructive and edifying stories. The life-stories of the five "Great Men" Ṛṣabha, Neminātha, Śāntinātha, Pārśvanātha and Vardhamāna Mahāvīra are contained in the epic Mahāpuruṣa Caritra[3] in five Sargas by Merutuṅga, the author of the Prabandhacintāmaṇi (1306 A.D.) The work has come down, in manuscripts, with a commentary which was probably written by the poet himself, and in this commentary the work is also called Upadeśaśataka and Dharmopadeśaśataka.

Not only the Tīrthakaras themselves, but other holy men too, have been glorified in Caritras. A famous legendary hero is Śālibhadra, a contemporary of Mahāvīra and King Śreṇika whose story is told briefly and simply in Hemacandra's Mahāvīra Caritra (Triṣaṣṭiśalākāpuruṣa-Caritra X, 57ff.) .Dharmakumāra treated this legend in 1277 A.D. in the epic Śālibhadra-Carita,[4] which was revised by Pradyumna Sūri[5] and supplied with all

1. Edited in Km, 8, 1888. Cf. *Peterson*, Report II, 77 f., 141 ff. It is impossible to determine the period of the poet, as there were several poets named Haricandra. As, however, he utilised not only Māgha but also Vākpati's Gauḍavaho (s. *Jacobi* WZKM 3, 1889, 136ff.) and as the Jīvandhara-Campū is based upon the Uttara-Purāṇa, he must have written later than 900 A.D. (s. E. *Hultzsch*, Ind. Ant. 35, 1906, 268).

2. *Cf.* A. *Ballini* in RSO I, 1906-07, 41ff. 169ff., 439ff. and II, 1908-09, 39 ff., 239 f.

3. *Cf. Weber* HSS Verz. II, 3, 1024 ff.; *Peterson*, 3 Reports, p. 266 f.; Report IV, p. xcviii and Report VI, 43 ff.

4. Edited in YJG No. 15, Benares 1910. Detailed treatment of it by M. *Bloomfield* in JAOS 43, 1923, p. 257 ff.

5. He was an excellent Sanskrit scholar and obviously a specialist in Kāvya. Among other things he worked up the Prabhāvaka-Caritra (1278 A.D.), the Śāntinātha-Carita by Devasūri (see above, p. 496, Note 5) and the Samarāicca-Kahā in a similar fashion, s. *Bloomfield loc. cit.*, p. 258. Pradyumna Sūri is also the author of the Vicārasāra-Prakaraṇa in Prākrit (edited with a chāyā by Māṇikyasāgara, Mehsana 1923). Cf. *Peterson*, 3 Reports, 270 ff.; Shankar P. *Pandit*, Gauḍavaho Ed. BSS, p. cliv.

the subtleties of ornate poetry. The story terms itself a Dāna-dharma-Kathā, "a narrative about the religious duty of giving alms," and also a Dānāvadāna,[1] "story of notable deeds of alms-giving." The subject-matter of the legend is as follows :

In his former incarnation Śālibhadra was the son of a poor widow, a shepherd boy named Saṃgama, who delighted in giving himself up to religious meditations while minding the flocks. On a feast-day he sees that delicious food is being prepared in all the houses, and he asks his mother to prepare a festive meal for him too. With great difficulty the poor woman succeeds in preparing a meal of this kind. However, before Saṃgama eats it, there comes an ascetic who is just about to break his fast, and the boy gives him the meal which has been prepared for himself. (According to the Jaina faith, it is the most meritorious form of alms-giving to offer food to an ascetic after his fast.) In consequence of this good deed, Saṃgama is reborn in Rājagṛha as Śālibhadra, the son of Bhadrā and Gobhadra, endowed with incomparable beauty and all virtues. When he had reached manhood, his father selects 32 beautiful virgins as his wives, and he leads a happy life. His father Gobhadra became an ascetic, died the voluntary death by starvation, and reached heaven. As a god, he procures immense wealth for his son Śālibhadra. "As rich as Śālibhadra" became proverbial, just as we say "as rich as Croesus." One day, however, owing to the sight of King Śreṇika who, in spite of all his power, is nevertheless only an ordinary mortal, he becomes enlightened, and becomes a Pratyekabuddha. He repairs to the teacher Dharmaghoṣa, who instructs him in the religion, and finally, after he has renounced the world, he is reborn as a god in heaven.

This simple legend is told in 7 cantos in the ornate style of Sanskrit poetry. Numerous sayings, maxims on morality and practical wisdom, are inserted into the narrative.

All these "life-stories" are purely legendary. Notwithstanding, in the life of Mahāvīra and perhaps also in that of

1. Avadāna is used here in the sense in which it is generally known to the Buddhists only. See above, p. 266f.

Pārśva we meet with many a historical trait. At any rate the stories of historical royal dynasties and personages in the history of the Order, as we found them in Hemacandra's Pariśiṣṭa-Parvan reveal a certain historical interest, which is also evinced already in the canonical texts in the beginnings of a biography of Mahāvīra and his first disciples, as well as in the list the Sthaviras and their schools with their branches, in Bhadrabāhu's Kalpa-Sūtra. There are many such lists of teachers (Paṭṭāvalīs in later centuries.[1] Semi-historical legends regarding the schisms are told in Haribhadra's and Śāntisūri's commentaries.[2] Works such as the Gurvāvalī-Sūtra,[3] a list of the teachers of the Tapāgaccha, by Dharmasāgara Gaṇin, and the Therāvalī[4] by Merutuṅga, deal exclusively with ecclesiastical history.

The so-called Prabandhas are also of semi-historical character, for they deal with historical personages, though they are collections of anecdotes rather than real biographies or history. Nevertheless they should not be entirely rejected as historical sources, even though they can be used only with extreme circumspection.[5] The Prabhāvaka-Caritra, "Life of the Prominent"[6] written by Prabhācandra or Candraprabha, and revised in the year 1277 A.D. by the well-known Kāvya specialist Pradyumna Sūri, is a continuation of Hemacandra's Pariśiṣṭa-Parvan. It contains the life stories of 22 Jaina teachers, poets and authors, including Haribhadra, Siddharṣi, Bappabhaṭṭi, Mānatuṅga, Śāntisūri and Hemacandra.

---

1. Paṭṭāvalīs have been edited, or extracted. by *J. Klatt*, Ind. Ant. 11, 245 ff.; 293 f.; 23, 169 ff.; *Hoernle*, Ind. Ant. 19, 233 ff.; 20, 341ff.; 21, 57ff.

2. See above. p. 466 and *Leumann*, Ind. Stud. 17, 91 ff.; *Jacobi*, ZDMG 38, 1ff. Jacobi also attributes historical value to the Bhadrabāhu-Carita by Ratnanandin (15th or 16th century).

3. Text in *Weber*, HSS. Verz. II, 2. 651 f. and 3, 997 ff. and *Guerinot* in JA 1912, s. 10, t. XIX, 605 ff.

4. *Bhau Dāji* in JBRAS 9, 1867, p. 147 ff.

5. Cf. Buhler, Hemachandra, p. 4 ff.

6. Edited by Hirānanda M. *Sharma*, Bombay NSP 1909. *Cf.* J. *Klatt* in WZKM 4, 1890, p. 63 ff. f. 67; *Bühler*, Hemachandra, pp. 4, 52 ff.; Sankar P. *Pandit* Gauḍavaho Ed., Introduction, p. cxlviii ff.; *Jacobi* The Upamitibhavaprapañcakathā, Edition, pp. xii, xcix ff. and S. Krishnaswami *Aiyangar* in JBRAS, N.S., 3, 1928, p. 101 ff.

The Prabandhacintāmaṇi or "Wishing-Jewel of Stories" by Merutuṅga,[1] completed in 1306 A.D. and the Prabandhakośa or "Treasury of Stories" by Rājaśekhara,[2] completed in 1349, can only be termed quasi-historical-biographical works. Under the semblance of "history," Merutuṅga's work contains a motley collection of stories, legends and anecdotes associated with historical and literary personages. Kings Bhoja, Vikramāditya and Śīlāditya are extolled as the patrons of the most excellent poets and scholars, and in doing this the author sticks at no anachronism. Thus for instance Varāhamihira, the great astronomer of the 6th century A.D. is made without further ado a contemporary of King Nanda in the 4th century B.C. Side by side with many naive little tales, there are, however, also many clever and witty anecdotes. Life at the courts of the Indian princes, and especially the literary contests which were organised at these courts, are very vividly described. The stories about Hemacandra and King Kumārapāla, personages not far removed from the period of the author, are also not devoid of a certain amount of historical value. Rājaśekhara's Prabandhakośa contains the life-stories of 24 persons, namely ten Jaina teachers (including Hemacandra), four poets (Śrīharṣa, Harihara, Amaracandra and the Digambara Madana Kīrti), seven kings and three other personages.

Another semi-historical work is the Tīrtha-Kalpa,[3] also called Kalpa-Pradīpa and Rājaprasāda, by Jinaprabha Sūri, written between 1326 and 1331 A.D. This work gives a description of the Jinistic places of pilgrimage, together with the names of their founders, the kings by whom they were restored,

1. Edited by Rāmacandra *Dīnānātha*, Bombay 1888; translated from Sanskrit by C. H. Tawney, Bibl. Ind. 1901. How unreliable Merutuṅga is, even in passages where he is apparently stating exact dates (day, month and hour) is shown by R. *Sewell* in JRAS 1920, 333 ff Cf. *Bühler*, Hemachandra, p. 4 ff.

2. We do not know of any edition of this work. Cf. *Bühler*, Hemachandra p. 4 ff. Shankar P. *Pandit*, Gauḍavaho Ed., Introduction, p. cliii ff.; E. *Hultzsch*, Report of Sanskrit MSS. in Southern India, Madras 1905, p. vif.

3. Edited by D. R. *Bhandarkar* and Kedarnath *Sāhityabhūṣaṇa* in Bibl. Ind., fasc. 1. 1923. *Cf. Peterson*, Report IV, pp. xxxvii, 91 ff. and G. *Bühler*, A Legend of the Jaina Stūpa at Mathurā in SWA 1897 and Ind. Ant. 26, 1897, 194 f.

and also the dates of the years. In spite of all the legendary matter which the work contains, we should nevertheless not be justified in denying that it has some slight historical significance, for in any case it is based upon earlier sources and in part tells of events belonging to the author's own period. It is written partly in bad Sanskrit and partly in Jaina-Māhārāṣṭrī.

The Jaina monks and authors have always been tellers of tales far rather than historians. We have already seen that the commentaries to the sacred texts contain not only a mass of traditions and legends, but also numerous fairytales and stories, and moreover that the legendary poems, the Purāṇas and Caritras were often only a frame in which all manner of fairy-tales and stories were inserted. Now, in addition to all this, the Jainas have produced a vast fairy-tale literature, in prose and in verse, in Sanskrit, Prākrit and Apabhraṃśa. All these works, be they stories in plain prose or in simple verse, or elaborate poems, novels or epics, are all essentially sermons. They are never intended for mere entertainment, but always serve the purpose of religious instruction and edification.

The earliest religious novel (dharmakathā) was Taraṅgavatī by Pādalipta (Pālitta) Sūri. "The author of the Taraṅgavatī" (Taraṅgavaīkāro) is already mentioned in the Aṇuogadāra, and for this reason the work must have been written before the 5th century A.D. However, the original has not come down to us but only a shorter version, written 1,000 years later, in 1643 Prākrit stanzas, entitled Taraṅgalolā.[1] The subject-matter of this romantic love-story, which ends in a pious sermon, is briefly as follows :

A nun who is conspicuous for her beauty, tells the story of her life. She was the charming daughter of a rich merchant. One day she sees a couple of ducks in a lotus pond, and falls into a swoon : for she remembers that in a previous life she had been a duck like this, and that, out of love for a drake killed by the hunter, she had burned herself with him. She

1. The Taraṅgalolā was translated into German by E. *Leumann*, "Die Nonne," in ZB III, 1921, 193 ff., 272 ff., (an off-print was also published). According to *Leumann*, Pādalipta lived as early as in the 2nd or 3rd century A.D.

longs for the husband of her previous life, and after many love-sorrows, she finds him, by the aid of a picture which she paints of the couple of ducks. The man carries her off, on their flight they are captured by robbers, and they are to be sacrificed to the goddess Kālī. They are rescued, and the parents agree to the marriage. The wedding takes place. Soon afterwards they meet a monk who delivers a lecture to them on the religion of the Jina. Through the encounter with the monk, who in his previous life had been the hunter who killed the drake, they are so much affected that they renounce the world, and become monk and nun.

The ancient Taraṅgavatī was one of the prototypes of the Prākrit poem Samarāiccakahā[1] by Haribhadra, described by the poet himself as a Dharmakathā, "religious novel." It is on this work that Haribhadra's fame as a poet primarily rests. The Samarāicca Kahā is a religious novel not only because the heroes and heroines after all sorts of adventures renounce the world at last, and enter the Order, and because copious instructions on religion are inserted in all convenient places, but also because, underlying the main narrative and most of the inserted narratives, there is the doctrine of Karman, according to which even the slightest peccadillo must have its effects in future rebirths. There is often a very great disparity, at least to our minds, between the sin and the atonement. The poet traces the fate of a hero and his opponent through nine rebirths (Bhava). In the introduction he quotes eight stanzas, in which the subject-matter of the main narrative is summarised very briefly. These stanzas are ascribed to "the ancient teachers whence it follows that Haribhadra took the main theme from earlier sources. In the numerous stories, parables and fairy-tales inserted, we come across many themes which we find often in Indian narrative literature, and some of which belong to universal literature.

1. Edited by H. *Jacobi* in Bibl. Ind. (1908) 1926, Vol. I. Text and Introduction. The introduction contains a detailed table of contents of the work. See also *Jacobi* in RSO II, 1909, pp. 233, 236, and Peterson, 5 Reports, 118ff. An abstract of Haribhadra's work was made by Pradyumna, in 1214 A.D., in his Samarādityasaṃkṣepa (ed. by H. *Jacobi*, Part 1, Ahmedabad 1905). *Cf.* A. *Guerinot*, JA 1909, s. 10, t. XIV, nr. 1078.

Thus in the course of a sermon the parable of the "man in the well"[1] is told. It is a very common occurrence in Indian ascetic poetry for a king to be forcibly reminded, by some chance sight, of the vanity of existence, and to renounce the world. For instance, a king sees a snake devouring a frog, but itself devoured by a sea-eagle, which in its turn is devoured by a boa constrictor. This sight causes him to renounce the world and become an ascetic. King Yaśodhara sees his first white hair[2] and resolves to become a monk. In the night he sees how his wife leaves the bedroom, approaches a hunchbacked watchman, who insults and misuses her, and how she gives herself up to this man.[3] In order to prepare his mother gently for his plan to become a monk, he departs somewhat from the truth, and tells her of a dream in which he had become a monk. Now, with a view to averting the evil consequences of the dream, his mother advises him to disguise himself as a monk and sacrifice a number of animals to the "family goddess" (obviously Kālī). The king naturally refuses to slaughter, but is prepared to make a compromise. He has a cock made of dough, and this fowl is beheaded in front of the image of the goddess, whereupon he eats the "meat" of the cock. Owing to this he brings upon himself a bad Karman,[4] in consequence of which he has to go through various animal births (peacock, antelope, fish, sheep) with his mother, until at length, reborn as a pair of fowls; they have the good fortune to hear the sermon of a famous monk, remember their previous births, and in their next existence, born as the twins of a queen, to become monk and nun. At the end of their lives they enter heaven as gods.

On the whole it is rather tiresome always to follow the wanderings of the same persons from one rebirth to another, the one always killing the other, the one going to heaven and

1. See above, Vol. I, p. 393f.

2. Thus also in Jātaka No. 9, see above, p, 141.

3. *Cf. Hertel,* Jinakirti's "Geschichte von Pāla und Gopāla," pp. 84 f., 92, where there is also reference to parallels from Indian and universal literature.

4. For, in the belief of the Jainas, even sins of thought have their consequences.

the other to hell or being reborn as an animal, in one instance even as a coconut-palm. However, we also meet with some interesting tales, romantic love-stories, such as that of Sanatkumāra and Vilāsavatī, who are reunited after a long separation and after inexpressibly sorrowful adventures (shipwrecks etc.). The story, too, of Dharaṇa and Lakṣmī is a pretty fairy-romance, full of adventures on land and sea, with many familiar fairy-tale motifs. Thus we find here the motif of the ungrateful wife : Dharaṇa and Lakṣmī are wandering in the forest. The woman is nearly dying of thirst. Dharaṇa draws blood from his arm, and cuts off some flesh from his thigh, so as to nourish his wife. Soon afterwards, nevertheless, she tries to get rid of her husband, in order to follow a robber, to whom she has taken a fancy.[1]

The destinies in the course of the reincarnations are often passing strange. A merchant is reborn as a pig in his own house and is slaughtered for the festive meal. Reborn in the same house as a snake, he remembers his previous existence, but is not angry with the cook who slaughtered him as a pig. Thereupon in his next rebirth he again becomes a man, in fact he is reborn as the son of his own son. When he is one year old, he remembers his previous existence. He sees that his daughter-in-law has now become his mother, and that his son is now his father, and is at a loss to know how to address them. Hence he does not speak at all, and is called "the dumb one." When he has reached the age of twelve years, an all-knowing monk invites him to come and be instructed by him. Then he breaks his vow of silence, and follows the monk into the religious life. The fate of the nun Susaṃgatā is tragic. In one of her former births she had given a female friend a love-potion for a lover. For this slight sin she was reborn, in succession, as an elephant, a monkey, a bitch, a cat, a Caṇḍāla girl and lastly as a Śabara girl. The savage Śabaras drove her away from their village. Whilst she is wandering in the forest, she meets some monks, to whom she does honour. For this she becomes a queen in her next existence, the consort of the king of Kosala. A remaining portion of the Karman was, however, still left. Thus it

1. See above, p. 126.

happened that a female demon (Yakṣī) who was in love with the king, assumed the form of the queen, and succeeded in persuading the king that the real queen was a demon. She is driven away, and is about to commit suicide. Then she meets a monk, who tells her previous existences. After some time the king, who had in the meantime discovered the truth, finds her again, but both of them now renounce the world, and enter the Jaina Order.

The Samarāicca Kahā is written in prose with inserted verse passages of varying length (usually in the Āryā metre). The language is Jaina Māhārāṣṭrī. In the verses it does not differ from the dialect used generally in Jaina-Prākrit, in the prose it is mingled here and there with peculiarities of Śaurasenī. On the whole the style is simple and lucid, not so elaborate as in the novels of Bāṇa and Subandhu; nevertheless long compound words in the descriptions, and the use of ornate poetical figures of speech show that the author was well-versed in the rules of poetic art.

This literary form, namely the Dharmakathā or religious novel, reaches its culmination in the allegorical Sanskrit novel Upamitibhavaprapañcakathā,[1] "the narrative in which the manifoldness of existence is presented in parable," by the poet Siddharṣi. The following anecdote about the poet is told in the Prabhāvaka-Caritra XIV :

Siddha was a cousin of the poet Māgha. He was married to Dhanyā, a woman of good family, but in the course of time he got into bad company, took to gambling and spent the nights with evil companions. One day his mother saw her young daughter-in-law weeping, and asked her what was the cause of her grief. The young woman said that her husband never came

1. Edited by P. *Peterson* and H. *Jacobi* in Bibl. Ind. 1899 to 1914; new edition Bombay 1918 and 1920 in JPU 46 and 49. German translation (Book I.III)by W. *Kirfel*, Leipzig 1924(Indische Erzähler Nr. 10).Italian transl., by A. *Ballini* in GSAI, vols. 17-19 and 21-24. See also *Jacobi*, Upamitibhavaprapañcae Kathae specimen, Bonnae 1891 (Festschrift der Universiät) and A. *Ballini*, Contributo alle studio della Upamitibhavaprapañcā Kathā di Siddharṣi (Rendiconti della Reale Accademia dei Linccei, Scienca morali, storichee filol. s. V, Vol. 15), Roma 1906. In the MSS. both Upamiti and Upamita occur as the title.

home before midnight. The mother-in-law comforted her, and promised to exhort her son. The next time that Siddha returned home late, she did not open the door to him, but told him to go to a place where doors were open at that time of night. Then Siddha went to the Jaina monks whose doors are always open. They recognised the future Prabhāvaka in him, and received him with due ceremony. He became a Jaina monk, and it was in vain that his father tried to dissuade him from his resolve. After he had learned with the Buddhists for some time and had become their adherent, he was brought back to the Jaina faith again by his old teacher.

As Siddharṣi completed his work, according to his own statement, in 906 A.D., whereas the poet Māgha lived in the second half of the 7th century, this pretty anecdote is devoid of any historical foundation. In the Praśasti, the appendix to his poem, Siddharṣi mentions in his genealogy of teachers the names of Sūryācārya of the Nirvṛtti Kula, Dellamahattara and Durgasvāmin, a wealthy Brahmin who had become a Jaina monk, and who died at Bhillamāla (the present-day Bhīnmāl in Southern Mārwāḍ),[1] but he then speaks with enthusiasm and great respect of the Ācārya Haribhadra as the teacher to whom he is indebted for the enlightenment in the true religion and of whom he has spoken in Book I of his poem as the "Awakener of the knowledge of the religion" (Dharmabodhakara).[2] These words would lead one to believe that Haribhadra must have been the immediate teacher of the poet. Nevertheless this is impossible, if the date for Haribhadra assumed above is correct. Neither has the later tradition, e.g., in the Prabhāvaka-Caritra, any knowledge of Haribhadra and Siddharṣi having been contemporaries. There is therefore, nothing for it but to assume that Siddharṣi pays Haribhadra so great a toll of veneration only because he has derived the greatest inspiration from his writings. Haribhadra's Samarāiccakahā did indeed serve as a model for Siddharṣi.

1. In the Jaina temple of the same town Siddharṣi first recited his poem and the nun Gaṇā, a pupil of Durgasvāmin, wrote it down.

2. He adds: "He who, foreseeing what is to come, wrote for my sake the Lalitavistarā, his commentary on the Caityavandana." On a MS. of this commentary, s. *Kielhorn* in Ind. Ant. 10, 1881, p. 101.

The work is a novel in prose with numerous verse passages, some long and others short, mostly Ślokas, only at the end of the individual books more elaborate metres also make their appearance.[1] Like all Indian novels it consists of a frame story with inserted tales. As in all narrative poems of the Jainas, here too destinies of a being are traced through numerous re-incarnations. The original trait of this poem is, however, that it does so in the form of an allegory, or rather of allegories : for it is not only the main narrative, but the separate stories also, which are in part allegories. On the other hand, the form of an allegory is not strictly adhered to.[2] The poet himself distinguishes between two kinds of personages : "outward" companions of the hero, and "inward" companions. It is only the latter which are personifications and they are indeed the main characters in the "drama of mundane existence" (saṃsāranāṭaka), which the poet intends to unroll before the pious hearer.

The poet commences with an allegory in which he describes his own career. In the city of "Without-beginning-and-without-end" there lives an ugly, wretched beggar, who is suffering from all diseases, and whose name is Virtueless (Niṣpuṇyaka). The wretched food which he was able to procure by begging, scarcely served to satisfy his hunger, and only increased his illness. In this city the famous king "Stand-firm" ruled. The beggar came to his palace, and was admitted by the door-keeper "Resolver-of-one's-own-Karman" out of pity. The beggar feels very happy indeed at the sight of the splendour of the palace. The cook "Awakener-of-the knowledge-of-religion" and his beautiful daughter "His pity" bring the beggar the tasty and curative food "The great good" and treat him with the eye-salve "Pure sight" and the mouth-lotion "Creating-joy-in-the-Truth." Little by little he is cured, but for a long time he is unwilling to give up his old bad diet. Then the cook "Awakener-of-the-knowledge-of-religion" engages "True Insight" as his nurse, and at length he realises the impurity of his former food, he cleans his begging bowl, and "Virtueless" is transformed into "Rich-in-Virtues."

---

1. *Cf. Jacobi*, Ed., Preface, p. xxiii ff.

2. This constitutes the difference of this work from Bunyan's "Pilgrim's Progress,', with which it has sometimes been compared.

He is now desirous of making this wondrous remedy available to others too, but as the people who had previously known him, do not want to listen to him, "True Insight" advises him to place the three remedies in a wooden bowl and place it in the courtyard of the royal palace, so that everyone may help himself. In the concluding verses of Book I the explanation of the allegory is then given : The city "Without-beginning-and-without-end" is Saṃsāra. The beggar "Virtueless" is the poet himself. The King "Stand-firm" is the Jina, his palace is the Jaina religion. The cook "A wakener-of-the-knowledge-of-religion" is "the Master who awakened me, and his daughter is the great pity which he extended towards me."[1] Knowledge is the eye-salve, the true faith is the salutary lotion, and the good life is the best diet. It is "True Insight" which allows one to find the path to virtue, and the wooden bowl with the food, the lotion and the eye-salve is the following story.

There is a city "Way-of-man," which has been in existence since all eternity, and in which, as in the narrative of Samarāditya,[2] many events take place. In this city there reigns the mighty king "Maturing-of-deeds" (Karmapariṇāma),[3] a ruler of unlimited powers, who mercilessly inflicts sever punishments. For his own entertainment he has the beings who act the drama of the world-wandering, wearing the most diverse masks. He makes them scream as denizens of hell, dance before him in agonies of pain, act the parts of crows, cats, mice, lions, elephants, buffaloes, lice, ants, and other large and small animals of all kinds; whilst others again are compelled to act human roles, such as hunchbacks and dwarfs, dumb and blind men, old men and invalids, the unfortunate, persons separated from their dear ones, poverty-stricken persons and tormented ones, as faithless women, ignoble men, etc. And this drama amuses the mighty king immensely. The principal wife of this

---

1. As the poet himself says in the Praśasti, this refers to the master Haribhadra.

2. An allusion to Haribhadra's Samarāiccakahā. We cannot help confessing that, after all this, we find it very difficult to believe the Haribhadra should not have been really Siddharṣi's teacher.

3. The law that every deed must have its consequences.

king is "Effect-of-Time" (Kālapariṇati), and he has to ask her advice on all occasions. She too takes delight with her husband in the drama of the world-wandering. She wishes for a son, and a son is born, who receives from his father the name "Man-as-he-should be" (Bhavyapuruṣa) and from his mother the name "Well-disposed" (Sumati). Now in the city of Way-of-man" there lives a great sage named Sadāgama, *i.e.*, "The true doctrine." The king is very much afraid of this man, because he spoils the king's drama, as he has already liberated many of the actors and taken them to a city called "Blissful-rest" (Nirvṛti, meaning Nirvāṇa) situated outside the realm, where they live in the greatest happiness. Nevertheless the female attendant "Rich-in-Insight" succeeds in effecting a meeting of the prince with Sadāgama. The parents give their consent to Sadāgama's undertaking the boy's education. Once when Sadāgama is reciting his doctrines on the market-place, a great tumult arises. It is seen that the thief "Wandering-Soul" (Saṃsārijīva) is being led to the judgment-seat. (It is the Emperor Anusundara who appears in the form of this thief, in order to relate his experiences in countless rebirths for the instruction of his relatives.) "Rich-in-Insight" takes pity on the thief, and advises him to seek the protection of Sadāgama. The executioners have to release him, and he now relates his experiences for the instruction of "Rich-in-Insight" and Prince "Well-disposed." Now there comes the story of Saṃsārijīva, *i.e.*, the soul wandering in the cycle of rebirths.

He relates how he was first of all born as a plant in the world "Motion-less," how he then came to the city "Home-of-beings-with-one-sense-organ" and ever and again wandered to and fro among the lowest organisms, the earth-bodies (stones, minerals, etc.), the water-bodies (hoar-frost, snow, fog, etc.), fire-bodies and wind-bodies,[1] and suffered many sorrows and torments. He was then reborn among the various animals from the very lowest insects, worms, etc., up to the elephants. At length he was reborn in the world of human beings as Nandivardhana, a king's son. Though he had an invisible friend "Dawn-of-virtue," to whom he was indebted for many successes

1. In the belief of the Jaina, all these are beings having souls.

in life, yet his most intimate "inner" friend was Vaiśvānara, *i.e.*, "Fire-of-anger." This friend always supplied him with the pill "Cruel Thoughts." For this reason the efforts of excellent teachers and counsellors, such as the sage Vidura, who sought to improve him by means of moral narratives (allegory of Sparśana, the sense of touch) and speeches, proved fruitless. The influence of Vaiśvānara grew even stronger, when he succeeded in marrying him to "Violence" (Hiṃsā), the daughter of King "Bad-Will" and Queen "Merciless."

Fortified by the pills of "Cruel Thoughts" and encouraged by the glances of his wife "Violence," he kills innumerable wild animals in the chase, but also wins great fame in fights with robbers and foes. After many adventures (the scene of some of them is laid, not in the world of allegory, but in the real world, love-stories, ete.) he becomes king. Under the influence of his evil "inner" friends he perpetrates many cruelties, he kills an ambassador, his father, his mother, his wives, and finally also his rescuer and benefactor. He flees and meets a young man : a quarrel ensues between them, the result of which is that they pierce each other with their swords. Thereupon both of them are reborn in the "Abode of the worst sinners," and after that, as lions, falcons, ichneumons, always as foes. At length Saṃsārijīva comes into the world as a prince again, Prince Ripudāraṇa. Now it is "Pride" and "Falsehood" that become his friends, and they exert paramount influence over him, so that "Dawn-of-virtue" does not stand much chance against them. After his father has become a monk, he becomes king, refuses to pay due respect to a ruler of the world, is humiliated by a sorcerer and slain by his servants. In the subsequent rebirths he pays the penalty of his misdeeds in hell and as animals, until he is once again reborn among human beings, this time as the son of the merchant Vāmadeva. "Falsehood," "Deceit" and "Theft" are now his friends. He robs a merchant, is hanged, and is then again reborn in hell and in the animal world. After a long time he again makes his appearance in the world as the son of a merchant, his "inner" companions now being "Dawn of Virtue" and "Avarice" (Sāgara). Through the latter he acquires enormous wealth. He makes friends with a prince, and goes on a sea-voyage with him. In order to secure the riches of this prince, he wants to kill him. The sea-god, however, rescues the prince, and throws the merchant into the sea. He is cast upon shore, wanders about in a wretched condition, and finally, when he wants to bury a treasure, he is devoured by a Vetāla. More rebirths in hell and in the animal world follow. Reborn as Prince Ghanavāhana, he grows up with his cousin Akalaṅka. The latter becomes a pious Jaina, and through him Ghanavāhana, too, comes into contact with Sadāgama. But Mahāmoha, *i.e.*, "The Great Infatuation," and Parigraha, *i.e.*, "Longing-for-possession" also seek his friendship, and finally obtain complete mastery over him. Hence he becomes a violent ruler, is deposed, and perishes miserably. After many rebirths in hell and in the animal world, he is at length reborn in Sāketa as Amṛtodara, and now begins Saṃsārijīva's ascent to higher forms of existence. He is converted to the Jaina faith, and attains to the world of gods and of men, by turns. Reborn as King Guṇadhāraṇa, he is reunited with Sadāgama and Samyagdarśana ("Right Faith" he becomes a pious layman and a good ruler, especially after he has brought home the ten virgins "Patience," "Pity," "Gentleness," "Love of Truth," "Straightness," "Honesty," "Chastity," "Liberation," "Science" and "Desirelessness" as brides. At the end of his life he becomes a monk, and is then reborn alternately as god or man. Finally, in his last incarnation Saṃsārijīvin is the world-ruler Anusundara. Now at length the retinue of the "Great Infatuation" is powerless, and only the good qualities are his "inner" companions; he attains to the highest knowledge, and remembers his former existences. Now, in the form of the thief condemned to death, he relates his fortunes in the cycle of rebirths. Then he becomes absorbed in meditation, and rises, as a god, to the highest heaven.

All this is told with great verbosity, and numerous stories and sermons are interwoven with the narrative wherever convenient. Siddharṣi says that he chose the allegory, in order to attract the readers and for the same reason he wrote in Sanskrit, and not in Prākrit, because Prākrit is for the uneducated, whilst even the educated are to be won over to the doctrine from their heretical views. He adds, however, that he wishes to write an easy Sanskrit which will be universally understood.

The language, is, indeed, smooth and clear, never bombastic and rarely obscure. As is usually the case with the Jainas who write in Sanskrit, he uses Prākritisms and popular expressions.[1] The great popularity which this poem enjoyed among the Jainas is shown by the fact that, only 100 years after its appearance, extracts and abridgments were made from it,[2] and that even Hemacandra uses names in one of the stories in the Pariśiṣṭa-Parvan[3] which presuppose that Siddharṣi's work was universally known.

There were also religious novels written entirely in verse. A romantic epic of this kind is the Bhavisatta Kahā[4] in Apabhraṃśa by a poet Dhaṇavāla (Sanskrit Dhanapāla), a Digambara Jaina layman, who belonged to the merchant caste of Dharkaṭa. The period of the author is unknown, but it is probable that he used Haribhadra's Samarāicakahā as a model. The explicit aim of the narrative is the glorification of the Pañcamīvrata, a vow which is fulfilled on the fifth day of one of the three months Kārttika, Phālguna or Āṣāḍha, and extends accompanied by various religious exercises, over 5 years. In order to show the fruits of the fulfilment of these religious exercises, the story of Bhavisatta (Bhaviṣyadatta) is told.

The main theme of the poem is a fairy-tale, the hero of which, Bhavisatta, experiences strange adventures. Deserted upon a lonely island by his treacherous step-brother, he comes to a deserted city, discovers a princess with the help of a god,

---

1. *Jacobi*, Ed., Preface, pp. xxii-xxvii-xxxv gives many examples of this.

2. Such as those by Vardhamāna (who suffered the voluntary death by starvation in about 1032 A.D.), Devendra Sūri and Haṃsaratna. *Cf. Jacobi* in JRAS 1909, 421; 'on Vardhamāna' s. *Peterson,* Report IV, p. cx.

3. II, 315 ff. It is said here of a wealthy merchant, that his father was "Ocean" (Samudra) and his mother "Deceitful" (Bahulā). In the Upamitibhavaprapañcakathā, Sāgara, "Ocean" is the personification of avarice and Bahulikā that of deceit. *Cf. Jacobi, loc. cit.*, 421 ff.

4. Bhavisattakahā von Dhanavāla, eine Jainalegende in Apabhraṃśa herausgegeben von H. *Jacobi* in ABayA XXIX, 4, München 1918; partly edited by the late C. D. *Dalal* and completed with Introduction, Notes, Glossary etc., by the late Pandurang Damodar *Gune* in GOS Nr. 20, Baroda 1923 ; *cf Gune* in Proc. I. OC Poona 1922, p. 158f. The work is especially important for our knowledge of the Apabhraṃśa language. The author is distinct from Dhanapāla, the author of the Pāiyalacchi.

marries her, and they live joyfully for 12 years. Bhavisatta is home-sick, and one day the ship of the wicked step-brother lands again on the island. Bhavisatta wishes to return to his home with his wife, but is again outwitted by the step-brother who carries off his wife, but leaves Bhavisatta himself on the island. With the help of a Yakṣa he is, however, brought home on the chariot of a god in the nick of time, and is reunited with his wife who has remained faithful to him throughout. In Part II fights after the manner of the Mahābhārata and the Rāmāyaṇa are described, whilst in Part III the preliminary stories of the principal characters in their former births are told.

The Malayasundarī Kathā,[1] in which an unknown poet has worked up popular fairy-tale themes into a Jaina legend, apppears to be a romantic epic in Prakrit of a similar nature. A veritable deluge of the most phantastic miracles and magic feats, almost takes away the reader's breath in this work. Countless motifs well-known in the fairy-tale literature are interwoven with the novel, which relates how Prince Mahābala and Princess Malayasundarī find each other, miraculously, how they are ever and again separated from each other and ever and again reunited. Since all the wonderful destinies are explained as the consequences of some deeds in previous existences, and as prince Mahābala finally attains to omniscience as a pious monk, and Malayasundarī becomes a famous nun, the magic fairy-tale comes to be a pious Jaina legend. This fairy-tale romance must have been very popular, for, as late as in the 15th century Māṇikyasundara wrote a Mahābala-Malayasundarī-Kathā, which, in its turn, served as a prototype for a Malayasundarī-Caritra in Sanskrit stanzas by Jayatilaka. The last-named work again formed the basis of a Gujarātī poem in the 18th century.[2]

---

1. We know the contents of the work only from *Hertel's* German translation of the Malayasundarikathoddhāra written by Dharmacakra in the 14th century an extract in Sanskrit prose with interspersed verse passages in Sanskrit and Prākrit, based upon the Prākrit epic, s. *Hertel,* Indische Mārchen, Jena 1919, pp. 185-268.

2. *Cf. Hertel, loc. cit.,* p. 377 ff.

Distinct from these novels there are the Campūs or ornate novels in prose and verse, written after the model of Bāṇa's "Kādambarī." Foremost among these is the Yaśastilaka[1] by the Digambara Jaina Somadeva Sūri, written in about 959 A.D. The contents of this religious poem in prose and verse, based upon Guṇabhadra's Uttara-Purāṇa, are briefly as follows :

King Māridatta has ascended the throne at an early age and is entirely given up to sensual pleasures. At the advice of his family priest he prepares to offer a great sacrifice to his family goddess Caṇḍamāridevatā, consisting of a pair of every living creature, including human beings. Māridatta himself is to perform the sacrifice. Then the servants drag in a youth and a maiden, a pair of ascetics whom they have selected for the human sacrifice. At the sight of them a change comes over the king. It occurs to him that these might be the twin children of his own sister, who were said to have renounced the world and joined the Jaina community. He asks these two to tell him their history, and it is revealed that they are indeed his relatives. The major part of the story deals with their experiences in various rebirths, but many explanations regarding the doctrines of the Jaina religion are interwoven. Many famous poets, such as Bhāravi, Bhavabhūti, Bhartṛhari, Guṇāḍhya, Vyāsa, Bhāsa, Kālidāsa, Bāṇa, and others, are mentioned, all of whom are supposed to have done honour to the Jaina religion. The last three sections also form an independent book, entitled Upāsakādhyayana ("Readings for Laymen"), which serves as a work of edification for Jaina laymen. The work ends with the conversion of Māridatta and his family goddess to the Jaina religion.

Poems of the same category are Tilakamañjarī[2] by the Śvetāmbara Jaina Dhanapāla who wrote about 970 A.D. and Gadyacintāmaṇi,[3] "Wishing-jewel of prose" by the Digambara

1. Edited with a Commentary in Km. 70, 1901. *Cf. Peterson*, Report II, 33 ff., 147 ff., and *Hultzsch* in Quarterly Journal of the Mythic Society, 1922, p, 318f.

2. Edited in Km. 85, Bombay 1903. *Cf. Jacobi* in GGA 1905, 379 Merutuṅga (Prabandhacintāmaṇi, Transl. by Tawney, p. 60f.) tells a pretty story about the origin of the work.

3. Edited by T. S *Kuppuswāmi Śāstrī*, Madras 1902.

Jaina Oḍeyadeva Vādībhasiṃha (beginning of the 11th century A.D.)[1] The subject-matter of this novel, as well as that of Kṣatracūḍāmaṇi[2] by the same author, is the legend of Jīvandhara with which we are familiar from the Uttara-Purāṇa. The same legend has also been treated in the form of a Campū by the Digambara Jaina poet Haricandra in his Jīvandhara-Campū.[3]

Just as the legends of the Jinas, thus other legends and fairy tale themes, too, have been worked up into ornate epics. Thus, for instance, the legend of King Yaśodhara, which we know already from Haribhadra's Samarāicca-Kahā has been treated byVādirāja Sūri[4] in the Yaśodhara-Carita,[5] and epic in 4 cantos. Vādirāja's source was, however, again Guṇabhadra's Uttara-Purāṇa. On the other hand, according to his own statements, Māṇikya Sūri used Haribhadra's narrative as a source, in his Yaśodhara-Caritra.[6] Surasundarī-Cariam[7] by Dhaneśvara, the

1. His teacher was Puṣpasena, a fellow-pupil of Vādirāja, the author of the Yaśodhara-Carita. Both were pupils of Somadeva Sūri, author of the Yaśastilaka. Vādibhasiṃha is an epithet of several teachers. *Cf. Hultzsch* in ZDMG 68, 1914, 697f. and A *Venkatasubbiah* in JBRAS, N. S., 3, 1928, 156 ff. According to him Śrīvijaya Oḍeyadeva is identical with Vādibhasiṃha.

2. Edited by T. S. *Kuppuswāmi Śāstrī*, Tanjore 1903 (Sarasvatī-vilāsa Series No. 3); *cf.* Ind. Ant. 36, 285 ff. and *Hultzsch* in Quarterly Journal of the Mythic Society, 1922, P. 318.

3. Edited by T. S. *Kuppuswāmi Śāstrī*, Tanjore 1905 (Sarasvatī-vilāsa Series No. 4); s. *Hultzsch* in Ind. Ant. 35, 1906, 268 and Quarterly Journal of the Mythic Society, 1922, p. 318. The author is probably identical with Haricandra, the author of the Dharmaśarmābhyudaya. A famous Tamil adaptation of the same legend is Jivakacintāmaṇi by the poet Tiruttakadevar, who probably lived before Oḍeyadeva. *Cf.* also *Glasenapp*, Der Jainismus, p. 119 f.

4. The same who wrote the Pārśvanātha-Carita in the year 1025; s. above p. 495.

5. Edited by T.A. *Gopinatha Rao*, Tanjore 1912 (Sarasvatī-vilāsa Series No. 5). *Cf. Hertel*, Jinakīrti's "Geschichte von Pāla and Gopāla," pp. 91 ff., 146 ff.

6. Edited by Hīrālāl *Haṃsarāj*, Jamnagar 1910. There were several authors named Māṇikya Sūri, one in the 13th and one in the 16th century, and it is not possible to ascertain which of them is the author of the Yaśodhara-Caritra. *Cf. Weber*, HSS. Verz., II, 3. 1067 ff.; *Hertel*, l. c., p. 81 ff., 138 ff.

7. Edited with Notes by *Muniraj Shree Raje Vijayjee*, Benares 1916 (Jaina Vividha Sahitya Shastramala No. 1).

pupil of Jineśvara Sūri and Buddhisāgara Sūri,[1] written towards the end of the 11th century, is a voluminous romantic epic in Prākrit. Mṛgāvatī-Caritra[2] by Maladhāri-Devaprabha, containing one of the many versions of the legend of Udayana and his wives Vāsavadattā and Padmāvatī, is another fairy-tale epic. The author, who probably lived in the 13th century, himself says that he drew upon the Siddhānta and its commentaries. He has indeed made use of Haribhadra's Āvaśyaka commentary and Hemacandra's Pariśiṣṭa-Parvan.

Mahīpāla, the hero of the Mahīpāla-Caritra[3] by Cāritrasundara, who probably wrote in the middle of the 15th century, is a genuine fair-tale king. All manner of narratives, fair-tales and legends are here combined to form an ornate epic in 14 cantos.

Mahīpāla is skilled in all arts, and gives numerous proofs of exceptional cleverness. For instance, when a Yakṣa, posing as the "double" of the real husband, tries to appropriate a woman, he decides who is the real husband, by saying that the real husband is the one who can crawl into a water-jug and out again. This can, of course, only be done by the Yakṣa, the demon, who is thus proved to be the false husband.[4] When he is cast into the ocean by a treacherous minister, he saves himself by swimming on the back of a large fish which carries him ashore. There he wins a beautiful wife, a magic bed which transports him to any place he desires, a magic staff which makes him invincible, and an incantation by means of which he can assume any form he desires. He changes himself into a hunchback, gives himself out as an astrologer, and shows the king a book which he says can be read by any person who has

---

1. These two were pupils of Vardhamāna Sūri, who died in 1031 A.D. so that Dhaneśvara must have lived not later than towards the close of the 11th century. However, there are five other teachers named Dhaneśvara.

2. Edited by Hīrālāl *Haṃsarāj*, Jamnagar 1909 ; *Cf. Hertel*, l. c., p. 105 ff., 150 ff.

3. Edited by Hīrālāl *Haṃsarāj*, Jamnagar 1909 ; *cf. Hertel*, l. c., p. 72 ff., 138 f.

4. Parallels from Indian and universal literature are cited by *Hertel*, l. c., p. 74, Note 2.

been legitimately begotten, but not by one who has been begotten in adultery. The king, the court priest and the prime minister in turn have a look at the book, none of them can read anything in it, but each one pretends that he can read it, and praises the clearness of the script.[1] Moreover, Mahīpāla is the only man who can weigh an elephant and also can tie up a post from the shore. Finally, of course, Mahīpāla becomes a monk and a saint, and attains to release, after having lived to the age of 500 years.

The Kathānakas or little stories, so many of which were included in the commentaries, were frequently also written down as independent works, and sometimes they were elaborat ed into ornate poems.

The Kālakācārya-Kathānaka,[2] which is generally recited by the monks at the end of the recital of the Kalpa-Sūtra, is a Prākrit poem in prose and verse. The narrative is probably based on an old tradition, and it is quite possible that it contains an historical nucleus.[3] It is the story of the king's son Kālaka, who is converted to the Jaina religion, and attains to the high degree of Superior of the Order.[4] His younger sister, the nun Sarasvatī, is abducted by Gardabhilla, ruler of Ujjayinī, and dragged into his harem. Kālaka feigns madness, incites the people to rebel against the ruler, and wanders to Śakakūla, whose rulers, the Sāhis, he causes to go to war against Gardabhilla and to conquer Ujjayinī. In the narrative portions the language is simple enough, but in the description an ornate style prevails, which reminds us of Subandhu and Bāṇa and the ornate Campūs. Unfortunately the date of the work is unknown, and not even the name of the author has come down.

Another work of unknown date is the Uttama (Kumāra)-Caritra-Kathānaka, "The Story of the Life of (Prince) Most

1. Parallels from universal literature are given by *Hertel*, l.c., p.77, Note 2.

2. Edited and translated by H. *Jacobi*, ZDMG 34, 1880, 247-318; supplements to it, ZDMG 35, 675 ff., and *Leumann*, ZDMG 37, 493 ff. There is also a Kālakācāryakathānaka by Bhavadeva Sūri in 102 Prākrit verses. On the same legend in Sanskrit *cf.* *Bhau Daji* in JBRAS 9, 1867, 139 ff.

3. *Cf.* Sten *Konow* in SBA 1916, p. 812 f.

4. He is identical with Ayya Sāma (Ārya Śyāma), who is said to have written the fourth Upāṅga. See above, pp. 416 and Note 1, 438.

Excellent,"[1] a fairy-tale full of the most wonderful adventures, inserted into the frame-work of a Jinistic sermon. It is to be found in one prose-version and several metrical ones. The language is Sanskrit, but the occurrence of dialectal words proves that the work originated in Gujarat.

A pious fairy and wonder tale of the same nature is the Pāpabuddhi-Dharmabuddhi-Kathānaka, "The Story of Evil-mind and Pious-mind."[2] King Evil-mind believes only in power and wealth and not in the consequences of religious merit. The minister Pious-mind, who, owing to his pious works in the previous life, attains to fabulous good fortune and wealth, with the help of all kinds of magic things (a wishing-pot which always supplies food, a cudgel which, itself invisible, drives all foes away, an umbrella which cures all diseases, etc.) proves the contrary to him. Finally a monk enlightens both of them as to their destinies in their former incarnations, and both the king and his minister become Jaina monks. In the case of this story also, the time and the author are unknown.

In the Campakaśreṣṭhi-Kathānaka, "Story of the merchant Campaka,"[3] by Jinakīrti, who wrote in about the middle of the 15th century,[4] we have the fairy-tale of the lucky child who is

1. The prose version edited and translated into German by A. *Weber* in SBA 1884, 1, 269 to 310, the metrical recension, Uttamakumāra-Caritra, in 686 Ślokas by Cārucandra the pupil of Bhaktilābha, is edited by Hīrālāl *Haṃsarāj*, Jamnagar 1908 (2nd Ed., 1911); *cf.* *Weber*, HSS Verz, II, 3, 1080 f. and *Hertel* in Festgabe Jacobi, p. 135 ff.

2. Edited and translated into Italian by E. *Lovarini* in GSAI 3, pp. 94-127 ; s. *Hertel, loc. cit.*, pp. 66 ff., 136, who quotes two recensions of the story in Sanskrit prose (one of these entitled Kāmaghaṭakathā, "Story of the Wishing-Pot," edited by Hīrālāl *Haṃsarāj*, Jamnagar 1909) and two in Gujarātī verses.

3. First analysed by A. *Weber* in SBA 1883, pp. 567 ff., 885 ff.; edited and translated into English by *Hertel* in ZDMG 65, 1911, pp. 1-51, 425-470; a German translation in "Indische Mārchenromane" I (Indische Erzāhler, Bd. 7, Leipzig 1922). The story is to be found among the Jainas also in Kathākośa (translated by C. H. *Tawney*, p. 169 ff.) and in Merutuṅga's Prabandhacintāmaṇi ; *cf.* J *Schick*, Das Glückskind mit dem Todesbrief (Corpus Hamleticum I,I), pp.; 75 ff.; 160 ff., and see above, Vol. I, 557; Vol. II, 195.

4. *Cf. Klatt.* Specimen of a lit-bibl, Jaina Onomasticon, p. 15; *Duff*, p. 254; *Peterson*, Report IV, p. xxxiii and *Hertel*, Jinakirti's "Geschichte von Pāla and Gopāla," p. 1.

saved from destruction by the fatal letter exchanged at the last moment. This is the tale, widely known both in the East and in the West, with which we are familiar from the Brahmanical and Buddhist literature, and with which we thus meet among the Jainas also. In this case it forms the frame-story for three inserted stories. The first of these is the fairy-tale of King Rāvaṇa, who vainly tries to defy a decree of fate. The third story of the merchant who has hitherto deceived every one, but, is himself at last deceived by a courtesan, is not lacking in humour.[1] Another work of the same author is the Pāla-Gopāla-Kathānaka, the "Story of Pāla and Gopāla," a pious Jaina legend, with which all kinds of well-known themes of novels and fairy-tales (of the two brothers who go on their wanderings, and after many adventures attain to honour and fame; of the grateful and helpful animals; of the woman who tries to seduce the chaste youth, and when she cannot succeed, accuses him of having made an attempt on her honour, etc.) are interwoven.[2] The same Jinakīrti is also the author of a didactic poem Dāna-Kalpa-Druma,[3] in which the importance of almsgiving is presented, and lavishly illustrated by means of stories.

The Aghaṭa-Kumāra-Kathā, the "Story of Prince Aghaṭa" is also based upon the fairy-tale of the lucky child and the fatal letter which is exchanged. There are three different recensions of this pretty fairy-tale, a longer and a shorter one in verse, and a prose version.[4]

The Ambaḍa-Caritra, "The Adventures of Ambaḍa,"[5] by Amara Sūri, is a very phantastic magical fairy-tale. The world

---

1. Similarly Gesta Romanorum Cap. 118. *Cf. Kohler* and *Gildemeister* in Weber, l.c., p. 591 f. 890 f.

2. Joh. *Hertel,* Jinakīrti's "Geschichte von Pāla und Gopāla, " Leipzig 1917 (BSGW 69. Bd. 1917, 4 Heft).

3. Edited in JPU No. 9, Bombay 1919.

4. The last-named is translated into German by Charlotte *Krause,* Indische Novellen I (Indische Erzahler Bd. 4), Leipzig 1922. The shorter metrical version appeared in Bombay NSP 1917 entitled Aghaṭa-Kumāra-Caritra. The two other versions were accessible to the translator in MSS.

5. Edited by Hīrālāl *Haṃsarāj,* Jamnagar 1910; translated into German by Charlotte *Krause,* l.c.

of ideas in which this fairy-tale moves, is Śivaite rather than Jinistic. Ambaḍa is a great magician, who can fly through the air, change men into animals and change them back again, and himself assume any form he likes. By means of his magic arts he succeeds in carrying out seven difficult tasks of the witch Gorakhā, and in winning 32 beautiful wives, untold wealth and a kingdom. It is not until the last chapter that the hero Ambaḍa is converted from the Śivaite faith to the Jaina faith; he becomes at first a pious layman and finally a monk, who, after his voluntary death by starvation, reaches heaven. It is true that a great magician Ambaḍa (or Ammada) is already mentioned in the Ovavāiya, the first Upāṅga, but the story itself is undoubtedly modern, and is associated with the "Thirty-two Throne-stories" (Siṃhāsanadvātrīṃśikā), which belong to the cycle of legends of King Vikramāditya.[1]

Another novel, consisting of a frame-story and a few inserted stories, is the Ratnacūḍa-Kathā, "Story of Ratnacūḍa,"[2] by Jñānasāgara Sūri, who lived in the middle and the second half of the 15th century. The framestory contains the witty and entertaining story of the city of rogues, Anītipura, in which King "Unjust" rules, whose prime minister is "Unwise" and whose court priest is "Restless," and in which only thieves, rogues and deceivers reside. Amongst the inserted stories we have that of the clever boy Rohaka, who, like Mahosadha in the Mahā-Ummagga-Jātaka,[3] is able to perform many seemingly impossible feats, owing to his intelligence. Here, too, we meet once more with the story of Somaśarman who builds castles in the air, which is familiar from the Pañcatantra. Some of the didactic passages inserted occasionally in these narratives, are also of interest : a long discussion on dreams and their interpretation; the instructions given by the father to his son Ratnacūḍa when the latter sets forth on his travels, and which present a curious mixture of worldly wisdom and superstition; an enumeration of the auspicious omens when going on a

1. *Krause*, l.c., 155 f. ; 162 ff.

2. Edited in YJG, Bhavanagar 1917 translated into German by *Hertel*, Indische Märchenromane, I. (Indische Erzähler, Bd. 7), Leipzig 1922, p. 97 ff.

3. See above, p. 133 ff.

journey, and an enumeration of the thirty-two characteristic marks of the body of a great man.

In later times the Jainas also compiled Books of stories, in which the stories either appear in the form of stories inserted into a frame-story, in the manner familiar in Indian narrative literature, or else they are just told one after another. A work belonging to the former category is Samyaktvakaumudī, "The Moonshine of Perfection," by an unknown author.[1] The only connection of this book of fairy-tales and stories with the Jaina religion is the frame, in which the merchant Arhaddāsa tells his eight wives, and they in turn tell him, how they attained to perfection (samyaktva) in the religion. At the same time these stories are overheard by a king, who roams about at night with his minister, after the fashion of Harun al Rashid, and by a thief. The story of King Suyodhana who, in order to set a trap for his faithful deputy, breaks into his own treasury, is recognised by the deputy as a thief, and is warned by seven stories told on successive days, but is finally unmasked as a thief and deposed by the people, reminds us of the "Arabian Nights" and still more of the Sindbad book.[2]

A rich mine of tales, part of which also belong to universal literature, is to be found in the Kathā-Kośa, the "Treasury of Stories," collected by an unknown compiler.[3] The language of the tales is bad Sanskrit with verses in Prākrit. Everywhere

---

1. A. *Weber.* Ueber die Samyaktvakaumudī, eine eventualiter mit Tausendundeinenacht auf gleiche Quelle zuruckgehende indische Erzählung, SBA 1889, 731 ff. According to *Weber*, l.c., p. 733, the time of the work would be limited by the date of the poet Bilhaṇa (end of the 11th century) who is mentioned in it, and by the date of one of the three MSS 1433 A.D. If, however, the Bilhaṇa referred to is not the Kashmiri poet, but the poet and minister whom Āśādhara mentions as his contemporary, then the work should be placed between the 13th and 14th centuries. As there are, however, two recensions of the text, the dating becomes even more uncertain.

2. The similarity with "The Arabian Nights" is very remote, but Jātaka No. 432 is very similar. *Cf.* also *Pulle,* GSAI 4, 161 ff.

3. Translated from Sanskrit MSS. by C. H. *Tawney*, London OTF, 1895. Unfortunately there are no clues whereby to determine the date of this compilation. It is certainly not old, though it probably made use of old sources.

there is a strong Jinistic tendency. For instance, a sea-faring story replete with wonderful adventures is transformed into a pious legend. The last story in the book, that of Nala and Davadantī is a curious Jinistic adaptation and extension of the Nala Episode of the Mahābhārata. Some of the stories are quite naive and even insipid through their tendency. However, along with them we find many a most charming fairy-tale, such as that of the maiden Garden-beautiful :

This maiden has a wicked step-mother, who makes her do all kinds of heavy work. Once when she has led the cows out to pasture, and has fallen asleep, she is awakened by a black snake, which begs her to protect it from the snake-charmer. The girl protects the snake, which then asks her to wish for something. She says, "Make a shade above my head, so that I can mind the cows in comfort." Then the snake conjures up a beautiful garden which accompanies Garden-beautiful wherever she goes. In this garden the king finds her one day, falls in love with her, and makes her his queen. The step-mother lies in wait for her, so as to make her own daughter the queen, but the snake rescues Gardenbeautiful from all dangers.[1]

As in other Indian narrative works, there are gnomic sayings to be found in the Kathā-Kośa too. One of these is worthy of mention :

"The father should cherish his little son until he is five,
And punish him until his fifteenth year he reaches;
But when the son has reached the sixteenth year of his life,
The father should ever treat him as a friend."

There is also a Kathā-Kośa in Apabhraṃśa, containing 53 tales in an equal number of chapters, by Śrīcandra, who wrote either in the 10th or 12th century,[2] also a Kathānaka-Kośa

1. *Tawney*, l.c., p. 85ff., where many parallels from fairy-tale literature are pointed out, among others No. 11 ("Brüderchen und Schwesterchen") in *Grimm*, Kinder- und Hausmärchen. But No. 13 in *Grimm*, Kinder- und Hausmärchen, has more in common with the Kathākośa story, as A. *Wesselski*, Versuch liner Theorie des Märchens, Reichenberg i. B., p.75ff., has shown.

2. According to the Praśasti, he wrote at about the period of King Mūlarāja of Anhilawāḍ : but there are two kings of this name in the Cālukya dynasty, the first of whom reigned from 941 to 996 A.D., and the second from 1176 to 1178 A.D. He traces his genealogy of teachers back to Kundakunda in the fifth degree; s. *Hiralal*, Catalogue, p. xlix ff.

written in 1092 A.D. by Jineśvara,[1] the pupil of Vardhamāna. In the 14th century Rājaśekhara wrote his Antara-Kathā-Saṃgraha, "Collection of various narratives,"[2] a book of stories which he took mostly from earlier works, especially from the commentaries on the canonical texts. Here, among other stories of the clever solver of riddles, of a "Judgment of Solomon"[3] etc., are to be found. The book Kathā-Mahodadhi, "The great ocean of stories,"[4] compiled in the year 1448 by Somacandra, contains 157 stories partly in Prākrit, partly in Sanskrit with Prākrit verses. In the year 1464 Śubhaśīla Gaṇin, pupil of Lakṣmīsāgara Sūri, wrote his Pañcaśatī Prabodha-Sambandha, "Book of 500 stories serving to awaken the Faith."[5] In spite of the title, the book contains nearly 600 stories, anecdotes, legends, fables, fairy-tales, etc., some of which allude to historical personages, kings and authors of both ancient and modern times, such as Nanda, Sātavāhana, Bhartṛhari, Bhoja, Kumārapāla, Hemasūri and others. The same Śubhaśīla Gaṇin also wrote the Bharatādi-Kathā[6] or Kathā-Kośa in the year 1452

1. The same author also wrote a Līlāvatī-Kathā in the year 1035 A.D. *Cf. Bhandarkar*, Report 1882-83, p. 46, and *Peterson*, Report IV, p. xliv.

2. Tales 7-14 have been given, and translated into Italian, by F. L. *Pulle*, Unoprogenitore Indiano del Bartoldo, Venezia 1888. The text of the first 22 tales has been edited by *Pulle* in SIFI I, 1 ff.; II, 1 ff., Firenze 1897-98. *Cf.* also *Weber*, HSS. Verz., II, 3, 1077 ff.

3. *Cf. Zachariae*, Kleine Schriften, pp. 65 ff., 190f.; *Garbe*, Indien und das Christentum, p. 25f.; *Glasenapp*, Der Jainismus, pp. 272, 472. The story of the "Judgment of Solomon" has been translated according to the Antarakathāsaṃgraha by L. P. *Tessitori* in Ind. Ant. 42, 1913, 148ff. together with another Jinistic recension (from Malayagiri's commentary on the Nandi-Sutta). *Hertel* (Geist des Ostens 1, 1913, 189 ff.) compares the Jinistic recensions with the Hebrew one, and endeavours to prove what, in our opinion, is impossible to prove, namely that the Jaina recension "is in contents the primary one, from which the other variants can then be derived."

4. *Cf. Weber*, Hss. Verz. II, 3, 1101 ff.; *Peterson*, 3 Reports, 18f; 316ff. *Alsdorf*, Kumārapālapratibodha, p. 201 f., gives the story of Sthūlabhadra.

5. *Cf. Weber*, Ind. Stud. 16, 159 f., and HSS. Verz., II, 3, 1112ff., *Pavolini* in GSAI 13, 89 ff., who deals with the stories of Draupadī, Kuntī-Devakī and Rukmiṇī which are told in this work, and A. *Ballini* in SIFI; Vol. VI, Firenze 1904 (Text and translation of the first 50 tales). A cycle of 16 tales deals with Suratrāṇa Pīroja, *i.e.*, Sultan Fīrūz II (1220-1296) and his friend Jinaprabha Sūri; s. *Ballini* in OC XIII, Hamburg 1902, p. 41 ff.

6. See *Weber*, l.c.

and several other narrative works. In about 1530 Nemidatta wrote a book of narratives entitled Ārādhanā-Kathā-Kośa.[1] In 1600 Hemavijaya wrote his Kathā-Ratnākara, "Ocean of Story"[2] a book of 258 stories. With the exception of a very few metrical narratives, the work is written in elaborate Sanskrit prose, in which stanzas in Sanskrit, Māhārāṣṭrī, Apabhraṃśa, old Hindī and old Gujarāti are interspersed. It is only the opening stanzas and the moralising introduction to the individual tales, and a very few edifying stories, which betray the fact that the compiler is a Jaina monk. Most of the narratives are similar to those in the Pañcatantra and other books of stories of this kind, tales of the artfulness of women, tales of rogues, tales of fools, fables and fairy-tales, anecdotes of all descriptions, including some which hold up Brahmins and other holy men to scorn. As in the Pañcatantra there are numerous wise sayings interspersed with the tales. The tales are, however, loosely strung together, and not inserted into a frame. There are also many interesting stories in the Dharma-Kalpa-Druma, "The wishing-tree of religion,"[3] a bulky narrative work in Sanskrit verses, written by a certain Udayadharma in about 1450 A.D. or later.

The mass of narratives and books of narratives among the Jainas is indeed vast.[4] They are of great importance not only to the student of comparative fairy-tale lore, but also because, to a greater degree than other branches of literature, they allow

1. *Peterson*, Report IV. p. 139 ff.; *Alsdorf*, Kumārapālapratibodha, p. 189 f. Nemidatta or Brahmanemidatta wrote a Śrīpālacarita in the year 1528 A.D.; s. *Bhandarkar*, Report 1883-84, pp. 123, 435.

2. Translated into German by Joh *Hertel* München 1920 (Meisterwerke orientalischer Literature 4 & 5). *Cf. Hertel*, Das Pañcatantra, p. 140 f; Ein altindisches Narrenbuch in BSGW 64, 1912, pp. 41, 43; Jinakirti's "Geschichte von Pāla und Gopāla," p. 58 ff. Geist des Ostens, 1, 1913, p. 249 ff., and Indische Märchen, pp. 90 f., 169 ff., 374 f., 377.

3. *Cf. Hertel* in ZDMG 65, 1911, 429 ff., 441 ff., Ein altindisches Narrenbuch, p. 58 ff., and Indische Mārchen, p. 111 ff. (*cf.* 375 f.) There was an Udayadharma, who wrote the Vākyaprakāśa (edited in the Stotra-Ratnākara, Mehsana 1913, Part I) in 1450 A.D., but also another who lived 99 years later; s. *Hertel* in ZDMG 65, 429 Note.

4. *Cf. Weber*, HSS. Verz. II, 3, 1090-1136. On the achievements of the Jainas in Indian narrative literature, s. *Hertel*. on the Literature of the Śvetāmbaras of Gujarat, Leipzig 1922.

us to catch a glimpse of the real life of the common people. Just as in the language of these narrative works there are frequent points of agreement with the vernaculars of the people, their subject-matter, too, gives a picture of the real life of the most varied classes of the people, not only the kings and priests, in a way which no other Indian literary works, especially the Brahminical ones, do.

As poets, the Jainas have also contributed their share to the literature of the Drama.[1] Only a few of the dramas written by Jainas can, however, be described as actually Jinistic. Rāmacandra, the pupil of Hemacandra, was an exceptionally prolific writer of dramas. He is supposed to have composed no less than 100 Prakaraṇas (dramas). One of his pieces, the Nirbhaya-Bhīma-Vyāyoga, "The spectacular play of the fearless Bhīma,"[2] treats the story of the giant Baka, who is killed by Bhīma, taken from the Mahābhārata. A theme from Mahābhārata is also treated by Vijayapāla, the son of Siddhapāla, a contemporary of Kumārapāla, in the drama Draupadī-Svayaṃvara.[3] Hastimalla, a pupil of Govindabhaṭṭa, wrote in about 1290 A.D. in the South of India several dramas, thus a Mahābhārata-drama, Vikrānta-Kaurava, in 6 acts, and a Rāma-Sītā-drama, Maithilī-Kalyāṇa in 5 acts.[4]

The Mudrita-Kumudacandra-Prakaraṇa[5] "The Drama of Kumudacandra who has been Silenced," by Yaśaścandra, is a genuine Jinistic drama. This five-act drama describes how the Digambara teacher Kumudacandra was defeated by the Śvetāmbara teacher Devasūri in a disputation which took place in the presence of King Jayasiṃha. This disputation is said to have taken place in the year 1124 A.D.[6] Thus the poet was probably

1. *Cf. Hultzsch in* NGGW 1921, 36 ff., and ZDMG 75, 1921, 61 ff.

2. Edited in YJG No. 19, s. *Hultzsch*, l. c., p. 62 f.

3. Edited by *Muni Jinavijaya*, Jaina-Ātmānanda-Sabhā, Bhavanagar 1918; s. *Hultzsch*, l.c. p. 67 f.

4. These two plays have been edited in MDJG, Nos. 1 and 5.

5. Edited in YJG No. 8, Benares 1905.

6. Thus according to the Prabhāvaka-Caritra, xxi, 86 ff., Deva Sūri, famous as the author of works on logic, died in 1169 A.D. *Cf. Hultzsch* in ZDMG 75, 1921, p. 61 f., and *Jacobi*, Sanatkumāracaritam, p. viii.

a contemporary of King Jayasiṃha who reigned in Gujarat from 1094 to 1142 A.D. The Jaina poet Jayasiṃha wrote in year 1229 A.D. the Hammīra-Madamardana,[1] "The Breaking of the Pride of Hammīra," a drama in 5 acts describing how the pride of Hammīra, that is, Amir Shikār or Sultan Samsu-d-dunyā, was broken, and the attack of the Mahomedans on Gujarat was repulsed. The piece is not Jinistic in itself, but the brothers Vastupāla and Tejaḥpāla, the famous ministers of the Caulukya-king Vīradhavala, who play a part in the drama itself, were pious Jainas. As such they are glorified by Jayasiṃha in a panegyric in verse, the Vastupāla-Tejaḥpāla-Praśasti, engraven on a stone slab in a temple founded by Tejaḥpāla, and by Udayaprabha Sūri in the panegyric Sukṛta-Kīrtikallolinī[2]

Between 1229 and 1232 A.D. Yaśaḥpāla wrote an allegorical drama Moha-Rāja-Parājaya, "The Defeat of King Delusion,"[3] in 5 acts, in which the conversion of King Kumārapāla to Jainism and his wedding with Princess Kṛpā-Sundarī, "Mercy Beautiful," daughter of King "Understanding" are presented, Hemacandra being named as the priest who consecrates the marriage before the Arhat. This play in which many characters, mostly allegorical, play a part, is of interest not merely from the literary point of view, but also as throwing light on the history and the social conditions of Gujarat in the 13th century.

The story of the robber Rauhiṇeya, well-known from the narrative literature, is treated in the drama Prabuddha-Rauhiṇeya[4] by Rāmabhadra Muni. This drama in 6 acts was performed at a festival in a temple of Ṛṣabha which had been erected by two contemporaries of the Cāhamāna prince Samarasiṃha in about 1185 A.D. Most probably the poet may be ascribed to about the same period. The Jaina teacher Bālacandra, who is

1. Edited by Ch. D. Dalal in Gos No. 10, Baroda 1920; cf. *Hultzsch* in NGGW 1921, p. 43 ff., and S. R. *Bhandarkar,* Report II, pp. 16 ff., 72ff.

2. Both Praśastis are edited in GOS No. 10 as appendices.

3. Edited by *Muni Chaturavijaya* with Introduction and Appendices by C. D. *Dalal* in GOS, No. 9, with English translation, Baroda 1918. *Cf. Bühler* Hemachandra, pp. 4, 32, 55, 81; *Kielhorn,* Report on the Search of Sanskrit, MSS. in the Bombay Presidency 1880-81, Bombay 1881, No. 50; *Hultzsch* in NGGW 1921, p. 39 ff.; *Munirāja Jinavijaya* in GOS, No. 14, p. xiv f., and *Dalal* in the introduction to the edition.

4. Edited in the Jaina-Ātmānanda Granthamālā, No. 60, Bhavanagar 1917; s. *Hultzsch* in ZDMG 75, 1921, p. 66 f.

also known as a writer of commentaries, is the author of a drama Karuṇā-Vajrāyudha,[1] in which the legend of the compassionate King Śibi, who protected the dove from the falcon, is treated. The name of the compassionate king is, however, Vajrāyudha here, as in an ancient Jaina legend.[2] It is also a Jinistic legend which constitutes the plot of the drama Dharmābhyudaya[3] by Meghaprabhācārya. This piece, which was acted at a festival in a temple of the Jina Pārśvanātha, calls itself at the end, a "Shadow-play" (chāyānāṭyaprabandha). The time of the author is unknown.

Since ancient times the Jainas have vied with the poets of other sects in another literary form also, namely the sphere of religious lyric poetry. There is a large number of hymns (Stutis, Stotras) in praise of Mahāvīra, the other Jinas, and some to the ancient Jaina teachers also, both in Sanskrit and in Prākrit; some of them were written solely for purposes of the cult, others, on the other hand, are worthy of being appreciated as lyrical poems too. Many of them are quite short, others are poems of considerable length.[4] The earliest known hymn is the Uvasaggahara-Stotra,[5] a hymn to Pārśva in 5 stanzas ascribed to Bhadrabāhu.

One of the most famous Stotras, used both in the cult and for purposes of magic, is the Bhaktāmara-Stotra[6] by Mānatuṅga. This poem enjoys a great reputation among both the Śvetāmbaras and the Digambaras, as both sects class the poet among

---

1. Edited by *Muni Chaturavijaya* in Jaina-Ātmānanda-Grantharatnamālā, No. 56, Bhavanagar 1916; s. *Hultzsch*, l. c., p. 68f.

2. Prākrit text by J. J. *Meyer*, Hindu Tales. p. 301 f.

3. Edited in the Jaina-Ātmānanda-Gratharatnamālā, No. 61, Bhavanagar 1918; s. *Hultzsch*, l. c., p. 69 f. Translated into German by H. *Jensen* in Das indische Schatten theater bear beitet von G. *Jacob*, H. *Jensen*, H. *Losch*, Stuttgart, 1931, p. 48 ff.

4. Collections of Jaina Stotras have been edited in Km., Part VII, 1890; Jaina-Stotra-Saṃgraha in YJG Nos. 7 and 9, 1905; Stuti-saṃgraha with Avacūri, Bombay NSP 1912; Stotra-Ratnākara I, II, edited by Yaśovijaya-Jaina-Saṃskṛta-Pāṭhaśālā, Mehsana, Bombay NSP 1913 and 1914; Pañcapratikramaṇādi-Sūtrāṇi in Sanskrit, Prakrit and Gujarāti, Ahmedabad 1915; some also in MDJG No. 21. *Cf. Weber* HSS. Verz. II, 3, 931-944; *Guerinot*, p. 203 ff.

5, *Jacobi*, Kalpasūtra of Bhadrabāhu, Introd., p. 12 f.

6. Edited and transl. into German by *Jacobi* in Ind. Stud. 14, p. 359 ff. Text also in Km., Part VII. The title is formed from the opening words of the first verse.

their own writers. This in itself seems to indicate that Mānatuṅga belongs to a comparatively early period. According to some lists of teachers, he might have lived as early as the beginning of the 3rd century A.D. Other traditions, on the other hand, point to the 5th, 7th, 8th or 9th century as his period.[1] The Bhaktāmara-Stotra is an ornate poem, but not so elaborate, by a long way, as the hymns of Bāṇa and Mayūra. In this hymn the Jina Ṛṣabha is extolled as the incomparable saint, set on a level with the highest deities, and his name is invoked as a protection in all perils. Thus we read of him :

"Hundreds of women bear hundreds of sons,
But no mother bore a son to equal thee :
Stars there are in every region of the sky, but,
Only the East brings forth the sun with its
Flaming network of rays, the thousand-rayed divinity." (22)

"Thou art Buddha, because the gods praise the awakening of thy mind.
Thou art Śaṃkara, because thou workest out the salvation of the three worlds;
Creator art thou,
Because through thy doctrine thou hast created a pathway to salvation;
Thou, O Lord, art Puruṣottama, the highest of all the beings." (25)

"He who bears thy name in his heart as a charm against snakes, can trample on the most furious poisonous snake with his bare feet; he who goes on pilgrimage to the lotus-grove of thy

1. The anecdote mentioned below, and related by Merutuṅga in Prabandhacintāmaṇi (transl. by *Tawney*, p. 66) makes Mānatuṅga a contemporary of Bāṇa, the friend of King Harṣadeva (606-647 A.D.), though also the friend of King Bhoja in the 11th century. In another Paṭṭāvali. Mānatuṅga is called "Mālaveśvara-Caulukya-Vayarasiṃha-devāmātyaḥ." If by Vayarasiṃha the Mālava Vairisiṃha I, the successor of Kṛṣṇa Upendra, who founded the Paramāra dynasty in the year 825, is meant, this brings us to the 9th century, whilst yet another tradition gives 743 A.D. as his date *Cf.* Note 1, p. 529 and above, p. 459 and Note 2.

feet, conquers the hosts of the enemy; with thoughts fixed on thee, the traveller sails fearlessly over the ocean" (38-40).

"Men whose bodies are fettered from head to foot in mighty fetters, and whose legs are sorely ground by thousands of heavy chains, are at once released of themselves from the pains of the prison, if they are ever mindful of thy name as an incantation." (42)

It is probably this verse 42 which gave rise to the legend that is related by the commentators. In order to purify himself of leprosy, so the story goes, Mayūra composed his 100 stanzas to the Sun-god (the Sūrya-Śataka). Bāṇa, who was zealous of him, hereupon had his hands and feet cut off, and composed 100 stanzas to the goddess Caṇḍikā (the Caṇḍikā-Śataka) by means of which his limbs were restored to him and grew on again. Then Mānatuṅga, in order to prove that the Jaina religion is also quite capable of performing great miracles, had himself fettered with 42 iron fetters and locked up in a house; then he composed the 44 verses of the Bhaktāmara-Stotra, and became free and quit of all his fetters. On the strength of this miracle he converted King Bhoja to the Jaina religion.[1]

Mānatuṅga is also the author of the Bhayahara-Stotra,[2] a hymn to the Jina Pārśvanātha, in Prākrit.

The celebrated Siddhasena Divākara, too, is among those Jaina writers who are claimed by both Digambaras and Śvetāmbaras. Just as the Bhaktāmara-Stotra, his Kalyāṇa-Mandira-Stotra[3] consists of 44 stanzas; it is also a hymn to Pārśvanātha,

---

1. *Cf. Bühler,* Ind. Ant. 1, 1872, 114 f.; *Klatt,* Ind. Ant. 11, 252; *Weber,* HSS. Verz. II, 3, 932 Note; *Peterson,* Report IV, p. xcii f,; *Jacobi,* Ind. Stud., 14, p. 360 f.; G. P. *Quackenbos,* The Sanskrit Poems of Mayūra, New York 1917, pp. 16 ff., 265f. In the 14th century, verses by Mānatuṅga were already used as incantations.

2. In 1309 A.D. Jinaprabha Sūri wrote a commentary on it. *Cf. Peterson,* Report 1882-83, p. 52; *Weber,* HSS. Verz. II. 3, p. 933 f. The text does not seem to be printed.

3. Edited and transl. into German by *Jacobi* in Ind. Stud. 14, 376 ff. Text also in Km., Part VII. The Paramajyoti-Stotra, an old metrical translation in the old Braj dialect, of the Kalyāṇamandira has been published by L. P. *Tessitori* in Ind. Ant. 42, 1913, 42 ff.

and is written in the same metre. It is however, far more artificial in style than the poem of Mānatuṅga, who never uses such ambiguities (Śleṣas) as Siddhasena, who has probably imitated his predecessor,[1] and is really more of a scholar than a poet. A less artificially elaborated poem is the Dvātriṃśikā-Stotra or Vardhamāna- Dvātriṃśikā,[2] a hymn to Vardhamāna Mahāvīra in thirty-two Sanskrit stanzas with the refrain : "He the only highest spirit, the prince of Jinas, is my refuge." In these verses all the qualities of the Jina are enumerated according to the Jaina theory, and the names and epithets of the great deities of Hinduism are attributed to him, though they are used in a different sense. He is "the Lord of the three worlds," "the Knower of the three times," he is Śiva ("the Bringer of Salvation"), he is Buddha ("He who has awakened to Knowledge"), he is the "Ancient One" and "Manifold, though he is but One",[3] he is Hṛṣīkeśa, Viṣṇu, Jagannātha, Jiṣṇu;[4] but he has no trident, no bow, no disc, no bird, no lion, no bull, there is no Gaṅgā on his head, he has no Lakṣmī etc.[5] In both poems Siddhasena Divākara shows himself to be a past master in the use of Sanskrit. A legend has it that by means of the Kalyāṇa-Mandira-Stotra the poet split the Liṅga (Phallus) of god Rudra in the Mahākāla temple at Ujjayinī, whereupon

1. Thus according to *Jacobi* l.c., p. 377 f. But the Jainācārya *Vijaya Dharma Sūri* wrote to me on 25th April 1922 : "Siddhasena, Divākara, the author of Kalyāṇamandira, lived before Mānatuṅga . . . I cannot say how far the argument of my old friend Dr. Jacobi "the Kalyāṇamandira appeared after Mānatuṅga," will hold good."

2. Edited with a commentary (Avacūri) by Udaya-Sāgara Sūri and explanations in Gujarātī, by the Jaina Dharma Prasāraka Sabhā, Bhavanagar 1903. The edition printed in 1922 is not known to me. I am not in a position to decide whether this Dvātriṃśikā is also a part of the Dvātriṃśad-Dvātriṃśika, "Treatise consisting of 32 with 32 verses each," as there is no text of the last-named accessible to me.

3. God (Brahman, Ātman) is thus described in the Brahmanical philosophy.

4. Names of the god Viṣṇu; but, according to the commentary, Viṣṇu also means "he who penetrates all things by his knowledge," Hṛṣikeśa, "Commander of all the organs of the senses," Jiṣṇu "Conqueror of the passions," Jagannātha "Lord of the world" is, of course. also the Jina.

5. Attributes of the god Viṣṇu.

the image of Pārśvanātha stepped forth out of the middle of it.[1]

Like Siddhasena Divākara, Samantabhadra and Vidyānanda (or Vidyānandin Pātrakesarin) also were the same time authors of learned works on logic, and of Stotras. Samantabhadra wrote a hymn in praise of all the 24 Jinas, entitled Bṛhat-Svayambhū-Stotra or Caturviṃśati-Jina-Stavana,[2] beginning with the praise of the first Jina who is here called Svayambhū, the Self-existent. Vidyānandin is the author of the Pātrakesari-Stotra,[3] an elaborate hymn in praise of Jina Mahāvīra in 50 stanzas.

There are quite a number of Stotras in which all the 24 Jinas are extolled. Thus the poet Bappabhaṭṭi,[4] who lived from 743 to 838 A.D. and is said to have converted King Āmarāja, the son and successor of Yaśovarman of Kanauj, wrote not only a Sarasvatī-Stotra,[5] but also a Caturviṃśati-Jina-Stuti[6] in 96 Sanskrit verses.

The most celebrated is the hymn in praise of the 24 Jinas by the poet Śobhana,[7] who lived in the second half of the 10th century. The poem is usually called, with intentional ambiguity "Śobhana-Stuti," which can mean "Hymn of Śobhana" as well as "Beautiful hymn." It is in very artificially ornate language with variegated metres and most perilous tricks in the matter of figures of speech. One such trick, for instance, consists of the second and fourth line of each verse being identical syllable by syllable, and yet having a different meaning.

---

1. Told in the Prabhāvaka-Carita, VIII, 144 ff. *Cf Peterson*, Report IV, p. cxxxi f.

2. Published in DJGK I. See also *Hiralal*, Catalogue, p. 639 f.

3. Published in DJGK I, and with (the author's own ?) commentary in MDJG No. 13 p. 100 ff. It is also called Bṛhatpañcanamaskāra-Stotra.

4. There are several "Life-stories of Bappabhaṭṭi," one in Prabandhakośa, one in the Prabhāvaka-Carita (XI) and an independent Bappabhaṭṭi-Sūri-Carita. *Cf. Shankar Pandurang Pandit*, Gauḍavaha, Ed., Introd., pp. cxxxv-clxi; *Bhandarkar*, Report 1883-84, b. 14 f.; *Peterson*, Report IV, p. lxxxii; S. Krishnaswami *Aiyangar* in JBRAS N.S., 3, 1928, p. 101ff. According to the Bappabhaṭṭi-Carita, Siddhasena Sūri was his teacher, and the poet Vākpati his contemporary.

5. *Peterson*, 3, Reports. p. 212.

6. Edited in Stutisaṃgraha with Avacūri, Bombay NSP 1912.

7. Edited and transl. into German by *Jacobi* in ZDMG 32, 1878, 509 ff. Text also in Km., Part VII.

Dhanapāla,[1] Śobhana's brother, wrote a commentary on the poem, and himself composed a hymn to Ṛṣabha, Ṛṣabha-Pañcāśikā.[2] This is a Prākrit poem in 50 stanzas. In the first 20 verses there are allusions to events in the life of Ṛṣabha whilst the following verses are exclusively devoted to the praise of Ṛṣabha. Though the style is very artificial, the poem is not lacking in warmth of imagination, and here and there we meet with beautiful metaphors. Thus the poet calls life an ocean, upon which Ṛṣabha is the boat, or a forest full of robbers, namely the passions, against which one can find protection only with Ṛṣabha, or a night of false belief, in which Ṛṣabha rises like the sun. The world is to him a chess-board[3] with human chess-men or a stage from which all the actors make their exit at the end. Dhanapāla was a Brahmin and it was not until after he had been converted to Jinism by his brother Śobhana that he wrote the hymn.

Ajiyasantithaya (Ajita Śānti-Stava) by Nandiṣeṇa,[4] who lived perhaps even earlier than the 9th century, is a Prākrit poem in rare, artificial metres. In this hymn, which is recited by special singers at the confession festivals, Ajita, the second, and Śānti, the 16th Tīrthakara, are glorified together because, according to the legend, both of them spent the rainy season in the caverns of the Śatruñjaya mountain, and, as the commentator tells us, the poet, while on a pilgrimage, was inspired to compose the hymn, by the sight of the shrines dedicated to them. The same two Tīrthakaras are also glorified by the very erudite Jinavallabha,[5] who died in 1110 A.D., in the

1. Probably he is the same author who wrote the Prākrit dictionary Pāiyalacchī in 972 A.D., and also the Tilakamañjarī.

2. Edited and transl. into German by *Klatt* in ZDMG 33, 1879, 445 ff. Text with Sanskrit translation in Km.; Part VII.

3. This is perhaps the earliest mention of the game of chess; s. *Klatt*, l.c., p. 465f.

4. *Cf.* W. *Schubring* in ZII 2, 1923, p. 178 ff.

5. Accordiug to Sumati Gaṇin, who was a pupil of Jinapati Sūri who died in 1221 A.D., and wrote life-stories of the heads of his school, Jinavallabha was versed in Pāṇini's grammar, in the Mahākāvyas and Alaṃkāra-Śāstras, in dramatic literature, in astronomy, logic and the works of Jayadeva and Abhayadeva. He was the successor of the last-named as head of the

Ullāsikkamathaya[1] by Vīra Gaṇin in the Ajiyasantithaya in Prākrit, and by Jayaśekhara in the Ajita-Śānti-Stava in Sanskrit. As late as in the 16th century Śānticandra Gaṇin imitated Nandiṣeṇa in his Ṛṣabha-Stava, perhaps also in his Ajita-Śānti-Stava.[2]

In the 11th century the celebrated commentator Abhayadeva wrote a Jayatihuyana-Stotra.[3] The legend has it that the poet, who was seriously ill, recovered his health through this hymn, and that he restored to the light of day a statue of Pārśvanātha which had been hidden for centuries.[4]

It is probably the same Vādirāja,[5] who wrote the Pārśvanātha-Carita in 1025 A.D. and later the Yaśodhara-Carita, who is also the author of some Stotras of philosophical contents, a Jñānalocana-Stotra,[6] an Ekībhāva-Stotra,[7] and an Adhyātmāṣṭaka.[8]

The great Hemacandra also indited few Stotras. At the request of King Kumārapāla he wrote a Vītarāga-Stotra,[9] "A

---

school, enjoyed a great reputation in Citrakūṭa (Chitore) and had various temples built in honour of the Jinas. *Cf. Klatt,* Jaina-Onomasticon, p. 34 f.; *Bhandarkar,* Report 1882-83, p. 47f., and L. G. *Gandhi* in the Introduction to GOS, No, 37, Baroda 1927.

1. It is also called Ajita-Śānti-Laghustavana. *Cf. Weber,* HSS. Verz. II, 3, 931 ff. and *Schubring.* l.c. Jinavallabha also wrote a Mahāvīra-Stotra (edited in Km., Part VII), a Praśnaśata, "A hundred questions," which are answered in the commentary (edited in Stotra-Ratnākara, Part II), and a number of erudite works; s. *Bhandarkar,* l.c.

2. *Schubring,* l.c.

3. Edited with a Sanskrit commentary, Ahmedabad 1890.

4. *Cf. Klatt* in Ind. Ant. 11, p, 248; *Peterson,* 3 Reports, pp. 25 f., 245ff.

5. This is Vādirāja II whose teacher was probably Kanakasena Vādirāja I who lived about 1000 A.D.; Vādirāja II wrote also a commentary on Akalaṅka's Nyāyaviniścaya; s. A. Venkatasubbiah in ZII 7, 1929, 179ff. and above, pp. 495, 515.

6. Published in MDJG No. 21, p. 124ff, In the last verse the author calls himself "the son of Pomarāja,"

7. Published in Km., Part VII.

8. Published in MDJG No. 13, p. 131.

9. Edited with two commentaries, the Vivaraṇa by Prabhānanda, Abhayadeva's pupil, and an Avacūri by a pupil (name not mentioned) of Viśālarāja, in JPU No 1, Bombay NSP 1911; in the title of the edition Viśālarāja is mentioned as the author of the Avacūri, but at the end of it, the author, who himself says that he wrote in 1455 A.D. does honour to Viśālarājā as his teacher.

poem in praise of the Passionless One," *i.e.*, Mahāvīra, which is at the same time a poetical manual of the Jaina religion and was perhaps Hemacandra's first attempt to make the king acquainted with the fundamental doctrines of Jinism.[1] The work consists of 20 short sections (Prakāśas or Stavas)[2] generally of 8 or 9 Ślokas each, or sometimes more. The language of the work is exceptionally lucid and simple. It being as follows:

"He who is the highest spirit, the highest light, the Highest of the Most High, whom they call the Sun-hued beyond the darkness;

from whom all trees of sin have been uprooted with their roots, before whom gods, demons and men bow their heads;

from whom proceeds all knowledge which furthers the welfare of men, whose wisdom illuminates the present, future and past forms of existence;

in whom knowledge, joy and Brahman are united—in him one should believe, about him one should meditate, in him do I take refuge."

The concluding verses (20, 6-9) read:

"These are eyes which take delight in thy countenance; these are hands which offer thee worship; these are ears which hear thy praises: May these ever be with me!

If this my speech, feeble though it be, but seek with ardent desire to comprehend thy excellence, then all hail to it! Why should I desire any other?

Thy servant am I, thy slave, thy footman, thy bondman. Say 'Yes' and give thy consent, O Lord! I say no more.

By this hymn to the Passionless One from the pen of the celebrated Hemacandra, may the King Kumārapāla attain the desired reward!"

In imitation of Siddhasena Divākara's Dvātriṃśika, Hemacandra wrote two Mahāvīra-Stotras, hymns to Mahāvīra, consisting of 32 verses (Dvātriṃśikas) each: the one is entitled

---

1. *Cf. Bühler*, Hemachandra, pp. 36 and 85.
2. N. G. *Javeri*, says in the Foreword to the Edition, that Hemachandra wrote 32 cantos at the request of Kumārapāla, of which 20 are contained in Vītarāga-Stotra and 12 in the Yoga-Śāstra.

Ayogavyavacchedā, and the other Anyayogavyavacchedā.[1] These two poems also contain instructions regarding the religion.

At the beginning of the 14th century Jinaprabha Sūri wrote a Caturviṃśati-Jina-Stuti and several other hymns.[2] Muni Sundara Sūri (died 1379 A.D.) wrote a large collection of hymns, entitled Jina-Stotra-Ratna-Kośa.[3] The first Prastāva contains 23 Stotras in praise of various Jinas in connection with their monuments at various sacred places. Mānatuṅga's Bhaktāmara. Stotra had many imitators. Bhāvaprabha Sūri wrote a Nemibhaktāmaram[4] with allusions to the legend of Neminātha and Rājīmatī. Dharmaghoṣa, a pupil of Devendra (died 1270 A.D.), is the author of a Yamaka-Stuti,[5] and probably also of a Caturviṃśat-Jina-Stuti.[6] Whether it is the same or a much earlier Dharmaghoṣa[7] who is the author of the Isimaṇḍala or Ṛṣimaṇḍala-Stotra,[8] must remain an open question. This work is a hymn in

---

1. Both texts are edited in Km., Part VII, pp. 102ff., 104ff.

2. They are printed in Km., Part VII, Caturviṁśatijina-Stuti also in "Stutisaṃgraha with Avacūri." In 1309 A.D. he wrote a commentary on Mānatuṅga's Bhayahara-Stotra. There is also a Caturviṃśatijinabhavotsava by Guṇavijaya Gaṇin, printed in Jaina-Stotra-Saṃgraha II, YJG 9, and a Jinacaturviṃśatikā by Bhūpāla Kavi in Km., Part VII.

3. Edited in Jaina-Stotra-Saṃgraha II, YJG No. 9. The third Stotra in dated Saṃvat 1476 (1419 A.D.): but the editor of the Adhyātmakalpadruma states Saṃvat 1436-1503 (1379-1446 A.D.) as the period of the author's life.

4. This and other Bhaktāmara Stotras, imitations of Mānatuṅga's celebrated Stotra, are printed in Stotra-Ratnākara, Part I, Bombay 1913, and in Bhaktāmara-Stotra, Part I, Bombay 1926 (AUS 45). Other Stotras by Bhāvaprabha Sūri are to be found in Jaina-Stotra-Saṃgraha I, YJG 7.

5. *Cf. Klatt* in Ind. Ant. 11, 255; *Peterson*, 3 Reports, pp. 17, 310 ff. The same author also wrote a Śrāddhajita-Kalpa, a work on atonements; s. *Weber*, HSS. Verz, II, 3, 881f.

6. Edited in Stotra-Ratnākara, Part I.

7. *Peterson*, Report IV, p. lxiii ff., names no less than 7 different Jaina writers by the name of Dharmaghoṣa.

8. A commentary written on this work in 1496 A.D. by Padmamandira, contains numerous legends on the Jaina teachers honoured in Isimaṇḍala. Some of these legends are also known from Hemacandra's Pariśiṣṭa-Parvan. *Cf. Peterson*, Report 1182-83, App. p. 93 f.; *Bhandarkar*, Report 1883-84, pp. 130 ff., 443 ff. : *Weber*, HSS. Verz. II, 3, 944 Note 2. Gāthās 155-218 and a portion of the commentary have been reprinted by *Jacobi* in the Edition of the Pariśiṣṭa-Parvan, Appendix, pp. 29 ff. and 37 ff.

Prākrit stanzas in praise of the ancient Jaina teachers Jambusvāmin, Śayyambhava, Bhadrabāhu, etc. A Vītarāga-Stotra in 25 verses, also entitled Ratnākara-Pañcaviṃśatikā, after the author Ratnākara, is of unknown date.[1]

As from the nature of the case, the glorification of the Jinas admitted of no variation as regards the subject-matter, the poets were at pains to introduce a change in the form. Hence it is precisely in this hymn poetry that the style of the ornate court poetry was most developed. Some of the hymns are very highly elaborated. A specimen of a very artificially constructed hymn is the Siddhipriya-Stotra[2] by Devanandin. Throughout this hymn the verses are rhymed in such a way that the same syllables in each of two consecutive lines, have a different meaning.[3] There is also a Mahāvīra-Stava in Prākrit, where the same words occur three times over with a different meaning each time, or a Nemi-Jina-Stava, in which no consonants occur except "l" and "m". In Jayatilaka Sūri's Caturhārāvalī-Citrastava there are verses in which the syllables are to be read in the shape of certain figures (of a cross, a lotus petal, a Svastika, etc.)[4] Attempts were also made to introduce a greater variety of metres, and poets went to the length of selecting a new metre for nearly every stanza in one and the same poem. What is still more curious is that these poems would be written in several languages, each stanza in a different language. Ṣaḍbhāṣānirmita-Pārśvajinastavana by Dharmavardhana (about 1200 A.D.) and Ṣaḍbhāṣāvibhūśita-Śāntināthastavana by Jinapadma (1325-1344 A.D.) are poems written in six languages, and belong to this category. The languages are Sanskrit, Māhārāṣṭrī, Māgadhī, Śaurasenī, Paiśācī and Apabhraṃśa. The first-named poem has even two stanzas written half in Sanskrit and half in Prākrit.[5]

---

1. Edited in "Stuti-Saṃgraha with Avacūri" and prefixed to the Edition of Muni Sundara's Adhyātmakalpadruma, Bombay NSP 1906.

2. Edited in Km., Part VII, p. 30ff.

3. In Verse 20 the relative pronoun ya is even extended by the suffix *ka*, only to make the rhyme muninā yakena, munināyakena possible. These tricks make it improbable that this Devanandin is identical with the old Pūjyapāda. As to the relattve pronoun *Yaka*, see M. *Bloomfield* in Lanmann Studies, p. 9ff.

4. These hymns are contained in Part II of the Stotra-Ratnākara, Bombay 1913.

5. *Cf. W. Schubring* in Festgabe Jacobi, p. 89ff.

Many of the Stotras mentioned above could equally well be termed didactic poems : on the other hand, it is not easy to separate the genus didactic poetry from the narrative literature, as this too is mostly instructive. The didactic poetry also forms the bridge to the purely learned works. For it is often difficult to decide whether to include certain manuals of religion and morals, as a rule written in verse, in the purely erudite literature or in the didactic poetry. In the Canon we already find aphorisms along with stories, and in many of the narrative works of the Jainas, as in Indian narrative literature in general, aphorism and narrative are closely interwoven.

One of the earliest non-canonical didactic poems is Praśnottara-Ratnamālā,[1] "The Jewel-Garland of Questions and Answers," consisting of brief questions and answers, and written in Ślokas, in the simplest possible style. The morality taught in these questions and answers, is general human morality and not specifically Jinistic, and it is as simple as the language in which it is couched. We find verses like the following :

8. "What does one fear ? Death. Who is in even worse plight than the blind man ? The passionate man. Who is a hero ? He who is not disconcerted by the arrows of the glances of beautiful women.

10. "What is unfathomable ? The conduct of women. Who is intelligent ? He who is not deceived by this. What is poverty ? Discontent. What is lack of dignity ? Entreating.

"What is hell ? Dependence upon another. What is good fortune ? The renunciation of all desires. What is truth ? The welfare of the beings. What do the beings like best ? Life.

26,27. "What shall I tell you, that is as difficult to find on earth as a wishing-jewel ? Certainly it is the fourfold good. And what is the special name given to it by those who have driven away the darkness of ignorance ? Gifts, accompanied by friendly

---

1. The title is also Vimala-Pr., *i.e.*, "Praśnottaramālā of Vimala," sometimes also "Ratnamālikā," edited in Km., Part VII, 121 ff.; a Prākrit recension by P. E. *Pavolini* in GSAI 11, 153-163. In 1373 A.D. Devendra and Maṇibhadra wrote a commentary on "Vimalacandrasūri's Praśnottararatnamālā," in which a story is told in connection with each question. *Cf. Weber*, HSS. Verz II, 3, 1118ff.

speech; knowledge without arrogance; heroism coupled with forbearance, and wealth hand in hand with self-sacrifice. This fourfold good is indeed difficult to find."

It is no wonder that this didactic poem is also claimed by Buddhists and Brahmins as belonging to their own writings.[1] The Jainas ascribe it to a Śvetāmbara Vimala[2] or Vimalacandra, but sometimes also to King Amogha-varṣa,[3] who reigned in the 9th century and was a friend of the Digambara Jinasena.

Another early work is Uvaẽsamālā, "Garland of Instruction,"[4] a didactic poem in 540 Prākrit stanzas, containing moral instructions for laymen and monks, by Dharmadāsa, who according to tradition is said to be a younger contemporary of Mahāvīra. This is scarcely possible, as the language of the Uvaẽsamālā corresponds to the later Jaina Māhārāṣṭrī. At all events, there were commentaries on this work as early as the 9th century and, as is proved by the numerous commentaries, it must have enjoyed considerable popularity.[5]

---

1. These is a Tibetan recension in the Tanjur with the title Praśnottararatnamālā, edited in Tibetan and German by *Schiefner*, Petropoli 1858; a Sanskrit and a Tibetan recension with French translation have been published by Ph. Ed. *Foucaux*, Paris 1867. *Cf.* A. *Weber*, Indische Streifen I, 210 ff., where two versions are translated into German, and Vidhushekhara *Bhattacharya* in Ind. Hist. Qu. 5, 1929, 143f. It is significant that the text in the Tanjur begins with an invocation to Mañjuśrī, a Bombay edition, in which Śaṅkara is mentioned as the author, with an invocation to Gaṇeśa, and the Jinistic version with that to Mahāvīra.

2. Haridas *Śāstri* (Ind. Ant. 19, 1890, 378f.) is of opinion that this Vimala is identical with the author of the Paumacariya. This admits of neither refutation nor proof. In the last verse the author is called simply Sitapaṭaguru *i.e.*, "the teacher clad in white." A Calcutta edition erroneously gives Asitapaṭa as the name of the author, s. *Weber*, l. c., p. 212, 220 Note 3.

3. *Cf. Bhandarkar*, Early History of the Dekkan, 2nd edition, p. 68f. J.F. *Fleet* in Ind. Ant. 33. 1904, 198ff.

4. Edited by L. P. *Tessitori* in GSAL 25, 1912, 167-297. *Cf. Jacobi*. AR 18, 1915, p. 285f. A number of stanzas are taken from the Mahānisiha-Sutta; s. *Schubring*, Das Mahānisiha-sutta, p. 51 ff.

5. The poet Siddharṣi, too, wrote a commentary on Uvaẽsamālā. This commentary is available in two recensions, one of which contains stories also s. *Jacobi*, Upamitibhavaprapañcā Kathā, Ed., Preface. p. xi; *Weber*, HSS. Verz. II, 3, 1082 ff, There is also an Uvaẽsamālā in 505 Prākrit stanzas by

There is also a Sīlovasamālā by Jayakīrti, the pupil of Jayasiṃha, in 116 Prākrit Gāthās, the date of which is not known. All we know is that in the years 1337 A.D. Somatilaka Sūri wrote a commentary on it, Śīlataraṅgiṇī, consisting of narratives.[1]

There are two didatic poems by the famous Pūjyapāda: Iṣṭopadeśa, "The desired Instruction,"[2] and Samādhiśataka, "A Hundred Verses on the Absorption (in meditation)."[3]

Haribhadra wrote 32 Aṣṭakāni,[4] poems of 8 verses each, on the "'Great God', (mahādeva) *i.e.*, the Jina free from all passions, on the cult, knowledge, renunciations etc. He is also the author of an Upadeśapada in Prākrit.[5]

Guṇabhadra, the author of the Uttara-Purāṇa, also wrote an ethical poem Ātmānuśāsana[6] in 270 stanzas.

The didactic poems of the Digambara Amitagati are greatly appreciated by the Jainas. An earlier work of his is Subhāṣitaratnasaṃdoha, "The Collection of Gems of Beautiful Aphorisms,"[7] in 32 chapters, each of which treats of a special subject, and is as a rule, written in a unified metre. The language, style and metres are those of the ornate poetry. In elaborate verses the poet deals with the entire ethics of the Digambara Jainas, gives rules of conduct for both monks and laymen and subjects the tenets of the Brahmanical religion to a severe and caustic criticism. It

---

Maladhāri-Hemacandra, the senior contemporary of the famous Hemacandra; s. *Weber*, l.c., 1081 f.

1. *Cf. Weber*, HSS. Verz. 11, 3, 1085 ff. The Sthūlabhadra legend from this commentary is given by *Alsdorf* Kumārapālapratibodha, p. 90ff.

2. Edited in DJGK I, in MDJG No. 13 (with Āśādhara's commentary), and in Granthatrayī, SJG No. 20, Calcutta V.S. 2449 (1922); translated into English by Champat Rai Jain, Hardoi 1925.

3. Edited in SJG, Vol. I Bombay 1905. The same volume also contains Puruṣārthasiddhyupāya by Amṛtacandra who, according to a Digambara Paṭṭāvali, wrote in 904 A.D. The two works are also printed in DJGKI.

4. Edited together with Yaśovijaya's Aṣṭakaprakaraṇa, Haribhadra's ṣaḍdarśanasamuccaya and Rājaśekhara's Ṣaḍdarśanasamuccaya, Surat 1918.

5. *Cf. Peterson*, 3 Reports, pp. 34f., Extract 46.

6. Edited in DJGK I, p. 55ff.

7. Edited in Km. 82; edited and transl. by R. *Schmidt* and J. *Hertel* in ZDMG 59, 1905 and 61, 1907, *Cf. Hertel*, WZKM 17, 1903, 105ff. and *Leumann*, ZDMG 59, 578 ff. According to Hertel (WZKM 17, 110 ff.) Amitagati was influenced by Bhartṛhari.

is but rarely, however, that we come across an original expression for those thoughts with which we are so familiar from the ascetic poetry, on the world of the senses and its dangers, on error and truth, the right mode of life, death and transitoriness, the wickedness of women, the sin of eat in flesh, drinking intoxicants, honey, e tc. A very few specimens will suffice to give an idea of this work which at any rate is important from the point of view of Jinistic ethics :

Chapter IV contains warnings against avarice, beginning with the verse :

"The sun grows cold, and hot the cool moon grows,
The cloud grows firm, the ocean is satiated with the water of the streams,
The wind stands still, the heat of the fire gives up its glow,—
But never does the ardour of avarice cease to glow."

Among the sins which are enumerated as following in the wake of avarice, are man's tilling the soil with a plough, sewing garments, producing paintings and doing other things which we should call useful professions. Chapter VI deals with the favourite theme of ascetic poetry, the "investigation of the virtues and faults of women." The female body is described by this poet-monk as the sum of all impurity, in his eyes woman is "the treasury of all sufferings," "the bolt barring the city of heaven, the path to the dwelling of hell," "the axe for the pleasant grove of piety, the hoar-frost for the lotus of virtues, the root of the tree of sins, the soil for the creeper of deceit" etc. The warning against the blandishments of courtesans takes up an entire chapter (XXIV). We read here, for instance (XXIV, 21) :

"As a thief of the wealth which bestows all delights, called penance,
As a man-murdering pest, skilled in bringing all sufferings,
As a snare to catch the mad elephant called man,
The whore, the saleable woman, was sent to earth by fate."

The Āptas, *i.e.*, the sinless beings who have cast off passion, hate and delusion are dealt with in Chapter XXVI. These "released ones" are the true gods; and here the poet indulges in the most damning expressions against the Brahmanical gods, who lust after women, drink intoxicating drinks and are entirely given up to sensual pleasures, and can therefore not be counted as Āptas. At the end of this chapter Amitagati protests that he has not laid such stress on the faults of the gods "from motives of eloquence, hate or passion," but he has merely endeavoured 'to know the all-knowing, faultless Āpta'. 'And yet the saviour of the three worlds, as he dwells in the Beyond, cannot be known in this world. As long as the sun does not rise, so long all darkness has not been banished." The essence of the true religion is shown in Chapter XXVIII, where, for instance, we read (V.6) :

"The king of hills may waver,
And cold the fire may grow,
The rock may swim in the water,
And the moon send forth rays of heat,
The sun may rise in the West—
But in the killing of beings
Religion can never consist."

Twenty years after the Subhāṣitaratnasaṃdoha, in 1014 A.D., the second great work of Amitagati, Dharmaparīkṣā,[1] "Examination of the Religion" was completed. This is a dogmatic-polemical work, which is, however, so closely interwoven with narratives, that it may be included among the narrative literature as well. The obvious aim of the author in this book is, not only to instruct and convert, but also to entertain at the the expense of adherents of other religions, the plan of the work being as follows : A Jaina converts his Brahmin friend by doing all kinds of absurd things or telling incredible stories, in order to bring home to his astonished friend that the Brahmanical legends tell even more incredible and more absurd things. This is a peg on which Amitagati succeeds in hanging a large number of popular anecdotes. They are gleaned either from oral tradition or from a book of tales in Prākrit. In the language, too, there are traces of their having been translated from Prākrit. Other tales are taken from the epic-Purāṇic tradition, but are sorely corrupted. Among the popular narratives, two

1. N. *Mironow*, Die Dharmaparikṣā des Amitagati. Diss. Leipzig 1903. See also *Bhandarkar*, Report 1884-87, pp. 13ff., 134ff.

interesting types are especially represented : stories of fools and marvellous tales of lies.

Among the first-named category the most interesting is the story of the four fools who meet with a saint, who greets them. The fools begin to quarrel as to who it was whom the saint had greeted. They ask the saint and he says : "The most foolish among you." Now they cannot agree as to who is the most foolish among them. So they go to the town, in order to ask the citizens to decide, and each of them relates some piece of stupidity which he has committed. The first one allowed his eyes to be burned out by a lamp, only in order not to disturb his two wives in their sleep. The second let his two bad wives break his legs. The fourth had his cheek pricked through, from fear of his mother-in-law. The third, however, behaved in a fashion similar to the man in Goethe's poem "Gutmann und Gutweib." Once he was lying in bed with his wife. Then they decided to act on his suggestion, that the one who spoke first must give the other ten sweet cakes. As they were thus lying quietly, a theif entered the house, and stole everything there was to steal. When the thief had already laid hands on the wife's undergarments, the wife said to the husband : "What ? Are you going to look on quietly even now ?" Then the husband demanded the promised ten cakes, because she had been the first to break the silence"[1]

As to the marvellous tales a la Münchausen (Münch-hausen), we mention only the following : A man sees a beautiful tree and wishes to taste its fruits. But the tree is too tall. So he cuts off his head, throws it on to the tree, where it eats as much fruit as it wants. Then he fastens his head on to his neck again.

---

1. *Mironow*, l.c., p. 21. *Cf.* R. *Pisechel*, ZDMG 58, 1904, 363ff.; *Hertel*, Ein altindisches Narrenbuch, p. 37ff. The story frequently recurs in India (*e.g.* Vetālapañcaviṃśati, ed. *Uhle*, 23, 63, and often in modern Indian versions). The earliest known version in the Chinese Tripiṭaka (E. *Huber*, BEFEO 4, 1091; cf *Zachariae*, ZVV 1906, 136 Note), takes us back as far as the year 492 A.D. The propagation of the anecdote, which is also known in Arabic variants and in Baluchi, has been traced, as far as Europe is concerned, by R. *Köhler* (Jahrbuch für romanische und englische Litteratur 12, 348 ff). *Goethe* took the theme from a Scottish ballad.

Remarkable are the sagas and legends which Amitagati cites from the Mahābhārata and the Rāmāyaṇa. Only few of these are told in the form in which we know them from the two epics. Most of them are pieced together from fragments of the most various traditions in such a way that they appear as absurd as possible. Yet most likely he did not invent these corruptions of the Brahmanical legends himself, but probably they had already been changed by the Jainas in this fashion at an earlier time.[1] Amitagati tells the following satirical story regarding the origin of the Mahābhārata :

Vyāsa certainly knew that his poem was full of lies, but he ventured do dish up the inconsistent and senseless stuff to mankind, after he had convinced himself, by an experiment, of the stupidity of men. He placed a pot on the bank of the Gaṅgā and began to heap sand over it. Immediately the people came along and followed his example, so that after a short time the place where the first pot stood, could no longer be determined.

Indeed Amitagati is none too scrupulous in his criticism of Brahmanism. The Brahmanical pantheon is condemned just as ruthlessly here as in the Subhāṣitaratnasaṃdoha.[2] Here, too, the narrator revels in dwelling on the infamous deeds of the gods, especially their amorous adventures. He is, moreover, very hard on Brahmanical ethics, and attacks the caste system in particular. He devotes far less space to the refutation of the Buddhist doctrines, and it is Mahāyāna Buddhism that he attacks. In his presentation of Jinistic ethics he tells, among other things, a version of the parable of the "Man in the Well." Most especially characteristic of Amitagati's standpoint are, however, the legends that he tells of the origin of Jinism and the heretical doctrines. This "historical" retrospect concludes with the statement that, though some good is certainly contained even in the heretical doctrines, this is always borrowed from Jinism.

1. According to *Mironow*, l.c., p. 49ff., he used Raviṣeṇa's Padma-Purāṇa and Śubhacandra's Pāṇḍava-Purāṇa (or "Jaina-Mahābhārata").

2. And this is additional proof of the fact that the two works are by one and the same author. According to *Mironow*, l.c, p., 41, the Subhāṣitaratnasaṃdoha appears to have been used in the last two sections of the Dharmaparikṣā.

A third book by Amitagati is Yogasāra.[1] This is a didactic poem in simple Ślokas, treating of various aspects of the religion, in 9 chapters, but consisting mainly of moral instructions. A few specimens are given here :

"An action performed by anger and the other passions counts as an action performed by the soul, just as a battle won by the foot-soldiers counts as a battle won by the king." (II, 34.)

"We see the soul-less body of our neighbour, but not his soul; whence then should affection come at a good deed, whence aversion at a harmful one ?" (V, 11.)

"Enemies, fathers, wives, relatives, brothers and children oppress and delight my body, not my soul." (V, 12.)

"The possessor of knowledge is not spotted by sins, any more than the sun by eclipses. Knowledge is not touched by the objects of the senses, any more than the mail-clad warrior is pierced by the enemy." (IX, 30.)

"Just as in spite of the difference among cows, there is no difference to be found in the milk, thus in spite of the difference among men, there is no difference in the true knowledge." (IX, 77.)

Among the works of Amitagati there is also a Dvātriṃśatikā,[2] a poem in 32 stanzas of highly ethical value, which partly has the form of a prayer in which the Āptā, the perfect saint or Jina, is invoked as "god" (deva) or "god of gods" (devadeva), and partly contains only religious-moral contemplations. It begins with the beautiful verses:

"May my self always have love (maitrī) for all beings, pleasure in the company of the virtuous, deepest compassion for the creatures in pain, and indifference towards him who is perversely inclined, O God !

"May I, by thy grace, O Lord of Jinas (Jinendra), possess the power to separate, like the sword from its sheath, my soul which is faultless and possessed of infinite power, from the body !

---

1. Edited with a Hindi explanation in SJG, No. 16, 1918.

2. Edited in MDJG No. 13, p. 132ff.; and in DJGK 1; also under the title Sāmayika Pāṭha, with an English translation by *Ajit Prasada* in the Jaina Scripture Gift Series No. 2. Yet another work of Amitagati, the Pañcasaṃgraha, is printed in MDJG No. 25.

"May my mind, O Lord, be always equal in sorrow and in joy, towards enemy and friend, in union and in separation, in the house and in the forest, and may all selfishness be banished from my heart !"

One of the most important didactic poems of the Jainas is the Yogaśāstra[1] by Hemacandra. The work consists of a text in simple Ślokas and a commentary short (vṛtti) in ornate Kāvya style, which also contains stories.[2] The first four chapters, which constitute more than three-quarters of the entire work, give a brief summary of the Jaina doctrine as far as it concerns laymen, "and the very copious commentary extends this summary into the clearest and most comprehensible presentation of the system which has ever been written."[3] The duties of a king of the Jaina faith are also often discussed here, for Hemacandra wrote this work at the request of King Kumārapāla, and it contributed largely towards winning the king over to the Jaina religion. In this "Yogaśāstra," Yoga does not, however, mean merely "meditation" or "absorption," but "religious exercise" in general, the whole "effort" which the pious must make. The work contains a complete doctrine of duties. The actual Yoga, the ascetic exercises and absorptions which lead to release, are

---

1. It is also called Adhyātmopaniṣad. The first four chapters belong to the daily reading of the Jaina monks, and are therefore frequently to be found copied out separately, whilst manuscripts of all 12 chapters are rare (*Peterson*, 3 Reports, p. 31; *Weber*, HSS. Verz., II, 3, 913ff.) ; they are edited and transl. into German by E. *Windisch* in ZDMG 28, 1874, 185-262. An edition with Italian translation has been begun by F. *Belloni-Filippi* in GSAI 21, 1908, 123 ff. The edition by Vijaya Dharma *Sūri* in Bibl. Ind. (fasc. 1, 1907 to fasc. 6, 1921) is also not complete. A complete edition with the author's own commentary was published by the Jaina Dharma Prasāraka Sabhā, Bhavanagar 1926.

2. These narratives look like brief summaries of the legends told in the Triṣaṣṭiśalākāpuruṣa-Carita, from which *Belloni-Filippi* concludes that this work was written earlier, whilst *Bühler* (Hemachandra, pp. 36, 43) agrees with the tradition (s. *Peterion,* Report IV, p. 7) in regarding the Yogaśāstra as the earlier work. On the Brahmadatta-Kathānaka in Hemacandra's commentary s. *Pavolini* in GSAI 7, 339 ff.; on the Abhayarājarṣi, Kathānaka in the same, which is connected with the Udayana legend, s. *Hertel,* Jinakīrti's "Geschichte von Pāla und Gopāla," p. 127ff.

3. *Bühler,* l.c., p. 36.

relegated to the last eight chapters, the explanation of which takes up only about one-tenth of the whole commentary. "It is remarkable that the Jaina-Yoga is preceded by a very lengthy exposition of those very exercises which, according to the explicit statement of the author, are useless to attain Mukti, though they enable one to catch a glimpse of the future and are supposed to endow one with supernatural powers. It appears that even Hemacandra believed in their efficacy, and perhaps gave himself up to them. If he devotes a long chapter to describing them, he probably did so with regard to the fondness of the king for Yoga exercises, of which he speaks in the commentary on XII, 55."[1] The subject-matter of the first four chapters coincides in the main with that of Amitagati's Subhāṣitaratnasaṃdoha. Though, however, Hemacandra moves in the same spheres of thought, he is certainly more ingenious and more original.[2] More often than in Amitagati's work we meet with ideas, images and metaphors which are not quite so stereotyped. For instance, the following invocation of Mahāvīra (1, 3) is very pretty :

> "Hail to the Jina hero's eyes
> Whose pupils are rigid with pity
> And wet with tears, from pity.
> Even for him who has committed sin."

He is very severe in his attack on Brahmanical morality as taught more especially in the Law-book of Manu. He is well versed in Brahmanical literature, and he quotes verses from Manu to show convincingly that they proclaim a morality which is incompatible with the command of Ahiṃsā (the sparing of all living creatures) and is therefore not worthy of the name of morality. This Ahiṃsā is inculcated again and again, for instance in II, 50f. :

> "Ahiṃsā is like a loving mother of all beings,
> Ahiṃsā is like a stream of nectar in the desert of Saṃsāra,
> Ahiṃsā is a course of rain-clouds to the forest-fire of

1. *Bühler*, l.c., p. 36.
2. Hence it is not so likely that he was influenced by Amitagati as is assumed by *Hertel* (WZKM 17, 106).

suffering.

The best healing-herb for the beings tormented by the disease

Called the perpetual return of existence, is Ahiṃsā."[1]

Of course, in the eyes of Hemacandra too, women are "the torchcs on the way to the gate of Hell, the root of all troubles and the primal cause of dissension" etc wherein he agrees not only with Amitagati, but with all monastic poets. In Hemacandra's work too we come across vivid and excellent metaphors of the kind so frequent in Indian gnomic poetry, thus when he says that "the tree of arrogance must be uprooted by the floods of the stream of gentleness" (IV, 14). Some of the verses on the transitoriness and vanity of human existence also remind us of the best sayings of Bhartṛhari, such as for instance IV, 58 :

"Fortune wavers like the wave,
The meeting of friends is like a dream;
Youth is like the particle of a blade of grass,
Whirled on high by each gust of wind."

A contemporary of Hemacandra is Jinadatta Sūri (1075-1154 A.D.), a pupil of Jinavallabha Sūri. He wrote Upadeśarasāyana Rāsa,[2] a didactic poem in the form of a dancing-song in 80 verses, Kālasvarūpakulakam, a didactic poem in 32 rhymed verses in Apabharaṃśa, and a Caccarī (Carcarī),[3] also a kind of dancing-song in praise of his teacher Jinavallabha Sūri, who had moral sayings engraven on various shrines.

---

1. It is, however, very characteristic of Hemacandra that, at the request of the same King Kumārapāla, whom he sought to win over to ascetic morality by the Yogaśāstra, he also wrote a Laghvarhanniti-Śāstra, "Short Manual of the Art of Governing for Jainas," which cannot be said to be entirely in conformity with the principle of Ahiṃsā. More will be said of this Niti-Śāstra in Vol. III.

2. Among the devotees of Kṛṣṇa, Rāsas are dancing-songs, in which the love of Kṛṣṇa and Râdhā is sung. Among the Jainas, they are ballads, often with a bearing on historical personages, frequently in Old Gujarātī.

3. All three poems are edited with a Sanskrit introduction by Lalchandra Bhagwandas *Gandhi*, Three Apabhraṃśa Works of Jinadatta Sūri with Commentaries, in GOS No. 37, Baroda 1927. In the same volume are published

A younger contemporary of Hemacandra and King Kumārapāla is Somaprabha, the author of the Kumārapāla-Pratibodha,[1] a didactic poem and collection of tales, in verse and prose, for the most part in Prākrit, but also partly in Sanskrit and Apabhraṃśa. According to the statement of the author himself, the work was written in the year 1184 A.D., and consists of five Prastāvas ("Recitals, sermons") by which Hemacandra who is made the speaker, is supposed to have converted King Kumārapāla. Prastāva I deals with the 5 commandments as to conduct : avoidance of killing, of gambling, adultery, fornication, drinking and theft; Pr. II with the worship of gods and teachers, Pr. III with the four duties : generosity, virtue, asceticism and meditation, Pr. IV on the 12 vows of the Jaina layman,[2] and Prastāva V on the four passions (anger, pride, deceit and greed)and various other points of the doctrine. The separate teachings are illustrated by stories, of which there are 54 in all. Most of the stories told here occur in other Jaina works too.[3]

As an example of the vice of gambling the story of Nala is told.[4] The story of King Pradyota of Ujjayinī serves to elucidate

---

as appendices : a Saṅghapaṭṭaka by Jinavallabha Sūri, a Gaṇadharasārdhaśataka (*cf.* also *Weber*, HSS. Verz. II, 3, 981 ff.) and a Sugurupāratantrya by Jinadatta, and a hymn written in 1113 A.D. by Jinarakṣita, the pupil of Jinadatta, in praise of his teacher. A Gaṇadharasaptati, written for the purpose of exorcising a man possessed by a spirit, is mentioned by *Bhandarkar*, Report 1882-83, p. 48f. Another Jinadatta, who lived in the first half of the 13th century, wrote an encyclopaedia Vivekavilāsa, s. *Bhandarkar*, Report 1883-84, pp. 156, 458 ff.

1. Edited by *Munirāja Jinavijaya*, Baroda 1920 (GOS No. 14). *Cf. Peterson*, Report IV, p. 12f.; P.D. *Gune* in Proce. I. OC, Poona 1922, p. 159ff., and Ludwig *Alsdorf* Der Kumārapālapratibodha, ein Beitrag zur Kenntnis des Apabhraṃśa und der Erzählungslitteratur der Jainas (Alt-und Neu-Indische Studien) Hamburg 1928. In the last verse the title is given as Jinadharmapratibodha, in the colophon Kumārapālapratibodha, which is probably to be explained as an abbreviation for Kumārapāla-Jinadharma-pratibodha, "Awakening of the religion of the Jina in Kumārapāla," Hemakumāracaritra also appears to be a title of the same work, s. *Alsdorf*. l.c., p. 1, Note I.

2. *Cf.* Mrs. S. *Stevenson*, The Heart of Jainism, p. 205ff.; *Glasenapp*, Der Jainismus, p. 202ff.

3. See *Alsdorf*, l. c., p. 7ff.

4. Pp. 47-76 of the edition.

the sin of adultery. The story belongs to the cycle of the Udayana legends. It is also told here how Prince Abhaya of Rājagṛha becomes the prisoner of King Pradyotạ owing to trickery. As a captive he does the king an important service on three occasions, and each time the king grants him a wish with the exception of his liberty. When he rescues the king from his distress the fourth time, and the king again offers to grant him a wish Abhaya says: "Whilst you sit upon the elephant Nalagiri as a driver and I sit on the lap of (your consort) Śivadevī, burn me with the (fire-proof) wood of the chariot Agnibhīru." By demanding such impossibilities, he indicates to the king that he has only the one wish for liberty. The king recognises this and sets him free, whereupon Abhaya takes leave of him with this oath : "If I do not take you prisoner, O King, in broad daylight in the middle of the town amidst loud cries, may I go into the fire." By means of a ruse he does actually take the king prisoner.[1]

As an instance of the vow of virtue, the story is told of Śīlavatī, the virtuous wife of the rich merchant Ajitasena. She understands the language of the birds and performs all kinds of seemingly absurd actions and gives seemingly absurd answers: it turns out, however, that the apparent absurdities are in reality proofs of great intellgence.[2]

Prastāva V contains two long narratives in Apabhraṃśa. The one is the Jīva-manaḥ-karaṇa-saṃlāpa-Kathā, "The Story of the Conversation between Soul, Mind and Senses."[3] This is an elaborately worked out allegory (105 stanzas), in which King Ātman (Soul), his consort Buddhi (Insight), his minister Manas (Mind) and his five court officials, the Five Senses appear: Manas and the five Senses carry on a heated debate as to the origin of suffering, whereupon Ātman takes the lead, and in a long speech describes the terrible sufferings of Saṃsāra and extols the happiness of those whose mind is directed towards the Jina, the Munis and pity on all beings, "who avoid the striving after possession, as one avoids robbery, which brings suffering in its

1. Pp. 76-83 of the edition; *cf. Alsodorf,* l.c., p. 140 f. and P.D. *Gune* in Ann. Bh. Inst. II, 1920, p. 1ff.

2. Pp. 221-229 of the edition; *cf. Alsdorf,* l.c., p. 141 f.

3. Pp. 422-437 of the edition; *cf. Alsdorf,* l.c., pp. 6, 10 ff., 80 ff., 92 ff.

wake, kingly power, as a snare or poison, sensual pleasure and a loving woman, as a piece of wood, wealth as a fetter, inclination to adornment as a burden; who, making no difference between themselves and others, have taken upon themselves the burden of the discipline of the Order."[1]

The second long story in Apabhraṃśa is the story of Sthūlabhadra[2] in 106 verses. Sthūlabhadra is the last successor of Mahāvīra, who still knew the 14 Pūrvas. Stories about him and his enemy, the learned Brahmin Vararuci, are already told in the Pariśiṣṭa-Parvan.[3] We also find here the story of the monks, each of whom fulfils another, more difficult vow, whilst Sthūlabhadra takes upon himself and fulfils the vow that he will spend four months in the house of the courtesan Kośā, without violating his vow of chastity. The vain attempts of Kośā to entangle the monk in the bonds of love, are described in accordance with all the rules of the Kāma-Śāstra. In the end the king gives Kośā to his charioteer as a wife. In order to amuse her, this man performs a remarkable trick : he cuts a mango from the tree with two arrows shot into one another, whereupon Kośā does a still more wonderful trick : she dances upon the point of a needle which is sticking at the top of a heap of mustard-seeds. Then the charioteer is astonished, but she says that Sthūlabhadra performed a far more marvellous trick, when he lived with her and yet did not violate his vow of chastity.

Somaprabha is a poet well versed in all the arts of the Alaṃkāra-Śāstra : this is evidenced by the extremely artificial hymn to Pārśva in Apabhraṃśa.[4] Another work by Somaprabha which is very artificial and at the same time reveals great Sanskrit erudition, is the Śatārthakāvya written between 1177 and 1179 A.D. This is a single verse in the Vasantatilakā metre, which is explained by the poet himself in 100 different ways.[5]

---

1. *Alsdorf.* l. c., p. 100.
2. Pp. 443-461 of the edition; *cf. Alsdorf,* l.c., pp. 6, 19ff., 100 ff., 113 ff.
3. Pariśiṣṭa-Parvan VIII, 110-193, see above, p. 487 ff.
4. P. 471 f. of the edition; *cf. Alsdorf,* l.c., pp. 45f., 126 ff.
5. *Munirāja Jinavijaya,* Kumārapāla-Pratibodha, Ed., Introduction, p. vii f.

The same Somaprabha is also the author of the didactic poem Sindūraprakāra or Sūktimuktāvalī,[1] written in 1199 A.D., a book of moral sayings very popular among the Jainas.

It is, on the other hand, a later Somaprabha, who wrote the Śṛṅgāravairāgya-Taraṅgiṇī[2] in about 1276 A.D. This is a didactic poem in 46 elaborate stanzas written in the most perfect Kāvya style. In this erotic-ascetic poem, the charms of women and the blandishments of love are described with all the arts of the Kāma-Śāstra, as a warning against them as being an obstacle to peace of mind and release.

Śīladūta, "Virtue as a Messenger,"[3] by Cāritrasundara, is a very elaborate didactic poem composed on the principle of the completion of verses (samasyāpūraṇa) in imitation of Kālidāsa's Meghadūta. In the last verse the poet mentions the date when his poem was completed, which corresponds to the year 1420 A.D.

Anthologies of moral sayings have also been compiled by Jainas. Thus the Gāthā-Kośa by Municandra Sūri[4] (died 1122), a book of Prākrit verses, from which Peterson has culled a few remarkable sayings, *e.g.* :

"Heaven and hell, the atmosphere and the whole earth
Do the wise ones know,—the doings of women they know not."

---

1. Edited in Km., Part VII, pp. 35-51 ; translated into Italian by *Pavolini* in SIFI II, 33-72, Firenze 1898 with Introduction by F.L. *Pullée* ; *cf. Weber*, HSS. Verz. II, 3, P. 1132 ff.; *Bhandarkar*, Report 1882-83, pp. 42, 225 f. *Munirāja Jinavijaya* 1. c., p. vi who says : "This work is well-known among the Jainas and is repeated by heart by many a man and woman of the Jain Community."

2. Edited in Km., Part V, 1888, 124 ff. Trans. into German as "A true Capuchin's Sermon against Women" by R. *Schmidt*, Liebe und Ehe im alten und modernen Indien, Berlin 1904, p. 36 ff. According to verse 33 (" he whose thoughts are bent on Śiva, should not even stay in the vicinity of women") and verse 39 ("the city of Śiva" in the sense of "release") it appears to be an originally Śivaite poem, which has been appropriated by the Jainas. The commentator explains Śiva as a synonym for mukti, "release."

3. Edited in YJG. No. 18, Benares 1909. *Cf.* F. *Belloni-Filippi* in GSAI, 28, 1916, 153 ff.

4. *Peterson*, 3 Reports, 12ff, 297 ff.

"The path of the fish in the water, the bird's flight through the air
The wise ones know,—the heart of a woman they know not."

Gāthāsahasrī by Samayasundara,[1] is a more comprehensive anthology of more recent date (1630). All of these "thousand stanzas," partly in Sanskrit, partly in Prākrit, are compiled from earlier works by Haribhadra, Devendra and others. There are also memorial verses among them, the contents of which deal with ecclesiastical history. A saying taken from a work by Devendra is deserving of mention :

"You cannot tread two paths at once,
You cannot sew with a needle with two points;
You cannot enjoy both at the same time :
The pleasure of the senses and release in the Beyond."

Bhavavairāgyaśataka,[2] a collection of a hundred verses on the vanity of existence, the inconstancy of all earthly goods, the wretchedness of Saṃsāra, etc., as the sole remedy for which the Jaina religion is recommended, is an anthology of Prākrit verses.[3]

Great is the number of the purely erudite works, some of which are works on the dogmas of the Jaina religion, others on philosophy, and more especially logic. The Jainas play by no means unimportant part in the history of Indian philosophy. The Upaniṣads taught the eternal existence of the soul, which is the only existing being. Earlier Buddhism taught that there

---

1. *Peterson,* 3 Reports, 3 ff., 284 ff. Samayasundara is also the author of Visaṃvādaśataka, a compilation of a hundred verses which contain discrepancies to be found in the sacred texts (l.c., p. 10).

2. Edited and translated by L. P. *Tessitori* in GSAI 22, 179-211 ; 24, 405 ff.

3. Other anthologies such as the earlier Vajjālagga by Jayavallabha (with Sanskrit version ed. by J. *Laber* in Bibl. Ind., Fasc. I, 1914, Fasc. II, 1923) and the more modern collection Prākrita-Sūktaratnamālā (Collection of Ancient Prakrit Popular Poems with Sanskrit Equivalents and English Translation) compiled by Puran Chand *Nahar,* Calcutta 1919 (Jaina Vividha Sāhitya Śāstra Mālā No. 11) are of quite general character, and not specifically Jinistic, though they are compiled by Jainas.

is no independent self, but only a constant becoming and passing away of psychical and physical phenomena, from which Mahāyāna Buddhism developed the doctrine of Śūnyavāda or Nāstivāda, "the doctrine of It is not."—Midway between these two stand the Jainas, who proclaim the Syādvāda, "the doctrine of It-can be," saying : "There is something which exists eternally, objects are eternal as matter, but this matter can assume all possible forms and qualities." At an early period the Jainas rendered very great services in the development of logic and atomism, the Nyāya and the Vaiśeṣika philosophy. Bhadrabāhu taught a syllogism consisting of ten parts already in the Āvaśyaka-Niryukti, and Syādvāda in the Sūtrakṛtāṅga-Niryukti.[1] According to the Āvaśyaka-Sūtra, the Jaina teacher Rohagutta is supposed to have occasioned a schism in the year 18 A.D. and founded the Vaiśeṣika.[2]

The earliest Digambara author who is also cited with esteem by the Śvetāmbaras, is Kundakunda, who wrote only in Prākrit. Of the 83 treatises (pāhuda, prābhṛta) which he is said to have written, only seven are known. Pañcatthiyasāra (Pañcāstikāyasāra)[3] or Pavayaṇasāra Pañcātthiyasaṃgaha (Pravacanasāra Pañcāstikāyasaṃgraha][4] consists of two parts, which are really independent works.[5] The first and longer section contains the doctrine of the 5 Astikāyas or groups of existence : souls (Jīva), non-souls (pudgala), principles of rest and motion (dharma and adharma) and space (ākāśa). The second section

---

1. *Cf. Jacobi* in Transactions of the Third Congress for the History of Religion, Oxford 1908, II, p. 59 ff. ; S. Ch. *Vidyābhūṣaṇa*, History of Indian Logic, p. 164 ff. ; H. *Ui*, Vaiśeṣika Philosophy (OTF). London 1917, p. 83. S. *Dasgupta*, History of Indian Philosophy I, Cambridge 1922, p. 173 ff.

2. *Cf. Weber* Ind. Stud. 17, 121 ff. ; *Jacobi* in SBE, Vol. 14, p. xxxvii. *Ui*, l. c., p. 35 ff.

3. The Building of the Cosmos or Pañcāstikāyasāra (The five Cosmic Constituents) by Svami Sri Kundakundācārya ed. with Philosophical and Historical Introduction, Translation, Notes and an Original Commentary in English by A. *Chakravartinayanar*, Arrah 1920 (SBJ, Vol. III). Text also edited by *Pavolini* in GSAI 14, 1901, pp. 1-40 and in Rāyacandra-Jaina-Śāstramālā, Bombay 1904.

4. The title of the work is given thus in the colophons.

5. Each of the two parts has an introductory formula and a conclusion of its own.

treats of the path to release. This work, together with Pavayanasāra, and Samayasāra, forms a "trilogy" (Prābhṛtatraya or Nāṭakatraya). Pavayaṇasāra (pravacanasāra)[1] in Prākrit Gāthās, is a much prized book on Jinistic dogmatics, psychology and ethics. On Samayasāra (Kernel or Essence of the Doctrine")[2] in 414 Prākrit stanzas, there are Sanskrit commentaries by Prabhācandra, the pupil of Akalaṅka, and Amṛtacandra, who commented on the principal works of Akalaṅka in abont 904 A.D. Niyamasāra[3] is a work on the discipline to which the seeker after salvation must submit himself. To Kundakunda is also ascribed Chappāhuḍa (Saṭprābhṛta),[4] six chapters on the Jaina doctrine, but this work contains views which differ from the views of the teacher known from his other works. The author calls himself "pupil of Bhadrabāhu," which may mean Bhadrabāhu II, who lived in the 1st century A.D., so that the author may nevertheless have been a contemporary of Kundakunda.

It was probably in one of the early centuries of the Christian era that Vaṭṭakera wrote his Prākrit works Mūlācāra and Trivarṇācāra on the moral conduct of a pious Jaina. There is a commentary Ācāravṛtti on the Mūlācāra, written by Vasunandin, who observes by way of introduction that Vaṭṭakera intended to give in his work a brief summary of the Āyāraṅga for his pupils.[5]

Kārttikeya Svāmin whose Kattigeyāṇupekkhā (Kārttikeyānuprekṣā)[6] enjoys a great reputation among the Jainas,

1. More recent editions have appeared in India. *Cf. Bhandarkar*, Report 1883-84. pp. 91 ff., 379 ff.

2. Edited with a Sanskrit commentary in SJG No. 3, Benares 1914. *Cf. Peterson* Report II, p. 161 ff., and *Hiralal*, Catalogue; p. 702; on Amṛtacandra Sūri s. *Peterson*, Report IV, p. ix.

3. *Cf. Bhandarkar*, Report 1883-84, p.102 f.

4. Edited with a Hindi commentary by *Bābu* Sūrajbhān *Vakil*, Benares 1910. Commentary on it by Amṛtacandra Sūri and by Śrutasāgara. *Cf. Peterson* Report II, pp. 80 ff., 158ff., and W. *Denecke* in Festgabe Jacobi. p. 163 f.

5. Mūlācāra with Vasunandin's commentary edited in MDJG Nos. 19 and 23. In one manuscript Mūlācāra is ascribed to Kundakunda. *Cf. Peterson*, Report II, pp. 74ff., 134 ff.; *Hiralal*, Catalogue, p. xiv f. and *Denecke*, l.c., p. 162. Vasunandin quotes Amitagati and is quoted by Āśādhara, and must therefore have lived between the 10th and 13th centuries.

6. Printed with a Hindī commentary in Bombay 1904. *Cf. Peterson*, Report IV, p. 142 ff.; *Bhandarkar*, Report 1883-84, pp. 113 ff., 398 ff. (where the text of Chapter XII is given) *Hiralal*, Catalogue, p. xiv.

probably also belongs to this earlier period. This work treats in 12 chapters of the 12 Anuprekṣās or meditations, to which both monk and layman must devote themselves, in order to emancipate themselves little by little from Karman.[1] These are reflections on the transitoriness of all things, the helplessness of all beings, the sufferings of the beings in the cycle of rebirths, the soul which goes on this journey alone and can only be released alone, the difference of everything else (body, friends, relatives and possessions) from the soul, the impurity of the body, the influx, (āsrava) of Karman and the means whereby one can stem this influx, the annihilation of Karman and the purification of the soul by mortifications, the countless uncreated worlds, the precious treasure of illumination, which is difficult of attainment, and lastly the duties of laymen and monks, which are set forth in Chapter 12.

The Digambara Umāsvāmin, who is called Umāsvāti by the Śvetāmbaras[2] and described as a pupil of Ghoṣanandi Kṣamāśramaṇa, was, according to tradition, a pupil of Kundakunda. The Digambaras also give him the epithet Gṛdhrapiccha, "Vulture's feather," which Kundakunda had too, and the title "Reciter" (Vācakaśramaṇa or Vācakācārya). According to the Digambara-Paṭṭāvalīs he lived from about 135 to 219 A.D., whilst the statements of the Śvetāmbaras not only contradict those of the Digambaras, but even contradict one another.[3] In any case he is earlier than Siddhasena Divākara, who wrote a commentary on the principal work of Umāsvāti. He is said to have written no less than 500 books, but his most famous work,

1. *Cf.* Mrs. S. *Stevenson,* The Heart of Jainism, p. 156ff. *Glasenapp,* Der Jainismus, p. 206. f.

2. He is said to be called so because his mother was called Umā Vātsī and his father Svāti.

3. *Cf. Klatt,* Jaina-Onomasticon, p. 4 f. *Peterson,* 3 Reports, p. 328 f.; Report IV, p. xvi f. ; *Jacobi,* in ZDMG 60, 1906, 288 f. ; *Vidyābhūṣaṇa,* History of Indian Logic, p.168ff,; L.*Suali* Introductione alla Studio della Filosofia Indiana, Pavia 1913, p. 36 ff.; J. L. *Jaini* in SBJ II, p. vii; *Farquhar,* Outline, p. 164 f. Neither are the statements of the Digambaras free from ambiguity. J.H. *Woods,* The Yoga-System of Patañjali (HOS Vol. 17), p. xix, makes it appear probable that Umāsvāti quotes from the Yoga-Sūtra.

which he wrote in Pāṭaliputra, is the Tattvārthādhigama-Sūtra,[1] "the Manual for the Understanding of the True Nature of Things," a Sanskrit manual, which is recognised as an authority by both Svetāmbaras and Digambaras, and even at the present day is read by all Jainas in private houses and temples. By reading this book once through one is said to acquire just as much religious merit as by fasting for one day. The logic, psychology, cosmography, ontology[2] and ethics of the Jainas, are treated in these Sūtras and the in the Commentary appended by the author himself, in the closest possible agreement with the Canon, more especially with Aṅga VI and Pūrva II. Even to-day it may still serve as an excellent summary of Jaina dogmatics. It is true that the Commentary, which expresses views that are not in harmony with those of the Digambaras, is not recognised by this sect as the work of Umāsvāmin. It is doubtful, therefore, whether the Digambaras are justified in claiming him as one of their own. He probably belongs to a period at which there was not yet so wide a gulf between the two sects as was the case later. The large number of commentaries which have been written on this work by both Śvetāmbaras and Digambaras, bear witness to its significance and great popularity; these include commentaries by such notable teachers as Siddhasena Divākara, Samantabhadra and Haribhadra. The last-named also wrote a commentary on Śrāvakaprajñapti,[3] a systematic treatise of the Jaina religion for lay adherents, in Prākrit. Praśamarati-Prakaraṇa,[4] "Treatise on the Joys of

1. Edited with the Commentary, by *Vakil* Keshavalal Premchand *Mody* in Bibl. Ind. 1903-1905, together with a few minor works of Umāsvāti in the appendices ; with a commentary in Hindi, also in Rāyacandra-Jaina-Śāstramālā, Bombay 1906 ; with Introduction, Translation, Notes and Commentary in English by J. L *Jaini*, Arrah 1920, SBJ, Vol. 2 ; Text of the Sūtras also in *Bhandarkar*, Report 1883-84, p. 405 ff. ; and in DJGK I; translated into German and explained by H. *Jacobi* in ZDMG 60, 1906, 287 ff., 512 ff. ; *cf. Peterson*, Report II, 78 ff., 156 ff.

2. On the classification of the animals according to Tattvārthādhigama, *cf.* B. N. *Seal* in the Appendix to B.K. *Sarkar*, The Primitive Background of Hindu Sociology, Allahabad 1914, p. 323 ff.

3. Ed. by B. K. Premchand (*Mody*), Bombay 1905.

4. Edited in the Appendix to the Edition of Tattvārthādhigama, Bibl. Ind.; also in Ahmedabad, Saṁvat 1960; with Ṭīkā and Avacūri, Bhavanagar,

Peace of the Soul," is a religious-philosophical work, also possessing literary merit.

Like Umāsvāti, Siddhasena Divākara, too, is regarded by both Śvetāmbaras and Digambaras as one of their own. He wrote a commentary on the Tattvārthādhigama-Sūtra,[1] and is said to have written 32 different works on logic, 21 of which are known.[2] His Nyāyāvatāra,[3] which treats of the means of acquiring knowledge (pramāṇa) and of methods (naya) in 32 Sanskrit verses, is a fundamental Jaina work on logic. It forms a part of the Dvātriṃśad-Dvātriṃśikā.[4] The Sammatitarka-Sūtra[5] is a general work on philosophy, which also deals with logic.

A commentary on Umāsvāti's work, entitled Sarvārthasiddhi[6] was also written by Pūjyapāda Devanandin.

In the first half of the 8th century A.D. lived the Digambara Samantabhadra,[7] who again wrote a commentary on Umāsvāti's

---

Saṃvat 1966 ; edited with Commentary and translated into Italian by A. *Ballini* in GSAI, 25, 1912, 117 ff. ; 29, 1918-20, 61 ff.

1. Tattvānusāriṇī Tattvārthaṭīkā was printed in Ahmedabad. Siddhasena Gaṇin, who also wrote a Tattvārthaṭīkā quotes Siddhasena Divākara. *Cf. Peterson*, 3 Reports, Extracts p. 83 ff.; *Hiralal*, Catalogue, p. xii ff. Distinct from these two is Siddhasena Sūri, who in 1185 A.D. wrote a commentary on Nemicandra's Pravacanasāroddhāra ; *cf. Weber* HSS. verz II, 3, 850; *Peterson* Report IV, p. cxxx ff.

2. Ekaviṃśatidvātrīṃśikā. Nyāyāvatāra and Sammatisūtra were published in Siddhasena-Divākara-Kṛta-Granthamālā, Bhavanagar 1909, Sammatitarka-prakaraṇa with commentary by Abhayadeva is published in YJG No. 13, Benares 1919. Abhayadeva's exhaustive commentary has also been published in Gujarātapurātattvamandira-Granthāvali 10, 16, 18, 19 Ahmedabad, 1923-1928.

3. Edited with Commentary and an English translation by Satis Chandra *Vidyābhūṣaṇa* Calcutta, 1909.

4. *Cf.* Ch. *Vidyābhūṣaṇa*, History of Indian Logic, p. 174 ff.

5. Edited with Abhayadeva's commentary Tattvabodhinī in YJG, No. 13; with Tattvārthavidhāyinī in the Ārhatamata-Prabhākara Series, Poona 1926.

6. Edited in Kolhapur 1904, s. *Jacobi* in ZDMG 60, 290.

7. Thus according to K. B. *Pathak* in Ann. Bh. Inst. XI, 1930, 149 ff., who proves that Samantabhadra lived after Dharmakīrti and before Kumārila S. Ch. *Vidyābhūṣaṇa*, History of Indian Logic, p. 182 f. states his period as 600 A.D. According to a Vaṃśāvali he is supposed to have lived in 419 A.D.; s. *Hiralal*, Catalogue, p. xff. On Samantabhadra's life, character, and time,

Tattvārthādhigama-Sūtra. The introduction to this commentary is entitled Devāgama-Stotra or Āptamīmāṃsā,[1] in which the Jinistic philosophy of Syādvāda is explained. The work was known to the philosophers Kumārila and Vācaspatimiśra. Another philosophical work by Samantabhadra is Yuktyanuśāsana.[2] Ratnakāraṇḍaśrāvakācāra,[3] also called Upāsakādhyayana, is a manual of morals for the lay adherent, in 150 Sanskrit verses.

Not far removed from Samantabhadra in point of time is Akalaṅka,[4] or Akalaṅkadeva, who wrote Tattvārtharājavārttika,[5] a commentary on the Tattvārthādhigama-Sūtra, and Aṣṭaśatī, a commentary on Samantabhadra's Āptamīmāṃsā. He is also the author of works on logic, Nyāyaviniścaya, Laghīyastraya and Svarūpasambodhana.[6] A treatise on expiatory rites, Prāyaścittagrantha (or Prāyaścittvidhi) is also ascribed to him.[7] His views are opposed by Kumārila, the great philosopher of Brahmanical orthodoxy, whilst Vidyānanda Pātrakesarin[8] and Prabhācandra defend Akalaṅka against Kumārila. Vidyānanda wrote Aṣṭasāhasrī,[9] a commentary on Aṣṭaśatī, also Tattvārthaślokavārttika,[10] a commentary on Umāsvāmin's work, Āptapa-

see Pandit Jugala Kiśora *Mukhtara* in MDJG No. 24, 1925, Samantabhadra is also called, "Kavi" and is the author of a Svayambhū-Stotra, s. above p. 531.

1. Edition in Jaina Grantha Ratnākara and in SJG Vol. I, Bombay 1905; in SJG 10, Benares 1914, and in DJGK I. On the contents of the Work, cf. *Vidyābhūṣaṇa* l. c., p. 184 f.

2. Edited in SJG Vol. 1 ; MDJG No. 15 ; and in DJGK I.

3. Text with English translation (after the Hindī translation) by Champat Rai *Jain*. The Householder's Dharma, Arrah 1917 ; text only DJGK I; text with commentary by Prabhācandra in MDJG No. 24.

4. *Cf. Hiralal*, Catalogue p. xxvi ff.

5. Edited in SJG 4, Benares 1915.

6. Laghīyastraya and Svarūpasambodhana are edited in MDJG No. 1.

7. Edited together with three other treatises on Prāyaścittas in MDJG No. 18 (Prāyaścitta-Saṃgraha). But it is doubtful whether Akalaṅka is really the author of this treatise ; s. *Hiralal*, Catalogue, p. xxvi.

8. *Cf. Hiralal*, Catalogue, p. xxviii f.

9. Edited in Gāndhīnāthāraṅga-Jaina-Granthamālā, Bombay 1915.

10. Edited in Gāndhīnāthāraṅga-Jaina-Granthamālā, Bombay 1918.

rīkṣā and Patraparīkṣā,[1] Pramāṇanirṇaya and Pramāṇaparīkṣā.[2] Based upon Akalaṅka's Nyāyaviniścaya there is a work on logic, the Parīkṣāmukha-Sūtra,[3] by Māṇikyanandin;[4] and Prabhācandra, who calls himself a pupil of Padmanandin (*i.e.*, Kundakunda), wrote a commentary on the last-named work : this commentary is entitled Prameyakamalamārtaṇḍa, and is a well-known work on logic. The same author also wrote another work on logic, Nyāyakumudacandrodaya. It has been believed hitherto that this is the same Prabhācandra who was a pupil of Akalaṅka in the 8th century. According to the epilogue (praśasti) of the first work, however, this work was written in Dhārā in the reign of King Bhoja (1019-1060 A.D.),[5] One Prabhācandra wrote commentaries on the Tattvārthādhigama-Sūtra by Umāsvāmin, the Samayasāra by Kundakunda, Pūjyapāda's Samādhiśataka and on Samantabhadra's Ratnakāraṇḍa and Svayambhū-Stotra.[6]

At the close of the 8th or the beginning of the 9th century the Digambara Śubhacandra wrote a philosophical treatise in

1. Edited in SJG 1, 2, Benares 1913; Āptaparīkṣā also in DJGK I.

2. Edited in SJG 10, 1914.

3. Edited in SJG I, Bombay 1905 ; also in DJGK I. *Cf.* S. Ch. *Vidyābhūṣaṇa* History of Indian Logic, p. 188 ff.

4. According to a Digambara Paṭṭāvali *Hoernle* in Ind. Ant. 20. 1891, p. 352) Māṇikyanandin lived in 528 A.D. *Cf.* also *Hiralal*, Catalogue p. xxviii. A later Māṇikyanandin was the teacher of Meghacandra, who died in 1163 A.D., s. Lewis *Rice*, Epigraphia Carnatica, Vol. XII, p. 134.

5. Thus according to A. *Venkatasubbiah* in JBRAS, N.S., 3. 1927, p. 144 ff, But according to K.B. *Pathak* in OC. IX, London 1892, I, 213 (s. above, p. 459 and note 4) Jinasena mentions Akalaṅka in the Ādi-Purāṇa (838 A.D.) and speaks of Prabhācandra as the author of Candrodaya. In the introduction to Nyāyakumuda-Candrodaya, Prabhācandra says that he is the pupil of Akalaṅka and that he also wrote Prameyakamalamārtaṇḍa. According to this, Prabhācandra lived at the end of the 8th or beginning of the 9th century. As the works themselves are not accessible to me, I am not in a position to settle the question.

6. Neither can I decide to which Prabhācandra these commentaries should be ascribed, or the short treatise Arhatpravacana, printed in MDJG Nr. 21, p. 114. ff. Jaina authors named Prabhācandra lived in the 12th, 13th and 16th centuries too. *Cf. Hiralal,* Catalogue, pp. xxviii, 625 f., 629 648, 671, 702, 704, 714. See above, p. 459 note 4.

Sanskrit verses, entitled Jñānārṇava, "The Ocean of Knowledge" or Yogapradīpādhikāra.[1]

Among the Śvetāmbaras we must mention the famous Haribhadra, who wrote a large number of works both on general philosophy and the Jaina doctrine. In the former category there is Ṣaḍdarśanasamuccaya, "A summary of the six Philosophical Systems."[2] Haribhadra here deals with the systems of Buddhism, Nyāya, Sāṃkhya, Vaiśeṣika and Jaimini, in a short appendix also with the materialism of Cārvāka, and only one short section, the fourth, is devoted to Jinistic metaphysics. Lokatattvanirṇaya ("Investigation of the True Nature of the World),"[3] a philosophical text in Sanskrit verses, is also not an exclusively Jinistic text. In fact Haribhadra goes to the length of saying that Lord Mahāvīra is not his friend and the others are not his foes; that he is not biased in favour of Mahāvīra and feels no hatred for Kapila and the other philosophers, but that he is desirous of accepting whosesoever doctrine is the true one.[4] He also proved his unbiasedness by writing a commentary on the Nyāyapraveśa of the Buddhist Dignāga.[5] On the other hand, other works such as Yogabindu,[6] Yogadṛṣṭisamuccaya,[7] Dharmabindu, etc., contain presentations of the Jaina doctrine. Dharmabindu[8] is a

1. Edited in Rāyacandra Jaina-Śāstramālā, Bombay 1907. *Cf. Weber*, HSS. Verz., II, 3, 907 ff. ; *Guerinot* in JA 1912, s. 10, t. XIX, 373 ff.

2. Edited by F.L. *Pullee* in GSAI 1, 47 ff.; 8, 159 ff., 9, 1 ff.; edited with Guṇaratna's (or Guṇākara Sūri's) Commentary, by L. *Suali* in Bibl. Ind. 1905 ff. ; edited together with Aṣṭaka-Prakaraṇa and with works of Yaśovijaya and Rājaśekhara, Surat 1918; also edited with Guṇaratna's Commentary in Jaina Ātmānanda-Granthamālā 49, Bhavanagar, V.S. 2444 (1917).

3. Edited and translated into Italian by L. *Suali* in GSAI Vol. 18. 263 ff. Text also edited, Bhavanagar 1902.

4. *Cf. La Vallee Poussin*, in JA 1911,, s. 10, t. XVII 323 ff.

5. See N.D. *Mironov* in Festgabe Garbe P. 37 ff.

6. Ed. with Comm. by L. *Suali*, Bhavanagar 1911,

7. Edited by L. *Suali* in JPU 12, Bombay 1912.

8. Edited and translated into Italian by L. *Suali* in GSAI, Vol. 21, 223 ff.; edited together with Municandra's Commentary by the same scholar in Bibl. Ind. 1912 (fasc. 1, Adhy, 1, 2); edited with Municandra's Commentary and detailed Indices, in AUS, Ahmedabad 1924. The title " Drop of the Religion" is an expression of modesty : As the drop of water is to the ocean, so is this work to the religion of the Jina. An abridgment of Haribhadra's Muṇivaicariya is Munipaticaritrasāroddhāra: s. F. *Belloni-Filippi* in GSAI, Vol. 25, 137 ff., 26, 163 ff.

manual of practical morals and asceticism in three sections, the first of which treats of the duties of the layman, the second of the rules for the monks, and the third of the bliss of the saint in Nirvāṇa. The author here uses the Sūtra style in the manner of the Brahmanical Dharma-Sūtras. He availed himself of Umāsvāti's works.[1]

In about 904 A.D. Amṛtacandra[2] wrote works Puruṣārtha-siddhyupāya or Jinapravacanarahasyakośa[3] in 226 Sanskrit verses, Tattvārthasāra,[4] Tattvadīpikā and commentaries on Kunda-kunda's works. In the year 933 A.D. Devasena, who was born in 894 A.D., wrote a manual of the Digambara faith entitled Darśanasāra,[5] and in the same year a Śrāvakācāra, a manual of rules of life for the layman.[6] He is also the author of an Ārādhanasāra, "Essence of Worship,"[7] and of a Tattvasāra.[8] All these books are written in Prākrit verses, Śrāvakācāra being in the Dohā metre which is otherwise not used in scientific works. The Ālāpapaddhati is a short manual of Jaina dogmatics in Sanskrit verses with commentary.[9]

Cāmuṇḍarāya, who won great fame by his warlike deeds as the minister and general of the Gaṅga princes Mārasiṃha II (died 974 A.D.) and Rācamalla or Rājamalla II (974-984

---

1. *Jacobi* in AR 18, 1915, 277 f. mentions also the following works of Haribhadra; Anekāntajayapatākā with the author's commentary printed in YJG, Ahmedabad; Śāstravārttāsamuccya (together with Saḍdarśanasamuccaya and Aṣṭakāni in one vol) Bhavanagar 1908; Aṣṭaka-Prakaraṇa with Abhayadeva's Aṣṭakavṛtti published in Ahmedabad; Upadeśapada, part I, Palitana 1909; Ṣoḍaśa-Prakaraṇa with Commentary, Bombay 1911.

2. *Cf. Peterson*, Report IV, p. ix.

3. Edited in Rāyacandra-Jaina-Śāstramālā Bombay 1905, and in SJG Vol 1, Bombay 1905.

4. Edited in SJG Vol. 8; also in DJGK I, where we find also a philosophical poem Nāṭakasamayasārakalaśāḥ by Amṛtacandra.

5. Edited by Nathuram *Premi*. Bombay 1920, *cf. Peterson*, 3 Reports, pp. 22 ff., 374 ff.

6. *Cf. Hiralal*, Catalogue. p. xlvii f.

7. Edited with Commentary in MDJG, No. 6, Bombay Vik. S. 1973 (1916).

8. Edited in MDJG, No. 13, p. 145 ff.

9. Printed in DJGK I.

A.D.), but devoted himself to pious works in his later years, erected the famous colossal statue of Gommaṭa[1] in Śravaṇa Belgola (Mysore) in about 980 A.D., and wrote the Cāmuṇḍarāya-Purāṇa in the Kanarese language[2] in the year 978 A.D., mentions Ajitasena and Nemicandra as his teachers. The last named who must thus have lived at the close of the 10th and the beginn'ng of the 11th century, has the epithet of Siddhānta-Cakravartin i.e., "He who like a ruler of the world, has a mastery over the totality of the sacred writings," and is a very erudite Digambara writer, who deals with the whole system of the Jaina religion in his works. He mentions Abhayanandin, Indranandin, Vīranandin[3] and Kanakanandin as his teachers. Davvasaṃgaha (Dravyasaṃgraha), "Compendium of Substances,"[4] in 58 Prākrit verses, deals not only with the substances, the living (jīva) and the lifeless (ajīva), but also with release, its causes and conditions, morals and the importance of meditation. Gommaṭasāra[5] is a bulky work, in which the author explains the essence (sāra) of the Jaina doctrine for Gommaṭarāya[6], *i.e.*, Cāmuṇḍarāya. The work, which has the title Pañcasaṃ-

1. Gommaṭa or Bāhubali, the son of the first Jīna Ṛṣabha is highly honoured especially by the Digambaras.

2. *Cf.* S.Ch. *Ghoshal* in SBJ, Vol. 1, Introduction, and A.*Venkatasubbiah* in Ind. Hist. Qu. VI, 1930, 290 f.

3. Vādirāja, author of the Pārśvanātha Kāvya. mentions Vīranandin as a celebrated author ; s. A. *Venkatasubbiah* in Ind. Hist. Qu. VI, p. 294.

4. With a Commentary by Brahmadeva, edited with Introduction. Translation, Notes and an original Commentary in English, by Sarat Chandra *Ghoshal*, Arrah 1917, SBJ, Vol. 1. Bṛhat-Dravyasaṃgraha, edited in Rāyacandra-Jaina Śāstramālā, Bombay 1906-07 ; Laghu-Dravyasaṃgraha is an abridgment made by the author himself; s. *Guerinot* in JA 1912. s. 10, t XIX, p. 377 f.

5. Edited in 4 vols. in Gāndhi-Haribhai-Devakaraṇa Jaina-Granthamālā No. 4 with the Sanskrit Commentaries by Abhayacandra (on Jīva Kāṇḍa) and Keśavavarṇin (on Karma-Kāṇḍa) and a Commentary in Hindī, Calcutta also with Introduction, translation in Sanskrit and English and with a Commentary in English by J.L. *Jaini* in SBJ, Vols. V and VI, Lucknow 1927. Karma-Kāṇḍa edited in Rāyacandra-Jaina-Śāstramālā, Bombay 1928; *cf. Hiralal*, Catalogue, p. xxxiv ff.

6. So called because he erected the Gommaṭa statue.

graha[1] also, consists of two parts, the Jīva-Kāṇḍa in 734 and the Karma-Kāṇḍa in 972 Prākrit verses. The Jīva-kāṇḍa deals with the Jīvas, the "souls," their classification, their origin and nature. It is a kind of natural history of the living beings and this word is to be taken in the comprehensive Jinistic sense.[2] On the whole it is nothing but dry-as-dust, purely scientific enumerations, descriptions and calculations. Only rarely do we light upon a simile, such as in Verse, 202: "As a bearer of burdens bears a burden in a shoulder-pannier, thus the soul bears the burden of Karman, for which the body serves as the shoulder-pannier." There is scarcely any detail in the religion and philosophy of Jinism which does not find a place in the Jīva-Kāṇḍa. Chapter IX deals with the activity of the soul in connection with thought, speech and action, and the origin of Karman, various kinds of speech and the ten kinds of truth (Verse 222). Chapter XI deals with the denizens of hell, which have their origin in sin, with the passions, etc. Chapter XII deals with knowledge, and the various types of knowledge. Space is also here devoted to the knowledge which is acquired by the reading of the sacred scriptures, and a survey of the sacred texts (Aṅgas, Pūrvas, etc.) is given. The Karma-Kāṇḍa treats of the nature of Karma and its relationship to the soul. Cāmuṇḍarāya himself wrote a commentary on the work in the Kanarese language.

The works Labdhisāra, "The Essence of attainment" (of the things which lead to perfection) and Kṣapaṇasāra, "The Essence of Annihilation" (of the Kaṣāyas or sinful passions: anger, pride, falseness and greed.),[3] which are connected with each other, form a sequel to Gommaṭasāra. Trilokasāra,[4] "The Essence of

1. "Compendium of the 5 Things," namely binding (bandha) of the soul to the Karman, that which is bound, that which binds, the cause of the binding, and the kinds of binding.

2. *Cf.* Mrs, *Stevenson*, Heart of Jainism, p. 94 ff. ; *Glasenapp* Jainismus, p. 252 f.

3. The two works are edited together, with Sanskrit and Hindi Commentaries, in Gāndhi-Haribhai-Devakaraṇa-Jaina-Granthamālā, No. 5, Calcutta.

4. *Cf.* Rajenralala *Mitra,* Notices of Sanskrit MSS., Vol, 6, 1882, p. 97ff.; S. Ch. *Ghoshal* in SBJ, Vol. I, p. xlii, f. The edition by Pandit

the Three Worlds," is a complete cosmology. Nemicandra is also said to have written a work Pratiṣṭhāpāṭha on the erection and consecration of statues.[1]

It is not Cāmuṇḍarāya, the pupil of Ajitasena and Nemicandra, but a certain Cāmuṇḍa-Mahārāja,[2] the pupil of Jinasena, who wrote Cāritrasāra,[3] a manual of morals and the path of salvation according to the faith of the Digambaras.

Vardhamāna Sūri[4] is the author of Ācāradinakara,[5] a work on the daily life of the Jaina with all details.

In the year 1015 A.D. Jinacandra Gaṇin, who later called himself Devagupta, wrote a Navapaya of (Navapada-Prakaraṇa) in Prākrit with a Sanskrit commentary. He is also the author of a Navatattva-Prakaraṇa,[6] a treatise on the nine Tattvas or fundamental truths : souls (Jīva), the lifeless (ajīva), merit (puṇya), sin (pāpa), influx (āsrava) of the Karman into the soul, warding off (saṃvara) this influx, binding (bandha) of the Karman, the gradual vanishing away (nirjarā) of the Karman and release (mokṣa).[7] The work consists of only 14 Prākrit Gāthās, on which Abhayadeva wrote a commentary in about 1063 A.D. and Yaśodeva between 1108 and 1117 A.D.

Manohara Lala *Śāstri* mentioned by A. *Venkatasubbiah* (Ind. Hist. Qu. VI, 1930, p. 298) is not accessible to me.

1. *Ghoshal,* l.c., p. xliii f.

2. It is true that both have the epithet Raṇaraṅgasiṃha, "Lion on the stage of battle." Hence both of them must have been generals. However, there were three political personages named Cāmuṇḍarāya in the 11th century, who are distinct from the founder of the Gommaṭa statue; s. A, *Venkatasubbiah* in Ind. Hist. Qu. VI, 1930, pp. 296ff., 299 note 1.

3. Edited with explanation in Hindī, by *Lālā Rāmaji* in SJG 20(Gāndhī-Haribhaī Devakaraṇa-Jaina-Granthamālā 6), Calcutta.

4. The same who, according to the Kharatara-Gaccha-Paṭṭāvali, died the voluntary death by starvation in Saṃvat 1088 (1031 A.D.)? (*Klatt* in Ind. Ant. II, 248.)

5. According to this work (edited several times in India) *Glasenapp* (Der Jainismus, p. 408ff.) describes the rites of the daily life of the Jainas.

6. Edited with the two Commentaries in Ātmānanda-Grantha-Ratnamālā, No. 10, Bhavanagar 1912. *Cf Peterson,* 3 Reports, p. 16, App, 280 ff.; Report IV, p. xxxiv.

7. *Cf.* Mrs. *Stevenson,* Heart of Jainism, p. 94 ff., 299 ff. Sometimes only 7 Tattvas are enumerated, *i.e.* puṇya and pāpa, being contained in āsrava and bandha, are not counted separately; *Cf. Jacobi* in ZDMG 60, 1906. p. 293.

It is perhaps only one of the recensions of the semi-canonical work Nava Tattva[1] on the nine fundamental truths.

Another semi-canonical work is Jīvaviyāra (Jīvavicāra),[2] "Investigation as to the Living Beings," in 51 Āryā verses by Śānti Sūri(died, 1039 A.D.). In this work the beings are classified into such as are in the state of release, and such as are still in the cycle of rebirths : the latter are again classified into lifeless and living, these being in their turn subdivided into denizens of hell, animals, human beings and gods. The work is therefore at one and the same time a treatise on Theology, Zoology, Botany, Anthropology and Mythology.

Maladhāri Hemacandra Sūri, the pupil of Abhayadeva, wrote a Jīvasamāsa[3] in the year 1107 A.D. and a Bhavabhāvanā[4] in 531 Prākrit Gāthās in the year 1113 A.D. He is also the author of commentaries on the Anuyogadvāra-Sūtra,[5] Haribhadra's Āvaśyakavṛtti,[6] and on Jinabhadra's commentary on the Āvaśyaka-Sūtra.[7]

The great Hemacandra is the author of a philosophical work Pramāṇa-Mīmāṃsā, "Examination of the Means of Proof."[8] Mahesara Sūri, who calls himself a pupil of Hema-

---

1. The author and the date of this work, of which there are recensions of 30, 50 and 60 Prākrit stanzas, are not known. An extended recension names Maṇiratna as the author. *Cf. Weber*, HSS. Verz., 11, 3, 841 f.; *Guerinot*. La religion Djaina. p. 85f. The Kalpa Sūtra and Nava Tattva, two works illustrative of the Jaina Religion and Philosophy, translated from the Māgadhi by J. *Stevenson*, London 1848. Neither this book nor the texts printed in Ahmedabad in 1871 and in Bombay in 1905 were accessible to me. The relationship of these texts to one another and to Devagupta's work should be investigated.

2. Edited and translated into French by A. *Guerinot* in JA, 1902, s. 9, t. XIX. pp 231ff. Edited with Pāṭhaka Ratnākara's Commentary by the Yaśovijaya-Jaina-Saṃskṛita Pāṭhaśālā, Ahmedabad 1915. A commentary by Kṣamākalyāṇa is mentioned by *Aufrecht* Bodl. Cat, p. 377.

3. *Cf. Peterson*, Report 1882-83, App., p. 63.

4. With an (anonymous) commentary in Sanskrit, s. *Peterson*, 3 Reports, p. 155f.; *Weber*, HSS. Verz. II, 2, 855ff.

5. Edited with text, Bombay 1924.

6. Edited in JPU 53, Bombay 1920.

7. *Cf. Bühler*, Leben des Hemachandra, p. 74 f.; *Peterson*, Report IV. cxl f.

8. Edited with the author's own commentary. in Ārhata-Mata-Prabhākara, No. 1, Poona 1925.

haṃsa Sūri, and who wrote Sañjamamañjarī,[1] a work on ethics, in Apabhraṃśa, is possibly a contemporary of Hemacandra, at all events earlier than 1309 A.D. The work consists of only 35 Dohā verses, but is furnished with an exhaustive commentary containing a great mass of quotations from Sanskrit, Prākrit and Apabhranṃśa works which make it valuable. The work teaches self-control (sañjama, Skr. Saṃyama) as the only "gate to release." Another Apabhraṃśa poem in 77 Dohā verses is Vairāgyasāra[2] by Suprabhācārya.

Syādvādamañjarī,[3] which was written in the year 1292 A.D. by Malliṣeṇa, is a commentary on the 32 verses of Hemacandra's Anyayogavyavacchedikā, but is at the same time an independent philosophical work which frequently levels criticism at other systems, for instance the Śūnyavāda of the Buddhists. When Malliṣeṇa completed the work, he had, as he himself tells us, the collaboration of Jinaprabha Sūri.

In the first half of the 13th century, Āśādhara, who is highly esteemed both as a poet and a scholar, wrote a number of Stotras, one narrative work and several learned works. According to the very detailed panegyric (praśasti) at the end of his Dharmāmṛta, he was friend of King Arjunadeva of Mālava. The sage Udayasena said of him : "Great is Āśādhara, the swan on the lotus of the Vyāghreravāla family, the son of Sallakṣaṇa, and the Kālidāsa of the Kali age of the world,"

1. Text with translation into Sanskrit by P.D. *Gune* in Ann. Bh. Inst. I. 1919-21, p, 157ff. Mahesara Sūri is also the author of a Kālakācārya-Kathānaka, of which there is a manuscript written in the year 1309.

2. Discovered and edited by H.D. *Velankar* in Ann. Bh. Inst. 9. 1928, p. 272 ff. Another author who wrote learned works in Apabhraṃśa (Yogasāra, Paramātmaprakāśa, Śrāvakācāra Dohaka and Dohāpāhuda) is Joindu (Yogīndra), who wrote before Hemacandra; s. A.N. *Upadhye* in Ann. Bh. Inst. 12, 1931, 132 ff. Yogasāra is published in MDJG No. 21, p. 55 ff. (with Sanskrit translation).

3. Edited in Chowkhambā Sanskrit Series, No. 9, fasc, 32,33, Benares 1900 and in YJG No. 30, Benares. Vīra S. 2438 (1911) and in-Ārhata-Mata-Prabhākara No. 3, Vīra S. 2452 (1925). The chapter which contains a criticism of the proofs of the existence of God, translated into German by H. *Jacobi*, Die Entwicklung der Gottesidee bei den Indern, Bonn 1923, p. 102ff. *Cf. Weber*, HSS. Verz. II, 3, 940ff.; *Peterson*, Report IV, p. lxxxix; *Barth*, RHR 45, 1902, p. 173=Oeuvres II, 376.

and the poet-prince Vilhaṇa,[1] the wa: and peace minister of Vijayavarman, King of the Vindhyas, said of him : "Noble Āśādhara ! Know that, as a son of Sarasvatī you are naturally my brother and friend." The principal work of Āśādhara is Dharmāmṛta, "Nectar of religion,"[2] which, in two parts, Sāgāra and Anāgāra-Dharmāmṛta treats of the duties of the layman living in the house and of the homeless ascetic. He himself wrote a commentary on his work in the year 1243. D.A.[3]

Devendra Sūri,[4] a pupil of Jagaccandra, wrote probably at the period of Vastupāla, minister of king Vīra Dhavala of Gujarat (died 1241 A.D.) and of his brother Tejaḥpāla (died 1251 A.D.) a Vandaru-Vṛtti, a commentary on the Śrāddha-pratikramaṇa-Sūtra.[5] He is also the author of a Siddhapañcāśikā,[6] an extract from the Diṭṭhivāya in 50 stanzas, and in the year 1241 A.D. he wrote Upamitibhavaprapañca-Kathā-Sāroddhāra,[7] an extract from Siddharṣi's famous poem. First and foremost, however, he is the author of the first 5 Karmagranthas.[8] The Karmagranthas are six books in Prākrit verses, in which the entire doctrine of Karman which is very intricate in

1. This Vilhaṇa, who is also mentioned in inscriptions of the kings of Mālava, has, of course, no connection with the Kashmiri poet Bilhaṇa who lived from about 1070 till 1090. *Cf. Kielhorn* in Ep. Ind. 9, 1908, 107f.

2. There appears to be no edition of the work, but manuscripts are existent. See for this and other works of Āśādhara, *Bhandarkar*, Report 1883-84, pp. 103 ff., 390 ff.; *Hiralal*, Catalogue, pp. XXXVI, 644, 669, 682, 706 (Sarasvatī-Stotra), 709 (Siddhacakra-Stotra). A Triṣaṣṭi-Smṛti contains stories of 63 great men according to the Jaina-Purāṇas.

3. His Jinayajña-Kalpa is dated 1228 A.D.. the Sāgāra-Dharmāmṛta 1239 A.D. Āśādhara was a contemporary of no less than five successive kings of Mālava, from Vindhyavarman to Devapāla's son Jaitugideva; s. *Kielhorn* in Ep. Ind. 9, 1908. 107 f.

4. *Cf. Peterson*, Report IV, p. lvii f. He is said to have died in the year 1270 A.D. in Mālava; s. *Klatt* in Ind. Ant. 11, p. 255.

5. Edited in JPU No. 8, Bombay 1912.

6. *Cf. Weber*, HSS. Verz. II, 2, 534ff.

7. *Cf. Peterson*, Report VI, pp. xf., 40 ff. On the basis of Chapter VIII of the Mahā-Nisīha he wrote a Susaḍha Kahā in 519 Āryā stanzas; s. W. *Schubring*, Das Mahānisīha, p. 48 ff.

8. Edited in Vol. 4 of Prakaraṇa-Ratnākara, Bombay 1880; with the author's commentaries on Books 1 to 5 and commentary by Malayagiri on Book 6, by the Śrī-Jaina-Dharma Prasāraka Sabhā, Bhavanagar 1909-1911. *Cf. Weber*. HSS. Verz. II, 3, 837 ff.

the religion of the Jainas, is treated in all its details. The books are as follows: Karmavipāka, Karmastava, Bandhasvāmitva, Ṣaḍaśītika, Śataka and Saptatikā. Book VI consists of 70 verses by Candramahattara, to which his teacher (?) Devendra Sūri added a further 19 verses. Candramahattara is also the author of the Pañcasaṃgraha,[1] a compendium of the whole doctrine of Karman. Śivaśarma Sūri's Karmaprakṛti[2] in 475 Gāthās, is a more exhaustive work. If the tradition is to be believed, all these works can be traced back to the Diṭṭhivāya. They have all been commented on by Malayagiri, who also wrote commentaries on several canonical works.[3]

In the 15th century Sakalakīrti, who probably died in about 1464 A.D., wrote Tattvārthasāradīpaka,[4] a large work in 12 chapters on the entire system of the Jaina religion. The first chapter teaches how the soul attains to the 5 kinds of knowledge by annihilating the Karman. One of these is attained through sacred books which on this occasion are completely enumerated, with exact information as to the number of words, and in the case of the Aṅgas and Pūrvas even the number of syllables. A second work by Sakalakīrti is Praśnottaropāsakācāra,[5] in which the duties of lay adherents are taught in the form of question-answers.

Round about 1494 A.D. Śrutasāgara, the pupil of Vidyānandin, wrote a Jainedrayajñavidhi, a ritual work after the style of the Brahmanical Prayogas, a Tattvārthadīpikā, and a commentary on Kundakunda's Ṣaṭprābhṛta.[6] Kupakṣakauśika-

1. Edited with Malayagiri's Commentary, by *Hīrālāla Haṃsarāja*, Jamnagar 1909. 4 vols.

2. Edited with Malayagiri's Commentary, JPU, No. 17, Bhavanagar 1912.

3. On Malayagiri *cf. Peterson*, Report IV, p. lxxxviii. A manuscript of Malayagiri's Commentary on Karmaprakṛti is dated 1395 A.D., a manuscript of the commentary on the Nandī-Sūtra is dated 1235 A.D., a MS. of the commentary on the Vyavahāra-Sūtra is dated 1253 A.D.; s. *Peterson*, 3 Reports, Appendix, pp. 35f., 49f., 70 f., 157. On all the works on the doctrine of Karma mentioned here, s. H. v. *Glasenapp*, Die Lehre von Karman in der Philosophie der Jainas nach den Karmagranthas zusammengestellt, Leipzig 1915; also *Glasenapp*, Der Jainismus, pp. 167, 184.

4. *Cf. Bhandarkar*, Report 1883-84, pp. 106ff., 393ff.

5. *Bhandarkar*, l. c., p., 116f.

6. *Cf. Bhandarkar*, l.c., p. 117 and *Peterson*, Report 11. pp. 8 ff., 158 ff. and Report IV, p. cxxiii f.

sahasrakiraṇa, "The Sun for the Owls of the heretical Doctrine,"[1] by the Śvetāmbara Dharmasāgara, is a polemic treatise against the Digambara Jainas. This treatise, written in 1573 A.D. in Prākrit, with a commentary in Sanskrit by the same author, violently refutes the doctrines of the Digambaras, especially their views on going naked and the exclusion of women from release.

We would also mention Vinayavijaya, the son of Tejaḥpāla, who in the year 1649 compiled Lokaprakāśa,[2] a comprehensive encyclopaedia of everything a Jaina needs to know.

Yaśovijaya (1624-1688) of the Tapāgaccha, is a prominent Jaina teacher, reformer and author of the 17th century.[3] He endeavoured to unite the two sects of the Digambaras and Śvetāmbaras, by seeking to prove that the Kevalin, the completely Enlightened, so long as he leads a physical life, must take nourishment, that women can attain to release, and that the ordinary objects of usage of the monks, garments etc., are not to be counted as "possessions," and that the saintly life does not exclude life in the world. Even at the present day he is still cited as a model and a saint. His name is borne by two educational institutions (Pāṭhaśālās) in Benares and Mehsana, and by the collections of texts (Granthamālās) published by them.[4] Among his works we mention Adhyātmaparīkṣā in Prākrit with a Sanskrit commentary by the author himself, Jñānabinduprakaraṇa[5] and Jñānasāra or Aṣṭakaprakaraṇa.[6] He also revised the Dharmasaṃgraha[7] which was written by Mānavijaya in the year

1. The title of the treatise is also Pravacana-Parīkṣā. It is dealt with by A. *Weber* in SBA 1882, p. 793ff.

2. Edited by *Hīrālāla Haṃsarāja* in 3 vols., Jamnagar 1910. The same author also wrote a commentary on the Kalpa-Sūtra in the year 1639. *Cf.* H. D. *Velankar*, Descriptive Catalogue of Sanskṛta and Prākṛta MSS. in the Library of the Bombay Royal Asiatic Society, Vols. III-IV, 1930, pp. 386f., 446.

3. On him *cf. Jacobi* in AR. 18, 1915, 271, 278 f. and *Glasenapp*, Der Jainismus, pp. 72, 109, 342.

4. Edited in JPU No. 5, Bombay 1911.

5. A manuscript written in the year 1675, described by *Peterson*, 3 Reports, p. 192f.

6. Published together with Haribhadra's Aṣṭaka and other works, Surat. 1918.

7. Edited in JPU, Nos. 26 and 45, Bombay 1915 and 1918. The work is very rich in quotations. According to the index 103 works and 26 authors are quoted.

1681. This is a bulky work on the duties of the householder and the ascetic.

In our own times, too, the Jainas not only turn their attention to the editing of texts, which are being published in numerous series, and are most generously made accessible to European scholars also, but they are still productive in literature proper, and are writing original works in Sanskrit and the vernaculars on Jaina philosophy and dogmatics, The publication of a series of valuable editions in the Yaśovijaya-Jaina-Granthamālā is the immortal legacy of the great Jaina saint and teacher Vijaya Dharma Sūri,[1] who also wrote a number of works in Gujarātī, Hindī and Sanskrit (Pramāṇa-Paribhāṣā, Jaina-Tattva-Jñāna). A pupil of this saint is Muni Nyāyavijaya, from whose pen two works in Sanskrit have appeared : Adhyātma-Tattvāloka[2] and Nyāya-Kusumāñjali.[3]

The Jainas have extended their activities beyond the sphere of their own religious literature to a far greater extent than the Buddhists have done, and they have memorable achievements in the secular sciences to their credit, in philosophy, grammar, lexicography, poetics, mathematics,[4] astronomy and astrology, and even in the science of politics. In one way or other there is always some connection even of these "profane" works with religion. In Southern India the Jainas have also rendered services in developing the Dravidian languages, Tamil and Telugu,

---

1. On the life and works of *Vijaya Dharma Sūri*; s. L.P. *Tessitori*, A Jain Āchārya of the present day, Calcutta 1917, A. J. *Sunavala*, Vijaya Dharma Suri, His Life and Work, Cambridge 1922; *Vijaya Indra Suri*, Reminiscences of Vijaya Dharma Sūri. Allahabad, 1924; Sayings of Vijaya Dharma Suri translated by Charlotte *Krause*, Bhavanagar 1930.

2. The Spiritual Light. with Gujarātī Translation and Explanatory Notes, translated into English by Motichand Jhaverchand *Mehata*, Bhavanagar 1920.

3. With Introduction in English and Translation and Notes in English and Gujarātī by Hiralal Rasikadās *Kapadia*, Baroda 1922.

4. On the great interest taken in Mathematics by Jainas of ancient and modern times, s. D. M. *Roy* in Ann. Bh. Inst. 8, 1926-27, p. 145 ff.; Bibhutibhusan *Datta*, The Jaina School of Mathematics, in Bulletin of the Calcutta Mathematical Society, Vol. XXI, 2. 1929, p. 115 ff.

and especially the Kanarese literary language. They have, besides, written a considerable amount in Gujarātī, Hindī and Marvārī. Thus we see that they occupy no mean position in the history of Indian literature and Indian thought.

APPENDIX (on page 4).

THE YEAR OF BUDDHA'S DEATH. DID A GOTAMA BUDDHA LIVE ?

Much as has already been written about the year of Buddha's death, it is by no means firmly established as yet. According to the Singhalese tradition, 544 B.C. would be the death-year, but this is rejected by most European scholars as incompatible with the chronology of the kings of Magadha. According to M. de Z. *Wickremasinghe*, there used to be in Ceylon too, an era beginning with 483 B.C. as the year of Buddha's death, whilst 544 B.C. as the death-year cannot be traced back further than about the middle of the 11th century.[1] However, all the seemingly convincing evidence which we thought we had acquired in favour of various dates between 477 and 487 B.C., has in every case proved to be uncertain and doubtful. *Cf.* J.F. *Fleet* JRAS 1909, 1 ff., 323ff. 981 ff., 1910, 1308, 1912 239ff.; *Oldenberg*, AR 13, 1910. 611 ff., V, Gopala *Aiyer* Ind. Ant.37,1908,341ff.; W. *Geiger*, The Mahavaṃsa, Transl., p. xxii ff.; J. *Charpentier*, Ind. Ant. 43, 1914, 130 ff.; T.W. *Rhys Davids* in Cambridge History I, 171 ff,; E. *Hultzsch*, Inscriptions of Aśoka (1925), p. xxxii f., xxxv, H. *Jacobi*, Buddhas und Mahāviras Nirvāṇa und die politische Entwicklung Magadhas zu Jener Zeit, in SBA 1930, p. 55 7ff. K. P. Jayswal (JBORS I, 1915, 67ff. 197ff; *cf.* III, 1917, 425 ff.; IV, 1918, 264 ff.) again endeavoured to prove, on the basis of a new reading of the Hāthīgumphā inscription of Khāravela, that the year 544 B.C. is the year of Buddha's death, and V.A. *Smith* (JRAS 1918, 543 ff.; Early History, 4th ed.. 49 f.) agreed with him, though he is also compelled to say : "I do not believe that the date can be fixed with anything like certainty." *Jayaswal's* readings and calculations have, however, been shown to be untenable, by R.C. *Majumdar* (Ind. Ant. 47, 1918, 223 f.; 48, 1919, 187 ff.; *cf.* R. P. *Chanda*, Ind. Ant. 48, 214 ff.; K.G. Śankara *Aiyar*, Ind. Ant. 49, 1920, 43 ff).

---

1. *Cf.* W. *Geiger*, The Mahāvaṃsa, Transl., p. xxviii.

A.B. Keith, too (Buddhist Philosophy, p. 32) refutes *Jayaswal's* argumentation, but even he declares the usual dating 487-477 to be uncertain, and says that "the case against the traditional date is insufficient to justify its rejection out and out."[1] When we take into consideration that there is sufficient evidence to show that Buddha was a contemporary of kings Bimbisāra and Ajātaśatru, whom we can place with a fair amount of certainty in the 6th and 5th centuries B.C., then we are at least justified in saying that the best working hypothesis is to place the life of Buddha into this period too.[2]

It is true that we are taking it for granted that Gotama Buddha did really live. R. Otto *Franke* ZDMG 69, 1915, 455 f.)—like E. *Senart* and A. *Barth.* before him—doubts even this, and is of opinion that "the so-called doctrine of Buddha is perhaps only the collection of a bundle of didactic elements from the vast treasury of philosophical thoughts" which came into being in India in the centuries preceding the Christian era. In another passage (OZ 4, 1915-16, p. 10) the same scholar says : "For me Gotama Buddha is not a bit less mythical than his six 'mythical predecessors'"; "Buddha" according to him is but a dogmatical conception, and all the seven Buddhas are but "paradigmata of the dogmatical Buddha," who to him is apparently nothing more than "a form, grown nebulous, of an ancient conception of the deity"' "perhaps of the philosophical conception of the pantheistic divinity," perhaps a form of this divinity, which was especially associated with trees. How improbable and how baseless is this hypothesis compared to the assumption that Gotama Buddha is an historical personage, who enjoyed such great veneration that myths and legends were woven around him ! True, we know very, very little about the real life of Gotama. On the other hand, tradition and even monuments afford us a few facts which there are no grounds to doubt. *Oldenberg* (Reden des Buddha, p. xx f.) is right when he says that there is no reason to doubt the accounts that Buddha

1. *Cf.* also E. J. *Thomas,* The Life of Buddha, p. 27; G. P. *Malalasekara,* The Pali Literature of Ceylon, London 1928, p. 15; Mrs. *Rhys Davids,* Sakya or Buddhist Origins, London 1931. p. 434.

2. *Cf.* also Appendix VI.

belonged to the Sakya race and was born at Kapilavatthu, in all other respects so insignificant a place. At any rate this tradition was already so firmly established in about 250 B.C., that king Aśoka went on a pilgrimage to Buddha's birthplace, and recorded the memory of his pilgrimage in an inscription on the column found in 1896 near the Nepalese village of Paderia. The inscription reads : "When King Piyadasi had been anointed 20 years, he came here in person and paid his devotion here, because the Buddha, the sage born of the Sakya race, was born here."

It was also in the vicinity of Kapilavatthu, near Piprāvā, on the Nepalese frontier, that Mr. W.C. *Peppe* found in 1898 a reliquary chest containing a crystal urn with remains of bones which were formerly regarded as actual relics of the Buddha.[1] The readings and explanation of the inscription which is written round the rim of the lid of the urn, certainly admits of various interpretations. Even if the explanation : "This is the reliquary treasure of the Lord Buddha of the Sakyas," is, as I believe, the correct one, this does not constitute a proof of the "authencity" of the relics; it only shows that at Aśoka's time (the script is that of Aśoka inscriptions) people *believed* that these were relics of the Buddha.[2] Yet this belief would scarcely have arisen, unless a man venerated as a saint, as a "Buddha," had actually lived in the days before Aśoka.

Even when we eliminate all legendary and mythical elements from the tradition, the Buddhist texts still afford us a life-like and very plausible picture of the personality of Gotama and his career as the founder of religion and as a preacher.[3] If the personality of the Buddha, with its strong reaction on the contemporaries, had never existed, it would indeed be passing strange that in Buddhist literature it is precisely the picture of the Master which is so living. "It is no exaggeration to say," says Sir Charles *Eliot* (I, 297), "that the Buddha is the most living

1. *Cf. e.g.* R. *Pischel.* Leben und Lehre des Buddha, 4th Ed., by J. *Nobel*, 1926, p. 48f.

2. *Cf.* R. O. *Franke* in OZ 4, 1915-16, 1ff.; E.J. *Thomas*, The Life of Buddha, 160ff.

3. See also E.J. *Thomas*, The Life of Buddha, p. 225f.

figure in Hindu literature. He stands before us more distinctly not only than Yājñavalkya and Śaṅkara, but also than modern teachers like Nānak and Rāmānuja, and the reason of this distinction can, I think, be nothing but the personal impression which he made on his age."

In addition to this, the accounts of the Buddhists regarding Gotama Buddha and his contemporaries are in striking agreement with those of the Jainas regarding Mahāvīra, and the two currents of tradition supplement each other.[1] Lastly, when we call to mind that it has repeatedly happened in India, down to quite modern times, that founders of a religion or of a religious sect are deified even during their own lifetime, then we can only call it exaggerated, barren scepticism to doubt that Gotama Buddha lived just as certainly as did Keshub Chunder Sen, the founder of the "Brahmo Samaj of India," who died in 1884, and who was worshipped as a deity by some of his adherents as early as in the year 1868.[2]

If we wish to regard Buddhism, with *Franke*, as "only a collected bundle of general Indian doctrines," we should still have to explain why this "bundle," in spite of all the changes of Buddhism, shows such individual traits, if there was not an individual, a creative personality, who bound this "bundle" into something entirely new and special, and stamped the impress of his personality upon it. Even if we were unable to give credence to the Buddhist chroniclers, and could not determine the exact date of the Buddha, but were compelled to limit ourselves to affirming that his doctrine came into being before Aśoka's time, we cannot doubt the personality of the founder[3] any

1. *Cf. Oldenberg*, Buddha, 5th Ed., Berlin 1906, p. 95 f. As to whether Buddha is historical, *ibid*, p. 93ff.

2. J.C. *Oman*, Brahmans, Theists and Muslisms of India, London 1907, p. 122f.

3. *Franke* admits in a later essay (ZDMG 69, 1915, p. 456) that such a personage existed, when he says : "Let us content ourselves with the conviction that it was no ordinary mind which evolved what we call earliest Buddhism, and with the fact that he was an Indian Aryan of (be it said provisionally) one of the pre-Christian centuries but not the latest of those centuries." Why this "Indian Aryan" should not have been called Gotama and received the epithet "Buddha," it is really difficult to see.

more than that of Kālidāsa, whose date we can also determine only approximately.

APPENDIX II (on page 14).

What is Pāli ?

Wilhelm Geiger, Pāli Literature und Sprache, p. 5, does not explain the words *anujānāmi bhikkhave sakāya niruttiyā buddhavacana pariyāpāpunituṇ* Culla Vagga V, 33) like the translators in SBE, Vol. 20, p. 150 f., "I allow you. O brethren, to learn the word of the Buddhas each in his own dialect," but according to the commentary of Buddhaghosa : "I order you to learn the word of the Buddha in *his* own language" (i.e. in Māgadhī, the language spoken by the Buddha). Consequently, *Geiger* regards Pāli as an attempt to re-construct the word of the Buddha in Buddha's own language. According to this the Pāli Canon would be identical with the Canon of Pāṭaliputra not only in content, but also in language. I do not think, however, that *Geiger's* explanation of Culla-Vagga V, 33 is tenable. *Geiger* is of opinion that, in the translation "I allow you" etc., we would expect a *vo* after *anujānāni*, to which *sakāya* would refer. However, this *vo* can, I think, be supplied easily enough from the vocative *bhikkave*, especially when we remember that the expression *anujānāmi bhikkhave* occurs on almost every page of the Vinaya-Piṭaka, and has become stereotyped. If *Geiger's* explanation were correct, we should also expect that not only the translation into Sanskrit, but also the learning of the word of Buddha in the dialects of the monks of various districts, would have been forbidden. Then again, the stern words attributed to Buddha, in which he rejects the suggestion that the word of Buddha should be translated into the language of the Veda or set in verse after the manner of the Veda, because that would not contribute to the conversion of the unconverted nor increase the number of the converted, are additional evidence that the chief concern was to propagate the word of Buddha as widely as possible, which is only possible if the monks in various districts preach the word of Buddha in languages of those districts.[1]

E. J. *Thomas* (The Life of Buddha, p. 253 f.) explains this passage differently. He translates *nirutti* by "grammar" and *chando* by "metre," and makes Buddha say : "I order you, monks, to master the word of Buddha (Buddhavacanam) in its own grammar." He does not think it possible that *sakāya nirut-tiyā* can mean "each in his own dialect," and believes that the passage in question only contains a prohibition to versify the Canon. Even if this explanation be accepted, it is difficult to see why a versification of the word of Buddha should be detri-mental to the propagation of the doctrine. Moreover, *nirutti* does not mean "grammar," but "linguistic expression."[2] *Chandas* may mean "metre" just as well as "Veda." *Chandas* has the latter meaning in *Sāvitthī chandaso mukhaṃ* too (Vinaya-Piṭaka, Mahā-Vagga VI. 35, 8 and Sutta-Nipāta 568). *Oldenberg* and *Rhys Davids* have taken it in the sense of "Veda dialect," and refer to the use of " *chandasi*" by Pāṇini. Buddhaghosa too says : *chan-daso āropemā ti vedaṃ viya sakkaṭa-bhāsāya vācanāmaggam āropema.*[3] The translation : "I allow you, O monks, to learn the word of the Buddha each in his own language" also accords well with Majjhima-Nikāya 139 (III, pp. 234f., 237) wherein it is said that the "middle way" which leads to rest, is for a man not to insist unduly on his own provincial dialect (janapada-nirutti) and at the same time not to diverge from general lingu-istic usage.[4]

The commentaries frequently use the word "Pāli " in the sense of "canonical text" in contrast to the Attha-Kathā, some-

---

1. *Geiger's i.e.,* Buddhaghoṣa's explanation of the passage is also rejected by Friedrich *Weller* in ZB, N. F. I, 1922, p. 211ff. (to which *Geiger* replies in the same publication, p. 213f.) and by A.B. *Keith* in Ind. Hist. Qu. 1, 1925, p. 501.

2. *Cf.* Digha I, 202; Saṃyutta III, 71; *Childers,* Dictionary of the Pāli Language s.v. nirutti : "use or expression of a language." PTS. Dic. s.v. : "way of speaking, expression."

3. The form chandaso from the neuter chando is difficult to explain.

4. It is said here that, for instance, a different word is used for "bowl": pāti patta, vittha, sarāva, dhāropa, poṇa, pisila, and that each one considers his word as the only correct one, but that in the interests of peace it is best for each one to use the word which is current in his land.

times also in the sense of "language of the canonical texts;" in the Jātaka commentary "Pāli" often means the Jātaka-Gāthās. Curiously enough the term "Pāli" is used at the present day by the country people of Eastern Bengal to denote the verse portions in their prose narratives (Rūpa-Kathās and Gīta-Kathās).[1]

Phonetic peculiarities of the Māgadhī dialect in Pāli have already been indicated by E. *Kuhn*, Beiträge zur Pāli-Grammatik, Berlin, 1875, p. 9, E. *Müller*. Grammar of the Pāli Language, London, 1884, and R. *Pischel*, SBA 1904, p. 807. E. *Windisch* (OC XIV, 1906, p. 252ff.) endeavoured to prove that Māgadhī forms the foundation of Pāli. S. *Levi* (JA 1912 10, t. XX, p. 495ff.) attempted to trace remnants of an earlier Māgadhī Canon. According to *Lüders* (Bruchstücke buddhistischer Dramen, p. 41) it would be more correct to speak of "Old Ardha Māgadhī" as the foundation of Pāli. "This dialect agrees in essentials with the Māgadhī of the Aśoka Inscriptions, but in part it already represents a more advanced stage of development" (*Lüders* in SBA 1927, p. 123). The demonstration by P. V. *Bapat* (Ind. Hist. Qu. 4, 1928, 23ff.) that Pāli cannot be derived from Ardha-Māgadhī, as the last-named shows a later stage of development of Prākrit than Pāli, refers only to Jaina Ardha-Māgadhī. Paiśācī elements in Pāli have been pointed out by *Konow* (ZDMG 64, 1910, 114ff.) *Grierson* (Bhandarkar Comm. Vol., p. 117 ff.) and Nalinaksha *Dutt* (Early History of the Spread of Buddhism, p. 249ff.). *Konow* localises Pāli and Paiśācī in the district of the Vindhya hills. This leads us to the district of Ujjain, where Pāli had already been localised by *Westergaard*, E. *Kuhn* and R. O. *Franke* (Pāli und Sanskrit, Strassburg 1902, 127 ff.). *Grierson* regards Paiśācī as the local dialect of Kekaya and Eastern Gandhāra. Kekaya, especially Takṣaśilā was at the time of the Buddha famous for learning. *Grierson* concludes from this that Pāli is the literary form of the Māgadhī language, which was in those days used in India as *Koiné*, and was in particular utilised in Takṣaśilā as the language of instruction. *Cf.* also *Eliot* I. 282 ff.

1. *Cf.* Ind. Hist. Qu. 4, 1928, 6 ff., and Dineshchandra *Sen*, Eastern Bengal Ballads Vol. III, part 1, Calcutta, 1928, p. lxv ff.

According to S.K. *Chatterji* (Origin and Development of the Bengali Language, 1926, I, 55 ff.) the phonetics and morphology of Pāli show most resemblance to Śaurasenī, but have adopted archaic forms from north-western and other Aryan dialects.

Oldenberg (Vinaya Piṭaka I, Introduction, p. 1 ff.) held the view that Buddhism was not introduced to Ceylon by Mahinda as related in the Singhalese chronicles, but spread gradually over the Island from the neighbouring Kaliṅga land, and that Pāli is the language of the Kaliṅga land. There are, however, no proofs for this.

T.W. *Rhys Davids* (PTS Dic., Foreword) is of opinion that Pāli is based upon the dialect of Kosala, as it was spoken in the 6th and 7th centuries B.C. But what do we know of the dialects of these centuries ?

Max *Walleser* (Sprache und Heimat des Palikanons, Heidelberg 1924, and ZB VII, 1926, 56 ff.) made an unfortunate attempt to explain Pāli as the "language of Pāṭaliputra" even by way of etymology.[1]

There is nothing to support the assumption that Pāli originated in Ceylon. Though Singhalese has much in common with Pāli, we should rather assume that it is the Pāli which influenced Singhalese. *Cf.* W. *Geiger*, Literature und Sprache der Singhalesen (Grundriss I, 10), p. 91.

Cf. Geiger, Pāli Literatur und Sprache, pp. 1-5; H. *Reichelt* in Festschrift fur Wilhelm Streitberg, 1924, p. 244 ff.; A.B. *Keith* in Ind. Hist. Qu. I, 1925, 501 ff.; W. *Wust*, Indisch (Grundriss der indogermanischen Sprach und Altertumskunde II .4,1), p. 44 f. Mrs. *Rhys Davids*, Sakya or Buddhist Origins, p.429ff.

The latest discussion on the problem of Pāli and its home are those by R. *Siddārtha*, Origin and Development of Pāli Language with special reference to Sanskrit Grammar, and by A.B. *Keith*, The Home of Pāli, in B.C. *Law*, Buddhistic Studies, p. 641 ff., and p. 728 ff.

1. E.J. *Thomas* (Ind. Hist. Qu. 4, 1928, 773 ff.) also rejects this hypothesis.

APPENDIX III (on page 17)

Bhābrū-Bairāt-Edict of Aśoka

The small boulder which contains the inscription of Bairat, is now preserved in Calcutta in the Asiatic Society of Bengal, and for this reason the inscription is described by E. *Hultzsch* (Corpus Inscriptionum Indicarum, Vol. I Inscriptions of Aśoka, New Edition, p. xxv) as "Calcutta-Bairat Rock-Inscription," as there is also another rock inscription of Bairat. The boulder was discovered in 1840 on an eminence in the neighbourhood of Bairat. As the discoverer stated that Bairat was not far from "Bhabra," the inscription was also called the "Bhabra edict." Bhabra is, however, only an erroneous name for Bhābrū, which is, as a matter of fact, 12 miles from Bairat. Many scholars have devoted themselves to identifying the texts mentioned in the inscription, in the Canon. and appreciating their historical significance, *Cf.* E., *Hultzsch,* l. c., pp. xliii f., 172ff.; *Senart* in JA 1884, s. 8, t. III, p. 478ff.; 1885, t. V, p. 391 ff.; and 1887, t. IX, p. 498ff. with an excellent facsimile of the inscription ; H. *Oldenberg*, Vinaya Piṭakam Ed., Vol. I, p. xl note; K.E. *Neumann,* Reden Gotamo Buddhos I, pp. 135, 324, 567 and WZKM 11, 1897, p. 159f.; T.W. *Rhys Davids* in JPTS 1896. p. 93ff.; JRAS 1898, p. 639f.; Buddhist India, p. 169f.; Dialogues of the Buddha, SBB II, 1899, Preface, p. xiii f.; S. *Levi* in JA 1896, s. 9, t. VII, p. 475ff.; E. *Hardy* in JRAS 1901, p. 311 ff. and Aśoka, p. 58ff. and V.A. *Smith* in JRAS 1901, p. 574; Aśoka, 3rd Ed., p. 157; *Kern*, Manual, pp. 2 and 113; *Pischel* in SBA 1904, p. 807f., A.J. *Edmunds* in JRAS 1913, 385 ff.; *Kosambi* in Ind. Ant. 41,40 ; *Barua* in JRAS 1915, p. 805; Ind. Ant. 48, 8ff.; *Eliot* I, 290f.; F. *Weller* in Asia Major 5, 1930, p. 166.

The texts recommended by Aśoka are :—

(1) *Vinaya-samukase*, probably "the principal sermon of the Vinaya-Piṭaka," *i.e.*, the sermon of Benares, which in numerous passages (Vinaya-P., Mahā-Vagga 1,7, 6; 8, 2 etc., Udāna V, 3) is called sāmukkaṃsikā dhammadesanā "the most excellent sermon." Thus according to A. J. *Edmunds* in JRAS 1913, p. 385. *Oldenberg* and *Rhys Davids* (SBE 13, p. xxvi f.)

explained it as "Abstract of the Vinaya" and assumed that this referred to the Pâtimokkha. B.M. *Barua* translates ; "Excellent treatise on Vinaya moral discipline."

(2) *Aliya-vasāṇi,* the dasa ariya-vāsā, "the ten rules of life of the noble one" which are taught in the Saṃgīti-Suttanta and in the Dasuttara-Suttanta of the Dīgha-Nikāya (III, pp. 269 and 291) and in the Aṅguttara-Nikāya X, 19 (Vol. V p. 29),

(3) *Anāgata-bhayāni,* "the five future dangers," which are taught in the Aṅguttara-Nikāya V, 77-80 (Vol. III, p. 100ff.).

(4) *Munigāthā,* probably the Muni-Sutta in the Sutta-Nipāta 206 to 220.

(5) *Moneyasute,* doubtless the moneyyāni in the Itivuttaka 67, also in Aṅgutt. III, 120 (Vol. I, p. 273).

(6) *Upatisapasine,* "Questions of Upatissa." As Upatissa is a name of Sāriputta, and as the Sāriputta-Sutta in Sutta-Nipāta 955-975 contains questions of Sāriputta, which are answered by Buddha, I have no doubt that this is what is meant. Thus already *Neumann* and now also *Walleser.*

(7) *Lāghulovāde musāvādam adhigichya bhagavatā Budhena bhāsite,* "the exhortations to Rāhula, which were uttered by the Lord Buddha in regard to lying," in Majjhima-Nikāya 61. As there is also a second Rāhulovāda-Sutta (Majjhima 62), Aśoka also states the subject-matter of the text recommended by him. Thus Aśoka must have known both texts.

The significance of the Bairat Edict should neither be overrated nor yet under-estimated. It is overrating it to conceive of it, as *Barua* l. c. has done, "as a rare historical document, which conclusively proves the existence of the Buddhist Canon in the third century B.C., in the same form, and with almost the same titles to its different passages, as we have now." On the other hand, it is under-estimating it, when *Barth* (RHR 5, 1882, 239 f. = Oeuvres, I, p. 342) declares that the titles do not prove that there was a Canon in existence in those days, but that on the contrary they show that though Buddhism had a literature, it had not yet a Canon. Similarly *La Vallee Poussin,* Bouddhisme, Études et Matériaux (Mémoires Acad. Belgique, 55, 1898), p. 32f., says that the titles prove nothing for the antiquity of the Pāli Canon : according to him they prove merely the antiquity of Sūtras and Vinayas which are related to the Pāli texts, and that Aśoka does not allude to a definite Canon. The very words of the edict : "Whatever has been uttered by the Lord Buddha, all that is well said."[1] make it appear probable that there was something in the nature of a Canon in existence, wherein that which was regarded as having been uttered by Buddha, was collected, and which, therefore, to the minds of believers, bore the stamp of genuineness. When Aśoka says that, though everything which the Lord uttered is good, he especially recommends a few selected texts not only to the monks and nuns, but also to the lay adherents of both sexes, it seems as though he must have been acquainted with a considerable number of such texts. We shall therefore not be unduly bold in arguing from the Edict that, at the time when it was written, there was a canonical collection of Sutta and Vinaya texts in the Māgadhī language. As the texts enumerated by Aśoka appear in various books of the Pāli Canon, it is, to say the least of it, very probable indeed, that the Pāli Canon, as far as the Sutta and Vinaya-Piṭaka are concerned, was very closely related to the Māgadhī Canon. The exaggerated scepticism of *Minayeff,* Recherches, p. 84 ff., has already been confuted by *Oldenberg*, ZDMG 52, 1898, 634 ff.

According to T. *Bloch*, ZDMG 63, 1909, 325 ff., the purpose of the inscription of Bairat was to institute public recitals of the texts named and to make a foundation for this. Unfortunately, however, there is nothing to this effect in the inscription.

As to the correctness of the readings and interpretations of the Edict given by Max *Walleser* (Das Edikt von Bhabra, Materialien zur Kunde des Buddhismus, Heft 1, Leipzig, 1923; Nochmals das Edikt von Bhabra, ibidem Heft 9, Heidelberg 1925 and ZII 3, 1924, 113ff.), I am just as little convinced as Joh. *Nobel* in OLZ 1924, 361ff., and E. *Leumann* in ZII, 2, 1923, 316f.

---

1. The dictum of Aṅguttara IV, 164: "All that is well said, that is the word of Buddha" (similarly Śikṣāsamuccaya, p. 15) represents a later stage of development.

APPENDIX IV (on page 185f)

Time and Life of Buddhaghosa

Th. *Foulkes* (Ind. Ant. 19, 1890, p. 122) already gave expression to the conjecture that Buddhaghosa never lived at all, but that the existing commentaries were ascribed to the 'Voice of Buddha." V. A. *Smith,* too (Ind. Ant. 34, 1905, p. 185) says, "Personally I do not believe in the existence of Buddhaghosa, 'The Voice of Buddha,' as an historical personage." L. *Finot* (La légende de Buddhaghosa, in Cinquantenaire de l' école pratique des hautes études, Paris 1921, p. 101ff.) goes further, and attempts to prove that there is no historical foundation for Buddhaghosa's journey from Magadha to Ceylon, and that the commentaries are the work of several Singhalese translators, who have been grouped by tradition around the more or less authentic name of Buddhaghosa. We admit that the accounts of Buddhaghosa which have come down to us are 800 years later than he himself, that they are full of legends, that the accounts of Buddhaghosa's journeys to Burma and Pegu have no sort of historical background, and likewise that some commentaries have been ascribed to him erroneously. However, in the case of Śaṅkara, too, there are only quite legendary so-called "biographies," and many works are ascribed to him, which he could not have written, and yet no one doubts that a philosopher Śaṅkara really existed. At all events the name Buddhaghosa is quite trustworthy, as this name already occurs in inscriptions of Mathurā in the first centuries of the Christian era (*Foulkes*, l. c., p. 105ff.). *Cf. P. Pelliot* in T'oung Pao 21, 1922, p. 243 f., and *Pe Maung Tin* in JRAS, 1923, 265 ff. *Pelliot* (l. c. and BEFEO 4, 149,412) has pointed out that, at the beginning of the fifth century Fa-hien and Tche-mong made the acquaintance of a Brahmin Raivata in Pāṭaliputra, who is possibly identical with Buddhaghosa's teacher. The fact that Buddhaghosa knew the Vedas and was versed in Sāṃkhya and Yoga, lends probability to the tradition that he was originally a Brahmin; s. *Maung Tin,* l.c.

The period of the reign of King Mahānāma of Ceylon was formerly assumed to be 410-432 or 413-435, and the life-time of Buddhaghosa was accordingly set in the first half of the 5th century. This view was still held by *Burlingame* (HOS Vol. 25, p. 58). According to the chronology of W. *Geiger* (The Mahāvaṃsa transl., p. xxxvi ff.), which is based upon the foundation of the date 483 B. C. as the year of Buddha's death, 458-480 A.D. would be the dates of Mahānāma's reign and thus also Buddhaghoṣa's time. This chronology, however, given only "provisionally" by *Geiger* himself, seems rather doubtful to me. The account of Chinese annals of an embassy which King Mahānāma of Ceylon sent to the emperor of China in the year 428 A.D. (S. *Lévi*, JA 1900, s. 9, t. XV, p. 412f.) speaks rather in favour of the date 410-432. *Geiger* refers to the fact that, according to his chronology King Meghavaṇṇa of Ceylon reigned from 352 to 379 A.D., and according to a Chinese account (*Lévi*, l. c., p. 316 f.) this king sent an embassy to Samudragupta, who reigned from 326 to 375 A.D. (*Smith*, Early History, in the 4th edit. gives 330-380). However, even the old dating of Meghavaṇṇa, *viz.*, 304-332 A.D. would not contradict the Chinese account, if the embassy had taken place between 330 and 332 A.D. *Smith*, Early History, p. 345, does, it is true (obviously on the basis of *Geiger's* chronology), give the date of about 360 A.D. for King Meghavaṇṇa's embassy.

APPENDIX V (on page 246)

The Date of Kaniṣka's Reign

The date of the reign of King Kaniṣka is of the utmost importance for the study of the History of Buddhism and Buddhist literature. Now though there are numerous dated coins of Kaniṣka, and inscriptions in which Kaniṣka is mentioned, there is no sure means of determining according to which era these dates should be reckoned. There are also traditions about Kaniṣka in Tibet, China and Mongolia. Deriving their material from Indian sources, the Chinese give much edifying information concerning Kaniṣka, but they do not give us any synchronisms with Chinese History. Hence even now we have nothing beyond hypotheses as to Kaniṣka's time. Epigraphical, numismatical, archaeological and literary evidence points more and more to the 2nd century A.D. as the time when Kaniṣka reigned, and to round about 125 A.D. as the probable date of his accession. The view, still maintained by a few scholars, that Kaniṣka is the founder of the Śaka era, which began in 78 A.D., is less likely to be correct.

In view of the importance and the difficulty of this question, I give below a summary of the almost overwhelming litertaure on the problem, which is still further complicated by the fact that there were probably two rulers named Kaniṣka.

(1) The view that Kaniṣka is *the founder of the Vikrama era in* 58 *B.C.* will find but few supporters now-a-days. It was represented by Alexander *Cunningham* (Archaeological Survey of India, Reports, Vol. II, 1871, p. 68 note, 159 ff.; III, p. 31),[1] J.F. *Fleet* in his Introduction to the English translation of G. Bühler's 'Indian Palaeography' in Ind. Ant. 33. 1904, and in JRAS 1906, 979 ff.; 1903,334; 1913, 95ff., 965ff.; 1914, 992ff.; O. *Franke* in ABA 1904, 61ff., J. *Kennedy* in JRAS 1912, 665ff.; 981ff.; 1913, 369ff·, 661 ff., 1054ff.; S. *Levi* JA 1896, s. 9, t. VIII, 444ff., 1897,s. 9. t. IX, 1ff.,[2] assumes the *1st century B.C. and the beginning of our era* as Kaniṣka's time. The same view is also held by L.D. *Barnett* in JRAS, 1913, 193, and in Calcutta Review, Feb. 1924, p. 252.

The view that Kaniṣka is *the founder of the Śaka era in* 78 *A.D.* was first put forward by *J. Fergusson* in JRAS, 1880, 259 ff. and by H. *Oldenberg* in Zeitschrift fur Numismatik 8, 1881, 289ff. (English translation in Ind. Ant. 10, 1881, 213 ff.), and is still defended at the present day by E.J. *Rapson* (Cambridge History I, pp. 581, 583ff.), Daya Ram *Sahni* in JRAS, 1924, 399 ff., L. *Bachhofer* in OZ, 1927, 21ff., 1930, 10ff. s. Hari Charan *Ghosh* in Ind. Hist. Qu. 4, 1928, 760 ff., 5, 1929, 49ff. *The*

1. *Cunningham* changed his opinion later, and placed Kaniṣka about 80 A.D.

2. The same Chinese sources on which *Levi* takes his stand, are utilised by Ed. *Specht* in JA 1897, s. 9,t. X, p. 152ff., for fixing the date as the end of 1st or the beginning of the 2nd century A.D.

first century A.D. is assumed as Kaniṣka's time by L. A. *Waddell* in JRAS, 1913, 947 ff., on archaeological grounds, and by J. Ph. *Vogel* in Ep. Ind., VIII, 173 ff. on palaeographical grounds.

(3) *The end of the* 1*st and the beginning of the* 2*nd century A.D.* is assumed by many scholars, s. H. *Oldenberg* in NGGW, 1911, 427 ff. (English translation JPTS, 1910-11, p. 1 ff.), AR, 17, 1914, 646 ff., Ed. *Specht in* JA 1897, s. 9, t. X. p. 152 ff., A. M. *Boyer* in JA 1900, s. 9, t. XV, 526 ff,, H. *Lüders* Die Inschrift von Āra in SBA, 1912, 824 ff. (English translation in Ind. Ant., 42, 1913, 132 ff.), F.W, *Thomas* in JRAS, 1913, 627 ff.; 1011 ff.; 1914, 748 ff., GGA, 1931, 1 ff., and M.A. *Stein* in Ind. Ant., 34, 1905, 77 ff. : "Palaeographical and other considerations make it appear probable that the date of Kaniṣka's accession may be somewhat later than the beginning of the Śaka era." According to R.D. *Banerji*, who has formulated all the theories advanced up to that time (Ind. Ant., 37, 1908, 27 ff.) Kaniṣka crossed the Indus in the year 91 A.D. and died in 123 A.D.

(4) *The* 2*nd century A.D.* is supported on archaeological grounds by A. *Foucher*, L art greco-bouddhique du Gandhāra I, 1905, p. 623, II, 1918, p. 505 ff., Sir John *Marshall* in JRAS 1914, 973 ff., 1915, 191 ff., Guide to Taxila, 2nd Ed., Calcutta 1921, p. 17, V.A. *Smith*, History of Fine Art in India and Ceylon, Oxford 1911, p. 99.[1] The most decided supporter of the view that Kaniṣka did not come into power until after the year 125 A.D. and that the Kaniṣka era begins with the years 128-29 A.D., is Sten *Konow* (ZDMG, 68, 1914, 97 ; SBA, 1916, 787 ff.; Ep. Ind., XIV, 1918, 130 ff. ; Acta Or., II, 1923, 130 ff.: III, 1924, 52 ff.; JBRAS, N.S. 1, 1, 1925, p. 1' ff.; Ind. Hist. Qu. 3, 1927, 851 ff. and lastly in Kharosthi Inscriptions, Corpus Inscriptionum Indicarum, Vol. II, part I, Calcutta, 1929, pp. lxxv ff., lxxx ff., xciii f.). V. A. *Smith*, Early History, 271 ff., gives approximately 120-160 A.D., and R. *Kimura* (Ind. Hist. Qu., 1, 1925, 415 ff) 140-180 A.D. as the time of Kaniṣka's reign. *Cf.* also A.V. *Staëll-Holtsein* in SBA, 1914, 643 ff. ; E.

1. Earlier views are discussed and criticised by *Smith* in JRAS 1903, p. 3 ff.

Windisch Philologie und Altertumskunde in Indien, Leipzig, 1921 (AKM, XV, 3), p. 26 ff., who again gives a survey of the various theories, and *Keith*, Hist. Sansk. Lit., p. xxvii.

(5) *The 3rd century A.D.* is supported only by D. R. *Bhandarkar* (JBRAS, 20, 1899, 269 ff.), R.G. *Bhandarkar* (JBRAS 20, 1900, 385 ff.), R. C. *Majumdar* (Ind. Ant., 46, 1917, 261 ff. and JDL, 1, 1920, 65 ff.).

For a second Kaniṣka, who was probably the grandson of the great Kaniṣka and lived in the 3rd century, *s. Lüders* l. c.; Satis Chandra *Vidyabhushana* in JASB 6, 1910, 477 ff. ; *Kimura* l. c.; Daya Ram *Sahni* l. c.; Hari Charan *Ghosh*, Ind. Hist. Qu., 5, 1929, p. 70, and Sten *Konow*, Kharoshthi Inscriptions, p. lxxx f.

APPENDIX VI (on page 408).

The Year of the Death of Mahāvīra

According to the usual chronology of the Śvetāmbara Jainas, Mahāvīra died 470 years before the beginning of the Vikrama era, *i.e.*, in 527 B.C., but according to the Digambaras, in 605 B.C. These dates are probably based upon erroneous calculations, for they are as difficult to reconcile with the one and only firmly established fact, namely that Buddha and Mahāvīra were contemporaries and lived in the reigns of Kings Bimbisāra and Ajātaśatru, as they are with other traditions of the Jainas themselves. There is a tradition of the Jainas, which can be traced as far back as the 11th century A.D., according to which Candragupta was anointed king 155 years after the death of Mahāvīra. Now it is true that even the date of Candragupta's coronation is by no means certain. Otto *Stein* (Archiv Orientálni 1, 1929, 354ff., 368 ff.) has shown that Candragupta cannot have been crowned king before 318-17 B.C. If we assume 317 B.C., hypothetically, as the coronation year, then the Nirvāṇa of Mahāvīra would have taken place in 473-72 B.C., and that of Buddha in 480-79 or 483-82 B.C., according to whether we assume

28 or 25 years as the length of Bindusāra's reign. J. *Charpentier* (Ind. Ant., 43, 1914, 118 ff., 125 ff., 167 ff. and Cambridge History, I, 150 ff.) has attempted to prove that Buddha died in 477 B.C. and Mahāvīra in 467 B.C. H. *Jacobi*, who formerly (The Kalpasūtra of Bhadrabāhu Ed., Introduction, p. 6 ff.) had likewise assumed the date 467 B.C., now accepts (Buddhas und Mahāvīras Nirvāṇa und die politische Entwickulung Magadhas zu jener Zeit in SBA, 1930, p. 557 ff.) 484 B.C. as the year of Buddha's death and 477 B.C. as that of Mahāvira, as a "sure foundation' for the history of Magadha, and he sets out from the year 322 B.C. as the year of Candragupta's coronation. S.V. *Venkateswara*, JRAS, 1917, 122 ff., has tried to prove that Mahāvīra could not have died earlier than 437 B.C.

None of these datings can be reconciled with the tradition, preserved in three different passages in the Pāli Canon (Dīgha III, 117, 210 ; Majjhima II, 243f.) and also in the Chinese Dīrghāgama (s. S. *Behrsing* in Asia Major VII, 1931, p. 1ff.), that the Nighaṇṭa Nātaputta died a short time before Gotama. *Jacobi* SBA 1930, 558 ff., assumes that this report was only invented in order to connect with it the story of the quarrels in the community of the Nighaṇṭas after the death of the Master. Of course, this is possible, but I have grave doubts that such a report which, as the Chinese translation shows, belongs to an earlier Canon, should be mere invention. I should prefer to say that the real date of Mahāvīra's Nirvāṇa is still unknown.

Cf. also K.B. *Pathak* in Ind. Ant. 12, 1883, p. 21f. ; *Hoernle* in ERE 1, 261; *Smith*, Early History (4th ed.), pp. 34, 48f., and *Guérinot*, La religion Djaina, p. 41.

ADDITIONS AND CORRECTIONS

P. 249 note 4, add ; On the style and language of Aśvaghoṣa's poems *cf. Keith*, HSL, p. 56ff.

P. 251 note 1, add : On the relation between Vālmīki and Aśvaghoṣa, s. Vol. I, p. 512f., and C. W. *Gurner* in JASB, Vol. XXIII, 1927, p. 347ff. (BB I, no. 102).

P. 252 note 1, L. 4, after "1928" add ; An English translation of the Saundarananda by E. H. *Johnston* has been published in the same series, London 1932.

P. 255 note 2, add : It seems to me quite impossible that such texts as the Nairātmya-paripṛcchā, the Gurupañcāśikā, and similar Mahāyāna and Tantra texts which are ascribed to Aśvaghoṣa (s. S. *Lévi* in JA 213, 1928, 204ff.; 215, 1929, 255 ff.) could be works of the poet. Either they are apocryphal, or their author is another Aśvaghoṣa. *Cf.* J. *Przyluski* in Acad. roy. de Belgique Bulletins de la classe des lettres, 1930, 425ff.

P. 256 note 3, add : It is possible that Aśvaghoṣa is also the author of a lyrical drama treating the legend of Rāṣṭrapāla, s. S. Lévi in JA 213, 1928, 200ff.

P. 256ff note 4, add : Pages 256 were already printed when I saw Joh. *Nobel's* paper "Kumāralāta und sein Werk" (NGGW, 1928, 295ff.; see also S. *Levi* in JA 213, 1928, 193ff.; 215, 1929, 271ff., and L. de *La Vallee Poussin*, Vijñaptimātratāsiddhi (Buddhica I, 1) Paris 1928, p. 223f.) which makes it most probable that Kumāralāta's Kalpanāmaṇḍitikā Dṛṣṭāntapaṅkti is not identical with the Sūtrālaṃkāra, but an imitation of it prepared for the use of the Sautrāntikas, and that Aśvaghoṣa is the author of the "Sūtrālaṃkāra" translated by Kumārajīva. On the other hand the colophons of the Turfan fragments leave no doubt that Kumāralāta is the author of the Kalpanāmaṇḍitikā, s. J, *Przyluski* in Acad. roy. de Belgique Bulletins de la classe des lettres, 1930, 425ff. H. *Lüders* (Kātantra und Kumāralāta, SBA 1930, 531f. has also discovered fragments of a grammar by Kumāralāta.

P. 274 note, 3, add : J. *Przyluski* (Ind. Hist. Qu. 5, 1929, p. 5) does not think it probable that the Vinaya is the source of the Divyāvadāna. He holds that "the compilers of the Vinaya of the Mūlasarvāstivādins are likely to have borrowed...from the ancient collection fables of which our Divyāvadāna is only a late recension."

P. 283 note 2, add : On the Bodhisattvapiṭaka see also Haraprasād *Śāstri* in B.C. *Law*, Buddhistic Studies, 1931, p. 846ff.

P. 283, L. 16, add : As there is no Mahāyāna Canon, there is also no special Vinayapiṭaka of the Mahāyāna, though there are Sūtras which treat of Vinaya subjects. Such Sūtras are the Chinese *Brahmajāla-Sūtra* (translated into French by M. *de Groot*, Le code du Mahāyāna en Chine (see p. 226 above, note 2) and the *Bodhisattva-Prātimokṣa-Sūtra*(edited by Nalinaksha *Dutt* in Ind. Hist. Qu. 7, 1931, 259ff.) See also N. *Dutt*, Aspects of Mahāyāna Buddhism and its relation to Hīnayāna, p. 290ff.

P. 293 note 4, add : On the great importance of the Saddharmapuṇḍarīka in Japan, see M. W. de *Visser*, Ancient Buddhism in Japan Sūtras and Ceremonies in use in the Seventh and Eighth Centuries A.D., Paris 1928 (Buddhica, ser. I, t. III), pp. 1ff., 43.

P. 302 note 2, add : See now also the valuable "Note on the Prajñāpāramitā" by Nalinaksha Dutt, Aspects of Mahāyāna Buddhism, London 1930 (Calcutta Oriental Series No. 23), p. 323ff., and the survey of the Prajñāpāramitā literature by Tokumyo *Mastumoto*, Die Prajñāpāramitā-Literatur nebst einem Specimen der Suvikrāntavikrāmi-Prajñāpāramitā (Bonner Orientalistische Studien Heft 1), Stuttgart 1932. N. *Dutt*, l. c., pp. 39f., 328 dates the Aṣṭasāhasrikā "as early as the first century B.C." According to *Matsumoto* (l. c., p. 22) the earliest Chinese translation of the Aṣṭasāhasrikā Pr. dates 172 A.D. He thinks (l.c., p. 31) that the Prajñāpāramitās originated in Kashmir between the birth of Christ and the time of Kaniṣka.

P. 302 note 3, add: On a list of Prajñāpāramitās in the Tibetan

Kanjur, see also Marcelle *Lalou* in JA 215, 1929, pp. 87-102.

P. 303 note 5, add : The Sanskrit text of the Saptaśatikā Prajñāpāramitā has been edited by G *Tucci* (Memorie della R. Accademia Nazionale dei Lincei, Vol. XVII). Roma 1923, and together with Hsuan Tsang's Chinese version by Jiryo *Masuda* in Comm. Wogihara, p. 185ff.

P. 304 note 2, add : N. *Dutt*, l. c., 328ff., by a comparison of the Prajñāpāramitā versions, comes to the conclusion that "the relation between the Aṣṭa. and the Śata. can be hardly that of abridgment or expansion, as it can be said between the Śata. and the Pañcaviṃśati." Verbal agreements show "that the Aṣṭa. and the Śata. deal with identical topics, but the arrangement and the emphasis laid on a particular topic are quite different. Besides this, the Śata. introduced new topics like bhūmis and expositions of the various śūnyatās, samādhis, etc., which were only enumerated or referred to in the Aṣṭa. So it may be said that the Śata. utilised the Aṣṭa. and not *vice versa*." On the other hand, "the Pañcaviṃśati is clearly an abridgment of the Śata. effected by an omission of set enumerations and repetitions." Dr. Dutt is certainly right in saying "that the generalisations regarding abridgment and expansion of the Prajñāpāramitās are not possible and that each book must be judged by its contents." About the Daśasāhasrikā and Aṣṭasāhasrikā in Chinese, s. *Dutt*, l.c., p. 323f. *Matsumoto*, in his list of prajñāpāramitā texts (l.c., p. 2ff.). does not mention a Daśasāhasrikā at all.

P. 310 note 1, add : N, *Dutt*, l.c., p. 332ff., would explain the tiresome repetitions in the Prajñāpāramitās as due to the desire of philosophical writers of first wiping out from the minds of the readers old ideas, in order to implant new ideas in their place, but who "sadly lacked the knowledge of *artful* repetitions," and therefore became tiresome. I think that the writers of the Pr. wrote for religious purposes rather than for philosophical teaching.

P. 314 note 4, add : See also J. *Rahder*, Glossary of the Sanskrit, Tibetan, Mongolian and Chinese Versions of the Daśabhūmika-Sūtra, Paris 1928 (Buddhica, ser. 2, tome I) and The Daśabhūmika-Sūtra (Gāthā portion) Edited by Johannes *Rahder* and Shinryu *Susa* in EB 5, No. 4, July 1931.

P. 315 note 1, add : On the Bhūmis and the literature on them see now N. *Dutt*, Aspects of Mahāyāna Buddhism, p. 238ff.

P. 319 note 2, add : The Ugradatta Paripṛcchā seems to have been a book of conduct for use by the lay Bodhisattvas, S.N. *Dutt*, Aspects of Mahāyāna Buddhism, p. 299.

P. 319 note 3, add ; The Sanskrit text of a Nairātmyaparipṛcchā, formerly only known in a Tibetan and in a Chinese version, has been discovered by S. *Levi* (see JA t. 213, 1928, p. 207ff.) A reconstruction of the Sanskrit text from the Tibetan version has been edited by Sujitkumar *Mukhopadhyaya* in Visva-Bharati Studies, No. 4, Calcutta 1931.

P. 320 note 4, add : See now also Daisetz Teitaro *Suzuki*, Studies in the Laṅkāvatāra Sūtra, London 1930 (*cf.* EB V, 1929, pp. 1-79), also Haraprasād *Śāstrī* and S. N. *Dasgupta* in B.C. *Law*, Buddhistic Studies, 1931, pp. 840ff., 859ff.

P. 320, L. 14 : The last chapter should not be called "Sagāthakam," but (if it had any title at all) it should be "Gāthāḥ." This is also the meaning of the colophon : ity āryasaddharma-Laṅkāvatāro nāma mahāyānasūtraṃ sagāthakaṃ samāptam. *Cf. Suzuki*, Studies in the Laṅkāvatāra Sūtra, p. 22.

P. 323 note 2, add : Of the 884 Gāthās of Chap. X, 200 occur also in the main part of the work. *Suzuki*, Studies in the Laṅkāvatāra Sūtra, p. 21ff., describes this Gāthā chapter as "nothing but a heap of rubbish and gems."

P. 326 note 3, add : The new edition of the Suvarṇaprabhāsa Sūtra, prepared by the late Professer Bunyiu *Nanjio* and after his death revised and edited by H. *Idzumi*, The Eastern Buddhist Society, Kyoto 1931, has since been published.

P. 329 note 1, L. 4, read : An Uiguric version of the Suvarṇaprabhāsa has been edited by W. W. *Radloff* and S. E.

Malov in Bibl. Buddh. XVII, 1913ff., and translated into German by the same in Bibl. Buddh. XXVII, 1930.

P. 331 note 2, add : A Sanskrit biography of the Siddhas, found by G. *Tucci* (JASB, N.S., XXVI, 1930, 138ff.), contains also some information on Nāgārjuna, or rather on the different authors and teachers of this name. On the confusion of the Mādhyamika Nāgārjuna and the Tāntrika Nāgārjuna s. also Nalinaksha *Dutt* in Ind. Hist. Qu. 7, 1931, 635ff.

P. 334, L.9 add : The Vigraha-Vyâvartanī is a polemical treatise; it has been translated from the Tibetan by Susuma *Yamaguchi* (JA 215, 1929, pp. 1-86), who also notes the differences of the Chinese translation. The Tibetan text and an English translation from the Chinese and Tibetan has been published by G. *Tucci* in Pre-Diṅnāga Buddhist Texts on Logic from Chinese Sources, GOS No. XLIX, 1929.

P. 334 note 1, L. 2-3, read : *Materialien zur Kunde des Buddhismus.*

P. 334 note 4, add : A reconstruction of the Sanskrit text from the Tibetan and Chinese versions, and an English translation, with Introduction and Notes, has been published by Vidhushekhara *Bhattacharyya* in Viśva-Bhāratī Studies No. 1, Calcutta 1931. The Pandit leaves it an open question whether the author of the work is the old Nāgārjuna of about 200 A.D., or the second Nāgārjuna who "is believed to have flourished in about the first half of the seventh century A.D."

P. 334 note 5, L. 2, after "Oxford 1885" add : Different from the Sanskrit Dharmasaṃgraha, but closely related to it is the Chinese Dharmasaṃgraha, see F. *Weller*, Der chinesische Dharmasaṃgraha, Leipzig 1923.

P. 337 note 4, add : See now also the Catuḥśataka Āryadeva Sanskrit and Tibetan texts with Copious Extracts from the Commentary of Candrakīrti. Reconstructed and edited by Vidhushekhara *Bhattacharyya*, Part II, Viśva-Bhārati Series, No. 2, Calcutta 1931. An English translation from the Chinese of Āryadeva's *Śataśāstra*, a work which is similar to the Catuḥśataka, though the subjects are differently arranged, has been published by G. *Tucci* in Pre-Diṅnāga Buddhist Texts on Logic from Chinese Sources, GOS No. XLIX, 1929. Another Madhyamaka text of Āryadeva, the *Akṣara-Śatakam*, has been translated after Chinese and Tibetan materials by Vasudev *Gokhale*, Heidelberg 1930 (Materialien zur Kunde des Buddhismus 14).

P. 341 note 1, add : The Sanskrit text and Tibetan translation of the Abhisamayālaṃkāra-Prajñāpāramitā-Upadeśa-Śāstra have been edited by Th. *Stcherbatsky* and E. *Obermiller* in Bibl. Buddh. XXIII, 1929. It is, according to *Stcherbatsky*, "the fundamental work for the study of the Buddhist doctrine of the Path towards moral perfection and the attainment of the condition of a Buddhist Mahāyānistic Saint, and of a Mahāyānistic Buddha in the blessed Nirvāṇa.' *Stcherbatsky* explains *abhisamaya* as a synonym of *mārga*, and says : "*Alaṃkāra* is the name for a literary form popular with the Buddhists. It means that the work in question contains no full and detailed exposition of the doctrine, it is not a mahāśāstra, like the Abhidharmakośa, but it is only a short summary of the salient points of the system contained in the prajñāpāramitā sūtras." The Alaṃkāras are always composed in memorial verses (kārikās) which, like the Brahmanical Sūtras, again require a commentary. See also *Tucci*, On some Aspects of the Doctrines of Maitreya (nātha) and Asaṅga, Calcutta 1930, p. 10ff., and in JASB N.S. XXVI, 1930, p. 127.

P. 341 note 2, add : See also Hakuju *Ui* Maitreya as an Historical Personage in Lanman Studies, p. 95 ff. Here he says (p. 99) that it "is still a question" whether the authorship of the commentary on the Mahāyāna-Sūtrālaṃkāra belongs to Asaṅga or to Vasubandhu. He ascribes to Maitreya the works ; Yogācārabhūmi, Yoga-vibhaṅga-śāstra (now lost), Mahāyāna-Sūtrālaṃkāra, Madhyānta-vibhaṅga, Vajracchedikā-Pāramitā-śāstra, and Abhisamayālaṃkāra. G. *Tucci*, on some Aspects of the Doctrines of Maitreya(nātha) and Asaṅga, Calcutta, 1930, and in JASB, N.S., XXVI, 1930, p. 125ff., supports, by new evidence, the view that Maitreya or Maitreyanātha is an historical personage and the author of six works, including the Mahāyāna-Sūtrālaṃkāra, and the Yogacaryā-bhūmi-śāstra (this is the correct title). He is of opinion that Maitreya is the author of the Kārikās of all the six works, while Asaṅga, his chief pupil, wrote the commentaries on them. E. *Obermiller*, in the introduction to his translation of the Uttaratantra of Maitreya (The Sublime Science of the Great Vehicle of Salvation, being A Manual of Buddhist Monism, The Work of Ārya Maitreya with a Commentary by Āryāsaṅga. Translated from the Tibetan, in Acta Orientalia, Vol. IX, 1931, pp. 81-306), states that the following five works are ascribed to Maitreya by Tibetan tradition, *viz.*, Sūtrālaṁkāra, Madhyānta-vibhaṅga, Dharma-dharmatā-vibhaṅga, Abhisamayālaṃkāra, and Uttaratantra. *Obermiller* gives a summary analysis of all these works. As the commentary on the Abhisamayālaṃkāra is ascribed to Asaṅga, and as both text and commentary must have been composed by the same author, *O.* inclines to the opinion that all the 5 treatises which show a great resemblance with each other as regards style, though they are written from different points of view (1-3 from Yogācāra-Vijñānavāda, 4 and 5 from Mādhymika point of view), were written by Asaṅga, and that the tradition of Asaṅga having heard them from Maitreya in the Tuṣita heaven is only meant to give a divine sanction to the works.

P. 342 note 1, add : An edition of the Bodhisattvabhūmi, being the 15th section of the Yogācārabhūmi, has been published by Unrai *Wogihara*, Tokyo 1930.

P. 342 note 2, add : The question of Vasubandhu's date has recently been discussed by J. *Takakusu*, Taiken *Kimura* and Genmyo *Ono* (in Lanman Studies, pp. 79ff., 89ff. 93f,) who agree in assigning the author of the Abhidharamakośa to the 5th century (420-500 A.D.). T. *Kimura* speaks here also of two Vasubandhus. *Takakusu's* chief arguments are *argumenta ex silentio* : Kumārajīva (383-414 in China) and Fa-hien (399-414 in India) know nothing of Vasubandhu and his Abhidharmakośa. The sources on which N. *Peri* relies, are declared by *Takakusu* to be "spurious." On the other hand, H. *Ui* (Lanman Studies, p. 101f.) gives the following dates : Maitreya 270-350, Asaṅga 310-390, Vasubandhu 320-400, which Takakusu considers too early by 100 years.

P. 344 note 1, Line 2, after "1918" add : Second Kośasthāna ed. by U. *Wogihara*, Th. *Stcherbatsky*, and E. *Obermiller*, Bibl. Buddh., 1931. The Tibetan version of the Abhidharmakośakārikāḥ and Abhidharmakośabhāṣyam has been edited by Th. *Stcherbatsky* in Bibl. Buddh. XX, 1917 and 1930.

P. 346 note 1, add : A similar work is the Śīlaparikathā, a moral treatise of 11 verses, which is ascribed to Vasubandhu, and preserved in the Tibetan Tanjur only, s. Anathanath *Basu* in Ind. Hist. Qu. 7, 1931, 28ff.

P. 348 note 1, add : A fragment of the Sanskrit text of the Commentary on the Pratītya-Samutpāda-Sūtra has been publishad by G. *Tucci* in JRAS, 1930, p. 611 ff. Instead of "According to G. *Tucci*," etc. read ; H.R. Rangaswamy *Iyengar* (JBORS 12, 1926, 587 ff. ; Ind. Hist. Qu. 5, 1929, p. 81ff.) and G. *Tucci* (Ind. Hist. Qu. 4, 1928, p. 630ff.) have proved that the Vādavidhi also is a work of Vasubandhu, and not as A. B. *Keith*, in agreement with Satis Chandra *Vidyabhushana*, tried to prove (Ind. Hist. Qu. 4, 1928, p. 221ff.) the work of Dharmakīrti.

P. 349 note 2, add; The whole extremely complicated problem of the authenticity of the Ta Tch'eng K'i Sin Louen (this is the Chinese title of the Mahāyāna-śraddhotpāda-śāstra) has been fully discussed by Paul *Demiéville*, Sur l'authenticite du Ta Tch'eng K'i Sin Louen (Extrait du Bulletin de la Maison Franco-Japonaise, tome II, No. 2, Tokyo 1929). Mr. *Demiéville* sees no reason to deny the Indian origin of the work which (he thinks) must be later than the Laṅkāvatāra, but earlier than Asaṅga and Vasubandhu. Else it would be difficult to explain why they are never quoted in the work. On the other hand, it is strange that the work, so famous in China and Japan, is never alluded to in any Sanskrit text, nor in any Chinese or Tibetan translations of Buddhist Sanskrit works.

P. 351, L. 14, add note to Prasannapadā: Chapters I and XXV of the Prasannapadā have been translated by Th. *Stcherbatsky* in his work. The Conception of Buddhist Nirvāṇa (Leningrad 1927), pp. 79-212 ; Chap. X by St. *Schayer* in Rocznik Orjentalistyczny, Lwow 1930, VII, 26-52, and Chapters V, XII, XIII-XVI by St. *Schayer*, Ausgewählte Kapitel aus der Prasannapadā in Polska Akademja Umiejetnośći. Memoires de la Commission Orientaliste Nr. 14, w. Krakowie 1931. An analysis of Chap. XXIV was given by *La Vallée 'Poussin* in Melanges Charles de Harlez, Leiden 1896.

P. 351 note 3 : An edition of the Sanskrit text of the Madhyamakāvatāra is now being published in the Journal of Oriental Research, Madras, Vol. VI, 1932 (Supplement).

P. 356, L. 13 : The Avalokita- Sūtra in the Mahāvastu II. 363ff.. agrees with the Avalokana-Sūtra quoted by Śāntideva in general, but differs from it in so many details that Śāntideva's text cannot possibly be a quotation from the Mahāvastu.

P. 356, L. 20, read *Tathāgataguhya-Sūtra.*

P. 357 note 1, add; A Mongolic translation of the Bodhicaryāvatāra ed. by B. J. *Vladimircov in Bibl.* Buddh. XXVIII, 1929.

P. 363 note 2, L. 1, read *The Tibetan text with a French translation*; and add at the end of the note : The first and the last of the four hymns, Sanskrit and Tibetan Texts, have been edited, with an English translation, by G. *Tucci* in JRAS, 1932, p. 309 ff,

P. 371 note 3, add : The Mahā-Māyūrī has been translated into Chinese by Kumārajīva, and three times more. See also G. *Tucci* in JASB, NS. XXVI, 1930, p. 129.

P. 378 note 1, add : G. *Tucci* also (JASB XXVI, 1930, p. 129ff) is of the opinion that the Tantras go back to the times of

Harivarman and Asaṅga (4th century A.D.) because they allude to a "Somasiddhānta" which he identifies with the "Tantric sect" of the Kāpālikas. I am afraid the use of the terms "Tantric" and "Tantras" is too vague to allow any safe dating of Tantra literature. In line 3 of the note read Sādhanamālā II (instead of III).

P. 379, L. 1, Uḍḍiyāna is probably not Orissa, but the Swat country ; s. P. C. *Bagchi* in Ind. Hist. Qu 6 1930, p. 580f.

P. 379 note 3, add : See also P.C. *Bagchi* in Ind. Hist. Qu. 6, 1930, 389ff. The Sandhā-bhāṣā is also used in the *Dohā-kośa*, Sahajayāna poems written in Apabhraṃśa, s. Les chants. mystiques de Kāṇha et de Saraha. Les Dohā-Koṣa (en apabhraṃśa avec les versions tibetaines) et Les Caryā (en vieuxbengali)...edites et traduits par M. *Shahidulla*, Paris 1928. Kāṇha lived about 700, Saraha about 1000 A.D.

P. 381 note 3, add : None of the passages quoted from a Tathāgataguhya-Sūtra in the Śikṣāsamuccayā occur in the Guhyasamāja Tantra or Tathāgataguhyaka edited by Benoytosh *Bhattacharyya*, Baroda 1931 (GOS No. 53). The latter is a genuine Tantra. In the colophons it is called "Guhyasamāja Mahāguhyatantrarāja." It is a work belonging to the Yogatantra class. Dr. Bhattacharyya would ascribe this Tantra to Asaṅga, but his arguments are very weak indeed.

P. 382 note 2, add : See also Marcelle *Lalou*. Iconographie des étoffes peintes (paṭa) dans le Mañjuśrīmūlakalpa, Paris 1930 (Buddhica, ser. 1, t. VI). B. *Bhattachryya* (GOS, Vol. LIII, p. xxxiii ff.) would ascribe the Mañjuśrīmūlakalpa in its original form to the second century A.D. But his arguments are by no means convincing.

P. 385, L. 14 : Some scholars (see *e.g.*, G. *Tucci* in JASB N. S. XXVI, 1930, p. 128 ff.) claim a higher antiquity for the Tantras. But no real Tantra can be proved to have existed before the 7th century A.D. Neither the Suvarṇaprabhāsa nor the Mahāmāyūrī can be called "Tantras." Nor are the Kāpālikas a "Tantric sect." All we can say is that some of the elements of Tantrism are already found in earlier works.

P. 386 note 3. add : A goddess Lāmā often appears in Buddhist Tantras connected with the cult of Dākinīs and Yoginīs. Lāmā is the same as Tibetan Lhamo, "she-devil." On this Lāmā and on Tibetan influence on the Tantras s. also G. *Tucci* in JASB N.S. XXVI, 1930, p. 155 ff.

P. 391 f. note 3, add : See also W. *Wüst,* Buddhismus und Christentum auf vorderasiatisch-antikem Boden, in Zeitschrift für Missionskunde und Religionswissenschaft, 1932, 33ff.

P. 413, L, 35-36, read *Ohanijjutti.*

After P. 483, L. 38, Add : Another "Mahāpurāṇa" is the *Tisaṭṭhimahāpurisagaṇālaṃkāra* in Apabhraṃśa by the poet *Pupphayanta* or *Puṣpadanta.* This Mahāpurāṇa also consists of two parts, an Ādipurāṇa in 37, and an Uttarapurāṇa in 65 Chapters. It was completed in 965 A.D. Puṣpadanta is also the author of two other Apabhraṃsa works, a *Nāgakumāracariu*, and a *Jasaharacariu* (Yaśodharacarita).[1] The subject of the latter is the life of Yasodhara, which has also been treated in Somadeva Sūri's Yaśastilaka and Vādirāja Sūri's Yaśodharacarita.

---

(1). Jasaharacariu of Puṣpadanta. Critically edited with an Introduction, Glossary and notes by P.L. *Vaidya* (The Ambādās Chaware Digambara Jain Granthamālā or Karanjā Jain Series edited by Hiralal Jain Vol. I) Karanjā, Berar 1931. On the Tisaṭṭhimahāpurisaguṇālaṃkāra, see introduction, p. 19ff. and also *Hiralal*, Catalogue, p. xliiiff.

INDEX

C

I

J

S

U

V

W

Y